# SQL
# Server 2000™
# Black Book

Patrick Dalton
Paul Whitehead

**President and CEO**
*Keith Weiskamp*

**Publisher**
*Steve Sayre*

**Acquisitions Editor**
*Charlotte Carpentier*

**Product Marketing Manager**
*Tracy Rooney*

**Project Editor**
*Karen Swartz*

**Technical Reviewer**
*Buck Woody*

**Production Coordinator**
*Carla J. Schuder*

**Cover Designer**
*Jody Winkler*

**Layout Designer**
*April Nielsen*

**CD-ROM Developer**
*Chris Nusbuum*

**SQL Server 2000™ Black Book**

**Limits of Liability and Disclaimer of Warranty**

The author and publisher of this book have used their best efforts in preparing the book and the programs contained in it. These efforts include the development, research, and testing of the theories and programs to determine their effectiveness. The author and publisher make no warranty of any kind, expressed or implied, with regard to these programs or the documentation contained in this book.

The author and publisher shall not be liable in the event of incidental or consequential damages in connection with, or arising out of, the furnishing, performance, or use of the programs, associated instructions, and/or claims of productivity gains.

**Trademarks**

Trademarked names appear throughout this book. Rather than list the names and entities that own the trademarks or insert a trademark symbol with each mention of the trademarked name, the publisher states that it is using the names for editorial purposes only and to the benefit of the trademark owner, with no intention of infringing upon that trademark.

The Coriolis Group, LLC
14455 N. Hayden Road
Suite 220
Scottsdale, Arizona 85260

(480) 483-0192
FAX (480) 483-0193
www.coriolis.com

Library of Congress Cataloging-in-Publication Data
Dalton, Patrick.
   SQL server 2000 black book / by Patrick Dalton and Paul Whitehead.
     p. cm.
   ISBN 1-57610-770-1
   1. Client/server computing. 2. SQL server. 3. Related databases. I. Whitehead, Paul.
II. Title.
QA76.9.C55 D36 2000
005.75'85--dc21
                                        00-050857

Printed in the United States of America
10  9  8  7  6  5  4  3  2  1

The Coriolis Group, LLC • 14455 North Hayden Road, Suite 220 • Scottsdale, Arizona 85260

Dear Reader:

Coriolis Technology Press was founded to create a very elite group of books: the ones you keep closest to your machine. Sure, everyone would like to have the Library of Congress at arm's reach, but in the real world, you have to choose the books you rely on every day *very* carefully.

To win a place for our books on that coveted shelf beside your PC, we guarantee several important qualities in every book we publish. These qualities are:

- *Technical accuracy*—It's no good if it doesn't work. Every Coriolis Technology Press book is reviewed by technical experts in the topic field, and is sent through several editing and proofreading passes in order to create the piece of work you now hold in your hands.

- *Innovative editorial design*—We've put years of research and refinement into the ways we present information in our books. Our books' editorial approach is uniquely designed to reflect the way people learn new technologies and search for solutions to technology problems.

- *Practical focus*—We put only pertinent information into our books and avoid any fluff. Every fact included between these two covers must serve the mission of the book as a whole.

- *Accessibility*—The information in a book is worthless unless you can find it quickly when you need it. We put a lot of effort into our indexes, and heavily cross-reference our chapters, to make it easy for you to move right to the information you need.

Here at The Coriolis Group we have been publishing and packaging books, technical journals, and training materials since 1989. We're programmers and authors ourselves, and we take an ongoing active role in defining what we publish and how we publish it. We have put a lot of thought into our books; please write to us at **ctp@coriolis.com** and let us know what you think. We hope that you're happy with the book in your hands, and that in the future, when you reach for software development and networking information, you'll turn to one of our books first.

Keith Weiskamp
President and CEO

Jeff Duntemann
VP and Editorial Director

## Look for these related books from The Coriolis Group:

**Data Modeling Essentials, 2nd Edition**
*By Graeme C. Simsion and Graham C. Witt*

**Exchange 2000 Server Black Book**
*By Marcus Goncalves*

**MCSE Administering SQL Server 7 Exam Prep**
*By Brian Talbert*

**MCSE Database Design on SQL Server 7 Exam Cram**
*By Jeffrey R. Garbus and David Pascuzzi*

**MCSE Windows 2000 Security Design Exam Prep**
*By Richard McMahon, Sr. and Glen R. Bicking*

**MOUS Access 2000 Exam Prep**
*By Lisa Friedrichsen*

## Also recently published by Coriolis Technology Press:

**Mac OS 9.1 Black Book**
*By Mark R. Bell and Debrah D. Suggs*

**Software Project Management: From Concept to Deployment**
*By Kieron Conway*

**Windows Admin Scripting Little Black Book**
*By Jesse M. Torres*

**Windows 2000 Active Directory Black Book**
*By Adam Wood*

**XML Black Book, 2nd Edition**
*By Natanya Pitts*

*I would like to dedicate this book to all those people who get frustrated with "the way it has always been done" and do not accept that as a viable excuse. The only true innovation happens through dedication and persistent effort. Individuals can make a difference when they do not give up!*
*—Patrick Dalton*

❧

*This book is dedicated to Barrie Whitehead, my wonderful wife; to Marie Lucas, my loving grandmother; and in loving memory of my Granny, Elizabeth Whitehead.*
*—Paul Whitehead*

❧

*To our children...*
*This is an example that no goal is unreachable. True failure is possible only when you accept defeat. Never stop trying to achieve your goals and we will always be proud of you!*

❧

# About the Authors

Here is a brief background on the people bringing this Black Book to you. Each has paid dues in some form or another in the IT industry and brings a unique perspective to this text.

### Patrick Dalton MCSD, MCT

Senior DBA, Senior Developer and Database Architect.

Patrick has spent his career solving complex design and process problems. He has focused on enterprise client/server and database solutions since 1982 and has worked as a consultant, trainer, and project manager for many of the Fortune 500 companies. His very large database experience is quite diverse and his knowledge of many database platforms gives him a unique perspective on what tools are best to get the job done. He has designed and developed applications in many industries ranging from satellite communications to food service and voice recognition.

### Paul Whitehead

Senior Developer, Team Lead

Paul has been working in the IT field since 1985 as a software developer, network administrator, database administrator, database architect, and analyst. He is an accomplished software and database developer utilizing primarily Delphi and Microsoft SQL Server. He has been working with SQL Server 6.5, 7.0, and now 2000, and has primarily focused his database efforts in the areas of database design and Transact-SQL programming, optimization, and troubleshooting. He also has an extremely strong Delphi background and experience with client/server and multi-tier development with Delphi and SQL Server.

## Contributing Authors

Each person contributes in different ways, some through direct efforts and others through support and guidance. Each of the contributing authors below has in some way directly helped to make this book a reality, and we owe them a great deal of thanks.

### Christopher Maddox MCSE, MCP+I, CCA
Information Systems Director, Senior Network Engineer

Chris is a very driven engineer who has been involved in developing client/server enterprise solutions from the hardware to the database and Web server. Enterprise applications place unique demands on the network and servers that require a great deal of expertise, which Chris has demonstrated time and time again. He continues to be a valued resource for bleeding-edge technology and possesses the know-how and determination to get it working.

### Jared Kirkpatrick MCSE, MCDBA
Database Administrator

Jared is relatively new to the database world but has done an incredible job of learning the complex administrative and programming tasks associated with supporting and developing an enterprise application. His networking and hardware skills have been a great asset and his dedication is something that is rare in today's workplace.

### Jeff Jones
Senior Database Administrator

With roots in the mainframe, Jeff crossed over to the Microsoft SQL Server world and has made it home (never looking back!). He has been through numerous database and application design cycles for large database solutions and has had to field developers' questions for years now on the best methods for accessing and manipulating data. Jeff's dedication and attention to detail are second to none. Jeff has been the go-to guy on many occasions and always finds an answer to even the toughest questions.

### Brad Haarer
Multimedia Developer

Brad is a freelance Web/multimedia developer who specializes in the development of user interfaces for computer applications. He has worked for several corporate clients and educational institutions developing CBT materials. He also specializes in digital publishing, media production, and IP-based videoconferencing. He is also a professional comedian, but because that has no bearing on this book, it probably shouldn't be mentioned.

# Acknowledgments

We would like to thank a few people who have been key to the success of this book. Without the help and support of each of these people, we would not have been able to write this book or to have the drive required to succeed in today's rapidly evolving technical environment.

## *Combined Thanks...*

First, we would like to thank Barrie Whitehead (Paul's wife). She has provided both support and patience throughout this process. Whether we invaded her home, or her husband disappeared for hours (and days) to make this project happen, she has faced each challenge with love and understanding. We would also like to thank our families and friends for their support and understanding as well. It may take us a while, but we'll manage to get caught back up on our personal lives now that this project has drawn to an end.

We would also like to thank several people who provided portions of the research and chapter work that allowed us to get this book done and keep the quality at as high a level as possible. Christopher Maddux, Jared Kirkpatrick, Jeff Jones, and Brad Haarer all contributed to the success of this project, and this project would have been much more difficult to complete without their help. A great deal of thanks is owed to each of you, and without your support (project or work-related) this book would not have been completed.

We owe a special thanks to the great team at The Coriolis Group. They are the ones responsible for making us look like authors in spite of ourselves. They have taken really good care of us and have worked diligently to see that the book you have in front of you is both technically accurate and easy to read and understand. Karen Swartz, our project editor, has been especially helpful in keeping us on schedule and making sure that we had everything we needed to produce a quality book (including the occasional kick in the seat of the pants!). Thanks go to Buck Woody, technical editor; Anne Marie Walker, copyeditor; Carla Schuder, production coordinator; Jody Winkler, cover designer, April Nielsen, layout designer; and Tracy Rooney, Product Marketing Manager, for their instrumental work behind the scenes. Thanks to Karen and the team at Coriolis for all your hard work!

We also need to acknowledge the support of our employer. We both work for The Ultimate Software Group in Weston, FL. We have both worked diligently to minimize the impact of this project on our normal work life, but some overlap is always unavoidable. We both thank them for their understanding and support of this endeavor.

### Pat's Acknowledgments

Having written my second book now, I am amazed at how hard it is to put into words the feelings I have for the people in my life. My parents have been a huge part of my life and have taught me that I can accomplish anything if I do not give up. I owe so much to them both and doubt I could ever repay them for what they have given me. I thank you from the bottom of my heart.

My children have taught me to be both proud and humble. I am amazed at how much they can learn and yet how much they teach me every day. They have had to deal with a part-time dad and have had to pay a far greater price for my ambition than I would like. Yet, through it all they are the most loving and understanding people. They are growing up so fast, and each becoming an individual. I just hope I can live up to the pedestal they place me on. I love you both more than words can ever say.

Paul Whitehead deserves a great deal of credit for this book. He has been a wonderful friend and partner in this endeavor, and for that I am thankful. His wife and personal life have taken the brunt of this project head on and yet he never gave up. I am proud to be associated with someone who places so much value on giving your word and sticking by it. He has been a technical sounding board for me and has troubleshooting skills second to none. A long time ago, I told him in jest that the definition of a guru was someone who knew just how much they did not know and was not afraid to say so. I guess now Paul has an understanding of what I meant. Each problem or task that has presented itself to us during the course of writing this book, Paul has tackled with dogged determination and Herculean effort. I have seen him tackle a subject with little or no guidance and produce some fine work that many people can use as a guide for years to come. We may joke around with each other about who is the "expert", but one thing is for sure: You are every bit the guru and then some. Thank you for your friendship.

Last but not least, I want to thank everyone who helped with the book. You all gave a piece of your time and lives to make this happen. I am fortunate to have friends and associates with your level of commitment. I know that I have not always told you how much I appreciate the help, but I will never forget what you have done for me.

## Paul's Acknowledgments

The first person that I need to thank is my wonderful, loving wife, who has stood by me and held me up throughout this entire process. I don't know how I got lucky enough to land her in the first place, but I sure am glad she's been willing to put up with me and stay around. She has not only managed to provide me with patience and support, but has also kept our house running in (what might as well have been) my absence. I have spent every spare minute for many months working on this project, and she has only pulled me away to take care of absolute necessities like eating, sleeping, and making sure the bills get paid. She is the light that guides me on my journey and the rock that I lean on when I need support. I love her more than I can put into words. Thank you, my love, for being the wonderful and loving person that you are!

Next, I need to thank Patrick for talking me into helping him with this book. There are still times when I am not sure whether I should hug him or slug him, but it has been a rewarding and educational experience. Being involved in a project like this is not something that everyone has the opportunity to do, and I am grateful that he selected me as his coauthor. I am privileged to have him as a friend and a coworker and hope that both continue for a long time to come. I now have a full understanding of something he told me not long after we met: "Writing a book was both the most difficult, and the most rewarding thing I have ever done." Not only do I understand the sentiment, but now I share it with him as well. The experience leaves me feeling both elevated and humbled at the same time. Thank you, my friend, for both the pain and the joy that accompany this project!

I would also like to thank all of the people who have provided me with the code (both good and bad) that I used as examples in this book. I have had the opportunity to learn not only from my own mistakes, but also from the mistakes of those I work and interact with professionally. I need to thank my friend and coworker Mike Lanyzs specifically for providing the SP that creates an SP in another database that I used in the Immediate Solutions in Chapter 19.

Finally, I want to thank my parents, and especially my grandmother, for the love and support that they provided me when I was growing up and first getting into this business. Without their guidance and support, I have no idea where I would be today. I have them to thank for my education and the support that kept me going in the early years when things didn't always turn out the way I planned. I love you, Mom and Dad, and I am glad that you are my parents. My grandmother will always occupy a special place in my heart. I spent several years living with her, and she spent a couple of years living with me. She moved in with my mother when we relocated to Florida from South Carolina, and I miss her a lot. She has always been there when I needed her and has supported me through all my successes and failures over the years. I hope she knows I will always be here for her if she needs me. I love you, Gram, and thank you for all your love and support!

# Contents at a Glance

# Table of Contents

**Chapter 7**
**Data Transformation Services (DTS)** ................................................................ 281

# Introduction

Thanks for buying *SQL Server 2000 Black Book*.

Welcome to the most exciting version of Microsoft SQL Server released to date. Whether this is your first exposure to Microsoft SQL Server or you are upgrading from a previous version, you are sure to find SQL Server 2000 a joy to work with. Over the years, Microsoft SQL Server has evolved from a state-of-the-art client/ server database platform into a word-class n-tier database platform that delivers all the power and functionality you need to produce both client/server and Web-enabled applications that will simply amaze your users. Here is the database platform that will take you into the new millennium in style. With new data types, user-defined functions, Internet support, and many more new features, this version of SQL Server is poised to take the market by storm.

*SQL Server 2000 Black Book* will help you make the most of this exciting new version of SQL Server, as well as provide you with many tips and techniques that can be applied to legacy systems back to at least SQL Server 6.5 and forward into future versions of SQL Server for years to come. This book provides help and guidance for building and configuring your SQL Server and designing rock-solid maintenance plans. Then it moves on to database design, development, and performance tuning topics that will help you make the most of this remarkable database platform.

## Is This Book for You?

*SQL Server 2000 Black Book* was written with the intermediate or advanced user in mind. One of the points emphasized in this book is that you can solve any technical problem you are faced with using the tools available to you. What are those tools? How do you research answers to questions? How do you know if you can trust the sources you consult? How do particular features really work, and will they work for you? We cover all of these questions and many more in the pages of this book. We hope that you enjoy reading it and learn as much from it as we did writing it.

This book is geared toward two basic groups of readers. The first group is the database administrators with an intermediate to advanced level of SQL Server knowledge and experience. The second group is SQL developers, also with an intermediate to advanced level of SQL Server knowledge and experience. The Tools chapter (Chapter 5), and the SQL chapter (Chapter 9) in particular are provided to ensure that readers have a solid grounding in these two areas, because this information is key to understanding the material presented in later chapters. Some beginners may find these chapters useful as well. You should possess a good working knowledge of SQL Server and Transact-SQL programming. This book also assumes a basic understanding of Windows NT and windows programs and utilities in general.

Among the topics that are covered are:

- Hardware choices for server planning

- Server maintenance routines every database administrator should know

- New features available in SQL Server 2000

- Advanced SQL programming techniques

- Advanced data manipulation routines

- Database design guidelines for enterprise-level databases

This book is written as an extension to the *Microsoft SQL Server Black Book* published by The Coriolis Group in 1997. While the first book focused mainly on installing and configuring SQL Server, this book delves deeply into what is required to take full advantage of the capabilities and features of SQL Server 2000. This book has a great deal more information about building good relational databases and using the Transact-SQL programming language to build robust applications.

We have tried to keep the language in this book as clear and matter-of-fact as possible. We have supplied you with a substantial technical background, while also supplying numerous hands-on examples to help you quickly become familiar with various topics. This book can be used as a tutorial or as a desktop reference to help you get the most from SQL Server 2000. With this book in hand, you will have no problem creating and maintaining enterprise-level solutions with SQL Server 2000 at their core.

# How to Use This Book

Each chapter in this book is broken into two sections. The first part of each chapter presents explanatory material about the topics covered in the chapter. The second part of the chapter (the Immediate Solutions) supplies you with some step-by-step examples that reinforce and expand on the information provided in the first part of the chapter as well as providing hands-on practice with the concepts being presented. Chapters 1 through 8 cover installation, configuration, tools and utilities, and setting up the sample databases used throughout the remainder of the book. After completing this section of the book, you should have a working SQL Server 2000 server with a solid maintenance plan in place and the sample databases installed and be ready to work through the examples in the remainder of the book.

# The *Black Book* Philosophy

Written by experienced professionals, Coriolis *Black Books* provide immediate solutions to global programming and administrative challenges, helping you complete specific tasks, especially critical ones that are not well documented in other books. The *Black Book*'s unique two-part chapter format—thorough technical overviews followed by practical immediate solutions—is structured to help you use your knowledge, solve problems, and quickly master complex technical issues to become an expert. By breaking down complex topics into easily manageable components, this format helps you quickly find what you're looking for, with the diagrams and code you need to make it happen.

Writing this book has been both difficult and rewarding. It is always interesting to work with a beta version of a product this complex, but writing a book using a product beta can be especially challenging. When the final release version of the product was reviewed, we made very effort to make sure we were up-to-date and that nothing had changed. If you find something that is perhaps a bit different than the actual product, we apologize.

We welcome your feedback on this book. You can either email The Coriolis Group at **ctp@coriolis.com**, or you can reach the authors on the Internet through email. Patrick can be reached at **pdalton@telocity.com**, and Paul can be reached at **prwhitehead@email.msn.com**. Please do not hesitate to send us feedback— whether positive or negative—concerning this book. Errata, updates, and more are available at **www.coriolis.com**.

# Chapter 1

## Server Hardware

Systems administrators face many challenges today in setting up a new server, regardless of the operating system (OS), application, and hardware manufacturer. An often difficult task is to adapt the installation to the needs of the environment. Administrators should look at as many factors as possible prior to setup to ensure that the machine is configured to the requirements of the users and the application load placed on the server. This approach will help spare administrators from having to upgrade the equipment almost immediately when their performance expectations are not met.

Understanding the basic components of server hardware is important for planning your first installation, reinstallation, or upgrade. The following pages will help clear the way and help you choose or configure your server hardware.

## Recommended System Configurations

There are many aspects of a system configuration that should be considered. You need to think about how much of a load the server needs to be able to handle. You also need to think about what part of the system will most likely be your bottleneck. And unfortunately, you'll probably need to keep an eye on the budget as well.

Microsoft's recommendations for your system and what most administrators have found to be a more realistic configuration for your server are quite different. Keep in mind that Microsoft's recommended minimum configuration is just that, the bare minimum that SQL Server will install on. Microsoft's recommendations should be implemented with care. Each environment is unique and is rarely a fit for minimums or guidelines. Likewise, other recommendations should also not be followed blindly. Recommendations are intended to give you an idea of where to start and should not be considered the end all solution for choosing your system or platform.

The system requirements for installing Microsoft SQL server are actually very easy to meet, and often lead the administrator into a false sense of security with regard to how well the server will perform. Table 1.1 contains Microsoft's minimum system requirements. Remember, these are the *minimum* system requirements.

The minimum CPU recommendation of an Intel-based Pentium 166 is usually a poor choice for a production machine. This kind of machine should only be considered for a development-type environment. Even then, it should only be used for very light loads. The preference is to use a Pentium II 400MHz or equivalent, at minimum. But depending on the application, processor speed will probably be much less important than memory or disk subsystems.

That's not to say that you should discard your current machine or scrap your plans for a cheaper alternative. Budgets and real-world requirements often do not allow a top-of-the-line machine for every project. The idea is to put your best performing machine as well as your money where it will do the most good.

If you are using existing hardware for your data server, take a good inventory of what makes the target machine tick. Know the specifics of the disk access time and memory configuration. Benchmark the machine wherever possible to get an idea of how well it is performing against others in the same class. You might find a less expensive alternative to the planned configuration. Sometimes, a simple memory upgrade is good enough to get a server performing reasonably well.

The minimum RAM recommendation of 32MB for Standard Edition and 64MB for Enterprise Edition is also usually a poor choice for a production machine or even a development machine. Development servers with a very light load should have

**Table 1.1   Microsoft's minimum system configuration.**

| Item | Requirement |
|------|-------------|
| Computer | Intel or Compatible |
| CPU | Pentium 166MHz or higher, Pentium PRO, Pentium III, or the minimum processor required for your operating system, which varies for SQL Server editions |
| Memory (RAM) | Enterprise Edition: 64MB, minimum<br>Standard Edition: 32MB minimum |
| Hard disk space | SQL Server 2000:<br>180MB (full)<br>170MB (typical)<br>65MB (minimum)<br>90MB (client tools only)<br>Analysis Services: 50MB<br>English Query: 12MB |

a minimum of 128MB of RAM, especially if you are running Windows 2000. Actually, the minimum amount of memory in *any* machine needs to be 128MB for Window NT 4 and 192MB for Windows 2000. You would be hard-pressed to even try to install Windows 9x on a system with 32MB of RAM. RAM is a very performance-sensitive item that can make a significant difference and is relatively cheap and easy to add to a system. Most newly installed production servers today are configured with 256MB to 2GB of RAM with the occasional 4GB machine. Current hardware and specific operating systems can even handle up to 16GB, whereas Windows 2000 DataCenter Server will recognize up to 64GB of RAM. DataCenter is not likely to be a widespread solution due to cost, but rather a hosting solution for only the larger installs.

Always specify more RAM than you think you will need for the server. Have at least 256MB of RAM for a production server. This amount of memory gives you plenty of spacc for Microsoft SQL Server and a good amount of data cache and procedure cache for performance. You cannot go wrong by adding RAM. Even on an old Pentium Pro processor, giving it additional RAM will allow it to run very well.

Adding RAM to a server is almost always the best starting point in improving performance. However, don't forget about multiprocessor machines. Machines that can hold four or more processors normally have a higher I/O bandwidth as well as improved upgrade paths. As important as RAM is—and it is *very* important—you also need to take a good look at your drive subsystem. Databases are by nature very I/O-intensive, and your drives can quickly become the bottleneck of the system.

With constant changes in hardware, any server purchase you make today will likely be outdated by the time you finally get your system up and running. This can be very frustrating. Consequently, you should buy servers with good expandability and lots of options. The potential expansion allows you to keep up with changes in the industry and react to changes in software requirements over time. You may want to purchase brand-name servers so that you don't invest money in machines that have poor technical support or that might not be supported the following year. *Always* check the Windows Hardware Compatibility List (HCL). This is a must. Check each component, from CPU to disk controller, when needed. This ensures that you will not have an operating system problem with the server you are configuring.

---

**NOTE:** *You can check the current HCL online at* ***www.microsoft.com/hcl/default.asp*** *to get up-to-date information on available options.*

---

You may want to configure your servers with a RAID disk subsystem for your data, which will be covered in detail later in the chapter. When reliable access to data is critical, you should require some sort of RAID configuration for the data to reside on. With the capability of Microsoft Windows NT to implement RAID at the operating system level, this is easily accomplished with even a limited budget. But keep in mind that a hardware solution is always going to perform much better than a software solution.

You may also want to try to keep the operating system and program files separate from the data and log files. Place these files on a separate disk and controller from the data files as well as the log files and mirror the disk when the budget allows. This provides the maximum amount of protection from hard drive failures while keeping performance at the highest possible levels. The number of disks in the RAID 5 array can be as few as three and as many as the disk subsystem can support.

Not everyone can afford this type of configuration for his or her hardware. Nevertheless, it is highly recommended for a fault-tolerant data server. If your budget is tight, cut the hardware mirror and RAID controller out of the plans for the operating system drives and transaction log drives. The data drive RAID subsystem should be the last system you relinquish. Use the built-in, software-driven, RAID option on Microsoft Windows NT servers only as a last resort. You should use this feature and set up your own fault-tolerant disk system for storing data only if no other option is available.

Given the many ways Microsoft SQL Server can write backups of databases to shared drives on other machines, a tape drive for backups is not required on the data server as well. However, this can be a nice feature if you run around-the-clock operations and need to keep performance at high levels 24 hours a day. Moving the backup software and hardware load to another machine is in keeping with the distributed-load concept, which is becoming popular in many enterprises today. You will find techniques in Chapter 5 that will allow you to keep the tape drives off your database server. If you must put your tape drive in the database server, remember *not* to attach it to the same controller as the data and log devices. (This could slow down performance unnecessarily.)

Invest in a good network interface card—a card with as much bus speed and bandwidth as possible. If you are setting up a cluster, it is recommended that you put two network cards in the server: one for user connections and the other for cluster communications. Standard 100BaseTx Bus Mastering network cards are considered a standard part of servers. Some administrators like to connect to their servers using a switch instead of a hub. Packet switches for heavily used servers are a must. They allow you to connect at full duplex as well as limit the bottleneck of slow networks. If you are setting up a large server environment, you may even want to consider Gigabit Ethernet or some other high bandwidth option for your backplane.

Most of the time you won't need to go overboard on the CD-ROM because you may rarely use it for production purposes. Try to use whichever speed comes with the server. You definitely want to watch where you connect your CD-ROM drive. Most brand-name servers are shipped with IDE CD-ROMs. This keeps the CD-ROM off the SCSI data channels. Placing the CD-ROM or other slow devices, like tape drives, on the same channel as the data slows the entire bus to a crawl. So, if you are going to install a tape backup drive directly on your server, put it on a separate bus from the data.

There is no need for expensive monitors, video cards, or sound cards. This is where you can save your money and buy more RAM. Keep it simple. Video memory is not an issue on a data server. And there is no reason for a sound card in a data server unless you want to hear the server say, "I am slowing down now. Please let your users know. Never mind, they already know." If you follow the recommendations in this book, your server will be just a data server, which is best for your users.

Verify that you have full functionality on the server before installing Microsoft SQL Server. One of the hardest things to do is troubleshoot problems when you have no idea what is working and what is not. Assume nothing. Always use the break-it-down-into-the-simplest-form approach in troubleshooting. If you cannot get out on the network, no one will be able to connect to your server for data.

Consider using a redundant power supply for your unit. Keeping the data available should be any systems administrator's primary focus. Use an uninterruptible power supply (UPS) that is reliable, and test it occasionally. An untested backup strategy is just that: untested. If you think you're under pressure now, wait until the backup won't restore and the system your boss has invested thousands of dollars in does not work. See Table 1.2 for an example of what is considered a minimum system configuration in today's production environment.

Now that you've been presented with the preliminary details and discussion, let's get into more in-depth detail about a question that always comes up when choosing a system: What goes under the hood?

**Table 1.2   Recommended minimum system configuration.**

| Item | Requirement |
| --- | --- |
| Computer | Intel or Compatible. |
| CPU | Pentium II 400MHz or higher. Dual capability. |

*(continued)*

**Table 1.2    Recommended minimum system configuration *(continued)*.**

| Item | Requirement |
|---|---|
| Memory (RAM) | Enterprise Edition: 256MB minimum<br>Standard Edition: 128MB minimum |
| Hard disk space | SQL Server 2000:<br>180MB (full)<br>170MB (typical)<br>65MB (minimum)<br>90MB (client tools only)<br>Analysis Services: 50MB<br>English Query: 12MB |

# RAID Configurations

Disk subsystem performance is not always easy to figure out. There are so many important questions to resolve. What type of drives should I use? If I use a RAID, what level should I use? Different levels of RAID have different performance characteristics, and for this reason, you need to consider what type of performance you need. Where do you need the best performance on a RAID set? Read or Write?

Let's consider what RAID is. RAID is an acronym for Redundant Array of Independent (or Inexpensive, depending on who you ask or what you consider inexpensive) Disks (or Devices, also depending on who you ask). A RAID array is a collection of drives that collectively act as a single storage system, which can, in most cases, tolerate the failure of a drive without losing data and can operate independently of each other.

A research group at the University of California at Berkeley coined the term "RAID," defining six RAID levels, 0 through 5. Each level provides a different way to spread data across multiple drives—a compromise between cost and speed. Understanding these levels is important because each level is optimized for a different use. Since the initial introduction of RAID, a few new RAID levels have been defined. Some of these are included in this section as well.

- *RAID 0*—Striped disk with no fault tolerance. See Figure 1.1. RAID level 0 is not redundant and so, does not truly fit the "RAID" acronym. In level 0, data is split across drives, resulting in higher data throughput. Because no redundant information is stored, performance is very good in both reading and writing operations, but the failure of just one disk results in the loss of all data in the array. This level of RAID should never be used in a mission critical environment. This level is commonly referred to as striping.

- *RAID 1*—Mirroring and duplexing. See Figure 1.2. RAID level 1 provides redundancy by duplicating all data from one drive to another drive. The

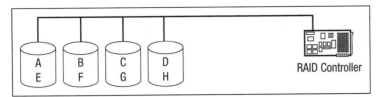

Figure 1.1    RAID 0.

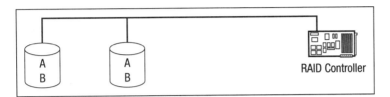

Figure 1.2    RAID 1.

performance of a level 1 array is only slightly better than a single drive, but if either drive fails, no data is lost. The biggest performance increase in this RAID level is in sequential reads and writes. It is a good entry-level redundant system because only two drives are required; however, because one drive is used to store a duplicate of the data, the cost per megabyte is high. This level is commonly referred to as mirroring.

- *RAID 0+1*—Mirroring of striped drives. See Figure 1.3. RAID level 0+1 provides redundancy and performance by mirroring two sets of RAID 0 stripes. Most current RAID controllers automatically provide redundancy and performance by mirroring if you configure an even number of four or more drives as a mirror set. This level is your best option for both Read and Write I/O performance.

- *RAID 1E*—Mirroring and spreading the "Hot Spare" across all drives. See Figure 1.4. RAID level 1E, recently created by IBM, takes a mirror set plus a Hot Spare drive and "stripes" the Hot Spare across all drives. This gives the performance of a RAID 0 by adding additional drives as well as the redundancy of RAID 1.

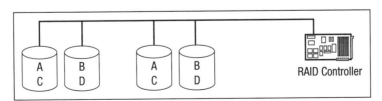

Figure 1.3    RAID 0+1.

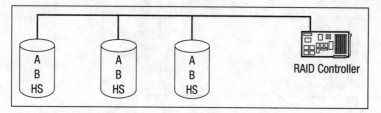

**Figure 1.4    RAID 1E.**

- *RAID 2*—Hamming code ECC. See Figure 1.5. RAID level 2, which uses Hamming error correction codes, is intended for use with drives that do not have built-in error detection. All SCSI drives support built-in error detection, so this level is of little use when using SCSI drives. This level is not used and not even supported in today's high-end RAID controllers.

- *RAID 3*—Parallel transfer with parity. See Figure 1.6. RAID level 3 stripes data at a byte level across several drives, with parity stored on one drive. It is otherwise similar to level 4. Byte-level striping requires hardware support for efficient use. This level is also not normally used or supported.

- *RAID 4*—Independent data disks with shared parity. See Figure 1.7. RAID level 4 stripes data at a block level across several drives, with parity stored on one drive. The parity information allows recovery from the failure of any single drive. The performance of a level 4 array is very good for Reads (the same as level 0). Writes, however, require that parity data be updated each time. This slows small random Writes, in particular, though large Writes or

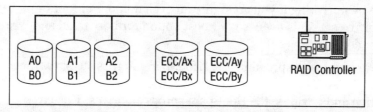

**Figure 1.5    RAID 2.**

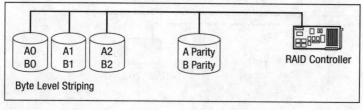

**Figure 1.6    RAID 3.**

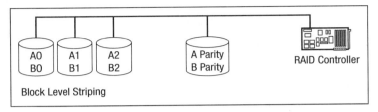

**Figure 1.7    RAID 4.**

sequential Writes are fairly fast. Because only one drive in the array stores redundant data, the cost per megabyte of level 4 arrays can be fairly low.

- *RAID 5*—Independent data disks with distributed parity blocks. See Figure 1.8. RAID level 5 is similar to level 4, but distributes parity among the drives. This can speed small Writes in multiprocessing systems because the parity disk docs not become a bottleneck. Because parity data must be skipped on each drive during Reads, however, the performance for Reads tends to be considerably lower than a level 4 array, but much higher than a level 1 array for random access. The cost per megabyte is the same as level 4. This is the most commonly used RAID level today.

- *RAID 5E*—Independent data disks with distributed parity blocks. See Figure 1.9. RAID level 5E, also recently created by IBM, is the same concept

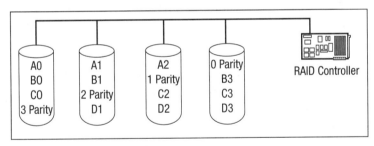

**Figure 1.8    RAID 5.**

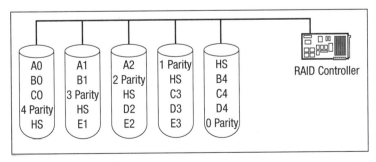

**Figure 1.9    RAID 5E.**

as RAID 1E. The Hot Spare drive is "striped" across all the drives in the array, and just like RAID 1E, gives you added performance of an additional disk in the array. Because the use of a Hot Spare drive is highly recommended, this level may very well become the most popular one to implement.

- *RAID 6*—Independent data disks with two independent distributed parity schemes. See Figure 1.10. RAID level 6 is very similar to level 5, the difference being that level six requires an additional drive for an additional parity scheme. The Write performance is even worse than level 5 or a single disk because of the overhead of writing two independent parity bits. (I do not know of any implementations of this type of RAID level.)

The most widely used RAID levels are levels 1, 0+1, and 5. But for any RAID level, you need to consider dropping in a Hot Spare. If a drive fails in a RAID 5 set, the performance hit is quite severe because the system has to calculate the parity bit every time the set is accessed. If you add a Hot Spare to the controller, when a drive fails, the controller automatically rebuilds the set using the Hot Spare. You still get a performance hit, but only when the set is rebuilding, not while it's waiting for you to replace the drive, then do the rebuild. This is especially useful if a drive fails late on a Friday night.

When deciding on the level of RAID to use, keep in mind the type of performance needed for your application. In the case of SQL Server, the log files are very Write-intensive. The data files are both Write- and Read-intensive. Because RAID 5 has good Read performance, and RAID 1 (or 0+1) has excellent Read and Write performance, the best configuration is to have the data files and the log files reside on RAID 0+1 sets. If a RAID 0+1 will not fit your budget, then the data files can be placed on a RAID 5 set, but you should still push to keep the log files on a RAID 0+1 set. You should always keep the data files and log files on separate channels. An even better configuration puts the OS, data files, and log files all on separate controllers. Sometimes this is not possible because of tight budgets, so you should at least try separate channels if you have to share a controller.

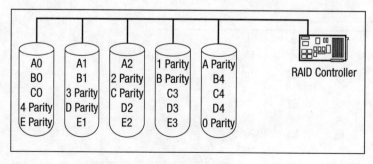

**Figure 1.10    RAID 6.**

# Disk Subsystems

Disk subsystems are typically the biggest bottlenecks in a SQL server. This is because most SQL applications are very I/O-intensive. The more I/O-intensive the database, the more disk subsystem bandwidth you need.

## Drive Types

There are very few options when it comes to drive types. As a result, it may make it easier to decide which one to choose. Basically you have three choices: Integrated Drive Electronics (IDE), Small Computer Serial Interface (SCSI), and Fiber Channel. For all intents and purposes, SCSI and Fiber Channel are basically the same drives with different interfaces.

### IDE

For almost all cases, IDE is out of the question. There are very few options for IDE that allow for more than four drives on a system, let alone enough options for a good RAID configuration. IDE also does no error correction internally and does not support asynchronous I/O. And until recently, IDE didn't even have a decent throughput for server use. By the time IDE got close to the throughput of SCSI, SCSI had doubled its throughput capacity with the advent of SCSI160. IDE works fine for a workstation, but for servers, go with a SCSI or higher throughput drive subsystem. If you must use IDE, try to separate the drives across both channels or use one of the new IDE RAID controllers.

### SCSI

SCSI channels have currently increased to 160MB/s, taking SCSI performance higher than Fiber Channel and Serial Storage Architecture (SSA) for now. This doesn't necessarily mean that SCSI160 is going to perform faster than Fiber Channel. SCSI is only half duplex and Fiber Channel is full duplex. One of the problems with SCSI is that it is unlikely to get much faster throughput. SCSI cables can only handle so much data, and they are limited in length. The channels are also still limited to 16 devices, including the controller. This can restrict the amount of drive space you can add to your server. Normally, this is not too much of a problem, but very large databases can grow quickly and fill up your SCSI drives.

Figure 1.11 illustrates what is probably your best bet for SCSI RAID configurations.

This configuration is not always possible, especially on low-end servers. Figure 1.12 represents a more feasible configuration for mid-range servers.

If you must put two or more RAID sets on a single RAID controller, be sure to separate the sets onto different channels of the controller.

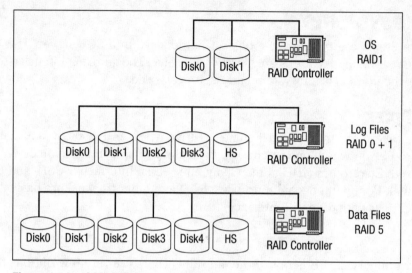

Figure 1.11    SCSI RAID—best configuration.

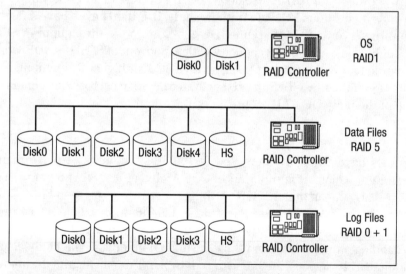

Figure 1.12    SCSI RAID—more affordable configuration.

The configurations shown in Figures 1.11 and 1.12 have the log file set on its own RAID controller. This allows you to set the controller cache to 100-percent Write, thus increasing the Write performance on an already fast system. The other controllers need to remain at 50-percent Read and 50-percent Write.

If you can only purchase one RAID controller, you might want to think about putting the two OS drives on a SCSI controller instead of the RAID controller, and setting up an OS level mirror. This gives you the redundancy on the OS drives that you should have as well as leaves the RAID controller for the drive sets that need the performance the most (data and log devices).

When shopping for a RAID controller, you need to make sure you get one that comes with a battery backup. This is essential to avoid loosing data that is in cache and not yet written to disk. If cache data is lost before being written to disk, it causes data corruption in your database.

# Fiber Channel

Fiber Channel drives don't have quite the limitation of SCSI. Fiber cables can handle gigabit speeds and long distances. And in time, the Fiber Channel drives and controllers will catch up to the current speed of Fiber Channel network devices. This kind of performance is exactly what you need for database servers. Currently, Fiber Channel disk subsystems are limited to 126 devices and 100MB/s throughput. Fiber Channel also uses 98 percent of the channel as opposed to SCSI, which uses only about 90 percent because of packet overhead. Fiber Channel is also full duplex, whereas SCSI is only half duplex. Basically, what this means is that communication to and from the fiber drives can occur simultaneously, whereas SCSI can only communicate in one direction at a time.

About the only problem with Fiber Channel drives is cost. Any item with fiber costs quite a bit more than SCSI. From the controllers to the drives and including the cables, there is a premium to pay. But for high-end servers, there is no question that you need the added performance and scalability. When considering Fiber Channel, keep in mind that your best bet is a Network Attached Storage (NAS) device or a Storage Area Network (SAN).

### NAS/SAN

A rising trend in enterprise storage is consolidation. Consolidating storage into very few areas can ease administration and management as well as lessen redundancy. What does enterprise storage have to do with SQL Server? It's pretty simple really. The need to consolidate storage and make it more expandable has created two new technologies: NAS and SAN. These two technologies have made it possible to expand data to almost limitless sizes.

NAS devices are storage appliances. Basically, they are large, single purpose servers that plug into your network. Think of them as high-speed file servers. Large NAS devices can grow to a multiterabyte size. There is a huge battle brewing between SAN and NAS technologies today, and in time, the database server will be the biggest winner.

SANs are multiple-server, multiple-storage networks and can grow to extremely large sizes, larger than 400TB. A SAN is basically a "private network" separated from the LAN running the SCSI protocol as opposed to a network protocol. All servers that need to access storage on the SAN have their own fiber connection to this private network. Backing up large files on the SAN has no effect on the LAN because all the traffic occurs within the SAN. Of course, you can always set up a "private LAN" for your NAS devices to limit the excess network traffic on your main LAN.

Let's take a look at both technologies to determine which one you should use if any at all. Let's first look at the difference between the two. There is only a slight difference between a NAS appliance and the function of a SAN. A NAS appliance uses protocols, such as Network File System (NFS) and NetBIOS, to serve files, and a SAN uses a SCSI protocol to serve data blocks. NAS appliances serve files on request, whereas a SAN grants direct access to the disks. This makes the SAN appear to be a locally installed drive, as opposed to the NAS, which looks just like a file server.

One way to compare these two technologies is to consider that a NAS appliance uses Ethernet or a network interface to connect the disk subsystem and server, whereas a SAN uses SCSI. This allows for different types of clients to connect to a high-performance NAS appliance.

SANs are a big improvement on a standard server storage model, providing high-speed data access as well as expandability well beyond almost all database needs. What a SAN does is join several storage devices into a pool that is partitioned. Each server in the SAN has its own assigned storage partition. This may look like a standard server storage model, but it is not. The difference is that a SAN lets you quickly retrieve data, change partitions, and assign storage space. A SAN also allows you to back up data without affecting your LAN.

These two technologies are becoming very important solutions for high-end servers. With the expandability and the performance of these solutions, NAS and SAN have quickly become the de facto standard, replacing SCSI-only solutions (I say SCSI-only solutions because the drives in most of the NAS/SAN solutions are usually SCSI).

How does the vendor squeeze Fiber Channel performance out of SCSI drives? The vendor spreads the SCSI drives across several RAID controllers and channels. Although SCSI drives are not as fast as Fiber Channel, this configuration uses less expensive SCSI drives, making the combined bandwidth perform pretty impressively as well as making the expandability quite amazing. The key is to have as many spindles as possible to spread the write operations across many drives.

### Nuts and Bolts of a NAS

A NAS appliance is basically a file server dedicated to storage only, which you plug into your network. As you can see in Figure 1.13, the NAS appliance plugs directly

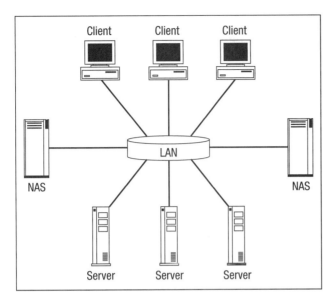

**Figure 1.13    NAS appliance.**

into your existing LAN, making it accessible to all types of clients. These clients send file requests directly to the NAS, bypassing all other servers on the network.

Most NAS appliances run a highly optimized OS that is embedded and a stripped down Unix-type kernel that only serves files to clients. The OS kernel is optimized to do nothing more than serve files and use a network connection. This makes the kernel very small and decreases complexity while increasing performance, because it doesn't have any excess drivers or services running. This also makes the kernel very stable and reliable, keeping uptime very high and allowing a system administrator to worry less about "Blue Screens of Death," AbEnds, and other OS crashes.

The appliances normally also include an I/O processor and a file processor to get the best disk and I/O performance possible. NAS appliances typically allow you to configure the RAID level of the array. In general, a NAS device gives you the options of RAID 0+1, 4, or 5. Refer to the "RAID Configurations" section earlier in this chapter for more information on RAID levels. A choice of RAID options in combination with the capability to use multiple Gigabit Ethernet cards gives you quite an impressive performance option for storage.

A NAS appliance normally has a proprietary file system and can serve files across platforms because it uses network redirectors, like NFS and NetBIOS, over TCP/IP networks. NAS appliances are less expensive than standard servers, so you can buy a NAS appliance for Windows NT at a very low price compared to any other type of file server. For this reason, a NAS appliance's cost for performance and scalability makes it a very promising package worth considering.

One last note about the NAS approach and what it means to the database community. Over the last few years, network bandwidth, which is at the base of the NAS system, has increased in throughput at incredible rates. Network bandwidth and speed will continue to increase due to the Internet and video requirements that are being placed on networks. These network improvements will mean that NAS systems may well be positioned to become a major player in the storage arena and a must-have for very large databases.

### Anatomy of a SAN

A SAN is unlike a NAS appliance in that a SAN is a network of devices as opposed to just a device itself. A SAN is a private network separated from the main LAN. Let's take a look at the characteristics of a SAN.

SANs are private storage networks that include normal devices, like servers, and storage devices, like disk drives and tape drives. Each server and storage device uses a SCSI or Fiber Channel connection to the SAN, so every server receives high-speed access to the data storage. Each server treats its portion of SAN space just like a directly connected disk, and the SAN uses the same communication protocol that servers use to communicate with their attached disks. The storage sits behind each server, so unlike the NAS model, clients must send file requests to the servers to receive data on the SAN storage devices.

SANs provide the benefit of storage flexibility as well as expandability. SANs give you the option to reallocate storage space from one server to another. You can also just add storage to your SAN, and then allocate it where needed. System administrators can manage the storage in a SAN fairly easily. The management tools that come with a SAN make it simple for the system administrator to repartition storage space, which in turn prevents too much wasted space on one server while another server is running out of space. When setting up a SAN, you can add tape systems to your SAN for your backups. This allows you to back up your data without affecting the main LAN as well as speed backups because the tapes will basically be "local" to your server.

# Clustering

Another consideration when configuring your Microsoft SQL Server 2000 server is clustering, which is becoming a very popular setup for SQL Servers. Microsoft Clustering Service is a failover, storage-sharing cluster. It requires the shared drives to be external. You especially need to check the HCL on Microsoft's Web site for Cluster Service because hardware compatibility is even more stringent for these services.

Starting with SQL Server 7.0, the option of an Active-Active cluster instead of just an Active-Passive cluster was introduced. This new option allows you to run two independent SQL Servers that "cover for each other" should one of them fail. They both have their own databases, but if one server fails, the other one takes over all the databases. This can make the larger expenditure of two big servers worthwhile by not having one server just sitting around mostly unused.

With the release of Windows 2000 DataCenter, Microsoft Clustering Service is now able to incorporate four servers. With SQL Server on a four cluster setup, you can run an Active-Active-Active-Passive cluster, which only leaves one out of four servers unused: A four-way Active cluster is also an option. This type of cluster requires the use of a NAS or SAN device to be able to share drive space among the four servers.

If you have servers that are mission critical to run at all times, clustering is the only way to go. If you are going to be using an Active-Active type configuration, you need to keep in mind that your memory requirements as well as other hardware requirements may be higher. This is because you will be running two instances of SQL Server on each machine—four in a four-way cluster. See Chapter 3 for more details on clustering.

---

**NOTE:** *Disk subsystem clustering is also available through some of the network appliance vendors and should not be overlooked when considering a 24/7 solution.*

---

# Backups

Why are backups important to consider when you're planning a hardware setup? You have to think about how you're going to back up the database. Large databases take a long time to back up. In view of the fact that you cannot make your databases smaller because data is always increasing, you have to think of ways to make your backups faster.

There are several options when it comes to backing up servers. You can back up directly to tape, to local disk drives, to a network share, to a NAS device, or even to a tape system on a SAN. Each option has different costs, speeds, and complexities. All of these factors have to be considered when you're setting up your backup solution.

Tape drives are only so fast. But there are ways around the slow speeds of these drives. Most of the current backup software can perform a "software RAID" with several drives. This includes redundancy as well as performance increases. Backing up your database to five different tape drives at once using a RAID 5 configuration gives you almost four times the performance, and it gives you some redundancy in case of tape media or drive failure. However, sometimes this solution isn't even good enough. Some databases grow to such immense sizes that large autoloading multidrive systems are required.

If you are going to be setting up a large NAS/SAN environment, the vendor you purchase the equipment from will most likely try to sell you a backup solution. If the vendor doesn't try to sell you some sort of backup solution, you may want to think about looking for another vendor.

Data always grows. A backup solution that barely fits the backup operation in your time window currently, surely won't in the near future. Keep the amount of time your backup operation will take in mind when planning your backup strategy. Make sure your backup solution can be expanded quickly and efficiently when needed.

# Specification of a New Server

Most people purchase servers with a dollar amount in mind and work backward from the price to the features that are available for that price. This often nets a slow server, which under performs when put under a load, or a machine that only provides minimal upgrades before becoming obsolete. The following list contains some helpful considerations when ordering hardware. If you stay focused on this list in its proposed order, you can meet most budgets and still provide adequate performance. Be sure to ask these questions when planning a server configuration:

1. Disk Subsystem

   a. How much disk space is required? Do not forget to allow for growth. Can you add drives easily?

   b. Availability? A server that is required to be up 24 hours a day and 7 days a week is harder to upgrade and change. Can the data be unavailable for high disk I/O operations? Does the subsystem need to support one-line spares? Will a shared disk subsystem work?

   c. Performance? What types of tasks will the disks support? If the tables are wide or large numbers of rows will be moved around, the speed of the drives and I/O will play a major role.

2. RAM

   a. How many large, in-memory operations will be performed? Will the application be performing large sort operations? Will there be a great deal of tempdb activity?

   b. Is this a single instance of SQL Server? If you are using the new multi-instance ability built into SQL 2000, you should plan for extra memory. (Static memory allocation will also prove helpful so one instance does not starve another for RAM.)

   c. Will this be a dedicated server? Will any other processes be run on this machine? Print Services, FTP, or file sharing can impede the performance of the server. If you are unable to off-load these types of activities, you will need more memory and CPU power than a dedicated server.

3. Internal Issues

   a. What kind of disk subsystem should I use? The new eight-way servers have incredible bus architecture and should be the first consideration for a high-speed system.

   b. How much activity will I have to deal with? If you are supporting a large number of users or processes that read and write a great deal of data from the disks, the bus architecture becomes more important than a server that supplies data to a report engine or a seldom written to database. If you are dealing with a batch processing application that handles the I/O in controlled bursts, the bus may play less of a role in your purchase decision.

   c. How many network cards should I put in the server? Will I be duplexing the network cards? Will I be putting a fiber controller in alongside network cards? Make sure the slots and available speeds make sense based upon the peripherals you are planning on purchasing.

4. CPU

   a. Will there be one or more processors? Can I add processors later without changing motherboards? Will I have to pay a contractor to come out and upgrade the server, or will I do it myself?

   b. Can I purchase additional processors later? Make sure the model you buy will be available for some time. Do not buy a model of processor that has been out for a few years because it may be hard to find additional processors six to eight months down the road when you need them.

   c. How scalable do I think the server will need to be? Some servers are just not planned to grow very much. It is rare, but it does happen. The server you are buying may be a stepping-stone to that "nice" server you can afford to buy when sales or business has provided the revenue to buy a new one. (Be careful, many of these servers become primary production boxes far longer than planned.)

   d. Will this be a dedicated server? If you are planning on having different applications share the space with SQL Server, you should consider a multiple CPU machine.

5. Backup strategy

a. What are the availability requirements for the database to the user community? How big is the window that a backup or restore must fit in? If you buy a small tape drive and have to throw a lot of data at it in a small window, you may find you will outgrow that hardware quickly. Think about the maintenance plans you will have to support when ordering hardware.

b. Should I choose a local or remote backup strategy for the database? Most of the backup software today has numerous services that run in the background and can perform many functions right on the server. Having these services on the server is easy, but can also impact performance. It is *highly* recommended that you choose a backup solution that migrates the load of backup to another server and disk subsystem.

c. How big of a window do I have to complete a backup? Whatever the amount of time, double it and use that to plan. (Data always grows.)

d. How big of a window do I have to restore the database? When you need to get some data back, how long will you typically have? Whatever amount of time you determine, divide it in half.

Many people buy servers that are "packaged" by a vendor without realizing they can order them to their specifications. You can ask for drives and controllers to be organized in a certain way, or you can order what you need from a single source and build it yourself. Always purchase servers from vendors that are well known and that have complete support for SQL Server. Take the time to ask other businesses their opinions and experiences working with certain vendors or certain servers. Check the newsgroups for tips on servers and reliability.

| Related solutions: | Found on page: |
|---|---|
| Cluster Installation | 60 |
| Creating a Maintenance Plan for the System Databases | 256 |
| Newsgroups and the Internet | 925 |

## Low-End Server

For low-end servers, a single processor server normally works well, but it would be best to at least buy a server that can be upgraded to a dual processor. When buying a new server, the slowest processor at the time of this writing, you are likely to find is a Pentium III 600MHz. This is more than enough CPU power for a low-end server. If you are using existing equipment, a Pentium II 400MHz or equivalent is sufficient.

For a low-end production server, 256MB of RAM should be the minimum. Today's memory prices are low enough to include this amount of RAM as a baseline. Low-end development servers, or any server for that matter, should never have less than 128MB of RAM.

Drive space always depends on the size of the database you will have. So, you will have to figure out the size of the drives needed. The configuration of the drives needs a bit more consideration and thought. See Table 1.3. Production servers need redundancy. For low-end servers, a single RAID 5 configuration provides decent performance as well as redundancy. If a RAID controller is unattainable, then a three-drive configuration will help performance (one drive for the OS, one drive for data files, and one drive for log files), but will be lacking in redundancy. The problem with this configuration is that if a drive fails, you'd better have a good recent backup.

## Mid-Range Server

For a mid-range server, a dual processor server will probably do the job. Your best bet may be to buy a server that can be upgraded to four processors in case you need extra power. This will also give you a machine with a decent system bus with good I/O.

These servers should start at 512MB of RAM and be upgradeable to at least 2GB. This is a very reasonable configuration for midsized servers.

Again, drive space will depend on what your needs are. But mid-range servers should definitely have at least one RAID controller. Two RAID controllers are desirable if you can squeeze it into your budget. Your data drive needs to be at

**Table 1.3   Low-end server minimum system configuration.**

| Item | Requirements |
|---|---|
| Computer | Intel or Compatible |
| CPU | Pentium II 400MHz or higher. Dual capable. |
| Memory (RAM) | 256MB minimum |
| Hard disk space | SQL Server 2000: <br> 180MB (full) <br> 170MB (typical) <br> 65MB (minimum) <br> 90MB (client tools only) <br> Analysis Services: 50MB <br> English Query: 12MB |

least a RAID 5 set, RAID 0+1 being the best for performance, and your log drive needs to be RAID 1 (or 0+1). Your OS should also be on its own RAID 1 if possible. Never put the OS on the same RAID set as your log files. And if you can avoid it, try to put the OS, data, and log files all on separate channels. The best configuration for this type of server is two RAID controllers with the OS and data drive on separate channels of one controller, and the log drive on its own controller with the cache set to 100% Write.

Table 1.4 lists the minimum server configuration for a mid-range server.

## High-End Server

High-end servers are intriguing to tune and configure. This is the type of server you can have a lot of fun with. As of this writing, the most Intel CPUs you can get in a single server, other than the IA-64 Itanium processors in beta, is eight. But the big companies are working on providing servers that contain thirty-two processors or more. That is quite a bit of power that most applications won't need. Current popular server configurations are 4- and 8-way servers with great system bus speed. The 8-way servers have twice the available bandwidth on the bus as the 4-way servers. This is a huge advantage for I/O-intensive applications, even if you only install 2 or 4 processors in the server. So, you may want to buy a system that is 8-processor capable, but only start with 4 processors.

Memory is quite important to SQL servers. A high-end server needs to start at 2GB of RAM and be capable of 8GB or more. Today's 8-way systems have this capability, and most of them are capable of handling 16GB.

Your best drive system for a high-end server is a NAS or SAN. These will provide you with the expandability and performance you need. These solutions also make it easier to set up clusters for redundancy.

**Table 1.4   Mid-range server minimum system configuration.**

| Item | Requirements |
| --- | --- |
| Computer | Intel or Compatible |
| CPU | Dual Pentium III 500MHz or higher. Quad capable. |
| Memory (RAM) | 512MB minimum |
| Hard disk space | SQL Server 2000: <br> 180MB (full) <br> 170MB (typical) <br> 65MB (minimum) <br> 90MB (client tools only) <br> Analysis Services: 50MB <br> English Query: 12MB |

If you are going to use SCSI drives, high-end systems need to have at least three RAID controllers: one with a RAID 1 set for the OS, one with a RAID 0+1 set for data files, and one with a RAID 0+1 set for log files. Spreading the drives on each controller across all possible channels also widens the I/O bandwidth.

Table 1.5 provides the minimum system configuration for a high-end server.

# Third-Party and Multiple Server Requirements

Purchasing software to run different applications can be very hard to do. One vendor assumes it is working with a pristine environment, while another uses non-standard naming conventions. Each vendor is not wrong for taking its approach; in fact many have valid reasons for how they arrived at the requirements for their software. Changing the environment of one software package to meet the needs of another can sometimes cause all kinds of tension and support problems. Here are some of the things you should look for when considering third-party software:

- If you are setting up a system for a third-party application, beware of the requirements for that system. Find out ahead of time how the special configurations will need to be set up to let a particular piece of software run well.

- You might find that a system configured to run one application well might not allow another application to run well at all. If this case arises, contact the vendor to determine how you can adjust your server configuration to best provide for both situations.

- Find out from the vendor what backup and recovery methods are recommended. This can help you determine how the server and hardware should be configured.

**Table 1.5    High-end server minimum system configuration.**

| Item | Requirements |
|---|---|
| Computer | Intel or Compatible |
| CPU | Quad Pentium III 600MHz or higher. Eight-way capable. |
| Memory (RAM) | 2GB minimum |
| Hard disk space | SQL Server 2000:<br>180MB (full)<br>170MB (typical)<br>65MB (minimum)<br>90MB (client tools only)<br>Analysis Services: 50MB<br>English Query: 12MB |

- Acquire a data model of the application before purchasing the server. A large number of tables do not always mean a complex system. Look for wide table structures that can cause I/O bottlenecks.

- If you have an existing NAS or a SAN setup or you are planning on installing one, you can use it with all your servers, from the low-end to the high-end. This is probably your best bet in a multiserver environment.

- Check the newsgroups for industry opinion on systems and applications. Other people have had to implement the products or systems you are considering.

The old saying "hindsight is 20/20" is a testament to being prepared. You cannot see all failures or issues ahead of time; everyone makes mistakes. By preparing yourself for these mistakes, you will know where to look, how to look, and what action to take to solve problems that arise. The fact that you are reading this book shows you are making an effort to be prepared.

| Related solutions: | Found on page: |
|---|---|
| Creating a Maintenance Plan for the System Databases | 256 |
| Newsgroups and the Internet | 925 |

# Hardware Hints

The information in this chapter might seem like a lot to think about before you install the OS and other software, but it will help you make better decisions about the type of machine you need. The following list contains the major factors to consider:

- More RAM is better. Use at least 256MB in a production server for best results.

- Disk I/O is a *very* important aspect of choosing a server.

- Think about your backup strategy beforehand. Make sure you can back up your database in the allotted amount of time.

- Use a RAID disk subsystem for your data when possible. The hardware-level RAID rather than the software-level RAID is the best choice in Windows NT.

- If you can afford Fiber Channel disk subsystems, use them. They will become the industry standard in the years to come.

- Use a separate drive set for OS and program files, and mirror that drive with a separate controller from the data if possible. If not, at least use a different channel on the controller. Also, use a separate drive set for data files and log files.

- Use a RAID 0+1 for data files and log files, and use separate controllers when possible setting the log files controller cache to 100% Write.

- When configuring high-end servers or multiserver environments, consider a NAS or SAN drive system. Don't forget to cluster the disk subsystem if the vendor supports that option.

- Always buy machines that can be upgraded in the future. If you are buying a 4-processor box, buy a machine that holds 8 processors to allow for an upgrade path.

- Remember: Databases always grow!

**1. Server Hardware**

# Chapter 2
## Windows Tuning

# In Depth

This chapter discusses tuning the Windows Operating System (OS) for optimal SQL Server performance. The considerations for both Windows NT 4 and Windows 2000 are very closely related. Although Microsoft did make many improvements in Windows 2000, many of the same tuning parameters still apply.

Because they are not server class operating systems, Windows 95 and Windows 98 are not covered in this chapter. You should not consider placing a production database on workstation operating systems. In both production and development environments, it is strongly recommended that you use a server class operating system for stability and performance. The workstation versions of Windows NT 4 and Windows 2000 do not have as robust a feature set as the server versions, but they still have the inherent stability of their server level counterparts. For this reason, the workstation versions of these operating systems are discussed in a few places.

For the sake of simplicity and to avoid the need to refer to both versions of the OS, the following references are used throughout this chapter to refer to the Windows Operating System. "Windows NT Server" is used to refer to the server versions of both Windows NT 4 and Windows 2000. "Windows NT Workstation" is used to refer to the workstation versions of these operating systems. "Windows NT" is used to reference Windows 2000 and Windows NT 4 without regard to edition. If a particular reference does not apply to a particular version, the exception is specified in the text.

## Deciding Which Windows Version to Install

The first step in tuning your server is to determine which version of Windows you are going to install. There are a number of considerations when making this decision, so this section covers the differences between versions in some detail to help you make the right choice for your environment.

Windows 2000 has several advantages over Windows NT 4, but the most important one is stability. Windows 2000 has proven itself to be more stable than previous versions of Windows NT. Even with the improvements made in Windows 2000, performance is still very similar to Windows NT 4. Windows 2000 supports Active Directory and will be the operating system of choice as we move forward, so you should consider using Windows 2000 when possible.  Upgrade paths and patches will be available for both operating systems for some time, but will eventually become Windows 2000-centric.

The number of editions of NT available can make selecting the appropriate one a daunting task. One consideration is the version of SQL Server 2000 that you will be installing. Table 2.1 shows the various editions of SQL Server 2000 and which versions and editions of Windows they are designed for.

Also, consider the number of processors you want to be able to use in your server when selecting the operating system. Table 2.2 lists the number of processors natively supported by the various editions of Windows NT.

The amount of memory supported by Windows NT varies between editions as well. Because memory is a key factor in system performance, you should review the information in Table 2.3 to determine which versions of Windows NT will support the amount of memory you plan to install. It is a good idea to leave room for future expansion if possible.

**Table 2.1   OS requirements listed by SQL Server 2000 Edition.**

| SQL Server 2000 Edition | Windows Version and Edition |
| --- | --- |
| Personal | Windows 2000 Millennium |
| | Windows 2000 Professional |
| | Windows NT 4 Workstation |
| | Windows 95 |
| | Windows 98 |
| Standard | Windows 2000 Server |
| | Windows NT 4 Server |
| Enterprise | Windows 2000 Advanced Server |
| | Windows 2000 DataCenter |
| | Windows NT 4 Enterprise |
| Windows CE | Windows CE |

**Table 2.2   Supported numbers of processors listed by operating system.**

| Windows Edition | Number of CPUs |
| --- | --- |
| Windows NT Workstation | 2 |
| Windows 2000 Professional | 2 |
| Windows NT Server | 4 |
| Windows 2000 Server | 4 |
| Windows NT Enterprise | 8 |
| Windows 2000 Advanced Server | 8 |
| Windows 2000 DataCenter | 32 |

Table 2.3    **Maximum supported memory.**

| Windows Edition | Memory |
| --- | --- |
| Windows NT 4 Workstation | 2GB |
| Windows 2000 Professional | 2GB |
| Windows NT 4 Server | 4GB |
| Windows 2000 Server | 4GB |
| Windows NT 4 Enterprise | 4GB |
| Windows 2000 Advanced Server | 8GB |
| Windows 2000 DataCenter | 64GB |

Although Windows NT 4 Enterprise Edition does not support more memory than the standard edition, it does handle memory differently. With the standard edition of Windows NT 4, a memory configuration of 4GB allows Windows to use 2GB and allows the application (in this case, SQL Server) to use 2GB, whereas the Enterprise edition of Windows NT 4 supplies 3GB of memory to the application and leaves 1GB for the OS. Because the memory allocated to SQL Server can make a significant difference in performance, this is an important fact to consider when choosing your operating system.

The combination of Windows 2000 DataCenter and SQL Server 2000 Enterprise Edition can support an impressive amount of RAM. There are no servers available as this is being written that can hold more RAM than the amount that is supported by Windows 2000 DataCenter. The good news is that Microsoft does not know when you start to receive diminishing returns from adding more memory to SQL 2000 because it has not yet been able to reach this point in testing. Depending on the application, you can quickly and easily find the performance curve that determines when you should add additional processors. With memory, as long as your database is larger than the amount of RAM in your server, adding memory will only help. Also, keep in mind that if you have plenty of RAM, there are tuning tricks in SQL Server that you can test on your applications to determine what improvements are available. Large in-memory sorts or pinning tables in memory are a couple of memory-intensive operations that only become viable if you have a large amount of memory to work with.

The number of processors supported as well as the maximum supported memory can provide sufficient information to make the necessary operating system selection; however, clustering capabilities can be another important factor. The Professional and Standard Editions of Windows NT Server do not support clustering of any kind. The Advanced Server Edition of Windows supports 2-node failover clusters as well as 32-node Network Load Balancing (NLB) clusters (NLB is primarily used for Web Servers). The DataCenter Edition of Windows 2000 supports 4-node failover clusters. Clustering is covered in more detail in Chapter 3.

When all of the preceding factors have been considered, your final decision will likely be a combination of the features you need, the features you want, and the budget you have available to cover the equipment and OS expenses. If you do not need clustering or support for more than four processors or 4GB of RAM, the Windows NT 4 Server Edition or Windows 2000 Server Edition is probably your best choice. If you need a 2-node cluster for your SQL Server, you will need to use either the Windows NT 4 Enterprise Edition or Windows 2000 Advanced Server Edition. If you require a 4-node cluster, or more than eight processors, or more than 8GB of RAM, then you need the Windows 2000 DataCenter Edition.

---

**NOTE:** *For the most efficient outcome in performance, the order in which you choose to purchase upgrades to your environment should be RAM first, bus and disk subsystem next, and then the type of processor configuration and upgrade path you want to have.*

---

# Installation

If you have set up a SQL Server before, there is a pretty good chance you have installed Windows NT as well. With this in mind, this section covers several important elements that can affect your system performance. Some of these factors you may not be aware of and others are details always focused on during a Windows NT installation.

There seems to be a lot of debate as to the best size allocation for your system partition. There are a few questions you should consider when making this decision. Do you normally install a parallel installation of Windows NT for troubleshooting? How much memory does your machine have?

---

**NOTE:** *Remember that your pagefile resides on your system partition unless you move it to another location.*

---

Does your budget provide enough resources to place the system partition on its own drive? Placing the system partition on a separate drive from your data and log files is highly recommended. Are you going to mirror the operating system drives?

It is also a good idea to install your applications on a separate partition from your OS installation to prevent your system partition from running out of space, which can cause the system to crash, and then be unable to boot. The application can share a physical device with the system partition, but the storage should be segregated to avoid filling up the system partition.

The minimum size that you should allocate for your system partition is 1.5GB plus the amount of RAM installed on your server. This configuration will provide enough space to install the OS, maintain your pagefile, and provide enough space for service packs and OS upgrades. With Windows NT 4, the largest partition that setup allows you to create is only 4GB, although Windows 2000 does not share this limitation. Although this was not a major concern a couple of years ago, today's servers are using much higher amounts of RAM. If the size of the system partition allowed by Windows NT 4 does not allow you enough space for this minimum space recommendation, you should plan to move the pagefile to a new partition once you have completed the installation. Take this extra partition into account when calculating the space to allocate for the system and application partitions.

Creating a parallel install can be extremely helpful for troubleshooting severe OS problems. This many not seem necessary with the Recovery Console that comes with Windows 2000, because most boot problems can be corrected from within the console. It is still a good idea to allocate enough space for a parallel install, to help you recover from catastrophic failures. Even if you do not initially create a parallel install, you might decide that it would be a good idea to do so in the future.

---

**NOTE:** *Some enterprises place the 1386 directory on the local drive along with service packs. This can be beneficial in a fluid and changing environment. However, a production machine may not need this because you are always able to boot from a CD if need be. Development servers or network shares containing a single copy of the 1386 directory are better choices and take up less disk space.*

---

Another consideration for the system and application partitions is fault tolerance. The best option is to create these partitions on a mirror set. If a hardware mirror is not possible, then setting up a software mirror after the OS is installed is suggested. This will allow you to recover much more quickly from a drive failure. A hardware fault-tolerance solution is always the preferred method, however.

---

**NOTE:** *Microsoft recommends that you never use software RAID on a SQL Server, even for the system partition.*

---

Normally, on small to midsized servers, a pair of 9GB hard drives is sufficient for the OS and application. Once you have created the system partition, you should still have ample space to install SQL Server and any administration tools that you need. The data and log files that SQL Server needs should be on a separate set of drives, usually RAID in nature. See Chapter 1 for an in-depth look at drive subsystems for data and log placement.

## Services and Components

When setting up a SQL Server, especially if it is a production server, you should keep all unnecessary services and applications off the server. During the installation, select only the minimum required components. Only install the services and applications needed for the server to run SQL Server and any needed administrative and monitoring tools. Excess services and applications consume valuable memory, processor, and thread resources. On large servers these small services may seem insignificant, but they do add up, and then your server becomes heavily utilized. When it comes to tuning your system for maximum performance, every little bit helps. The following are a few details people tend to forget about their database server, but should not be overlooked:

- Do not hang a printer or share a printer from your database server. Print services (spooler) occasionally take large amounts of RAM and disk I/O away from SQL Server.

- Plan on monitoring your server remotely. You should never leave your server logged in at the management console or running *any* application other than SQL Server.

- Try to avoid a backup solution that resides on the database server or places services on the machine.

By default, Windows 2000 selects Internet Information Server (IIS) to be installed. In most cases, this application is not needed unless you are going to make use of the new XML support in SQL Server 2000. Most of the other services that are selected are required, so you should leave them as they are unless you are sure that you will not need them.

---

**NOTE:** *Even if you are going to make use of the new XML support features, IIS should be installed on a server separate from SQL Server 2000.*

---

Windows 2000 now includes Terminal Services in all Server Editions. Terminal Services has two different modes: Administrative mode and Application mode. Administrative mode uses very few resources and is much less of a strain on your server than most other desktop sharing applications available today. If you need to access your server remotely for administrative purposes, you should consider enabling the Administrative Mode Terminal Services. If you do not need to administer your server remotely, Terminal Services should be disabled completely to conserve resources.

Another factor that many people do not consider carefully enough is network protocol selection. Even though installing all available protocols may yield the highest flexibility, each enabled protocol consumes additional resources. You should enable only those protocols that are needed to support your environment. Consider the advantages of consolidating your network on a single protocol if possible to simplify administration and reduce server resource consumption. If you are using multiple protocols, move the most commonly used protocol to the top of the binding order.

All disk I/O settings can be tested using SQL Server Simulator tools. These tools allow you to quickly test any settings that you make without having to design an entire application to exercise your server. Remember to make one change at a time so that you know how each change affects your server's performance.

# Drivers and Service Packs

You should always obtain the latest drivers for your components from the hardware manufacturer. Check the vendor's Web site for any BIOS, firmware, or device driver updates for your SCSI or RAID controllers as well as any other devices that are installed in your machine. Compare them to what you are running and read the release notes carefully.

Check the full disclosure report for the latest set of TPCC/D numbers (an industry standard test) that the server vendor has posted. Vendors must make available to the public any tweaks they have made to the standard setup, that is, any trace-flags, driver versions, driver parameters, and so on. These "tweaks" may be important because they may not provide options for the software package you are planning on purchasing. It is all too easy to have system problems caused by fairly major bugs that are quietly fixed with a firmware update when the vendor finds them. These include failures to hot-swap properly as well as failures to multiple drives in a RAID 5 configuration when one drive fails (thus losing the data). In addition to functionality corrections, you may find fixes for performance enhancements or additional features on a vendor's Web site.

As an example, Compaq provides two sets of drivers for some of its controllers. The controllers with updated firmware can run the Enhanced Command Interface (ECI) drivers that reduce the CPU requirement at the host and increase performance. Also, check with Microsoft for any security fixes and bug fixes for your selected OS version. Critical updates are available from **http://windowsupdate.com**. Most vendors take the approach that the majority of customers will periodically check their Web sites for postings of fixes and patches.

---

**NOTE:** *When you purchase hardware and software of any kind, it is a good idea to become a frequent visitor to those vendors' Web sites!*

---

# Server Usage

It is strongly recommended that SQL Server be installed on a server with no other function or duties. This is especially important for production SQL Servers. Adding additional workload, like a mail server, domain controller, or Web server, will take valuable resources away from SQL Server and can greatly impact the performance of your database. In addition to consuming system resources, each additional process on the server adds to the possibility of a system problem, which could result in the loss of mission-critical data or significant downtime.

Development servers can normally be used for multiple purposes unless you want to do some load/stress testing. If you have a development server running SQL Server as well as another application, like IIS, you will need to monitor the memory usage on the server closely. The memory requirements will grow as the load on the server increases. The same resource and stability issues that were mentioned earlier still apply to development servers, but these servers are often not as critical as production servers. You should also look for memory paging activity. Paging memory to and from disk is an easy way to kill the performance of your SQL Server!

If you do decide to add additional services to the server running SQL Server, you should consider the following: Adding additional RAM can make a big difference in how all the services on the server perform. Depending on the load, you may need to add additional processors to the server as well to help offload the work for the additional services. It is extremely important to make a plan for recovery if one or more of the services on the server stops working. Consider the steps you will have to take to get that service back online and the impact on your business if you have to interrupt the other services in order to do it.

Third-party backup solutions always provide powerful backup functionality, but will kill your performance if you run them on your SQL Server. Use a separate server for backups. Because backups to a drive are much faster than backups to tape, have a separate partition on your server for performing local backups so they can be backed up to tape remotely, thereby limiting the performance impact on your SQL Server. See Chapter 6 for more information on choosing a backup strategy for your servers.

Never use a production server as a workstation. Your server should be logged off unless you need to do something specific to that server. However, if you are going to have the server logged on, make sure the screen saver is set to None or Blank. You don't want a screen saver consuming your resources. Some screen savers are quite processor-intensive. The 3GL screen savers are very nice to look at, but can produce 30–35 percent processor load and create disk activity that interferes with SQL disk reads.

# Services

Running unnecessary services on your server will tie up valuable system resources, such as memory, threads, and processes. This section provides a list of the services that are not needed for SQL Server to help you determine which ones can be disabled in your environment to conserve resources. In most cases, you will not be able to disable all of these services. You may need some of them for administration and monitoring of your server. You should carefully consider the function of each service and decide whether or not it is needed in your environment.

## Windows NT 4 and Windows 2000 Services

The following is a list of the services installed with both Windows NT 4 and Windows 2000. This list provides information about the purpose of each service to help you determine which ones may be able to be disabled in your environment.

- *Alerter*—This service is used to collect administrative or performance alerts. You should use SQL Agent for alerts on your SQL Server. This service is sometimes used to perform an orderly shutdown of a server that is running on an Uninterruptable Power Supply (UPS).

- *Computer Browser*—This service is used to resolve NetBIOS names in the network and maintain the list of machines in the network segment as well as their network protocols. It is included in Windows 2000 only for backward compatibility with older clients because Active Directory has other services for this purpose. This service should almost always be disabled on your SQL Server. (Some third-party backup software packages require this service to be running, so be careful not to disable this service if you need it.)

- *License Logging Service*—This service is used to log license usage of BackOffice applications, such as SQL Server and Exchange Server, to include Windows NT. Your domain controller should run this service to keep track of licenses, but depending on the license type used for SQL Server, this will probably not be needed on your SQL Server. We recommend the per-seat licensing method, which renders this service unnecessary.

- *Messenger Service*—This service is used to send messages across the network. It is useful only for NET SEND commands, alerts from the Alerter service, and UPS error messages. This service should almost always be disabled on your SQL Server.

- *MS DTC*—This service is used to coordinate distributed transactions. This service is only needed if you are using distributed transactions for your applications. If you are setting up a database server for a Web server or any other application running COM, COM+, or Microsoft Transaction Server (MTS) objects, you may need this service. This service is required if you will be using MTS.

- *Plug and Play*—This service is no longer needed after the server is up and running. In the event that you add new hardware devices, you can then restart the service. Once your SQL Server is configured properly, you should disable this service.

- *Remote Access Services*—These services are used to dial into remote networks or for clients to dial into the server. If your SQL Server is on a Local Area Network (LAN) with no modem installed, then these services are not needed and should be disabled. If you need Remote Access Services (RAS) dial in capability, it is strongly recommended that you run this service on a separate server rather than bogging down your SQL Server with this type of load. It may not seem like much to have a couple of low-speed connections on the server, but this type of application will probably impact your server's performance more than you think.

- *Schedule Service/Task Scheduler*—This service can be used to execute any scripts or run scheduled jobs on the server, but you will probably want to disable this service and use the SQL Agent instead. The SQL Agent is designed to perform these tasks for SQL Server and is well integrated for use with your SQL Server.

- *Server*—This service is used mainly for file and printer sharing. You should only disable it for security reasons. Disabling it prevents making a connection to the Windows NT Server and creates an ultra-secure server. It does not affect your SQL Server connections.

- *Spooler/Print Spooler*—This service is used to spool print jobs either from the server itself or from clients using the server as a print server. You should never use a production SQL Server as a print server as it can greatly affect the performance of your server. Setting this service for manual startup allows you to temporarily start the service in the event you need to print something from the server for tracking or debugging purposes.

- *Telephony*—This service is only useful if you have a modem installed on your server. For security and performance reasons, you should never have a modem installed on your production server. If you do not have a modem installed on the server, you should disable this service. Some SQL Server solutions use a modem for sending pages for certain error conditions. If this is the case, you should configure the modem for dial-out purposes only.

## Additional Services for Windows 2000

The following is a list of the additional services installed with Windows 2000. This list provides information about the purpose of each service to help you determine which ones can be disabled in your environment.

- *Distributed File System*—This service was a post-install add-on for Windows NT 4, but comes standard on Windows 2000. This service is only needed if you are taking advantage of the distributed file system features on your network.

- *Distributed Link Tracking*—This service is used for tracking file movements between NTFS volumes in a domain. It does not do you much good on a SQL Server that is not moving files around. This service should usually be disabled on your SQL Server.

- *Indexing Service*—This service is useful for indexing files on local drives, but only if you constantly search your drives for files. This service normally isn't needed on a SQL Server.

- *Infrared Monitor*—This service is only needed if you have an infrared port and are planning to attach infrared devices to your server. In most cases, this service should be disabled on your SQL Server.

- *Removable Storage*—This service is used to manage removable storage devices. In most cases, you will not have any of these devices attached to your SQL Server, so this service can be disabled.

Look at the other services installed on your SQL Server. If you're not sure what a service does, you can look it up in the Microsoft knowledgebase at **http:// search.support.microsoft.com**. If you cannot find any information about a particular service in the knowledgebase, try stopping the service, and then checking the server to see if any other services or applications are affected. Do this for one service at a time, so that if stopping a service breaks the server, you know which one did it. If the server functions normally, you can then disable the service.

---

**NOTE:** *Test the services on a test server by turning them on and off before making changes to your production server. Always reboot the server, and make sure the normal boot sequence and SQL Server service accounts start properly before assuming the service is not required.*

---

# Vendor Services

All major computer manufacturers that build servers include many services to monitor their hardware. These services can become resource hogs and can seriously hamper your server performance, or they can be vital to catching impending hardware failures or other potential problems with your server. If you don't use these services, don't install them. If they are installed automatically, disable them. The server will run the same without these services and will most likely perform better without them.

However, if you do use these services, make sure you have the latest version of the software. Some older versions of these monitoring tools have memory leaks as well as bugs that can monopolize your processor and memory. Even well-known vendors have created monitoring tools that can consume a great deal of server resources.

# *Immediate Solutions*

## Installation

Most people install Windows with all the default settings and only change minor personal settings. For workstations this may work well, but for servers, you need to really tune the server for the best performance. Putting some effort into tuning Windows allows you to get the most bang for your buck with the performance of your machine. If you stay focused on the list provided in this section, you will be able to tune your server for optimal performance. Be sure to check out the following areas when setting up your OS:

1. OS Version

   - Is your server a production or development server? Never use a workstation OS for a production server.

   - Should you choose Windows NT 4 or Windows 2000? Future support of Windows NT 4 is questionable. It's best to keep fairly up-to-date. Windows 2000 is more advanced, but can take up a lot of memory on low-end servers.

2. OS Edition

   - How many processors does your server support? Standard Editions only support four, Advanced/Enterprise Server supports eight, and DataCenter supports 32.

   - How much RAM do you have installed? Standard Editions only support 4GB, Enterprise Edition of Windows NT 4 supports 4GB (1GB for the OS and 3GB for an application), Advanced Server supports 8GB, and DataCenter supports 64GB.

   - Do you need clustering? Clustering is only available on Advanced/Enterprise Server and DataCenter. Advanced Server and Enterprise Edition support two-node failover clustering, whereas DataCenter supports four-node failover clustering.

3. System Drive

- How large should your system drive be? It must be large enough for service pack upgrades and possibly a parallel install for troubleshooting.

- What is the availability of your drive? Hardware RAID 1 is best, but OS RAID 1 is better than nothing if you cannot afford a RAID controller.

- Which file system should you choose? NTFS is always your best bet for security and reliability.

4. Pagefile

- What size pagefile do you need? Installed RAM + 12MB is all that is needed for a pagefile. Make the minimum and maximum sizes of the pagefile the same size to prevent resizing and fragmentation.

- Which pagefile placement should you choose? Spreading the pagefile across several dedicated physical drives is best. On low-end and development servers, placement of the pagefile on the OS drive works well, but for mid- to high-end production servers, the pagefile needs to be separate from the OS and data drives.

| Related solution: | Found on page: |
|---|---|
| Installing MSSQL Server 2000 | 110 |

## Install

This section provides a few details to keep in mind during the Windows installation.

Don't worry about the fact that during setup only one processor is detected. Setup is only capable of running in single-processor mode. After the last boot, you will notice that Windows will see all of your processors. In most cases, if your system supports multiple processors but you only have one installed, setup still recognizes it as a multiprocessor system and installs the correct Hardware Abstraction Layer (HAL). The auto-detect will not actually recognize the additional processors until they are installed in the server, but usually you do not need to reinstall Windows when you add a second processor. If this is not the case, you will still have the option to specify this during the Windows installation process.

During the first part of the install process, you are asked where you want the OS to be installed. You should have answered this question in the previous section. After selecting the location to install the OS, you are then asked how to format the partition. For security and reliability, you should always select NTFS no matter which version of Windows NT you are using.

During the installation, it is always a good idea to perform a custom install. This allows you to install only the components that you need. A custom install should be chosen not only with the OS, but also with all applications.

During the installation of Windows NT 4 Server, you are asked if you want to install IIS. Even if you plan on running a Web server, you don't want to install this version of IIS. During the Windows 2000 install, you are given options for the components that come with Windows 2000 Server. If you will not be using XML, deselect IIS in Windows 2000 Server. If you plan on clustering your servers, don't select clustering services during the installation; clustering should be installed later. Clustering is covered in more detail in Chapter 3.

For Windows 2000, select Terminal Services to be installed. Scroll all the way to the bottom and select Terminal Services. Don't worry about selecting Terminal Services Licensing Services. That is only needed if you are running Terminal Services in Application mode, which you never want to do on a SQL Server.

After clicking on Next, if you selected Terminal Services, a screen appears asking which mode you want for Terminal Services. Leave the default selection of Administrative mode and just click on Next.

## Installation Files

After finishing the install, in order to eliminate future need of the install disk, just copy the install files to the local or network shared drive. Copy the appropriate directory (i.e., i386) from the CD to the hard disk. Modify the Registry to point to the hard disk copy of the original files. Change the following Registry key:

```
HKLM\Software\Microsoft\WindowsNT\CurrentVersion\SourcePath
```

Modify the value to the appropriate drive and directory; for example, C:\i386.

To prevent becoming annoyed with having to reapply the service pack to your server every time you have to access the install files, follow the next tip.

Uncompress the latest service pack. At the command prompt in a temp directory where the service pack files exist, type the file name followed by "/x" (e.g., c:\temp\<SP> /x, where <SP> is the name of the file). Then copy the expanded files into C:\i386, and overwrite all files.

This allows for the direct installation of a file without reinstalling the entire service pack. So, every time you make a change that requires files from the i386 directory, you no longer need to reapply the service pack afterwards.

*WARNING! It is highly recommended that you apply the service pack before copying the files.*

## Boot.ini

The default setting of 30 seconds for the boot menu is not needed unless you plan on booting into different operating systems on a regular basis.

All you have to do is edit the boot.ini file in the root of the system drive to speed up your boot times. There are only a couple of lines in this file; just change the timeout to equal 3. This only saves you 27 seconds, but there really is no reason to keep this setting at 30 seconds. You will then only have 3 seconds to select any boot option other than the default, but this should be plenty of time.

## Hard Drive

The disk subsystem is one of the biggest bottlenecks of a SQL Server. Little adjustments in this subsystem can make a big difference in performance.

### Fragmentation

The normal process of creating, modifying, and deleting files can cause fragmentation. Fragmentation, if left unchecked, can and will seriously degrade the performance of your drives. Defragmenting your drives will reorder the files so that they are contiguous. This increases the speed in which files are read, written, updated, and created.

Windows NT 4 does not include any defragmentation software, but Windows 2000 comes with Diskeeper Lite, which is built-in but has limited functionality. If you want to schedule weekly defragmentation runs on your drives, you need to obtain a full version of some third-party software like Diskeeper.

**NOTE:** *Schedule defragmentation time on the server during weekly or monthly maintenance periods, so it does not interfere with day-to-day operations.*

The Master File Table (MFT) is a part of the disk you don't want to ignore. The MFT keeps track of the files and empty space on an NTFS partition. Whenever a file is read, written, created, or modified, its location is read from the MFT. Most applications read and write to many files, resulting in heavy I/O for the MFT. A heavily fragmented MFT can cause performance to degrade severely.

Unfortunately, defragmenting the MFT is no easy task. The cleanest way is to format the drive as NTFS from within Windows NT. Even during the install of Windows NT 4, setup formats the system drive as FAT, and then converts it to NTFS the next time you reboot, causing the MFT to start out fragmented. Windows 2000 setup does, however, format the drive as NTFS.

The only other option is to use the latest version of Diskeeper. Starting with v5.0, Diskeeper is able to defragment the MFT as well as the files and directories.

### NTFS Cluster Sizes

When formatting a drive, you can choose the cluster size you want to use. Changing the cluster size can increase disk performance by optimizing the disk clusters for the types of files on the partition. Don't worry about the system partition; the default works best for that drive. NTFS supports cluster sizes of 512 bytes, 1KB, 2KB, 4KB, 8KB, 16KB, 32KB, and 64KB.

---

**NOTE:** *Increasing the cluster size does not always increase disk performance. If the partition contains a lot of small files, a smaller cluster size might be better.*

---

### Compression

You should not compress the data and log drives on your SQL Server. On development servers and in special cases, you may be able to compress a drive to get more disk space. You can, however, compress some directories and other drives to allow for improved storage.

Microsoft does not want you to compress SQL Server drives and will not support your server if it is installed on compressed drives. SQL Server installs and operates on a compressed drive with little or no problem on a laptop or development server, however. You will see some performance drop-off in a compressed environment, but you will be able to fit much larger databases on your mobile and development environments.

# The Paging File

You can't stop your server from using the pagefile, so you need to optimize it. Placement of your pagefile is important. Normally, leaving your pagefile on your system partition works well, but when you start using larger, more heavily used servers, you need to move your pagefile over to its own drive or sets of drives. Although placement of the pagefile is not an easy decision to make, Table 2.4 can make it easier on you with its pagefile placement options.

Even though leaving the pagefile on the system drive works well, Table 2.4 illustrates the best-performing options. Keep in mind that if you move your pagefile off the system drive, the system is no longer able to dump the memory to disk. If your server is giving you problems and keeps blue screening, you may need to

**Table 2.4    Pagefile placement.**

| Choice | Placement |
| --- | --- |
| Optimal | Spread the pagefile across several dedicated hard drives. |
| Good | Place the pagefile on a dedicated hard drive. |
| Adequate | Place the pagefile on a RAID set. |
| Worst | Place the pagefile in the default location on the system drive. |

place the pagefile back on the system drive so you can capture a memory dump to send to Microsoft Technical Support. Never put multiple pagefiles on the same physical disk. Placing multiple pagefiles on different partitions of the same physical disk defeats the purpose of spreading it out.

Once you have figured out where to place the pagefile, you need to decide how large to make it. Always make the minimum and maximum pagefile sizes the same size. This prevents the OS from having to resize the pagefile and also prevents fragmentation of the pagefile. You don't need to worry about making your pagefile very large. SQL Server will only use the available memory, it will never consume more memory than is available. If you have less than 1GB of memory installed, your pagefile size should total the amount of your RAM + 12MB.

# Tweaking the Registry

Some tweaking can be done within the Windows Registry. These changes can sometimes be small, but result in big performance boosts. Unfortunately, most of these modifications are hit-or-miss type changes, and you will have to experiment with the settings to find the best ones for your system. When making changes in the Registry, you need to heed the following warning.

**WARNING! Using the Registry Editor incorrectly can cause serious, systemwide problems that may require you to reinstall Windows NT to correct them. Microsoft cannot guarantee that any problems resulting from the use of the Registry Editor can be solved. Use this tool at your own risk.**

Either regedt32.exe or regedit.exe will work for editing your Registry, but with Windows NT 4, regedit.exe does not connect to remote Registries. Also, regedit.exe does not contain all of the functionality of regedt32, for instance, it does not include the capability to change Registry security settings. Regedit.exe allows you to rename keys, copy keys, and use the right mouse button to access an editing menu, whereas regedt32.exe does not.

## Tagged Command Queuing

Similar to SQL, SCSI and RAID controllers work on the same asynchronous I/O concept. The only difference is that they do it at the hardware layer. In SCSI terms, this is called *tagged command queuing*. The default depth for most drivers and controllers is between 8 and 32. You need to check the controller documentation or contact the vendor to see what the default depth is for your particular configuration.

If you set this value too high, you can overload the disk subsystem, but if it is too low, you may be limiting the throughput of the disk subsystem. Unfortunately, there is no way of determining the correct value without benchmarking the performance of your drive system. The more powerful the controller and the more disks connected to it, the higher the tagged command queue depth can be set.

It can be manually overridden by editing the Registry:

```
KLM\System\CurrentControlSet\Services\<DRIVERNAME>\Parameters\Device<n>\
NumberOfRequests
```

If this entry does not exist, you will need to create it. This entry should be a DWORD value. Try starting with a decimal value of 128.

Before setting the value of this entry above 255 on Windows NT Server 4, make sure that you have Windows NT SP6a applied; otherwise, your server will blue screen due to a Windows NT bug.

**WARNING!** *Changing this setting can be extremely dangerous. You should not make this type of change without adequate testing on a development server running identical hardware. It is also strongly recommended that you contact the vendor for your controller and ask it for recommendations before embarking on this type of change.*

## Disabling Paging Executive

Normally, user mode and kernel mode drivers as well as kernel mode system code are written to either pageable or nonpageable memory. It is possible to configure Windows NT and Windows 2000 to never page out drivers and system code to the pagefile that are in the pageable memory area. This should only be done on systems with large amounts of RAM or severe performance problems could develop.

```
KLM\SYSTEM\CurrentControlSet\Control\Session Manager\Memory
Management\DisablePagingExecutive\<n>
```

Set the value of this key to 1.

## Disabling 8.3 File Names

When creating files, Windows NT automatically generates 8.3 file names, which is only useful if you plan on booting in DOS or Windows 9x. For servers, booting in DOS or Windows 9x should never happen. Disabling this file-naming feature can give you some added drive performance because Windows NT will no longer have to generate an extra file name.

To change this setting, modify the following Registry setting:

```
HKLM\System\CurrentControlSet\Control\FileSystem
```

And set the following value: NtfsDisable8dot3NameCreation=1

## Memory Used for File Cache

Windows NT does not allow much tuning of caching except for the following Registry entry:

```
KLM\SYSTEM\CurrentControlSet\Control\Session Manager\Memory Management\
LargeSystemCache
```

Set the value of this key to 0.

If you start the Network Control Panel applet and select the Services tab, you can select Server and click on Properties. Select Maximize Throughput For Network Applications to use less memory (this actually sets LargeSystemCache to 0).

There is a freeware utility available from Sysinternals called CacheSet (**www. sysinternals.com**), which allows you to more specifically set the amount of memory used for caching. Full source code is included with this utility. Visit its Web site for more information about this product.

# Configuring Network Protocols

The fewer network protocols you have installed, the better. You don't want your SQL Server listening on protocols that it's not using. Having fewer protocols will also cut down on network traffic. If your server is only going to use TCP/IP, just install TCP/IP. In some cases, it may be necessary to install multiple protocols. In such cases, put the most commonly used protocol at the top of the binding order.

To change the binding order in Windows 2000:

1. Select Start|Settings, and then click on Control Panel.

2. Double-click on Network and Dial-Up Connections.

3. On the Advanced menu, click on Advanced Settings.

4. In the Connections box, select the adapter you want to change the binding order on. After you select the adapter, the Bindings For Local Area Connection box displays the current binding order.

5. Use the arrows on the right side of the box to move the protocol you choose to the top of the list, and then click on OK.

6. If you are prompted to restart the computer, click on Yes.

To change the binding order in Windows NT 4:

1. Select Start|Settings, and then click on Control Panel.

2. Double-click on Network.

3  Click on the Bindings tab.

4. In the Show Bindings For drop-down menu, select all adapters.

5. In the box below this drop-down you will see all network cards listed. Click on the + next to the network adapter and a list of all protocols will appear.

6. Select the protocol you want to move, use the buttons on the bottom to change the order in which the protocols are listed, and then click on OK.

7. If you are prompted to restart the computer, click on Yes.

| *Related solution:* | *Found on page:* |
| --- | --- |
| Changing the Default Protocol | 202 |

# The Browser Service

The master browser is the service that maintains the list of all the systems in the domain or workgroup the server resides in. All Windows NT and Windows 2000 systems, Workstation Editions, and all Server Editions can maintain this list.

The primary function of the browser service is to provide a list of computers sharing resources in a client's domain along with a list of other domain and workgroup names across the wide area network (WAN). This list is provided to clients that view network resources with Network Neighborhood or the NET VIEW command.

The master browser is responsible for collecting host or server announcements, which are sent as datagrams every 12 minutes, by default, by each server on the network segment of the master browser. (The interval for these announcements is configurable and may be different in your environment.) The master browser instructs the potential browsers for each network segment to become backup browsers. The backup browser on a given network segment provides a browse list to the client computers located in the same segment.

Microsoft Active Directory services in Windows 2000 replaces the Computer Browser service used in earlier versions of Windows, which provided NetBIOS name resolution. The browser service in Windows 2000 is only provided for backward compatibility with client systems that are running earlier versions of Windows.

In a Windows NT domain structure, the primary domain controller (PDC) is always selected as the domain master browser. Only the PDC can be a domain master browser. If a PDC is not present, a domain master browser is not available, and you are unable to obtain browse lists from workgroups other than the workgroup you are located in.

To prevent your SQL Server from becoming the domain master browser, change the following Registry keys. Ensure that this key is set to **FALSE**:

```
HKLM\SYSTEM\CurrentControlSet\Services\Browser\Parameters\IsDomainMaster
```

Make this value of this key equal to **NO**:

```
KLM\SYSTEM\CurrentControlSet\Services\Browser\Parameters\
MaintainServerList
```

You can also stop the Computer Browser service and disable it if you do not need NetBIOS name resolution, which will have the same effect.

# Windows Tuning Hints

The following list contains some of the most important items to consider when installing and tuning Windows NT Server:

- Consider the number of processors and amount of memory you need. This helps narrow the choice of Windows Edition to use.

- Install the latest service packs and drivers. But always test them before installing them on production servers.

- Leave your server logged off, but if you are going to be logged on to the server, make sure your screen saver is None or Blank.

- Spread your pagefile across several dedicated drives if you can; otherwise, at least one dedicated drive is suggested.

- Set your pagefile maximum and minimum settings to the same amount to prevent resizing.

- Keep your hard drives defragmented on a periodic basis.

- Disable any and all services not being used.

- Test one change at a time, so you can determine exactly which changes cause what effects.

- Never use your production SQL Server for anything other than a SQL Server.

- Once every month or so, you should cycle the SQL Server and/or Windows to make sure your server does not page or load other services or applications into memory, which would cause SQL server to page.

# Chapter 3

# Clustering and Multi-Instances

*(continued)*

# *In Depth*

In this chapter, clustering and multi-instances are discussed in detail, and then step-by-step procedures are provided for setting up a cluster as well as multi-instances. The reason for discussing these two topics in the same chapter is that some clustering cases require the use of multi-instances. The "Immediate Solutions" section of this chapter is very lengthy due to the examples that need to be covered. Each of the immediate solutions builds on previous solutions, so take the time to review each one before jumping into a solution for your server(s).

## What Is Clustering?

In the case of SQL Server, clustering is the capability to provide failover for an instance of SQL Server to maintain the highest possible uptime in spite of any hardware or software failures. SQL Server 2000 failover clustering increases server availability by allowing a system to automatically switch the processing for an instance of SQL Server from a failed server to a working server. For example, an instance of SQL Server can quickly restore database services to a Web site or enterprise network even if the server running the instance fails. SQL Server 2000 implements failover clustering based on the failover-clustering features of the Microsoft Clustering Service (MSCS) in Windows NT 4 and Windows 2000.

The type of MSCS failover cluster used by SQL Server 2000 consists of multiple server computers, two on Windows NT 4.0 Enterprise Edition and Windows 2000 Advanced Server and up to four on Windows 2000 DataCenter Server, which share a common set of cluster resources, such as disk drives. Each server in the cluster is called a node. Each server, or node, is connected to the network, and each node can communicate with every other node. Each node must be running the same version of MSCS.

The shared resources in the failover cluster are collected into cluster groups. For example, if a failover cluster has four clustered disk drives, two of the drives can be collected in one cluster group and the other two in a second cluster group. Each cluster group is owned by one of the nodes in the failover cluster, although the ownership can be transferred between nodes.

Applications can be installed on the nodes in the failover cluster. These applications are typically server applications or distributed Component Object Model (COM) objects that users access through network connections. The application executables and other resources are typically stored in one or more of the cluster groups owned by the node. Each node can have multiple applications installed on it.

The failover cluster nodes periodically send each other network messages called *heartbeat messages*. If the MSCS software detects the loss of a heartbeat signal from one of the nodes in the cluster, it treats the server as a failed server. MSCS then automatically transfers the cluster groups and application resources of that node to the other nodes in the network. The cluster administrator specifies the alternate nodes to which cluster groups are transferred when any given node fails. The other nodes then continue processing user network requests for the applications transferred from the failed server.

**NOTE:** For more information about MSCS, see the Windows NT Server, Windows 2000 Server, Windows 2000 Advanced Server, or Windows 2000 DataCenter documentation.

# What Is Multi-Instance?

SQL Server 2000 supports multiple instances of the SQL Server database engine running concurrently on the same computer. Each instance of the SQL Server database engine has its own set of system and user databases that are not shared between instances. Applications can connect to each SQL Server database engine instance on a single computer in much the same way that they connect to SQL Server database engines running on different computers. There are two types of instances of SQL Server: *default* and *named*.

## Default Instances

The default instance of the SQL Server 2000 database engine operates in the same way as the database engines in earlier versions of SQL Server. The default instance is identified solely by the name of the computer on which the instance is running; it does not have a separate instance name. When applications specify only the computer name in their requests to connect to SQL Server, the SQL Server client components attempt to connect to the default instance of the database engine on that computer. This preserves compatibility with existing SQL Server applications.

There can be only one default instance on any computer. The default instance can be any version of SQL Server. Configurations that can operate as a default instance include the following:

- An installation of SQL Server version 6.5.

- An installation of SQL Server version 7. A SQL Server 7 installation can coexist with one or more named instances of SQL Server 2000 running at the same time.

- A default instance of SQL Server 2000.

- A default instance of SQL Server 2000 that can be version-switched with an installation of SQL Server version 6.5 using the SQL Server 2000 vswitch utility.

- An installation of SQL Server version 7 that can be version-switched with an installation of SQL Server version 6.5 using the SQL Server version 7 vswitch utility.

---

**NOTE:** *You must apply SQL Server 6.5 Service Pack 5 to any instance of SQL Server 6.5 before installing instances of SQL Server 2000 on the same computer.*

---

## Named Instances

All instances of the database engine other than the default instance are identified by an instance name specified during the installation of the instance. Applications must provide both the computer name and the instance name of any named instance to which they are attempting to connect. The computer name and instance name are specified in the format *computer_name\instance_name*.

---

**NOTE:** *Depending upon the network topology in your enterprise, naming conventions may restrict the length and content of the names you can choose. Always choose a naming convention that meets the least common denominator for all environments you anticipate.*

---

There can be multiple named instances running on a computer, but only the SQL Server 2000 database engine can operate as a named instance. The database engines from earlier versions of SQL Server cannot operate as a named instance. Instances apply primarily to the database engine and its supporting components, not to the client tools. When you install multiple instances, each instance gets a unique set of:

- System and user databases.

- SQL Server and SQL Server Agent services. For default instances, the names of the services remain MSSQLServer and SQLServerAgent. For named instances, the names of the services are changed to MSSQL$*instancename* and SQLAgent$*instancename*, allowing them to be started and stopped independently from the other instances on the server. The database engines for the different instances are started and stopped using the associated SQL Server service. The SQL Server Agent services manage scheduled events for the associated instances of the database engine.

- Registry keys associated with the database engine and the SQL Server and SQL Server Agent services.

- Network connection addresses, so that applications can connect to specific instances.

## Shared Components

The following components are shared between all instances running on the same computer:

- There is only one SQL Server 2000 program group (Microsoft SQL Server) on the computer and only one copy of the utility represented by each icon in the program group. There is only one copy of SQL Server Books Online.

- The versions of the utilities in the program group are from the first version of SQL Server 2000 installed on the computer. For example, if you install the French version of SQL Server 2000 as a default instance, and then install the U.S. English version of SQL Server 2000 as a named instance, there is one SQL Server 2000 program group. All of the utility icons and the SQL Server Books Online icon in the program group start the French versions of the tools.

- All of the SQL Server 2000 utilities work with multiple instances. You can start and stop each of the instances from a single copy of the SQL Server 2000 Service Manager. You can use a single copy of the SQL Server 2000 SQL Server Enterprise Manager to control objects in all instances on the computer and use a single copy of the SQL Server 2000 Server Network Manager to manage the network addresses with which all of the instances on the computer communicate.

- There is only one copy of the MSSearchService, which manages full-text searches against all instances of SQL Server on the computer.

- There is only one copy each of the English Query and Microsoft SQL Server 2000 Analysis Services servers.

- The Registry keys associated with the client software are not duplicated between instances.

- There is only one copy of the SQL Server development libraries (include and .lib files) and sample applications.

## Switching Between Versions of SQL Server

You cannot version-switch between an installation of SQL Server version 7.0 and a default instance of SQL Server 2000. Only a number of named instances of SQL Server 2000 are allowed on a server in addition to the default instance, up to a total of 16 instances. You are not required to run a default instance on a computer before you can run named instances, which means it is possible to run named instances on a computer that has no default instance. SQL Server version 6.5 and SQL Server 7.0 cannot operate as named instances, only as default instances. Microsoft supports only 16 instances on a single computer or failover cluster.

If you run SQL Server version 6.5 as a default instance and run one or more named instances of SQL Server 2000 on a single computer, the computer has two SQL Server program groups instead of one SQL Server program group:

• A SQL Server 2000 program group executes the SQL Server 2000 tools.

• A SQL Server version 6.5 program group runs the SQL Server 6.5 tools.

If you are running SQL Server version 7.0 with SQL Server 2000, the icons in the SQL Server 7.0 program group will execute the SQL Server 2000 tools.

# Multiple Instances of SQL Server on a Failover Cluster

You can run only one instance of SQL Server on each virtual server of a SQL Server failover cluster, although you can install up to 16 virtual servers on a failover cluster. The instance can be either a default instance or a named instance. The virtual server looks like a single computer to applications connecting to that instance of SQL Server. When applications connect to the virtual server, they use the same convention as when connecting to any instance of SQL Server—they specify the virtual server name of the cluster and the optional instance name (only needed for named instances): *virtualservername\instancenam*.

# Checklist for Windows 2000 Cluster Service

The following sections provide a checklist of requirements to assist you in preparing to set up and configure your Microsoft Cluster Service. Step-by-step instructions on setting up a failover cluster are then presented in the "Immediate Solutions" section.

## Software Requirements

Windows 2000 Advanced Server or Windows 2000 DataCenter Server must be installed on all nodes of the cluster. A name resolution method, such as Domain Name Service (DNS), Windows Internet Naming Service (WINS), HOSTS or LMHOSTS files for TCP/IP, and so on, is also required. To allow for remote administration, Terminal Services in Admin Mode is recommended.

## Hardware Requirements

The hardware for a Cluster Service node must meet the hardware requirements for Windows 2000 Advanced Server or Windows DataCenter Server. These requirements can be found at the Product Compatibility Search page.

Cluster hardware must be on the Cluster Service Hardware Compatibility List (HCL). The latest version of the Cluster Service HCL can be found by going to the Windows HCL and searching on the keyword "Cluster".

You will need two HCL approved computers, each with the following:

- A boot disk with Windows 2000 Advanced Server or Windows 2000 DataCenter Server installed. (The boot disk cannot be on the shared storage bus.)

- A separate PCI storage host adapter (SCSI or Fiber Channel) for the shared disks. This is in addition to the boot disk adapter.

- Two PCI network adapters in each machine in the cluster.

- An HCL approved external storage unit that connects to all computers in the cluster.

- Storage cables to attach the shared storage device to all computers. Refer to the manufacturers' instructions for configuring storage devices.

- All hardware should be identical, slot for slot, card for card, for all nodes. This makes configuration easier and eliminates potential compatibility problems.

## Network Requirements

The network requirements are fairly simple. Some of the requirements can be considered suggestions, but to ensure optimal performance, you should follow all of the guidelines presented in the following list:

- A unique NetBIOS cluster name.

- Five unique, static IP addresses: two for the network adapters on the private network, two for the network adapters on the public network, and one for the cluster itself.

- A domain user account for Cluster Service. All nodes must be members of the same domain.

- Each node should have two network adapters—one for connection to the public network and the other for the node-to-node private cluster network. If you use only one network adapter for both connections, your configuration is unsupported. A separate private network adapter is required for HCL certification.

- Each node should have a third network adapter for network failover. This adapter transmits public and private traffic, so it needs to be connected to the public local area network (LAN).

# Shared Disk Requirements

The shared disk requirements may seem a little strict, but they must be followed very closely. Remember, this is where your data is stored, so the last thing you want to do is put your data at risk.

- All shared disks, including the quorum disk, must be physically attached to a shared bus.

- Verify that disks attached to the shared bus can be seen from all nodes. This can be checked at the host adapter setup level. Please refer to the manufacturer's documentation for adapter specific instructions.

- SCSI devices must be assigned unique SCSI identification numbers and be properly terminated, as per the manufacturer's instructions. (If the SCSI devices are on a shared backplane, all device IDs are set to 0 and the backplane handles the numbering and termination.)

- All shared disks must be configured as basic (not dynamic).

- All partitions on the disks must be formatted as NT File System (NTFS).

- Although not required, the use of fault-tolerant RAID configurations is strongly recommended for all disks. The idea is to provide fault-tolerant RAID configurations like RAID 0+1, 1, or 5—not stripe sets without parity.

# *Immediate Solutions*

## Cluster Installation

The following sections provide step-by-step instructions for installing your cluster. It is very important that your Windows cluster is set up and operating correctly, so let's start with the Windows cluster and then proceed to the SQL 2000 cluster.

### Installation Overview

Before going into the step-by-step instructions, let's take a moment for a quick overview of the process. During the installation process, some nodes will be shut down and some nodes will be rebooted. These steps are necessary to guarantee that the data on disks that are attached to the shared storage bus is not lost or corrupted. This can happen when multiple nodes try to simultaneously write to the same disk that is not yet protected by the cluster software.

Use Table 3.1 to determine which nodes and storage devices should be powered on during each step. The steps in this guide are for a two-node cluster. However, if you are installing a cluster with more than two nodes, you can use the Node 2 column to determine the required state of other nodes.

Several steps must be taken before installing the Cluster Service software. Perform these steps on every cluster node before proceeding with the installation of Cluster Service on the first node:

1. Install Windows 2000 Advanced Server or Windows 2000 DataCenter Server on each node.

2. Set up networks.

3. Set up disks.

To configure the Cluster Service on a Windows 2000-based server, your account must have administrative permissions on each node. All nodes must be member servers, or all nodes must be domain controllers within the same domain. It is not acceptable to have a mix of domain controllers and member servers in a cluster.

**Table 3.1    Power sequencing for cluster installation.**

| Step | Node 1 | Node 2 | Storage | Comments |
|---|---|---|---|---|
| Setting Up Networks | On | On | Off | Verify that all storage devices on the shared bus are powered off. Power on all nodes. |
| Setting Up Shared Disks | On | Off | On | Shut down all nodes. Power on the shared storage, and then power on Node 1. |
| Verifying Disk Configuration | Off | On | On | Shut down Node 1. Power on the second node and repeat for nodes 3 and 4 if applicable. |
| Configuring the First Node | On | Off | On | Shut down all nodes and power on the first node. |
| Configuring the Second Node | On | On | On | Power on the second node after the first node is successfully configured. Repeat this process for nodes 3 and 4 if applicable. |
| Post Installation | On | On | On | At this point, all nodes should be powered on. |

## Installing the Windows 2000 Operating System

Refer to the documentation you received with the Windows 2000 operating system packages to install the system on each node in the cluster. You can also refer to Chapter 2 of this book for more information on installing Windows 2000.

---

**NOTE:** *This step-by-step guide uses the naming structure from the "Step-by-Step Guide to a Common Infrastructure for Windows 2000 Server Deployment" found at the following address:* **www.microsoft.com/windows2000/library/ planning/server/serversteps.asp**. *You can use any names or naming convention you desire, but using a standard naming convention is recommended.*

---

## Setting Up Networks

Each cluster node requires at least two network adapters—one to connect to a public network and one to connect to a private network consisting of cluster nodes only. The private network adapter establishes node-to-node communication, cluster status signals, and cluster management. Each node's public network adapter connects the cluster to the public network where clients reside. Verify that all network connections are correct; with private network adapters connected to other private network adapters only, and public network adapters connected to the public network. Perform these steps on each cluster node before proceeding with shared disk setup.

---

**NOTE:** *For this section, power down all shared storage devices, and then power up all nodes. Do not let both nodes access the shared storage devices at the same time until the Cluster Service is installed on at least one node and that node is online.*

---

### Configuring the Private Network Adapter

Perform these steps on the first node in your cluster:

1. Right-click on My Network Places, and then click on Properties.
2. Right-click on the Local Area Connection 2 icon.

---

**NOTE:** *Which network adapter is private and which is public depends upon your wiring. For the purposes of this example, the first network adapter (Local Area Connection) is connected to the public network, and the second network adapter (Local Area Connection 2) is connected to the private cluster network. This may not be the case in your network.*

---

3. Click on Status. The Local Area Connection 2 Status window shows the connection status as well as the speed of connection. If the window shows that the network is disconnected, examine cables and connections to resolve the problem before proceeding. Click on Close.

4. Right-click on Local Area Connection 2 again, click on Properties, and click on Configure.

5. Click on Advanced to display the network adapters for the private network.

6. Network adapters on the private network should be set to the actual speed of the network rather than the default automated speed selection. Select your network speed from the drop-down list. Do not use an auto-select setting for speed. Some adapters may drop packets while determining the speed. To set the network adapter speed, click on the appropriate option, such as Media Type or Speed.

7. All network adapters in the cluster that are attached to the same network must be identically configured to use the same Duplex Mode, Flow Control, Media Type, and so on. These settings should remain the same even if the hardware is different.

---

**NOTE:** *It is highly recommended that you use identical network adapters throughout the cluster network. It will make failover less complex.*

---

8. Click on Transmission Control Protocol/Internet Protocol (TCP/IP).

9. Click on Properties.

10. Select Use The Following IP Address, and type in the following address: "10.1.1.1" (use 10.1.1.2 for the second node).

11. Type in a subnet mask of 255.0.0.0.

12. Click on Advanced, and select the WINS tab. Select Disable NetBIOS over TCP/IP. Click on OK to return to the previous menu. *Do this step for the private network adapter only.*

### Configuring the Public Network Adapter

Although the public network adapter's IP address can be automatically obtained if a Dynamic Host Configuration Protocol (DHCP) server is available, this is not recommended for cluster nodes. Setting static IP addresses for all network adapters in the cluster, both private and public, is strongly recommended. If IP addresses are obtained via DHCP, access to cluster nodes could become unavailable if the DHCP server goes down. If you must use DHCP for your public network adapter, use long lease periods to assure that the dynamically assigned lease address remains valid even if the DHCP service is temporarily lost. In all cases, set static IP addresses for the private network connector. Keep in mind that Cluster Service recognizes only one network interface per subnet. If you need assistance with TCP/IP addressing in Windows 2000, see the Windows 2000 Online Help found at **www.microsoft.com/windows2000/library/resources/onlinehelp.asp**.

### Rename the Local Area Network Icons

It is recommended that you change the names of the network connections for clarity. For example, you might want to change the name of *Local Area Connection (2)* to something like *Private Cluster Connection*. The naming helps you identify a network and correctly assign its role.

1. Right-click on the Local Area Connection 2 icon.

2. Click on Rename.

3. Type "Private Cluster Connection" into the text box, and press Enter.

4. Repeat steps 1 through 3, and rename the public network adapter as Public Cluster Connection.

5. Close the Networking and Dial-up Connections window. The new connection names automatically replicate to other cluster servers as they are brought online.

### Verifying Connectivity and Name Resolution

To verify that the private and public networks are communicating properly, perform the following steps for each network adapter in each node. You need to know the IP address for each network adapter in the cluster. If you do not already have this information, you can retrieve it by using the **ipconfig** command on each node:

1. Select Start|Run and type "cmd" in the text box. Click on OK.

2. Type "ipconfig /all", and press Enter. IP information should display for all network adapters in the machine.

3. If you do not already have the command prompt on your screen, select Start|Run, and type "cmd" in the text box. Click on OK.

4. Type "ping ipaddress", where *ipaddress* is the IP address for the corresponding network adapter in the other node. For example, assume that the IP addresses are set as indicated in Table 3.2.

5. In this example, type "ping 172.16.12.14" and "ping 10.1.1.2" from Node 1, and type "ping 172.16.12.12" and "10.1.1.1" from Node 2.

6. To verify name resolution, ping each node from a client using the node's machine name instead of its IP number. For example, to verify name resolution for the first cluster node, type "ping hq-res-dc01" from any client.

### Verifying Domain Membership

All nodes in the cluster must be members of the same domain and be able to access a domain controller and a DNS Server. They can be configured as member servers or domain controllers. If you decide to configure one node as a domain controller, you should configure all other nodes as domain controllers in the same domain as well. In this example, all nodes are configured as domain controllers.

1. Right-click on My Computer, and click on Properties.

2. Click on Network Identification. The System Properties dialog displays the full computer name and domain. In this example, the domain name is reskit.com.

3. If you are using member servers and need to join a domain, you can do so at this time. Click on Properties and follow the on-screen instructions for joining a domain.

4. Close the System Properties and My Computer windows.

**Table 3.2   IP address settings.**

| Node | Network Name | Network Adapter IP Address |
|------|--------------|----------------------------|
| 1 | Public Cluster Connection | 172.16.12.12 |
| 1 | Private Cluster Connection | 10.1.1.1 |
| 2 | Public Cluster Connection | 172.16.12.14 |
| 2 | Private Cluster Connection | 10.1.1.2 |

*Setting Up a Cluster User Account*

The Cluster Service requires a domain user account under which the Cluster Service can run. This user account must be created before installing Cluster Service because setup requires a user name and password. This user account should not belong to a user on the domain.

1. Select Start|Programs|Administrative Tools|Active Directory Users And Computers.

2. Click on the plus sign (+) to expand reskit.com (if it is not already expanded).

3. Click on Users to select that node in the tree view.

4. Right-click on Users, and select New|User.

5. Type in the cluster name, and click on Next.

6. Set the password settings to User Cannot Change Password and Password Never Expires. Click on Next, and then click on Finish to create this user.

---

**NOTE:** *If your administrative security policy does not allow the use of passwords that never expire, you must renew the password and update the cluster service configuration on each node before password expiration.*

---

7. Right-click on Cluster in the left pane of the Active Directory Users And Computers snap-in. Select Properties from the context menu.

8. Click on Add Members To A Group.

9. Click on Administrators, and then click on OK. This gives the new user account administrative privileges on this computer.

10. Close the Active Directory Users And Computers snap-in.

## Setting Up Shared Disks

To proceed, power off all nodes. Power up the shared storage devices, and then power up node one.

**WARNING!** *Make sure that Windows 2000 Advanced Server or Windows 2000 DataCenter Server and the Cluster Service are installed and running on one node before starting an operating system on another node. If the operating system is started on other nodes before the Cluster Service is installed, configured, and running on at least one node, the cluster disks can be corrupted.*

*About the Quorum Disk*

The quorum disk is used to store cluster configuration database checkpoints and log files that help manage the cluster. You should adhere to the following quorum disk recommendations:

1. Create a small partition (a minimum of 50MB) to be used as a quorum disk. (It is generally recommended that a quorum disk be 500MB.)

2. Dedicate a separate disk for a quorum resource. Because the failure of the quorum disk causes the entire cluster to fail, it is strongly recommended that you use a volume on a RAID disk array.

3. During the Cluster Service installation, you must provide the drive letter for the quorum disk. In this example, the letter Q is used.

### Configuring Shared Disks

To configure shared disks, follow these steps:

1. Right-click on My Computer, click on Manage, and then click on Storage.

2. Double-click on Disk Management.

3. Verify that all shared disks are formatted as NTFS and are designated as Basic. If you connect a new drive, the Write Signature And Upgrade Disk Wizard starts automatically. If this happens, click on Next to go through the wizard. The wizard sets the disk to dynamic. To reset the disk to Basic, right-click on Disk # (where # specifies the disk you are working with) and click on Revert To Basic Disk.

4. Right-click on Unallocated Disk Space.

5. Click on Create Partition.

6. The Create Partition Wizard begins. Click on Next twice.

7. Enter the desired partition size in megabytes, and click on Next.

8. Accept the default drive letter assignment by clicking on Next.

9. Click on Next to format and create the partition.

### Assigning Drive Letters

After the bus, disks, and partitions have been configured, drive letters must be assigned to each partition on each clustered disk using the following steps:

---

**NOTE:** *Mountpoints is a feature of the file system that allows you to mount a file system using an existing directory without assigning a drive letter. Mountpoints is not supported on clusters. Any external disk used as a cluster resource must be partitioned using NTFS partitions and must have a drive letter assigned to it.*

---

1. Right-click on the desired partition, and select Change Drive Letter And Path.

2. Select a new drive letter.

3. Repeat steps 1 and 2 for each shared disk.

4. Close the Computer Management window.

### Verifying Disk Access and Functionality

It is important to verify disk access and functionality once everything is configured. The following steps help you perform basic verification checks:

1. Select Start|Programs|Accessories|Notepad.

2. Type some text into Notepad, and select File/Save As to save it as a test file called test.txt. Close Notepad.

3. Double-click on My Documents.

4. Right-click on test.txt, and click on Copy.

5. Close the window.

6. Double-click on My Computer.

7. Double-click on a shared drive partition.

8. Select Edit|Paste.

9. A copy of the file should now reside on the shared disk.

10. Double-click on test.txt to open it on the shared disk. Close the file.

11. Highlight the file, and press the Delete key to delete it from the clustered disk.

12. Repeat the process for all clustered disks to verify that they can be accessed from the first node.

13. At this time, shut down the first node, power on the second node and repeat the preceding steps. Repeat these steps for any additional nodes. When you have verified that all nodes can read and write from the disks, turn off all nodes except the first and continue with this guide.

## Installing Cluster Service Software

The following sections provide you with the steps to install the Microsoft Cluster Service.

---

**NOTE:** *During installation of Cluster Service on the first node, all other nodes must either be turned off or stopped prior to Windows 2000 booting. All shared storage devices should be powered up.*

---

### Configuring the First Node

In the first phase of installation, all initial cluster configuration information must be supplied so that the cluster can be created. This is accomplished by using the Cluster Service Configuration Wizard:

1. Select Start|Settings|Control Panel.

2. Double-click on Add/Remove Programs.

3. Double-click on Add/Remove Windows Components.

4. Select Cluster Service. Click on Next.

5. Cluster Service files are located on the Windows 2000 Advanced Server or Windows 2000 DataCenter Server CD-ROM. Enter "x:\i386" (where $x$ is the drive letter of your CD-ROM). If Windows 2000 was installed from a network, enter the appropriate network path instead. (If the Windows 2000 Setup splash screen displays, close it.) Click on OK.

6. Click on Next.

7. Select I Understand to accept the condition that Cluster Service is supported on hardware from the HCL only.

8. Because this is the first node in the cluster, you must create the cluster itself. Select The First Node In The Cluster, and then click on Next.

9. Enter a name for the cluster (up to 15 characters), and click on Next. (In this example, the cluster is named MyCluster.)

10. Type the user name of the Cluster Service account that was created during the preinstallation. (In this example, this user name is cluster.) Leave the password blank. Type the domain name, and click on Next.

---

**NOTE:** *You would normally provide a secure password for this user account.*

---

11. At this point, the Cluster Service Configuration Wizard validates the user account and password.

12. Click on Next.

13. The Add Or Remove Managed Disks page specifies which disks on the shared SCSI bus will be used by Cluster Service. Add or remove disks as necessary to reflect your configuration, and then click on Next.

---

**NOTE:** *By default, all SCSI disks not residing on the same bus as the system disk will appear in the Managed Disks list. Therefore, if the node has multiple SCSI buses, some disks may be listed that are not to be used as shared storage (for example, an internal SCSI drive). Such disks should be removed from the Managed Disks list.*

---

14. Note that because logical drives F: and G: exist on a single hard disk, they are seen by Cluster Service as a single resource. The first partition of the first disk is selected as the quorum resource by default. Change this to denote the small partition that was created as the quorum disk (in this example, drive Q). Click on Next.

---

**NOTE:** *In production clustering situations, you must use more than one private network for cluster communication to avoid having a single point of failure. Cluster Service can use private networks for cluster status signals and cluster management. This provides more security than using a public network for these roles. You can also use a public network for cluster management, or you can use a mixed network for both private and public communications. In any case, make sure at least two networks are used for cluster communication, as using a single network for node-to-node communication represents a potential single point of failure. It is recommended that multiple networks be used, with at least one network configured as a private link between nodes and other network connections established through a public network interface. If you have more than one private network, make sure that each uses a different subnet, as Cluster Service recognizes only one network interface per subnet.*

*This example assumes that only two networks are in use. It shows you how to configure these networks as one mixed and one private network. The order in which the Cluster Service Configuration Wizard presents these networks may vary. In this example, the public network is presented first.*

---

**3. Clustering and Multi-Instances**

15. Click on Next in the Configuring Cluster Networks dialog box. Make sure that the network name and IP address correspond to the network interface for the public network. Select the Enable This Network For Cluster Use checkbox. Select the option All Communications (mixed network). Click on Next. This dialog box configures the private network. Make sure that the network name and IP address correspond to the network interface used for the *private* network. Select the Enable This Network For Cluster Use checkbox. Select the option Internal Cluster Communications Only. Click on Next.

16. In this example, both networks are configured in such a way that they can be used for internal cluster communication. The next wizard page offers an option to modify the order in which the networks are used. Because Private Cluster Connection represents a direct connection between nodes, it is left at the top of the list. In normal operation, this connection is used for cluster communication. In case of the Private Cluster Connection failure, cluster service automatically switches to the next network on the list—in this case, Public Cluster Connection. Make sure the first connection in the list is the Private Cluster Connection, and click on Next.

---

**NOTE:** *Always set the order of the connections so that the Private Cluster Connection is first in the list.*

---

17. Enter the unique cluster IP address (172.16.12.20) and Subnet mask (255.255.252.0), and click on Next. The Cluster Service Configuration Wizard automatically associates the cluster IP address with one of the public or mixed networks. It uses the subnet mask to select the correct network.

18. Click on Finish to complete the cluster configuration on the first node. The Cluster Service Setup Wizard completes the setup process for the first node by copying the files needed to complete the installation of Cluster Service. After the files are copied, the Cluster Service Registry entries are created, the log files on the quorum resource are created, and the Cluster Service is started on the first node. A dialog appears telling you that Cluster Service has started successfully. Click on OK. Close the Add/Remove Programs window.

### Validating the Cluster Installation

Use the Cluster Administrator snap-in to validate the Cluster Service installation on the first node.

1. Select Start|Programs|Administrative Tools|Cluster Administrator.

2. You are now ready to install Cluster Service on the second node.

### Configuring the Second Node

Installing Cluster service on the second node requires less time than on the first node. Setup configures the Cluster Service network settings on the second node based on the configuration of the first node.

---

**NOTE:** *For this section, leave node one and all shared disks powered on. Power up the second node.*

---

Installation of Cluster Service on the second node begins exactly as it did for the first node. During installation of the second node, the first node must be running. Follow the same procedures used for installing Cluster Service on the first node, with the following differences:

1. In the Create or Join A Cluster dialog, select The Second Or Next Node In The Cluster, and click on Next.

2. Enter the cluster name that was previously created (in this example, MyCluster), and click on Next.

3. Leave the Connect To Cluster checkbox cleared. The Cluster Service Configuration Wizard automatically supplies the name of the user account selected during the installation of the first node. Always use the same account used when setting up the first cluster node.

4. Enter the password for the account (if there is one), and click on Next.

5. Click on Finish to complete the configuration.

6. The Cluster Service starts. Click on OK.

7. Close Add/Remove Programs.

8. If you are installing additional nodes, repeat the previous steps to install Cluster Service on all other nodes.

## Verifying the Installation

There are several ways to verify a successful installation of Cluster Service. For example:

1. Select Start|Programs|Administrative Tools|Cluster Administrator.

---

**NOTE:** *The presence of two nodes shows that a cluster exists and is in operation.*

---

2. Right-click on the group Disk Group 1, and select the option Move. The group and all its resources are moved to another node. After a short period of time, the Disk containing logical drives F: and G: will be brought online on the second node. If you watch the screen, you can see this shift. Close the Cluster Administrator snap-in.

Congratulations, you have completed the installation of Cluster Service on all nodes. The server cluster is fully operational. You are now ready to install cluster resources, like file shares and printer spoolers; cluster-aware services, like Microsoft Internet Information Services (IIS), Message Queuing, Distributed Transaction Coordinator, DHCP, and WINS; or cluster-aware applications, like Exchange or SQL Server.

# SCSI Drive Installation Considerations

This section is provided as a generic instruction set for SCSI drive installations. If the SCSI hard disk vendor's instructions conflict with the following instructions, always use the instructions supplied by the vendor.

The SCSI bus listed in the hardware requirements must be configured prior to installation of Cluster Services. This includes:

- Configuring the SCSI devices.
- Configuring the SCSI controllers and hard disks to work properly on a shared SCSI bus.
- Properly terminating the bus. The shared SCSI bus must have a terminator at each end of the bus. It is possible to have multiple shared SCSI buses between the nodes of a cluster.

In addition to the information on the following pages, refer to the documentation from the manufacturer of the SCSI device or the SCSI specifications, which can be ordered from the American National Standards Institute (ANSI). The ANSI Web site at **www.ansi.org** contains a catalog that can be searched for the SCSI specifications.

## Configuring the SCSI Devices

Each device on the shared SCSI bus must have a unique SCSI ID. Because most SCSI controllers default to SCSI ID 7, part of configuring the shared SCSI bus will be to change the SCSI ID on one controller to a different SCSI ID, such as SCSI ID 6. If there is more than one disk that will be on the shared SCSI bus, each disk must also have a unique SCSI ID.

Some SCSI controllers reset the SCSI bus when they initialize at boot time. If this occurs, the bus reset can interrupt any data transfers between the other node and disks on the shared SCSI bus. Therefore, SCSI bus resets should be disabled if possible.

**WARNING! Each disk controller may have vendor-specific recommendations that should be followed. The example above may not be valid for your particular environment.**

## Terminating the Shared SCSI Bus

*Y* cables can be connected to devices if the device is at the end of the SCSI bus. A terminator can then be attached to one branch of the Y cable to terminate the SCSI bus. This method of termination requires either disabling or removing any internal terminators the device may have.

*Trilink* connectors can be connected to certain devices. If the device is at the end of the bus, a Trilink connector can be used to terminate the bus. This method of termination requires either disabling or removing any internal terminators the device may have.

Y cables and Trilink connectors are the recommended termination methods because they provide termination even when one node is not online.

**NOTE:** Any devices that are not at the end of the shared bus must have their internal termination disabled.

| Related solution: | Found on page: |
|---|---:|
| RAID Configurations | 6 |

# Failover Clustering Support

In SQL Server 2000 Enterprise Edition, the number of nodes supported in SQL Server 2000 failover clustering depends on the operating system you are running:

- Windows NT 4.0 Enterprise Edition and Windows Advanced Server support two-node failover cluster only.

- Windows 2000 DataCenter Server supports up to four-node failover clustering including an active/active/active/active failover clustering configuration.

The following tools, features, and components are supported with failover clustering:

- *Microsoft Search Service*—For more information, see the "Using SQL Server Tools with Failover Clustering" section.

- *Multiple Instances*—For more information, see the "What Is Multi-Instance?" section.

- *SQL Server Enterprise Manager*—For more information, see the "Using SQL Server Tools with Failover Clustering" section.

- *Service Control Manager*—For more information, see the "Using SQL Server Tools with Failover Clustering" section.

- *Replication*—For more information, see the "Creating a Failover Cluster" section.

- *SQL Profiler*—For more information, see the "Using SQL Server Tools with Failover Clustering" section.

- *SQL Query Analyzer*—For more information, see the "Using SQL Server Tools with Failover Clustering" section.

- *SQL Mail*—For more information, see the "Using SQL Server Tools with Failover Clustering" section.

The SQL Server 2000 Analysis Services component is not supported for failover clustering.

---

**NOTE:** *Microsoft Data Access Components (MDAC) 2.6 is not supported for SQL Server version 6.5 or SQL Server 7.0 when either version is in a failover cluster configuration.*

---

Before using failover clustering, consider the following:

- Failover clustering resources, including the IP addresses and network name, must be used only when you are running an instance of SQL Server 2000. They should not be used for other purposes, such as file sharing.

- In a failover-cluster configuration, SQL Server 2000 supports Windows NT 4.0 Enterprise Edition, but requires that the service accounts for SQL Server services (SQL Server and SQL Server Agent) be local administrators of all nodes in the cluster.

---

**NOTE:** *SQL Server 2000 supports both Named Pipes and TCP/IP Sockets over TCP/IP within a failover cluster. However, it is strongly recommended that you use TCP/IP Sockets in a clustered configuration.*

---

3. Clustering and Multi-Instances

| Related solution: | Found on page: |
|---|---|
| Enterprise Manager | 178 |

## Using SQL Server Tools with Failover Clustering

You can use SQL Server 2000 failover clustering with a variety of SQL Server tools and features. However, review the following usage considerations.

### Full-Text Queries

To use the Microsoft Search service to perform full-text queries with failover clustering, consider the following:

- An instance of SQL Server 2000 must run on the same system account on all failover cluster nodes in order for full-text queries to work on failover clusters.

- You must change the startup account for SQL Server 2000 in the failover cluster using SQL Server Enterprise Manager. If you use Control Panel or the Services Application in Windows 2000, you will break the full-text configuration for SQL Server.

### SQL Server Enterprise Manager

To use SQL Server Enterprise Manager with failover clustering, consider the following:

- You must change the startup account for SQL Server 2000 in the failover cluster by using SQL Server Enterprise Manager. If you use Control Panel or the Services Application in Windows 2000, you could break your server configuration.

- When creating or altering databases, you will only be able to view the cluster disks for the local virtual server.

- If you are browsing a table through SQL Server Enterprise Manager and lose the connection to SQL Server during a failover, you will see the error message, "Communication Link Failure." You must press Esc and undo the changes to exit the SQL Server Enterprise Manager window. You cannot click on Run Query, save any changes, or edit the grid.

- If you use Enterprise Manager to reset the properties of the SQL Server service account, you are prompted to restart SQL Server. When SQL Server is running in a failover cluster configuration, this brings the full text and SQL Agent resources offline, as well as SQL Server. However, when SQL Server is restarted, it does not bring the full text or SQL Agent resources back online. You must start those resources manually using the Windows Cluster Administrator utility.

### Service Control Manager

Use the Service Control Manager to start or stop a clustered instance of SQL Server. You cannot pause a clustered instance of SQL Server. To start a clustered instance of SQL Server:

1. Type the name of the virtual SQL Server in the Server box. If it is a default instance, you only need to specify the virtual server name. If it is a named instance, you must enter VIRTUALSERVER\Instance.

2. In the Services box, click on SQL Server.

3. Click on Start/Continue.

To stop a clustered instance of SQL Server:

1. Type the name of the virtual SQL Server in the Server box. If it is a default instance, you need only specify the virtual server name. If it is a named instance, you must enter VIRTUALSERVER\Instance.

2. In the Services box, click on SQL Server.

3. Click on Stop. This pauses the cluster resource, and then stops the SQL Server service, which does not cause a failover of SQL Server.

### SQL Profiler

You can use SQL Profiler with failover clustering. However, if you experience a failover on a server where you are running a SQL Profiler trace, you must restart the trace when the server is back online to continue tracing.

### SQL Query Analyzer

You can use SQL Query Analyzer with failover clustering. However, if you experience a failover on a server where you are executing a query, you must restart the query when the server is back online to continue execution.

### SQL Mail

To use SQL Mail with failover clustering, consider the following:

- An instance of SQL Server 2000 must run on the same Windows NT 4 and Windows 2000 account on all failover cluster nodes in order for SQL Mail to work on failover clusters.

- Each failover cluster node must have a Messaging Application Programming Interface (MAPI) profile with an identical name and settings.

| Related solutions: | Found on page: |
|---|---|
| Windows Tuning Hints | 48 |
| Query Analyzer | 193 |

## Before Installing Failover Clustering

Before you install a SQL Server 2000 failover cluster, you must select the operating system on which your computer will run. You can use Windows NT 4.0 Enterprise Edition, Windows 2000 Advanced Server, or Windows 2000 DataCenter Server. You also must install Microsoft Cluster Service (MSCS).

### Preinstallation Checklist

The following items should be verified before beginning the installation of failover clustering:

- There is no IRQ sharing between network interface cards (NICs) and drive/array (SCSI) controllers. Although some hardware may support this sharing, it is not recommended.

- Your hardware is listed on the Windows NT HCL. For a complete list of supported hardware, see the HCL on the Microsoft Web site at **www.microsoft.com/hcl**. The hardware system must appear under the category of cluster. Individual cluster components added together do not constitute an approved system. Only systems purchased as a cluster solution and listed in the cluster group are approved. When checking the list, specify cluster as the category. All other categories are for Original Equipment Manufacturer (OEM) use.

- MSCS has been installed completely on at least one node before you run Windows NT 4.0 Enterprise Edition or Windows 2000 Advanced Server or Windows 2000 DataCenter Server simultaneously on all nodes. When using MSCS, you must make certain that one node is in control of the shared SCSI bus prior to the other node(s) coming online. Failure to do this can cause application failover to go into an online pending state. As a result, the cluster either fails on the other node or fails totally. However, if your hardware manufacturer has a proprietary installation process, follow the hardware manufacturer's instructions.

- WINS is installed according to the Knowledge Base article Q258750 "Recommended Private 'Heartbeat' Configuration on Cluster Server."

- The disk drive letters for the cluster-capable disks are the same on both servers.

- You have disabled NetBIOS for all private network cards before beginning SQL Server Setup.

- You have cleared the system logs in all nodes and viewed the system logs again. Ensure that the logs are free of any error messages before continuing.

## Requirements for Creating a Failover Cluster

To create a SQL Server 2000 failover cluster, you must create and configure the virtual servers on which the failover cluster runs. You create virtual servers during SQL Server Setup. Virtual servers are not provided by Windows NT 4 or Windows 2000.

To create a failover cluster, you must be a local administrator with rights to log on as a service and to act as part of the operating system on all computers in the failover cluster.

### Elements of a Virtual Server

A virtual server contains:

- A combination of one or more disks in a Microsoft Cluster Service (MSCS) cluster group. Each MSCS cluster group can contain at most one virtual SQL Server.

- A network name for each virtual server. This network name is the virtual server name.

- One or more IP addresses that are used to connect to each virtual server.

- One instance of SQL Server 2000 including a SQL Server resource, a SQL Server Agent resource, and a full-text resource. If an administrator uninstalls the instance of SQL Server 2000 within a virtual server, the virtual server, including all IP addresses and the network name, is also removed from the MSCS cluster group.

A failover cluster can run across one or more actual Windows 2000 Advanced Server, Windows 2000 DataCenter Server, or Windows NT 4.0 Enterprise Edition servers that are participating nodes of the cluster. However, a SQL Server virtual server always appears on the network as a single Windows 2000 Advanced Server, Windows 2000 DataCenter Server, or Windows NT 4.0 Enterprise Edition server.

### Naming a Virtual Server

SQL Server 2000 depends on distinct Registry keys and service names within the failover cluster so that operations continue correctly after a failover. Therefore, the name you provide for the instance of SQL Server 2000, including the default instance, must be unique across all nodes in the failover cluster as well as across all virtual servers within the failover cluster. For example, if all instances failed over to a single server, their service names and Registry keys would conflict. If INST1 is a named instance on virtual server VIRTSRV1, there cannot be a named instance INST1 on any node in the failover cluster, either as part of a failover cluster configuration or as a stand-alone installation.

Additionally, you must use the VIRTUAL_SERVER\Instance-name string to connect to a clustered instance of SQL Server 2000 running on a virtual server. You cannot access the instance of SQL Server 2000 by using the computer name that the clustered instance happens to reside on at any given time. SQL Server 2000 does not listen on the IP address of the local servers. It listens only on the clustered IP addresses created during the setup of a virtual server for SQL Server 2000.

## Usage Considerations

If you are using the Windows 2000 Address Windowing Extensions (AWE) API to take advantage of memory greater than 3GB, make certain that the maximum available memory you configure on one instance of SQL Server is still available after you fail over to another node. If the failover node has less physical memory than the original node, instances of SQL Server may fail to start or may start with less memory than they had on the original node. You must:

- Give each server in the cluster the same amount of physical RAM.

- Ensure that the summed value of the max server memory settings for all instances is less than the lowest amount of physical RAM available on any of the virtual servers in the failover cluster.

---

**NOTE:** For more information about AWE, see the "Using AWE Memory on Windows 2000" section.

---

If you need high-availability servers in replication, it is recommended that you use an MSCS cluster file share as your snapshot folder when configuring a Distributor on a failover cluster. In the case of server failure, the distribution database will be available and replication will continue to be configured at the Distributor.

Also, when creating publications, specify the MSCS cluster file share for the additional storage of snapshot files or as the location from which Subscribers apply the snapshot. This way, the snapshot files are available to all nodes of the cluster and to all Subscribers that must access it.

If you want to use encryption with a failover cluster, you must install the server certificate with the fully qualified DNS name of the virtual server on all nodes in the failover cluster. For example, if you have a two-node cluster, with nodes named test1.redmond.corp.microsoft.com and test2.redmond.corp.microsoft.com and a virtual SQL Server "Virtsql", you need to get a certificate from "virtsql.redmond.corp.microsoft.com" and install the certificate on both nodes. You can then select the Force Protocol Encryption checkbox on the Server Network Utility to configure your failover cluster for encryption.

**WARNING! You should not remove the BUILTIN/Administrators account from SQL Server. (BUILTIN refers to the Windows NT Administrator account.) The IsAlive thread runs under the context of the cluster service account, and not the SQL Server service account. The Cluster Service must be part of the administrator group on each node of the cluster. If you remove the BUILTIN/Administrators account, the IsAlive thread will no longer be able to create a trusted connection, and you will lose access to the virtual server.**

## Creating a Failover Cluster

To create a failover cluster using the Setup program, use the following basic steps:

1. Identify the information you need to create your virtual server (for example, cluster disk resource, IP addresses, and network name) and the nodes available for failover. The cluster disks to use for failover clustering should all be in a single cluster group and be owned by the node from which the Setup program is run. This configuration must take place before you run the Setup program. You configure this through Cluster Administrator in Windows NT 4 or Windows 2000. You need one MSCS group for each virtual server you want to set up.

2. Start the Setup program to begin your installation. After all necessary information has been entered; the Setup program installs a new instance of SQL Server binaries on the local disk of each computer in the cluster and installs the system databases on the specified cluster disk. The binaries are installed in exactly the same path on each cluster node, so you must ensure that each node has a local drive letter in common with all the other nodes in the cluster. In SQL Server 2000, during a failover only the databases fail over. In SQL Server version 6.5 and SQL Server version 7.0, both the SQL Server databases and binaries fail over during a failover. If any resource (including SQL Server) fails for any reason, the services (SQL Server, SQL Server Agent, Full-Text Search, and all services in the failover cluster group) fail over to any available nodes defined in the virtual server.

3. Install one instance of SQL Server 2000, creating a new virtual server and all resources.

# Creating a New Failover Cluster

Use the following steps to create a new failover cluster:

1. On the Welcome screen of the Microsoft SQL Server Installation Wizard, click on Next.

2. On the Computer Name screen, click on Virtual Server and enter a virtual server name. If Setup detects that you are running MSCS, it defaults to Virtual Server. Click on Next.

3. On the User Information screen, enter the user name and company. Click on Next.

4. On the Software License Agreement screen, click on Yes.

5. On the Failover Clustering screen, enter one IP address for each network configured for client access. That is, enter one IP address for each network on which the virtual server will be available to clients on a public (or mixed) network. Select the network for which you want to enter an IP address, and then enter the IP address. Click on Add.

6. The IP address and the subnet are displayed. The subnet is supplied by MSCS. Continue to enter IP addresses for each installed network until you have populated all desired networks with an IP address. Click on Next.

7. On the Cluster Disk Selection screen, select the cluster disk group where the data files will be placed by default. Click on Next.

8. On the Cluster Management screen, review the cluster definition provided by SQL Server 2000. By default, all available nodes are selected. Remove any nodes that will not be part of the cluster definition for the virtual server you are creating. Click on Next.

9. On the Remote Information screen, enter login credentials for the remote cluster node. The login credentials must have administrator privileges on the remote node(s) of the cluster. Click on Next.

10. On the Instance Name screen, choose a default instance or specify a named instance. To specify a named instance, clear the Default checkbox, and then enter the name for the named instance. Click on Next.

---

**NOTE:** *You cannot name an instance DEFAULT or MSSQLSERVER. For more information about naming instances of SQL Server 2000, see "Working with Named and Multiple Instances of SQL Server 2000" in the Books Online. Names must follow rules for SQL Server identifiers. For more information about naming conventions for identifiers, see "Using Identifiers" in the Books Online.*

---

11. On the Setup Type screen, select the type of installation to install. The Setup program automatically defaults to the first available cluster disk resource from the group you previously selected. However, if you need to specify a different clustered drive resource, under Data Files, click on Browse, and then specify a path on a clustered drive resource. You will be required to select a clustered drive resource that is owned by the node on which you are running the Setup program. The drive also must be a member of the cluster group you previously selected. Click on Next.

12. On the Services Accounts screen, select the service account(s) that you want to run in the failover cluster. Click on Next.

13. In the Authentication Mode dialog, choose the authentication mode to use. If you change the selection from Windows Authentication Mode to Mixed Mode (Windows Authentication and SQL Server Authentication), you need to enter and confirm a password for the sa login.

14. On the Start Copying Files screen, click on Next.

15. On the Setup Complete screen, click on Finish.

If you are instructed to restart the computer, do so. It is important to read the message from the Setup program when you are done with the installation. Failure to restart any of the specified nodes may cause failures when you run the Setup program in the future on any node in the failover cluster.

## Installing a One-Node Failover Cluster
To install a one-node failover cluster, follow these steps:

1. On the Welcome screen of the Microsoft SQL Server Installation Wizard, click on Next.

2. On the Computer Name screen, click on Virtual Server and enter a virtual server name. If SQL Server Setup detects that you are running MSCS, it defaults to Virtual Server. Click on Next.

3. On the User Information screen, enter the user name and company. Click on Next.

4. On the Software License Agreement screen, click on Yes.

5. On the Failover Clustering screen, enter one IP address per installed network for the virtual server. Select the network for which you want to enter an IP address, and then enter the IP address. Click on Add.

6. The IP address and the subnet are displayed. The subnet is supplied by MSCS. Continue to enter IP addresses for each installed network until you have populated all desired networks with an IP address. Click on Next.

7. On the Cluster Disk Selection screen, select the cluster disk group where the data files will be placed by default. Click on Next.

8. On the Cluster Management screen, review the failover cluster definition provided by SQL Server 2000. By default, all available nodes are selected. Remove any nodes that will not be part of the cluster definition for the virtual server you are creating. Click on Next.

9. On the Remote Information screen, enter login credentials that have administrator privileges on the remote node of the cluster. Click on Next.

10. On the Instance Name screen, choose a default instance or specify a named instance. To specify a named instance, clear the Default checkbox, and then enter the name. Click on Next.

---

**NOTE:** *You cannot name an instance DEFAULT or MSSQLSERVER. The name must follow the rules for SQL Server identifiers.*

---

11. On the Setup Type screen, select the type of installation to install. Setup automatically defaults to the first available clustered disk resource from the group you previously selected. However, if you need to specify a different clustered drive resource, under Data Files, click on Browse, and then specify a path on a clustered drive resource. You will be required to select a clustered drive resource that is owned by the node on which you are running Setup. The drive must also be a member of the cluster group you previously selected. Click on Next.

12. On the Services Accounts screen, select the service account(s) that you want to run in the failover cluster. Click on Next.

13. In the Authentication Mode dialog, choose the authentication mode to use. If you change the selection from Windows Authentication Mode to Mixed Mode (Windows Authentication and SQL Server Authentication), you must enter and confirm a password for the sa login.

14. On the Start Copying Files screen, click on Next.

15. On the Setup Complete screen, click on Finish. If you are instructed to restart the computer, do so. It is important to read the message from the Setup program when you are done with the installation. Failure to restart any of the specified nodes may cause failures when running the Setup program in the future on any node in the cluster.

# Maintaining a Failover Cluster

After you have installed a SQL Server 2000 failover cluster, you can change or repair the existing setup. For example, you can add additional nodes to a virtual server in a failover cluster, run a clustered instance as a stand-alone instance, remove a node from a clustered instance, or recover from failover cluster failure.

## Adding a Node to an Existing Virtual Server

During SQL Server Setup, you are given the option of maintaining an existing virtual server. If you choose this option, you can add other nodes to your failover cluster configuration at a later time. You can add up to three additional nodes to an existing virtual server configured to run on one node. Use the following steps to add nodes to an existing virtual server:

1. On the Welcome screen of the Microsoft SQL Server Installation Wizard, click on Next.

2. On the Computer Name screen, click on Virtual Server and specify the virtual server to which you want to add a node. Click on Next.

3. On the Installation Selection screen, click on Advanced options. Click on Next.

4. On the Advanced Options screen, select Maintain A Virtual Server For Failover Clustering. Click on Next.

5. On the Failover Clustering screen, click on Next. You do not need to enter an IP address.

6. On the Cluster Management screen, select the node, and click on Add. If the node is listed as unavailable, you must modify the disk resources in the cluster group of the virtual server so the disk is available for the node you want to add to the SQL Server configuration. Click on Next.

7. On the Remote Information screen, enter login credentials that have administrator privileges on the remote node of the cluster. Click on Next.

8. On the Setup Complete screen, click on Finish.

## Removing a Node from an Existing Failover Cluster

You can remove a node from a virtual server (for example, if a node is damaged). Each node in a virtual SQL Server is considered a peer, and you can remove any node. A removed node can be added back to a failover cluster at any time. For example, a removed node can be rebuilt after a failure and added back to the failover cluster. Alternately, if a node is temporarily unavailable and later comes back online and an instance of SQL Server 2000 from the affected virtual server is still in place, the Setup program removes this instance from the computer before installing the binaries on the node again. Use the following steps to remove a node from an existing failover cluster:

1. On the Welcome screen of the Microsoft SQL Server Installation Wizard, click on Next.

2. On the Computer Name screen, click on Virtual Server, and specify the name of the server from which to remove the node. Click on Next.

3. You may see an error message saying that one (or more) of the nodes of the Windows NT 4 or Windows 2000 cluster are unavailable. This may be because the node(s) you are attempting to remove is damaged. The node(s) can still be removed. Click on OK.

4. On the Installation Selection screen, click on Advanced Options. Click on Next.

5. On the Advanced Options screen, select Maintain A Virtual Server For Failover Clustering. Click on Next.

6. On the Failover Clustering screen, click on Next. You do not need to modify any IP address(es).

7. On the Cluster Management screen, select the node, and click on Remove. Click on Next.

8. On the Remote Information screen, enter login credentials that have administrator privileges on the remote node(s) of the cluster. Click on Next.

9. On the Setup Complete screen, click on Finish.

If you are instructed to restart the computer, do so. It is important to read the message from SQL Server Setup when you are done with the installation. Failure to restart any of the specified nodes may cause failures when you run the Setup program in the future on any node in the failover cluster.

---

**NOTE:** *A damaged node does not have to be available to be removed, but the removal process will not uninstall any of the binaries from the unavailable node.*

---

## Running a Clustered Instance of SQL Server as a Stand-Alone Instance

Usually, you run a clustered instance of SQL Server under the control of MSCS. However, it may be necessary to run a clustered instance of SQL Server as a stand-alone instance (for example, when you want to perform administrative operations such as running an instance of SQL Server in single-user mode). To connect to a clustered instance of SQL Server 2000 in stand-alone mode using sockets, both the IP address and network name resources must be online for the virtual server on which the instance was installed.

If these resources cannot be online, connect using Named Pipes. However, you must create an alias on the client side to talk to the pipe name on which the instance of SQL Server is listening. Use SQL Server Network Utility to find out the pipe name. For more information, see "Failover Cluster Troubleshooting" in the Books Online.

## Recovering from Failover Cluster Failure

Typically, there are two situations that cause failover cluster failure. To recover from this failure, first remove the failover cluster using the Setup program. Use the following steps to remove a failover clustered instance:

1. On the Welcome screen of the Microsoft SQL Server Installation Wizard, click on Next.

2. On the Computer Name screen, click on Virtual Server, and specify the name of the server from which to remove a clustered instance. Click on Next.

3. On the Installation Selection screen, click on Upgrade, Remove, Or Add Components To An Existing Instance Of SQL Server.

4. On the Instance Name screen, for a default instance, click on Default. For a named instance, specify the name of the instance to remove. Click on Next.

5. On the Existing Installation screen, select Uninstall Your Existing Installation. Click on Next.

6. On the Remote Information screen, specify the password that is a valid administrator password on all nodes in the cluster. Click on Next.

7. In the Setup message "Successfully uninstalled the instance . . .", click on OK.

8. On the Setup Complete screen, click on Finish.

If you are instructed to restart the computer, do so. It is important to read the message from SQL Server Setup when you are done with the installation. Failure to restart any of the specified nodes may cause failures when you run the Setup program in the future on any node in the failover cluster.

### How to Recover from Failover Cluster Failure in Situation 1

In Situation 1, failure is caused by hardware failure in Node 1 of a two-node cluster. This hardware failure could be caused by a failure in the SCSI card or the operating system. To resolve this problem, use the following steps:

1. After Node 1 fails, the SQL Server 2000 failover cluster fails over to Node 2.

2. Run SQL Server Setup, and remove Node 1. For more information, see the "Remove a Failover Clustered Instance" section.

3. Evict Node 1 from MSCS. To evict a node from MSCS, from Node 2, right-click on the node to remove, and then click on Evict Node.

4. Install new hardware to replace the failed hardware in Node 1.

5. Install the operating system. For more information about which operating system to install and specific instructions on how to do this, see the "Before Installing Failover Clustering" section.

6. Install MSCS and join the existing cluster. For more information, see the "Before Installing Failover Clustering" section.

7. Run the Setup program on Node 2, and add Node 1 back to the failover cluster. For more information, see the "Adding Nodes to an Existing Virtual Server" section.

*3. Clustering and Multi-Instances*

### How to Recover from Failover Cluster Failure in Situation 2

In Situation 2, failure is caused by Node 1 being down or offline, but not irretrievably broken. This could be caused by an operating system failure. However, recovering from operating system failure using the following steps can take time. If the operating system failure can be recovered easily, avoid using Situation 2. Should you have no other recourse, follow these steps:

1. After Node 1 fails, the SQL Server 2000 failover cluster fails over to Node 2.

2. Run SQL Server Setup, and remove Node 1. For more information, see the "Remove a Failover Clustered Instance" section.

3. Resolve the problem with Node 1.

4. Ensure that the MSCS cluster is working and all nodes are online.

5. Run the Setup program on Node 2, and add Node 1 back to the failover cluster. For more information, see the "Adding Nodes to an Existing Virtual Server" section.

## Changing Service Accounts

You should not change the passwords for any of the SQL Server service accounts when a failover cluster node is down or offline. If you have to do this, you need to reset the password again using Enterprise Manager when all nodes are back online. If the service account for SQL Server is not an administrator in a cluster, the administrative shares cannot be deleted on any nodes of the cluster. The administrative shares must be available in a cluster for SQL Server to function.

# Failover Cluster Troubleshooting

In the following sections, some of the common problems that you may run into with a failover cluster as well as some optimizing tips are discussed.

## Resolving Common Usage Issues

To resolve some common usage problems, consider the following:

- SQL Server 2000 cannot log on to the network after it migrates to another node. SQL Server service account passwords must be identical on all nodes or else the node cannot restart a SQL Server service that has migrated from a failed node. If you change the SQL Server service account passwords on one node, you must change the passwords on all other nodes. However, if you change the account using SQL Server Enterprise Manager, this task is done automatically.

- SQL Server cannot access the cluster disks. A node cannot recover cluster disks that have migrated from a failed node if the shared cluster disks use a different drive letter. The disk drive letters for the cluster disks must be the same on both servers. If they are not, review your original installation of the operating system and MSCS. For more information, see the Windows NT 4.0 Enterprise Edition, Windows 2000 Advanced Server, or Windows 2000 DataCenter Server documentation.

- You do not want a failure of a service, such as full-text search or SQL Server Agent, to cause a failover. To prevent the failure of specific services from causing the SQL Server group to fail over, configure those services using Cluster Administrator in Windows NT 4 or Windows 2000. For example, to prevent the failure of the Full-Text Search service from causing a failover of SQL Server, clear the Affect The Group checkbox on the Advanced tab of the Full-Text Properties dialog box. However, if SQL Server causes a failover, the Full-Text Search service restarts.

- SQL Server does not start automatically. You cannot start a failover cluster automatically using SQL Server. You must use Cluster Administrator in MSCS to automatically start a failover cluster.

- The error message "No compatible resource groups found" is displayed during SQL Server Setup. This error is caused by the Microsoft Distributed Transaction Coordinator (MS DTC) Setup on Windows NT 4.0 Enterprise Edition. MS DTC requires a group containing a network name, IP address, and shared cluster disk to be owned by the local node when the Setup program is run. If this error is displayed, open Cluster Administrator, and make certain there is a group that meets those requirements and is owned by the local node. The easiest way to do this is to move a disk into the cluster group that already contains a network name and IP address. After you have this group on the local node, click on Retry.

- The error message "All cluster disks available to this virtual server are owned by other node(s)" is displayed during Setup. This message is displayed when you select the drive and path for installing data files, and the local node does not own the drive you have selected. Move the disk to the local node using Cluster Administrator to resolve this issue.

- The error message "Unable to delete SQL Server resources. They must be manually removed. Uninstallation will continue." is displayed during SQL Server Setup. This message is displayed if SQL Server Setup cannot delete all of the SQL Server resources. You must go into the Control Panel and uninstall the instance you were trying to remove on every node.

- You cannot enable the clustering operating system error log. The operating system cluster error log is used by MSCS to record information about the cluster. Use this error log to debug cluster configuration issues. To enable the cluster error log, set the system environment variable **CLUSTERLOG=<*path to file*>** (for example, **CLUSTERLOG=c:\winnt\cluster\cluster.log**). This error log is on by default in Windows 2000.

- If the Network Name is offline and you cannot connect using TCP/IP, you must use Named Pipes. To connect using Named Pipes, create an alias using the Client Network Utility to connect to the appropriate computer. For example, if you have a cluster with two nodes (Node A and Node B), and a virtual server (Virtsql) with a default instance, you can connect to the server that has the Network Name resource offline by doing the following:

  1. Determine on which node the group containing the instance of SQL Server is running by using the Cluster Administrator. For this example, it is Node A.

  2. Start the SQL Server service on that computer using *net start*. For more information about using net start, see the "Starting SQL Server Manually" section.

  3. Start the SQL Server Network Utility on Node A. View the pipe name on which the server is listening. It should be similar to \\.\$$\VIRTSQL\pipe \sql\query.

  4. On the client computer, start the Client Network Utility.

  5. Create an alias, SQLTEST1, to connect via Named Pipes to this pipe name. To do this, use Node A as the server name and edit the pipe to be \\.\pipe\$$ \VIRTSQL\sql\query. Connect to this instance using the alias SQLTEST1 as the server name.

## Optimizing Failover Clustering Performance

To optimize performance when using failover clustering, consider the following:

- If your disk controller is not external to your clustered computer, you must turn off write-caching within the controller to prevent data loss during a failover.

- Write-back caching cannot be used on host controllers in a cluster without hindering performance. However, if you use external controllers, you continue to provide performance benefits. External disk arrays are not affected by failover clustering and can sync the cache correctly, even across a SCSI bus.

- It is recommended that you do not use the cluster drive for file shares. Using these drives impacts recovery times and can cause a failover of the cluster group due to resource failures.

## Using Extended Stored Procedures and COM Objects

When you use extended stored procedures with a failover clustering configuration, all extended stored procedures need to be installed on the shared cluster disk. This is to ensure that when a node fails over, the extended stored procedures can still be used.

If the extended stored procedures use COM components, the administrator needs to register the COM components on each node of the cluster. The information for loading and executing COM components must be in the Registry of the active node in order for the components to be created. Otherwise, the information remains in the Registry of the computer on which the COM components were first registered.

## Using AWE Memory on Windows 2000

SQL Server 2000 Enterprise Edition uses the AWE API to support very large amounts of physical memory. SQL Server 2000 Enterprise Edition can access amounts of memory approaching 8GB on Windows 2000 Advanced Server and approaching 64GB on Windows 2000 DataCenter Server.

Standard 32-bit addresses can map a maximum of 4GB of memory. The standard address spaces of 32-bit Microsoft Windows NT 4 and Windows 2000 processes are therefore limited to 4GB. By default, 2GB is reserved for the operating system, and 2GB is made available to the application. If you specify a /3GB switch in the boot.ini file of Windows NT Enterprise Edition or Windows 2000 Advanced Server, the operating system reserves only 1GB of the address space, and the application can access up to 3GB. For more information about the /3GB switch, see the documentation for Windows NT Enterprise Edition or Windows 2000 Advanced Server Help.

AWE is a set of extensions to the memory management functions of the Microsoft Win32 API, which allows applications to address more memory than the 4GB that is available through standard 32-bit addressing. AWE lets applications acquire physical memory as nonpaged memory, and then dynamically map views of the nonpaged memory to the 32-bit address space. Although the 32-bit address space is limited to 4GB, the nonpaged memory can be much larger. This enables memory intensive applications, such as large database systems, to address more memory than can be supported in a 32-bit address space. For more information about AWE, see the MSDN page on the Microsoft Web site.

## Enabling AWE Memory

You must specifically enable the use of AWE memory by an instance of SQL Server 2000 Enterprise Edition by using the **sp_configure** option *AWE enabled*. When AWE enabled is set to 0, AWE memory is not used, and the instance defaults to using dynamic memory in standard 32-bit virtual address spaces.

When an instance of SQL Server 2000 Enterprise Edition is run with AWE enabled set to 1:

- AWE memory is used, and the instance can access up to 8GB of physical memory on Windows 2000 Advanced Server and 64GB on Windows 2000 DataCenter Server.

- The instance does not dynamically manage the size of the address space.

- The instance holds all memory acquired at startup until it is shut down.

- The memory pages for the instance come from the Windows nonpageable pool, meaning that none of the memory of the instance can be swapped out.

You must carefully manage the memory used by an instance of SQL Server when AWE enabled is set to 1. If the instance acquires most of the available physical memory as nonpaged memory, other applications or system processes may not be able to access the memory they need to run. Use the max server memory configuration setting to control how much memory is used by each instance of SQL Server that uses AWE memory. For more information, see the "Using AWE Memory on Windows 2000" in this chapter.

| *Related solution:* | *Found on page:* |
|---|---|
| Specification of a New Server | 18 |

# Chapter 4

# Installing and Upgrading to Microsoft SQL Server 2000

# In Depth

This chapter covers the basic information you need to install Microsoft SQL Server 2000 or upgrade an existing SQL Server to SQL Server 2000. There are a number of details that you need to consider before starting the upgrade or installation process, which are also covered in this chapter. Using the information provided, you should be able to successfully complete the installation or upgrade process painlessly and safely.

## SQL Server Instances

An installation of Microsoft SQL (MSSQL) Server 2000 is known as an *instance*. You can run multiple instances of SQL Server on one computer. Each instance operates independently with its own name, services, Registry entries, and databases. There are two types of instances that can be installed on MSSQL Server 2000: a Default Instance and Named Instances.

### Default Instance

A Default Instance is identified by the name of the computer. There can only be one Default Instance per computer. If you are installing MSSQL Server 2000 on a computer that already contains a copy of MSSQL Server 7, you have the option to leave the MSSQL Server 7 installation as the Default Instance and install a Named Instance of MSSQL Server 2000. If you are installing on a computer that contains a copy of MSSQL Server 6.5, you must install SQL Server 2000 as a Default Instance. The SQL Server 6.5 installation can be left on the machine, but it cannot be run at the same time. To run each version, you would have to switch between the two using the MSSQL Server 2000 Version Switch (VSwitch) command prompt utility. The Default Instance of MSSQL Server 2000 operates in the same way as previous versions of MSSQL Server. When more than one instance is installed on a single computer, client applications will attempt to connect to the Default Instance if only a computer name is supplied.

**NOTE:** *If you intend to have MSSQL Server 7 installed as the Default Instance, the MSSQL Server 7 icons in the program group will execute the MSSQL Server 2000 files including the MSSQL Server Books Online.*

# Named Instances

All installations of MSSQL Server 2000 on a machine, other than the Default Instance, are known as Named Instances. These are identified by the computer name plus an instance name in the format of computer_name\instance_name. An instance name can consist of up to 16 characters. The name can start with a letter, an underscore, or an ampersand and can contain any combination of letters, numbers, and other characters. MSSQL Server 2000 supports a total of 16 instances per machine, but the number of instances that can actually be installed depends on the available resources of the machine. Although MSSQL Server allows up to 16 instances on a single system, only the MSSQL Server 2000 database engine can operate as a Named Instance. If an installation of MSSQL Server 7 will be run concurrently with MSSQL Server 2000, it must run as the Default Instance.

## Independent Components of Each Instance

Some components of the installation must be maintained separately for each instance installed on the server. The following list provides a description of these components:

- *SQL Server Name*—Computer_name\instance_name identifies the name of an MSSQL Server 2000 instance.

- *System Databases*—Each instance has its own set of system databases.

- *User Databases*—The user databases created for an instance are owned by the instance under which they are created. These databases can be detached and then reattached to a different instance if you need to move them.

- *SQL Services*—Every instance contains its own MSSQLSERVER Service and SQLSERVERAGENT Service.

- *Registry Keys*—Each service has its own set of keys associated with that particular instance that is recognized by the MSSQL database engine.

- *Network Connection Address*—Each instance creates its own network connection address, so that applications can connect to the associated instance.

- *Directory Structure*—The directory structure is the path in which the databases, backups, and Dynamic Link Libraries (DLL) can be segregated from every other instance running on the system.

## Shared Components of MSSQL Server 2000 Instances

Although each instance of MSSQL Server 2000 is recognized independently, certain components are still shared by all instances.

- *Program Group*—There is only one set of the MSSQL Server 2000 utilities that is used for every instance (Enterprise Manager, Query Analyzer, MSSQL Profiler, etc.).

- *Services*—Although each instance runs on its own services, some services are shared among all MSSQL Server 2000 instances. These services include:

  - MSSQLSearchService

  - English Query Service

  - MSSQL Server 2000 Analysis Service

- *Registry Keys*—The Registry keys are the keys associated with the client software.

- *Development Libraries*—The Development Libraries contain the Include and .lib files.

### Multiple Instances

There are some advantages to being able to run multiple instances of MSSQL Server 2000 on a single machine. Separate instances can be installed to segregate different front-end applications that rely on MSSQL Server 2000 as the back-end. It is now possible to separate SQL Servers by department, region, quarter, or development version without the need to purchase additional hardware. Multiple instances of MSSQL Server 2000 can also be set up to accommodate different languages. For example, the Default Instance can be installed with the English Version, whereas another instance can be installed with the Japanese Version.

A couple of issues to keep in mind when installing multiple instances of MSSQL Server 2000 are:

- Each Instance utilizes resources on the system. Although having multiple instances on a single computer may seem cost-effective, it is also resource-intensive. The performance penalties of running multiple instances on your server may cost more than the additional hardware.

- The utilities installed to administrate MSSQL Server 2000 are from the Default (or first) Version of MSSQL Server 2000.

---

**NOTE:** The Books Online defaults to the language installed for the Default Instance of SQL Server.

---

- Because the licensing of SQL Server is controlled either by licensing each processor or by client access licenses, the number of instances of SQL Server installed on a server does not affect licensing. For an explanation of Microsoft's licensing and price structures for SQL Server 2000, refer to the following page on its Web site: **http://www.microsoft.com/sql/productinfo/pricing.htm**.

## SQL Server Services

Windows services are processes that perform system functions to support other programs. Three services are created when MSSQL Server 2000 is installed. The following sections detail each of these services and provide descriptions of their function.

### MSSQLSERVER

MSSQLSERVER is MSSQL Server's database engine. It manages all of the files that make up the databases. There is an MSSQLSERVER Service for each instance of MSSQL Server 2000 on a machine. The Default Instance of MSSQL Server uses the default service name of MSSQLSERVER. All Named Instances install their own server services, which are identified as MSSQL$instance_name.

### SQLSERVERAGENT

MSSQL Server uses the SQLSERVERAGENT process to schedule activities and notify system administrators of server problems. The Default Instance installs the server agent as SQLSERVERAGENT. Each Named Instance uses the naming format of SQLAGENT$instance_name to distinguish each server agent service associated with the instance.

### Microsoft Search

Microsoft Search is a full-text indexing and search engine that allows MSSQL Server to do more complex string searches. All instances of MSSQL Server utilize one single MSSearchService running on the system.

# SQL Server Editions

Microsoft has included several different editions with the release of SQL Server 2000. Consequently, you will need to decide which version of SQL Server 2000 you are going to install. The following list contains a description of each edition offered.

- *Personal Edition*—This version is used on a client computer that is running a standalone application that requires SQL Server data storage. The user who is running applications that need SQL Server data storage but who cannot be connected to the network full-time will prefer this edition. This is also the edition of choice for users needing a mobile solution.

- *Standard Edition*—This edition is used as a small to mid-size database server.

- *Enterprise Edition*—This edition is the choice for larger production database servers. Its performance levels are scalable enough to support the largest application loads. The Enterprise Edition also supports data warehousing systems.

- *Desktop Engine*—This is the version of SQL Server 2000 that software vendors can package and distribute with their applications.

- *Developer Edition*—This is the edition that programmers use while designing and developing applications. It supports all the features of the Enterprise Edition, but cannot be licensed as a production database server.

- *Windows CE Edition*—This edition is used for data storage on a Windows CE device. The data can then be kept current with the database server through the use of replication.

# Installation

This section covers the actual installation of MSSQL Server 2000. The information provided is intended to help you become familiar with the installation process. It also provides insight into the details you will need to consider before starting the actual installation of your server.

## Requirements

There are several items that must be taken into account before installing MSSQL Server 2000. The following list contains some of these items as well as a description of each:

- *Computer*—Your computer must have an Intel or compatible processor. The processor must be a Pentium 166 or higher, Pentium III, or Pentium Pro. There is no Hardware Compatibility List (HCL) for SQL Server 2000. As long as your computer meets all requirements necessary to run your version of Windows, you should be fine.

- *Memory*—The Enterprise Edition of SQL Server 2000 requires a minimum of 64MB RAM, whereas the Standard Edition requires a minimum of 32MB RAM.

- *Disk Space*—For a full install, 180MB are required. For a typical install, 170MB are required. For the minimum install, 65MB are required, and 90MB are required if you are only installing the client utility tools.

- *Internet Requirements*—Microsoft Internet Explorer 5.0 and higher is required for all SQL Server 2000 installations.

- *Operating System*—The Enterprise and Standard Editions of SQL Server require a minimum of Windows NT Server 4.0. There are some features of the Enterprise Edition that can only be taken advantage of with Windows 2000 Server. The Personal Edition can be installed on Windows 98 or higher. Although an instance of MSSQL Server 2000 can be installed on MS Windows 95, it is recommended to have MS Windows 98 installed before installing MSSQL 2000. If an instance of MSSQL 2000 is going to be installed on a MS Windows 95 system, the Winsock2 must be updated before installation. The Developer Edition can be installed on Windows NT Workstation or higher.

**Table 4.1   SQL Server edition that can be installed by operating system.**

| SQL Server Edition or Component | Operating System Minimum Requirement |
| --- | --- |
| Enterprise Edition | Microsoft Windows NT Server 4.0, Microsoft Windows NT Server Enterprise Edition 4.0, Windows 2000 Advanced Server, and Windows 2000 DataCenter Server. |
| Standard Edition | Microsoft Windows NT Server 4.0, Windows 2000 Server, Microsoft Windows NT Server Enterprise Edition, Windows 2000 Advanced Server, and Windows 2000 DataCenter Server. |
| Personal Edition | Microsoft Windows 98, Windows NT Workstation 4.0, Windows 2000 Professional, Microsoft Windows NT Server 4.0, Windows 2000 Server, and all the more advanced Windows operating Systems. |
| Developer Edition | Windows NT Workstation 4.0, Windows 2000 Professional, and all other Windows NT and Windows 2000 operating Systems. |
| Client Tools Only | Windows NT 4, Windows 2000 (all versions), and Windows 98. |
| Connectivity Only | Windows NT 4 or Windows 2000, Windows 98, and Windows 95. |

The Client Utility Tools can be installed on Windows 98 or higher. Table 4.1, which is based on information in the MSSQL Server 2000 Books Online, distinguishes the requirements of each operating system and the edition of MSSQL Server 2000 that can be installed.

## Pre-installation

Before you begin the installation of SQL Server 2000, there are some matters that should be considered. This section lists a number of requirements that must be met and other issues based on the previous version (if any) of SQL Server you have installed. Also listed are other tasks that should be completed prior to starting the installation of SQL Server 2000, regardless of whether this will be a new installation or an upgrade of an existing installation.

### MSSQL Server 6.5

If you want to install MSSQL Server 2000 on a machine with an existing installation of MSSQL Server 6.5, Service Pack 5 or higher *must* be applied to your MSSQL Server 6.5 installation prior to beginning the install process. MSSQL Server 6.5 will not run concurrently with MSSQL Server 2000. The MSSQL 6.5 Server must be accessed by means of the MSSQL VSwitch.

### MSSQL Server 7.0

MSSQL Server 7.0 can run concurrently alongside MSSQL Server 2000 as the Default Instance without accessing the MSSQL VSwitch. If a system contains both MSSQL Server 6.5 and MSSQL Server 7.0, then the MSSQL Server 7.0 Version must be the active version before installation of MSSQL Server 2000 is initiated.

### Creating a User Account

A user account is needed to start the MSSQL Services when the system is booted. There are two types of accounts that can be set up in a Windows server environment: a local account and a domain user account. A local account starts the services without the requirement of a password, but it does not have access to the network. If a local account is desired, the setup can create a local system account at the time of installation. A domain account is usually used because some options can only be utilized when the system is logged on to with an account that can access the network. Some of these options include:

- Backing up to network drives
- Replication
- MSSQL Mail
- Remote Procedure Calls

### Checklist

The following is a pre-installation checklist that should be completed prior to beginning an installation of SQL Server 2000:

- Back up all databases if MSSQL Server 2000 will not be the first instance installed on the server.
- If the server will participate in a failover cluster, then the administrator must disable NetBIOS on all private network cards before the installation of MSSQL Server 2000.
- Know which collation settings are required by your company before installation. More often than not, these settings will be the default.

**WARNING! If regional, character set, or sort order settings are changed after the installation of any MSSQL Server, the databases will have to be rebuilt, and the data will have to be repopulated!**

- Set up a user account on the domain so the MSSQL Services can start with this account.
- Log on to the server with the local administrator account or an account that has similar permissions.
- Shut down all services that depend on the MSSQL Service.

---

**TIP:** Shut down any services that are using Open Database Connectivity (ODBC), such as Internet Information Server (IIS).

---

- Review all MSSQL Server 2000 installation options and make the appropriate decisions before starting the installation.

# Installing MSSQL Server 2000

The installation of MSSQL Server 2000 is pretty simple and straightforward. Depending upon the preparation and environment SQL Server will reside within, the complete setup of an MSSQL Server 2000 instance takes approximately 20 minutes.

### MSSQL Server 2000 Splash Screen

Insert the MSSQL Server 2000 CD into the CD-ROM drive. It should start automatically, but if it doesn't, you can double-click autorun.exe in the root directory of the CD. The first screen that appears is the default splash screen. Within the splash screen are options to prepare for the installation of MSSQL Server 2000 as well as the option to start the installation.

The first option, Install SQL Server 2000 Prerequisites, is an important one if the system targeted for installation happens to be a Microsoft Windows 95 computer. The options under prerequisites include a Winsock2 Update for Windows 95 and an option to install the Common Controls Library Update.

The second option is the setup for MSSQL Server 2000.

The third option is a Help menu that contains a list of articles specifically related to the installation process. This can be an extremely useful tool and should be examined prior to starting the installation process.

The fourth option is the release notes that document the product and touch base on some of the new features of the product.

The fifth and last option is a shortcut to an Internet site that has last minute notes, fixes, or other documentation related to the product. It is strongly recommended that you visit this site prior to the installation to obtain any information and updates available. This can save you hours of headaches troubleshooting a problem that has already been identified and corrected by Microsoft.

After you have reviewed the previous checklist, you're ready to start the installation, Click on Install SQL Server Components, and the Edition screen appears. Select the edition of MSSQL Server 2000 that is desired. If you are unsure which version to install on the target computer, refer back to the "Requirements" section in this chapter.

### Installing SQL Server 2000 Components

The next screen presents the component options of MSSQL Server 2000:

- *Database Server*—This is the first component; it installs SQL Server 2000.

- *Analysis Services*—This component is designed to facilitate Online Analytical Processing (OLAP) applications.

- *English Query*—English Query allows developers to build applications that provide end users with the ability to pose questions in English rather than forming questions with a SQL statement.

## Computer Name

After continuing through a couple of screens by clicking on Next, the computer name dialog is presented with three options:

- *Local Computer*—This is the default. Leave the setting as is if SQL Server is going to be installed on the local computer.
- *Remote Computer*—This option should be chosen if the installation of SQL Server is intended for a computer located on the network.
- *Virtual Server*—This option is available if the administrator is intending to install MSSQL Server 2000 on a virtual system.

If the installation of SQL Server is not going to be located on the local machine, enter the name of the computer on which you want to modify or create a new instance of SQL Server.

## Installation Selection

The installation dialog offers three options: Create A New Instance Of SQL Server, Upgrade (remove is included with the upgrade option), or Advanced Options. The Advanced option allows you to perform advanced functions with regards to modifying an installation or creating an unattended installation file.

## User Selection

The user selection has two sections that expect user information. The first, which is required, is a field presented for your name. The second option is a field designated for the company name. The company name field is optional and can be left blank.

## Software License Agreement

Scroll through and read the license agreement. Click on Yes if you agree to the terms. If you do not agree to the terms, the installation is aborted.

## Installation Definition

Under the Installation Definition, one of three options is available:

- *Client Tools Only*—This option is used if you do not want to install SQL Server, and you will be connecting to an existing server.
- *Server and Client Tools*—This is the option to choose if you wish to install SQL Server and have administrative privileges to the server. This is the default.
- *Connectivity Only*—This option installs only the Microsoft Data Access Components (MDAC) and Network Libraries.

## Instance Name

The Instance Name dialog prompts you for a name that will be used to identify the server. If this is the first instance, then the Default Instance is selected and the name of the local computer is used. Otherwise a name must be supplied to identify the Named Instance.

## Setup Type

There are a couple of decisions to be made in the Setup Type box. Select the type of setup you prefer. Typical is recommended for most users and is the default. Minimum is used to install the minimum required options needed to run SQL Server and is recommended for users who have minimum disk space available. Custom allows you to change any of the default options and is recommended for the more advanced user. You will also need to choose the location of the program and data files. The program files typically do not change as you use SQL Server, so their space requirements shouldn't change.

The data files should be stored on a drive that has plenty of space for growth as SQL Server is used. If you want to change the default directory where the program files and data files are stored, simply click on the Browse button to specify the desired location. At the bottom of the dialog, the amount of space that is required for each particular set of data is listed along with the amount of space that the directory currently has available. In an ideal environment, the data and log files should be put on separate partitions, preferably on separate physical devices. For clarity, it is a good idea to specify a different path name for each instance's data.

## Service Accounts

The Service Accounts dialog allows the administrator to set a domain user account to start the SQL Services every time MSSQL Server 2000 starts. A domain user account is not mandatory, but there are certain aspects of SQL Server that cannot be accomplished if the system account is selected to start the SQL Services (for more information, see the "SQL Server Accounts" section earlier in this chapter).

At the top of the dialog, there is an option to select the same user account to start both the MSSQLSERVER Service and the SQLSERVERAGENT. The other choice is to select a user for each service individually. If Customize The Settings For Each Service is chosen, select Auto Start Service if you want the MSSQLSERVER service and the SQLSERVERAGENT service to automatically restart after a system shutdown.

## Authentication Mode

The Authentication Mode determines the security validation method used by client applications to connect to a SQL Server. The Windows Authentication Mode simply restricts all SQL logins to valid domain user accounts, which have been set within SQL Server. Mixed Mode is a combination of Windows authentication and SQL Server authentication. Previous versions of SQL Server installed sa with no password, leaving it to be assigned after the installation process. It was discovered that many sites did not assign an sa password, which was a huge security risk. As a result, you must now either assign a password for sa or explicitly indicate in a checkbox that you are going to leave the sa password blank. A blank password is not recommended.

---

**NOTE:** *The sa account is the SQL Server system administrator account, so a password should be added to keep this access secure.*

---

### Completing the Installation

After the Authentication Mode information has been entered, Setup then starts copying the files to install MSSQL Server. After the installation process has finished, you will see the Setup Complete screen. Click on Finish, and you will have successfully installed SQL Server 2000 on your computer.

## SQL Server Program Group

Let's take a quick look at the MSSQL Server program group that is added during the installation process. Figure 4.1 shows the icons for the tools and utilities installed with SQL Server 2000. These tools are covered in more detail in Chapter 5.

### Books Online

The Books Online is the complete documentation for SQL Server 2000. You should take a few minutes to explore the Books Online and get acquainted with the types of information it contains, how it is structured, and how it can be searched. The

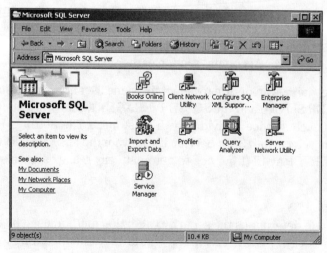

Figure 4.1    Program icons.

Books Online will probably be your best source of information for troubleshooting any SQL Server problems.

### Client Network Utility Program

The Client Network Utility program is where you can configure the Net-Libraries used by client applications to connect to an instance of SQL Server 2000.

### Configure SQL XML Support in IIS

The Configure SQL Extensible Markup Language (XML) Support in IIS program defines and registers a virtual directory before accessing a SQL Server 2000 database by way of Hypertext Transfer Protocol (HTTP).

### Enterprise Manager

The Enterprise Manager is a client utility that can be run locally or remotely to administer your SQL Server machines.

### Import and Export Data

The Import and Export Data icon is a shortcut to the Data Transformation Services Import/Export Wizard. This tool allows you to Import/Export data between like and heterogeneous data sources.

### SQL Profiler

Profiler is a tool that captures SQL Server events either to the screen or to a trace file. Profiler can be filtered to capture only a select few events or every event that occurs on the server. A primary use for Profiler is to troubleshoot the server. Slow running or problem queries can be captured and diagnosed. Profiler can also be used to determine what steps are required to perform certain tasks. For example, let's say you want to write a script to automate the task of adding users and granting database access but don't know the system-stored procedures necessary to do that. You can enable Profiler, and then use Enterprise Manager to add a user and grant database access. You can then look at the trace file that was created by Profiler and see what procedures were called to perform the task you are interested in.

### Query Analyzer

The Query Analyzer is a graphical query tool that allows you to query tables on the server you are connected to.

### Server Network Utility

The Server Network Utility configures the Net-Libraries your server is listening on.

### Service Manager

The Server Manager is a utility that performs the same functions as the Services icon in the Administrative Tools. It is an easy way to start and stop SQL Server-related services. After installation, an icon appears in the tool tray on the left of the taskbar. This is a shortcut to the Server Manager.

# Upgrading to SQL Server 2000 from Previous SQL Versions

There are some hardware and software issues you should take into consideration when performing an upgrade. The requirements for installing SQL Server 2000 that were described earlier are all still necessary. If you are upgrading a version of SQL Server 6.5 to SQL Server 2000 on the same machine, you will need to make sure you have applied Service Pack 5 or higher to your copy of SQL Server 6.5. If you're doing the upgrade on a different computer, you must have applied Service Pack 3 or higher to your copy of SQL Server 6.5. You will also need about one and one-half times the hard disk size of all your SQL Server 6.5 databases to complete the upgrade. On the MSSQL Server 6.5, make sure that there is 25MB set for Tempdb and 3MB free in the master database. If you're upgrading from SQL Server 7.0, there are no Service Pack or hard disk requirements. All versions of SQL Server must be set to use the Named Pipes protocol when doing an upgrade.

Note that you cannot upgrade directly to SQL Server 2000 from SQL Server 6.0. If you happen to be running 6.0, you have a couple of options to get you to SQL Server 2000. First, you can upgrade to SQL Server 7.0 using 7.0's Upgrade Wizard. It allows you to go straight from 6.0 to 7.0. Then, you can use Setup and go from your copy of SQL Server 7.0 to SQL Server 2000. Second, you can convert your 6.0 data to 6.5, and then use the Upgrade Wizard to go from 6.5 to SQL Server 2000.

In order to upgrade your databases from SQL Server 6.5 to SQL Server 2000, you must already have an instance of SQL Server 2000 installed on either the same server as the SQL Server 6.5 installation or another server. After the upgrade is finished, you will have two completely separate copies of the database, one owned by each version of SQL Server. You can leave the SQL Server 6.5 version running as long as you need it. It is a good idea to keep the SQL Server 6.5 version available until you are sure that your data was upgraded successfully, and you no longer have a need for the older version.

Once you have an installation of SQL Server 2000 up and running, it is an easy task to upgrade one or more databases to SQL Server 2000 from SQL Server 7. You have the option of performing this task manually, or by using the Copy Database Wizard. The manual process involves detaching the database from your SQL Server 7 server and copying or moving the data to your SQL Server 2000 server. Once the data has been copied or moved, you simply need to attach the database and it will be upgraded automatically. This is actually the process performed internally by the Copy Database Wizard. The major advantage to using the Copy Database Wizard is that logon information, jobs, and user-specific objects can be automatically transferred along with the database.

Before doing any upgrade, make sure that you make backups of all your databases. No matter how good the upgrade process may be, there is always the possibility of failure, and you need to make sure you have backups of everything so you can completely restore your system if necessary.

### Upgrading the Catalog Stored Procedures

MSSQL Server uses a set of stored procedures known as *catalog stored procedures* to attain vital information from the system catalog. MSSQL Server 2000 installs the catalog stored procedures when an install or upgrade has been successfully completed.

The file that holds the update to the catalog stored procedures is called an instcat.sql file. If an instance of SQL Server is connecting to an MSSQL Server 6.5 or earlier edition, then the catalog stored procedures must be upgraded. To upgrade the catalog stored procedures, back up the master database first. The instcat.sql file can then be run from the Query Analyzer, ISQL window, or from the command prompt (preferred). To run the instcat.sql file from the command prompt, open a command prompt window and type:

```
C:>ISQL /Usa /P<password> /S<server name> /I<path>\Instcat.sql
```

## Rebuilding the Master Database

The master database is an MSSQL system database that holds vital information about the meta data and has entries for every database that is configured within that particular database. If the master database is dysfunctional, then that instance of MSSQL Server is dysfunctional as well. If the master database becomes corrupt, it does not necessarily mean that MSSQL Server has to be uninstalled, reinstalled, or upgraded. The master database can be rebuilt. The master database has to be rebuilt if any collation settings are changed on an instance of MSSQL Server. To rebuild the server, use the rebuild master utility (rebuildm.exe), which is located in <drive>:\program files\Microsoft SQL Server\80\Tools\Binn.

## Unattended Installation

An unattended installation is supported with MSSQL Server 2000. This can provide an easy and convenient solution for installing several similar instances of SQL Server. Performing an unattended installation allows you to bypass the prompts and user intervention and allows an administrator the ability to configure the installation according to standards that may be set within a company. Before an unattended installation can be executed, the setup process needs an initialization file, which can be created in several different ways.

### Initialization Files

A number of initialization files are provided on the MSSQL Server 2000 CD. They include:

- *Sqlins.iss*—This file installs a typical installation of MSSQL Server.

- *Sqlcli.iss*—This file installs the client tools only.

- *Sqlcst.iss*—This file installs a custom installation in which all components are installed.

- *Sqlupg.iss*—This file allows an upgrade from MSSQL Server 7.0 to MSSQL Server 2000.

- *Sqlupsku.iss*—This file upgrades from MSSQL Server 2000 Standard Edition to MSSQL Server 2000 Enterprise Edition.

- *Sqlrem.iss*—This file is the unattended installation that removes MSSQL Server 2000 from the computer.

- *Setup.iss*—This is the file created when an installation of the Default Instance is performed on the server.

An .iss file retains the components and configuration that were installed on the local computer. The file is placed in the system root directory <%windir%>. The setup.iss custom file can be created without installing an instance of MSSQL Server by using the Record Unattended .iss option in the Setup program. The file is created as you select the options for installing an instance of MSSQL Server; however, the SQL Server files are not actually installed.

To run an unattended install, run the Setup program \msolap\install\setup.exe on the CD that ships with MSSQL Server using the following parameters:

- **-r**—Allows Setup to generate a silence response file (installation input) in the Microsoft Windows folder.

- **-s**—Performs a silent unattended installation.

- **-f1**—Is the alternate path and name of the response file. If omitted, the response file has to be in the same directory as the Setup executable.

- **-f2**—Is the alternate path and name of the log file (optional); the default log file (setup.log) is located in the Winnt folder.

### Batch Files

There are the same numbers of batch files (with the same prefix and installation types described previously) as there are initialization files to initiate an unattended installation. The batch file tries to locate the response file (.iss file) in the same directory as the batch file that is executed if the –f1 option is omitted. A batch file can also be used with an smssql.pdf file (a format file used to create a SQL Server package in Software Management System [SMS]). For more information about an SMS installation, refer to "Installing SQL Server using SMS" in the MSSQL Server 2000 Books Online.

## Post Installation

After the installation of MSSQL Server 2000, it is a good idea to check the MSSQL Server thoroughly to verify that the installation completed successfully.

The first sign that an installation has completed successfully is to start the MSSQLSERVER Service. To start the service from a command prompt, type:

```
Net start mssqlserver
```

The MSSQLSERVER Service can also be started within the services applet in the Control Panel or the Server Manager, which both provide a GUI interface to start the service. If the service starts successfully, launch the Enterprise Manager, and check the SQL Server Logs located in the management folder under the new instance. The Event Viewer is another tool that will indicate any problems during the installation. If SQL Server does not start as expected, the Application Log in the Event Viewer is one of the first places to start gathering information for troubleshooting a bad installation.

When you are satisfied that the server has in fact started successfully, open the Query Analyzer with the sa login to query the integrity of the system databases installed with SQL Server. If the Query Analyzer opens, then a connection is established to the server and the sa account is a valid administrative login. The first query that you execute should check the server name (this ensures that the instance can be identified as you intended, and it also assures you that a connection to an already existing server is not giving you a false sense of security):

```
SELECT @@SERVERNAME
```

The next query should check the version of SQL Server to ensure that the component was installed as expected:

```
SELECT @@VERSION
```

After these checks prove to be legitimate, run a fast and easy test on all the system databases with a simple query to check database integrity, such as:

```
SELECT *
  FROM sysobjects (NOLOCK)
```

Once the installation has been completed to your satisfaction, check the database options within the Enterprise Manager to ensure that the databases will run as expected. The database options are accessed by expanding the instance, navigating to Databases, right-clicking on the desired database, left-clicking on Properties, and then left-clicking on the Options tab. If the server will be creating new databases, it might be a good idea to set the database options for the model database, which will decrease the administrative overhead when setting up a number of new databases.

## Model Database

The model database is a template for the creation of any new databases. When a database is created with all the defaults, it has the same properties the model has at the time of its creation. The size is the same, database options like Automatic File Growth At 10 Percent and Truncate Logon Checkpoint are set the same, and even the users in the model database are carried over to the new database. Once again, if a number of databases will be created on the server and the databases are similar to one another, take the time at the outset to set up the model database accordingly.

## Compatibility Level

If MSSQL Server 2000 was applied as an upgrade to a previous version, it is a good idea to check the compatibility level of each database. Even though the database is running on an MSSQL Server 2000 database engine, it can still emulate (to a certain degree) a previous version of MSSQL Server. To check the database compatibility level, open the Query Analyzer, choose the master database from the drop-down menu if it is not already the target database, and type:

```
EXEC sp_dbcmptlevel <'database_name'>
-- The results look like ...
The current compatibility level is 80.
```

If the compatibility level is not at the expected or desired level, the database can be changed with the same syntax:

```
EXEC sp_dbcmptlevel <'database_name'>, <65|70|80>
```

Included on the CD accompanying this book is a script called usp_cmptlevel.sql, which checks all databases within a given instance for their compatibility level.

For more information on the different compatibility levels of MSSQL Server, refer to the MSSQL Server 2000 Books Online and search for sp_dbcmptlevel.

After verifying the state of an installation or an upgrade, *back up all databases*!

# Uninstalling SQL Server 2000

SQL Server 2000 can be uninstalled or removed from your computer in a few ways. The following sections describe each method.

## Control Panel

You can remove SQL Server 2000 by using the Add/Remove feature of the Control Panel. Select the name of the SQL Server instance you want to delete, and click on Remove. Each instance has to be removed separately. If you want to delete all instances on a computer, repeat the removal process for each one. Some directories may still exist when you're finished, so you will need to delete them manually.

## Setup CD

You can remove SQL Server 2000 by using the Setup option on the installation disk. Insert the SQL Server 2000 CD into the CD-ROM drive. It should automatically start, but if it doesn't, you can double-click on the autorun.exe file in the root directory of the CD. Select Install SQL Server 2000 Components, and then select the edition you want to install or actually uninstall in this case. In the Computer Name box, choose either Local Computer or Remote Computer. In the Installation Selection box, choose upgrade, remove, or add components to an existing instance of SQL Server, and click on Next. In the Instance Name box, click on Next. In the Existing Installation box, choose Uninstall Your Existing Installation. Setup will then remove the existing installation.

## Registry

A complete uninstall sometimes calls for the removal of keys associated with an application using the Registry Editor (RegEdit). Always back up the Registry before attempting to make any changes. The keys associated with MSSQL Server are as follows:

**HKEY_LOCAL_MACHINE\SOFTWARE\MICROSOFT\MICROSOFT SQL SERVER\MSSQL SERVER**

# *Immediate Solutions*

## Installing MSSQL Server 2000

This section provides the steps required to install a Default Instance of Microsoft SQL Server 2000 Enterprise Edition on a local production server. Make sure you are logged on to the system as a user who has local administrative privileges.

1. Insert the compact disk into the CD-ROM drive. If MSSQL Server 2000 does not start the installation automatically, double-click autorun.exe in the root directory of the compact disk.

2. Select SQL Server 2000 Components to bring up the Install Components page of the install, which is shown in Figure 4.2.

3. Select Install Database Server.

4. Click Next on the Welcome dialog.

5. Select Local Computer, which is the default, on the Computer Name dialog and click Next to continue.

6. Choose Create A New Instance Of SQL Server in the Installation Selection dialog, which is shown in Figure 4.3. Click Next to continue.

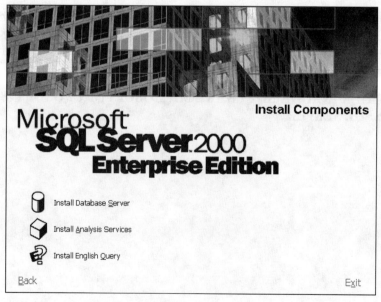

Figure 4.2    Install Components page.

4.  Installing and Upgrading to Microsoft SQL Server 2000

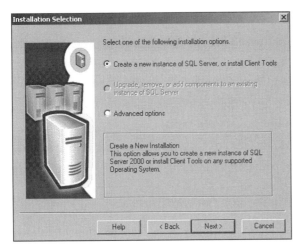

Figure 4.3    Installation Selection dialog.

7. The User Information box will now appear. Enter your name in the Name Edit box. This is a required entry. The Company Edit box is an optional entry that you can complete or leave blank. Click Next to continue.

8. On the Software License Agreement dialog you must click the Yes button in order to continue.

9. In the Installation Definition dialog, select the Server And Client Tools option and click Next to continue.

10. The Instance Name dialog is shown in Figure 4.4. Once the Instance Name dialog appears, check the box to select Default For The First Installation Of MSSQL Server 2000 On This Computer.

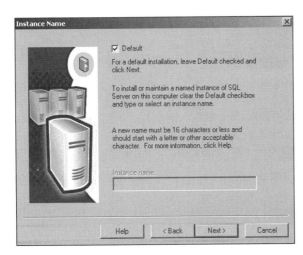

Figure 4.4    Instance Name dialog.

11. Click Next to continue.

12. In the Setup Type dialog, shown in Figure 4.5, choose Custom and then click Next to continue.

13. Figure 4.6 shows the Select Components dialog, where you select the components you want to install for SQL Server.

14. Select Server Component under Components.

15. Under Sub-Components, select the following sub-components: SQL Server, Replication Support, and Performance Counters. Make sure all other sub-components are deselected.

16. Select Management Tools in the Components list box.

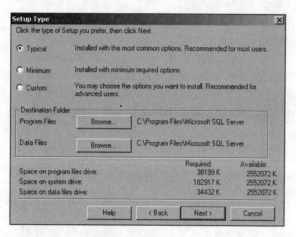

Figure 4.5   Setup Type dialog.

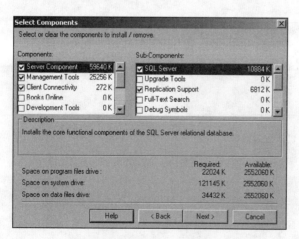

Figure 4.6   Select Components dialog.

17. Under Sub-Components, select all sub-components except Profiler.

18. Make sure that Client Connectivity is selected under Components.

19. Make sure the following options under Components are deselected: Books Online, Development Tools, and Code Samples.

20. Click Next to continue.

21. In the Services Accounts dialog, shown in Figure 4.7, Select Customize The Settings For Each Service.

22. Select SQL Server under Services.

23. Select Use a Domain User account under Service Settings.

24. Enter the Username, Password, and Domain for a user account that was created for the MSSQLSERVER service before the MSSQL Server 2000 installation was started.

25. Check the box for Auto Start Service.

26. Select SQL Server Agent under Services.

27. Select Use A Domain User Account under Service Settings.

28. Enter the Username, Password, and Domain for a user account that was created for the MSSQLSERVERAGENT service before the MSSQL Server 2000 installation was started.

29. Check the box for Auto Start Service.

30. Click OK on the warning dialog that pops up.

31. Click Next to continue.

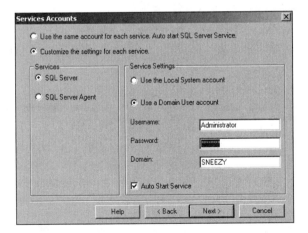

Figure 4.7    Services Accounts dialog.

32. Select Mixed Mode (Windows Authentication and SQL Server Authentication) in the Authentication Mode dialog and type in a password for the sa login.

33. Click Next to continue.

34. Leave the default selections on the Collation Settings dialog and click Next to continue.

35. Keep the default selections on the Network Libraries dialog and click Next to continue.

36. Click Next on the Start Copying Files dialog to continue.

37. Select the appropriate option in the Choose Licensing Mode dialog for the licensing strategy you will employ. This example will select the Processor License for 1 processor. Click Continue.

38. If the Microsoft Data Access Components (MDAC) 2.6 Setup detects any tasks that need to be shut down in order to complete the installation, a dialog will be displayed listing the tasks that will be shut down automatically. If this dialog appears, you should review what is being shut down and click Next to continue.

39. Click the finish button to begin the installation of MDAC 2.6.

*Warning! There are currently a number of compatibility issues between this version of MDAC and some existing applications. Prior to installation, you may want to verify that the software you are using will not be negatively impacted by this new version.*

40. Once the MDAC installation is complete, the SQL Server installation will continue and begin copying files to the server.

41. When the Setup Complete dialog appears, click the Finish button to complete the installation.

# Upgrading Databases from Microsoft SQL Server 7

If you have an existing installation of Microsoft SQL Server 7, you will most likely, at some point, find it necessary to move or copy some of your existing databases from SQL Server 7 to SQL Server 2000. There are two easy ways to accomplish this task, and this section will provide you with step-by-step instructions for each of them.

## Manually Upgrading Microsoft SQL Server 7 Databases

Manually transferring your data from SQL Server 7 to SQL Server 2000 is a fairly easy task, once you know the procedure. This section will walk you step-by-step through the manual process of performing this upgrade on a database.

1. From a machine with the SQL Server 2000 tools installed, open the Query Analyzer.

2. Connect to your SQL Server 7 server.

3. Select the database that you want to move or copy to SQL Server 2000.

4. Execute the code shown in Listing 4.8 to generate a script to detach and reattach the database.

5. Copy the output of this SQL into your clipboard.

6. Switch to the MASTER database.

7. Paste the generated code into the query window.

8. Execute the **SP_DETACH_DB** command.

9. Manually copy the files shown in the **SP_ATTACH_DB** command from the SQL Server 7 Server to the SQL Server 2000 server.

10. If you are leaving the database on your SQL Server 7 server, run the **SP_ATTACH_DB** command in the generated code to reattach the database.

11. Your database is now available on your SQL Server 7 server if you need to access it for any reason.

12. Select File | Connect from the menu.

13. Connect to your SQL Server 2000 server.

14. Paste the generated code into the new query window that is connected to your SQL Server 2000 server.

15. Change the path information in the **SP_ATTACH_DB** command to the location that you copied the files on your SQL Server 2000 server.

16. Execute the **SP_ATTACH_DB** command to attach the database to your SQL Server 2000 server.

17. The database is upgraded automatically when it is attached. You now have a functional copy of the database on your SQL Server 2000 server.

18. You will need to set the permissions for the database to make it accessible to your client applications.

19. It is recommended that you run **SP_UPDATESTATS** on the database once it has been transferred. The SQL Server 7 statistic information may negatively impact the performance of the database on SQL Server 2000.

20. You should set the compatibility of the database to make use of all the new features of SQL Server 2000. By default, the compatibility level that was set for the database on the SQL Server 7 server will be preserved. The valid compatibility levels for a database are 60, 65, 70, or 80. The command to set the compatibility level for a database is:

```
sp_dbcmptlevel [ [ @dbname = ] name ]
               [ , [ @new_cmptlevel = ] version ]
```

21. Close the Query Analyzer.

**Listing 4.1    Code to Generate Attach and Detach Commands for a Database.**

```
/* Declare Variables */
DECLARE @v_DB VARCHAR(30),
        @v_DBFile VARCHAR(255),
        @v_FilCt INT,
        @v_SQLLine VARCHAR(400)

/* Get Database Name */
SELECT @v_DB = DB_Name()

/* Generate Detach Code */
PRINT '/* Detach '+@v_DB+' Database */'
PRINT 'SP_DETACH_DB '+@v_DB
PRINT 'GO'
PRINT ''

/* Generate Re-Attach Code */
PRINT '/* Re-Attach '+@v_DB+' Database */'
PRINT 'SP_ATTACH_DB @v_dbname = N'''+@v_DB+''', '

/* Initialize File Counter */
SELECT @v_FilCt = 0

/* Create Cursor to Retrieve Database Filenames */
DECLARE c_MyCursor CURSOR FOR
  SELECT FileName
    FROM sysfiles (NOLOCK)

/* Open Cursor */
OPEN c_MyCursor
FETCH NEXT FROM MyCursor INTO @v_DBFile
```

```
/* Get Filenames for the Database */
WHILE (@@FETCH_STATUS <> -1)
  BEGIN
  IF (@@FETCH_STATUS <> -2)
    BEGIN
    /* Write the FaleName Parameter Line With a Comma */
    IF (@v_SQLLine IS NOT NULL) PRINT @v_SQLLine + ','

    /* Increment the File Counter */
    SELECT @v_FilCt = @v_FilCt + 1

    /* Build the FaleName Parameter Line */
    SELECT @v_SQLLine = '          @v_FileName' + CONVERT(VARCHAR, @v_FilCt) +
                  ' = N''' + RTRIM(@v_DBFile) + ''''
    END
  FETCH NEXT FROM c_MyCursor INTO @DBFile
  END

/* Write the last FaleName Parameter Line Without a Comma */
IF (@v_SQLLine IS NOT NULL) PRINT @v_SQLLine

/* Close and Deallocate the Cursor */
CLOSE c_MyCursor
DEALLOCATE c_MyCursor
```

| Related solution: | Found on page: |
| --- | --- |
| Detaching and Attaching Databases | 189 |

## Using the Database Copy Wizard

The Database Copy Wizard actually makes use of the same technique employed to move the data manually. The advantage of using the wizard is that SQL Server does most of the work for you. You select the source and target information and the transfer is done using a DTS task. This section will walk you step-by-step through the process of moving the data using the wizard.

1. From a machine with the SQL Server 2000 tools installed, open the Enterprise Manager.

2. If you have not already done so, you will need to register both the SQL Server 7 server that you want to copy a database from and the SQL Server 2000 server that you want to copy the database to. Refer to the Immediate Solutions in Chapter 5 for step-by-step instructions to register a server in the Enterprise Manager.

3. Expand the tree and select the SQL Server 7 server in the treeview.

4. Select Tools | Wizards… from the menu.

5. Expand the Management node in the tree.

6. Double-click on Copy Database Wizard in the tree view to launch the Copy Database Wizard shown in Figure 4.8.

7. Click Next to continue.

8. Select your SQL Server 7 server in the "Source server" drop-down box.

9. Provide the necessary authentication information for your SQL Server 7 server.

10. Click Next to continue.

11. Select your SQL Server 2000 server in the "Target server" drop-down box.

12. Provide the necessary authentication information for your SQL Server 2000 server.

13. Click Next to continue.

14. The next page presents you with a list of the databases on the selected source server. This list will indicate whether or not the database can be copied to the target server. The wizard will not allow you to rename a database, so a database of that name must not exist already on the target server.

15. Locate the database that you wish to copy to the SQL Server 2000 server.

16. Check either the Copy or Move box in the list box for the database you wish to transfer.

17. If you select more than one database to transfer in the list, the databases will be copied one after another by the DTS task generated by this wizard.

18. Click Next to continue.

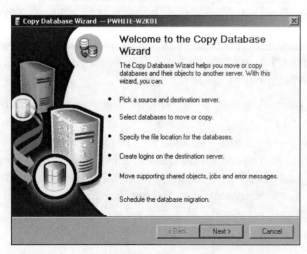

Figure 4.8   Copy Database Wizard—page one.

19. This page indicates the size and drive letter information for the database and log files on the target server. You can change the destination path by clicking the Modify button near the bottom of the page. The default path for data and log information that was set during the installation of SQL Server 2000 will be used automatically unless you modify that information now.

20. When you have finished changing the path information and closed the Database Files dialog, click Next to continue.

21. Select the related objects that you want to transfer along with the database from SQL Server 7 to SQL Server 2000.

22. Click Next to continue.

23. The next page allows you to schedule the execution of the DTS package that is being generated by this wizard. Select the option that best meets your needs. Remember that the database will not be available on either server during the copy process.

24. Click Next to continue.

25. Click Finish on the last page to schedule or execute the DTS Package generated by the wizard. This page provides you with the details of your selections for a final review before completing the wizard.

26. If you scheduled the package for immediate execution, a Log Detail dialog will appear that shows the progress of the transfer process. Once the transfer has completed, click the Close button to close the dialog.

27. Expand the Databases folder under your SQL Server 2000 server in the tree view in the Enterprise Manager.

28. If your new database does not appear in the list, right-click on the Databases folder and select Refresh from the context menu to update the display.

29. Right-click on the database in the tree view.

30. Select Properties from the context menu.

31. Select the Options tab.

32. At the bottom of this tab, the compatibility level for this database is displayed. You should select "Database compatibility level 80" to allow full access to the new features of SQL Server 2000 for this database.

33. Click the OK button to close the database Properties dialog.

34. Close the Enterprise Manager.

35. It is recommended that you open the Query Analyzer and run **SP_UPDATESTATS** on the database you just transferred. The SQL Server 7 statistic information may negatively impact the performance of the database on SQL Server 2000.

# Chapter 5

## Microsoft SQL Server Tools

# In Depth

The tools that ship with Microsoft SQL Server 2000 are worth serious study by the database administrator (DBA) and the developer alike. They include functionality to maintain, configure, and optimize a server with an easy-to-use graphical interface. Database design and maintenance are also extremely well supported by the standard set of tools shipped by Microsoft. All of the tools needed for the tuning and optimization of the server, database, and queries possess astonishing power and are easy to use. Taking the time to become familiar with these tools early in the implementation phase of Microsoft SQL Server 2000 will save time and increase productivity for any and all projects on this platform. Let's begin with a brief look at the available tools and their major uses.

## Enterprise Manager

The most important tool for managing servers and databases is the Enterprise Manager. This tool encompasses all of the server configuration and maintenance functionality as well as database design and maintenance. It is a comprehensive set of graphical interfaces to all of Microsoft SQL Server 2000's management functionality. It also contains a host of wizards to help the novice and the expert alike perform a variety of tasks, such as server registration, setting up maintenance schedules, and database replication. In addition to these management functions, the Enterprise Manager can also serve as a launching point for almost all of the other tools. The amount of flexibility in this tool creates a multitude of paths that can be taken to accomplish almost any given task.

This section walks you through all the core functionality contained in the Enterprise Manager, but it is by no means complete. Be sure to spend some time working with the menus and toolbars as you go through this section to become familiar with the various options available to complete certain tasks.

The Enterprise Manager is built as a snap-in for the Microsoft Management Console (MMC). MMC provides a common console framework for server and network management applications. These applications are known as snap-ins and allow administrators to more effectively manage network resources. All of the Microsoft BackOffice products, like SQL Server and Exchange, use this method for server management. There are also third-party vendors developing snap-ins for managing their backend server applications. These add-ins can add nodes to the structure in the tree pane as the user selects or expands a node and can augment node menus with items that will cause their program to be called when those items are selected. You can also use this technology to build your own snap-ins for more effective management of your environment.

The technology used to create the functionality in Enterprise Manager is available in an Application Programming Interface (API) called SQL Distributed Management Objects (DMO). You can use SQL DMO to create your own custom management applications. These objects are a set of ActiveX Dynamic Link Libraries (DLLs) that can be called from languages like Visual Basic (VB) or Delphi to create an application for server management. This allows you to create an application to perform automated tasks that provide a Graphical User Interface (GUI) for monitoring progress. You can also use this API to create applications that expose only the tasks that you want the users in your organization to have access to without providing them the full capability of the Enterprise Manager.

*NOTE: The screen shots is this section were taken using the Taskpad view for server and database related functions. This view can be turned on by right-clicking on the server and selecting View|Taskpad from the context menu.*

# Managing Servers

This section will introduce you to the features in the Enterprise Manager that provide access to server management functionality. The interfaces provided for managing SQL Servers in the Enterprise Manager will allow you to perform most if not all of your configuration and maintenance work for servers from this one centralized location.

## Registering a Server

In the Enterprise Manager tool, you first need to register the server or servers you will be working with. This can be accomplished either through the Register SQL Server Wizard (the default) or by using a simple dialog to provide the needed information. Step-by-step instructions for registering a server using the Server Registration Wizard are provided in the "Immediate Solutions" section of this chapter. The first screen of the wizard gives you the opportunity to turn off the wizard for server registration. This allows you to perform the entire registration using a single dialog. The information needed to register a server is fairly simple, so an experienced user will appreciate the ability to use a single dialog (shown in Figure 5.1) and complete the registration very quickly.

## Editing Properties for a Previously Registered Server

The dialog shown in Figure 5.1 is used to edit the registration properties of a previously registered server. The registration information consists of the server name and the login information. SQL Server can be configured to use either Windows NT or SQL Server login authentication. Microsoft SQL Server 2000 can be configured to support either Windows NT authentication only or both of these methods of authentication. You may need to contact your DBA to determine which of these

Figure 5.1    Registered SQL Server Properties dialog.

methods is available in your environment. Once you have established the server and appropriate login information, you need to choose a group to have the server added to. If you have a large number of servers, it is a good idea to group them according to some logical scheme to make it easier to find the server you need. You also have a few connection options that you can select. These options consist of displaying the server state in the console, displaying the system databases and objects, and starting the server on connection if it is not already running.

---

**NOTE:** *Displaying the system databases and tables can be useful, but carefully consider the dangers before turning them on for non-DBAs because doing so allows the opportunity to inflict accidental harm on the system information in the database. It is recommended that you leave the display of system tables disabled during normal operations to avoid unintentional alteration of this critical data.*

---

### SQL Server Properties

Once you have successfully registered at least one server, you are ready to use the other features of the Enterprise Manager. The left pane of the display allows you to drill down into the server groups, servers, and databases in a treelike fashion similar to Windows Explorer. This allows you to select the server, database, or table (or other database object) that you will be performing tasks on. Selecting the server displays some basic server and configuration information in the right pane. Holding the cursor over the yellow button in the Server section in the right pane brings up a menu. This menu allows you to register another server, edit the registration properties (like login information or whether or not to display system databases and tables) of a server that was previously registered, and change the configuration properties for the selected server.

Selecting the Properties option on the menu brings up a dialog that allows adjustment to the configuration settings of SQL Server. The SQL Server Properties [Configure] dialog has eight tabs that allow you to change various settings of the server. This dialog provides an easy-to-use graphical interface to many of the Microsoft SQL Server 2000 configuration options. Please refer to the "Immediate Solutions" section for detailed instructions on using this dialog and some recommended changes to the default settings.

Notice that some tabs have radio buttons at the bottom for the configured values and running values. These allow you to see what is configured and which options are currently in use by Microsoft SQL Server 2000. Some configuration options require Microsoft SQL Server 2000 to be restarted before they take effect. Changing from the Configured values to the Running values allows you to see if any changes that have been made require the server to be restarted before they will take effect. The information shown for running values is read-only.

### Configuring Multiserver Administration and Replication

Figure 5.2 shows the configuration menu for SQL Server Multiserver Administration and Replication. Multiserver Administration participation is configured by using the first two options on this menu. First, use the Make A Master Server option to allow one instance of SQL Server to declare itself a multiserver administration master server (MSX) by creating an administering operator. Second, use

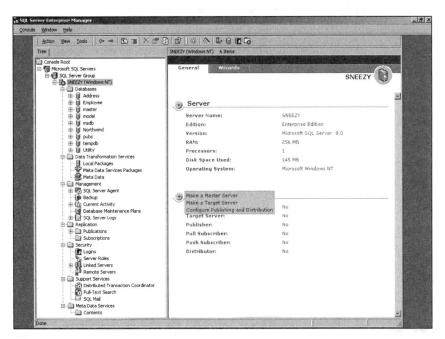

Figure 5.2    The Enterprise Manager.

the Make A Target Server option for other servers to enlist with the configured MSX. These servers then become administration target servers (TSX). The multiserver administration for SQL Server is implemented using a hub and spoke technology, which means that one MSX cannot enlist as a target of any other MSX in the organization. It is also not allowed for a TSX to enlist as the target of any other MSX. The MSXEnlist and MSXDefect methods can be used to establish and break the master-target relationships. You must use MSXDefect to break the relationship prior to enlisting the target server in a new multiserver administration group. The Configure Publishing And Distribution option on the menu launches the Configure Publishing and Distribution Wizard, which walks you through setting up replication for the current SQL Server.

### Wizards View

The Wizards view, shown in Figure 5.3, provides easy access to the available configuration wizards as well as other tools, like the Query Analyzer, Profiler, and Books Online. Numerous wizards are provided to simplify the process of managing databases and servers. These wizards can be used to decrease the amount of time required to manage the server and databases, thus allowing a single DBA to manage a greater number of servers effectively. They can also be used to allow a greater level of involvement in the maintenance of the server by non-DBAs. This can be especially useful in development and testing environments,

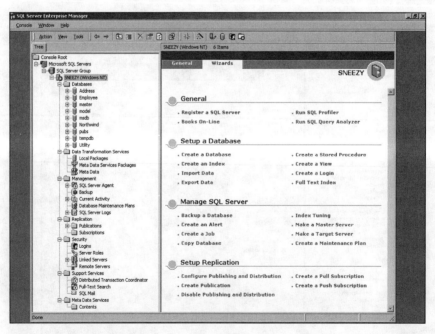

Figure 5.3   Wizards view.

which can require a greater number of servers than a normal production environment. It is fairly easy to train the development and testing staff to perform the basic maintenance functions, like backup and restore operations, using the wizards and tools provided.

The wizards available in Microsoft SQL Server 2000 make administering a server easier than any previous version of Microsoft SQL Server. In fact, they make common server administration so easy that some companies have been able to implement and manage a server without having a DBA on staff. You can obtain adequate performance from a server using this method, but there is really no substitute for a qualified DBA for servers running in any type of critical production environment. There are a number of software companies that advertise their software as not really needing a DBA, but this situation leaves you at the mercy of the technical support group of your software vendor to resolve any problems that arise that are outside of the normal routine. A good DBA also works to keep the server tuned to maximize the performance of applications running against it as well as monitor for conflicts between various applications to resolve any problems that arise as quickly as possible.

### DTS and Replication

Enterprise Manager is where the majority of the setup and maintenance for DTS and Replication are performed. It is a good idea to become familiar with the available options and where they can be accessed in the tools. Figure 5.3 shows these options expanded in the tree for the selected server. These options can be configured and administered for each registered server in Enterprise Manager.

### Management

Management gives you access to several key areas of server management. The various management features are shown expanded in the tree in Figure 5.3. This is where you can access most of the functionality you need to manage and administer the servers for your enterprise. The options in this section cover normal maintenance and administration tasks that you need to perform on a regular basis. Refer to Chapter 6 for more detailed information on maintaining your server.

The SQL Server Agent is responsible for running scheduled jobs, monitoring server activity, and sending alerts to configured operators of the status of the server and the scheduled tasks. Alerts can be configured to notify the administrator of server problems to allow quick resolution before the problem grows out of control. You can configure an Operator to get the configured Alerts as well as configure the Alert to launch a configured job. Because the DBA will often be away from his desk, the best method to notify him will probably be via pager. This can be accomplished using email on most modern paging systems. Errors can be monitored by specific number, severity, or message text. The alerts can pertain to all databases or a specific database. In addition to the capability to notify an operator, the alert can also be used to fire off a maintenance job that may be able to correct the problem without human intervention, like backing up the transaction log to free the space in use for committed transactions. Operators can be configured to allow notifications by the configured alerts and jobs. The operator setup includes the operator's name, email address, pager number, and net send address. There is also a setup for the pager "on duty" schedule to determine when paging will occur. In addition to notifications when a configured alert occurs, any scheduled job can be configured to notify an operator on the completion of the job or an error in the job. This can be especially useful when the administrator has several locations to manage and may not be able to check the jobs directly on a daily basis. Jobs are maintenance tasks that can be scheduled to run as needed. These tasks can include regular backups, database consistency checks, and so on. This can also be useful for scheduling and running off-hour tasks on the server, like large reports or replication tasks. Jobs can also be set up to run tasks on demand. This allows the DBA to create tasks that can be run by a non-DBA if needed or to set up complicated processes that are used on an irregular basis to make them easier to run when needed. Each job consists of a series of one or more steps. Each step can specify whether or not the job should continue if the step fails. This provides a great deal of flexibility in configuring jobs that have both dependent and independent steps. Jobs have their own notification configuration that can be set up to notify an operator on successful completion or failure. The job can also be configured to write to the NT Application Event Log. If you have a job that you need to run only once, but you need to make sure it successfully completes, you can schedule the job to run at intervals and delete itself if it finishes successfully.

Backup allows you to create, delete, and rename backup devices. You can also perform database backups from this section. This is also where you can look at the contents of the backup devices you have created. The context menu in this section allows you to perform database backups and customize the view to suit your personal taste. You even have the option to export the list of backup devices to a text file, which can easily be imported into a spreadsheet or database.

Current activity provides information on the users connected to the server. With this feature, you can find out which users are connected, which machines they are connected from, and what applications they are using to connect to the server. You can also obtain information about database locks. The locks are shown by connection and also by object. This information can be helpful in spotting deadlocks, blocking, or lock-related slowdowns. You can kill a process from this feature, allowing you to remove a user that has been left "hung" in the system after an abnormal system shutdown or other error. This function can also be useful for terminating a process that is blocking or preventing the execution of a necessary maintenance task.

Database Maintenance Plans allows you to establish regular scheduled server maintenance in a wizard-driven fashion. This is a simple way of establishing and scheduling reasonable periodic maintenance. You may need to perform some additional steps for your particular environment, but this wizard covers the basic steps that should be performed in most environments. Integrity checking, reorganizing data, shrinking the database (if possible), and regular database and transaction log backups are all covered by this wizard.

SQL Server Logs let you look at what has been happening with the server since it was last started. Microsoft SQL Server 2000 also keeps backups of the last six or fewer logs (you can configure a lower number). Chapter 6 provides details on how to modify the registry to allow storing more than the default number (six) of old error logs. The SQL Server logs are a good place to start looking if you suspect any type of server problem. This section also provides access to archived logs for the previous six server logs. It gives you plenty of history for diagnosing most problems that occur in the environment as well as makes it easy to determine when a problem first appeared in the system if you have not checked the log recently. It is strongly recommended that you check the log for problems at least once a day as a DBA. The earlier a problem is discovered, the better the chance of correcting it before it becomes a major problem.

### Security

Security allows you to configure the users, logins, and roles for the server and their associated database permissions. The expanded list of available options is shown in Figure 5.3. This section provides access to the basic features for managing security for SQL Server. Logins, Server Roles, and Linked Servers are all managed in this section.

Logins is where everyone who has permission to log in to the server must first be set up. The login contains a name and password, the default database to attach to, and the default language. In addition, the login can also be associated with one or more server roles to grant server-wide security privileges to the login. Specific database access and database roles can also be associated with the login. This only applies to SQL Server authentication. If you are using Windows NT authentication, you will not need to set up the logins for the users in SQL Server.

Server Roles shows the list of predefined server roles and the access privileges granted by each role. You can also add logins to the roles from this area. The predefined roles cover a reasonable range of access levels to make it easier to establish the security for logins and to allow multiple levels of administration.

Remote Servers is included for backward compatibility. Setting up a remote server allows you to run stored procedures on the remote server. If you do not already have remote servers configured, it is suggested that you set up a linked server instead because linked servers support running both stored procedures and distributed queries.

Linked Servers can be established to allow queries against OLE DB data sources on different servers. This provides the capability to run distributed queries, transactions, updates, and commands across the entire enterprise on heterogeneous data sources. This also allows different data sources to be accessed in a more uniform fashion. The OLE DB provider, which is shipped as a DLL for the data source that is returning data, must be present on the same server as Microsoft SQL Server 2000. Refer to Books Online for a list of the providers that have been tested for use as Linked Servers. If you are setting up Federated servers for data partitioning, you will need to create Linked Servers for the other servers in the federation to allow the partitioned views to access them. Federated servers will be explained in Chapter 10 and Chapter 17.

### Support Services

Support Services consist of the Distributed Transaction Coordinator (DTC), Full-Text Search, and SQL Mail. These are additional services that work in conjunction with SQL Server to provide enhanced capabilities. These services can be stopped, started, and configured from this section.

MS DTC is the Microsoft facility for a two-phase commit, which is the protocol for coordinating transaction atomicity across multiple resource managers. A list of the scenarios that can be enabled for distributed transactions is available in Books Online. Distributed transactions must be atomic, which means that they must either commit all resource managers or abort all of them. No portion of a distributed transaction can be allowed to commit unless all of them can be committed successfully. If you will be using MTS, you should configure this service to be started automatically, because this is required for MTS to work with SQL Server.

The Full-Text Search service must be configured and running in order to access the database using full-text indexes. Queries that perform full-text search operations pass the full-text search request to the Full-Text Search service for processing, and this service returns the results to SQL Server for further processing or returns the results to the client.

SQL Mail must be set up and running to allow email notifications for alerts and job completion status. It is also possible to process incoming mail and to send mail from a query using xp_sendmail and sp_readmail. SQL Mail can be a real time-saver for the DBA because it can be used to help monitor the server's performance and the success or failure of jobs without having to check the logs for each job to make sure it ran successfully. Refer to Chapter 6 for instructions on setting up SQL Mail.

### Meta Data Services

Microsoft SQL Server 2000 Meta Data Services is a set of services that allows you to manage meta data. An understanding of meta data characteristics is required in order to use Microsoft Meta Data Services. If you are new to the concept of meta data, you should refer to Books Online and Chapter 18 of this book to get a good understanding before attempting to use this feature. Meta data describes the structure and meaning of data as well as the structure and meaning of applications and processes. Meta data is abstract, has a context, and can be leveraged in a development environment.

# Managing Databases

Now that the server management tools in Enterprise Manager have been reviewed, it is time to take a look at the database management tools. Enterprise Manager provides the graphical interface to all of Microsoft SQL Server 2000's database management functionality. Most of these functions are available through Transact-SQL, but the graphical interfaces provided by Enterprise Manager make these tasks much easier and more intuitive to work with.

Figure 5.4 provides a look at basic database status and configuration information. The Table Info view gives the number of rows in each table, its size, and how the space is allocated between data and indexes. The Wizards view is the same one provided at the server level and grants access to all of the wizards for database and server configuration. Each of the yellow "buttons" in this view provides access to a menu for managing features related to the section in which it appears. The features on these menus are also accessible from other areas of the Enterprise Manager, but this view provides a centralized place to manage them. You can display the menus by positioning the mouse cursor over the yellow button.

The Database section provides information about the database owner, the date the database was created, the size of the database, the remaining available space in the database, the database options, and the number of users configured for the database. The Maintenance section displays information about the most recent backups and the most recently run maintenance plan. The menu for this section provides access to the common tasks associated with database maintenance. The Space Allocated section shows the space allocated to the database and its transaction log and how much free space is remaining in each. The space usage is shown as a graph to make it easy to see when you are getting tight on database space. If you have set up your database to grow dynamically, available space is less of an issue, but it still bears watching to see how often the database is being expanded. If it is being expanded too frequently, you may want to adjust the amount of space that is being added when the database is expanded. For this expansion, you may want to consider selecting a fixed increment to provide better control

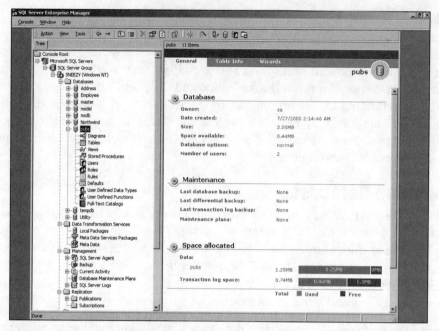

**Figure 5.4   Database information view.**

than a percentage, which will vary as the database size changes. The other item that needs to be monitored regularly is free disk space, especially when you have databases configured to expand as needed. It's easy to forget that you can run out of disk space and an automatic expansion will no longer be possible.

### Database Properties

The Database Properties dialog, shown in Figure 5.5, provides a graphical interface to examine and configure a database. The General tab provides a look at the same basic information that is displayed on the General View, which is displayed when you select a database. This tab provides a quick look at the current status of the database.

---

*TIP: The yellow buttons to the left of each section heading in this view will provide access to a context menu of functions related to that section. Place the mouse cursor over the button for a second or two and the context menu will appear, which will allow you to access these functions without having to find them elsewhere in the Enterprise Manager.*

---

The Data Files tab provides the list of files used to store the data for the database. Additional files can be added on this tab if needed. The file's location, name, size, and file group are displayed in a grid for ease of use. The Delete button allows removal of one or more of the database files if they are not needed. Removing files should be done with extreme care because any data in files that are deleted

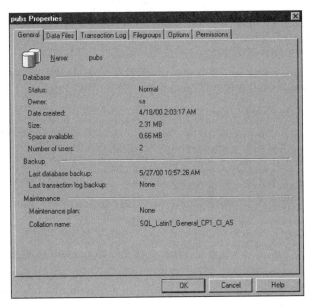

Figure 5.5   Database Properties dialog—General tab.

will be lost. For each file, you can allow the file to grow dynamically or not. If you allow dynamic growth, there are several other options that you can use to determine how the file will grow and how large it can become. The file can either be increased by a number of megabytes at a time or by a percentage of the exiting size. The file can also be allowed unrestricted growth, or a maximum size can be assigned to the file.

The Transaction Log tab is nearly identical to the Data Files tab. It gives the list of files used to store the data for the database's transaction log. The file handling for data and transaction log files is basically identical except for the information contained within them.

The File Groups tab allows you to create or remove file groups from the database. These named groups allow you to specify a file or files for data to reside in when performing certain database tasks, like adding indexes. Indexes are created on the same file group as the base table on which the index is created by default. It is possible to create nonclustered indexes on a file group other than the one used by the base table. By using a different file group, you can create the indexes on different physical drives with their own controllers to realize performance gains. Index information and data can then be read in parallel by multiple disk heads. This same type of strategy can be applied to the placement of tables in different file groups to allow parallel reads and speed query execution. This type of setup can require more maintenance, but the performance gains might prove to be worth the effort. The same basic benefit can actually be achieved by creating a single file on a RAID 0, 1, or 5 device with much less effort and administration overhead. Microsoft recommends placing the data on a RAID 5 set and the log on a RAID 1 set for optimal performance, because RAID 5 is optimized for random reads and writes, and RAID 1 is optimized for sequential writes.

The Options tab allows you to access configuration options for the database. This tab provides the capability to limit access to the database, which can be helpful in some debugging situations and is required for some maintenance operations, like restoring the database. You can also mark the database as read-only to prevent the data from being altered, or when using removable media such as a CD-ROM database. The database settings determine basic default behaviors of the database. The ANSI NULL default setting determines whether or not newly created columns allow null values by default. Enabling recursive triggers allows changes made in a trigger to activate the same trigger. If this setting is enabled, the trigger design process has to take the possibility of recursion into account to prevent an endless loop. The Select Into/Bulk Copy setting determines whether or not these types of functions can be performed against the database. These operations are not logged, so there is no way to roll back this type of operation in the event of a problem. The Truncate Logon Checkpoint setting determines whether or not the log is truncated when a checkpoint operation occurs. The checkpoint operation writes all committed transactions to the database, and these transactions can then be removed from the log. This option can be used to save disk space, but it prevents you from being able to make transaction log backups periodically between database backups because the log will not contain all of the transactions since the last backup, only the ones since the last checkpoint. Refer to Chapter 6 for more information on backup strategies and Point In Time Recovery before enabling this option. Torn page detection can be enabled to provide another level of logical data security for certain types of system failure. When this option is true, Microsoft SQL Server 2000 marks units of a database page prior to attempting a write and checks page marking on every read. Turning on the Auto Close option causes the database to be shut down after its resources are freed and all users exit. This can be used to preserve server resources for databases that are seldom used. Using this option on a database that is used frequently may result in performance degradation by forcing the database to be constantly closed and reopened when it is needed.

If you have a database that may shrink over time or is inclined to grow larger than needed because of certain occasional processes that require additional storage, you can enable the Auto Shrink option, which causes the server to periodically regain disk space by shrinking the database. This option should not normally be enabled for performance reasons. For example, suppose the log is reduced to 8MB, and you then run a process that needs a large amount of log space. If your process needs 20MB of log space to complete and you have the database set to grow dynamically by 10 percent, the log will have to be expanded 10 times to complete the task. Refer to Books Online for the factors that influence how the database is reduced and how the minimum size is determined.

Auto Create Statistics allows the server to generate any missing column statistics during the optimization process to allow building better query plans. These statistics require some additional storage space, but the space required is usually minimal, and the performance gains can be tremendous. Unless you have an exceptionally good strategy for creating the necessary statistics and indexes for the database, this option should be enabled. Chapter 11 discusses these automatically generated statistics in more detail. Enabling the Auto Update Statistics option specifies that out-of-date statistics needed by a query for optimization should be built automatically during optimization. This is another good option to leave enabled unless you have a good understanding of the process and take adequate steps to maintain the statistics in your maintenance plan. Microsoft SQL Server 2000 generally does a better job of making this determination, but the overhead to update the statistics may be inappropriate in some environments unless it is performed in a controlled manner. The option to Use Quoted Identifiers changes the behavior of Microsoft SQL Server 2000 to enforce ANSI rules regarding quotation marks. This option specifies that double quotation marks may only be used for identifiers, such as column and table names. Character strings must be enclosed in single quotation marks. The final option on this tab allows you to select the Compatibility Level. This can be helpful if you will be running software that was written for older versions of Microsoft SQL Server 2000, but it will also limit the features that are available when accessing this database. The compatibility level should probably be set to the highest level at which any existing software will still function to provide as much access to the power and features of Microsoft SQL Server 2000 as possible.

The Permissions tab puts each database user in a grid to allow easy selection and viewing of the available database permissions granted to the user. Enabling and disabling permissions for a user should be done with care. Removing permission to perform a task that is vital to the user's work can disrupt productivity and cause tension in the workplace. Allowing too much access to the database opens the door for accidental damage by persons who should not be performing certain tasks. The security and integrity of your data may depend on how well you manage user access to the database.

### Creating Database Diagrams
The Database Diagram option on the menu takes you through the Create Database Diagram Wizard. The tool includes the capability to generate a model from an existing database structure, which was the method used to generate the sample

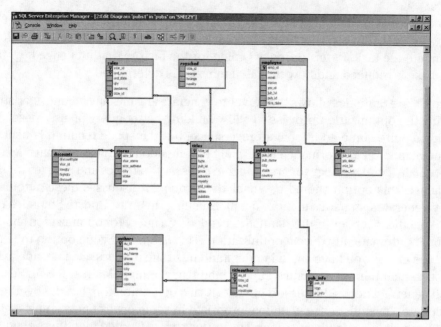

Figure 5.6    Database diagram for Pubs database.

model shown in Figure 5.6. This model was generated from the existing Pubs database that ships with SQL Server. The wizard allows selection of the tables to be included in the model. In general, system tables should probably not be included in the database model, but they will appear in the selection list as available if system tables are displayed for the database you are modeling. Database diagrams allow you to see the tables and their relationships in a graphical way. You can also create and manage tables and relationships in this view and save the changes to the underlying database when you are done. This wizard is not as full-featured as the many third-party modeling tools that are available to help with this task, but it does have the advantage of being included and available when the SQL Client Tools are installed. A database diagram is an invaluable asset when developing applications to work with the database effectively and efficiently. Even the basic modeling functionality provided by Enterprise Manager can be far superior to ignoring the need for at least basic database diagrams. This tool has the capability to manage multiple diagrams for a single database to allow modeling the database in logical pieces instead of requiring an extremely large database to be managed in one huge piece. A model can also be useful to provide information on specific tables and relationships that the user or developer needs to complete his work. Once you have created and organized the model, you need to save the diagram and give it a name. Be sure to give it a descriptive name, so that you can identify it from multiple diagrams that may be created for the same database.

When the database node is expanded in the left pane of Enterprise Manager, the first option in the list allows access to the previously created database diagrams.

### Creating a New Database User

The New User option on the menu displays the Database User Properties—New User dialog, which is shown in Figure 5.7. This dialog allows you to add a new user to the database and assign the user's role or roles in the database. You must first select a login name to associate with the user, and then enter a user name for the database. You can access the permissions for the selected login by clicking on the Permissions button next to the login name selector. You can also select New to launch the SQL Server Login Properties—New Login dialog and add a new login to the server for this user. The available database roles are listed with checkboxes that can be used to select which roles are granted to the user. The Properties button gives you access to the properties of the highlighted role. You can use this button to view or modify the user list and permissions of the selected role in a database.

### Creating a New Table

The New Table option on the menu displays the Table Designer dialog to allow you to design a new table for the database. Figure 5.8 shows the Table Designer, which is divided into two sections. The top section contains a grid; each row of the grid describes one column of the table. For each column, the grid displays its fundamental characteristics: column name, data type, length, and nulls-allowed setting. The bottom section shows additional characteristics for whichever data

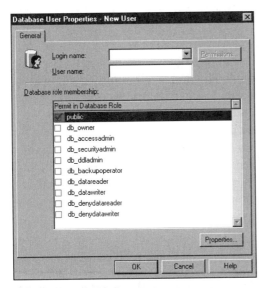

Figure 5.7    Database User Properties—New User dialog.

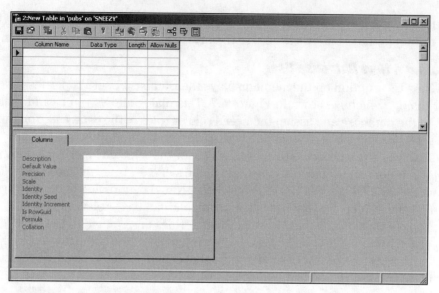

**Figure 5.8   New Table dialog.**

column is highlighted in the top section. You can also access property pages through which you can create and modify relationships, constraints, indexes, and keys for the table from this dialog using the toolbar buttons.

### Creating a New Database View

The New View option on the menu brings up the View Designer dialog to allow you to design a new view for the database. As you can see in Figure 5.9, this designer is very similar in look and functionality to the query designer available in Microsoft Access 2000. A view is used similarly to a table in SQL. A view is defined by creating a select statement that retrieves columns from one or more tables in the database. There are two main uses for views. The first is to simplify complex joins by establishing a view that presents the data to the user or developer in a simplified and denormalized fashion. The second is to enhance security by allowing users access to the views with the columns they are allowed to interact with and not the underlying tables in the views. The top section displays the tables that are used in the view and the relationship(s) by which they are joined. The next section allows selection of the columns that will either be returned or used in the selection criteria of the query. You can select the criteria, sorting, sort order, and whether or not the column will be included in the output from the view. This is also where column names can be aliased if needed. The third section displays the actual SQL code generated for the query. This section can be used to enter the needed SQL directly, rather than using the top two sections to design the query. The final section is the result pane for the query, which displays data returned the last time the query was executed in this view. Any of these sections can be hidden to provide just the information you want to be able to see while designing the view.

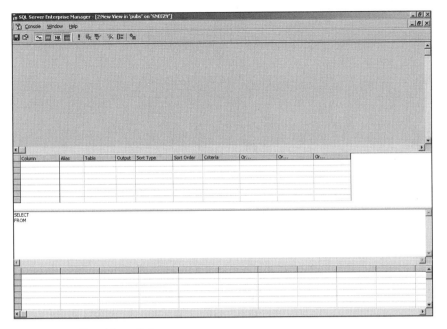

Figure 5.9    New View dialog.

## Import Data and Export Data

Both the Import and Export options on the menu launch the DTS Import/Export Wizard. This wizard walks you step-by-step through using DTS to import data from another server or database or to export data to another server or data source. DTS is a powerful tool for moving data between servers, platforms, or databases. The only difference between these two menu options is the defaults assigned in the wizard for the source and destination of the data being transferred. Refer to Chapter 7 for a more complete explanation of the functionality and capability of this feature.

## Generating SQL Scripts

The Generate SQL Script option on the menu launches the Generate SQL Script dialog, which can be used to generate SQL scripts to create or re-create any or all objects in the database. This dialog is shown in Figure 5.10. The General tab allows selection of the objects to be scripted. This selection can be made by selecting the Script All Objects checkbox, by selecting specific checkboxes for the categories of objects to script, or by selecting specific objects to be scripted from the selector at the bottom of the tab. The Preview button allows you to see the script that was generated prior to running or saving it. Generating scripts provides an easy way to migrate table structures and stored procedures between databases or servers. It also allows you the ability to make modifications to the table structure or procedure before applying it to the new database. It is a good

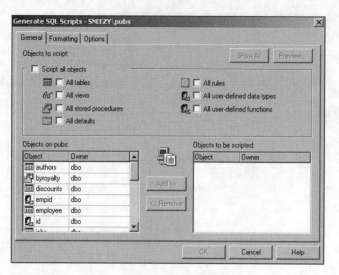

**Figure 5.10    Generate SQL Scripts dialog.**

idea, especially in a development environment, to make periodic backups of the structure by scripting the entire database. This allows you to make comparisons of structure and procedure changes and to restore a previous version of the structure without the need to revert to a database backup. Using a script, you can create a new table with the old structure, migrate the existing data to the new table using DTS, and then replace the existing table with the new one. If you restore the old structure using a backup, you will lose any new data that has been added since the backup was taken.

The Formatting Tab allows you to determine how the script is generated. The default options are to generate the drop object commands for the objects if they already exist and to generate the create object command for each selected object. There is also an option that causes the script to include any dependent objects in the script that are not otherwise selected. This can be helpful if you know which tables you want to create, but are not sure what other objects may be required to create the tables properly. There is an option to include descriptive comments with each SQL statement in the script. Enabling this option can be helpful if you are creating the scripts as part of your backup strategy (recommended) and may not refer back to them in the near future. This can also be useful for less advanced users to better understand what each step of the script is intended to accomplish. The Include Extended Properties option determines whether or not these properties are included in the script. This option should only be used if you are generating the script for use on another server of the same version. These scripts can be modified to create the database on another platform, in many cases, with minimal changes. Only Script 7.0 Compatible Features should be used if you are creating the database on a Microsoft SQL Server 7.0 server to avoid the need to make manual modifications to the script to fix compatibility problems. As the options are selected, the script template at the bottom is updated to display how the changes will affect the final script.

The Options tab is used to determine which features are included in the script when it is generated. The Security Scripting options allow you to select whether or not to generate the code necessary to re-create the existing database schema, users and roles for the database, SQL Server logins, and object level permissions. If the script is being generated as part of a disaster recovery plan, these options can be extremely helpful in fully re-creating your database. The Table Scripting options allow you to determine what elements of the tables should be included in the script. You can select whether or not to include indexes, full-text indexes, triggers, primary keys, foreign keys, defaults, and check constraints. Any or all of these may need to be excluded depending on where you are planning to re-create the table and whether or not you will have any or all of its related tables in the new location. The File Options section of this tab allows you to determine how the script output will be stored. You have two decisions to make: The first is the format that you want the script to be stored in, and the second is whether you want a single script file or one file per object.

### Creating a Database Maintenance Plan

The New Maintenance Plan option on the menu launches the Database Mainte-nance Plan Wizard, which guides you step-by-step through the process of setting up a database maintenance plan. This wizard covers the steps to set up database integrity checks, update statistics, back up the database, and ship transaction logs to another server. The wizard makes it easy to set up regularly scheduled database maintenance, which is a key part of keeping a well-tuned and protected database. These tasks can be combined into a single maintenance plan for the server or can be broken down into one or more plans for each database or groups of databases.

### Checking Maintenance Plan History

The Maintenance Plan History option on the menu brings up the Database Main-tenance Plan History dialog, which is shown in Figure 5.11. This dialog provides the historical log of maintenance plan activity for all plans run on this server. The filter criteria section allows you to limit the amount of information in a number of ways to make it easier to find the steps you are looking for. The filters allow you to select a specific plan, server, database, status, or activity, and can additionally filter criteria based on keywords in the message text. The plan name, server name, database, activity, status, end date, and message are displayed in a grid for each log entry that matches the filter criteria. You can access properties for the entry and delete the entry from this dialog. The Refresh button can be used to update the view for any plans that may be in progress or for plans started while the view is open.

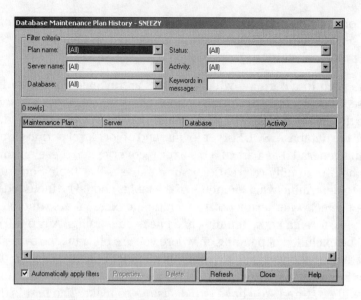

Figure 5.11    Database Maintenance Plan History dialog.

## Backing Up a Database

The Backup Database option on the menu brings up the SQL Server Backup dialog, which is shown in Figure 5.12. This dialog provides an easy-to-use interface for performing manual backups of the database. You select the database to back up, give the backup a name, and provide a description for the backup. This

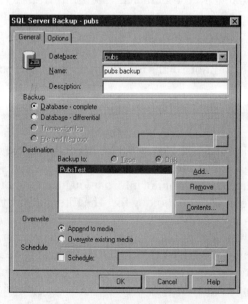

Figure 5.12    SQL Server Backup dialog.

information should be descriptive enough to allow you to select the appropriate backup if you need to restore it at some point. You can back up the complete database, perform a differential backup, back up the transaction log, or perform a backup of a specific file or file group. The destination allows you to select whether the output should be directed to tape (if installed) or disk. The wizard does not allow performing a backup to a network device, so you will have to resort to using T-SQL is you want to back up to a network drive. The destination shows the SQL Backup Device or file to contain the backup. If more than one device or file is listed, the backup will be striped across the listed devices. Using a stripe set for the backup requires that the devices be used only as a part of this set. All of the devices for a stripe set must always be used together. To change the device, you must remove the existing device(s) from the list, and then add the device(s) you wish to use for this backup. The Contents button allows you to view the current contents of the device(s) you are going to use for the backup. The Add button allows you to select an existing device or file, or create a new device or file for the backup. If you have an existing backup device, you can choose whether to Append this backup to the device or to Overwrite existing media, which will delete any existing backups on the device. Note that the Overwrite option removes *all* backups on the device, not just the ones for the currently selected database. You also have the option of scheduling the backup or performing it immediately. This option allows you to schedule a special backup to run overnight or to schedule a recurring backup to run at a designated time. This dialog also allows scheduling backups independently from other maintenance options.

The Options tab provides additional options for backing up the database. The Verify Backup Upon Completion option causes Microsoft SQL Server 2000 to read the entire backup after it is completed to verify media integrity. If you are backing up to a tape device, you can select Eject Tape After Backup to prevent another scheduled backup from overwriting the current one before the tape is changed. Remove Inactive Entries From Transaction Log causes all log entries for completed transactions to be removed from the log when the backup is completed. Check Media Set Name And Backup Set Expiration checks the identity and expiration of the media to prevent accidental overwrites. You need to provide the media set name for this option to verify. You can set the number of days or a specific date that the current backup set will expire. You can also choose to initialize the media set label and give the set a name and description.

### Restoring a Database

The Restore Database option on the menu brings up the Restore Database dialog. This dialog is shown in Figure 5.13 and provides an easy-to-use interface for performing manual database restores. This option is more likely to be used in a development and testing environment to reset the database to rerun a series of tests

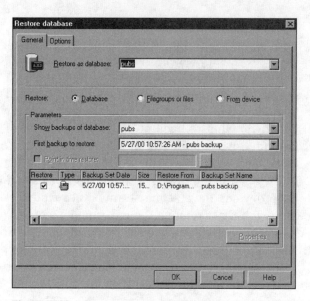

Figure 5.13    Restore Database dialog.

to verify that a process is working correctly or to aid in the debugging process. You first select a database to restore the backup to. It is possible to restore a backup from one database to another database, but this should only be done with careful consideration of the consequences. In a development environment, this feature can be helpful for moving testing environments around to multiple servers or setting up multiple test environments on the same server. The Restore option determines the options you are presented with on the remainder of the dialog. The Database option allows you to select which database to restore backups from. Once you have selected the database, you need to select the device or file that contains backups for the selected database. The dialog presents a list of backups that exist for the selected database and allows you to choose the proper one to restore. Selecting an entry in the backup list and clicking on the Properties button gives you more detailed information about that particular backup. The description, start and end dates, time, size, and so on, are included on the form that is displayed. The only item that can be changed from this form is the location of the backup file, which may have changed since the previous backup was performed. The file location is stored in the backup log, but Microsoft SQL Server 2000 has no way of knowing when a file is moved using the operating system tools. This dialog provides the necessary functionality to allow you to easily tell Microsoft SQL Server 2000 what the new location of the backup file is before attempting the restore. The File Groups option also allows you to specify what database you wish to restore a backup of. You can then select a subset of backup sets, which allows selecting only backup sets of files on a particular drive, only the backup sets completed after a certain date, or only the backup sets for a particular file or group of files. Once the subset selection is made, you are presented with a list of backups that match the selection criteria. The backup properties for these are available in the same fashion as the ones displayed for the Database option. The From Device option allows you to select one or more files or devices to restore from, and then select the backup number to restore from that device. You can use the View Contents button to list the contents of the device or file and make the proper selection. You then have the option to either restore from the backup set or to read the backup set to update the backup history. If the backup was made on another server or if the history log was lost or damaged, it can be updated in this way. If you are restoring from the backup set, you have the option to restore the entire database, a differential backup of the database, the transaction log, or a specific file or group of files.

The Options tab provides additional options for restoring the database. You can choose the Eject Tapes (if any) After Restoring Each Backup option, so that the tape will be ejected to prevent the backup from being overwritten by another scheduled backup before the tape is changed. You can select the Prompt before restoring each backup option to allow you to change media or do other tasks that may be required in between these operations. You can select the Force restore over existing database option to allow overwriting a database other than the one the database was created from. There is a grid in the middle of this tab that shows the original file name and the file name that the restore will be directed to. The Restore As file name can be changed in this grid to force the restore to a different file. The lower section of the tab allows you to select the appropriate Recovery Complete state. There are three options for the state that the database will be left in once the restore operation is completed. The first two options are fairly self-explanatory. The third option, Leave The Database Read-Only And Able To Restore Additional Transaction Logs, can be used to allow query access to the database before it is fully restored. This may be needed in a critical production environment where at least this minimal functionality could allow a company to continue doing business for a short time until the database is fully restored. This option also allows specifying an undo file.

### Truncating the Transaction Log

The last option on the Maintenance section menu is Truncate Log. This option allows you to truncate the transaction log for the selected database, which removes all entries for completed transactions from the database log. It is strongly recommended that a full database backup be made after this operation. This operation should only be run by a knowledgeable DBA, especially in a production environment. Before truncating the log, make sure you fully understand how this operation will impact your backup strategy and your ability to recover in the event of a system failure.

**5. Microsoft SQL Server Tools**

### Shrinking a Database

The Shrink Database option allows you to remove unused space from a database that has expanded to a size that is no longer needed, especially if new data will no longer be added to the database. This option brings up the Shrink Database dialog, which is shown in Figure 5.14. Databases that have large amounts of history information stored in them, like payroll or accounting databases, may need to be shrunk when old history data is purged or archived from the database. Books Online has information on what factors influence how much you can shrink a database and what the minimum size of the database can be. The dialog allows you to select an amount of free space to remain in the database after it has been resized. Unless you are no longer going to use the database in a production environment, it is probably best to leave at least a little free space allocated to it. You can select to move the pages to the beginning of the database, which rearranges the database pages to move the free space to the end of the file(s). This may impact performance, but it allows the most space to be reclaimed by this process. The Schedule section of this dialog allows you to establish a schedule for the shrinking to be performed on a regular basis. The Files button allows you to configure the shrinking process for individual database files. You can choose to shrink the file by compressing the pages and truncating the free space from the end of the file, just truncating the free space from the end of the file, emptying the file (which would force the data to migrate to other files in the group), or setting a minimum size for the file to shrink to. You also have the ability to defer the shrink to a specified date and time. The natural tendency for most databases is that they continue to grow as long as they are used in a production environment, but this tool addresses the occasional need to reclaim some of the space that is no longer needed by the database.

Figure 5.14    Shrink Database dialog.

### Modifying Data and Log File Sizes

The Modify Data File Sizes option on the menu brings up the Database Properties dialog with the Data Files tab selected. The Data Files tab lists the files used to store the data for the database. Additional files can be added on this tab if needed. The file's location, name, size, and file group are displayed in a grid for ease of use. The Delete button allows you to remove one or more of the database files if they are not needed. This should be done with extreme care because any data in files that are deleted will be lost. For each file, you can allow the file to grow dynamically or not. If you allow dynamic growth, there are several other options that you can use to determine how the file will grow and how large it can become. The file can either be increased by a number of megabytes at a time or by a percentage of the existing size. The file can also be allowed unrestricted growth, or a maximum size can be assigned to the file. The same process applies to the Modify Log File Sizes option on the menu, which displays the Transaction Log tab. These tabs are nearly identical except for which files they affect.

### Managing Database Diagrams

Figure 5.15 shows the existing Database Diagrams for the current database. This is where the database diagrams that you have created for the database can be viewed and edited. These diagrams provide a graphical look at the tables and their relationships within the database. This is one of the best forms of documentation for any database. It can also be very beneficial to use this view of the

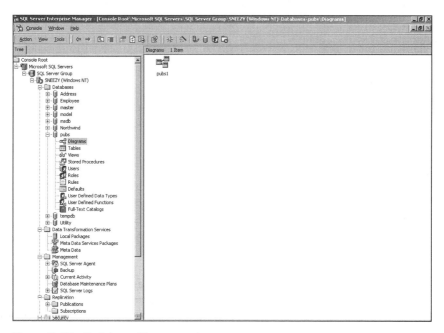

Figure 5.15    Database Diagrams view.

database during the design phase. The graphical representation of the tables and relationships can help you determine if something is missing or not relating correctly. Good up-front database modeling can save time not only in the database development and implementation, but also in the development cycle of the applications that will use the database.

In the designer, you can alter the view of the tables to provide as much or as little information about the table as you need for the particular diagram. The default view for tables just shows the column names, which allows the complete diagram to be viewed or printed in a relatively compact fashion. For development purposes, the standard view is more beneficial because it also displays the data type, length, and nullability of each column. The standard view generates a larger diagram, but it is more practical for use by programmers and DBAs that are not intimately familiar with the database. You can customize this view to provide exactly the information that you need or want for your particular use. All aspects of table design and maintenance can be accessed from this view and are applied to the underlying data. You can create and manage indexes, statistic sets, triggers, primary and foreign keys, dependencies, constraints, relationships, and permissions. You can remove a table from the diagram and/or from the database and add and remove columns from the table. You can also generate the SQL scripts needed to create the objects in the diagram from this view. This tool is not as full-featured as some of the tools available on the market, but it is tailored specifically for use with Microsoft SQL Server 2000, and as such, it meets the needs of many DBAs. Another advantage to using the database diagramming capability of Microsoft SQL Server 2000 is that anyone who is using Enterprise Manager in the organization can gain access to the diagrams to work with as needed. This feature does not give anyone access to change table structures or add tables who does not already have that level of access for the database, so it provides a safe way to keep the latest diagrams instantly available across the enterprise. The tool also includes the capability to print the diagrams for those who still like to work from a hard copy for certain tasks.

### Managing Tables

The tables contained in the database can be managed from the Tables view, which is accessed by clicking on the Tables node in the tree. The table name, owner, type (system or user), and date created are all displayed in this view for easy reference. Right-clicking on a table will bring up a context menu, which provides access to the table management features.

The New Table option on the menu brings up the Design Table dialog and allows you to define columns and relationships for the table. The same dialog is displayed by the Design Table option on the menu, but it allows you to modify an existing table structure instead. You can even alter the column length or data type for existing database columns. Enterprise Manager warns you when a change affects related changes, and then makes the changes to all of the tables for you. If there is a chance that the change will result in data loss, you will receive a separate warning detailing which tables may be affected. You must then decide whether or not to continue with the modification to the table. Some structure changes actually require the table to be re-created and the old data migrated into the new structure, but Enterprise Manager takes care of this process automatically when you save the changes to the database. The Design Table dialog also has a toolbar, which provides access to the management dialogs for triggers, permissions, dependencies, relationships, indexes, keys, and constraints.

The Open Table option provides another menu that allows you to return all the data in the table or just the specified number of rows. It also allows you to design a query using an interface very similar to the one found in Access 2000. The data is displayed in a grid for easy viewing and contains one record per row in the grid. All three of these options actually use the same interface with different default panes selected and different default queries. Once you have selected an option and you are looking at the data, the additional panes can be hidden or displayed and all of the functionality is available to design or change the query and redisplay the resulting data.

The Full-Text Index option provides a menu of tools for creating and maintaining full-text indexes for the table. Full-text indexes provide efficient support for sophisticated word searches in character data. The full-text index stores information about significant words and their position within a given column. This information is used to allow the quick completion of full-text queries that search for rows with particular words or word combinations. Full-text indexes are contained in full-text catalogs. A database can contain one or more full-text catalogs, but a full-text catalog can belong to only one database. A full-text catalog can contain full-text indexes for one or more tables, but a table can have only one full-text index. This means that each table with a full-text index belongs to only one full-text catalog. The catalogs and indexes are managed separately by the Microsoft Search service and are not contained within the database to which they belong. A full-text index cannot be defined on a view, system table, or temporary table. These indexes can only be defined for base tables. A full-text index definition includes a unique key for the table (primary or candidate key) that does not allow nulls and one or more character fields that are covered by the index. The entry for each key in the index has information about the significant words that are associated with the key, the column that contains them, and their position in the column. Noise-words or stop-words, which can be defined, are not included in the index. Full-text indexing implements two Transact-SQL predicates for finding rows using a full-text search condition. These new predicates are **CONTAINS** and **FREETEXT**, both of which can be found in the Transact-SQL reference in

Books Online. Two new functions have also been added to Transact-SQL to return the set of rows that match a full-text search condition. These functions are **CONTAINSTABLE** and **FREETEXTTABLE**, which can also be found in the Transact-SQL reference in Books Online. Internally, Microsoft SQL Server 2000 sends the search condition to the Microsoft Search service, which finds all the matching keys and returns them to Microsoft SQL Server 2000. Microsoft SQL Server 2000 then uses the list of keys to determine which rows to process.

The All Tasks option provides a menu with options for table management, DTS, replication, and other functions. The first section of this menu provides access to dialogs for managing indexes, triggers, and permissions for the selected table. The Import Data and Export Data options launch the DTS Import/Export Wizard to allow transferring data between the database and other databases or platforms. The Create New Publication option launches the Create New Publication Wizard, which allows you to publish tables from the database for replication to other servers. The Generate SQL Script option provides access to the Generate SQL Scripts dialog that was discussed in detail earlier in this chapter. The Display Dependencies option brings up a dialog that lists all of the objects that depend on the current table and all of the objects that the current table depends on. All of the functions on this menu can be accessed from multiple locations.

The Properties option brings up the Table Properties dialog, which gives you information about the columns included in the table and their configuration as well as a tab to see the full-text indexing setup (if any) for the current table. The Permissions button brings up a dialog that allows you to view and edit the user permissions for the current table. This dialog is also launched by double-clicking on the table in the list.

The final menu option is Help, which launches Books Online and takes you to Tables in the table of contents under Creating and Maintaining a Database. Books Online is the best place to look for any information you may need about tables, databases, Microsoft SQL Server 2000 tools, and so on.

### Managing Database Views

Selecting the Views node in the tree provides the functionality for creating and managing database views. Database views are basically queries that can be used like tables in other queries. Views are normally utilized for one of two reasons. One reason is security, which can be more tightly controlled by giving users access to views that encompass the columns that they are allowed to view and edit instead of allowing them access to the entire table or tables that are used to create the view. The other main reason for using a view is to simplify data access in other queries. A view can be used to simplify complex joins needed to retrieve data by including one or more views in the join so that each view performs a portion of the work for the join. Another benefit that can be provided by a view is the capability to present a highly normalized structure in an easier-to-understand, denormalized way. Views can also be used to generate total information that needs to be included in other queries. Writing such a query without using a view can be extremely difficult if not impossible for the average developer. In Microsoft SQL Server 2000, a new type of view has been introduced that can be even more useful than the traditional standard views. The new type of view is called an *indexed view*. The indexed view can have a clustered index (these are explained in Chapter 10) associated with it to improve the performance of the view. Standard views must be rebuilt by executing the defined query each time the view is referenced. Indexed views create a permanent clustered index in the database, which is maintained like any other index, and this index is used to dramatically improve the performance of the indexed view. The query optimizer can use an index created for an indexed view to improve the performance of a query that references the base tables within the view and not the actual view. This new functionality should be used carefully, however, to make sure that the increase in query performance outweighs the overhead of maintaining the index. Indexed views should normally only be used for relatively static data because the lack of changes will minimize the upkeep required for the index. For more complete information on views and indexed views, refer to Books Online. The context menu that can be accessed by right-clicking on a view provides access to the view management features.

The New View option on the menu brings up the View Designer dialog to allow you to design a new view for the database. This designer is very similar in look and functionality to the query designer available in Microsoft Access 2000. The top section displays the tables that are used in the view and the relationship(s) by which they are joined. The next section allows selection of the columns that will either be returned or used in the selection criteria of the query. You can select the criteria, sorting, sort order, and whether or not the column will be included in the output from the view. Column names can be aliased in this section if needed. The third section displays the actual SQL code generated for the query. This section can be used to enter the needed SQL directly, rather than using the top two sections to design the query. The final section is the result pane for the query, which displays data returned the last time the query was executed in this view. Any of these sections can be hidden to provide just the information you want to see while designing the view.

The Design View option brings up the same dialog as the New View option, but with the existing view already contained in the dialog. This dialog allows you to edit the existing view using the same functionality that was available during the creation process. Some views may be too complex to make use of the graphical designer functionality, but any valid Transact-SQL statement can be entered in the view pane and used to define the view.

**5. Microsoft SQL Server Tools**

The Open View option works exactly like the Open Table option.

The All Tasks option provides a menu with options for view management and other functions. These options are the same as the corresponding options explained in the "Managing Tables" section.

The Properties option brings up the View Properties dialog, which displays the SQL used to define the current view. You can modify the SQL in this dialog to make changes to the view. The Check Syntax button allows you to verify that the SQL code is valid prior to applying the changes to the view. The Permissions button brings up a dialog that allows you to view and edit the user permissions for the current view. Double-clicking on a view in the list also launches this dialog.

### Managing Stored Procedures

Selecting the Stored Procedures node in the tree provides the functionality for creating and managing stored procedures (SPs) in the database. SPs can be used to enhance database security by restricting insert, update, and delete access to the database from the users and making these operations available only through the use of SPs. These procedures can then control what data is changed and manage any dependencies that may be affected by the data changes. This option also allows restricting this access to specific rows or columns based on what SPs the user has access to. Another benefit of SPs is that they provide a reusable library of code that can be used by many applications to affect changes in the database. If the applications and SPs are properly designed, any changes that need to be made to how information is accessed in the database can be made in a single SP that is used everywhere to perform updates on the data affected by the SP. The other main benefits of SPs are that they are precompiled, and their query plans are stored in cache. Unlike running normal queries, the SP does not have to be compiled every time it is run and can therefore provide a significant performance benefit for an application. Right-clicking on a stored procedure brings up a context menu, which provides access to additional stored procedure management features.

The New Stored Procedure option on the menu brings up the Stored Procedure Properties dialog, which is basically a text box for editing the SQL code for the SP. This version of Enterprise Manager provides syntax highlighting in the stored procedure editor similar to the one provided in the Query Analyzer. This makes the task of creating and editing SPs much simpler by making it easier to spot syntax problems in the editor before you attempt to create or modify the SP. A Check Syntax button is provided to allow you to ensure that all of the syntax is correct prior to making a permanent change to the procedure. This check can prevent you from dropping a procedure that may be needed by running applications, when you are unable to replace it with a new valid procedure. Double-clicking on the SP in the list displays the same dialog to allow you to edit existing SPs.

The All Tasks option provides a menu with options for managing permissions, replication, and other functions. The first section of this menu provides access to the dialogs for managing Permissions for the selected SP. The Create New Publication option launches the Create New Publication Wizard, which allows you to publish information from the database for replication to other servers. The remaining options are the same as those discussed in the "Managing Tables" section.

The Properties option brings up the same dialog that is accessed by double-clicking on the SP in the list or accessing the New Stored Procedure option on the menu.

The Help option launches Books Online and takes you to Stored Procedures in the table of contents under Creating and Maintaining a Database.

### Managing Database Users

Clicking on the Users node in the tree provides a list of the database users, their associated database logins, and whether or not they have permission to access the database. Managing user permissions is a key ingredient in maintaining the security and integrity of your data. The roles and permissions assigned to each user should be carefully planned to provide the access required by the user to perform his or her function within the organization. Some organizations have a need to restrict view access to sensitive information like employee salary, sales information, or any information deemed sensitive by the organization. It is therefore up to the DBA to take all of these factors into account when designing and implementing the permission scheme for all databases and servers in the environment. The context menu provides access to the user management features.

The New Database User option on the menu brings up the Database User Properties—New User dialog, which was covered in the "Creating a Database User" section of this chapter.

The All Tasks option provides a menu with an option for managing permissions. This option provides access to the dialogs for managing Permissions for the selected user.

The Properties option brings up the Database User Properties dialog, which allows you to edit the properties assigned to the selected user. This is the same dialog that is used to create new users for the database. You can use the Properties button to view or modify the user list and permissions of the selected role in the database. The user name and login name cannot be changed for an existing user. If you need to change either of these options, the user must be deleted and re-created with the corrected login name or user name.

### Managing Database Roles

Roles are used to simplify the administration of security for the database. Clicking on Roles in the tree will access the view that allows you to manage the database roles and the permissions assigned to each one. The permissions for the database can be designed around these roles to simplify the process of security management with less chance of human error rather than assigning all of the permissions for each user individually. The context menu provides access to the role management features.

The first option on the menu is New Database Role, which launches the Database Role Properties dialog. This dialog allows you to create a new role for the current database. You assign a name for the role, and use the Permissions button to assign the permissions to the new role. The role can be defined as either a standard role with a list of associated users or an application role that requires a password to be used. If it is a standard role, you can add or remove user associations by using the Add and Remove buttons.

The Properties option on the menu brings up the same dialog as the New Database Role option, but you cannot change the name or type of role from this dialog. You can use this dialog to alter the permissions for the role and add and remove user associations.

### Managing Database Rules

Rules are provided for backward compatibility and perform some of the same functions as **CHECK** constraints. **CHECK** constraints are the preferred, standard way to restrict the values allowed for a column. **CHECK** constraints are also more concise than rules. Multiple **CHECK** constraints can be applied to a single column, but there can only be one rule applied to each column. It is possible to have one rule and multiple **CHECK** constraints on the same column. **CHECK** constraints are specified as part of the **CREATE TABLE** statement, whereas rules are created as separate objects, and are then bound to the desired column. For more information about rules, refer to Books Online.

### Managing Database Defaults

Defaults are used to specify what values should be assigned to a column if you do not specify a value for the column when inserting a row. Defaults can be any entity that evaluates to a constant, such as constants, built-in functions, and mathematical expressions. Defaults can be applied to a table in two ways. The first method is to use the **DEFAULT** keyword in the **CREATE TABLE** command to assign a constant expression as a default on a column. This is the preferred method and is more concise than the second method. The second method is to create a default object using the **CREATE DEFAULT** statement and bind it to columns using the **sp_binddefault** SP. The second method is included for backward compatibility. Defaults can be established when creating a new table in Enterprise

Manager and can also be added or changed in the Design Table dialog. The view accessed by clicking on the node in the tree is provided to allow you to manage the default objects that are created using the second method. For more information about default objects, refer to Books Online.

### Managing User-Defined Data Types

The list of user-defined data types for the database is displayed by clicking on the User-Defined Data Types node in the tree. The name, owner, base type, length, nullability, default, and rule associated with the type are visible in this view. User-defined data types allow you to manage specialized data types in the database without having to change the SQL code associated with them. Common types are phone numbers, ZIP codes, names, and so on. Using a user-defined type allows you to create columns in various tables that share a defined set of characteristics beyond that of a standard data type. You can set up defaults and rules for a user-defined type, and any changes you make will be applied to all columns that are defined to be of that type. This can save a tremendous amount of time changing the setup of fields in various tables when a change needs to be made to how a particular type of field is stored or handled in the database. The context menu provides access to the user-defined data type management features.

The first option on the menu is New User-Defined Data Type. This option allows you to create a new data type, which can be used when creating or modifying tables in the database. This option launches the User-Defined Data Type Properties dialog. The name of the new data type must be specified. You then select the base data type, length (if applicable), whether or not to allow nulls, the rule to associate with the data type (if any), and the default for the data type (if any).

The Properties option brings up the same dialog that is accessed by double-clicking on the data type in the list or by accessing the New User-Defined Data Type procedure option on the menu. The main difference between using this dialog for an existing data type rather than a new one is that you can only edit the rule and default information for the data type. The Where Used button will be available if you have used the selected data type. It provides a list of what fields are using the data type in the database.

### Managing User-Defined Functions

Clicking on the User-Defined Functions node in the tree displays the view used to manage user-defined functions for the current database. User-defined functions are new to Microsoft SQL Server 2000. They are created and managed similarly to SPs. Functions are subroutines made up of one or more Transact-SQL statements that can be used to encapsulate code for reuse. With Microsoft SQL Server 2000, you are no longer limited to the built-in functions defined as part of the Transact-SQL language. You now have the ability to create your own user-defined functions. User-defined functions are created using the **CREATE FUNCTION** statement, modified using the **ALTER FUNCTION** statement, and dropped using the **DROP FUNCTION** statement. Function names must be unique. You must have **CREATE FUNCTION** permissions to create, alter, or drop user-defined functions. Users other than the owner must be granted appropriate permissions on a function before they can use it. You must also have REFERENCES permission on the functions in order to create or alter tables with references to user-defined functions in the **CHECK** constraint, **DEFAULT** clause, or computed column definition. User-defined functions are covered in more detail in Chapter 10. The context menu provides access to the user-defined function management features.

The New User-Defined Function option on the menu brings up the User-Defined Function Properties dialog, which is basically a text box for editing the SQL code for the function. Syntax highlighting is provided in the function editor similar to that provided in the Query Analyzer. This makes the task of creating and editing functions much simpler by making it easier to spot syntax problems in the editor before you attempt to create or modify the function. A Check Syntax button is provided to allow you to ensure that all of the syntax is correct prior to making a permanent change to the function. This check can prevent you from dropping a function that may be needed by running applications, when you are unable to replace it with a new valid function. Double-clicking on the function in the list displays the same dialog to allow you to edit existing functions. You can use the Save As Template button on the dialog to change the template that is used to create new functions. This overwrites the existing template with the new one.

The Properties option brings up the same dialog that is accessed by double-clicking on the function in the list or accessing the New User-Defined Function option on the menu. The Save As Template button is not available when editing an existing function.

### Managing Full-Text Catalogs

Click on the Full-Text Catalog node in the tree to display the full-text catalogs defined for the current database. A full-text catalog can contain full-text indexes for one or more tables, but a table can have only one full-text index. This means that each table with a full-text index belongs to only one full-text catalog. The catalogs and indexes are managed separately by the Microsoft Search Service and are not contained within the database to which they belong. A full-text index cannot be defined on a view, system table, or temporary table. These indexes can only be defined for base tables. The context menu provides access to the full-text catalog management features.

The first option on the menu is New Full-Text Catalog, which launches the New Full-Text Catalog dialog. You specify the name and location of the catalog on the New Full-Text Catalog tab. The Schedules tab is used to view or modify the list of full or incremental population schedules for the new full-text catalog. Each row represents a full or incremental population schedule. A full-text catalog can be assigned one or more full or incremental population schedules. Buttons are provided below the list of schedules to allow you to add, edit, and delete schedules.

The Rebuild Catalog option deletes and rebuilds the selected full-text catalog. The re-created catalog is not populated but is ready for population. After performing this task, you need to use either the Start Full Population or Start Incremental Population option on the menu to repopulate the catalog.

The Stop Population option can be used to stop a previously started full or incremental population of the full-text catalog.

The Start Full Population starts population of the catalog with all rows in the tables included in the full-text catalog.

The Start Incremental Population causes the full-text catalog to be populated as rows are inserted or modified in the tables covered by the full-text catalog. This option requires that the indexed table have a column of the timestamp data type. If the table does not have a timestamp column, only full population can be performed. Requests for incremental population on tables without timestamp columns result in a full population operation. If a new full-text index is defined for a table that has not been previously associated with the catalog, the next incremental population request for the catalog builds all the entries for the table.

The Properties option brings up the Full-Text Catalog Properties dialog. The Status tab displays the name, location, physical catalog, status, item count, catalog size, unique key count, and last population date for the selected catalog. The Tables tab shows a list of tables with full-text indexing enabled in the catalog.

## Wizards

The Select Wizard dialog can be accessed from the Tools menu in Enterprise Manager. It provides a list of the available wizards and the capability to launch any of them from this centralized location. The wizards are provided to help DBAs perform their associated tasks more easily by taking them through a process in an intuitive step-by-step manner. Most, if not all of these tasks, can be performed without using the associated wizards, but the wizards are designed to help DBAs, who may not be familiar with a specific task, successfully complete it with a minimum amount of time and effort. The available wizards in Enterprise Manager are:

- Register Server Wizard
- Create Database Wizard
- Create Index Wizard

- Create Login Wizard
- Create Stored Procedure Wizard
- Create View Wizard
- Full-Text Indexing Wizard
- DTS Export Wizard
- DTS Import Wizard
- Backup Wizard
- Copy Database Wizard
- Create Alert Wizard
- Create Job Wizard
- Database Maintenance Plan Wizard
- Index Tuning Wizard
- Make Master Server Wizard
- Make Target Server Wizard
- Web Assistant Wizard
- Configure Publishing and Distribution Wizard
- Create Publication Wizard
- Create Pull Subscription Wizard
- Create Push Subscription Wizard
- Disable Publishing and Distribution Wizard

# Query Analyzer

The Query Analyzer is the place where most, if not all query construction, debugging, and optimization takes place. The Query Analyzer includes syntax highlighting, the capability of viewing the query plan, an object browser (new), and configurable output for easier use with ad hoc queries. There is also a new template area that contains some easy-to-use templates for common maintenance or query tasks. This template set can be expanded to include your own commonly used (or less frequently used) queries for quick access.

As the name implies, this tool is much more than an environment for running queries, it is also a tool for analyzing the query and its impact on the server. The tool has a wealth of features that help you optimize your queries for better performance. Whether you are working on SPs for the server or dynamic SQL that will be generated from an application, this tool is a great place to start. A good understanding of the concepts of relational databases and a working knowledge of the Transact-SQL language are invaluable for making the most of Microsoft SQL Server 2000. This tool provides the perfect environment for study and experimentation with query building. The full Transact-SQL reference is contained in Books Online, which can be launched directly from this tool. The version shipped with SQL Server 2000 also includes an object browser and templates, which can help make the query process easier than ever.

## The Query Window

Figure 5.16 shows a basic view in the Query Analyzer. The query window allows you to type in SQL statements to be executed. All of the Transact-SQL commands can be entered and used from this window. The syntax highlighting is especially helpful for spotting typos in commands as well as problems with improper quotation around character strings. Six different colors are used to distinguish between SQL keywords, built-in functions and system variables, string constants, system stored procedures, punctuation, and other text in the query. The results returned from the query can be configured from the Query menu or the Execute button on the toolbar. The query output can be text or a grid, or you can choose to send the output straight to a file. There are also additional output options that display the query execution plan, a server trace, and client statistics. Selecting these additional options causes the result pane to have additional tabs for each of the types

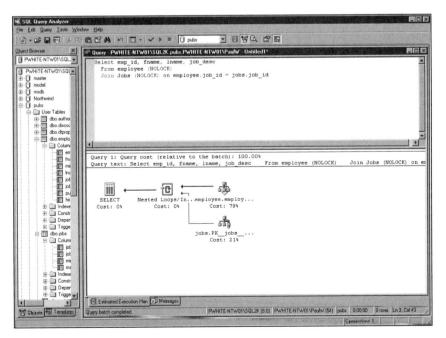

Figure 5.16    Query Analyzer.

of output requested. These tabs are normally located below the result pane, although the location of these tabs can be changed in the editor options. You also need to become familiar with the current connection properties, which can be used to modify the way a query is run and what information is provided thereafter.

## Connection Properties

The Current Connection Properties button is located on the right side of the toolbar. The available configuration options are:

- **Set nocount**—This option suppresses the row count messages that appear at the end of each statement.

- **Set noexec**—This option parses and compiles the query without actually executing it. It allows you to validate both the syntax and the referenced objects without running the query.

- **Set parseonly**—This option parses the query, but does not compile or execute it. It does not verify the objects referenced by the query.

- **Set concat_null_yields_null**—This option causes the query to return null for a concatenation operation if any of the operands in the operation are null.

- **Set arithabort**—This option indicates that the query should terminate if an arithmetic overflow or division by zero error occurs in the query.

- **Set showplan_text**—This option provides a text version of the query plan, but does not execute the query.

- **Set statistics time**—This option provides a listing on the time in milliseconds required to parse, compile, and execute each statement.

- **Set statistics IO**—This option provides the disk activity (reads, writes, and scans) for every table referenced in each statement.

- **Set rowcount**—This option specifies the maximum number of rows to be returned by each statement in the query.

- **Set ansi_defaults**—This option turns on or off the remaining options in the list as one unit. If the other options are set individually, this option appears checked and grayed.

- **Set ansi_nulls**—This option causes the query to return UNKNOWN for any null value in a comparison. If this option is off, comparisons with null values always return **TRUE**.

- **Set ansi_null_dflt_on**—This option overrides the default nullability for new columns.

- **Set ansi_ padding**—This option determines whether or not trailing blanks are trimmed automatically. If this option is on, trailing blanks for varchar data and trailing zeroes for varbinary data are not automatically trimmed.

- **Set ansi_warnings**—This option causes the server to issue warning messages for conditions that violate the ANSI rules but do not violate the rules for Transact-SQL.

- **Set cursor_close_on_commit**—This option causes cursors to be closed when a transaction commits.

- **Set implicit_transactions**—This option begins transactions without **BEGIN TRANSACTION** statements being used explicitly.

- **Set quoted_identifier**—This option causes characters enclosed in double quotation marks to be interpreted as identifiers.

# Execution Plans

You can view the execution plan that will be used to run a query to see if it is behaving as expected. Figure 5.16 shows a query execution plan in the bottom window. The Display Estimated Execution Plan button on the toolbar displays the execution plan without actually running the query. The query plan is displayed in an easy-to-read graphical diagram. You can use this diagram to see what indexes (if any) for each table are being used to perform the requested query. The order in which the tables are accessed is determined by looking at the direction of the arrows in the diagram. The first table used in the query will be on the far right at the top. The diagram also indicates any places in the query plan where the server could use parallelism to speed the query execution on multiprocessor servers. In addition, the diagram indicates any place that column statistics are missing. These statistics should be generated to allow the parser to build an accurate query plan. Moving the mouse cursor over an object in the diagram brings up a hint window that displays more information about that object in the query plan. For a table, you can see what index (if any) is being used, statistical information (including the estimated cost of that step), and the query argument that the table is referenced in. Right-clicking on the table objects provides a context menu that can be used to manage indexes and statistics for the table. There is also a menu option to create missing statistics on the table if the analyzer has determined that this operation is needed. This menu also provides the basic zoom functions and access to help in Books Online. You should become familiar with the execution plan diagrams and watch how different queries perform in your environment. The execution plan is often the only tool you need to diagnose and correct slow-running queries once you are familiar with the information that it presents and have done some experimentation on how to change a query's execution plan. Some items to experiment with when trying to adjust a query plan are creating new indexes and statistics that cover the fields used in both the where clause and any fields referenced in the join conditions. If you have multiple tables that are joined on the same key field, changing which table the successive joins use to pull the key field from can make a difference. The join order specified in the query can also make a difference in the query plan, so you should experiment with moving the order of joined tables and see if the query plan changes. These last two items will often not make a difference in the query plan because the query optimizer attempts to determine the best join order internally, but does not always appear to try every possible combination. Reorganizing the join order seems to become more effective as the number of tables in the join increases. Pay attention to the indexes that are being used for each table and see if they are the ones you expect to be used. If they are not, you can try hinting the index using the optimizer hints (see the **SELECT** statement in Books Online for details) to force the optimizer to use a different index. As a general rule, the optimizer makes the best selections, but sometimes it can be beneficial to force it to choose a different strategy.

## The Object Browser

The Object Browser, which is shown in the left pane in Figure 5.16, is a new feature in the Query Analyzer for Microsoft SQL Server 2000. This option can be displayed or hidden by clicking on the Object Browser button on the toolbar. The Object Browser provides access to all of the databases located on the connected server. You can expand the database to gain access to the objects contained within it. This makes looking up the table or field name you need for a query much simpler than either going to the Enterprise Manager or using the system catalog to retrieve the desired information. Once you have located the table or field you need, it can be placed in the query pane using standard drag-and-drop techniques. All of the server objects (like views, functions, and SPs) are available in this browser and can be dragged into the query pane in the same fashion. The server objects that are available are:

- User Tables
- System Tables
- Views
- Stored Procedures
- Functions
- User-Defined Data Types

You can also right-click on the objects to bring up a context menu that provides some additional functionality, such as scripting options. In addition to having the databases and their objects at your fingertips, the Object Browser also provides access to all of the system-defined functions and server variables under a folder called common objects. These functions and variables can be added to your queries using drag and drop. These functions are grouped by category to make them easier to find, and there is an available list of the parameters for each function, which can be accessed by expanding the desired function. The parameter information includes the data type and whether the parameter is an input or output parameter. The Object Browser can save you a great deal of time in the query construction process, especially when you need to use an object or function that you are not entirely familiar with.

The categories of common objects are:

- Configuration Functions
- Cursor Functions
- Date and Time Functions
- Mathematical Functions
- Aggregate Functions
- Meta Data Functions
- Security Functions
- String Functions
- System Functions
- System Statistical Functions
- Text and Image Functions
- Rowset Functions
- System Data Types

## Query Templates

With the Object Browser displayed, you can change from the Objects tab to the Templates tab and access the available templates to provide a framework to aid in the construction of certain types of queries. The templates are also arranged by category and are extremely easy to use. Clicking on the Insert Template button on the toolbar can also provide access to the templates. Using the Insert Template button, a standard Open dialog is presented with the templates arranged in folders. You can use this dialog to determine where the template files are stored on your system and view their arrangement. Once you become familiar with how the templates are constructed, you may wish to add your own templates for tasks that you perform frequently. You may also want to create templates for tasks that you do not perform frequently enough to remember the syntax, so that you do not have to look up the commands every time you want to use them. The template files are standard query files and use the .tpl extension instead of .sql. Once you have inserted the template into the query pane, you can use the Replace Template Parameters option on the Edit menu and the Query Analyzer will give you an easy-to-use dialog to enter the appropriate values to substitute for each of the template parameters. This feature makes the templates even more useful and intuitive to work with. The available template categories are:

- Create Database
- Create Function
- Create Index
- Create Procedure
- Create Statistics
- Create Table
- Create Trigger
- Create View
- Manage Extended Property
- Manage Linked Server
- Manage Login Role User
- Using Cursor

All of these categories contain multiple templates that cover basic to advanced versions of the syntax. You can add additional categories by creating new folders in the base template directory, and then adding your own templates to the new folders.

## Object Search Dialog

The Object Search button on the toolbar provides access to the Object Search dialog, which is shown in Figure 5.17. This dialog allows you to locate a database object when you are not sure of the name of the object or which database the object resides in. The criteria that can be specified are:

- Object Name
- Database Name
- Hit Limit (the maximum number of matches returned)
- Object Type(s)
- Extended Properties

This search can be used to locate any of the objects available in the Object Browser and once located, the objects can be transferred to the query window using drag and drop.

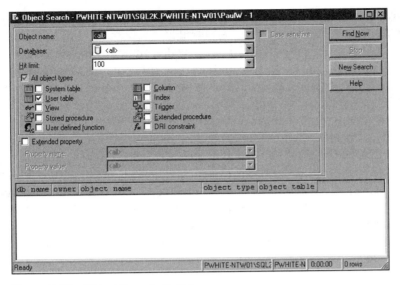

Figure 5.17    Object Search dialog.

## SP Debugger

Figure 5.18 shows the new SQL debugger for SPs, which can be used to step through an SP and examine the contents of variables as the procedure is run. This can be an invaluable debugging tool for working with SPs. Prior to the introduction of this feature, the only way to debug an SP was to pull the code into the

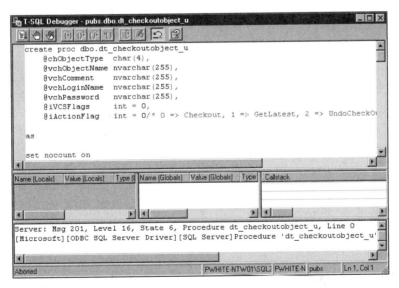

Figure 5.18    SP Debugger.

Query Analyzer and execute it in pieces until you found the piece that was not working as intended. This tool provides debugging capability similar to that of most modern programming languages, including the capability to watch variables and set break points in the code. The code for the procedure is displayed in the top pane for tracing. Two additional panes provide information showing the values of both local and global variables. The call stack is shown in a separate pane to allow the tracking of multiple levels of procedure nesting. The bottom pane displays the results generated by the procedure as it is run. This debug mode is available by right-clicking on the SP in the Object Browser and selecting the Debug option at the bottom of the context menu. The first dialog that comes up obtains the values for any input parameters needed for the procedure and has a checkbox that allows all work done by the procedure in debug mode to be rolled back when the execution is complete. This allows you to debug procedures without actually making permanent database modifications. More information on this debugger is available in Books Online.

# SQL Server Profiler

The SQL Server Profiler is a full-system debugging tool that allows you to monitor all or portions of the activity being sent to the server. With this tool, you can monitor a production environment to see what queries or SPs are executing slowly. You can filter the amount of data that you are capturing to obtain only the events that you are interested in. You can include or exclude specific users, hosts, and/or applications. Once you have captured a trace, the SQL Profiler allows the event data to be replayed against an instance of Microsoft SQL Server 2000, which reexecutes all of the saved events as they occurred originally. SQL Profiler can be used in the following ways:

- You can monitor the performance of a SQL Server or instance.

- You can locate the long-running queries that are executing against your server.

- You can step through statements to confirm that the code works as expected to test and debug your SQL statements and SPs during development. This feature can also be extremely helpful for locating problems in a production system.

- You can use the trace to audit security information, like logins, failed logins, and permission changes.

- You can capture events on a production system and replay them on a test server to allow you to troubleshoot a problem without disrupting the production environment.

## Setting Up a New Trace

Once you have loaded the Profiler, you will need to start a trace. Select File|New|Trace from the menu to start tracing a server. You will first be asked to select the server you want to trace and log in to the server. Once you have connected to a server, you are presented with the Trace Properties dialog, which is used to configure the options for your trace.

The Trace Properties dialog is used to set the trace options. First, select a name for the trace. The server that you connected to is displayed as the trace server, but you can change servers using the button to the right of the name. Second, select the template to use for the default trace settings. You can select the template by name or by using the file browser, which allows you to select templates that been saved in an alternate location. The template is used to determine the starting values of all trace options. You can save the trace to a file, which reduces the memory overhead of the Profiler as well as allows you to review the data at a later time. You can set a maximum size for the trace file. The Enable File Rollover option causes a new file to be created each time the maximum file size is reached and appends a number to the file name to keep the names unique. The Server Processes SQL Server Trace Data option requires the server to process the trace data. If this option is enabled, you will receive every event, even when the server is stressed. Enabling this option may have a negative effect on the server's performance. Turning this option off means that the client handles the trace processing, and you may miss events if the server is stressed. You also have the option of saving the trace to a table. You can configure a maximum number of rows to capture to the table. The last option on this tab allows you to configure a stop time for the trace. You can use this feature to trace a particular time of day that the server was experiencing problems. You can set up and run the trace, and it will end at the specified time. This option allows tracing overnight processes without having to stay late to stop the trace at the desired time.

The Events tab allows you to select the particular events that you want to monitor in the trace. It is unlikely that you will want to monitor every possible event in a single trace. The number and type of events that you select plays a large role in the amount of space required to save the trace. You should have some idea of what you are looking for in a particular trace before you make the event selections. The events are arranged by category to make the selection process easier. You can select the entire category to watch or just specific members. The available event categories are:

- Cursors
- Database
- Errors and Warnings
- Locks
- Objects
- Performance

- Scans
- Security Audit
- Server
- Sessions
- Stored Procedures
- Transactions
- T-SQL
- User Configurable

You can create user-defined trace events using the **sp_trace_generateevent** stored procedure. This can be an extremely useful debugging tool. Instead of is-suing print statements in an SP to help you follow the progress in a complicated script, you can use the SP to generate trace events that are ignored unless there is a trace running. This allows you to insert this type of debugging code without affecting the output of the script(s) you are working with. When you have compli-cated procedures that involve multiple nested SPs, this technique can save you a lot of time and trouble in the debugging process. You must include the User Configurable events that you will be using for them to show up in the trace. The event numbers passed to the SP are 82 through 91, which correspond to the User Configurable events 0 through 9.

The Data Columns tab allows you to configure what information is captured for each event. Based on the type of trace you are running, you can choose the appro-priate statistical information to be captured. The only two required columns are EventClass and SPID (Server Process Identifier). These columns must be included in every trace; the tool will not allow you to remove them from the list. Any of the other available columns may be removed or reordered to suit your needs. Some of the columns may become less useful depending on the filters that you impose for the trace. For example, displaying the login name if you are tracing a single login would be a bit redundant.

This tab presents you with a list of the event criteria that you can use to filter the trace. The events are presented in a tree view, and if you expand the event, you have a list of the types of filters that can be applied to that event. The Numeric and Date/Time events allow you to set filters that specify equal to, not equal to, greater than or equal to, and less than or equal to a specified value. The Character Type events allow you to filter the trace based on whether they are like or not like a specified value. You can specify multiple values to apply the same filter criteria against. Boolean events are treated like numeric events and have a value of zero or one. The filter criteria include most of the available columns that can be dis-played by the profiler.

## Creating Trace Templates

You can create your own templates for use with the profiler. This allows you to define the standard traces that you need to perform in your environment, so that you do not have to make major modifications to the trace properties every time you want to run a trace. For a step-by-step example of setting up a template, please refer to the "Immediate Solutions" section of this chapter. The only differences between this dialog and the one presented when you start a new trace are that you do not connect to a server, and you have far fewer options on the General tab. The General tab displays the current template name and presents a Save As button to allow you to change the name for the new template. You can then use the remaining tabs to establish default trace values for the template you are creating. This is a real time-saving feature if you will be running traces on a regular basis with configurations not present in one of the provided templates. Once you have created a template and have given it a descriptive name, you will be able to select it the next time you are ready to start a trace. (I have several templates that I use regularly to run a trace that only require the selection of the server, which template to use, and where to store my trace file.)

## Running a Trace and Interpreting the Output

Once you have configured and started a trace, it is time to start looking at the output that you will be evaluating. Figure 5.19 shows the output of a common trace used for query optimization. Let's examine the output of this simple trace to

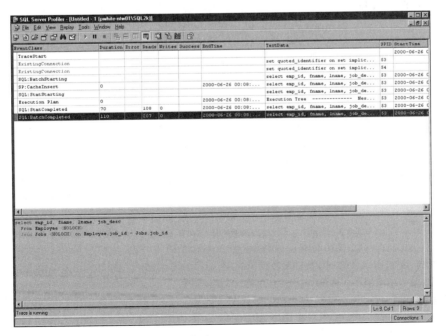

Figure 5.19    SQL Profiler Trace window.

get a basic understanding of the information provided. The first and last items in a trace are the Trace Start and Trace Stop lines. You always have a Trace Start at the beginning of a trace. If you pause and resume a trace, you will receive a Trace Stop entry when the trace is stopped and a Trace Start entry when the trace is resumed. If you are monitoring the start and stop times in a trace, these entries allow you to see the reasons there might be a gap in time at some point in the trace. If there is a gap that was not caused by pausing the trace, you might need to do some investigation as to what happened. The entries can also help you understand the reason a trace captured the beginning of a process, but not the end. If you stop a trace instead of just pausing it, the trace is cleared and is started over if you run it again. In the trace shown in Figure 5.19, two existing connections are shown to the database. This knowledge can be useful if you are monitoring the connection information and you start getting activity from someone that you did not actually see connect. This entry allows you to see the connections that existed prior to starting the trace. The next event is the **SQL: BatchStarting** event, which denotes the beginning of the current batch of statements. This provides the start time for the batch as well as the batch text. The **SP:ChaheInsert** event denotes the fact that plan is being placed in the cache to allow later reuse without the need for it to be prepared and compiled before being run again. The **SQL:StmtStarting** event denotes the start of a single statement in the batch and provides a test of that statement. In this case, the statement and batch are the same, so this information is a bit redundant but is very helpful when you have several statements executed as a single batch. For each statement that is executed, you can obtain the Execution Plan event that displays how Microsoft SQL Server 2000 decided to process that statement. The chosen indexes and join methods are presented in a text format that can be used to make tuning and query restructuring decisions. This execution plan, in conjunction with the duration of the statement, can be invaluable in determining which statements need work and what needs to be changed to improve the performance of the batch. The **SQL:StmtCompleted** and **SQL:BatchCompleted** events denote the stop time and duration of each statement individually and the batch as a whole. The duration is presented in milliseconds and can be used to determine which statements occupied significant amounts of the total batch time. When optimizing the batch, it is generally best to focus on the longest-running piece first. As you improve each statement's performance, the focus will shift to another statement until the total batch performance is acceptable. There are two additional columns that can be very enlightening in the optimization process. These columns contain the numbers of reads and writes performed against the database by the given statement. This information generally helps to explain the reason the duration was longer than expected. As a general rule, the duration will follow increases and decreases in these values. There is a great deal of additional information provided that allows you to pinpoint problem queries to the workstation, user, and application that is running them. If a particular user is running intensive ad hoc queries during a heavy production cycle and bogging down the server, the Profiler can help you track down the problem. Another handy feature is found in the bottom pane of the trace file. This pane is used to display the actual SQL code that corresponds to the highlighted statement or batch. This is also where the execution plan for the statement is displayed when the Execution Plan event is highlighted.

## Trace Playback

When you are working to resolve a problem in a query, it can be extremely useful to play back all or portions of a trace that you previously captured. This can be done on any server where the appropriate data is located and does not have to be the server where the capture was originally taken. Playback can also be a useful feature when you are working to tune the server settings of a particular server. The best evaluation of the effect of adjustments to the server is to replay the same steps after each change and see if the changes have any effect on performance. The profiler gives you an easy way to capture real-world production activity to use in this process, which allows you to do a much better job of tuning the server to a particular environment. The replay can be accomplished by stepping through the capture one event at a time or by running the entire capture again just as it was recorded. You also have the option to replay the events using multiple threads to speed performance, but this disables the debugging features. If you are tuning a server, replaying with multiple threads can be used to more accurately represent multiple clients accessing the server simultaneously. A new trace is generated to allow you to monitor the current performance of the operations as they are played back. It also allows you to monitor the effect of any environmental or load differences on the performance of the playback. In addition, the new trace allows you to monitor the status of each statement to see if there are any errors in the playback.

## Index Tuning Wizard

Once you have captured a trace, you can use the Index Tuning Wizard, which is shown in Figure 5.20, to perform an analysis of the queries being run and make recommendations for adding and removing indexes to improve performance. Removing indexes should only be done if you have captured a complete and accurate workload sample of the system activity. If you do not have a complete sample, the wizard may recommend removing indexes that are needed by other processes. The wizard also gives you an estimate of the performance increase that can be gained by making the suggested changes. This can be another extremely useful tool for tuning the environment for maximum performance. Along with its recommendations, the wizard provides a number of analysis reports to

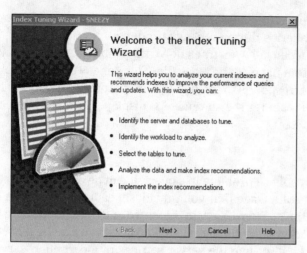

Figure 5.20    Index Tuning Wizard.

help you understand the choices that were made and also gives you a picture of how the various pieces of the database are being used by the sample workload. The wizard gives you two options for making the suggested changes if you so desire. The first option is to have the wizard apply the changes automatically, either immediately or scheduled for a later time. The second option is to generate a script that you can use to apply the changes later. The script gives you the option of making modifications before applying the changes to the database. Generating a script also gives you the ability to apply the same changes to another server or servers in the environment without having to rerun the wizard. It is important to understand that the wizard is not always right. There is no substitute for empirical testing to determine the effects of any change on your environment.

# Client Network Utility

The Client Network Utility allows you to configure how the clients on the current workstation connect to the various servers in your environment. You can select and configure which protocols you want to have available for connections. You can also create aliases for servers to allow connecting to the same server with different protocols from different tools. Aliases can also allow clients that do not support new features, like the named instances introduced in Microsoft SQL Server 2000, to be able to connect. The options for DB Library can be configured using this utility as well. You can view the list of library files (.dlls) that are being used and their locations and versions.

The General tab allows the selection of the protocols that can be used by the clients on a workstation to connect to Microsoft SQL Server 2000 servers. You can also click on the Properties button to change certain configuration options for the enabled protocols (like the default port number for TCP/IP connections). The order in which the enabled protocols are listed determines the order in which the client will attempt to use them for a connection. The Enable Protocol Encryption checkbox is used to turn on encryption using Secure Socket Layer (SSL). The Enable Shared Memory Protocol checkbox allows the use of the shared memory protocol for connections within the same computer.

The Alias tab allows you to define aliases for one or more servers to allow applications to connect to a server with overridden parameters. You can specify the network option to use for the connection, create a name that is usable by applications that do not support instance names, or make changes to the default options for the selected protocol. Creating aliases can allow you to support multiple applications on the same client machine that would otherwise require different client network configuration setups.

The DB Library tab displays the file name, version, date, and size of the DLL that is being used for DB Library support by the client. There are two configuration options available for DB Library. The Automatic ANSI to OEM Conversion checkbox specifies that DB Library should automatically convert the character set from OEM to ANSI when going from the client to the server and from ANSI to OEM when going from the server to the client. The Use International Setting checkbox causes DB Library to obtain date, time, and currency formats from the system rather than using hard-coded parameters.

The Network Libraries tab provides a list of the network libraries that are registered including their file names, locations, versions, dates, and sizes. This can be useful information if you are experiencing a problem and need to make sure you have the correct version of a particular library installed. You may have multiple versions of the same library residing on the system, but this tab shows you the one actually being used.

# Server Network Utility

The Server Network Utility is only available if the server is installed on the machine. You can configure the protocols that are available to connect to the current server as well as the properties of each allowable protocol. These settings can be changed for each server instance that is running on the machine independently. You can also view the list of library files (.dlls) that are being used and their locations and versions.

The General tab allows the selection of the protocols that can be used by clients to connect to this Microsoft SQL Server 2000. There is also a checkbox to Enable Winsock Proxy for the SQL Server. If you enable Winsock proxy support, you must provide the address and port for the proxy server.

The Network Libraries tab provides the same information about installed network libraries that is found on this tab in the Client Configuration Utility.

# Service Manager

The Service Manager is simply an easy-to-use graphical interface for starting, stopping, and checking the status of the various services related to Microsoft SQL Server 2000. In addition to the server service itself, the DTC, SQL Server Agent, and Microsoft Search Services can be monitored and controlled. Because the tool can be run remotely and also allows the capability to change the server that is being monitored, it permits a level of centralized control of all servers in the environment.

# Import and Export Data

The DTS Import/Export Wizard can be accessed from several different locations, including the Microsoft SQL Server Menu and the Enterprise Manager. This wizard takes you through the process of transferring data between Microsoft SQL Server 2000 and another data source step-by-step. This data can simply be copied, or it can be transformed to fit the environment to which it is being transferred. This wizard can even be used to copy data between different versions of Microsoft SQL Server within your environment. Refer to Chapter 7 for more detailed information on DTS. Whether you are a developer or a DBA, Books Online provides you with a wealth of valuable information in an easy-to-use, searchable database. It may well be the most important tool that ships with Microsoft SQL Server 2000.

# Books Online

Books Online is an invaluable set of documentation for Microsoft SQL Server 2000. It is a one-stop shop for all the help you need relating to topics from installation through development and maintenance. There is a "What's New" section that is especially helpful to users of previous versions of SQL. It helps you get a feel for new features as well as changes to existing functionality, which may need to be addressed in existing applications before upgrading to Microsoft SQL Server 2000. There are sections on installation, architecture, and administration of the server. There are guides for optimizing database performance and troubleshooting that can be of great benefit to the DBA and the developer. Also included in Books Online is a full Transact-SQL Reference. The APIs shipped with Microsoft SQL Server 2000 are covered as well. DB Library, Open Database Connectivity (ODBC), and SQL DMO are covered in detail with examples in C++ and Visual Basic. Books Online can easily become the developer or DBA's best friend when working with Microsoft SQL Server 2000. You can locate information by browsing through the table of contents, searching the index, or using the full search engine to locate words or phrases in the help text. There is also a Favorites tab that allows you to save quick links to pieces of the help that you need to refer to on a regular basis. Books Online is now the default help available in the tools when you press F1 for help.

The main table of contents for Books Online is shown in Figure 5.21. You can drill down into each topic to find the information you need. The "Getting Started" and "What's New" sections should probably be read by those who are using Microsoft SQL Server 2000 and its related tools. If you are not sure where to start looking in the table of contents, you can perform a keyword search in the index to find a particular topic. If the topic is located in several places, a menu is displayed listing the choices, and you can select the one that you are looking for. If you still cannot find the word or phrase you are looking for in the index, you can try using the full search engine to locate any help that contains them. You will be presented with a list of articles containing the word or words you specified, and you can select the one you want to read. The words in the search will be highlighted in the text to make them easier to find. You may have to try several promising sounding articles to find the information you are looking for. If your search does not return the information you intended, you can change or refine the search and try again. You can add articles that you need to use on a regular basis to the Favorites tab

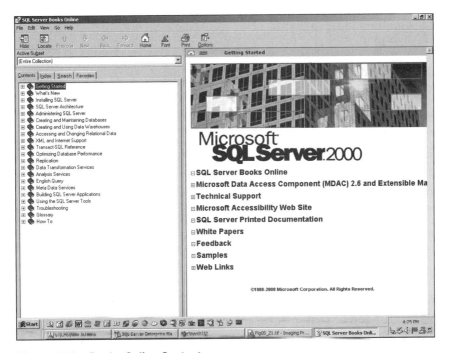

**Figure 5.21**  Books Online Contents.

for easy access. You may also want to add articles to this list that have information that was not easy to find, which can save you time when you need to refer to this information again in the future. Articles can be added to and removed from the Favorites list to correspond to your changing focus and needs.

# Nongraphical Utilities

There are several nongraphical utilities provided with the SQL Server tools. These tools are referred to in Books Online as Command Prompt Utilities because they are intended to be run from a DOS command prompt. These utilities can be quite useful for automating tasks using DOS batch files or running commands in a job using **xp_cmdshell**. The following is a list of the available nongraphical utilities and a brief description of each.

- *Bcp*—Used to copy data between SQL Server and a data file in a user specified format. Refer to Chapter 15 for details on using this utility.

- *Console*—Used to display backup and restore messages when backing up to or restoring from tape dump devices. This utility must be running before the backup or restore process is initiated on the server.

- *Isql*—Used to run queries against SQL Server with the option to save the query output to a text file. This utility uses DB Library to access the server.

- *Osql*—Used to run queries against SQL Server with the option to save the query output to a text file. This utility uses ODBC to access the server.

- *Sqlagent*—Used to start the SQL Server Agent from the command prompt.

- *Sqldiag*—Used to gather and store diagnostic information and the contents of the query history trace (if applicable).

- *Sqlmaint*—Used to perform a specified set of maintenance operations on one or more databases.

- *Sqlservr*—Used to start, stop, pause, and continue an instance of SQL Server.

- *Vswitch*—Used to switch the active version of Microsoft SQL Server between 2000, 7.0, and 6.5.

- *Dtsrun*—Used to retrieve, execute, delete, and/or overwrite a package created using DTS.

- *Dtswiz*—Used to start the DTS Import/Export Wizard using command prompt options.

- *Itwiz*—Used to execute the Index Tuning Wizard from a command prompt.

- *Odbccmpt*—Used to enable or disable the 6.5 ODBC compatibility option for an ODBC application executable file.

- *Rebuildm*—Used to fix a corrupted master database or to change the collation settings for an instance of Microsoft SQL Server 2000.

- *Sqlftwiz*—Used to execute the Full-Text Indexing Wizard from a command prompt.

- *Distrib*—Used to configure and start the Distribution Agent.

- *Logread*—Used to configure and start the Log Reader Agent.

- *Replmerg*—Used to configure and start the Merge Agent.

- *Snapshot*—Used to configure and start the Snapshot Agent.

- *Scm*—Used to create, modify, start, stop, or pause any of the Microsoft SQL Server 2000 services that run under Microsoft Windows NT. This utility can also be used to start, stop, or pause the equivalent SQL Server applications under Microsoft Windows 98.

# *Immediate Solutions*

## Enterprise Manager

This section provides step-by-step instructions for some of the tasks that can be performed using the Enterprise Manager. These tasks will provide you with a general idea of how simple it is to perform management tasks using the Enterprise Manager.

### Registering a Server Using the Register SQL Server Wizard

You will not be able to connect to a server using the Enterprise Manager until you have registered the server. This section provides a walk-through of the registration wizard to help you become familiar with this process.

1. Open Enterprise Manager.

2. Expand the Microsoft SQL Servers node in the tree.

3. Right-click on SQL Server Group, and select New SQL Server Registration from the menu. This launches the Register SQL Server Wizard, which is shown in Figure 5.22.

4. Make sure the From Now On, I Want To Perform This Task Without Using A Wizard checkbox is cleared. This checkbox allows you to turn off the wizard as the default method for registering a server. If you select this

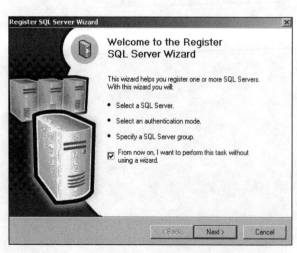

Figure 5.22   Register SQL Server Wizard page 1.

checkbox, the wizard stops when you advance to the next page, and the Register SQL Server Properties dialog is launched instead. Once you are familiar with the registration process, you may wish to turn off the wizard and use the dialog.

5. Click on Next.

6. The second page of the wizard allows you to add one or more servers to the list on the right, which will contain the servers to be registered this session.

7. The edit box on the left allows you to type in the name of the server to be added. If you have created any aliases using the Client Network Utility, these names will be displayed in the list below the edit box. You can either select a name from the list on the left, or type a new name to add, and then click on the Add button to populate the list on the right. If you select more than one server to register, all of the registration properties for the servers must match. These properties include the group name and login information for the servers.

8. Once you have selected the server or servers you wish to add, click on Next.

9. The third page of the wizard is where you must choose the correct login method to attach to the server or servers you selected on the previous page. If you do not know the authentication method that was installed for the server to which you are attaching, you will need to contact your DBA to find out how to log in to the server. If you specify Windows NT Authentication, you will not be asked to provide a user name and password to attach to the server. This example uses SQL Server Authentication because it is supported on all servers.

10. Click on Next.

11. The next page of the wizard is only used for SQL Server Authentication. Because SQL Server Authentication was selected, you have the choice of being logged in automatically or having the tool prompt for a user name and password every time you connect to the server.

12. Select Login Automatically Using My SQL Server Account Information. This causes the tool to automatically log in when you connect to the server.

13. Enter your SQL login name.

14. Enter your password.

15. Click on Next.

16. The Select SQL Server Group page allows you to select the group to which you want to add the server or to create a new top-level group. Select Create A New Top-Level SQL Server Group.

17. Enter a new group name. This creates a new group by the selected name for the server(s) you are registering to be added to. This is especially useful if you are managing more than a few servers. Putting too many servers in a single group can make it more difficult to find the one you need to work with.

18. Click on Next.

19. The final page of the wizard shows you the list of servers that you are about to register. Click on Finish to perform the registration for the server(s) listed. Once the registration and login information has been verified, the servers will appear in the selected group and you are ready to start managing them using Enterprise Manager.

## Registering a Server Using the Registered SQL Server Properties Dialog

Once you have become familiar with the registration process, you may wish to disable the Register SQL Server Wizard and use this dialog instead. The dialog allows you to enter all of the information needed to register a server on a single page instead of having to walk through all the pages of the wizard. In most environments, you will only need to provide a small amount of information and take the defaults for the rest, so the dialog will often allow you to complete the registration more quickly than the wizard.

1. Open Enterprise Manager.

2. Expand the Microsoft SQL Servers node in the tree.

3. Right-click on SQL Server Group, and select New SQL Server Registration from the menu. This launches the Register SQL Server Wizard, which is shown in Figure 5.22.

4. Select the From Now On, I Want To Perform This Task Without Using A Wizard checkbox. This checkbox turns off the wizard as the default method for registering a server.

5. Click on Next. The wizard stops, and the Register SQL Server Properties dialog is launched instead.

6. Figure 5.23 shows the Registered SQL Server Properties dialog, which is where you can enter the information needed to register the server. Enter the name of the server you want to register in the Server prompt. The ellipsis […] button next to the server name provides access to the SQL Active Directory Search dialog, which can assist you in locating the server you want to register.

7. The next section allows you to select the authentication method used to connect to the server. Select the appropriate authentication type and provide the user name and password if applicable.

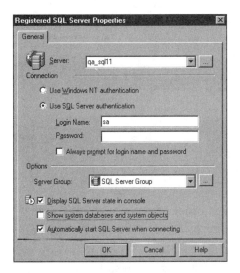

**Figure 5.23    Registered SQL Server Properties dialog.**

8. You must provide a group name for the server to be added to. This is done by using a drop-down list of the configured server groups. Select the group that this server should be added to. The ellipsis [...] button next to the drop-down box allows you to create a new top-level group or subgroup to add the server to.

9. Select the Display SQL Server State In Console checkbox to cause this information to be displayed as part of the icon in the normal console window. This is useful for keeping an eye on the servers to make sure they are started, and so on.

10. Clear the Show System Databases And System Objects checkbox. This option should be disabled unless you are currently working with it for some reason. Removing these objects from the view helps eliminate accidental modifications of this data.

11. If you want the server to be started automatically if it is stopped when you attempt to connect to it, select the Automatically Start SQL Server When Connecting checkbox. This option can be useful in some environments, but is not really needed for production servers because it is unlikely that they will be stopped without an extremely good reason.

12. Click on OK to compete the registration process for the server.

## Modifying SQL Server Properties

This section provides step-by-step instructions for modifying the configuration properties of an existing SQL Server. This is the easiest way to check or modify these properties once the server installation is complete. This is not something that will need to be modified on a regular basis, but it is important to know how and where to access this information if you need it.

1. Open Enterprise Manager.

2. Expand the Microsoft SQL Servers node in the tree.

3. Expand SQL Server Group.

4. Select a server from the list.

5. Hold the cursor over the yellow button in the Server section in the right pane until the menu pops up.

6. Select Properties from the menu. This launches the Server Properties dialog from which you can change a number of server configuration options. This should definitely be done with care and *only* by the DBA or with the DBA's knowledge and consent.

7. The General tab, shown in Figure 5.24, gives some basic configuration information about the server. From this tab, select the checkboxes for the services you want to have started automatically when the system is rebooted.

8. Click on Network Configuration to bring up the SQL Server Network Utility and make sure that only the protocols that you actually need to use are enabled for this server. Remember that Named Pipes must be enabled to use the SQL Server Profiler on this server. If you make any changes, click on Apply.

Figure 5.24   SQL Server Properties (Configure) dialog—General tab.

9. Click on OK to close the SQL Server Network Utility and return to the SQL Server Properties (Configure) dialog.

10. Select the Memory tab to display the configuration of Microsoft SQL Server 2000's memory usage and allow you to change this configuration. You have the option of either letting Microsoft SQL Server 2000 dynamically allocate memory as needed (you can set minimum and maximum values for this) or allocating a fixed amount of memory to Microsoft SQL Server 2000. If your server is dedicated to SQL Server (recommended), you should select Use A Fixed Memory Size and allocate as much memory as possible to SQL Server. The colored graph indicates the amount of memory that should be safe to allocate to SQL Server based on what is in the machine.

**NOTE:** *If you are allocating a fixed amount of memory to SQL Server, you should also select the Reserve Physical Memory For SQL Server checkbox. The combination of these options improves performance by eliminating the need for SQL Server to request and release memory as its needs change based on the workload.*

The radio buttons for the Configured values and Running values allow you to see what is configured and which options are currently in use by Microsoft SQL Server 2000. Changing from Configured values to the Running values allows you to see if any changes that have been made require the server to be restarted before they take effect. The information shown for Running values is read-only.

11. Select the Processor tab, which displays the available processors in the server and allows you to select processors to be used by Microsoft SQL Server 2000. If there is only one processor in the machine, no selection is allowed. If you have more than one processor in the machine and the server is dedicated to Microsoft SQL Server, make sure that all processors are selected.

**NOTE:** *The maximum worker threads should normally be set to around 100 (the default is 255).*

You can elect to boost the priority of Microsoft SQL Server 2000 under Windows NT/2000, but it is not recommended. Microsoft SQL Server 2000 should be installed on a server set up specifically as a SQL Server and no other software or network services (like domain controller or email) should be installed on that server. Issuing the priority boost can lead to the server not responding to management tools and can make it difficult to properly administer the server.

You can also elect to use Windows NT fibers instead of threads. This option can be tested in your environment to see which yields the best performance.

**5. Microsoft SQL Server Tools**

Select the number of processors to use for parallelism. The parallel processing of a single query can be broken into multiple parallel steps, which are then executed simultaneously to speed the execution time on multiprocessor systems.

12. Select the Security tab. The authentication model should be considered carefully to make sure it meets the needs of your organization. This interface is an easy and convenient place to change this model if you determine after installation that the chosen model does not meet your needs.

You can set the Audit Level for the server to determine what login events are written to the log on this server. The four options provided determine the level of detail that will be tracked in the log as well as attempted logins to the server.

You can also configure the startup account used by SQL Server to log in to the machine on which it is running. Configuring the server startup account is very important because the startup account determines what resources (both local and network) the service has access to. Giving the server too little access can be detrimental to the performance of required tasks, but too much access may present a security risk, especially if you allow the use of tools like **xp_cmdshell**.

13. The Connections tab is used to set the maximum number of concurrent user connections.

A list of default connection options that can be set at the server to establish default properties for all connections is provided. Study the help for each of these options and determine the best setting for your environment. The settings that relate to ANSI compatibility should be carefully considered to avoid problems in the future. Changing the ANSI settings once a system is running in production can have unpredictable side effects.

This dialog also allows for configuration of remote access. Remote Procedure Calls (RPC) can be enabled so that other servers can connect to the current one remotely. If you do not need this option, disable it to prevent any possible security risk as well as to save the required resources for other tasks.

A query timeout can be established for remote connections. You need to consider any timeout value carefully because the server is not selective concerning the processes it stops. If you have any long running queries, perhaps in nightly or weekend jobs, you need to consider them when you set this value. If you can find a manageable setting, it can provide great protection for the server from runaway queries.

The Enforce Distributed Transactions (MTS) option causes the MSDTC to be used to coordinate server-to-server procedures. If you will not be performing server-to-server procedures, disable this option.

14. Select the Server Settings tab. The Server Settings tab allows for some general configuration of the server. Specify the default language for the users.

15. Clear the Allow Modifications To Be Made Directly To The System Catalogs checkbox. Direct modifications to the system catalog should be allowed only in extreme circumstances and only by a knowledgeable DBA. Use of this capability in an inappropriate manner can easily damage or destroy your database or cripple your server.

    You should decide whether or not to enable the Allow Triggers To Be Fired Which Fire Other Triggers (Nested Triggers) option. Nested triggers can be enabled if needed, but you will need to be extremely careful to prevent endless loops with this option enabled.

    Enabling the Use Query Governor To Prevent Queries Exceeding Specified Cost: option can provide another safeguard for the server to prevent runaway queries, but again you *must* be sure that you allow sufficient margin for all of the queries that are required in your environment. Pay special attention to long-running overnight or weekend processes before setting this option. If you enable this option, you need to provide a value for the maximum cost.

    The SQL Mail login name is also displayed, which allows you to verify that it is set correctly.

    You can modify the "sliding window" Microsoft SQL Server 2000 uses to determine the century for two-digit years entered for dates in queries. Depending on your environment, you may want to adjust this window to provide more accurate defaults for the most common dates your users will be entering.

16. Select the Database Settings tab. The Database Settings tab allows you to set the default fill factor for indexes. When this option is cleared, it allows SQL Server to select the optimum setting. You should leave the option cleared unless you have an extremely good understanding of how the fill factor will affect the performance in your environment and are sure that SQL Server is not making the best selection.

    The default timeout for tape devices used in Backup and Restore operations can be set to determine how long SQL Server will attempt to access the device before failing the operation. Normally, these operations should have alerts configured to notify the DBA in the event of a failure.

You can also determine the Default Backup Media Retention time for a backup. This option can be set when the backup is performed, but you can configure the default value on this tab to prevent having to change it for standard backups.

The Recovery interval determines how many minutes SQL Server needs to complete its recovery per database. The default is 0 minutes, which is also known as "fast recovery." For performance reasons, this value should be set to the maximum amount of time that can be tolerated in your environment.

Setting the default location for newly created database and log files helps you to avoid accidentally creating a new database or log file on the wrong drive and eliminates the aggravation of having to edit the path every time. It is recommended that you separate the log and data files on different drives if possible to boost performance. This works even better if the drives are on separate controllers.

17. Select the Replication tab, which allows for the configuring and disabling of publishing and distribution for the current server. The Configure button on this tab launches the Configure Publishing And Distribution Wizard for the server.

   When publishing and distribution has been configured for the server, a new option is displayed on this tab that allows adding the server to the Replication Monitor group.

   The Disable button on this tab launches the Disable Publishing And Distribution Wizard for the server.

18. When you are done making changes, click on OK to return to the Enterprise Manager. If you have made any changes to the configuration that require SQL Server to be restarted, you can either use the Start and Stop options on the context menu in the Enterprise Manager or launch the Service Manager to stop and restart the server.

*TIP:* Be sure to have everyone log off the server before you stop it to prevent loss of work. If the server is stopped while any transactions are pending, they are automatically rolled back when the server is restarted, and users will have to start them again from the beginning.

## Modifying a Table Structure

This section provides a step-by-step example of modifying the structure of an existing table using the Enterprise Manager. This task can also be performed using T-SQL commands, but the GUI provided by the Enterprise Manager makes the task much simpler to perform.

1. Open Enterprise Manager.
2. Expand the Microsoft SQL Servers node in the tree.
3. Expand SQL Server Group.
4. Select a server from the list, and expand it in the tree.
5. Expand the Databases node in the tree.
6. Expand the pubs database in the tree.
7. Select Tables under pubs in the tree.
8. Right-click on the sales table in the right pane, and select Design Table from the context menu. This launches the Design Table dialog shown in Figure 5.25.
9. Click in the Column Name column of the empty row beneath **table_id**, and enter a new field name.
10. Tab to the Data Type column, and select int for the data type.

   The Length tab defaults to 4 for an integer. You cannot change the length of fixed length fields, such as integers and money.

   You can select or clear the Allow Nulls column to determine whether or not the new columns will accept null values.

   The tab at the bottom of the dialog allows you to change additional properties for the column.

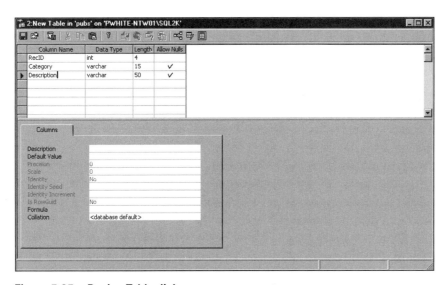

Figure 5.25    Design Table dialog.

11. Click on Save on the toolbar to save the changes to the database for this table.

12. Close the dialog when you have finished making changes to the table.

## Scripting Database Objects

This section will show you how to generate SQL Scripts for your database objects using the Enterprise Manager. It is a good idea to keep scripts available to re-create your database schema as part of your backup plan. The Enterprise Manager provides a simple interface to generate scripts for any or all of your database objects that you can save for later use. These scripts can also be useful for creating copies of one or more objects on another database or server.

1. Open Enterprise Manager.

2. Expand the Microsoft SQL Servers node in the tree.

3. Expand SQL Server Group.

4. Select a server from the list, and expand it in the tree.

5. Expand the Databases node in the tree.

6. Expand the pubs database in the tree.

7. Select Tables under pubs in the tree.

8. Right-click on the sales table in the right pane, and select All Tasks from the context menu.

9. Select Generate SQL Script from the submenu to launch the Generate SQL Scripts dialog shown in Figure 5.26.

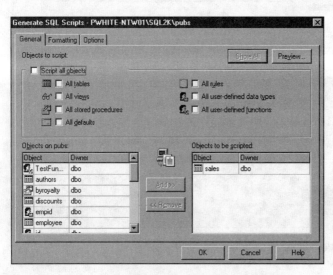

Figure 5.26    Generate SQL Scripts dialog—General tab.

The dialog launches with the General tab selected and has the selected table in the bottom-right pane under Objects to be scripted. To display the full list of database options, click on the Show All button.

10. Select the Formatting tab.

11. Select the following checkboxes: Generate CREATE <object> Command For Each Object checkbox and Generate DROP <object> Command For Each Object checkbox.

12. Select the Options tab.

13. Select the following checkboxes: Script Indexes, Script Triggers, and Script PRIMARY Keys, FOREIGN Keys, Defaults, and Check Constraints.

14. Select the General tab again, and click on Preview to see the script that will be generated. The Copy button copies the contents of the preview window to the clipboard for you to paste into another application, such as the Query Analyzer.

15. Close the preview window.

16. Click on OK to generate the script. The Save As dialog appears and prompts you for the file name to save the generated script.

## Detaching and Attaching Databases

This section will provide a step-by-step walk-through of the process of detaching and reattaching a database. This can be extremely useful for moving or copying data from one server to another, either as a backup or to create an offline testing environment. The ability to attach and detach databases was introduced in SQL Server 7 and makes moving data between servers extremely easy. The Enterprise Manager provided with SQL Server 2000 make this process even easier by providing a graphical interface for the attach and detach processes instead of forcing the use of T-SQL commands.

1. Open Enterprise Manager.

2. Expand the Microsoft SQL Servers node in the tree.

3. Expand SQL Server Group.

4. Select a server from the list, and expand it in the tree.

5. Expand the Databases node in the tree.

6. Select the pubs database in the tree.

7. Right-click on pubs, and select All Tasks from the context menu.

8. Select Detach Database from the submenu to launch the Detach Database dialog shown in Figure 5.27.

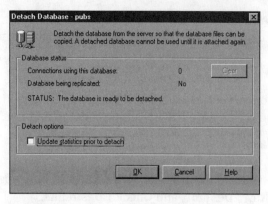

Figure 5.27   Detach Database dialog.

If there are any current connections to the database shown in the Database Status section of this dialog, click on Clear to remove the connections. You cannot detach a database until all connections to the database have been closed or removed.

9. Click on OK to detach the database. Notice that it is no longer shown in the list of databases for the server.

10. Right-click on the Databases node in the tree, and select All Tasks from the context menu.

11. Select Attach Database from the submenu to launch the Attach Database dialog shown in Figure 5.28.

12. You must provide the path and file names for the database to reattach. Click on the ellipsis […] button next to the edit box to browse for the file to add.

13. Locate the .mdf file for the pubs database on your server using the file browser, and select it (pubs.mdf). Notice that the log file for the pubs database is also included in the Original File Name(s) grid automatically.

14. Click on OK to reattach the database and close the dialog.

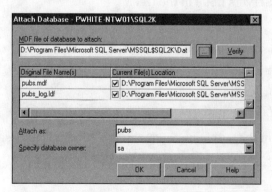

Figure 5.28   Attach Database dialog.

| Related solution: | Found on page: |
|---|---|
| Creating a Stored Procedure That Will Detach, Zip, Copy, and Attach the Inventory Database | 270 |

## Creating a Database Diagram from Existing Data

This section will show you how easy it is to create a database diagram for your existing databases using the GUI provided by the Enterprise Manager.

1. Open Enterprise Manager.

2. Expand the Microsoft SQL Servers node in the tree.

3. Expand SQL Server Group.

4. Select a server from the list, and expand it in the tree.

5. Expand the Databases node in the tree.

6. Expand the pubs database in the tree.

7. Select Diagrams under pubs in the tree.

8. Right-click on Diagrams, and select New Database Diagram from the context menu to launch the Create Database Diagram Wizard.

9. Click on Next.

10. Select all available nonsystem tables, and click on Add.

11. Click on Next.

12. Once you have reviewed the list of tables to be added to the diagram, click on Finish to generate the diagram.

13. In the New Diagram dialog, you can rearrange the tables to make them easy to read. Notice that all FOREIGN key relationships are automatically added to the diagram for you.

14. Click on Save on the toolbar to save the diagram and any changes to the arrangement that you have made. You are prompted for a name for the new diagram, which can be especially helpful if you will be creating more than one diagram for different aspects of the database.

15. Close the New Diagram dialog to return to the Enterprise Manager. You will see the diagram displayed in the right pane when you select Diagrams in the tree.

## Modifying Table Structures from a Database Diagram

The ability to modify table structures from the Database Diagram makes these diagrams in the Enterprise Manager even more useful. This section provides step-by-step instructions to help you become familiar with this method of modifying your table structures.

1. Open Enterprise Manager.

2. Expand the Microsoft SQL Servers node in the tree.

3. Expand SQL Server Group.

4. Select a server from the list, and expand it in the tree.

5. Expand the Databases node in the tree.

6. Expand the pubs database in the tree.

7. Select Diagrams under pubs in the tree.

8. Double-click on an existing diagram in the right pane.

9. Right-click in the empty space in the table, and select New Table from the context menu.

10. Enter a name for the new table.

11. Enter properties for one or more fields for the new table.

12. Right-click on the table, and select Modify Custom from the Table View submenu to gain access to additional properties for the columns.

13. Click on Save to save the changes to the diagram. You will be asked if you wish to save these changes to the database.

14. Click on Yes to add this table to the Pubs database. You can add, delete, or modify tables using the Database Diagram and save the diagram changes to the database.

| Related solutions: | Found on page: |
|---|---|
| Installing the Book Databases from Scripts | 369 |
| Database Design Steps | 725 |

## Adding External Tools

The ability to add external tools to the menu in the Enterprise Manager will allow you to centralize access to all the tools you need for database and server management. Once you have added the additional tools that you use on a regular basis to this menu, the Enterprise Manager can become the central focus of most of your work. This section provides the detailed steps needed to add access to external tools from inside the Enterprise Manager.

1. Open Enterprise Manager.

2. Select Tools|External Tools to launch the External Tools dialog shown in Figure 5.29.

3. Click on Add to launch the Add External Tool dialog.

4. Click on Browse to search for the .exe file of the tool you wish to add.

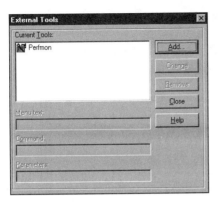

Figure 5.29    External Tools dialog.

5. Once you have selected the application you want to add in the Open dialog, you can enter any parameters that should be passed to the application when it is launched in the Parameters edit box.

6. Click on OK to add the tool, and return to the External Tools dialog.

7. Click on Close when you are done adding and modifying external tools.

8. Click on the Tools menu to see the tools you have added displayed at the bottom of the menu.

# Query Analyzer

The following solutions will help you make better use of the Query Analyzer as well as introduce you to some of the new features available in the version shipped with SQL Sever 2000. These examples cover some basic functionality to help you become familiar with the tool and its available features.

## Using a Template

The following steps are intended to make you familiar with the new templates available in the Query Analyzer provided with SQL Server 2000. This is a simple example of using a template to create a user-defined function, which is another new feature in SQL Server 2000.

1. Open the Query Analyzer.

2. Connect to a server.

3. Select Tools|Object Browser. The Object Browser can also be accessed by pressing F8 or by clicking on the Object Browser on the toolbar, which is the second button to the right of the Database Selection drop-down box.

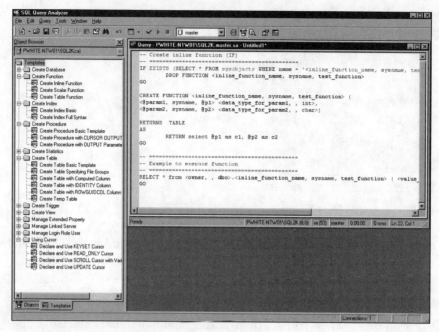

**Figure 5.30   Templates in the Query Analyzer.**

4. Figure 5.30 shows the Query window with the Templates tab selected in the Object Browser. Select the Templates tab at the bottom of the Object Browser.

5. Expand the Create Function node in the tree. Click on the Create Inline Function template, and drag it into the query window. You can also select Insert Template from the Edit menu, and select the template you want to work with.

6. Once the template text is in the query window, you can replace the template parameters to create a functional query. To replace the parameters, select Edit|Replace Template Parameters.

7. The Replace Template Parameters dialog, shown in Figure 5.31, makes it simple to replace the template parameters with the values you need for your script. The parameters for an Inline Function are shown in the dialog. To replace each parameter, just enter the required information in the Value column of the grid. Enter a name for the function.

8. Provide the name and type of the parameters for the function. The dialog only allows for using two parameters, but once this text is in the script, it will be obvious how to add additional parameters.

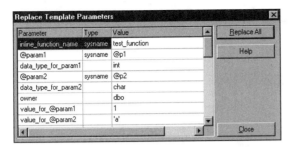

**Figure 5.31**   Replace Template Parameters dialog.

9. The last two parameter items in the dialog allow you to supply values to pass to your function when it is called. Enter the values you want to pass to the function in the "example" code inserted by the template.

10. Once you have entered the new values for the parameters, click on Replace All to insert these values into the script. You then have the basic shell for the function in the script window. You can further modify the parameter list to add or remove parameters and insert the code for your function.

## Changing Current Connection Properties

The following instructions will help you become familiar with some of the available connection level settings that can be changed in the Query Analyzer, as well as how and where to make these changes.

1. Open the Query Analyzer.

2. Connect to a server.

3. Select Query|Current Connection Properties to launch the Current Connection Properties dialog shown in Figure 5.32. This dialog can also be accessed by clicking on the Current Connection Properties button on the toolbar.

4. Select the Set Statistics Time checkbox to cause the Query Analyzer to show the duration of each statement in the query.

5. Select the Set statistics IO checkbox to cause the Query Analyzer to show the number of reads and writes performed against each table referenced in the query.

6. Click on Apply to apply the new settings to this connection.

7. Click on OK to close the dialog and return to the Query Analyzer.

8. Enter a simple query, such as "SELECT * FROM pubs..sales" and execute it.

9. Look at the query results to see the output of the two options that you turned on for this connection.

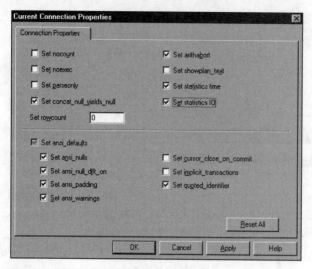

**Figure 5.32   Current Connection Properties dialog.**

## Using the Object Browser

These instructions will help you become familiar with what this author considers to be the best enhancement to the Query Analyzer shipped with SQL Server 2000. Once you have used the Object Browser, you will never want to go back to an older version of the Query Analyzer. Fortunately, the Object Browser is available for connections to SQL 6.5 and 7 Servers as well as SQL 2000 Servers. Some of the options are not supported for the older versions of SQL Server, but 90 percent of the features in the Object Browser are available for all of them.

1. Open the Query Analyzer.

2. Connect to a server.

3. Press F8 to display the Object Browser if it is not already displayed.

4. In the query window, type "SELECT * FROM".

5. In the object browser, expand the pubs node in the tree.

6. Expand the User Tables node in the tree.

7. Left-click on the titles table, and drag it into the query window at the end of the text you just entered. This places the titles table in the query window for you. You can use the Object Browser to locate table names, field names, views, SPs, user-defined functions, system variables, and system functions. This can be a real time-saver when constructing queries.

8. Once you have typed or copied all of the information you need to construct a query, you can execute it normally.

## Displaying and Examining a Query Plan

Examining the query plan that is being used by the SQL Server to execute your query can help you determine what changes you need to make to improve performance. This section provides instructions on how to display and interpret the query plan for a simple query using the Query Analyzer. The "Adding an Entry to Favorites" section in the immediate solutions section of this chapter will help you locate the legend that lists all of the icons used to display a query plan and their meanings.

1. Open the Query Analyzer.

2. Connect to a server.

3. Type the following query into the query window:

```
SELECT au_fname + ' ' + au_fname as Name,
    title as Book
  FROM pubs..authors a (NOLOCK)
  JOIN pubs..titleauthor ta (NOLOCK) on a.au_id = ta.au_id
  JOIN pubs..titles t (NOLOCK) on ta.title_id = t.title_id
  ORDER BY title
```

4. Select Query|Display Estimated Execution Plan to display the graphical query plan in a second pane below the query pane. This can also be accomplished by clicking on the Display Estimated Execution Plan button on the toolbar or by pressing Ctrl+L.

    The execution plan shows each referenced table and what the percentage of the total query cost is to read from each one.

5. Hold the mouse cursor over one of the table icons in the execution plan to see more detailed information about the operation performed on the table and the associated statistics.

    You can use the statistics and estimated query cost to determine what areas of a query to look at for the purposes of optimization. You may be able to change a join condition or add an index to improve the query performance. When optimizing, it is best to concentrate on the pieces of the query with the highest cost because those will have the greatest impact on the overall query time.

| Related solutions: | Found on page: |
|---|---|
| Examining an Execution Plan in the Query Analyzer | 516 |
| Improving Query Performance Using a Covering Index | 523 |

# SQL Server Profiler

This section includes some examples to help you become familiar with the Profiler. The Profiler is an invaluable tool for debugging and optimizing your SQL code, and these examples will show you how to make use of some of these features.

## Creating a Trace Template for Optimization

Creating templates will allow you to more quickly set up a trace. You can create templates with the selections you use most frequently. Since you will find it useful to highlight or filter different information depending on the purpose of the trace, the Profiler allows you to create as many templates as you need to cover these various situations. Once you have created a template, you can use it to set the default properties of a new trace and greatly reduce the amount of work that must be repeated to start a trace.

1. Open the SQL Server Profiler.

2. To create a new trace template, select File|New|Trace Template from the menu. For this example, let's set up a template that will be used in Chapter 11. Creating trace templates saves you time and aggravation when you want to run a trace. You can set the properties in the template that you want to use in a trace, and then select the template when you create a new trace to automatically use those properties. You will want to create templates for any set of trace properties that you use regularly. You may want to use a different trace setup for debugging than the one you use for optimization.

3. Figure 5.33 shows the General tab of the Trace Template Properties dialog. Click on Save As to choose a file name for the template. Once the file name is set, it will be displayed on this tab. If you do not select a file name, you will receive the Save As dialog the first time you click on Save at the bottom of the dialog.

4. Select the Events tab. This tab is where you select the events you want to see in the trace. The events you leave out of the trace can be as important as the events you include. If you include too many events, the trace can become difficult to follow, and you may not be able to find the information you are looking for. You will need to spend some time experimenting with the various events to find out which ones do and don't provide meaningful information in your environment. The events that you will want to watch also vary depending on the purpose of the trace you are running. The events that should be added to the optimization template are:

   a. *Cursors*—Add the entire list, which can be accomplished by selecting the main node and clicking on Add or by double-clicking on the main node in the left pane.

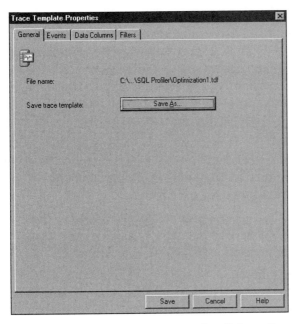

**Figure 5.33    Trace Template Properties dialog—General tab.**

    b. *Errors and Warnings*—Add the entire list.

    c. *Locks*—Add the entries for Deadlock and Deadlock Chain.

    d. *Performance*—Add the entries for Execution Plan and Show Plan Statistics.

    e. *Sessions*—Add the entire list.

    f. *Stored Procedures*—Add the entire list.

    g. *TSQL*—Add the entire list.

5. Select the Data Columns tab to configure the columns you want to have displayed in the trace window. This is also where you select the order in which the columns are presented in the view. The order the columns are presented affects how easy it is to interpret the trace results, especially while the trace is running. As with the events, it is important to choose the columns you want to display with sufficient care to prevent overloading the view and making it unusable. You will need to experiment with the columns to determine which ones provide useful information in various situations. The columns that will be used for the optimization template should be added in the order shown in the following list:

    a. *EventClass*—Displays the type of event captured.

    b. *Duration*—The time in milliseconds to complete a process. This time is normally displayed for the final event in a process, like a select statement, which may generate multiple events. In some cases, the time will be displayed for some of the events between the beginning and ending of a process, but the final event will display the cumulative time for the process. This column allows you to determine which steps in a procedure are taking the majority of time to allow you to focus your tuning efforts in the areas where they will be most beneficial. This column also allows you to see the timing effect of any changes that you make in the tuning process.

c. *Reads*—The number of logical database reads performed by the event. This column can be helpful in determining why a particular query is taking a longer time to execute than anticipated.

d. *Writes*—The number of logical database writes performed by the event. This column can be helpful in determining why a particular insert, update, or delete operation is taking longer than anticipated.

e. *Success*—The success or failure of an operation. This column displays a 1 for success and a 0 for failure. This is useful for making sure that all of the pieces of a procedure are executing properly.

f. *Error*—The error number (if any) generated by the event.

g. *EndTime*—The time at which the event ended.

h. *StartTime*—The time at which the event started.

i. *TextData*—The text value corresponding to the event. The text of each query statement is displayed in this column. This is also where the execution plan and other text values are displayed. When you select an event in the list, the text value is also displayed in the pane at the bottom of the window.

j. *SPID*—The Server Process ID assigned to the client that generated the event.

k. *HostName*—The name of the computer on which the client application is running.

l. *ApplicationName*—The name of the client application that created the connection that generated the event.

m. *LoginName*—The login name used to connect to the server for the connection.

n. *NTUserName*—The Windows NT User Name using the client connection.

o. *DatabaseName*—The name of the database that the statement that generated the event is running against.

6. Select the Filters tab to create filters that allow you to eliminate traffic from the trace that is not relevant to the information you are trying to gather. One of the filters that you will normally want to use is Application Name Not Like SQL%. This filter prevents the messages generated by the SQL Server Agent and other related services from showing up in the trace mixed in with the information from the application you are trying to trace. This filter should be set for the optimization template. The other filters can be used to limit the trace to only those events generated by a specific application, login ID, host, database, and so on. You should spend some time examining these options because they will be invaluable in generating meaningful traces in a production environment.

7. Click on Save to save the template and close the dialog.

## Saving a Trace to a File

The ability to save a trace to a file allows you to keep information for comparison to later trace results and provides you with the ability to perform the trace and move the file to another machine for evaluation. These trace files also provide the workload information required for the Index Tuning Wizard to make recommendations for your indexing scheme.

1. Open the SQL Server Profiler.

2. To start a new trace, select File|New|Trace.

3. Connect to the server you are going to run the trace against. You will need to provide the server or alias name and login information.

4. Enter a name for the trace.

5. Select a template from the Template Name drop-down list.

6. Select the Save To File checkbox.

7. Select the file name and directory for the trace file in the Save As dialog.

8. Click on Run to start the trace.

9. With the trace running, either run an application against the server or run a query from the Query Analyzer to capture the trace information.

10. Click on Stop on the toolbar. You can pause a trace and continue it later, but once you have stopped a trace, the fill will be cleared and re-created if you restart the trace.

11. Close the trace window.

12. You can then access the saved trace file by clicking on Open on the toolbar and selecting the file from the Open dialog. You can change the events and columns that are available by editing the trace properties, but you will not be able to add any columns or events that were not present in the original trace.

**5. Microsoft SQL Server Tools**

| Related solution: | Found on page: |
| --- | --- |
| Running Traces for Optimization | 518 |

# Client Network Utility

The examples in this section show you how and why to use the Client Network Utility. These examples provide step-by-step instructions on how to perform the tasks that will normally require you to make use of this utility.

## Changing the Default Protocol

Configuring the default connection protocol for a workstation is the most common use of the Client Network Utility. In many environments, all applications used on a workstation will use the same protocol to connect to the SQL Server. The protocol used to connect to the server can affect the performance of the applications on the workstation as well as prevent a connection if the server does not support the selected protocol.

1. Open the Client Network Utility.

2. Select the General tab.

3. The SQL Server 2000 client utilities allow you to specify more than one connection protocol, and the utilities will attempt the connection in the order that the protocols are listed. Not all applications will support this functionality immediately, so the protocol that is required for the majority of your applications should be placed at the top of the list.

4. Select a protocol in the Disabled Protocols list.

5. Click on Enable. This moves the protocol to the Enabled Protocols list.

6. Use the up and down arrow buttons below the Enabled Protocols list to move the selected protocol to the desired order in the list.

7. Click on Properties to change the configuration options for the selected protocol.

8. When you have finished selecting protocols and have the list in the order that you need, click on OK to save the changes and close the Client Network Utility.

## Creating an Alias for Use with SQL Server Profiler

Many of the applications that run on Microsoft SQL Server have specific connectivity requirements. These can easily be addressed on the server by enabling the protocols required for the applications you will be using. Problems can arise on the client when you need to access the same SQL Server with multiple applications that have different protocol requirements. A good example of this might be running an application that requires TCP/IP for connectivity and needing to run the SQL Server Profiler against the server while you are running the application. The Profiler requires Named Pipes or Multi-Protocol for connectivity to the server. In order to facilitate connecting to the server with a protocol other than the default, you need to create an alias for the server on the client machine that specifies the correct protocol for one of the applications.

1. Open the Client Network Utility.

2. Select the Alias tab, shown in Figure 5.34, to establish a server alias. Let's create an alias for the Profiler example mentioned previously. Because the application that is running uses TCP/IP for connectivity, it will be the most-likely default protocol configured on the machine. In order to access the server using Named Pipes, create an alias to allow connectivity using Named Pipes. Because the trace will be run on the same server as the application, you need to create an alias that uses a different name from the actual server name. If you create an alias with the same name as the server, all applications, including the application that you want to trace, will use Named Pipes to connect to the server.

3. Click on Add to bring up the Add Network Library Configuration dialog shown in Figure 5.35.

4. Enter the name of the alias you want to use for the server.

5. Because you are using an alias that differs from the actual server name in this example, you need to change the server name under Connection Parameters. If you have selected Named Pipes in the Network Libraries group, you will see that the Pipe Name is set automatically to match the server name instead of the alias name.

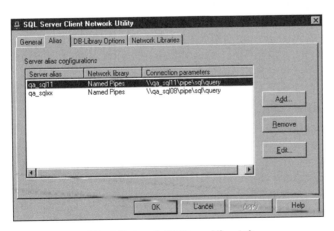

Figure 5.34    Client Network Utility—Alias tab.

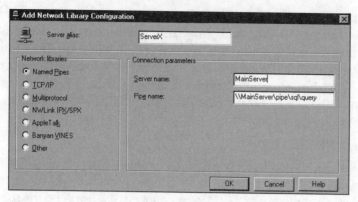

**Figure 5.35   Add Network Library Configuration dialog.**

6. Click on OK to add the alias.

7. To use this alias in the SQL Server Profiler, you would specify the alias name as the server name when prompted for the server to connect to. Any application that you are running should provide a way to select the proper server to connect to. The dialog allows you to specify the alias name to use for any connection that needs to be made using a protocol other than the one you have configured as a default. The alias can also be used to specify any nonstandard properties needed for the protocol you are using, such as a nonstandard port for TCP/IP.

# Books Online

The Books Online is probably the most complete reference on SQL Server 2000 available. Learning to make effective use of the available features will help you increase your productivity by enabling you to find the information you need more quickly and easily. This section provides instructions to help you become familiar with two tasks that will help you find and keep critical information.

## Adding an Entry to Favorites

Books Online has the capability to create a Favorites list for easy access to items that you find and want to be able to get back to without having to repeat the search process. This feature can be extremely useful for keeping track of helpful topics that were difficult to locate when you initially tried to find them. How many times have you spent a significant amount of time trying to find help on a particular topic and then needed the information again at a later time and was not able to remember how you found it the first time. You have probably wasted hours trying to relocate a piece of information that you needed for a particular project. The following instructions will familiarize you with the process of adding an entry to your "Favorites" list:

1. Open Books Online.

2. Select the Search tab.

3. Type "execution plan" as the words to search for, and press Enter.

4. Double-click on the "Graphically Displaying the Execution Plan Using SQL Query Analyzer" entry in the result list returned by the search. Figure 5.36 shows Books Online with the search performed to locate the legend for the icons used in the graphical query plan displayed in the Query Analyzer. This information is not actually difficult to locate, but it is very useful, so it makes for a good example.

5. Select the Favorites tab, which is displayed in Figure 5.37. Notice that the entry that was selected from the search in Figure 5.36 is displayed in the Current Entry box at the bottom of the tab.

6. Click on Add to add the entry to the list.

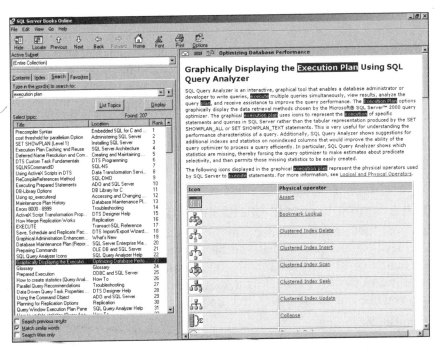

**Figure 5.36   Books Online—Search tab.**

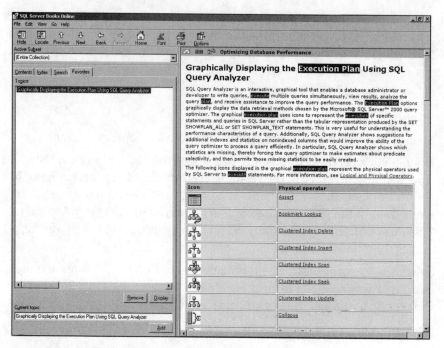

**Figure 5.37    Books Online—Favorites tab.**

7. You also have the ability to remove entries from the list if it gets too cluttered and the entries are no longer needed. Some topics will become less useful as you get more familiar with the subject matter. To remove an item from the list, select the item, and click on Remove.

8. Once you have added one or more items to the list, you can switch to the Favorites tab to access them quickly at any time. Just select the item you are looking for and either click on Display or double-click on the item in the list to display the topic in the right pane.

## Refining a Search to Locate Useful Information

The amount of information available in the Books Online can make locating the specific piece of information that you need a daunting task. It is important to become familiar with how the search engine can be used to refine a search to eliminate entries that are not useful for your present situation. These instructions will help you become familiar with the process of refining a search.

1. Open Books Online.

2. Select the Search tab.

3. Type "DTS" as the word to search for, and press Enter. This produces a list of 500 topics that match the search criteria.

4. Select the Search Previous Results checkbox at the bottom of the form.

5. Type "custom" as the word to search for, and press Enter. This reduces the original list to 178 entries that match the new search criteria.

   You can continue entering more distinct criteria until you find the information you are looking for.

6. Once you have located the information you need, double-click on the entry in the list that you need and the help will be displayed in the right panel.

**5. Microsoft SQL Server Tools**

# Chapter 6

# Server Maintenance

(continued)

# *In Depth*

Maintenance is often overlooked in product development and software purchase decisions. As a result, it often causes problems when implementing a software solution or handling the minor issues that *all* systems face in day-to-day operations. Any development effort or purchase that is made in today's information technology area should consider maintenance and fail-over requirements. This chapter covers some of the features that SQL 2000 offers and how those features can be used to provide a good foundation to your maintenance planning.

## A DBA Tale

The following story describes an incident with a new database administrator (DBA) that you should be able to relate to. This tale is not far removed from fact in many enterprises today. Read through this anecdote and see if it brings to mind any memories in your present or past situations.

Bob pranced into his new office with overwhelming confidence as the exiting DBA finished packing his belongings. As Bob walked into the room, the DBA stopped for a moment, walked to his desk, and took out three envelopes. Bob could see that the envelopes were blank other than the labels, which read "#1", "#2", and "#3". The DBA smiled for a moment and was about to place the envelopes into his box, when he looked at Bob. The DBA walked over to Bob and handed him the three envelopes. Bob immediately started to open the first envelope when the DBA stopped him and instructed him not to open any of them until the appropriate time. The DBA told him that the database administrator before him had done the same thing to him and these were a gift of knowledge that would be effective only if Bob opened them at the right time. As the exiting DBA finished packing his things, he said, "When you get into a situation where you don't know what to do, open the first letter before you go to the boss." Bob laughed arrogantly and asked, "How do you know I won't open the letters when you walk out that door?" Without turning around, and heading towards the door, the DBA's last words were, "You will have bad luck for six months, and you will be out of a job if you open them now!" So Bob placed the envelopes in his drawer and forgot about them.

Bob began to get himself situated in his new surroundings, and in about a week, felt 10 feet tall and bulletproof. Systems were running pretty well, and Bob had completed every task handed to him without a problem. Then, his world came crashing down around him. He needed to get some data from a backup, and the nightly backups were failing. Remembering the envelopes, Bob rushed to his office and desperately tore open the envelope labeled #1. It simply read...*Blame it on the last administrator!*

Bob walked into his boss's office pondering what to say and thought of how easily this whole situation could have been avoided. He checked the SQL Mail setup, and it looked like it was set up correctly. He even tested it. How was he supposed to know that the MIS department would change something on the mail server that would cause mail to stop working? They are the ones to blame! (Of course, Bob could not say that because he did not want to start any problems with MIS.) So Bob blindly took the advice of letter #1. His boss looked at him and agreed that the fault did not lie with Bob, but that from that point on Bob was responsible for any and all SQL Server issues no matter what the environment was or would be. Bob had learned a valuable lesson just as the previous DBA said he would. And Bob swore that he would be more responsible and pay more attention to detail. His first resolution was to have SQL Mail send him an email on success as well as failure. This way if he did not receive an email, he would know things were not working well.

Two weeks went by, and Bob was a legend in his own mind. He marveled at the new backup strategy that he implemented. It was so sleek and flexible that there was no possible way he would lose data. Then, it was put to the test, and the recovery operation failed. Bob had had two successful emails and couldn't understand how this could happen. Was it the drive or the server? He had little idea why he could not restore his backups. He then remembered the envelopes. Bob rushed to his office and violently ripped open envelope #2. It said...*Blame it on the hardware!*

Bob did not need this note to see that this was a great revelation. In fact, he had not fully tested his recovery plan from start to finish and never restored a backup in a test before going live. Bob tried to defuse the blame and used the note to guide him once again. He blamed it on the hardware. The director agreed, but brought up the fact that the company had just lost 48 hours of work. Bob humbly exited his office and thought to himself, "Why did I trust the backups when I never restored one of them into a test database?" "How could I have been so arrogant?" Bob decided he would test these functions to make sure they would work before he needed them again. He would also test them periodically to make sure they continued to work.

Bob was just about to turn in his resignation when he remembered that he had one more envelope in his desk. He seriously doubted that it could have anything to say that would help him feel better about the hole he had dug for himself, but he had nothing to lose. Bob opened the last letter and smiled. It read…*Take three envelopes and label them #1, #2, and #3. Place a note in the first envelope that reads, "Blame it on the last administrator!" In envelope #2 write, "Blame it on the hardware," and in the third envelope, place this note and start looking for a new job…You are the only one to blame!*

This story may seem all too familiar to some of you or perhaps a joke. All too often this is the norm rather than the exception. As the DBA, you are responsible for all aspects of the database. You can create the best database model, tune the server so it runs faster than a new Porsche, and create stored procedures that make life for programmers a breeze, but if you cannot maintain your database and recover after a disaster, then all of your work is futile.

# Maintenance Planning

Before jumping into implementation of a maintenance strategy, there is some premaintenance planning that you should consider. Although your maintenance plan will probably change as your company changes, it is important to lay a solid foundation at the outset that is flexible for inevitable growth.

A maintenance strategy should be based upon the environment of the database server or servers. Once you have an intimate knowledge of your server and its dependencies, you can effectively evaluate what needs to take place in order for your server to be stable, accessible, and recoverable. Try to divide your maintenance into many small, easy steps instead of tackling one all-or-nothing task. This will allow you to add additional small tasks into your schema without having to work around one large task that is not very flexible. This plan of attack also gives you a simple way of debugging your plan if it does not work as anticipated upon implementation. You can then run one task at a time and focus on only the portion that fails instead of debugging the entire plan. Write down the goal you want to achieve and ask yourself what steps you will have to complete in order to accomplish the task. Next, write down the steps in the most simplistic manner, and then execute them. The following questions will help guide you through this process:

- How many database servers are there that need to be included in your plan?
- Are there multiple servers that must have an up-to-date copy of the same database?
- Does your database exist within a cluster?
- What kind of network topography exists to support your plan?

- Do you have access to a large capacity share on the network?

- Do you have the appropriate network permissions in order to implement your proposed maintenance plan?

- How many employees are accessing the server and during what timeframes throughout the day?

- Does your environment allow your database to be taken offline at any time?

Start by writing down your questions without concern for their answers. Remember that some of your questions will answer themselves depending upon other issues. Don't worry if you do not have a long list of questions or answers. Keep in mind the fact that you want to generate a set of small tasks that make up the bigger job.

## The Databases

There are three main factors with regard to the actual database that you need to consider when creating a maintenance plan. You should answer the following questions for any database before attempting to create a backup plan:

- What is the current and estimated size of the database?

- Where is the database physically located?

- What kind of information is in the database? (Is it static or dynamic in nature, or what kind of availability does the data require?)

The obvious concern with the size of the database is where you are going to store a backup and/or copy in case the database needs to be recovered. Is the database small enough to be zipped and placed on removable media? Do you have a network share that will hold the backup? Is there enough room on the local server to keep a copy for easy replacement?

Location of the database can pertain to directories, file grouping, and data or log organization. You can query the system tables to determine what organization the database files have. See Listing 6.1 for a sample query listing file organization. The output from this query gives you the logical name of the file and the physical name of the files that make up the database. You can run this query in any database to find out how and where the files are stored.

---

**NOTE:** *Microsoft recommends using views and stored procedures to access information in the system tables because they are subject to change in future releases. The information provided by the query in Listing 6.1 can also be obtained using **sp_helpdb**, but this query provides a shorter result set for listing in this book.*

---

### Listing 6.1 Query of **sysfiles** table.

```
/* Query of sysfiles */
SELECT CONVERT(VARCHAR(15),name) AS Name,
       CONVERT(VARCHAR(50), SUBSTRING(filename, 1, 17) + '...' +
                       SUBSTRING(filename, 38, 40)) as filename
  FROM sysfiles (NOLOCK)
/* Output */
Name            filename
--------------  -------------------------------------------
master          C:\Program Files\...\MSSQL\data\master.mdf
mastlog         C:\Program Files\...\MSSQL\data\mastlog.ldf


(2 row(s) affected)
```

The **sysdatabases** table holds summary information for each database just as **sysfiles** does except that only the mdf (primary data file) is stored in sysdatabases. This can be helpful for processing in a cursor, but typically the log file location (ldf) or file group information that **sysfiles** stores is more beneficial. See Listing 6.2 for the **sysdatabases** query and output.

### Listing 6.2 Query of **sysdatabases** table, and sample output.

```
/* Query of sysdatabases */
SELECT CONVERT(VARCHAR(15),name) AS DBName,
       CONVERT(VARCHAR(50), SUBSTRING(filename, 1, 17) + '...' +
                       SUBSTRING(filename, 38, 40)) as filename
  FROM sysdatabases (NOLOCK)


/* Output */
DBName          filename
------------    ------------------------------------------------------------
address         C:\Program Files\...\MSSQL\Data\Address_Data.MDF
employee        C:\Program Files\...\MSSQL\Data\Employee_Data.MDF
master          C:\Program Files\...\MSSQL\data\master.mdf
model           C:\Program Files\...\MSSQL\data\model.mdf
msdb            C:\Program Files\...\MSSQL\data\msdbdata.mdf
Northwind       C:\Program Files\...\MSSQL\data\northwnd.mdf
pubs            C:\Program Files\...\MSSQL\Data\pubs.mdf
tempdb          C:\Program Files\...\MSSQL\data\tempdb.mdf
Utility         C:\Program Files\...\MSSQL\Data\Utility_Data.MDF
```

The key to understanding system tables is to know what data is stored where and what it can be used for. If you know where to find data, it is that much simpler to manipulate and copy it. You can write queries that manipulate databases and files

**6. Server Maintenance**

(see the "Immediate Solutions" section of this chapter) very easily if you study these tables and others.

---

**NOTE:** *Refer to the Books Online for more information on system tables and their column definitions.*

---

Many of the questions about size and location of databases can be answered through the Enterprise Manager, which is covered in Chapter 5. The key is to ask the right questions before developing your plan. If you ask the right questions, the plan you design will be more complete and easier to implement.

## The Budget

When planning a maintenance strategy, you need to consider your budget. Do you have the means to have a dedicated backup server? What kind of tape/disk drives can you afford that will be large enough to hold one or more databases? Can you use a RAID tape drive subsystem to back up all your data? Is there a need to keep a copy of your data offsite? Always ask yourself how important your database is to the livelihood of the company. The answer to that question should shed some light on how much money to set aside for disaster recovery.

---

**NOTE:** *The most expensive backup system is the one that is not adequate the day you need it most!*

---

## The Backup and Restore Windows

You should have some idea of how long a backup of the data will take under normal circumstances in order to allow for enough time to perform the backup without stepping on other tasks or network access. This window of time often increases because databases normally grow in size. You should check your backup routines often to make sure they still fit in the window you have set aside. If you are backing up your data while users are in the system, try to schedule your backups around peak activity periods to reduce the chances of slowing down user activity.

The restore window, the length of time it takes to restore a database from backup, is often overlooked. If the time frame is not acceptable, an alternative method may be required. Often, you have to restore your database under a great deal of external pressure. You should have some idea of how long it will take, so that you can set valid expectations for the user community.

---

**NOTE:** *If you practice the restore process occasionally, you should know how long a restore will take.*

---

# Backup Strategies

Microsoft has introduced some new twists in the conventional backups of previous versions. The new recovery models allow a DBA or system designer greater flexibility and higher data protection than ever before. Let's first recap the previous, tried-and-true methods and how they work. The standards they set are still very useful and will be used for a long time to come. Microsoft has added database recovery methods to your suite of solutions. The new recovery models are designed to be easier to understand and more flexible in the ever-changing enterprise. After comparing the features and benefits of both types of strategies, you should be able to choose the method that best suits your environment. See Table 6.1 for a summary of the Microsoft backup and restore requirements for certain operations.

There are some definite advantages to each of these models. One goal in the new backup design is to simplify the process of choosing which method is best for each situation. When you know what your limitations and requirements are for your server or system, you should be able to compare the options and make a reasonable choice of which method to use. See Table 6.2 for a feature benefit comparison.

**Table 6.1    Microsoft backup and restore requirements.**

| Model | Database | Differential | Transaction Log | File or File Differential |
|-------|----------|--------------|-----------------|---------------------------|
| Simple | Required | Optional | Not allowed | Not allowed |
| Full | Required (or file backups) | Optional | Required | Optional |
| Bulk-Logged | Required (or file backups) | Optional | Required | Optional |

**Table 6.2    Cost benefit comparisons.**

| Model | Benefit | Cost | Point in Time Available |
|-------|---------|------|-------------------------|
| Simple | High-performance bulk copy operations and small transaction log impact. | Changes to data since last database or differential backup must be reapplied. | Can recover to the point of last backup operation with any edits after that point lost. |
| Full | No work lost from damaged data file and can restore to an arbitrary point in time. | Normally none. (If the transaction log is damaged, you could lose some work.) | Can recover to any point in time. |
| Bulk-Logged | High-performance bulk copy operations and small transaction log impact. | Only problem is when most recent transaction log is damaged. (Same as full.) | Can recover to the end of any backup. |

# Previous Methods

In the early versions of SQL Server, there were three main strategies for creating a stable solution to disaster recovery. These are still available in SQL 2000 and are still the best methods for securing some types of data on your servers:

- A full database backup
- A differential backup
- A transaction log backup

## Full Database Backup

A full database backup creates a complete copy of the database at the time the backup is started. Any changes applied or committed within the database after the backup has been initiated will not be included in the backup. A full database backup does take more time and is more resource-intensive than the other types of backups.

---

**NOTE:** *The differential and transaction log backups are dependent on a full backup being restored first.*

---

The restore process for a full database backup is faster and simpler than the differential or transaction log backups. Only a single step is needed for the restore. Managing the files is easier because there are fewer files to worry about. The downside of this method is that the database is only recoverable to the point that the last full backup was executed. If you perform a full backup each night and the database fails near the end of the day, you could lose a full day's work. This option is best for static databases that do not change often in a system. Master and model databases are typical candidates for this method.

---

**NOTE:** *Only a full backup can be performed on the master database.*

---

## Differential Database Backup

A differential backup copies only the changes that have been committed since the last full backup was performed. If a full backup is planned every Sunday, with differential backups each day during the week, you would have to apply the full backup, and then the differential backup from the night before in order to properly restore the database.

---

**NOTE:** *For example, if the database went down on Thursday, you would restore the full backup from Sunday, and then restore Wednesday evening's differential backup to recover the data.*

---

The differential backup takes less time to complete because it only backs up the changes made rather than the entire database, however, your transaction log will have some growth that you should account for in space planning. The longer the time between full backups, the longer a differential backup takes to complete. Towards the end of the week, you will find that Friday's and Saturday's backups will be your longer-running backups.

A combination of differential backups and transaction log backups is commonly used to reduce the impact of running backups during the day and having long running operations take up processor time in 24/7 operations. See the "Immediate Solutions" section of this chapter for an example of how to make this backup method work for your environment.

### Transaction Log Backup

A transaction log backup makes a complete copy of the transaction log, and then removes committed transaction entries from the log to save space. The transaction log backup takes the least amount of time as long as you perform the backup operation at fairly close intervals (15 to 60 minutes depending on workload). It also is the only backup method that allows you to restore a server to a specific point in time. To restore from this method, you must apply the log backups in the same order as they were performed. This means that if four transaction log backups have been completed since the last full or differential backup, all log backups must be restored sequentially to get back the data to the point of failure.

---

**NOTE:** *For example, a full backup runs every Sunday at 12:00 A.M., with differential backup operations taking place every night at 3:00 A.M. Transaction log backups are performed every hour during each day. Your server hard drive fails on Thursday at 2:00 P.M. You would need to restore Sunday's full backup, Wednesday's differential backup, and all the log backups up to 2:00 P.M. in order to recover the database.*

---

You cannot have the Truncate Log On Checkpoint option enabled for a database that is using transaction log backups. Some third-party applications require this setting to reduce the amount of disk space required for their product, so you should always ask about this option when making a purchasing decision.

If your transaction log backups are taking longer to run than you would like, you can increase the frequency they are run (reducing the time between dumps), so that fewer transactions have to be backed up.

### Full Recovery Model

The Full Recovery Model provides the least amount of risk for losing data. The Full Recovery Model's success is dependent on the transaction log. All operations are fully logged in this model including the Bulk Copy Program (BCP), **BULK INSERT**, **SELECT INTO**, and **CREATE INDEX**. This model provides a performance gain when recovering from a transaction log backup because earlier versions of SQL server only recorded the fact that an index was created, so now the index does not have to be rebuilt after recovery.

To recover to the point of failure in the Full Recovery Model, the active transaction log must be backed up first. Next, restore the last full backup or differential without recovering the database (use the **WITH NORECOVERY** option). Next, restore each transactional log backup since the last full or differential backup in order without recovering the database. Then, restore the active transaction log that was just backed up using the **WITH RECOVERY** option. The Transact-SQL syntax is shown in Listing 6.3.

**Listing 6.3   Transaction log recovery using WITH RECOVERY option.**

```
RESTORE LOG <Database_name>
   FROM <backup_device>
   WITH RECOVERY
```

Transaction logs can become large if you do not back them up often. Every committed transaction is written to the transaction log (before-and-after images). For that reason, the transaction log must have some sort of fault tolerance at the disk subsystem level in order to guarantee its success. It is recommended that you place your logs on a RAID controller that is dedicated to the log files and that is part of a mirror set. This will speed up the write process and give the log files the fault tolerance they deserve.

### Log Marks

A new feature many developers will be able to add to their processing logic is an enhanced option for the **BEGIN TRANSACTION** statement called log marks. You can now add the **WITH MARK** clause to put a label in the transaction log that can be used to identify a point of recovery other than the current point in time. The name of the mark is supplied in quotes and can be a more descriptive name than that of the transaction. You can then restore a set of databases to a specified point that is logically consistent rather than an actual date and time. Programmers must use **WITH MARK** in their transactional code to facilitate this, but it is a small price to pay for the added capability. For an example of using log marks, see Listing 6.4.

---

**NOTE:** *Each marked transaction that is committed places a row in the **msdb..Logmarkhistory** table for reference purposes.*

---

**Listing 6.4   Example of a transaction using the WITH MARK option.**

```
BEGIN TRANSACTION AddressUpdate
 WITH MARK 'Update Address Values'
GO
UPDATE tbl_Address
   SET Line2 = NULL
 WHERE Address_ID = 234
```

```
GO
COMMIT TRANSACTION AddressUpdate
```

You can then use the **RESTORE** with the **STOPATMARK = '*<name of mark>*'** option, which restores the transaction to the point of the mark. Another option would be to restore the transaction and include **STOPBEFOREMARK = '*<name of mark>*'**. This method rolls forward all transactions before the mark mentioned in the clause. You can also use the **AFTER DATETIME** option in your restore statement. If **AFTER DATETIME** is not included, the recovery stops at the first log mark with the specified name. If it is included, then the recovery process stops at the log mark on or after the date and time.

### Bulk Logged Recovery Model

The Bulk Logged Recovery Model provides the best performance using the least amount of log space for most bulk procedures like BCP and **BULK INSERT**. Although the Bulk-Logged Recovery Model allows you to provide point-in-time recovery, it depends upon certain conditions and is not as reliable as the Full Recovery Model. The Full Recovery Model writes an operation completely to the transaction log, whereas the Bulk Logged Recovery Model logs only the occurrence of the bulk operation. This allows bulk operations to occur much faster, which is also a bonus. Unfortunately, the performance is lost during the backup of the log in this model, which usually requires more time and space. This may seem odd and on the surface downright alarming. However, the reason this occurs is because SQL 2000 has an additional allocation page within every file called a MINLOG page.

MINLOG pages are represented as groups of bits, and each bit on a MINLOG page represents an extent. A bit value of 1 means that a minimally logged bulk operation has changed the extent since the last full database backup. A MINLOG page is located in the eighth page of every data file and every 256,000 pages thereafter. All the bits on a MINLOG page are reset every time a full database backup or log backup occurs. Setting the bits in the appropriate MINLOG page requires some overhead, but compared with the cost of logging each change to a data or index row, the cost of flipping bits is negligible. SQL server scans the MINLOG pages and backs up all the modified extents along with the transaction log. Using MINLOG pages to track bulk operations makes this option a viable solution.

Restoring a backup that is on the Bulk Logged Recovery Model is exactly the same as restoring a database in the Full Recovery Model if there have been *no* bulk operations since the last backup (full/differential/log). If there has been a bulk operation, then the point of recovery is to the last completed backup.

---

***TIP:*** *When a bulk operation has occurred, it is a good idea to make a backup so the log files can be stored along with the affected extents.*

---

### Simple Recovery Model

As its name implies, the Simple Recovery Model is the simplest of the recovery models. It incorporates the full and differential backups that you are accustomed to along with transaction log backups at regular intervals. Of the three models, this model is the fastest model for bulk operations. The Simple Recovery Model is the one used by prior versions of SQL Server.

When trying to decide which model to use, keep in mind that your decision is not absolute. You may change the model at any time by changing two database options: Select INTO/Bulkcopy and Trunc. Log On CHKPT. In order to understand the combinations of these options and how they affect your recovery model, see Table 6.3.

Changing recovery models can become a normal activity when using the Full Recovery Model. Toggling the options gives you the flexibility of using the most secure of the three models while allowing your server to complete fast bulk operations. You can then switch to a more flexible option after completing the operations.

SQL Server has implemented a new function called **databasepropertyex**, which allows you to determine the recovery model your database is currently using. See Listing 6.5 for an example of how this function is used to check a database recovery setting.

**Listing 6.5    Syntax to determine current recovery model used by the master database.**

```
SELECT databasepropertyex('master', 'recovery') AS 'Recovery Mode'

/* Output */
Recovery Mode
-------------------------------------------------------------------
SIMPLE
```

## Backup Locations

Once you have considered all the questions that should be asked before choosing a recovery model, you can then turn your attention toward where you will place the backup files. Backup files are typically smaller than the database itself. Ensure that

**Table 6.3    Comparison of database options and their impact on recovery models.**

| Trunc. Log On CHKPT | Select INTO/Bulkcopy | Model |
|---|---|---|
| Off | Off | Full |
| Off | On | Bulk_Logged |
| On | Off | Simple |
| On | On | Simple |

you have enough free disk space to store the backup files wherever you decide to save them. One way to estimate the size of the backup is to use the **sp_spaceused** stored procedure to see how much room is currently being used in the database. See Listing 6.6 for the syntax of the stored procedure.

Listing 6.6    Code and output from **sp_spaceused**.

```
EXEC sp_spaceused

/* Output */
database_name
------------------------------------------------------------
master

reserved            data           index_size          unused
------------------  -------------  ------------------  ----------
10592 KB            8928 KB        1248 KB             416 KB
```

A backup does not compress the database, but it does reclaim the space not used or no longer in use. You can also keep the unused space at a minimum by running maintenance procedures on your system. See the section "Database Consistency Checks (DBCC)" for more details.

---

**NOTE:** *Be sure to allow for backups to grow in size and the capability to store more than one backup in your backup location. It is always a good idea to keep the previous night's copy of the database backup in a handy location, either on the server or on a network share point for easy access in the event of hardware failures. One option that may prove useful is to compress the backups to conserve space, which will allow you to keep backups for a longer period of time.*

---

Some networks have more than enough bandwidth to support a large backup share on the network that your server will use as a repository for its database backups. This method helps centralize the backup operation and removes the overhead from the database server. You can write your backups locally, and then copy them across the network to the share point so that they can be placed on removable media or archived without impacting your day-to-day operations. The network repository also allows you to write the information to tape without regard to the system load on the database server, because once the files are offloaded to the network, the backup will not affect the performance of your database server.

### Backup Devices

Microsoft SQL Server 2000 writes its backups to files called backup devices. These devices are created and written to when the backup is performed. They can then be backed up to tape, removable media, or a network share. Storing backups to a device rather than using one of the popular software packages is a great alternative that is often overlooked by many organizations. There are many packages that have the capability to back up your database files while the server is running, and most are very reliable. However, a fact that is ignored is that backing up while the server is running puts an additional load on the server and uses additional resources that could be used by SQL Server to respond to user load.

### Database Backup with Transact SQL

Backing up a database is simple and convenient with the Enterprise Manager, but sometimes it is necessary to create a backup routine programmatically. When you have many databases to manage on many servers, writing a scripted procedure to perform backups is very reasonable. See Listing 6.7 for the syntax to create a database backup.

**Listing 6.7    BACKUP DATABASE syntax.**

```
BACKUP DATABASE { database_name | @database_name_var }
TO < backup_device > [ ,...n ]
[ WITH
    [ BLOCKSIZE = { blocksize | @blocksize_variable } ]
    [ [ , ] DESCRIPTION = { 'text' | @text_variable } ]
    [ [ , ] DIFFERENTIAL ]
    [ [ , ] EXPIREDATE = { date | @date_var }
        | RETAINDAYS = { days | @days_var } ]
    [ [ , ] PASSWORD = { password | @password_variable } ]
    [ [ , ] FORMAT | NOFORMAT ]
    [ [ , ] { INIT | NOINIT } ]
    [ [ , ] MEDIADESCRIPTION = { 'text' | @text_variable } ]
    [ [ , ] MEDIANAME = { media_name | @media_name_variable } ]
    [ [ , ] MEDIAPASSWORD = { mediapassword | @mediapassword_variable } ]
    [ [ , ] NAME = { backup_set_name | @backup_set_name_var } ]
    [ [ , ] { NOSKIP | SKIP } ]
    [ [ , ] { NOREWIND | REWIND } ]
    [ [ , ] { NOUNLOAD | UNLOAD } ]
    [ [ , ] RESTART ]
    [ [ , ] STATS [ = percentage ] ]
]
```

Creating a backup is only half of the Disaster Recovery Model. You can create as many backups as you want, but if you cannot restore them with confidence, the plan will fail. Verify your backups regularly to make sure your plan is working properly.

### Restoring a Database

Most restore operations are handled through the Enterprise Manager (see Chapter 5) in most organizations. Usually, you are restoring a database while people are looking over your shoulder or waiting to start work again. Practice the restore process regularly, even if you restore to a temporary database just for the practice. You will be glad you did practice when you are under pressure.

Occasionally, you will need to have a server that is forcibly refreshed to a backup state. You can use SQL to create a set of restore commands to facilitate this refresh. You can then restore the target database through a scheduled or on demand job. See Listing 6.8 for an example of the restore syntax.

### Listing 6.8 **RESTORE DATABASE** syntax.

```
RESTORE DATABASE { database_name | @database_name_var }
[ FROM < backup_device > [ ,...n ] ]
[ WITH
    [ RESTRICTED_USER ]
    [ [ , ] FILE = { file_number | @file_number } ]
    [ [ , ] PASSWORD = { password | @password_variable } ]
    [ [ , ] MEDIANAME = { media_name | @media_name_variable } ]
    [ [ , ] MEDIAPASSWORD = { mediapassword | @mediapassword_variable } ]
    [ [ , ] MOVE 'logical_file_name' TO 'operating_system_file_name' ]
            [ ,...n ]
    [ [ , ] KEEP_REPLICATION ]
    [ [ , ] { NORECOVERY | RECOVERY | STANDBY = undo_file_name } ]
    [ [ , ] { NOREWIND | REWIND } ]
    [ [ , ] { NOUNLOAD | UNLOAD } ]
    [ [ , ] REPLACE ]
    [ [ , ] RESTART ]
    [ [ , ] STATS [ = percentage ] ]
]
```

### *Detaching a Database*

Reliable as the backup processes are, detaching and attaching databases is quickly becoming a favorite method to perform backups among database administrators and developers alike. This feature first appeared in SQL 7 and is simplified in SQL 2000 with graphical interfaces that can be used to perform this task, which has been added to the Enterprise Manager. (See the "Immediate Solutions" section in Chapters 5 and 8 for examples of how to perform this task.) Migrating data to a repository or another server has never been easier than it is now. A backup scheme that uses detach and attach methods to supply a backup solution for your databases is even shipping with this book. Some of the benefits of detaching a database, and then attaching it again include:

- Manual control when deleting a database
- Renaming a database
- Transferring a database to a different server
- Archiving
- Creating multiple databases with the same files
- Managing a development or testing environment

**6. Server Maintenance**

When a database is detached, it is also removed from the **sysdatabases** table in the master database. Likewise, when the database is attached, it adds a row in the same table. Because this process deletes the row in sysdatabases, you can use this feature to rename a database. However, you can use the **sp_renamedb** stored procedure as an alternate method of renaming a database. See Listing 6.9 for an example of the **sp_renamedb** syntax.

---

**NOTE:** *Some third-party tools or scripting methods may not work as expected if you use **sp_renamedb**. To avoid this problem, you can create a new database with the desired name and import the objects and data into the new database with DTS or use the attach and detach method.*

---

**Listing 6.9    Renaming a database with sp_renamedb.**

```
EXEC sp_renamedb @old_name = 'old_name',
                 @new_name = 'new_name'
```

A database consists of a primary data file, typically with the file extension MDF. The transaction log file usually has an LDF extension. You may also see NDF extensions for secondary files used to make up a file group for your database. You need to know what types of files make up your database before you detach them if you are going to effectively attach them at a later time. If you use the Enterprise Manager to attach the database, you only need to select the MDF file. The server will then read the information on other files from the MDF file when it is loaded. See Listing 6.10 for an example of the syntax used to detach a database.

**Listing 6.10    Detach database syntax.**

```
EXEC sp_detach_db <database_name>
```

Once the database has been detached, the files can be moved, copied, zipped, or even deleted. In a development or testing environment, detaching a database provides a perfect solution to perform tests and comparisons of code execution between the same data on two separate platforms. You can also test changes and if they do not work or break other code when tested, you can detach the copy of the database that is broken and reattach the previous database file in seconds to back out the changes. Another use for this feature is that developers can copy the files to their personal systems, and then attach them for working data.

If a share is made available on your network that can store versions of a database, you can create a scheduled job that detaches a database and makes a copy in some repository for later use. See Listing 6.11 for an example of the **xp_cmdshell** code that can provide the **copy** command.

**Listing 6.11    External procedure xp_cmdshell copy example.**

```
EXEC xp_cmdshell 'copy <file_name_&_path> \\<server_name>\<share_name>'
```

### Attaching a Database

After detaching a database and moving or compressing it, you need a way to reattach the database to the server for use. The **sp_attach_db** stored procedure provides this capability. See Listing 6.12. All of the information that is needed to attach a database file programmatically can be retrieved from the system catalog.

---

**NOTE:** *Refer to the Books Online for more information on system tables as well as the data that is stored in each table.*

---

### Listing 6.12    Attaching a database.

```
EXEC sp_attach_db '<database_name>',
                  '<file_name_&_path_for_mdf_file>',
                  '<file_name_&_path_for_ldf_file>'
```

The attach and detach procedures provide a powerful combination of tools that give you alternatives to the standard backup and restore methods of many database systems.

### Bulk Copy Program

BCP is a command-line utility that allows an administrator or developer to copy data from a table to a file or from a file to a table. If you are going to use BCP as an option to migrate data in and out of tables, you will need to occasionally move structures between servers before moving the data. You can generate the scripts for any objects in the database through the Enterprise Manager, and then run those scripts on the target server or database. If you need to import data from BCP files that are a different format than the target structure, you will need to use a format file to specify where the data in the file maps to the table structure. BCP operations are discussed in detail in Chapter 15. One technique that is useful for programmers and database administrators is to use a stored procedure or **SELECT** statement to generate the BCP statements for you. See Listing 6.13 for an example of a query to generate BCP statements and the sample output.

---

**NOTE:** *The line breaks in the output are to allow proper printing in this book.*

---

### Listing 6.13    BCP string to collect all tables within a database.

```
SET NOCOUNT ON

SELECT 'bcp address..' +
       name +
       ' out c:\temp\' +
       name +
       '.bcp /SSNEEZY /Usa /P /n /E'
  FROM sysobjects (NOLOCK)
```

```
WHERE type = 'U'
  AND name NOT LIKE 'dt%'
ORDER by name

/* Output */
bcp address..tbl_Address out c:\temp\tbl_Address.bcp /SSNEEZY /Usa
/P /n /E
bcp address..tbl_addressDN out c:\temp\tbl_addressDN.bcp /SSNEEZY /Usa
/P /n /E
bcp address..tbl_City out c:\temp\tbl_City.bcp /SSNEEZY /Usa
/P /n /E
bcp address..tbl_State out c:\temp\tbl_State.bcp /SSNEEZY /Usa
/P /n /E
bcp address..tbl_ZipCode out c:\temp\tbl_ZipCode.bcp /SSNEEZY /Usa
/P /n /E
```

To use this query to create a batch file, you should make the following modifications in other areas before executing it against your server:

- Change the options in the Query Analyzer to not print headers.

- Edit the string in the select list to contain the server name of your server.

- Edit the string in the select list to provide your sa account password.

- Make sure the database context you run the query in is correct. (The example uses the Address database.)

- Run the query, and save the results to a file named "bcpout.bat" in the same directory as the output files (c:\temp\).

Once you have created the batch file that runs via the command prompt and have taken the data out of all the tables, you can generate the import side of the batch file at the same time. Change the word "out" to "in", update the server and login information to reflect the target server, and repeat the previous process. Save the new output as "bcpin.bat". The batch files will create all the individual BCP files that hold the data from the tables. When you run the batches, they will pull the data out and put it in the new server.

---

**TIP:** *The database must have the Bulk Copy option set in the database in order for the BCP utility to load the data properly.*

---

### Data Transformation Services

Data Transformation Services (DTS) is a useful alternative to BCP for keeping data updated across servers. DTS works with predefined packages that can copy data to another server as a scheduled job or on demand. An entire chapter is dedicated to this process; see Chapter 7. DTS is quickly becoming a standard in the industry for data mart and data warehouse population routines.

### Log Shipping

Many database administrators are asked to produce some sort of fail-over option for their mission-critical data at some point in their careers. Log shipping has been added to SQL 2000 to provide an easy to configure, reliable method of keeping a standby or reporting server online and ready to go in the event of production system failure. The "Immediate Solutions" section of this chapter guides you through the process of configuring log shipping on a SQL 2000 server.

---

**NOTE:** *You are able to use log shipping only on SQL Server 2000 Enterprise and Developer Editions.*

---

The premise of log shipping is rather similar to the replication model that SQL server has used for years. A source server is configured to participate in log shipping that holds the read/write data. A monitoring server should be set up as a different server than the production data server. The processing load and backup requirements for the monitoring server preclude placing these operations on top of your production server. The monitoring server's role is to coordinate the log backup, copy, and distribution to the target backup servers. These servers can be used for read-only reporting purposes and still be used as standby servers. See Figure 6.1 for an illustration of the log shipping model.

The SQL Server Database Maintenance Plan Wizard can be used to configure log shipping. (See the "Immediate Solutions" section at the end of this chapter.) The number of target or standby servers is flexible. You do not need to have as many servers as Figure 6.1, but you should make sure you place the monitor activity on a different server than the production data server.

The roles of the servers in this model are very important to consider. You must create a DTS package that transfers the syslogins information from one server to the standby server. Then, follow these steps to switch the servers' roles in your enterprise:

1. Run the stored procedure **sp_change_primary_role** on the current primary server, so that it no longer acts as the primary source for the transaction logs.

2. On the secondary server, run **sp_change_secondary_role**.

3. On the monitor server, run **sp_change_monitor_role**.

4. Run **sp_resolve_logins** on the new primary server.

See the SQL Server Books Online for the step-by-step instructions, parameters, and the remarks associated with performing this task. Be sure to read through the directions thoroughly before attempting to perform this operation. Each procedure has specific locations that they must be run from, parameter lists, and requirements that are *not* listed in this section.

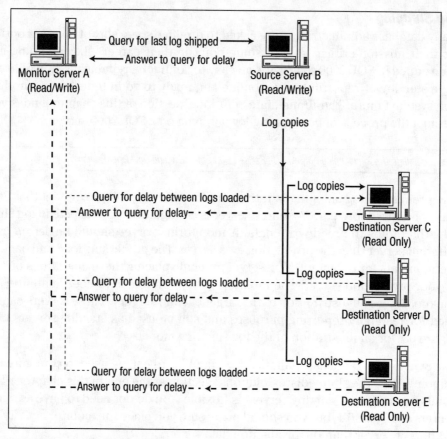

**Figure 6.1    Log shipping model.**

# Maintenance Code

Many servers running today operate without thorough maintenance routines. Attention to the small, routine maintenance tasks can determine the difference between a corrupted database and a smooth recovery from a problem. Microsoft has provided a few pieces of code that allow you to save space on your server and make sure your databases are healthy.

### *Database Consistency Check*

Database consistency check (DBCC) statements are used to perform a number of tasks. Most of them should be scheduled to run on a periodic basis against your databases. Some should run nightly, whereas others should be run anytime you perform bulk insert operations. Table 6.4 lists each of the commands and their uses.

---

**NOTE:** *See the "Immediate Solutions" section of this chapter for examples of how these commands should be used on your server.*

---

**Table 6.4  DBCC commands.**

| DBCC Command | Use | Recommended Frequency |
|---|---|---|
| CHECKDB | Checks the allocation and structural integrity of *all* the objects in the database. | Nightly |
| CHECKALLOC | Checks the space allocation in the specified database for consistency errors. | Nightly |
| DBREINDEX | Rebuilds the indexes dynamically including indexes created by constraints. | Nightly (If not **INDEXDEFRAG**) |
| CLEANTABLE | Reclaims space after a variable length column or text column is removed from a table. **(ALTER TABLE DROP COLUMN)** | As Needed, On Demand |
| INDEXDEFRAG | Defragments and reorders the index pages, and compacts the index. This process is less intrusive than **DBREINDEX**, but takes longer than rebuilding a highly fragmented index. This can be run online and is transaction-oriented. | Nightly (if not **DBREINDEX**) |
| ERRORLOG | Recycles the server error log and starts a new, clean copy. Used when the logs fill up or you want to trim the log space without cycling the server. | On Demand |
| CHECKIDENT | Used to check or correct the **IDENTITY** value for a table to ensure consistent auto-incremented values are returned from **INSERT** statements. Should be run anytime a large number of rows are inserted into a table with **IDENTITY** columns. | Nightly, On Demand |
| SHOWCONTIG | Displays fragmentation information for data and indexes in a database for a specified table. | On Demand |

## *Microsoft SQL Server Jobs*

The concept of "jobs" is similar to scheduled tasks in SQL Server version 6.5 and earlier. Jobs were introduced in SQL Server 7.0 and take on an even bigger role in server maintenance in SQL 2000. Jobs are divided into three areas: the job itself, job steps that make up the job, and a job schedule.

All the data pertaining to jobs are stored in the msdb database on your server. The SQL Agent runs as a service on the server checking for jobs to execute on a scheduled basis. The agent executes the jobs in the context they are stored and reports historical data like runtime, success and failure, and scheduled execution plans. You can create a job through the Enterprise Manager or through SQL with the stored procedure **sp_add_job** (see Listing 6.14). Creation of a job produces an entry in the **msdb..sysjobs** table containing the high-level details about the job.

**6. Server Maintenance**

### Listing 6.14   **sp_add_job** syntax.

```
EXEC sp_add_job @job_name = '<job_name>'
  ,@enabled = <enabled>
  ,@description = '<description>'
  ,@start_step_id = <step_id>
  ,@category_name = '<category>'
  ,@category_id = <category_id>
  ,@owner_login_name = '<login>'
  ,@notify_level_eventlog = <eventlog_level>
  ,@notify_level_email = <email_level>
  ,@notify_level_netsend = <netsend_level>
  ,@notify_level_page = <page_level>
  ,@notify_email_operator_name = '<email_name>'
  ,@notify_netsend_operator_name = '<netsend_name>'
  ,@notify_page_operator_name = '<page_name>'
  ,@delete_level = <delete_level>
  ,@job_id = <job_id> OUTPUT
```

Once you have added a job, you should add job steps for that job with the stored procedure **sp_add_jobstep**. See Listing 6.15 for the syntax of the stored procedure **sp_add_jobstep**. Job steps represent the actual work the job is performing broken down into logical steps. Some jobs only need one job step, whereas others may require four or five steps to complete the job. When the **sp_add_jobstep** is called, there is a row added to the **msdb..sysjobsteps** table.

### Listing 6.15   **sp_add_jobstep** syntax.

```
EXEC sp_add_jobstep @job_id = <job_id> | @job_name = '<job_name>'
  ,@step_id = <step_id>
  ,@step_name = '<step_name>'
  ,@subsystem = '<subsystem>'
  ,@command = '<command>'
  ,@additional_parameters = '<parameters>'
  ,@cmdexec_success_code = <code>
  ,@on_success_action = <success_action>
  ,@on_success_step_id = <success_step_id>
  ,@on_fail_action = <fail_action>
  ,@on_fail_step_id = <fail_step_id>
  ,@server = '<server>'
  ,@database_name = '<database>'
  ,@database_user_name = '<user>'
  ,@retry_attempts = <retry_attempts>
  ,@retry_interval = <retry_interval>
  ,@os_run_priority = <run_priority>
  ,@output_file_name = '<file_name>'
  ,@flags = <flags>
```

Once you have added the appropriate steps for a job, you must then determine the job's schedule. The scheduling facility in SQL Server is very robust and allows you to create a schedule that fits your needs. Scheduling a job may be only for the purpose of placing it in the list of predefined jobs on the server. Not all jobs run at a given time, but rather can be executed on demand by a user or DBA. Placing the job on the server allows you to remove some of the user error that can be introduced and save historical run data for processes. The stored procedure executed, providing you are not using the Enterprise Manager, is **sp_add_jobschedule**, which adds a row to the **msdb..sysjobschedules** table. See Listing 6.16 for the syntax used for **sp_add_job_schedule**.

**Listing 6.16   sp_add_job_schedule syntax.**

```
EXEC sp_add_jobschedule @job_id = < job_id>, | @job_name = '<job_name>'
  ,@name = '<name>'
  ,@enabled = <enabled>
  ,@freq_type = <freq_type>
  ,@freq_interval = <freq_interval>
  ,@freq_subday_type = <freq_subday_type>
  ,@freq_subday_interval = <freq_subday_interval>
  ,@freq_relative_interval = <freq_relative_interval>
  ,@freq_recurrence_factor = <freq_recurrence_factor>
  ,@active_start_date = <active_start_date>
  ,@active_end_date = <active_end_date>
  ,@active_start_time = <active_start_time>
  ,@active_end_time = <active_end_time>
```

Automating tasks programmatically is fairly daunting, and most database administrators use the Enterprise Manager to set them up. You can set up a central server as well and manage jobs on multiple servers from one location. This feature is covered in detail in the Books Online. See the "Multi-Server Administration" section for more information on centralized management enhancements in SQL 2000.

### SQL Mail

SQL Mail can be used to notify you of the successes and failures of your system. To use SQL Mail, the SQL Server has to have a Messaging Application Programming Interface (MAPI)-compliant mail client. To set up SQL Mail, the user has to create a working mail profile in the mail client before configuring SQL Server. Test and verify that you can send and receive mail through that client, and then tell SQL Server to use that mail profile for sending and receiving mail messages. The easiest mail system to use with SQL Mail is Microsoft Exchange (naturally). But other mail systems can be used providing they have MAPI-compliant clients to place on the server. (Internet mail and a simple MAPI client, like Outlook Express, are good alternatives if all you have is an Internet mail application.)

6. Server Maintenance

---

**NOTE:** *See the Books Online for the step-by-step details of how to configure SQL Mail to work with your mail system.*

---

Once you have SQL Mail running, you can send and receive mail that is driven by data events, or jobs. You can also use SQL Mail to return query or stored procedure results in mail messages. The notification mechanism is your mail system, but your server will actually send the messages. Combine this mailing capability with scheduling jobs and you have a powerful tool for creating a proactive database management environment.

### Multi-Server Administration

Centralized administration through the Enterprise Manager is a concept that has been around for quite some time. The capability to register all your servers in the Enterprise Manager is a wonderful feature. You can even create a forwarding server for error handling in a central location. Another giant step forward has been taken to provide the capability to create and manage tasks across servers in your enterprise. Microsoft has introduced the concept of master and target servers to SQL Server. The master server can monitor jobs and tasks, and report on many servers in your enterprise with greater ease than ever before. You can manage the information flow from your Online Transaction Processing (OLTP) system to your Warehouse or DataMart through one central server. Configuring a server as a master server is very easy and is accomplished through the Enterprise Manager. See Chapter 5 for more information on the enhancements to the standard tools delivered with SQL 2000.

To set up a master server, expand the management node in the Enterprise Manager, expand the server that will become the master server, right-click on SQL Server Agent, and select Multi-Server Administration to start the MSX Server Wizard.

---

**NOTE:** *The target servers should be registered before launching the MSX Wizard.*

---

In order to use the master server feature, you must be running SQL Server and the SQL Agent under a domain user account and not the local system account. The first steps in the wizard allow you to define the contact information of the operator that will be notified via email in the event of errors or problems with the server jobs.

---

**NOTE:** *The operator can be notified by email, pager, or through the **NET SEND** command.*

---

The operator has to be set up under the SQL Server Agent operators on the master server. After the contact information has been supplied, the next screen allows the administrator to choose the target servers. The master server is then ready to set up tasks either through jobs or through the SQL Maintenance Plan Wizard. There are a few details to take into account when establishing a master/ target server environment:

- All servers participating in the master/target server configuration must be running Windows NT 4 or Windows 2000 operating systems.

- Each target server can report to only one master server at a time. You must defect (unenlist) a target server before having it managed by another master server.

- You must defect a target server before changing the name of that server, and then reenlist it with the new name.

- If you want to stop using the multi-server management feature, you must defect each target server from the master server.

# *Immediate Solutions*

## Useful Server Administration SQL

The following sections contain some useful SQL, which are either a script snippet or a stored procedure that can be used to make the administration and maintenance tasks on your server easier. Not all scripts are required to perform all the maintenance tasks, but rather should be used to create a proactive server management environment, which is each database administrator's goal. All of the listings that create stored procedures are located in a file named allprocs.sql in the Chapter 6 directory of the CD-ROM accompanying this book.

### usp_KillUsers

Some operations require that no active user connections exist in a database before the operation can take place, for example, detaching a database. If you plan on using detach and attach methods for scheduled backups, you need a way to ensure that no one is in the target database so your backup does not fail. Listing 6.17 shows the source SQL used to remove any active user's connection from a target database. This procedure is written to be run from the master database.

**Listing 6.17    usp_KillUsers.**

```
CREATE PROC usp_KillUsers
  @p_DBName sysname = NULL
AS
/* Must be run from master           */

/* Check Paramaters                  */
/* Check for a DB name               */
IF (@p_DBName IS NULL)
BEGIN
  PRINT 'You must supply a DB Name'
  RETURN
END -- DB is NULL
IF (@p_DBName = 'master')
BEGIN
  PRINT 'You cannot run this process against the master database!'
  RETURN
END -- Master supplied
```

```
SET NOCOUNT ON

/* Declare Variables                  */
DECLARE @v_spid INT,
        @v_SQL  NVARCHAR(255)

/* Declare the Table Cursor (Identity) */
DECLARE c_Users CURSOR
   FAST_FORWARD FOR
 SELECT spid
   FROM master..sysprocesses (NOLOCK)
  WHERE db_name(dbid) = @p_DBName

OPEN c_Users

FETCH NEXT FROM c_Users INTO @v_spid
WHILE (@@fetch_status <> -1)
BEGIN
  IF (@@fetch_status <> -2)
  BEGIN
    SELECT @v_SQL = 'KILL ' + convert(NVARCHAR, @v_spid)
--    PRINT @v_SQL
    EXEC (@v_SQL)
  END -- -2
  FETCH NEXT FROM c_Users INTO @v_spid
END -- While

CLOSE c_Users
DEALLOCATE c_Users
GO
```

| Related solutions: | Found on page: |
|---|---|
| Query Analyzer | 193 |
| Identifying Autogenerated Statistics on All User Tables | 604 |
| Building and Executing Dynamic SQL | 834 |
| **sp_MSforeachtable** | 668 |

## usp_BCP

The **usp_BCP** procedure can be used to simplify the exporting and importing of data using the command-line executable BCP. You can specify a database and export all the tables' data from that database or supply a single table name to create a single BCP file holding data for that table. The code takes identity values into account and uses native format files by default. You can edit the strings to change to character format or add additional switches to the BCP command. See Listing 6.18 for the source SQL for **usp_BCP**. This procedure is placed in the master database in the allprocs.sql file contained on the CD-ROM.

*WARNING! This procedure should be used carefully because it will optionally truncate a table before importing data. Read through the source SQL before running it to be sure you fully understand how it works!*

### Listing 6.18    usp_BCP source SQL.

```
CREATE PROC usp_BCP
  @p_DBName     sysname,
  @p_TableName  sysname       = NULL,
  @p_FilePath   VARCHAR(255)  = NULL,
  @p_Direction  CHAR(3)       = 'out',
  @p_Truncate   INT           = 0,
  @p_Server     VARCHAR(50)   = @@servername,
  @p_PW         VARCHAR(30)   = ' '
AS
/* @p_Truncate 0 = false, 1 = true      */
/* Check Params                          */
IF (@p_FilePath IS NULL)
BEGIN
  PRINT 'You must supply a path to use usp_BCP'
  RETURN
END -- Path is NULL

/* Declare Varables                     */
Declare @v_Table      SYSNAME,
        @v_SQL        VARCHAR(255)

/* Check for Physical DIR */
SELECT @v_SQL = 'DECLARE @v_RESULT INT ' +
                'EXEC @v_result = master..xp_cmdshell ''dir ' +
                @p_FilePath +
                ' /A:D /B'', no_output ' +
                'IF (@v_Result <> 0) ' +
                'BEGIN ' +
                  'EXEC master..xp_cmdshell ''md ' + @p_FilePath + ''' ' +
                'END'
EXEC(@v_SQL)

/* Cursor to loop through each table */
SELECT @v_SQL = 'DECLARE c_Tables CURSOR FAST_FORWARD FOR ' +
```

```
                    'SELECT name ' +
                      'FROM ' + @p_DBName + '..sysobjects (NOLOCK) ' +
                      'WHERE type = ''U'''

SELECT @v_SQL = CASE
                  WHEN @p_TableName IS NULL THEN
                    @v_SQL
                  ELSE
                    @v_SQL + ' AND name = ''' + @p_TableName + ''''
                  END

SELECT @v_SQL = @v_SQL + ' ORDER BY name'

EXEC(@v_SQL)

OPEN c_Tables

FETCH NEXT FROM c_Tables INTO @v_Table
WHILE (@@fetch_status <> -1)
BEGIN
  IF (@@fetch_status <> -2)
  BEGIN
    IF (@p_Truncate = 1)
    BEGIN
      SELECT @v_SQL = 'TRUNCATE TABLE ' + @p_DBName + '..' + @v_Table
      EXEC(@v_SQL)
    END -- Truncate table
    SELECT @v_SQL = 'EXEC master..xp_cmdshell ''BCP ' +
                    @p_DBName + '..' + @v_Table + ' ' +
                    @p_Direction + ' ' + @p_FilePath + '\' +
                    @v_Table + '.bcp /S' + @p_Server +
                    ' /Usa /P' + @p_PW + ' /n /b5000 /E'', no_output'
    EXEC(@v_SQL)
  END -- -2
  FETCH NEXT FROM c_Tables INTO @v_Table
END -- WHILE

CLOSE c_Tables
DEALLOCATE c_Tables
GO
```

**6. Server Maintenance**

**NOTE:** *For security reasons, you may not want to use the password as a parameter in this procedure, but rather hard code the password in the procedure to make this process more secure and prevent publishing the sa password accidentally.*

## usp_DBCCCheckIdent

Anytime you move a large number of records into a table that has an identity column, there is a chance that the values returned from an **INSERT** statement can conflict or become disorganized. This does not happen often, but when it does, it typically causes applications to stop functioning properly. The **usp_DBCCCheckIdent** procedure automatically obtains a list of tables that have identity columns and runs this DBCC command to check if there is a problem. If values are incorrect, it fixes the numbers so they work properly in the future. Having this procedure run as a scheduled task each night is strictly a preventative measure. See Listing 6.19 for the source SQL for **usp_DBCC CheckIdent**. This procedure is scoped to the database in which it resides, so you will have to create it in the database in which you want to use it.

---

**NOTE:** *You may need to run **DBCC CHECKIDENT** on individual tables after performing a bulk load operation even if this task runs each night.*

---

**Listing 6.19   usp_DBCCCheckIdent source SQL.**

```
CREATE PROC usp_DBCCCheckIdent
AS
SET NOCOUNT ON
/* Declare Variables                    */
DECLARE @v_table SYSNAME,
        @v_SQL   NVARCHAR(2000)


/* Declare the Table Cursor (Identity) */
DECLARE c_Tables CURSOR
   FAST_FORWARD FOR
 SELECT obj.name
   FROM sysobjects obj (NOLOCK)
   JOIN syscolumns col (NOLOCK) ON obj.id = col.id
  WHERE col.colstat & 1 = 1
    AND obj.type       = 'U'


OPEN c_Tables

FETCH NEXT FROM c_Tables INTO @v_Table
```

```
WHILE (@@fetch_status <> -1)
BEGIN
  IF (@@fetch_status <> -2)
  BEGIN
    SELECT @v_SQL = 'DBCC CHECKIDENT(' + @v_Table + ')'
--      PRINT @v_SQL
    EXEC(@v_SQL)
  END -- -2
  FETCH NEXT FROM c_Tables INTO @v_Table
END -- While

CLOSE c_Tables
DEALLOCATE c_Tables
GO
```

| Related solutions: | Found on page: |
|---|---|
| Query Analyzer | 193 |
| Identifying Autogenerated Statistics on All User Tables | 604 |
| **sp_MSforeachtable** | 668 |
| Building and Executing Dynamic SQL | 834 |

### usp_DBCCReindex

Rebuilding the indexes in a database can be *extremely* useful when it comes to keeping performance of any application at its best. This operation should be scheduled once each night or on the weekend to ensure that your index pages are clean and well organized. There is one other new procedure that can be used in conjunction with **DBCC REINDEX** and that is **DBCC INDEXDEFRAG** (see the "**usp_DBCCIndexDefrag**" section later in this chapter). The **DBCC DBREINDEX** command is very intrusive and can block other processes, so be careful when you run this process. See Listing 6.20 for the SQL behind the stored procedure that runs **DBCC REINDEX** against all the user tables in a database. This procedure is scoped to the database in which it resides, so you will have to create it in the database in which you want to use it.

Listing 6.20   Source SQL for **usp_DBCCReindex**.

```
CREATE PROC usp_DBCCReindex
AS
/* Declare Variables                  */
DECLARE @v_table SYSNAME,
        @v_SQL   NVARCHAR(2000)

/* Declare the Table Cursor (Identity) */
DECLARE c_Tables CURSOR
   FAST_FORWARD FOR
```

```
SELECT name
  FROM sysobjects obj (NOLOCK)
 WHERE type = 'U'

OPEN c_Tables

FETCH NEXT FROM c_Tables INTO @v_Table
WHILE (@@fetch_status <> -1)
BEGIN
  IF (@@fetch_status <> -2)
  BEGIN
    SELECT @v_SQL = 'DBCC DBREINDEX(' + @v_Table + ')'
--    PRINT @v_SQL
    EXEC(@v_SQL)
  END -- -2
  FETCH NEXT FROM c_Tables INTO @v_Table
END -- While

CLOSE c_Tables
DEALLOCATE c_Tables
GO
```

| Related solutions: | Found on page: |
|---|---|
| Query Analyzer | 193 |
| Identifying Autogenerated Statistics on All User Tables | 604 |
| **sp_MSforeachtable** | 668 |
| Building and Executing Dynamic SQL | 834 |

## usp_DBCCIndexDefrag

Index fragmentation can occur over time and should be addressed by periodic rebuilding of the indexes in a database. There are times when running **DBCC DBREINDEX** is not convenient to system load or processing time. The new **DBCC INDEXDEFRAG** command is designed to reorganize the index pages of an index with less locking than **DBCC DBREINDEX** and regain some of the lost performance. You can run this procedure nightly and only run **DBCC DBREINDEX** on the weekend when processing loads are typically reduced and blocking is less of an issue. See Listing 6.21 for a stored procedure that defragments the indexes in a database. This procedure is scoped to the database in which it resides, so you will have to create it in the database in which you want to use it.

---

**NOTE:** *If you want to see how fragmented an index is, use **DBCC SHOWCONTIG**.*

---

The **usp_DBCCIndexDefrag** stored procedure uses nested cursors to iterate through not only the tables in a database, but also the indexes for each table. You may find other places where using a nested cursor or knowing what indexes are defined for a particular table may be useful. Feel free to use this code as an example in other stored procedures or SQL scripts.

**Listing 6.21  Source SQL for usp_DBCCIndexDefrag.**

```
CREATE PROC usp_DBCCIndexDefrag
AS
SET NOCOUNT ON
/* Declare Variables                   */
DECLARE @v_table SYSNAME,
        @v_Index INT,
        @v_SQL   NVARCHAR(2000)


/* Declare the Table Cursor            */
DECLARE c_Tables CURSOR
   FAST_FORWARD FOR
 SELECT name
   FROM sysobjects obj (NOLOCK)
  WHERE type = 'U'


OPEN c_Tables


FETCH NEXT FROM c_Tables INTO @v_Table
WHILE (@@fetch_status <> -1)
BEGIN
  IF (@@fetch_status <> -2)
  BEGIN
/* Declare the Index Cursor            */
    DECLARE c_Indexes CURSOR
      READ_ONLY FOR
     SELECT idx.indid
       FROM sysobjects obj (NOLOCK)
       JOIN sysindexes idx (NOLOCK) ON obj.id = idx.id
      WHERE obj.name  = @v_Table
        AND idx.indid > 0
        AND idx.indid < 255


    OPEN c_Indexes


    FETCH NEXT FROM c_Indexes INTO @v_Index
    WHILE (@@fetch_status <> -1)
    BEGIN
      IF (@@fetch_status <> -2)
```

```
        BEGIN
          SELECT @v_SQL = 'DBCC INDEXDEFRAG(0,' +
                          @v_Table + ', ' +
                          CONVERT(VARCHAR,@v_Index) + ') WITH NO_INFOMSGS'
--        PRINT @v_SQL
          EXEC(@v_SQL)
        END -- Index -2
        FETCH NEXT FROM c_Indexes INTO @v_Index
      END -- Index While

      CLOSE c_Indexes
      DEALLOCATE c_Indexes

    END -- Table -2
    FETCH NEXT FROM c_Tables INTO @v_Table
END -- Table While

CLOSE c_Tables
DEALLOCATE c_Tables
GO
```

| Related solutions: | Found on page: |
|---|---|
| Query Analyzer | 193 |
| Identifying Autogenerated Statistics on All User Tables | 604 |
| **sp_MSforeachtable** | 668 |
| Building and Executing Dynamic SQL | 834 |

## usp_DBCCCheckTable

Running **DBCC CHECKDB** is a very intrusive process. There are times when this process just will not complete in an acceptable timeframe, or you cannot run it because users are in the system. **DBCC CHECKTABLE** actually performs the same checks as **CHECKDB**, but only runs against the table specified. If you need to research an error reported by a nightly process, **DBCC CHECKTABLE** may be the only way to check errors without kicking everyone out of the system. Listing 6.22 is the source SQL for a DBCC loop that runs **DBCC CHECKTABLE** against each table in a database. This is essentially the same as running **CHECKDB**, but will not drain server resources as severely because it only checks one table at a time. You can schedule this procedure instead of **CHECKDB** and be just as safe.

Listing 6.22    Source SQL for **usp_DBCCCheckTable**.

```
CREATE PROC usp_DBCCCheckTable
AS
/* Declare Variables              */
DECLARE @v_table SYSNAME,
        @v_SQL   NVARCHAR(2000)
```

```
/* Declare the Table Cursor (Identity) */
DECLARE c_Tables CURSOR
   FAST_FORWARD FOR
 SELECT name
   FROM sysobjects obj (NOLOCK)
  WHERE type = 'U'


OPEN c_Tables

FETCH NEXT FROM c_Tables INTO @v_Table
WHILE (@@fetch_status <> -1)
BEGIN
  IF (@@fetch_status <> -2)
  BEGIN
    SELECT @v_SQL = 'DBCC CHECKTABLE(' + @v_Table + ')'
--     PRINT @v_SQL
    EXEC(@v_SQL)
  END -- -2
  FETCH NEXT FROM c_Tables INTO @v_Table
END -- While

CLOSE c_Tables
DEALLOCATE c_Tables
GO
```

| Related solutions: | Found on page: |
|---|---|
| Query Analyzer | 193 |
| Identifying Autogenerated Statistics on All User Tables | 604 |
| **sp_MSforeachtable** | 668 |
| Building and Executing Dynamic SQL | 834 |

# DBCC Commands

There are an unfortunate number of SQL Servers running in production today that do not have consistency checks run against them. This fact alone should raise some eyebrows in the database community. Many third-party applications are not being shipping with thorough maintenance plans. Companies are opting to purchase database applications without having trained database administrators in house to support the applications on their servers. The list of commands in the following sections can be valuable and may make the difference between having data on Monday morning or not.

You should be running DBCC commands against your servers on a regular basis. Many of the supposed "black marks" associated with SQL Server can be overcome by making sure you head off problems as early as possible. DBCC commands can be seen as "preventive medicine" for your database problems.

## DBCC CHECKDB

The **DBCC CHECKDB** statement checks the structural integrity and performs a few repair operations on any inconsistencies found in the database. This command is a bit intrusive and can cause consistency problems if it is run while the server is busy. The amount of tempdb workspace is also a factor to consider when running **CHECKDB** on a large database.

---

**NOTE:** *Run **DBCC CHECKDB** with the Estimate Only option to determine how much space is going to be required to successfully run the command.*

---

This command essentially runs **CHECKALLOC** and **CHECKTABLE** commands against the target database. When needed, you can run the **CHECKALLOC** and **CHECKTABLE** commands by themselves to reduce the amount of contention on your server, but remember that **CHECKDB** is the most comprehensive and thorough method of testing. You should check the health of your database each night and fix any errors as soon as detected to ensure your ability to keep the data online for the user community. See Listing 6.23 for the SQL syntax needed to run **DBCC CHECKDB**.

---

**NOTE:** *See the Microsoft SQL Server Books Online for more details on **DBCC CHECKDB**.*

---

**Listing 6.23    DBCC CHECKDB** syntax.

```
DBCC CHECKDB ('database_name'
             [, NOINDEX | {REPAIR_ALLOW_DATA_LOSS
                         | REPAIR_FAST
                         | REPAIR_REBUILD}])
      [WITH [[ALL_ERRORMSGS]
             [, [NO_INFOMSGS]]
             [, [TABLOCK]]
             [, [ESTIMATEONLY]]
             [, [PHYSICAL_ONLY]]]}]
```

## DBCC CHECKALLOC

Checking the disk space allocation structures is extremely important to any database. Microsoft SQL Server relies on the space allocation information to manage the objects within the database files on your server. If this data becomes unsynchronized, your server will have trouble working with the objects in that database. **DBCC CHECKALLOC** is a subset of the tests performed by **DBCC CHECKDB**. The main focus of **CHECKALLOC** is not data storage, but allocation of space for objects in the database. You can run **DBCC CHECKALLOC** with the Estimate Only option to make sure you will have enough space to expand tempdb to support the command operation. See Listing 6.24 for the SQL syntax needed to run **DBCC CHECKALLOC**.

---

**NOTE:** *See the Microsoft SQL Server Books Online for more details on* **DBCC CHECKALLOC**.

---

Listing 6.24    **DBCC CHECKALLOC** syntax.

```
DBCC CHECKALLOC ('database_name'
                [, NOINDEX |{REPAIR_ALLOW_DATA_LOSS
                            | REPAIR_FAST
                            | REPAIR_REBUILD}])
        [WITH {[ALL_ERRORMSGS | NO_INFOMSGS]
            [, [TABLOCK]]
            [, [ESTIMATEONLY]]}]
```

## DBCC CHECKTABLE

**DBCC CHECKTABLE** is a subset of **DBCC CHECKDB**. It tests the integrity of the data pages associated with the target table or view. Typically, **CHECKTABLE** is run against a server to interrogate a single table that is causing problems in a database. You can reduce the contention of **DBCC CHECKDB** by running **CHECKTABLE** in a table driven cursor against a database instead of running **CHECKDB**. See Listing 6.22 for the stored procedure code to loop through the user tables in a database and run **DBCC CHECKTABLE**.

You can further tune the impact on consistency and server load by using the optional parameters of **DBCC CHECKTABLE**. See Listing 6.25 for the SQL syntax needed to run **DBCC CHECKTABLE**. The Physical Only option can greatly reduce the amount of time and processing load of **DBCC CHECKTABLE** on the rest of the server. It skips the nonclustered indexes associated with the table and limits the checks to the page and record headers, the object ID, and index ID relationships for the target table.

---

**NOTE:** *See the Microsoft SQL Server Books Online for more information on* **DBCC CHECKTABLE**.

---

Listing 6.25    **DBCC CHECKTABLE** syntax.

```
DBCC CHECKTABLE ('table_name' | 'view_name'
                [, NOINDEX | index_id
                            | {REPAIR_ALLOW_DATA_LOSS
                            | REPAIR_FAST
                            | REPAIR_REBUILD}])
```

**6. Server Maintenance**

```
[WITH {[ALL_ERRORMSGS | NO_INFOMSGS]
      [, [TABLOCK]]
      [, [ESTIMATEONLY]]
      [, [PHYSICAL_ONLY]]}]
```

## DBCC CHECKIDENT

There are occasional errors returned from **INSERT** statements that just plain baffle many programmers. When an identity column defined on a table and a primary key or unique index uses the identity column, periodically an **INSERT** will generate a key violation error stating that you are attempting to **INSERT** a duplicate value.

What has happened is that the next value to be inserted into the identity column has become invalid and out of sync with the actual data in the table. This usually happens during a bulk operation and can be fixed by running **DBCC CHECKIDENT**. See Listing 6.26 for the SQL syntax needed to run **DBCC CHECKIDENT**. The New Reseed option allows you to specify a value if the automatic fix is not your desired result. See Listing 6.19 for a stored procedure that runs **CHECKIDENT** on all the tables in a database as a preventive measure.

---

**NOTE:** *See the Microsoft SQL Server Books Online for more information on **DBCC CHECKIDENT**.*

---

**Listing 6.26   DBCC CHECKIDENT syntax.**

```
DBCC CHECKIDENT ('table_name'
                [, {NORESEED | {RESEED [, new_reseed_value]}}])
```

## DBCC DBREINDEX

In any database, the indexing of the data is paramount to the speed of queries. No database engine can perform well without properly maintained indexes. In SQL Server's case, the health of the index statistics and the periodic restructuring of the index data pages make a world of difference in performance.

**DBCC DBREINDEX** rebuilds all indexes for the target table including indexes associated with constraints. This is a wonderful feature, but it has one major drawback to consider. The index is offline during the rebuild process as far as the query optimizer is concerned. This can bring some queries to their knees and have users scratching their heads. Run this command during off hours to reduce the impact on the user community when rebuilding indexes.

Many maintenance plans fail to maintain the indexes in a database in a complete manner because it can take time to code a solution that rebuilds all the indexes in a database. In Listing 6.20, there is a stored procedure that runs on *any* database and rebuilds the indexes in a single command. The stored procedure can be scheduled to run overnight to reduce the impact on the server and users. If the amount of time it takes to rebuild indexes is an issue, you may want to rebuild the indexes once a week and use the new **DBCC INDEXDEFRAG** command nightly. **DBCC INDEXDEFRAG** is discussed in the next section. See Listing 6.27 for the SQL syntax needed to run **DBCC DBREINDEX**.

---

**NOTE:** *See the Microsoft SQL Server Books Online for more information on **DBCC DBREINDEX**.*

---

Listing 6.27  **DBCC DBREINDEX** syntax.

```
DBCC DBREINDEX (['database.owner.table_name'
                [, index_name
                [, fillfactor]]])
        [WITH NO_INFOMSGS]
```

## DBCC INDEXDEFRAG

New to SQL Server, **INDEXDEFRAG** can be used to defragment and compact index data associated with tables and views. **DBCC INDEXDEFRAG** affects both clustered and nonclustered indexes. Indexes are compacted by reorganizing the leaf-level of an index. Any empty pages are then free to be used elsewhere in the database and reduce the scan time of the indexes for query operations. **DBCC INDEXDEFRAG** is the only operation that can be run online while indexes are being used. It does not take the indexes offline while rebuilding them. Locks are not held for very long using this method and therefore do not become blocking operations to other queries nearly as often as other index manipulation does.

---

**NOTE:** *The more fragmented an index is, the longer **DBCC INDEXDEFRAG** will run. There is a point at which rebuilding the index takes less time than defragmenting one.*

---

See Listing 6.28 for the SQL syntax needed to run **DBCC INDEXDEFRAG**. One interesting fact to point out about **INDEXDEFRAG** is that it accepts names or ID values as parameters. You can even mix and match them if required.

---

**NOTE:** *See the Microsoft SQL Server Books Online for more information on **DBCC INEXDEFRAG**.*

---

Listing 6.28  **DBCC INDEXDEFRAG** syntax.

```
DBCC INDEXDEFRAG ({database_name | database_id | 0 }
                ,{table_name | table_id | 'view_name' | view_id }
                ,{index_name | index_id })
        [WITH NO_INFOMSGS ]
```

6. Server Maintenance

## DBCC SHOWCONTIG

The fragmentation of data in an index or table can cause an unnecessary amount of disk I/O and page reads. Reducing this fragmentation can improve performance across all queries that access the data in a database. In earlier sections of this chapter, the capabilities of commands to reduce fragmentation was discussed, but not how to identify a fragmentation problem when it exists. The **DBCC SHOWCONTIG** command analyzes your database, table, or indexes and reports the statistics of the target object(s) via a text or tabular report.

Report servers and highly active data that is **INSERTED**, **UPDATED**, and **DELETED** will most likely be the places where your tables and indexes become fragmented. You should be able to analyze your code or the queries running against the server to get a list of "hot spots" that you should monitor with **DBCC SHOWCONTIG**. See Listing 6.29 for the SQL syntax needed to run **DBCC SHOWCONTIG**.

---

**NOTE:** *See the Microsoft SQL Server Books Online for more information on **DBCC SHOWCONTIG**.*

---

**Listing 6.29    DBCC SHOWCONTIG syntax.**

```
DBCC SHOWCONTIG
    [({table_name | table_id | view_name | view_id}
    [, index_name | index_id ])]
        [WITH {ALL_INDEXES
              | FAST [, ALL_INDEXES]
              | TABLERESULTS [, {ALL_INDEXES}]
              [, {FAST | ALL_LEVELS}]}]
```

## DBCC CLEANTABLE

Reclaiming space with **DBCC CLEANTABLE** is seldom an activity that is performed against a production system. It does bear mention, however, in development environments. Any time you use the **ALTER TABLE DROP COLUMN** statement, it is a good idea to run **CLEANTABLE** to reclaim the space any variable length character or text column would have used.

You only need to run **CLEANTABLE** after removing a variable length character field or a text field in a table. There is no need to run **CLEANTABLE** when removing any other column data types. Be sure to specify a batch size on larger tables because the **CLEANTABLE** operation will attempt to perform its operations as one large transaction. Failing to use the **batch_size** parameter could cause the transaction log to grow at an incredible rate and impact other operations on the server. See Listing 6.30 for the SQL syntax needed to run **DBCC CLEANTABLE**.

---

**NOTE:** *See the Microsoft SQL Server Books Online for more information on **DBCC CLEANTABLE**.*

---

Listing 6.30 **DBCC CLEANTABLE** syntax.

```
DBCC CLEANTABLE ({'database_name' | database_id}
                , {'table_name' | table_id | 'view_name' | view_id}
                [, batch_size])
```

## DBCC ERRORLOG

Often, during the day-to-day operation of your database server, you can forget about the amount of space your server error log is consuming. Depending on trace flags, your log can grow to over 1GB in size and become too large to open in many text editors. Every time a SQL Server is shut down and restarted the error log is detached and stored in the logs directory. This default behavior is not always easy to work with. Development environments that are performing a large number of tests or placing a server under a heavy load may generate more information than some text editors can read. A little-known DBCC command, **DBCC ERRORLOG**, cycles the log so that the current log does not grow any larger.

By cycling the error log, you move the current log into the first history position and each subsequent log down one place in history. The default of six logs worth of history is usually adequate for most installations, but sometimes it needs to be adjusted. You can "tweak" the default of six logs worth of history by adding a key value to the Registry telling SQL server how many logs to keep available. See Listing 6.31 for an example of the code to add the key and value to the Registry on your server. The key is absent from the Registry by default.

Listing 6.31 Add a key to the Registry to allow for more than the default number of logs to be kept. (Change the number 10 to a value equal to the total number of logs to keep.)

```
EXEC master..xp_regwrite 'HKEY_LOCAL_MACHINE',
                         'SOFTWARE\Microsoft\MSSQLServer\MSSQLServer',
                         'NumErrorLogs',
                         'REG_DWORD',
                         10
```

Once you have told SQL Server that you want to keep 10 logs worth of history, you can cycle the active log to history with a daily scheduled task that runs either **sp_cycle_errorlog** or **DBCC ERRORLOG** in the master database. As a rule, try not to over-complicate the code. Some people prefer to use the DBCC command directly rather than mask the call with a stored procedure. See Listing 6.32 for the SQL syntax needed to run DBCC ERRORLOG.

*WARNING! The DBCC ERRORLOG command and methods of using it are not documented in the online documentation. It is referenced online in article Q196909 on Microsoft's support Web site.*

Listing 6.32 **DBCC ERRORLOG** syntax.

```
DBCC ERRORLOG
```

# Using the Maintenance Plan Wizard

A popular method of creating a maintenance plan for a database running on SQL Server is to use the Maintenance Plan Wizard. This method is reliable and very good at providing a simple plan to protect your data. The wizard is best used for conventional database backup plans and may not suit all application requirements. If you have not performed server maintenance in the past, this is an excellent solution to start you down the path of maintaining your databases. It also exposes you to the tasks that must be performed in order to successfully safeguard valuable data. The Maintenance Plan Wizard performs four main tasks:

- Runs database integrity checks
- Updates database statistics
- Performs database dumps
- Ships transaction logs to another server (Enterprise Edition)

To access the wizard:

1. Expand the server within Enterprise Manager, navigate to the Management folder, and then right-click on Database Maintenance Plans.

2. Select New Maintenance Plan from the pop-up menu, which launches the Maintenance Plan Wizard. See Figure 6.2 for the location of the database maintenance plans item in the Enterprise Manager.

3. The initial screen of the wizard describing what the wizard does appears. Click on Next.

4. Select a combination of databases that you want to create a plan for. For this example, select a single database by making sure that the These Databases radio button is selected, and select the checkbox next to the Northwind database. See Figure 6.3.

5. Click on Next.

6. This wizard screen supplies the optimization and scheduling information. You can elect to rebuild your indexes, update statistics, and reclaim unused space from the database files. Depending on the nature of your data, you may choose to rebuild your indexes and remove unused space, as shown in Figure 6.4.

7. Once the checkboxes are selected, the additional options, like scheduling and percentages for this plan, are enabled.

---

**NOTE:** *The default schedule of once per week on Sunday at 01:00 hours is probably not the schedule you want for all your plans, so be sure to update the schedule by selecting the Change button.*

---

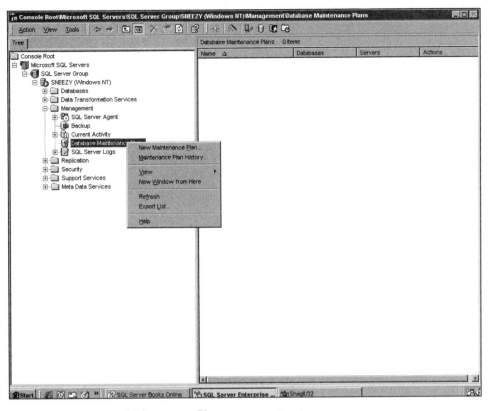

Figure 6.2   Database Maintenance Plans pop-up menu.

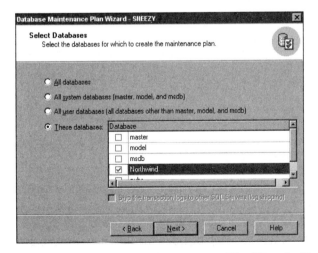

Figure 6.3   The Database Maintenance Plan Wizard with the Northwind database
selected.

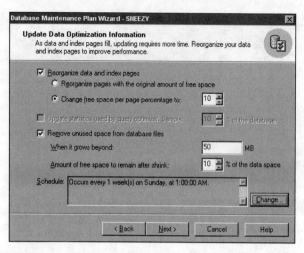

**Figure 6.4    Data optimization page of the Maintenance Plan Wizard.**

8. Once you have verified that the schedule works within your backup window, click on Next. (The default remains as is in this example.)

9. The next part of the wizard deals with database integrity. You should always perform integrity tests on your databases. Select the checkbox for Checking Database Integrity.

10. Include indexes, and select the Attempt To Repair checkbox.

11. Select the Perform These Checks Before Doing Backups checkbox. You do not want to perform a backup of corrupted data that may overwrite a good backup.

**NOTE:** *It is possible that you might actually want to keep a backup of the database before it is fixed so that you have enough information to determine what changes were made. Care must be exercised with a "corrupt" backup to ensure that it is not accidentally used to replace good data.*

12. Click on Next.

**NOTE:** *You can change the schedule of the integrity checks on this screen as well.*

13. You are then presented with the Backup Plan screen. Adjust the schedule to fit your backup window. You have the option of not performing the actual backup as part of this plan. You would want to select this option if you were using one of the other backup options discussed in this chapter to create your backups, but wanted to run the optimization and integrity portions under a separate job.

14. Let's assume for this exercise that you will actually perform the backup. Make sure you leave the verification checkbox selected.

15. Click on Next.

16. Choose the directory in which you want to place the backup.

17. Fill in the appropriate information for your server environment, and click on Next.

18. Optionally, you can create the transaction backups for this database. For the sake of this example, select the Back Up The Transaction Log checkbox. The defaults will be filled in for you, but you do have the ability to modify them. See Figure 6.5 for the transaction log backup page.

19. Click on Next.

20. As with the database backups, you can specify a location for the transaction log backup files. Fill in the same settings as you did for the database backup, and click on Next.

21. On the Reports screen of the wizard, select the directory in which you want to store the plan reports and the number of week's worth of reports you want to keep. (The defaults are used in this example.)

22. Click on Next.

23. The local and remote server options screen appears. Accept the default for this example.

24. Supply a name for this plan so it can be saved and the appropriate scheduled jobs created.

25. Review the summary report generated by the wizard, and click on Finish.

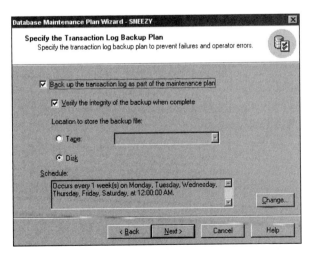

Figure 6.5   Transaction log backup page of the Maintenance Plan Wizard.

| *Related solution:* | *Found on page:* |
| --- | --- |
| Enterprise Manager | 178 |

# Creating a Maintenance Plan for the System Databases

The system databases seldom change. You may add a job to the system and create some entries in msdb or add a login that creates additional data in the syslogins table in the master database. This type of activity is not automated in most environments, so you can create a backup strategy that better suits the type of data you are trying to protect.

The data in the system databases requires a backup plan that runs in two situations: when the data is known to change and on a periodic basis. You should run the plan manually when you make changes to the data as described previously or once a week or so to cover yourself in the event you forget to run it manually.

The backups do not require a great deal of space, so disk utilization is not an issue. Should the backup fail for some reason, you will have to use the RebuildM utility to rebuild the master database and re-create your user login information manually, which is generally an extremely undesirable position to find yourself in.

1. From the Enterprise Manager main window, expand the server node for the server you are creating a maintenance plan for.

2. Navigate to the Database Maintenance Plans icon under the Management folder.

3. Right-click on the icon, and select New Maintenance Plan to display the Maintenance Plan Wizard.

4. Click on Next to go to the second page of the wizard.

5. This page is where the database selection occurs. Choose the second option from the top called All System Databases. See Figure 6.6 for the database selection page of the wizard.

6. Click on Next.

7. This screen of the maintenance wizard deals with updating data optimization. This activity is seldom required on the system catalog.

8. Click on Next to go to the Database Integrity Check screen.

9. Select the option to perform the database integrity check.

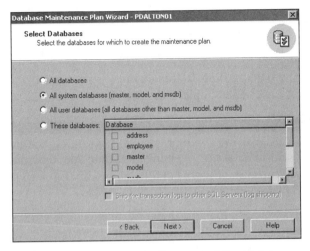

Figure 6.6    Database selection page of the Maintenance Plan Wizard.

10. Do *not* select the option Attempt To Repair Any Minor Problems. This will fail on the system databases.

11. Select the option Perform These Tasks Before Doing Backups.

12. Set the schedule for the integrity check if you require it to be different from the default of Sunday at 12:00 A.M. (Remember that this plan is a once-a-week plan.) Leave the default as is for this example. Your screen should look like Figure 6.7.

13. Click on Next.

14. Leave the default settings.

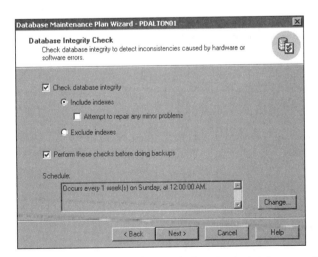

Figure 6.7    Integrity check window of the Maintenance Plan Wizard.

**NOTE:** *The selections verify the integrity of the backup, and the backup runs at 2:00 A.M. by default.*

15. Click on Next.

16. Specify where to place the backup files. In this example, there is a backups directory, so this directory is chosen to place the files in.

17. For organizational purposes, choose the option Create A Subdirectory For Each Database.

18. Because these backups seldom change, you can save some space by only keeping two weeks of backups. See Figure 6.8 for the Specify Backup Disk Directory screen.

19. Do not bother with the transaction logs for these databases. Leave the default state of the transaction log backup step, which is a cleared checkbox.

20. Click on Next.

21. Ensure that you have the Write Report To A Text File In Directory checkbox selected. (The default path of the SQL Server log directory is usually a good place to store this file.)

22. Select the Delete Text Report Files Older Than option, and change the number of weeks to match your backup plan (two weeks). See Figure 6.9, Reports To Generate, to ensure you have each option selected properly.

23. Click on Next.

24. Leave the defaults for the maintenance history unless your environment requires them to be edited.

25. Click on Next.

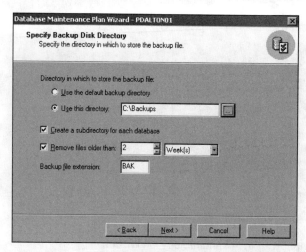

Figure 6.8    Specify Backup Disk Directory screen.

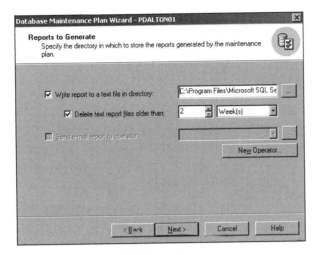

Figure 6.9    Reports To Generate.

26. Name the maintenance plan, and click on Finish to complete the maintenance wizard. Be sure to use a descriptive name for your plan, so that you can easily distinguish it from the other jobs on your server.

This plan creates two jobs on your server (depending upon the options you select, more than two jobs can be created for this plan). One job performs the integrity checks for the databases on a weekly basis, whereas the other performs the backup tasks. You can verify these new jobs by going to the jobs listing and running the newly created jobs. If either of the jobs fails to run, check the output report in the SQL Server log directory to find out what the problem was, correct it, and make sure the job runs successfully before assuming you have a successful maintenance plan established.

---

**NOTE:** *The SQL Server Agent must be running on the server to run the jobs. If the agent is stopped, your backups will never run.*

---

| *Related solution:* | *Found on page:* |
| --- | --- |
| Enterprise Manager | 178 |

# Creating a Transaction Log Backup Solution

The keys to creating a successful transaction log backup solution are to understand the schedule and type of activity on your server and the amount of data loss you can absorb without having your user community disturbed.

## Activity

The activity that is occurring in the database determines how large a transaction log will become and how long the actual dump of the log will impact users. Activity means **INSERT**, **UPDATE**, and **DELETE** traffic. Highly volatile data that changes often will create a large amount of log growth. The transaction log essentially stores the information needed to "undo" the edits made to the data. If your data is segmented into discrete databases, as recommended in this book, you have greater control over your backup routine. You can choose different routines for each database and tailor the scheduled dumps at different intervals to minimize the user impact.

Most workplaces have a schedule that can be graphed to determine when most work is done and critical times you will need the ability to restore information if a problem occurs. Workloads run similar to the illustration in Figure 6.10, but are based upon the type of application and data you are working with. Take the time to determine your own workload timeline before committing to a backup strategy.

Typically, at the beginning of each workday, the transaction load is increased because each user is starting the day and is fresh. The load then drops off over lunch with periodic spikes of activity around coffee breaks. After lunch, the load picks up again and levels off around the time people start thinking about going home. The transaction load drops off until nightly tasks and maintenance

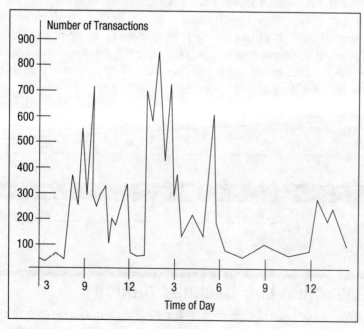

**Figure 6.10    Typical daily workload.**

routines and reports are run. You should plan your schedule not to be performing a transaction log dump during one of the peak times, but rather just before and just after a peak.

---

**NOTE:** *You can use the Windows Performance Monitor application to get more exact numbers and samplings than the chart in Figure 6.10 shows. Usually, lots of detail is not needed for planning purposes, but may be required to verify your estimates.*

---

## Data Loss

Data loss is always a touchy subject for any enterprise. When asked, "How much data can you afford to lose?" many managers will say "*None!*" This is seldom the actual fact when you start planning your backup strategy. You can create an incredibly fault-tolerant solution if you have enough money. Clustering hardware, servers, and standby servers are expensive. Some organizations cannot afford this expense, so they have to learn to ask questions in such a way as to get the answer they really need. For instance, if a major failure occurs, how hard would it be to redo or repeat the work accomplished in the last 15 or 30 minutes, or even the last hour? The more frequently you back up the transaction log, the closer you get to a zero data loss scenario, but the more impact the routine will have on users and performance.

Table 6.5 illustrates some of the data activity metrics that you can use in conjunction with the workload graph to come up with a schedule that best fits your server. These numbers are intended as guidelines only. Only you can determine what is best for your enterprise or application.

## The Plan

A transaction log backup plan entails creating a full database backup to use as a starting point for a restore operation, and then creating a scheduled task that dumps the transaction log on a regular schedule to provide the point-in-time recovery you desire. There are two steps to this method. The Employee database is used for this example: The data may change moderately and the target risk level is medium. You would then schedule hourly transaction log dumps during the day.

**Table 6.5   Data activity matrix.**

| Risk of Loss | Highly Changed | Moderately Changed | Seldom Changed |
|---|---|---|---|
| Low | 10-15 Minutes | 30-60 Minutes | 60-90 Minutes |
| Medium | 15-30 Minutes | 60-90 Minutes | 90-120 Minutes |
| High | 30-60 Minutes | 90-120 Minutes | 120 + Minutes |

**6. Server Maintenance**

### Creating a Database Dump

The following steps illustrate how to create a scheduled backup of the Employee database. This task will be scheduled to run each morning at 2:00 A.M.

1. Right-click on the Employee database in the Enterprise Manager.

2. Select the All Tasks menu option.

3. Select the Backup Database menu item.

4. In the dialog box presented, change the name to "Employee DB BU".

5. Fill in a description, such as "Employee DB Maintenance Plan".

6. Click on Add to choose the backup device.

7. When the Select Backup Destination dialog appears, click on the radio button for the appropriate backup device. Select the drop-down menu item New Backup Device. You are then presented with a backup device Properties dialog.

8. Fill in a descriptive name. (In this example, "EmployeeDB_BU" is used.) This automatically completes the file name in the location text box below.

9. Ensure that the path for the device file is correct. It should match your server's backup directory location. The default will be C:\Program Files\Microsoft SQL Server\MSSQL\BACKUP\EmployeeDB_BU.BAK. Change the path to match your server environment. See Figure 6.11 to verify your entries.

10. Click on OK.

11. In the Select Backup Destination dialog, click on OK.

12. Select Overwrite Existing Media.

13. Select the Schedule checkbox.

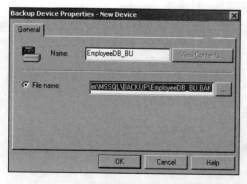

Figure 6.11   Backup device file information for database.

14. Click on the ellipsis [...] button next to the default schedule supplied when you selected the Schedule checkbox. This displays the Edit Schedule dialog.

15. Supply a name for this new schedule. For this example, use "Employee DB BU Schedule."

16. Click on Change, so that the default schedule can be edited.

17. In the Occurs group, select Daily.

18. In the Daily Frequency group box, change the time to 2:00:00 A.M.

19. Click on OK to close the Edit Recurring Job Schedule dialog.

20. Click on OK to close the Edit Schedule dialog.

21. Your backup dialog should look like Figure 6.12.

22. Select the Options tab to display the backup operation options.

23. Select the Verify Backup Upon Completion checkbox.

---

**TIP:** *Do not use expiration data for your backups unless you fully intend to invalidate a backup after a specific timeframe. For safety reasons, do not use this option.*

---

24. Click on OK to complete the process of creating the backup scheduled job. A nightly job is automatically created for you.

25. Go to the Jobs Management screen in the Enterprise Manager, and run this job to ensure that it is successful.

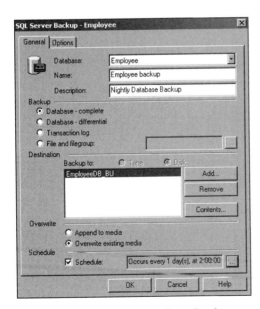

Figure 6.12   Employee database backup.

6. Server Maintenance

### Creating Dumps That Append to the Initial Dump

The next set of steps involved in a transaction log backup is to create a job that dumps the transaction log after the database dump job completes and before the daily workload starts to pick up. Let's use 7:00 A.M. as the log starting point. Follow these steps to create this job on your server.

1. Right-click on the Employee database in the Enterprise Manager.

2. Select the All Tasks menu option.

3. Select the Backup Database menu item.

4. In the dialog box presented, change the name to "Employee Log BU".

5. Fill in a description, such as "Employee DB Maintenance Plan".

6. Select Transaction Log.

7. Append the transaction log dumps to the existing backup device, EmployeeDB_BU. See Figure 6.13 to verify your entries.

8. Do *not* select Overwrite Existing Media. Leave the default Append To Media selected.

9. Sclect the Schedule checkbox.

10. Click on the ellipsis […] button next to the default schedule supplied when you selected the Schedule checkbox. This displays the Edit Schedule dialog.

11. Supply a name for this new schedule. For this example, use "Employee Log Dump Schedule".

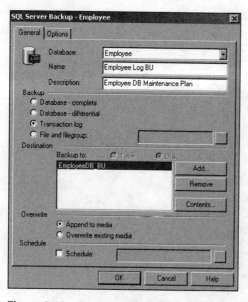

**Figure 6.13    Backup device file information for the transaction log.**

12. Click on Change, so that the default schedule can be edited.

13. In the Occurs group, select Daily.

14. In the Daily Frequency group box, select Occurs Every.

15. Change the start time to 7:00:00 A.M.

16. Click on OK to close the Edit Recurring Job Schedule dialog.

17. Click on OK to close the Edit Schedule dialog.

18. Your backup dialog should look like Figure 6.14.

19. Select the Options tab to display the backup operation options.

20. Select the Verify Backup Upon Completion checkbox.

21. Clear the Check Media Set checkbox.

22. Your option selections should match Figure 6.15.

23. Click on OK to complete the process of creating the backup scheduled job. A nightly job is automatically created for you.

24. Go to the Jobs Management screen in the Enterprise Manager, and run this job to ensure that it is successful.

As with any backup plan, test the restore to ensure that you can actually get what you need from your backups *before* you need them! Perform a walk-through verification of your backup plan at least once per month to ensure that all aspects are working correctly and that it is still viable.

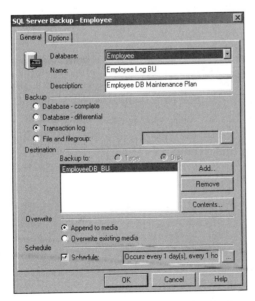

Figure 6.14   Employee database log backup.

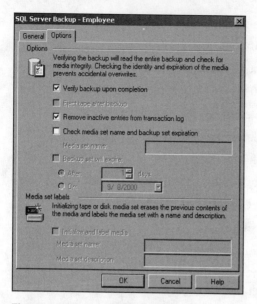

**Figure 6.15    Log backup options.**

**NOTE:** *For more information on backup and restore options and methods, see the Microsoft SQL Server Books Online.*

| Related solution: | Found on page: |
|---|---|
| Enterprise Manager | 178 |

# Creating a Differential Backup Solution

The differential backup solution plan is similar to a transaction log plan, but it does not require as much activity during the day. This plan works best for data that changes little during the day and can be backed up once per day during the week. The Utility database is used for this example.

## Creating a Database Dump

The following steps illustrate how to create a scheduled backup of the Utility database. This task will be scheduled to run each morning at 2:00 A.M.

1. Right-click on the Utility database in the Enterprise Manager.

2. Select the All Tasks menu option

3. Select the Backup Database menu item.

4. In the dialog presented, change the name to "Utility DB BU".

5. Fill in a description, such as "Utility DB Maintenance Plan".

6. Click on Add to choose the backup device.

7. When the Select Backup Destination dialog appears, click on the radio button for the appropriate backup device. Select the drop-down menu item New Backup Device. You are then presented with a backup device Properties dialog.

8. Fill in a descriptive name. (For this example, use "UtilityDB_BU".) This will automatically complete the file name in the location text box below.

9. Ensure that the path for the device file is correct. It should match your server's backup directory location. The default will be C:\Program Files\ Microsoft SQL Server\MSSQL\BACKUP\UtilityDB_BU.BAK. Change the path to match your server environment. See Figure 6.16 to verify your entries.

10. Click on OK.

11. In the Select Backup Destination dialog, click on OK.

12. Select Overwrite Existing Media.

13. Select the Schedule checkbox.

14. Click on the ellipsis [...] button next to the default schedule supplied when you selected the Schedule checkbox. This displays the Edit Schedule dialog.

15. Supply a name for this new schedule. For this example, use "Utility DB BU Schedule".

16. Use the default of Sunday and 12:00:00 A.M. Click on OK to close the Edit Schedule dialog.

17. Your backup dialog should look like Figure 6.17.

18. Select the Options tab to display the backup operation options.

19. Select the Verify Backup Upon Completion checkbox.

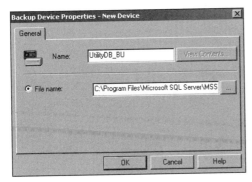

Figure 6.16   Backup device file information for database.

**6. Server Maintenance**

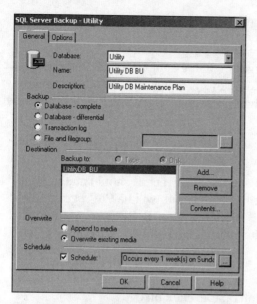

**Figure 6.17    Utility database backup.**

---

**TIP:** *Do not use expiration data for your backups unless you fully intend to invalidate a backup after a specific time frame. For safety reasons, do not use this option.*

---

20. Click on OK to complete the process of creating the backup scheduled job. A nightly job is automatically created for you.

21. Go to the Jobs Management screen in the Enterprise Manager, and run this job to ensure that it is successful.

## Creating Dumps That Append to the Initial Dump

The next set of steps creates a job that performs a differential backup each night. Follow these steps to create this job on your server.

1. Right-click on the Utility database in the Enterprise Manager.

2. Select the All Tasks menu option.

3. Select the Backup Database menu item.

4. In the dialog presented, change the name to "Utility Diff BU".

5. Fill in a description, such as "Utility DB Maintenance Plan".

6. Select Differential.

7. Append the differential dumps to the existing backup device, UtilityDB_BU.

8. Do *not* select Overwrite Existing Media. Leave the default Append To Media selected.

9. Select the Schedule checkbox.

10. Click on the ellipsis […] button next to the default schedule supplied when you selected the Schedule checkbox. This displays the Edit Schedule dialog.

11. Supply a name for this new schedule. For this example, use "Utility Differential Dump Schedule".

12. Click on Change, so that the default schedule can be edited.

13. Do *not* change the Occurs option from weekly.

14. Select the days of the week this backup should occur. (Clear Sunday and select the remaining days.)

15. There is no reason to change the time, so click on OK to close the Edit Recurring Job Schedule dialog.

16. Click on OK to close the Edit Schedule dialog.

17. Your backup dialog should look like Figure 6.18.

18. Select the Options tab to display the backup operation options.

19. Select the Verify Backup Upon Completion checkbox.

20. Clear the Check Media Set checkbox.

21. Click on OK to complete the process of creating the backup scheduled job. A nightly job is automatically created for you.

22. Go to the Jobs Management screen in the Enterprise Manager and run this job to ensure that it is successful.

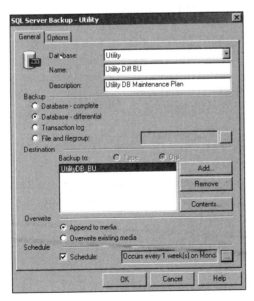

Figure 6.18    Utility database differential backup.

6. Server Maintenance

As with any backup plan, test the restore to ensure that you can actually get what you need from your backups *before* you need them! Perform a walk-through verification of your backup plan at least once per month to ensure that all aspects are working correctly and that it is still viable.

---

**NOTE:** *For more information on backup and restore options and methods, see the Microsoft SQL Server Books Online.*

---

| Related solution: | Found on page: |
|---|---|
| Enterprise Manager | 178 |

# Creating a Stored Procedure That Will Detach, Zip, Copy, and Attach the Inventory Database

One method of performing database backups that can be very flexible and fast is to detach, copy, and attach the data files associated with a database. Creating a stored procedure to automate this process can be a huge time-saver and allow you to have yet another option in your arsenal of database management tools.

The example will use the Inventory database that ships with this book. The distribution of the database to development servers, remote sites, or having an instant recovery option in the event of database failures are very important needs for any environment. Occasionally, you will want to add a compression routine to the file to make it more portable. In this example, PKUNZIP version 2.5 is used to zip and unzip the files. WinZip can also uncompress files that were initially zipped with PKUNZIP, so you have a reliable method of compressing files that is flexible enough to create small, manageable files for archival or storage. The support procedures are included in a single installation script named allprocs.sql on the CD-ROM for your convenience.

## Support Procedures

Let's walk through the support procedures first, so that you can understand the supporting code. You will need three stored procedures to use this technique. Each one is a utility in nature and can be stored in the Utility database:

- **usp_DBListUpdate**
- **usp_KillUsers**
- **usp_DBZip**

The primary need is to obtain a list of the files associated with each database that you are going to manipulate. The stored procedure **usp_DBListUpdate**, gathers database and file information and stores it in the Utility database for use at a later time. See Listing 6.33 for the SQL source code behind the stored procedure **usp_DBListUpdate**.

---

**NOTE:** *Listing 6.33 assumes that the default file extensions are used for all database files. If this is not the case, the code will need to be modified accordingly.*

---

**Listing 6.33   Source SQL for usp_DBListUpdate.**

```
CREATE PROC usp_DBListUpdate
AS
SET NOCOUNT ON
/* Declare variables                      */
DECLARE @v_SQL    NVARCHAR(2000),
        @v_DBName SYSNAME


/* Check for Utility database             */
IF NOT EXISTS (SELECT name
                  FROM master..sysdatabases (NOLOCK)
                  WHERE name = 'Utility')
BEGIN
  RAISERROR('Utility database is missing. Please install the Utility
database.',16,1)
  RETURN
END -- DB Check


/* Make sure DBList exists                */
IF NOT EXISTS (SELECT name
                  FROM Utility..sysobjects (NOLOCK)
                  WHERE name = 'tbl_DBList')
BEGIN
  SELECT @v_SQL = 'Create Table Utility..tbl_DBList (' +
                  'DBName    sysname, ' +
                  'DataFile VARCHAR(255), ' +
                  'LogFile   VARCHAR(255))'
  EXEC(@v_SQL)
END -- DBList Check


/* Check for new databases                */
IF (SELECT COUNT(DBName)
      FROM Utility..tbl_DBList                (NOLOCK)
      LEFT OUTER JOIN master..sysdatabases (NOLOCK) ON DBName = name
    WHERE name IS NULL) > 0
```

```
BEGIN
/* New databases exist, update list     */
   TRUNCATE TABLE tbl_DBList
END -- New DB


/* Filter out the DB names               */
/* Cursor to loop through each database */
DECLARE c_dblist CURSOR FAST_FORWARD FOR
 SELECT name
   FROM master..sysdatabases          (NOLOCK)
   LEFT OUTER JOIN Utility..tbl_DBList (NOLOCK) ON DBName = name
  WHERE DBName IS NULL
    AND name NOT IN ('master',
                     'model',
                     'msdb',
                     'tempdb',
                     'pubs',
                     'northwind')


OPEN c_dblist

FETCH NEXT FROM c_dblist INTO @v_DBName

WHILE(@@fetch_status <> -1)
BEGIN
  IF(@@fetch_status <> -2)
  BEGIN
/* Populate dblist */
    SELECT @v_SQL =
   'DECLARE @v_mdf VARCHAR(255), ' +
          '@v_ldf VARCHAR(255) ' +
   'SELECT @v_mdf = RTRIM(filename) ' +
     'FROM ' + @v_DBName + '..sysfiles (NOLOCK) ' +
     'WHERE filename LIKE ''%mdf%'' ' +
   'SELECT @v_ldf = RTRIM(filename) ' +
     'FROM ' + @v_DBName + '..sysfiles (NOLOCK) ' +
     'WHERE filename LIKE ''%ldf%'' ' +
   'INSERT Utility..tbl_DBList ' +
   'VALUES (''' + @v_DBName + ''', @v_mdf, @v_ldf)'
    EXEC(@v_SQL)
  END -- -2
  FETCH NEXT FROM c_dblist INTO @v_DBName
END -- WHILE

CLOSE      c_dblist
DEALLOCATE c_dblist
Go
```

This procedure checks for the existence of the Utility database on the server before it runs and creates the table **tbl_DBList** if it cannot find it. If the number of databases changes, the procedure automatically updates the table with current values for each database not in the filter portion of the **WHERE** clause highlighted in the previous script. If you want to change the databases manipulated by this procedure, edit the list of databases in the procedure to match your needs.

The second procedure needed is one that removes any active users in the target database, because you cannot detach a database with users working in it. In an earlier section, the procedure **usp_KillUsers** was discussed, which will do just that, issue a **KILL** statement for each user in a database. See "**usp_KillUsers**" earlier in the "Immediate Solutions" section for the source SQL (Listing 6.17) and an explanation of how the procedure works.

Let's now discuss the actual procedure that will drive the process, **usp_DBZip**. See Listing 6.34 for the source SQL. There are a few steps performed in this procedure that should be mentioned in a bit more detail. PKZIP is used as the compression application to keep the files as small as possible to reduce file copy time and save space on the repository share. You may substitute any similar application as long as it supports a command-line interface. Make sure you have an appropriately licensed copy of the application. A copy of PKZIP 2.5 is provided on the CD-ROM for you to test and evaluate for purchase. Make sure you copy the PKZIP.EXE to a location in your path so that it can be found by SQL Server when the **xp_cmdshell** call is made.

Also, it is a good idea to create your own file name for the zip file based upon the existing name of the database files. This process assumes that there is only one data and log file for each database to process. You must add the logic to handle multi-file databases before using this procedure to back up your databases.

*WARNING! Do not use this technique for the master database!*

**6. Server Maintenance**

### Listing 6.34   Source SQL for **usp_DBZip**.

```
CREATE PROC usp_DBZip
AS
SET NOCOUNT ON

/* Check for usp_DBListUpdate          */
IF NOT EXISTS (SELECT name
               FROM master..sysobjects (NOLOCK)
               WHERE name = 'usp_DBListUpdate')
BEGIN
 RAISERROR('usp_DBListUpdate must be loaded for this procedure to run
properly.',16,1)
 RETURN
END
```

```
/* Check for usp_KillUsers            */
IF NOT EXISTS (SELECT name
               FROM master..sysobjects (NOLOCK)
               WHERE name = 'usp_KillUsers')
BEGIN
 RAISERROR('usp_KillUsers must be loaded for this procedure to run
properly.',16,1)
 RETURN
END

/* Make sure we have a fresh list     */
EXEC master..usp_DBListUpdate

/* Declare Varables */
DECLARE @v_DBName    SYSNAME,
        @v_DataFile VARCHAR(255),
        @v_LogFile  VARCHAR(255),
        @v_mdfzip   VARCHAR(255),
        @v_ldfzip   VARCHAR(255),
        @v_SQL      NVARCHAR(2000)

/* Cursor to loop through db's that will be backed up */
/* List the DB names to NOT use this procedure on!    */
DECLARE c_dblist CURSOR FAST_FORWARD FOR
 SELECT DBName,
        DataFile,
        LogFile
   FROM Utility..tbl_DBList (NOLOCK)
  WHERE DBName NOT IN ('Utility',
                       'Employee')
   ORDER BY DBName

OPEN c_dblist

FETCH NEXT FROM c_dblist INTO @v_DBName, @v_DataFile, @v_LogFile
WHILE (@@fetch_status <> -1)
BEGIN
  IF (@@fetch_status <> -2)
  BEGIN
/* Kill Users in each database */
    EXEC usp_KillUsers @v_db
/* Detach Database */
    SELECT @v_SQL = 'EXEC sp_detach_db ''' + @v_DBName + ''''
    EXEC(@v_SQL)
    PRINT 'Detached DB :' + @v_DBName
```

```
/* Create zip name from mdf/ldf */
    SELECT @v_mdfzip = STUFF(@v_DataFile,(DATALENGTH(RTRIM(@v_DataFile))-3),
(DATALENGTH(RTRIM(@v_DataFile))), '.zip'),
          @v_ldfzip = STUFF(@v_LogFile,(DATALENGTH(RTRIM(@v_LogFile))-3),
(DATALENGTH(RTRIM(@v_LogFile))), '.zip')
/* Zip the files */
    SELECT @v_SQL = 'xp_cmdshell ''pkzip25 -add -silent -over=all ' +
                    @v_mdfzip + ' ' + @v_DataFile + ''''
    EXEC(@v_SQL)
    SELECT @v_SQL = 'xp_cmdshell ''pkzip25 -add -silent -over=all ' +
                    @v_ldfzip + ' ' + @v_LogFile + ''''
    EXEC(@v_SQL)
/* Attach Database back to the server */
    SELECT @v_SQL = 'sp_attach_db @dbname = ''' + @v_DBName + ''', ' +
                    '@filename1 = ''' + @v_DataFile + ''', ' +
                    '@filename2 = ''' + @v_LogFile + ''' '
    EXEC(@v_SQL)
  END -- -2
  FETCH NEXT FROM c_dblist INTO @v_DBName, @v_DataFile, @v_LogFile
END -- WHILE

CLOSE c_dblist
DEALLOCATE c_dblist
GO
```

Zipping the database will work for files under 4GB, but care should be taken to test the compression application you choose because some applications will have varied results when dealing with large files. In testing this method, it has been found that larger databases can create compressed files that cannot be uncompressed without generating errors.

---

**NOTE:** *Test the process from compression through reattachment to assure that there are no problems!*

---

The last item that bears discussion is the database list table. The procedure **usp_DBZip** depends on a reliable source for database information for the data and log files for each database. If a new database is created, **usp_DBZip** automatically adds it to the list of databases being backed up with this method. This feature is intended to make supporting a development environment easier to manage. You can very easily edit the code to back up only the databases in a specific list; for this reason, that approach is not shown in the example. Each environment is different and has unique needs, so take the time to look at this process and edit it to meet your needs. All that is required at this stage is to schedule a job that will run this stored procedure on a nightly basis.

| Related solutions: | Found on page: |
| --- | --- |
| Enterprise Manager | 178 |
| Query Analyzer | 193 |

# Creating Backup Scripts That Will BCP Data Files from the Utility Database to a Network Share

Occasionally, a database administrator or a programmer may need to transfer data from a source server to a standby or development server on a scheduled basis. You could create a DTS package, which is covered in Chapter 7, or you could use a stored procedure that uses the bulk copy program to create text files that can be used as needed to move data between servers or other analysis applications.

Earlier in the "Immediate Solutions" section of this chapter, a stored procedure was created that generated BCP files for an entire database in an easy to use package (stored procedure). The procedure **usp_BCP** can be scheduled as a job and the output path can be specified as a network share that other servers or applications can pull the files from for loading into another server or application. To create a job to export BCP files on a nightly basis, follow these steps.

1. Under the Management node of the Enterprise Manager, expand the tree under the SQL Server Agent.
2. Right-click on the Jobs icon, and select the New Job menu item.
3. In the name text box, fill in a name for this job. For this example, use "Export BCP Files".
4. Select the Steps tab at the top of the dialog.
5. Click on New.
6. In the Step Name box, fill in "Create BCP Files".
7. In the command window, type the following code, substituting your server name and sa password:

```
EXEC usp_BCP 'Utility', NULL, 'C:\temp', 'out', 0,
        <Server Name>, <sa password>
```

**NOTE:** *For security reasons, you may not want to use the password as a parameter in this procedure, but rather hard code the password in the procedure to make this process more secure and prevent publishing the sa password accidentally.*

8. Click on OK to close the Job Step dialog.

9. Select the Schedules tab from the top of the dialog.

10. Click on New Schedule.

11. Fill in a name for this schedule, such as "Utility BCP Schedule".

12. Click on Change to edit the default schedule for this job.

13. Select Daily in the Occurs group.

14. Change the time to 10:00:00 P.M.

15. Click on OK to close the Schedule Editing dialog.

16. Click on OK to close the New Job Schedule dialog.

17. Click on OK to close the Job dialog and create the BCP job on your server.

18. Test the job by running it and making sure the files are created in the correct location.

---

**NOTE:** *This immediate solution depends on having the **usp_BCP** stored procedure in the master database as described in an earlier solution.*

---

| Related solutions: | Found on page: |
|---|---|
| Enterprise Manager | 178 |
| Creating Custom Packages with the DTS Designer | 322 |
| Creating a Login Data File with BCP | 702 |

# Configuring Log Shipping

One of the new features of Microsoft SQL Server 2000 is the native support for log shipping between servers. You could perform a similar operation previously with SQL Server, but the hoops that you had to jump through were many and it was far more difficult to set up than the new solution.

---

**NOTE:** *There appears to be a bug in the wizard that disables the log shipping checkbox if you select a different database once inside the wizard. To work around this problem, select the database you want to configure log shipping for in the Enterprise Manager, and right-click on the target database to select the All Tasks menu option. Then, select the Maintenance Plan menu option to launch the wizard with the database preselected.*

---

Log shipping is easy to configure through the Database Maintenance Plan Wizard. You can create a shipping plan only for a single database through the wizard, and you are not allowed to re-create a log shipping plan for a database that already has a plan in place. You should have a network share that both servers participating in the log shipping operation can read and write files to. (Save yourself some headaches and test this before trying to set this process up.) Both servers must be running SQL Server 2000 Enterprise Edition and be registered in the Enterprise Manager. You can only configure log shipping to write to disk devices and not tape with the wizard interface. Follow these steps to configure log shipping:

1. Open the Database Maintenance Plan Wizard as described previously, and click on Next.

2. Make sure the appropriate database is selected, select the Log Shipping checkbox, and click on Next.

3. Specify the database maintenance options, which were discussed in earlier solutions, that you would like to be performed. Fill out each page of the wizard with the appropriate options until you are presented with the Specify Transaction Log Share page.

4. Fill in the network share name that will hold the shipped transaction logs, and click on Next.

5. Click on Add to add a destination database. (You can add multiple databases.)

6. In the Add Destination Database dialog, select the server you want to ship to. (This list will filter out any non-SQL Server 2000 servers.)

7. Enter the transaction log destination from the previous screen.

8. If the target database does not exist already on the target server, you can select the Create New Database option. It is recommended that the database already exist on the target server before configuring log shipping. You should restore the target database with the STANDBY option. See the "In Depth" section of this chapter for more information on restore syntax.

---

**NOTE:** *You can select a different name for the target database than the one on the source database, so be careful that you do not accidentally overwrite valid data. For report server purposes, you may want to use a different name for clarity.*

---

9. The data and log paths on the destination server will be filled in when you select the target database.

10. Select the Terminate Users checkbox if you want to have the users dropped from the database before the restore operation.

11. Select the Allow To Assume Primary Role checkbox if the target server is being used for disaster recovery. (You must then supply a network share path for the target server's log files to be written to.)

12. Click on OK to add this database.

13. Click on Next and create the log shipping schedule. If the default is not appropriate, select Change to edit the schedule to meet your needs. For this example, use the defaults.

14. Specify the copy and load frequency, the load delay, and file retention periods. The defaults may suit your needs. Refer to the SQL Server Books Online for more information on these options and their impact on performance.

15. Click on Next to set some threshold information.

16. The default values of 45 minutes before generating an alert that there is a problem may be too long, so change both values to 30 minutes.

17. Click on Next.

18. Choose the authentication model you want to use. Use the default for this cxample.

19. Click on Next.

20. The Reports page of the wizard allows you to write reports of the log shipping maintenance plan to a directory for monitoring purposes or to generate an email report to a specified operator if you have SQL Mail running on your server.

---

**NOTE:** *Remember to delete these reports periodically or use the retention options on this page to keep a specific age threshold of reports in the target directory.*

---

21. Click on Next.

22. Specify the history records threshold and/or select a remote server to store the same information. Use the default options for this example, and click on Next.

23. Name the maintenance plan that will be created on the server. Fill in a descriptive name, and click on Next.

24. This is all there is to configuring the log shipping functionality. Click on Finish to start the background tasks that SQL Server will perform to set everything up on each server and schedule the job to run the plan.

| *Related solution:* | *Found on page:* |
| --- | --- |
| Enterprise Manager | 178 |

# Chapter 7

## Data Transformation Services (DTS)

# In Depth

The need to improve corporate decision making in many organizations has led a push to centralize data from numerous sources. This data is likely to be stored in multiple formats and locations throughout the enterprise. DTS is designed to address this critical business need by providing a set of tools to allow you to transform, extract, and consolidate data from multiple sources. The data can be copied to a single or multiple destinations. You can use these tools to create custom data movement solutions that are tailored to the specific needs of your organization. These custom solutions can be created using the graphical tools provided with SQL Server or by using the set of programmable objects that provide access to the same functionality from languages such as C++, Visual Basic (VB), and Delphi.

## Enhancements

Several enhancements have been made to DTS for SQL Server 2000. This section provides information about these enhancements and how they affect the functionality of DTS in SQL Server 2000.

### Support for Keys and Constraints

Support for *keys* and *constraints* has been added to DTS. You can use the Import/Export Wizard to move primary keys, foreign keys, and constraints from the source to the destination in addition to the data being transferred.

### New Custom Tasks

The DTS Object Model and the DTS Designer introduce new custom tasks that can be used to set variables based on the runtime environment or to create packages that perform tasks. You can run packages asynchronously, build packages that send messages to one another, and build packages that execute other packages. You can also import data from and send data and completed packages to Internet and File Transfer Protocol (FTP) sites. These tasks also provide the capability to join multiple package executions as part of a single transaction.

### Saving Packages to Visual Basic Files

Packages created with the Import/Export Wizard or the DTS Designer can now be saved to Visual Basic programs. These programs can be used "as is" or as prototypes for developing applications that need to reference the components in the DTS Object Model. A package created using the Import/Export Wizard or DTS Designer and saved as a VB application can be an excellent starting point for programmers who are not yet familiar with using Visual Basic to create custom DTS packages, and it can also eliminate the need to code the basic functionality of a package before making custom modifications.

# DTS Packages

DTS packages are used to store DTS tasks for reuse. A DTS package consists of connections, tasks, transformations, and workflow constraints. These packages can be created with a DTS tool or programmatically. Packages contain one or more steps that are executed either sequentially or in parallel when the package is run. Packages can also be transferred from one server to another to help automate maintenance tasks. Tools are provided to simplify the creation of basic packages, but custom packages can also be created using the DTS Object Model with programming languages like Microsoft Visual Basic. You can save a package to Microsoft SQL Server 2000, a structured storage file, Microsoft SQL Server 2000 Meta Data Services, or a Microsoft Visual Basic source file. Packages can be edited, retrieved by version, password protected, and scheduled for execution. You can create custom data movement solutions tailored to suit the specific needs of your environment either by using the DTS tools or by programming a package with the DTS Object Model.

# DTS Package Elements

Each DTS package consists of one or more of the following elements: tasks, transformations, workflow, and connections. Each of these elements needs to be studied to understand how they fit together to create a useful package.

## Tasks

Each task is a single step defined within the package. A task defines a single work item to be performed as part of the data movement or transformation or as a job to be executed. A number of tasks are supplied as part of the DTS Object Model and can be accessed programmatically or graphically through the DTS Designer. Each task can be configured individually. The tasks cover a wide variety of transformation, copying, and notification scenarios. Some examples of common tasks are:

- *Copying database objects*—In addition to copying the data, you can also transfer indexes, views, stored procedures, rules, triggers, logins, user-defined data types, constraints, and defaults. You can also generate scripts to copy database objects. If both the source and destination data sources support the necessary OLE DB options, you can copy heterogeneous database objects, such as views and constraints, as well as table structures and data.

- *Data transformation*—You can select the data from a source connection, map the columns to a set of transformations, and send the transformed data to a destination connection. This functionality allows you to transfer data between versions of a database or between product databases with relative ease. This feature can also be used to eliminate inconsistencies in data types between the source and destination.

- *Importing and exporting data*—DTS can be used to import data from text files, Microsoft Access databases, and other sources into SQL Server databases. Data can also be exported to numerous sources, such as a Microsoft Excel spreadsheet. OLE DB provides the interface for both source and destination data.

- *Executing Transact SQL statements or ActiveX scripts*—You can write your own SQL statements and scripting code and execute them as a step in a package workflow. This functionality gives you the flexibility to accomplish almost any needed task as part of a DTS package.

- *Sending and receiving messages*—A Message Queue task allows you to use Microsoft Message Queuing to send and receive messages between packages. An Execute Package task can be used to execute another package as a step in the original package. A Send Mail task sends an email notification of the completion status of the step. This task can also be used to send email notifications of any other appropriate information.

DTS is based on an extensible Component Object Model (COM) model. This means that you can create your own custom tasks, integrate them into the user interfaces of DTS Designer, and save them as part of the DTS Object Model.

## Transformations

DTS transformations provide a powerful way to manage data across your enterprise. Using data transformation, data can be moved from very dissimilar sources into a single data warehouse for easy centralized access. A DTS transformation is one or more operations or functions applied to a piece of data before it reaches its destination. The source data is not changed in a transformation process, only the destination data is actually affected. Transformations can also be used to implement complex data validations, conversions, and data scrubbing during the import process. You can easily change the type, precision, scale, or nullability of a column using a transformation. There are a number of built-in transformation functions supplied with DTS, such as various string manipulation functions. You can also use functions written as ActiveX scripts, or create your own custom transformations as COM objects and apply them against column data.

# Workflow

DTS steps and precedence constraints impose order to the work items in a DTS package. The DTS Designer can be used to graphically design DTS package workflow. This process can also be performed programmatically. In addition, ActiveX scripts can be used to customize step execution.

## Steps

Steps represent the execution units in a DTS package. These steps define the order in which the tasks are executed when the package is run. The DTS Designer does not allow you to work with steps directly. Instead, you use precedence constraints to control the task execution sequence. A step is automatically added to the package for each task. For debugging purposes, the DTS Designer allows you to execute a single step in a package.

The relationship between a step and a task can be controlled more precisely when creating a package programmatically. You can create multiple steps for different operations that are all associated with a single task. For example, you could create a standard task to send an email when an error occurs and have all steps for handling errors refer to your standard task to send a message to the database administrator (DBA).

## Precedence Constraints

Precedence constraints are used to link tasks in a DTS package. There are three types of precedence constraints, which can be accessed either through the DTS Designer or programmatically.

- *Unconditional*—An Unconditional constraint is used to make a task wait for the completion of another task and then run regardless of the outcome of the original task.

- *On Success*—An On Success constraint causes a task to run when the linked task completes successfully. This type of constraint prevents the second task from running unless the first task completes successfully.

- *On Failure*—An On Failure constraint causes the linked task to be run when the original task fails to complete successfully. This can be used to link a task that will notify the DBA when the original task is unable to complete successfully.

Figure 7.1 illustrates how precedence constraints determine step execution. Step 1, Step 2, and Step 3 represent package steps. Step 1 is executed to perform a task such as dropping a table from a database. If Step 1 completes successfully, then Step 2 is launched by the On Success constraint. In the event of a failure running

7. Data Transformation Services (DTS)

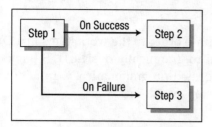

**Figure 7.1 Precedence constraints.**

Step 1, the On Failure constraint launches Step 3, which might notify the DBA or perform some other task depending on the criticality of the original task being performed.

You can issue multiple precedence constraints on a single task. Figure 7.2 shows Step C, which is called by an On Success constraint from Step A and an On Failure constraint from Step B. DTS assumes a logical AND operation for this situation, which means that Step A must complete successfully AND Step B must fail before Step C is executed.

## Connections

As with any other operation, successful completion of a DTS task relies on the ability to make a successful connection to both the source and destination data. Additional connections might also be required for lookup tables, and so on. The architecture used by DTS to make connections is OLE DB, which provides access to a variety of compliant data sources. Some of the currently supported data sources for an OLE DB connection are:

- Microsoft SQL Server
- Microsoft Access
- Oracle
- dBase
- Paradox

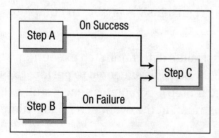

**Figure 7.2 Multiple precedence constraints on a single task.**

- ODBC Data Sources
- Microsoft Excel
- HTML
- Text Files in several formats

You can refer to the Books Online for a list of "OLE DB Providers Tested with SQL Server." This entry provides a chart of the providers that have been tested and any notes about limitations discovered with regard to using each provider.

There are three options for configuring connections in DTS. The first option is a data-source connection. Using a data-source connection requires you to select the OLE DB provider and set the configuration options in the DTS package. As a second option, you can use Microsoft Data Link (.udl) file connections, which are useful for resolving the connection information at runtime. These allow you to handle a situation where the source or destination of a package needs to vary regularly. A custom package can be created to retrieve the necessary information from the user to select the source, destination, or both for a particular run and update the connection file appropriately without having to modify the package. One possible use of a Microsoft Data Link file might be updating multiple test servers in an on-demand fashion with a single DTS package. The third option is a file connection. When connecting to a text file, you must use this option, because you need to specify file format information.

There are a number of considerations that need to be made prior to configuring connections for your DTS package. Connections are single-threaded, so only one DTS task can use a connection at any given time. If you are going to run tasks in parallel, you need to create separate connections for each task. If you plan to run a package on more than one server, you may have to edit the direct connections made in a package. You should consider using Microsoft Data Link connections in this case to allow for modifying the connection to the package externally. Your other option would be to use the Dynamic Properties task to change the connection information at runtime. Another item that needs to be considered for connections is Security. If you configured the connection using Windows Authentication, then the SQL Server Agent login information (rather than the account information you were using when you configured the package) is used to make the connection.

# DTS Tools

Microsoft provides several tools to assist you in working with DTS. These tools implement graphical interfaces to the functionality supported by the DTS Object Model. They also allow the DBA to make use of virtually all of the available DTS features without having to resort to programming. There are some tasks that simply cannot be accomplished without writing a custom application, but most tasks can be accomplished by using the tools provided with Microsoft SQL Server 2000. You should become familiar with these tools and understand their uses and limitations so that you can determine whether or not you need to devise a custom programming solution. Other sections of this chapter present a number of options available for adding custom functionality, which you should become familiar with because they can affect the type of resources needed to complete a particular task.

## DTS Browser

The DTS Browser is accessed from the Enterprise Manager. Under Data Transformation Services, select the Meta Data leaf to run the DTS Browser. The DTS Browser allows you to look at the meta data information and data lineage generated by the DTS Designer. It also allows you to explore the version history and meta data of a package and look up the specific version of a package that generated a particular row of data. This tool makes use of the fact that you can store catalog meta data for databases referenced in a package as well as accounting information about the package-version history of a particular row of data.

## DTS Designer

The DTS Designer allows you to create DTS packages with a wide range of functionality by graphically implementing the DTS Object Model. This is the tool that you can use to create most if not all of the DTS packages you will need for your environment. You can create simple packages or packages that contain complex workflows. This is also the tool that you can use to modify your existing packages to enhance or change functionality. The DTS Designer is accessed from the Enterprise Manager by right-clicking on the Data Transformation Services node in the tree and selecting New Package or Open Package from the context menu.

DTS Designer provides an easy-to-use and intuitive interface for creating and editing packages by displaying available tasks in a pallet. When you select a task, it is automatically dropped in the designer window, and the configuration dialog for that task is launched to allow you to configure the necessary settings for the task. You can modify the configuration options for a task that you previously configured by double-clicking on the task in the designer, which then displays the appropriate dialog again. You can link the tasks by selecting two or more tasks and then choosing the desired constraint type from the Workflow menu. The order in which you select the tasks determines how the constraint is applied to the tasks. You can move the tasks around in the designer to make it easy to follow the general flow of the steps in the package.

The first pallet allows you to set up and configure connections for the package. You can select from the standard connection types and set the configuration options for the connection. Regardless of the type you select from the pallet, you can change the properties of the connection at a later time if you need to.

The second pallet contains the available tasks that you can select to add to your package. When you click on a task in this pallet, it is added to the designer window and you are presented with a dialog that allows you to define the properties for the new task.

Once you have created a package, you have several options for saving it. You can save it to a SQL Server table, SQL Server Meta Data Services, a structured storage file, or a Visual Basic file. Saving the package to a Visual Basic file allows you to use the package created in the designer as a base for creating a custom package programmatically. You may find this option extremely useful to simplify getting the more mundane aspects of the package coded before working on the pieces that you want to customize with VB. This option can also be used to provide you with examples of how various tasks can be performed programmatically with VB and the DTS Object Model.

## Import/Export Wizard

The Import/Export Wizard tool provides the simplest interface for creating packages to copy data between OLE DB data sources. You connect to the source and destination, and then select the data to import or export. You can also use the wizard to apply a wide range of transformations to the data that you are copying. You can copy data that is generated as the result of a query, which will allow you to perform joins on multiple tables to get the information you want to populate a single table on the destination. The wizard automatically creates the destination table for you if it does not exist. You can use ActiveX scripts to transform column level data.

If the source connection supports copying Primary Key and Foreign Key constraints, the wizard automatically copies Primary Key and Foreign Key constraints along with the data being copied. If you are copying data between instances of Microsoft SQL Server 2000 and/or Microsoft SQL Server 7.0, you can also use the wizard to transfer database objects, such as views, referential integrity constraints, indexes, roles, and stored procedures.

After you complete the wizard, you can save the task and scheduling information as a DTS package. This package can be saved in the same formats provided by the DTS Designer. Once you have saved a package using the Import/Export Wizard, you must use the DTS Designer to make any needed changes to the package.

# Managing DTS Packages

This section provides details on the functionality provided with SQL Server 2000 for managing your DTS packages. Package management is broken down into various tasks and the available options for each of these tasks is discussed.

## Creating a Package

DTS Packages can be created graphically by using the Import/Export Wizard or the DTS Designer, or programmatically using the DTS Object Model. Packages created on an instance of SQL Server 2000 cannot be loaded or run on earlier versions of SQL Server.

## Saving a Package

Once you have created a DTS Package, you can save it for reuse in the future. Saving a DTS package saves all connections, tasks, transformations, and workflow elements as well as the graphical layout of these objects in the DTS Designer. You have several options for how and where to save the packages you create.

### Saving to SQL Server

Saving to SQL Server is the default option for saving packages. The package is saved as a table in the msdb database. This option allows you to store packages on any instance of SQL Server on your network, keep an inventory of saved packages in the Enterprise Manager, and create, delete, and branch versions of a package during the development process. This option also allows you to secure the package with one or more passwords.

### Saving to Meta Data Services

Saving to Meta Data Services allows you to maintain historical information about data modifications made by the package. Meta Data Services and the repository database must be installed and operational on your server in order to use this option. It allows you the ability to track the column and table information used for both the source and destination of the package. The package version used to change a particular row can be tracked using the data lineage feature. This type of information can be useful in decision support applications. This option does not support the package security features, but Meta Data Services contains its own security, which can be used to secure the packages.

### Saving to a Structured Storage File

A structured storage file format allows you to maintain multiple packages and multiple package versions in a single file. This option allows you to transfer packages across the network without having to store them in a SQL Server database. It also allows you to secure the package with one or more passwords.

### Saving to a Visual Basic File

Saving the package to a Visual Basic file allows you to programmatically customize a package that was created using the Import/Export Wizard or the DTS Designer. This option generates Visual Basic source code for the package, which can later be opened and modified in your development environment. This option does not provide any security choices for the package. The only way to secure the package with this option is to use some type of source control package such as Microsoft Visual Source Safe to store the Visual Basic code. Most source control packages contain some type of security that can be used to secure the package.

## Editing a Package

A previously created and saved package can be edited in one of two ways. If the package was saved to a Visual Basic file or created programmatically using the DTS Object Model, then the package can only be edited using the appropriate development environment. If any of the other three save options were used, the package can be edited using the DTS Designer.

To edit a package with the DTS Designer, you must have authorization to open the package. If the package was saved with an owner password, you are required to provide this password to edit the package. The user password provides access to execute the package, but not the ability to edit it. If the package is saved to the Meta Data Services, then the DTS password protection is not set. In this case, security is handled through either Windows Authentication or SQL Server Authentication.

## Deleting a Package

Any DTS package can be deleted. The format in which the package was saved dictates the method used to delete the package. If the package was saved to SQL Server or Meta Data Services, you can delete the package through the Enterprise Manager. These formats require you to be either the package creator or a member of the sysadmin fixed server role. If you saved the package to a structured storage file or a Visual Basic file, the package can be deleted using your file manager.

Deleting package versions is also dependent on the method used to save the package. No version information is kept for packages saved as a Visual Basic file unless you are using some type of source control application to save the version information. If you are using a source control application, you have to use that application to delete a version of the Visual Basic source file. If you saved the package to a structured storage file, you cannot delete individual versions of the package; you must delete the entire file. If the package was saved to SQL Server, you can delete any version. For packages saved to the Meta Data Services, you can only delete the most recent version of the package.

**7. Data Transformation Services (DTS)**

## Scheduling Package Execution

DTS packages can be scheduled to execute at specific times either once or at recurring intervals. The SQL Server Agent is responsible for executing the scheduled packages. Because automation for scheduling is handled by the SQL Server Agent, it must be running for any scheduled packages to be executed.

## Executing a Package

When a DTS package is executed, all of its tasks, transformations, and connections are run in the order described by the package workflow. Packages can be executed from the Import/Export Wizard after they are created. The DTS Designer can be used to execute a package that you create or edit. When you run a package using one of these tools, a summary of the execution progress and execution status of each step is displayed. You can check the progress of the execution and see if any steps failed to execute successfully. You can also execute a package from the Data Transformation Services node in the Enterprise Manager. It is not necessary to open a package in order to execute it from the Enterprise Manager.

Packages created programmatically or saved as Visual Basic files must be run using a compiled executable created in the appropriate development environment. The progress and status information for these packages is determined by the application that contains the package. These packages might provide visual summary information or simply write the status information to a log file for later review.

## Using Package Logs

The DTS package log can be used to troubleshoot problems that occurred during the package execution. This log contains information about the success or failure of each step in the package and can be helpful in determining the step at which the failure occurred. The execution information is appended to this log each time the package is run. If the log does not exist, it is created. Information is written to the log about each step in the package whether or not the step is executed. For each step that is executed, the log records the start and end times and the execution time for the step. If a step is not run, the log lists the step and notes that it was not executed.

DTS exception files can also provide useful debugging information. The Data Transformation task and the Data Driven Query task use exception files to save error information about rows that were not successfully copied to the destination. The actual source and destination rows that failed to copy are also stored in these files.

# Managing Package Properties

Package properties can be set or retrieved either graphically or programmatically. Using the DTS Designer, you can monitor or configure the following package properties:

- Errors
- Global Variables
- Transactions
- Package Identification
- Properties related to Microsoft Windows NT and Windows 2000

There is also a feature called Disconnect Edit included in the DTS Designer, which can be used to modify any property in a package. This feature should be used only as a last resort when other methods of modifying the package properties are unavailable. Disconnect Edit can be useful for reconfiguring package connections to enable the package to be run in a new environment.

# Handling Package Security

The issues that affect package access, permissions, and connections should be understood in order to view, edit, execute, and protect DTS packages on your network.

### Package Passwords

Packages saved to SQL Server or a structured storage file can use package passwords. These passwords are in addition to the authentication model used to connect to the SQL Server. There are two types of package passwords: the owner password and the user password. If the owner password is set, it is required to edit or execute the package. If the user password is set, it can be used to execute the package, but the owner password must be used to edit the package. To ensure both package and database security, package passwords are recommended for all packages. Package passwords are especially needed if connection information is saved, and Windows Authentication is not used.

### Scheduling and Security Issues

Packages run from the DTS Designer, the Import/Export Wizard, or from the command prompt, generally use the security context of the user who is currently logged in. When a package is run automatically based on a schedule, the package uses the security context of the SQL Server Agent job that runs the package. The owner of that job may or may not be the user that was logged in when the package was created and tested. For packages created using Windows Authentication, the job runs under the security context of the account used to start the SQL Server Agent. Otherwise, the owner of the job determines the security context. If the owner is a member of the sysadmin role, the job executes under the account used to start the SQL Server agent. If the owner of the job is not a member of the sysadmin role, the job executes under the SQLAgentCmdExec Windows NT user account.

Ownership conflicts can generate a number of problems. Files and paths specified in the package may not be visible or accessible to the new security context. COM components called by the package must exist on the same workstation on which the package is running. Copying all external files used by the package to the same server running the package can help preempt package failures caused by ownership problems. COM components used by a scheduled task must be loaded on the computer on which the instance of SQL Server is installed, and the SQL Server Agent account must have permission to use the objects.

---

**NOTE:** *If you schedule a package with a user password instead of an owner password, the scheduled job does not report a step failure unless the package is set to fail on the first step that fails to execute successfully. The step failure will not be reported because the user does not have permission to read the package status after it is run. This is not a problem if the package is scheduled using the owner password.*

---

### Data Link Files and Security

Microsoft Data Link (.udl) files are unencrypted text files that you can use to provide the connection information for the package. It is strongly recommended that you do not provide password information in the link file because unencrypted files are visible to anyone who opens the file. If you intend to use data link files to provide the connection information, you should consider using Windows Authentication for the connection. Windows Authentication does not require login information to be placed in the link file. This connection method is secure for use in conjunction with the link files.

### Saving Package Security Information

The authentication information used to connect to a data source is saved along with a package by default. To change this behavior, you can use the Persist Security Info option in the Advanced Connection Properties dialog box from the DTS Designer. This option exists only for SQL Server connections. To increase package portability and maintain security, use data link files and Windows Authentication to make package connections.

# Adding Functionality to a Package

There are a number of features included in DTS that provide capabilities for extending DTS packages. In this section, you learn about these features and gain some insight into how they can be used to create the custom packages that will be needed to make your job easier.

# Using ActiveX Scripts

You can use ActiveX scripts that implement the objects in the DTS Object Model to extend the capabilities of your packages. There are three basic types of scripts that you can write for DTS: ActiveX scripts, workflow scripts, and transformation scripts. ActiveX scripts that function as tasks can be written to perform tasks that are not available in the other tasks provided in the DTS Designer. These scripts are run each time the task is called by the package. ActiveX scripts can also be written to act as workflow scripts. Workflow scripts can extend the decision-making process of the workflow to look for specific return codes and activate alternative processing or prevent specific tasks from being run. These scripts are run each time the task to which they are attached is executed. The final type of script is the transformation script. You can write scripts that are used to transform data row by row. These scripts get added to a DTS task that transforms data and are executed once for each row of data processed by the task. Transformation scripts can adversely affect the speed of package execution, so this option should be used carefully if speed is an issue.

ActiveX scripts can be added to a package using the Import/Export Wizard, the DTS Designer, or programmatically. The ActiveX Script Transformation Properties dialog in the DTS Designer is used to define an ActiveX script transformation for a Transform Data task or a Data Driven Query task. An ActiveX Script Task can be added in the DTS Designer by dragging an ActiveX Script Task icon onto the design sheet and adding the script while configuring the task. The Workflow Properties dialog associated with a package step in the DTS Designer can be used to add ActiveX workflow scripts.

ActiveX scripts can make use of a wide range of functionality. You can make use of all Transact-SQL commands and have full access to SQL Server tables. Familiar data access interfaces like ActiveX Data Objects (ADO), Remote Data Objects (RDO), and Data Access Objects (DAO) can be used to make connections and execute SQL commands from your scripts. You can access and make use of any COM objects available on the server running the package including any custom COM objects that you create. You also have full use of the inherent functionality of whichever scripting language you are using. Looping, conditional logic, built-in functions, and other language features are all available and allowable for use in your ActiveX scripts. If you choose a scripting language other than VBScript or JScript, it is important to make sure that the language library for the language you are using is installed on the server that will be running the package.

# Incorporating Transactions

DTS packages use functionality provided by the Microsoft Distributed Transaction Coordinator (MS DTC) to provide the benefits of distributed transactions to the developer. In order to use DTS transactions, the MS DTC must be running on the computer that is executing the package. DTS transactions can be used to:

- Ensure consistent updates by combining the results of several tasks into a single transaction
- Ensure update consistency across multiple database servers
- Provide guaranteed updates in an asynchronous environment by combining database modifications with message queue operations
- Control multiple transactions from a single task

DTS transactions can be managed using the DTS Designer or programmatically. The properties for controlling transaction initiation, step participation, and commit or rollback are found in either package properties or in the workflow properties of a package step. Package settings are global and affect the behavior of the transaction across the entire package, whereas step properties only affect an individual task.

During the execution of a package, transactions are initiated, joined, and either committed or rolled back. Once a transaction is committed or rolled back, this cycle can be repeated. A transaction does not exist for the package until a step attempts to join it. When this happens, a new transaction is created for the package, and the step continues its attempt. If other steps attempt to join a package transaction before the first transaction is either committed or rolled back, they are enlisted into the existing transaction. It is possible to have multiple transactions initiated during the execution of a package, but only one package transaction can be active at any given time. Any workflow script is processed before the attempt to join a transaction. Updates made by a step that joins the package transaction are accumulated in the transaction. If a step is not part of the package transaction, updates are committed one at a time as they are requested.

In order for a step to join a transaction, certain criteria must be met. The step must be one of the several supported task types, and the step must use supported connection types for all outputs. When a step joins a transaction, all connections used by the step are enlisted in the transaction. This means that all updates for the connection, even those that originated from a step that did not explicitly join the transaction, are accumulated in the transaction. This also means that you need two separate connections to allow transactional and nontransactional updates from the same package.

When the package transaction is committed, all accumulated updates to the database are made permanent. If the transaction is rolled back, all accumulated updates are reversed. There are two events that trigger a transaction to be committed. The first event occurs when a step completes successfully with the Commit Transaction On Successful Completion Of This Step option selected. The second event occurs when the package completes successfully and the Commit On Successful Package Completion option is selected. Transaction rollback is also triggered by one of several events. If the package fails, the transaction is rolled back. If the package completes without the Commit Transaction On Successful Completion option selected, the transaction is rolled back. And finally, if a step fails with the Rollback Transaction On Failure option selected, the transaction is rolled back.

It is possible to leave the current transaction in an invalid state. Any attempt to join or commit an invalid transaction causes the package to fail. This state can be caused by situations like failure during a commit or rollback, or rollback occurring in a subpackage. Triggering a rollback in the controlling package terminates the invalid transaction, which allows a new transaction to be started.

## Using Parameterized Queries

Parameterized queries use parameter markers as placeholders for data that changes from one execution to the next in a reusable SQL query. For DTS tasks that use parameterized queries, the syntax for these placeholders is a question mark. The following example shows a parameterized query with the proper syntax for use in a DTS package.

```
INSERT INTO authors (au_lname, au_fname, address, city, state,
                 zip, contract)
         VALUES (?, ?, ?, ?, ?, ?, ?)
```

Lookup queries, which can be used to retrieve information from additional connections, often make use of parameters to control the data being retrieved. Parameterized queries can also be used in Data Driven Query tasks, Execute SQL tasks, and Transform Data tasks. These tasks can make use of parameterized queries as long as the data source that the query is running against supports it. Lookup Queries and Data Driven Query tasks can make use of data from a text file, global variable, or other source data fields as input for a parameterized query. The Execute SQL task and the Transform Data task can use only global variables as inputs for a parameterized query.

## Lookup Queries

Lookup Queries can be used in Data Driven Query tasks and Transform Data tasks. Lookup queries allow you to run queries and stored procedures against a connection other than the source and destination connections. They allow you to make a new connection during a query in order to retrieve additional information to include in the destination table. These queries include execution of a stored procedure or any of the **SELECT**, **INSERT**, **UPDATE**, and **DELETE** commands. This type of query can also be used to facilitate moving some portion of the data into one or more additional destinations other than the original destination connection. The results from a Lookup Query can be loaded into destination columns or used for further script processing. Lookup Queries can be used to perform the following tasks:

- Validate input before loading it into the destination table
- Use global variable values as query input parameters
- Invoke stored procedures depending on certain input conditions
- Look up tabular information from another data source
- Perform parallel updates on more than one database

Lookup Queries can actually share the source or destination connections, but this is not recommended for best performance. Although Lookup Queries can be useful and even necessary in many situations, they result in slower performance than tasks that do not use a Lookup Query. It is generally faster to execute two separate Data Transformation tasks than it is to execute a Lookup Query to update two tables. It is always faster to join two tables from the source connection than it is to look up values from the second table.

## Sharing Meta Data

Features for saving package meta data and information about data lineage to Microsoft SQL Server 2000 Meta Data Services are provided by the DTS Designer. You can store the catalog meta data for databases referenced in a package as well as accounting information about the package version used to modify a particular row of data in your data warehouse. The DTS Information Model is used for structuring and storing this information to the Meta Data Services. The DTS Browser found in the Enterprise Manager can be used to browse the meta data and data lineage information generated by the DTS Designer. You can use the DTS Browser to examine the meta data and version history of a package. This tool also provides a means to look up the specific package version that generated a particular row of data.

The DTS Information Model is based on the Transformation package of the Open Information Model. The DTS Information Model describes the types of data accessed as well as the data transformations and how they are grouped into larger execution units. This model allows the storage of data transformation meta data in one central location, which allows existing transformation to be reused when rebuilding a data warehouse. This central storage of meta data also facilitates sharing data transformation information across multiple tools. It is possible to use tools from multiple vendors sharing this information during the building and maintenance of a data warehouse.

Data Lineage can be tracked at the row level, the column level, or both. Before implementing this feature, you should take the time to design a plan for the information you need to track. There are several factors that should be carefully considered before putting this tracking in place:

- Determine your auditing needs
- Determine the amount of lineage information that can be managed
- Consider the performance impact of this tracking
- Determine whether you need to track changes at the row level, column level, or both

Row-level data lineage can be tracked at the package and row levels of a table to provide a complete audit trail of data transformation and package execution information. Row-level data lineage reveals the source of each piece of data and the transformations applied to it. The information contained in an object associated with this type of lineage contains the package execution Globally Unique Identifiers (GUIDs), the user name and server name for package execution, and the execution time.

Column-level data lineage provides information about a package version, and the tables and columns the package uses as a source or destination. You can check to see if a specific column is used as a source or destination for any package saved in the Meta Data Services. You can also browse packages and package versions that use the column as a source or destination.

# Usage Considerations

There are a number of issues that can arise when performing data conversions and transformations. When implementing DTS, you need to consider driver support, performance requirements, and heterogeneous data sources, among a number of other issues. The following sections provide some information on issues that should be considered as well as some helpful hints.

## Enhancing Performance of DTS Packages

A number of factors can affect the performance of a DTS package. Using ActiveX transformation scripts can be up to four times slower than straight copy operations, depending on the type of transformation and the scripting language used. Using ordinal values for column references is faster than referring to the columns by name. This speed difference is not really significant when the column count is less than 20, but it can become quite significant when the transformation contains many columns. If the scripting language you are using supports named constants, you can use them to maintain code readability without sacrificing performance. You should choose your scripting language carefully. Scripts written with Microsoft VBScript execute about 10 percent faster than the same scripts written with Microsoft JScript, which are approximately 10 percent faster than scripts written in PerlScript.

The data pump is the transformation component of the Data Driven Query task and the Transformation task. It may be possible to enhance the performance of the data pump when the scripting code is complex, when there are numerous transformations, or when there are large amounts of data. In these situations, you should use many-to-many mappings whenever possible. This avoids the need to map a separate transformation function for each column. Performance is increased because the script engine does not need to be invoked for each individual column. The Import/Export Wizard creates packages with many-to-many mappings, but the DTS Designer assigns one-to-one column mappings by default to improve readability. To improve performance, you should consider remapping as many transformations as possible to a many-to-many configuration when using the DTS Designer. The number of transformations generally determines the amount of speed increase that you experience. As with the ordinal values for column selection, you can see a noticeable speed increase when you have over 20 transformations.

The following list contains some other miscellaneous considerations for enhancing the performance of DTS packages:

- The Bulk Insert task creates and executes a Transact-SQL **BULK INSERT** statement, which is faster than Bulk Copy Program (BCP) or the data pump for performing text file import operations. If no transformations are necessary, you can use the Bulk Insert task to achieve as much as double the throughput for these operations.

- When exporting data, BCP can be approximately three to six times faster than DTS copy operations.

- A Transact-SQL query is the fastest method to move data between tables without transformations or validations.

- If your primary task is copying just the database information that has changes, you should consider using SQL Server Replication instead of DTS.

## Driver Support for Heterogeneous Data Types

DTS uses the OLE DB providers and Open Database Connectivity (ODBC) drivers supplied by Microsoft SQL Server 2000 to access heterogeneous data sources. Microsoft Technical Support helps you resolve any problems that you encounter when using the drivers supplied with SQL Server. If you are using other providers or drivers, you should contact the vendor that supplied the driver or provider for support. Table 7.1 lists the supplied drivers and providers for each of the major data sources and indicates whether or not it is supported for use with DTS.

**Table 7.1    OLE DB providers and ODBC drivers supplied with SQL Server.**

| Data Source | Driver or Provider | Supported for Use with DTS |
| --- | --- | --- |
| Oracle 8 | Microsoft ODBC for Oracle version 2.573.3401.00 | Yes |
| Microsoft OLE | DB Provider for Oracle version 2.0010.3401.000 | Yes |
| Microsoft Jet Version 4.0 | Microsoft OLE DB Provider for Jet version 4.0000.2115.0004 | Yes |
| Microsoft Excel Spreadsheet | Microsoft OLE DB Provider for Jet version 4.0000.2115.15 | Yes |
| IBM DB2/MVS | StarSQL 32 version 2.52.0501 | Yes |
| IBM DB2/AS400 | StarSQL 32 version 2.40.0805 | Yes |
| Microsoft Jet Version 3.5 | Microsoft OLE DB Provider for Jet version 4.00.3401.00 | No |

# Programming DTS Applications

This section contains information related to creating custom DTS packages using the Object Model provided by SQL Server 2000. Details about the Object Model and the enhancements made in SQL Server 2000 are covered as well as some specific programming topics to help you make the most of this power feature. The following sections also provide the basic information you need to start writing custom DTS applications as well as to extend the standard DTS Object Model with your own custom objects.

## Extended DTS Objects in SQL Server 2000

SQL Server 2000 provides some extended objects that enhance the objects that were available in SQL Server 7.0. These extended objects are named by appending a 2 to the name of the existing object. The extended objects inherit the properties of the original object and provide some extended functionality. One important consideration when working with these new objects is the fact that they are not compatible with SQL Server 7.0 or earlier servers. If you are programming DTS packages for SQL Server 7.0 servers, you need to use the original objects instead. Be careful when you are programming for earlier versions of SQL Server, because the new extended properties are available through the properties collection of the existing objects when you are working with SQL Server 2000.

## The Object Model

The following list contains the structure of the objects and collections of the DTS Model supplied with SQL Server 2000. There are three additional "submodels" provided, which are Pump Task Elements, Pump Rowset Elements, and Data

Driven Query (DDQ) Elements. Submodels are provided for some of the objects that are used in multiple places to eliminate duplication of this information.

- **Package2** object—This is the parent object of a DTS package. Several extended properties and methods have been added to the Package object to produce this extended object.

- **Package2.Connections** collection—This is a collection of Connection objects that contain information about connections to OLE DB service providers. This collection facilitates connection pooling as well as connection reuse across steps in the package.

- **Package2.Collection2** object—This object contains information about a connection to a data source through an OLE DB service provider.

- **Package2.Collection2.ConnectionProperties** property—This property is used to return a reference to an **OLEDBProperties** collection, which is used to establish the characteristics of a connection.

- **Package2.Collection2.ConnectionProperties.OLEDBProperty** object— These objects are used to set the connection properties for an OLE DB service provider.

- **Package2.GlobalVariables** collection—This collection is a group of GlobalVariable objects that contain information about variants to allow data to be shared across steps and Microsoft ActiveX scripts used in the package.

- **Package2.GlobalVariables.GlobalVariable** object—This object defines a variable that allows data to be shared across steps and Microsoft ActiveX scripts in a DTS package.

- **Package2.SavedPackageInfos** collection—This collection contains a group of **SavedPackageInfo** objects, which contain information about DTS packages saved in files.

- **Package2.SavedPackageInfos.SavedPackageInfo** object—This object contains information about a DTS package stored in a COM-structured storage file. This information is returned by the **GetSavedPackageInfos** method of the Package object.

- **Package2.Steps** collection—This is a group of **Step2** objects that contain information about the execution and flow of the steps within a DTS package.

- **Package2.Steps.Step2** object—This object controls the flow and execution of a task within a DTS package. Each **Step2** object can be associated with a single task, although it is possible to have no task association at all. The order of step execution is determined by the precedence constraints.

- **Package2.Steps.Step2.PrecedenceConstraints** collection—This collection contains a group of **PrecedenceConstraint** objects, which contain information about the conditions that must occur before a step can be released for execution.

- **Package2.Steps.Step2.PrecedenceConstraints.PrecedenceConstraint** object—These objects contain information about the conditions that must occur before a step can be released for execution. The precedence constraints of all step objects control the order in which the steps are executed in the package.

- **Package2.Tasks** collection—This collection contains all the **Task** objects defined in the package.

- **Package2.Tasks.Task** object—This object defines a unit of work to be performed as part of the DTS package.

- **Package2.Tasks.Task.CustomTask** object—This object is an interface that all DTS tasks must implement. It allows programmers to create their own custom tasks, which can be controlled by a DTS package.

- **Package2.Tasks.Task.CustomTask.PackageLog** object—This object allows **CustomTask** or **ActiveScriptTask** objects to write task log records in the database or to write log messages to the log file.

- **Package2.Tasks.Task.CustomTaskUI** object—This object is an interface that allows you to specify a custom dialog for a custom task that can be used in the DTS Designer. If you do not implement a **CustomTaskUI** object for your custom task, the DTS Designer displays a default user interface for the task properties in a simple grid format.

- **Package2.Tasks.Task.PersistPropertyBag** object—This object defines a persistent property storage interface for an object implementing a DTS custom task.

- **Package2.Tasks.Task.PersistPropertyBag.PropertyBag** object—This object defines a name-indexed container for property values for an object implementing a DTS custom task. Use this object as part of a custom task object when the custom task needs to maintain storage for task properties. DTS supports only simple data types, such as string, in a **PropertyBag** object. You cannot use objects or other complex data types as values in a **PropertyBag** container.

- **Package2.Tasks.Task.ActiveScriptTask** object—This object defines a task that is a Microsoft ActiveX script. Because ActiveX scripts do not use the data pump, they do not have access to the Connections collection or DTS source and destination collections. These objects do have full access to the **GlobalVariables** collection, however, which can be used to share information across multiple tasks in the package.

- **Package2.Tasks.Task.BulkInsertTask** object—This object provides the fastest method for copying large amounts of data from a text file to SQL Server. The **BulkInsertTask** object is based on the Transact-SQL **BULK INSERT** statement. Use this task for copying operations and in situations where performance is the most important consideration. This task is not used in conjunction with transformations during data import operations. A **Connection2** object must be used to access the database into which the data is being inserted.

- **Package2.Tasks.Task.CreateProcessTask2** object—This object is used to run a Win32 executable or batch file in the context of a DTS package. It is called the Execute Process Task in the DTS Designer.

- **Package2.Tasks.Task.DataDrivenQueryTask2** object—This object transforms data from a source connection and invokes user-defined queries to write the data to a destination connection. Any sequence of SQL action statements and stored procedure calls can be used for any of the queries. A **DataPumpTransformScript** object returns an indicator that determines which of four parameterized queries is executed on the destination connection. The query parameters are columns from the destination connection. If more than one **DataPumpTransformScript** object returns an indicator, all but the last is overwritten and lost.

- **Package2.Tasks.Task.DataDrivenQueryTask2** Pump Task Elements—See submodel.

- **Package2.Tasks.Task.DataDrivenQueryTask2** Pump Rowset Elements—See submodel.

- **Package2.Tasks.Task.DataDrivenQueryTask2** DDQ Elements—See submodel.

- **Package2.Tasks.Task.DataPumpTask2** object—This object is used to import, export, and transform data between heterogeneous data sources. The DataPumpTask2 object makes the features of the data pump available as a DTS task.

- **Package2.Tasks.Task.DataPumpTask2** Pump Task Elements—See submodel.

- **Package2.Tasks.Task.DataPumpTask2** Pump Rowset Elements—See submodel.

- **Package2.Tasks.Task.DTSFTPTask** object—This object is used to transfer one or more files from an Internet FTP site or network path to a specified destination directory.

- **Package2.Tasks.Task.DTSMessageQueueTask** object—This object is used to send and receive messages to and from a queue of Message Queuing. It allows participation in a distributed transaction when the MS DTC is running. A single instance of the **DTSMessageQueueTask** either sends one or more messages to a specified queue or receives a single message from a specified queue, waiting, if necessary, for the message to arrive.

- **Package2.Tasks.Task.DTSMessageQueueTask.DTSMQMessages** collection—This is a collection of **DTSMQMessage** objects that contain the messages to be sent by the **DTSMessageQueTask** object.

- **Package2.Tasks.Task.DTSMessageQueueTask.DTSMQMessages. DTSMQMessage** object—This object is used to define a message to be sent by the **DTSMessageQueTask** object.

- **Package2.Tasks.Task.DynamicPropertiesTask** object—This object is used to change the values of package properties at runtime. This is especially useful for packages created in the DTS Designer or using the Import/Export Wizard, because some properties may not be known at design time.

- **Package2.Tasks.Task.DynamicPropertiesTask. DynamicPropertiesTaskAssignments** collection—This collection contains the **DynamicPropertiesTaskAssignment** objects that define the source of the new value and the properties to be changed by a **DynamicPropertiesTask** object.

- **Package2.Tasks.Task.DynamicPropertiesTask. DynamicPropertiesTaskAssignments.DynamicPropertiesTaskAssignment** object—This object holds the definition of a single package object property to be modified by a **DynamicPropertiesTask** object and the source of the new property value.

- **Package2.Tasks.Task.ExecutePackageTask** object—This object is used to run another DTS package. If the MS DTC is running, steps in child packages can join the transactions of parent packages.

- **Package2.Tasks.Task.ExecutePackageTask.GlobalVariables** collection—Global variables can be passed to the target package in an **ExecutePackageTask**. For each such global variable, a **GlobalVariable** object, which defines the name of the variable and value, is added to the **GlobalVariables** collection of the **ExecutePackageTask** object. Use the **InputGlobalVariableNames** property to specify members of the parent package **GlobalVariables** collection that are to be created or set in the child package.

- **Package2.Tasks.Task.ExecutePackageTask.GlobalVariables.Global Variable** object—This object defines a variable that allows data to be shared across steps and Microsoft ActiveX scripts in a DTS package.

- **Package2.Tasks.Task.ExecuteSQLTask2** object—This object allows you to execute a sequence of one or more SQL statements on a connection.

- **Package2.Tasks.Task.ExecuteSQLTask2.CommandProperties** property—This property returns a reference to an **OLEDBProperties** collection, which contains an **OLEDBProperty** object for each OLE DB command property for the connection.

- **Package2.Tasks.Task.ExecuteSQLTask2.CommandProperties. OLEDBProperty** object—These objects are used to set the connection properties for an OLE DB service provider.

- **Package2.Tasks.Task.ParallelDataPumpTask** object—This object is used to copy and transform data from source to destination rowsets. It performs the same functions as the **DataPumpTask2** and **DataDrivenQueryTask2** except that it also copies and transforms hierarchical rowsets.

- **Package2.Tasks.Task.ParallelDataPumpTask** Pump Task Elements—See submodel.

- **Package2.Tasks.Task.ParallelDataPumpTask.TransformationSets** collection—This collection contains the **TransformationSet** objects that define the transformations to be performed by a **ParallelDataPumpTask** object on the columns of a component rowset in a hierarchical rowset.

- **Package2.Tasks.Task.ParallelDataPumpTask.TransformationSets. TransformationSet** object—This object defines the transformations to be performed by a **ParallelDataPumpTask** object on the columns of a component rowset in a hierarchical rowset.

- **Package2.Tasks.Task.ParallelDataPumpTask.TransformationSets. TransformationSet** Pump Rowset Elements—See submodel.

- **Package2.Tasks.Task.ParallelDataPumpTask.TransformationSets. TransformationSet** DDQ Elements—See submodel.

- **Package2.Tasks.Task.SendMailTask** object—This object lets you send an email as a DTS task. For example, if you want to notify the DBA about the success or failure of a particular task (such as a backup), you can link a **SendMailTask** with a precedence constraint to the previous task. To use a **SendMailTask**, the computer must have the Microsoft messaging Application Programming Interface (API) installed and configured with a valid user profile. A **SendMailTask** can include attached data files. You can point to a location for an attached file to send a dynamically updated file rather than a static copy of the file fixed when you create the task. This feature is useful for sending attachments, such as log and exception files, which contain information that changes constantly and for which the file may not exist when the package is created. If the attachment file does not exist when the package is run, you may receive an error message. This message can also be received if the package does not have rights to access the specified file.

- **Package2.Tasks.Task.TransferObjectsTask2** object—This task is used to transfer objects between instances of Microsoft SQL Server.

### Pump Task Elements

The following list describes the objects that make up the Pump Task Elements submodel:

- **DestinationCommandProperties** property—This property references an **OLEDBProperties** collection whose elements define the properties of the destination connection OLE DB provider.

- **DestinationCommandProperties.OLEDBProperty** object—These objects are used to set the connection properties for an OLE DB service provider.

- **SourceCommandProperties** property—This property references an **OLEDBProperties** collection, which contains the properties of the OLE DB provider used by the source connection.

- **SourceCommandProperties.OLEDBProperty** object—These objects are used to set the connection properties for an OLE DB service provider.

### Pump Rowset Elements

The following list describes the objects that make up the Pump Rowset Elements submodel:

- **DestinationColumnDefinitions** property—This property returns a reference to a **Columns** collection that contains the column definitions for a **DataPumpTask2**, **DataDrivenQueryTask2**, or **ParallelDataPumpTask** destination connection.

- **DestinationColumnDefinitions.Column** object—This object contains information about a destination column. If no destination columns are specified for a transformation, then all columns are implied by default.

- **Lookups** collection—This collection is a group of **Lookup** object definitions. In a Microsoft ActiveX script, the lookup should be referenced with the **Execute** method of an element of the **Lookups** collection. If the lookup rowset has more than one column, the **Execute** method returns a Variant array. The script may need to iterate through the array to use multiple values.

- **Lookups.Lookup** object—This object allows a data pump consumer to specify one or more named parameterized query strings that allow a transformation to retrieve data from locations other than the row being transformed. For example, a **Lookup** object might reference data in a Microsoft Excel worksheet.

**7. Data Transformation Services (DTS)**

- **Transformations** collection—This collection is a group of **Transformation2** objects that specifies the collection of transformations that transfer data from the data source to the data destination.

- **Transformations.Transformation2** object—This object contains information about the class specific transformation object and the source and destination columns it manipulates.

- **Transformations.Transformation2.DataPumpTransformCopy** object—This object converts a source column to the destination column data type and moves the data to the destination column. **DataPumpTransformCopy** supports multiple source and destination columns. It is possible to truncate the destination by setting **DTSTransformFlag_AllowStringTruncation** in the **TransformFlags** property of the **Transformation2** object. There are no transformation properties.

- **Transformations.Transformation2.DataPumpTransformDateTime String** object—This object is used to convert a datetime string in one format to another datetime format. It requires one source and one destination column, both of which must have data types compatible with the OLE DB data type **DBTIMESTAMP**. The transformation properties **InputFormat** and **OutputFormat** are used to specify the formats of the source and destination columns, respectively.

- **Transformations.Transformation2.DataPumpTransformLowerString** object—This object converts a source column to lowercase characters and, if necessary, to the destination column data type. It requires source and destination columns to be of string data types (**char**, **varchar**, **text**, **nchar**, **nvarchar**, **ntext**, and **flat file strings**).

- **Transformations.Transformation2.DataPumpTransformMidString** object—This object extracts a substring from the source column and converts it, if necessary, to the destination column data type. This object requires one source column and one destination column, both of a string data type. The properties **CharacterStart** and **CharacterCount** specify the position of the substring. Optionally, the transformation converts the extracted substring to uppercase or lowercase characters, as specified by the **UpperCaseString** and **LowerCaseString** properties. This object also optionally trims white space characters, as specified by the **TrimLeadingWhiteSpace**, **Trim TrailingWhiteSpace**, and **TrimEmbeddedWhiteSpace** properties. It is important to note that substring extraction occurs before the trimming of white space characters.

- **Transformations.Transformation2.DataPumpTransformReadFile** object—This object copies the contents of a file, the name of which is specified by a source column, to a destination column. Data conversion is controlled by the **OEMFile** and **UnicodeFile** properties. If the file named by the source column contains the Unicode prefix bytes (hex FFFE), the file is assumed to be Unicode regardless of the value of **UnicodeFile**, and the prefix bytes are skipped. If the file name column contains a path, it can use either a drive letter or a Universal Naming Convention (UNC) file specification. If no path is present, the **FilePath** property can be used to supply the path. Note that the **FilePath** is always used when it is specified, even if the file name column contains a path.

- **Transformations.Transformation2.DataPumpTransformScript** object—This object transforms source columns and moves data to the destination columns using a Microsoft ActiveX script. Columns can be transformed in any way supported by the scripting language. Valid script languages available on a particular system can be determined by enumerating the **ScriptingLanguageInfos** collection of the **Application** object. This object supports properties that are used to specify the script text, scripting language, and entry point name.

- **Transformations.Transformation2.DataPumpTransformTrimString** object—This object converts the source column to uppercase or lowercase characters, as specified by the **UpperCaseString** and **LowerCaseString** properties. It trims white space characters, as specified by the **TrimLeadingWhiteSpace**, **TrimTrailingWhiteSpace**, and **TrimEmbeddedWhiteSpace** properties. If necessary, it converts the data to the destination column data type. It requires one source column and one destination column, both of a string data type.

- **Transformations.Transformation2.DataPumpTransformUpperString** object—This object converts a source column to uppercase characters and, if necessary, to the destination column data type. It requires source and destination columns to be of string data types.

- **Transformations.Transformation2.DataPumpTransformWriteFile** object—This object converts a field from one source column into a file, the path of which is specified by another source column. Columns in the destination connection of the task are not written, although the connection must exist. Data conversion is controlled by the **OEMFile** and **UnicodeFile** properties. If **UnicodeFile** is set to **TRUE**, the Unicode file header (hex FFFE) is added to the beginning of the file, if it is not already there. The default behavior is to overwrite the destination file if it already exists. The data column must be a string or binary data type. If the column data is **NULL**, no file is written. If **AppendIfFileExists** is set to **FALSE** and the file exists, it is deleted. If the file is empty, a zero length file is created. The file name column cannot be **NULL** or empty. If the file name column contains a path, it can use either a drive letter or a UNC file specification. If no path is present, the **FilePath** property can be used to supply the path. Note that the **FilePath** is always used when it is specified, even if the file name column contains a path.

- **Transformations.Transformation2.DestinationColumns** property—This property returns a reference to a **Columns** collection that contains the definitions for the columns to which the transformation writes data.

- **Transformations.Transformation2.DestinationColumns.Column** object—This object contains information about a destination column. If no destination columns are specified for a transformation, then all columns are implied by default.

- **Transformations.Transformation2.SourceColumns** property—This property returns a reference to a **Columns** collection that contains the definitions for the columns from which the transformation reads data.

- **Transformations.Transformation2.SourceColumns.Column** object— This object contains information about a source column. If no source columns are specified for a transformation, then all columns are implied by default.

- **Transformations.Transformation2.TransformServerProperties** property—This property returns a reference to a **Properties** collection containing the properties of the **TransformServer** object.

- **Transformations.Transformation2.TransformServerProperties. Property** object—This object exposes the attributes of a DTS object property.

- **Transformations.Transformation2.TransformServer** property—This property returns a reference to the **TransformServer** object through which the properties of that object can be accessed directly.

### DDQ Elements

The following list describes the objects that make up the DDQ Elements submodel:

- **DeleteQueryColumns** property—This property returns a reference to a collection of columns whose values are to be placed into parameters, in sequential order, for the **DeleteQuery** property.

- **DeleteQueryColumns.Column** object—This object contains information about a Data Driven Query parameter.

- **InsertQueryColumns** property—This property returns a reference to a collection of columns whose values are to be placed into parameters, in sequential order, for the **InsertQuery** property.

- **InsertQueryColumns.Column** object—This object contains information about a Data Driven Query parameter.

- **UpdateQueryColumns** property—This property returns a reference to a collection of columns whose values are to be placed into parameters, in sequential order, for the **UpdateQuery** property.

- **UpdateQueryColumns.Column** object—This object contains information about a Data Driven Query parameter.

- **UserQueryColumns** property—This property returns a reference to a collection of columns whose values are to be placed into parameters, in sequential order, for the **UserQuery** property.

- **UserQueryColumns.Column** object—This object contains information about a Data Driven Query parameter.

## Using the Object Model

Any programming language that supports COM objects can be used to create DTS packages with the object hierarchy described in the previous section. After creating the objects and setting their properties, you can invoke the methods of the **Package2** object to run your package. The following sections summarize building DTS packages and using the DTS objects and features without regard to a specific programming language.

### Creating Package Objects

The **Package2** object is the base object for working with the DTS object hierarchy. You need to begin by creating one of these objects. The method used to create the **Package2** object depends on your programming environment. You then need to add one or more **Connection2** objects to enable the package to access databases and other data sources.

### Creating Connections

Normally, you create a **Connection2** object for each data source you want to access, although it is possible to reuse the **Connection2** objects. You need an OLE DB provider for the data source you want to access. You use the **New** method of the **Connections** collection of the **Package2** object to create a **Connection2** object, and then set the properties as needed. You then use the **Add** method of the **Connections** collection to add the connection to the collection. Properties unique to the specific OLE DB provider you are using can be referenced through the **ConnectionProperties** collection of the **Connection2** object.

### Creating Package Workflow and Tasks

DTS package workflow is implemented by creating steps. Steps are the units of functionality within the package. Precedence relationships are created between steps to determine the sequence in which the steps are executed. Tasks are the components the steps use to perform their functions.

You need to create a **Step2** object for each operation the package is to perform. You create a Task object of the appropriate type for each step. The Task object actually performs the work for the step. To create a **Step2** object, use the **New** method of the **Steps** collection of the **Package2** object, and then set the **TaskName** property of the Step object to the name of the associated task. Next, use the **Add** method of the **Steps** collection of the **Step2** object to add the step to the collection.

When a package is executed, DTS attempts to execute steps in parallel up to the limit established by the **MaxConcurrentSteps** property of the **Package2** object. You alter this behavior by using precedence constraints to order the steps. A **PrecedenceConstraint** object is used to inhibit the step with which it is associated from starting execution until an event by another named step occurs. If precedence constraints are used, a step begins execution only when all of its precedence constraints have been satisfied.

Use the **New** method of the **PrecedenceConstraints** collection of the Step object to create a **PrecedenceConstraint** object. Then, set its **StepName** property to the name of the preceding task, and set the **PrecedenceBasis** and **Value** properties to specify the type of event. Use the **Add** method of the **Precedence-Constraints** collection of the associated Step object to add the **Precedence-Constraint** to the collection.

To implement a DTS task, you need to create a generic Task object and a Task object specific to the task class being created. Use the **New** method of the **Tasks** collection of the **Package2** object to create both of these objects. Configure the properties of these objects according to the processing you want them to perform. The elements of the generic Task object manipulate information generic to all tasks, and those of the class specific Task object manipulate information unique to the class. The **CustomTask** property of the Task object returns a reference to the class specific Task object. The Properties collection of the generic Task object can also be used to reference the properties of the class specific Task object. Use the **Add** method of the **Tasks** collection of the **Package2** object to add each Task object to the collection.

### Adding Transformations

The data pump uses DTS transformations to perform various operations that you specify. The data pump is the engine used by the **DataPumpTask2**, **DataDriven-QueryTask2**, and **ParallelDataPumpTask** objects. Transformations are implemented as callbacks from the data pump. Task classes that do not host the data pump, do not use transformations.

The data pump fetches data rows from a source connection and writes data rows to a destination connection. Table 7.2 describes the phases of the data pump operations for which transformations can be specified. These phases are listed in the order in which they are invoked by the data pump.

In the case of the **ParallelDataPumpTask**, the PreSourceData and Post SourceData phases occur at the beginning and end of each rowset of the hierarchical rowset, but the OnPumpComplete phase occurs only once.

The **DTSTransformScriptProperties2** transformation can support multiple phases by providing a script function for each supported phase. **DTSTransform**

**Table 7.2    Data pump operation phases.**

| Phase | Description | Possible Uses |
|---|---|---|
| PreSourceData | Occurs before the first row is fetched from the source connection. | Writing header records to the destination or initializing objects, connections, or memory for use in later phases. |
| Transform | Occurs after each source row is read, but before the destination row is written. | Conversion and validation of data columns. |
| OnTransformFailure | Occurs after a failure in the Transform phase and is indicated by the return of DTS_TransformStat_Error or DTS_TransformStat_ExceptionRow. This is typically caused by conversion errors. | Handling custom data based on the Transform failure. |
| OnInsertSuccess | Occurs after each row is successfully written to the destination connection. | Maintaining aggregation when this function cannot be done by a transform phase transformation. |
| OnInsertFailure | Occurs after each failed attempt to write a row to the destination connection. | Handling custom data based on the insert failure, like writing error log information to a table. |
| OnBatchComplete | Occurs in DataPumpTask2 after each batch is written using the FastLoad option whether or not the batch was successful. | Recording the current position within the source rowset to allow for restarting the task at this point if needed. |
| PostSourceData | Occurs after the last row is written to the destination connection. | Writing trailer records, freeing up resources, or committing data held in global variables. |
| OnPumpComplete | Occurs at the end of the task execution. | Freeing up resources or committing data held in global variables. |

**ScriptProperties2** transformations or custom transformations must be used for transformations on phases other than Transform.

At least one transformation is required for the Transform phase. Transformations for the other phases are optional. When multiple transformations are supplied for a phase, they are executed in the order the **Transformation2** objects were added to the Transformations collection.

To implement a transformation, you need a generic **Transformation2** object and a **TransformServer** object. The **TransformServer** object is specific to the transformation class. To create both of these objects, use the **New** method of the Transformations collection of the **DataPumpTask2**, **DataDrivenQueryTask2**, or the **TransformationSet** object of the **ParallelDataPumpTask**.

To access the **TransformServer** object, use the **TransformServer** property of the **Transformation2** object to return a reference to the object. The properties of the **TransformServer** object also can be referenced through the **Transform-ServerProperties** collection of the generic **Transformation2** object. Set the **TransformPhases** property of the **Transformation2** object to the sum of the codes from **DTSTransformPhaseEnum** for the phases it is to support. Use the **Add** method of the **Transformations** collection to add the **Transformation2** object to the collection.

### Adding Column Objects

You create **Column** objects to specify the source and destination columns referenced by a transformation. These objects are also used to specify the destination column parameters for the queries of the **DataDrivenQueryTask2** object. Typically, transformations reference columns of the source and destination connections.

To create a **Column** object, use the **New** method of the **SourceColumns** or **DestinationColumns** collections of the **Transformation2** object. Set properties as appropriate, and then use the **Add** method of the appropriate collection. You can use the **AddColumn** method of the collection to create and add the column in a single step.

If the following conditions are met, you do not need to define column objects:

- Only a single **Transformation2** object has been defined for the task.
- The number of columns in the source and destination tables is the same.
- The source and destination tables have the same column ordering.

Table 7.3 shows the access permitted on the column based on the phase in which it is run. This information helps you determine the appropriate types of actions that can be performed on the data for each phase.

**Table 7.3   Column accessibility by data pump operation phase.**

| Data Pump Operation Phase | Source Column Access | Destination Column Access |
|---|---|---|
| PreSourceData | Read access to meta data | Write access to columns |
| Transform | Read access to columns | Write access to columns |
| OnTransformFailure | Read access to columns | Write access to columns |
| OnInsertSuccess | Read access to columns | No access to columns |
| OnInsertFailure | Read access to columns | No access to columns |
| OnBatchComplete | Read access to meta data | Write access to columns |
| PostSourceData | Read access to meta data | Write access to columns |
| OnPumpComplete | No access to columns | No access to columns |

To assign destination column parameters to the **DataDrivenQueryTask2** and **ParallelDataPumpTask** object queries, use the same procedure to create Column objects, and then add them to the **DeleteQueryColumns**, **InsertQuery Columns**, **UpdateQueryColumns**, or **UserQueryColumns** collections as appropriate.

### Adding Lookups

**Lookup** objects are used when you need a transformation to look up data in another query rowset through a separate connection. To create a **Lookup** object, use the **New** method of the **Lookups** collection of a class-specific Task object that uses transformations, set the appropriate properties, and then use the **Add** method of the **Lookups** collection to add the **Lookup** object to the collection. You can also create and add the **Lookup** object to the **Lookups** collection in a single step using the **AddLookup** method.

You access the lookup in the script of a **DataPumpTransformScript** or **DTSTransformScriptProperties2** object through the **Execute** method of a **DTSLookup** object. The **DTSLookup** object is the DTS Scripting Object Model counterpart of the **Lookup** object. Usually, you refer to the lookup by name from the **DTSLookups** collection.

### Adding Global Variables

Global variables provide a means for tasks within a package to exchange data. When using the **ExecutePackageTask** object, global variables also provide a means for tasks to exchange data between packages. To create a global variable in a DTS package prior to package execution, use the **New** method of the **Package2** object **GlobalVariables** collection, set the **Value** property, and then **Add** the object to the collection. The **AddGlobalVariable** method of the **Global Variables** collection can be used to create and add the new **GlobalVariable** in one step.

You need to create **GlobalVariable** objects before package execution if the **ExplicitGlobalVariables** property of the **Package2** object is set to **TRUE**. If **ExplicitGlobalVariables** is set to **FALSE**, however, you do not need to create **GlobalVariable** objects, and the package will automatically create global variables that do not exist at their first reference.

You can create and assign values to global variables in the **ExecuteSQLTask2** object. Specify a list of global variable names with the **OutputGlobalVariable Names** property. Values from the first row of the rowset generated by the **ExecuteSQLTask2** query are stored in the named global variables. Set the **OutputAsRecordset** property to store the entire rowset as a disconnected ADO recordset in the global variable named first in the list.

You can also use global variables as input parameters for the queries of the **Data DrivenQueryTask2**, **DataPumpTask2**, **ExecuteSQLTask2**, and **ParallelData PumpTask** objects. Specify a list of global variable names with the **InputGlobal VariableNames** property.

In order to transfer the information contained in **GlobalVariables** from a parent package to a child package, you must create and add global variables, as previously described, to the **GlobalVariables** collection of the **ExecutePackageTask** object. This allows you to export these global variables to the target package. These global variables are independent of the global variables in the **Global Variables** collection of the calling package. Use the **InputGlobalVariableNames** property of **ExecutePackageTask** to specify global variables from the collection that are to be exported.

### Adding ActiveX Scripts

Microsoft ActiveX scripts can be used to add functionality to DTS packages. Typical supported scripts are Microsoft VBScript, Microsoft JScript, PerlScript, and XMLScript. The **Step2** object can use an ActiveX script, which runs before the step's task executes. The **ActiveScriptTask** object requires an ActiveX script to perform the functionality of the task. The **DataPumpTransformScript** and **DTSTransformScriptProperties2** transformation objects require ActiveX scripts that perform the transformations. The ActiveX scripts are assigned as a single text string to a property of the objects that use scripts. This string can include embedded carriage return/line feed pairs. Each scripted object also has properties for the script language and the script function name.

The **DTSTransformScriptProperties2** object extends the functionality of **DataPumpTransformScript** by providing multiple transformation phases. The script specified by the **Text** property must have a function for each supported phase. Table 7.4 lists the property you use to specify the entry point for each phase supported by the **DTSTransformScriptProperties2**.

### Adding Query Strings

Many DTS tasks and objects require queries to access or store database information. Queries are assigned as a text string to a property of the object that uses the query. You can also include carriage return/line feed pairs in the string. Depending on the parent object, you can define query sequences and parameter placeholders for the query. Table 7.5 describes the types of queries supported for the objects that use queries.

### Handling Events

The **Package2** object raises events to report the package status during execution. If you implement handlers for any of the events, you must supply handlers for all the events. If you do not need a specific event handler, the code for the

**Table 7.4   Function entry points for data pump operation phases.**

| Data Pump Operation Phase | Function Entry Point Property |
|---|---|
| PreSourceData | **PreSourceDataFunctionEntry** |
| Transform | **FunctionEntry** |
| OnTransformFailure | **TransformFailureFunctionEntry** |
| OnInsertSuccess | **InsertSuccessFunctionEntry** |
| OnInsertFailure | **InsertFailureFunctionEntry** |
| OnBatchComplete | **BatchCompleteFunctionEntry** |
| PostSourceData | **PostSourceDataFunctionEntry** |
| OnPumpComplete | **PumpCompleteFunctionEntry** |

**Table 7.5   Query types supported by objects.**

| Object | Query Type | Query String Attributes |
|---|---|---|
| **DataPumpTask2**, **DataDrivenQueryTask2**, and **ParallelDataPumpTask** | Source Query | Must be a single select or stored procedure that returns a rowset and can use the **?** placeholder for global variable parameters defined in the **InputGlobalVariableNames** property. |
| **DataPumpTask2**, **DataDrivenQueryTask2**, and **ParallelDataPumpTask** | Destination Query | Must be a single select or stored procedure that returns a rowset. Parameters are not supported. |
| **DynamicPropertiesTask-Assignment** object of the **DynamicPropertiesTask** | Property Value Query | Must be a single select or stored procedure that returns a rowset consisting of a single row and only one column. |
| **ExecuteSQLTask2** | ExecutedQuery | Sequence of one or more SQL statements or stored procedures, which can be separated by the Transact SQL **GO** statement and can use the **?** placeholder for global variable parameters defined in the **InputGlobalVariableNames** property. |
| **DataDrivenQueryTask2** and **TransformationSet** objects of the **ParallelDataPumpTask** | Action Queries | Sequence of one or more SQL statements or stored procedures, which cannot be separated by the Transact-SQL **GO** statement, but can use the **?** placeholder for global variable parameters defined in the **InputGlobalVariableNames** property. |
| **Lookup** | Lookup Query | Must be a single select or stored procedure that returns a rowset and can use the **?** placeholder for parameters specified with the **Execute** method of the **DTSLookups** scripting collection. |

7. Data Transformation
Services (DTS)

event handler can consist of a single statement that simply exits the callback function called by the event. Table 7.6 lists the events that can be raised by the **Package2** object, the condition that causes the event to be raised, and the information returned to the application by the event.

### Handling Errors

Good programming practice requires your application to handle any errors that are raised by the **Package2** object's **Execute** method. During the phase of your program where you are creating DTS objects and setting their properties, you should implement error handling that is typical for your programming environment. Errors that occur during the **Execute** method of the **Package2** object are not sent back to the caller unless you set the **Package2** object **FailOnError** property or the **Step2** object **FailPackageOnError** property to **TRUE**. **FailPackageOnError** causes an error in the referenced step to fail the package, whereas **FailOnError** causes an error in any step to fail the package.

You must retrieve errors that occur within individual steps with the **GetExecutionErrorInfo** method of the **Step2** object. **GetExecutionErrorInfo** provides information only about errors that cause a step to fail. For more detailed information, you must implement handlers for the **OnError** and **OnProgress** events, which require you to provide at least stub handlers for the other events. The **OnError** event describes the error, whereas the **OnProgress** event indicates the step and the row being processed. The **ProgressRowCount** property of the **DataPumpTask2**, **DataDrivenQueryTask2**, and **TransformationSet** objects can be used to specify how frequently **OnProgress** is raised.

### Managing Package Programs

Once you have created a package programmatically, you have two basic options. You can either run the configured **Package2** object or save it in one of several formats. You also have the ability to load a saved DTS package into a **Package2** object in your application. After you have created the hierarchy of DTS objects

**Table 7.6   Package events.**

| Event | Condition | Information Returned |
|---|---|---|
| **OnStart** | A step has started. | Step Name |
| **OnQueryCancel** | Gives the application a chance to cancel the step. | Step Name |
| **OnProgress** | Occurs periodically during step execution. | Step Name, Progress Count (usually row count), Percent Complete, Description |
| **OnFinish** | A step has completed. | Step Name |
| **OnError** | An error occurred during package execution. | Step Name, Error Code, Error Description, Help File, Help Context, Interface ID |

and have set their properties as needed, use the **Execute** method of the **Package2** object to execute the package. Use the methods described in the previous two sections to handle any errors and events generated by the package during its execution. If you plan to do anything further with the **Package2** object after execution has completed, you need to release all references to other DTS objects, and then call the **UnInitialize** method before proceeding.

You can save the package you created as a project in your current development environment, or you have the option to save it in the formats in which DTS tools save packages. Table 7.7 provides a list of the methods of the **Package2** object that can be used to save a package. To load a **Package2** object with the state of a previously saved package, you can use the **LoadFromSQLServer**, **LoadFrom Repository**, or **LoadFromStorageFile** methods. Saved packages can be deleted by using the **RemoveFromSQLServer** and **RemoveFromRepository** methods.

### Retrieving DTS System, Package, and Log Data

DTS provides features for requesting information about registered components and saved packages as well as retrieving the contents of log records. The **Application** object provides access to the system, package, and log data, as well as allowing for versioning. This object is created independently of a DTS package. You can use the collections of the Application object to obtain information about several different types of registered components used by DTS.

Normally, DTS must scan all the registered classes in the operating system Registry to determine the membership of each of these collections, which can take a significant amount of time. However, DTS also maintains a cache of each component type in the operating system Registry. You can use the **Refresh** method of these collections to update the cache for that component from a full Registry scan. Set the **UseCache** property before iterating through the collection to initiate a scan of the cache rather than the system Registry.

DTS packages can be saved to an instance of SQL Server 2000 Meta Data Services. These packages have lineage information saved for them if the **LineageOptions**

**Table 7.7   Package2 object package save methods.**

| Methods | Description |
|---|---|
| **SaveToRepository, SaveToSQLServer, SaveToStorageFile** | Saves the package using the specified storage type. |
| **SaveToRepositoryAs, SaveToSQLServerAs, SaveToStorageFileAs** | Assigns a new name and Package ID to the package and saves it using the specified storage type. |
| **SaveAs** | Assigns a new name and Package ID to the package, but does not actually save it to storage. |

property of the package specifies this to be done. A package lineage record is generated each time a package is executed, and a step lineage record is generated for the execution of each step.

Use the **GetPackageRepository** method, specifying the server, database, and login information to return a **PackageRepository** object. This object provides access to an instance of Meta Data Services. The following methods of the **PackageRepository** object are used to return package and lineage information:

- The **EnumPackageInfos** method returns a **PackageInfos** collection with information about all or a subset of the packages saved in the Meta Data Services instance.

- The **EnumPackageLineages** method returns a **PackageLineages** collection with lineage data for a particular package version.

- The **EnumStepLineages** method returns a **StepLineages** collection with step lineage data for a particular package lineage.

- The **RemovePackageLineages** method can be used to remove some or all of the lineage data for a package version.

All DTS packages have the capability to log to an instance of SQL Server. Log records are written to the msdb database on the server specified by the package **LogServerName** property. A package log record is written by DTS for each package execution, and a step log record is written for the execution of each step each time a DTS package is executed if the package **LogToSQLServer** property has been set. Use the **PackageLog** object methods when custom tasks and **ActiveScriptTask** objects need to write task log records. A reference to **PackageLog** is passed as a parameter of the task's **Execute** method. In task ActiveX scripts, the package log is available using the **DTSPackageLog** scripting object.

The **GetPackageSQLServer** method, specifying server and login information, is used to return a **PackageSQLServer** object that provides access to the package and log data on the server. Use the **EnumPackageInfos** method of the **PackageSQLServer** object to return a **PackageInfos** collection with information about all or a subset of the packages in SQL Server storage on that server. Table 7.8 lists the methods of the **PackageSQLServer** object that are used to return the corresponding collection containing data for all or a subset of the log records of the indicated type on the server. The removal methods listed can be used to selectively remove log records of the indicated type. In addition, the **RemoveAllLogRecords** method is used to remove all log data for all packages from the server.

**Table 7.8    PackageSQLServer methods.**

| Method | Returned Collection | Removal Method |
|---|---|---|
| EnumPackageLogRecords | PackageLogRecords | RemovePackageLogRecords |
| EnumStepLogRecords | StepLogRecords | RemoveStepLogRecords |
| EnumTaskLogRecords | TaskLogRecords | RemoveTaskLogRecords |

You can retrieve information about the contents of a DTS package storage file, which can contain multiple packages each with multiple versions. Create a **Package2** object, and then use the **GetSavedPackageInfos** method to return a reference to a **SavedPackageInfos** collection with information about all the package versions contained in the file.

# Immediate Solutions

## Creating a Custom Package with the DTS Designer

This section provides a walk-through for creating an extremely simple package using the DTS Designer. The package copies the Employee database into a new database that is created during the design of the package. This example helps you become familiar with the interface used in the DTS Designer.

1. Open Enterprise Manager.

2. Expand the Microsoft SQL Servers node in the tree.

3. Expand SQL Server Group.

4. Select a server from the list, and expand it in the tree.

5. Expand the Data Transformation Services node in the tree.

6. Select the Local Packages node.

7. Right-click in the right pane, and select New Package from the context menu.

8. The DTS Designer, shown in Figure 7.3, is launched.

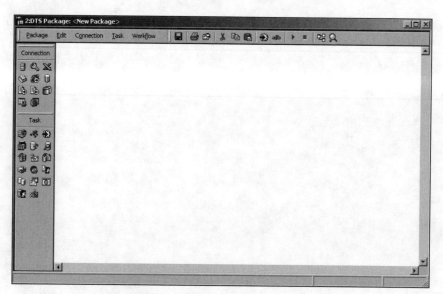

Figure 7.3    The DTS Designer.

9. On the Task toolbar, select the icon with the tool tip caption of Copy SQL Server Objects Task.

10. The Copy SQL Server Objects Task Properties dialog, shown in Figure 7.4, is launched.

11. On the Source tab, enter the server you are currently connected to and provide valid authentication information for the connection. Remember that the connection information determines the database access available to the package on this connection.

12. Select the Employee database.

13. Switch to the Destination tab.

14. Set the same properties for the server as were used in the source connection. Select <New> for the database.

15. Figure 7.5 shows the Create Database dialog that is launched when you select <New> for the database.

16. Enter "TestDTS1" for the new database name in the dialog, and click on OK. The database is created for you, using the default size.

17. Switch to the Copy tab.

18. The default options copy all database objects and properties except the extended properties. Select the Include Extended Properties checkbox to have the extended properties included in the copy.

19. Click on OK to close the Copy SQL Server Objects Task Properties dialog.

20. Select Save As on the Package menu.

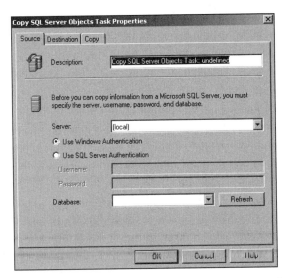

Figure 7.4    Copy SQL Server Objects Task Properties dialog.

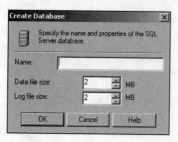

**Figure 7.5    Create Database dialog.**

21. Enter "Copy Employee to TestDTS1" as the task name.

22. Click on OK to save the package to SQL Server.

23. Close the DTS Designer.

24. Right-click on the Copy Employee to TestDTS1 package, and select Execute from the context menu to test the package. Figure 7.6 shows the Executing Package dialog that provides status information for the package during execution.

25. Close Enterprise Manager.

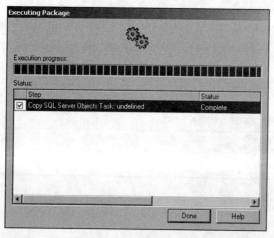

**Figure 7.6    Executing Package dialog.**

# Creating a Custom Package with Visual Basic

In this section, you go through the process of creating a simple custom package with Visual Basic. The package you create is designed to copy the data from the normalized address tables to the denormalized structure for reporting. Creating a denormalized structure for reporting is sometimes beneficial to the query processing time for these reports.

This section presents a number of source listings that are combined into a single source file on the CD accompanying this book. The code is saved as a standard Visual Basic source file named "TestPackage1.bas."

For your custom package, you first need to create a **Package2** object, because it is at the top of the DTS object hierarchy. For ease of use, a global variable is created to hold the reference to the **Package2** object. The code to declare and create a **Package2** object is shown in Listing 7.1.

### Listing 7.1  Declare and create a **Package2** object.

```
'----------------------------------------------
' Declare and create a Package2 global object
'----------------------------------------------
Public goPackage As New DTS.Package2
```

Next, you need to set the properties for your Package object. Because this is a simple application, error and event handling have been omitted for brevity. It is a good idea to add at least the necessary handling code for errors if you use this code as a model for your own applications. The code to set Package properties is shown in Listing 7.2.

### Listing 7.2  Set Package properties.

```
'------------------------
' Set package properties
'------------------------
goPackage.Name = "TestPackage1"
goPackage.WriteCompletionStatusToNTEventLog = False
goPackage.FailOnError = False
goPackage.PackagePriorityClass = 2
goPackage.MaxConcurrentSteps = 4
goPackage.LineageOptions = 0
goPackage.UseTransaction = True
goPackage.TransactionIsolationLevel = 4096
goPackage.AutoCommitTransaction = True
goPackage.RepositoryMetadataOptions = 0
goPackage.UseOLEDBServiceComponents = True
goPackage.LogToSQLServer = False
goPackage.LogServerFlags = 0
goPackage.FailPackageOnLogFailure = False
goPackage.ExplicitGlobalVariables = False
goPackage.PackageType = 0
```

**7. Data Transformation Services (DTS)**

Once the Package properties have been set, you need to create some connections for your source and destination data. Listing 7.3 shows the code to declare a variable for a Connection object. This listing also shows the code to create an out source connection, which points at a SQL Server database.

Listing 7.3    Declare and create a source connection.

```
'--------------------------------
' Declare connection variable
'--------------------------------
Dim oConnection as DTS.Connection2


'--------------------------
' Create Source connection
'--------------------------
Set oConnection = goPackage.Connections.New("SQLOLEDB")
```

After the connection has been declared and created, you need to set the source connection properties. The server name, database name, user name, and password for the connection can be set in this section of the code. This is also where you establish the connection timeout for the source connection. The name of the database is set in the **Catalog** property of the Connection object. The **ConnectionProperties** collection is used to set properties that are specific to the OLE DB provider that you are using. The **Data Source** property is set to the server name where your source data is located. The code used to set the properties for your source connection is shown in Listing 7.4.

Listing 7.4    Set source connection properties.

```
'----------------------------------------
' Set the Source connection properties
'----------------------------------------
oConnection.ConnectionProperties("Persist Security Info") = True
oConnection.ConnectionProperties("User ID") = "sa"
oConnection.ConnectionProperties("Password") = ""
oConnection.ConnectionProperties("Initial Catalog") = "Address"
oConnection.ConnectionProperties("Data Source") = "sneezy"
oConnection.ConnectionProperties("Application Name") = _
    "PackageExample"

oConnection.Name = "Source Data Connection"
oConnection.ID = 1
oConnection.Reusable = True
oConnection.ConnectImmediate = False
oConnection.DataSource = "sneezy"
oConnection.UserID = "sa"
```

```
oConnection.Password = ""
oConnection.ConnectionTimeout = 60
oConnection.Catalog = "Address"
oConnection.UseTrustedConnection = False
oConnection.UseDSL = False
```

Once the connection properties for the source connection have been set as desired, you need to add this connection to the **Connections** collection of the **Package2** object that you initially created. Listing 7.5 shows the code required to add the connection to the **Connections** collection.

**Listing 7.5   Add source connection to Connections collection.**

```
'----------------------------------------------------------
' Add the Source connection to the Connections collection
'----------------------------------------------------------
goPackage.Connections.Add oConnection
Set oConnection = Nothing
```

You can reuse the connection variable you declared earlier to create the destination connection for your package. Listing 7.6 shows the code used to create the destination connection. The only difference between the listing for the source and destination connections is that you do not need to re-declare the connection variable.

**Listing 7.6   Create destination connection.**

```
'------------------------------
' Create Destination connection
'------------------------------
Set oConnection = goPackage.Connections.New("SQLOLEDB")
```

Next, set the properties for your destination connection. Because the source and destination tables for this package are located in the same database, the only difference is the fact that you have pointed the destination to your report server. This allows you to copy the data to the report server to eliminate the server load caused by reporting from your production server. The code used to set the destination properties is provided in Listing 7.7.

**Listing 7.7   Set destination connection properties.**

```
'-------------------------------------------
' Set the Destination connection properties
'-------------------------------------------
oConnection.ConnectionProperties("Persist Security Info") = True
oConnection.ConnectionProperties("User ID") = "sa"
oConnection.ConnectionProperties("Password") = ""
```

```
oConnection.ConnectionProperties("Initial Catalog") = "Address"
oConnection.ConnectionProperties("Data Source") = "reportsrv"
oConnection.ConnectionProperties("Application Name") = _
    "PackageExample"

oConnection.Name = "Destination Data Connection"
oConnection.ID = 2
oConnection.Reusable = True
oConnection.ConnectImmediate = False
oConnection.DataSource = "sneezy"
oConnection.UserID = "sa"
oConnection.Password = ""
oConnection.ConnectionTimeout = 60
oConnection.Catalog = "Address"
oConnection.UseTrustedConnection = False
oConnection.UseDSL = False
```

Once again, you need to add the connection to the **Connections** collection of your **Package2** object. Listing 7.8 shows the code used to add the destination connection to the **Connections** collection.

**Listing 7.8   Add the destination connection to the Connections collection.**

```
'-----------------------------------------------------------
' Add the Destination connection to the Connections collection
'-----------------------------------------------------------
goPackage.Connections.Add oConnection
Set oConnection = Nothing
```

Once you have a **Package2** object with connections for the source and destination data, it is time to start coding the actual work to be performed by the package. For this, you need to declare and create a Step object. The code to declare and create a package step is provided in Listing 7.9.

**Listing 7.9   Declare and create package step.**

```
'--------------------
' Create package step
'--------------------
Dim oStep as DTS.Step2

'--------------------
' Define package step
'--------------------
Set oStep = goPackage.Steps.New
```

Next, set the properties for your Step object. Once these properties are set, you need to add your step object to the **Steps** collection of the **Package2** object. Listing 7.10 shows the code used to set the properties of the Step object and add it to the **Steps** collection.

**Listing 7.10   Set step properties and add the step to the Steps collection.**

```
'- - - - - - - - - - - - - - - - - - - -
' Set step properties
'- - - - - - - - - - - - - - - - - - - -
oStep.Name = "Denormalize_Address"
oStep.Description = "Build DN Table for Reporting"
oStep.ExecutionStatus = 1
oStep.TaskName = "Denormalize_Address"
oStep.CommitSuccess = False
oStep.RollbackFailure = False
oStep.ScriptLanguage = "VBScript"
oStep.AddGlobalVariables = True
oStep.RelativePriority = 3
oStep.CloseConnection = False
oStep.ExecuteInMainThread = False
oStep.IsPackageDSORowset = False
oStep.JoinTransactionIfPresent = False
oStep.DisableStep = False
oStep.FailPackageOnError = False


'- - - - - - - - - - - - - - - - - - - - - - - - - - - - - - - -
' Add the step to the Steps collection
'- - - - - - - - - - - - - - - - - - - - - - - - - - - - - - - -
goPackage.Steps.Add oStep
Set oStep = Nothing
```

Because the creation and definition of the Task object was quite long, a subroutine was used to create and define the object. Listing 7.11 shows the code in the main procedure used to call the **Create_Task** subroutine that was created.

**Listing 7.11   Call to Create_Task subroutine.**

```
'- - - - - - - - - - - - - - - - - - - - - - - - - - -
' Call sub to create Package Task
'- - - - - - - - - - - - - - - - - - - - - - - - - - -
Call Create_Task( goPackage )
```

The **Create_Task** subroutine shown in Listing 7.12 is used to create and set the properties for the task that will perform the work for your step. You first need to declare and create the Task objects. Next, set the properties for the **CustomTask** object. The commented code segregates the general properties from the properties for source and destination data. The source data is specified by a query that pulls data from the various tables used to store the normalized address and combines it into a result set that mirrors the denormalized data you want to create. The destination properties specify the table name that the data from your task will be written to when the transformation is complete. The source and destination properties also specify which of the Connection objects created earlier will be used to send and receive the data. The individual column transformations have each been placed in a separate subroutine for readability. The calls to these subroutines are shown in the listing. Once all of the properties have been set for the task and the transformations have been defined, you add the task to the **Tasks** collection of your **Package2** object.

### Listing 7.12   **Create_Task** subroutine.

```
'---------------------
' Create package task
'---------------------
Public Sub Create_Task(ByVal goPackage As Object)

    '----------------------
    ' Declare Task Objects
    '----------------------
    Dim oTask As DTS.Task
    Dim oCustomTask As DTS.DataPumpTask2

    '----------------------
    ' Create Task Objects
    '----------------------
    Set oTask = goPackage.Tasks.New("DTSDataPumpTask")
    Set oCustomTask = oTask.CustomTask

    '----------------------------
    ' Set CustomTask properties
    '----------------------------
    oCustomTask.Name = "Denormalize_Address"
    oCustomTask.Description = "Build DN Table for Reporting"
    oCustomTask.ProgressRowCount = 1000
    oCustomTask.MaximumErrorCount = 0
    oCustomTask.ExceptionFileName = "TestPkg1Log"
    oCustomTask.FetchBufferSize = 1
    oCustomTask.UseFastLoad = True
    oCustomTask.InsertCommitSize = 0
    oCustomTask.ExceptionFileColumnDelimiter = "|"
    oCustomTask.ExceptionFileRowDelimiter = vbCrLf
    oCustomTask.AllowIdentityInserts = False
```

```
oCustomTask.FirstRow = "0"
oCustomTask.LastRow = "0"
oCustomTask.FastLoadOptions = 2
oCustomTask.ExceptionFileOptions = 1
oCustomTask.DataPumpOptions = 0


'----------------------
' Set Source properties
'----------------------
oCustomTask.SourceConnectionID = 1
oCustomTask.SourceSQLStatement = "SELECT a.Line1," & vbCrLf
oCustomTask.SourceSQLStatement = oCustomTask.SourceSQLStatement & _
    "a.Line2," & vbCrLf
oCustomTask.SourceSQLStatement = oCustomTask.SourceSQLStatement & _
    "c.Name," & vbCrLf
oCustomTask.SourceSQLStatement = oCustomTask.SourceSQLStatement & _
    "s.State_Code," & vbCrLf
oCustomTask.SourceSQLStatement = oCustomTask.SourceSQLStatement & _
    "z.Zip5," & vbCrLf
oCustomTask.SourceSQLStatement = oCustomTask.SourceSQLStatement & _
    "z.Zip4" & vbCrLf
oCustomTask.SourceSQLStatement = oCustomTask.SourceSQLStatement & _
    "FROM tbl_Address a (NOLOCK)" & vbCrLf
oCustomTask.SourceSQLStatement = oCustomTask.SourceSQLStatement & _
    "JOIN tbl_City c (NOLOCK) on a.City_ID = c.City_ID" & vbCrLf
oCustomTask.SourceSQLStatement = oCustomTask.SourceSQLStatement & _
    "JOIN tbl_State s (NOLOCK) on c.State_ID = s.State_ID" & vbCrLf
oCustomTask.SourceSQLStatement = oCustomTask.SourceSQLStatement & _
    "JOIN tbl_ZipCode z (NOLOCK) on a.Zip_ID = z.Zip_ID"


'---------------------------
' Set Destination properties
'---------------------------
oCustomTask.DestinationConnectionID = 2
oCustomTask.DestinationObjectName = "Address.dbo.tbl_addressDN"


'--------------------------------------------------
' Call subs to add transformations for each column
'--------------------------------------------------
Call Transform_Line1( oCustomTask )
Call Transform_Line2( oCustomTask )
Call Transform_City( oCustomTask )
Call Transform_State( oCustomTask )
Call Transform_Zip5( oCustomTask )
Call Transform_Zip4( oCustomTask )
```

```
'---------------------------------
' Add task to Tasks collection
'---------------------------------
goPackage.Tasks.Add oTask
Set oCustomTask = Nothing
Set oTask = Nothing

End Sub
```

The code needed to transfer the Address **Line1** column from your source query to the destination table is in the **Transform_Line1** subroutine, which is shown in Listing 7.13. You first need to declare the Transformation and **Column** objects you will be using in this routine. Next, you create the Transformation object you will use for this column and set the needed properties. As you can see from the code, this is a simple copy transformation, so no actual data modifications are needed. Next, you create the source **Column** object and set the properties to define the source data. Then, you add the source **Column** object to the **Columns** collection of the Transformation object. You then reuse the **Column** object variable to reference the new destination **Column** object that you need to create. Once you have created the destination **Column** object and have set the needed properties, add it to the **DestinationColumns** collection of the Transformation object. Once the transformation properties are set and the source and destination columns have been defined and added to their respective collections, you can add the Transformation object to the **Transformations** collection of your **CustomTask** object.

### Listing 7.13    **Transform_Line1** subroutine.

```
Public Sub Transform_Line1(ByVal oCustomTask As Object)
'---------------------------------------------------
' Set up transformation for Address Line 1
'---------------------------------------------------

    '---------------------------------------------------
    ' Declare transformation and column objects
    '---------------------------------------------------
    Dim oTransformation As DTS.Transformation2
    Dim oColumn As DTS.Column


    '-----------------------------------------------------------
    ' Create transformation object and set needed propeties
    '-----------------------------------------------------------
    Set oTransformation = _
        oCustomTask.Transformations.New("DTS.DataPumpTransformCopy")
    oTransformation.Name = "Address_Line1_Transformation"
```

```
oTransformation.TransformFlags = 63
oTransformation.ForceSourceBlobsBuffered = 0
oTransformation.ForceBlobsInMemory = False
oTransformation.InMemoryBlobSize = 1048576
oTransformation.TransformPhases = 4


'-----------------------------------------------------
' Create source column object and set needed properties
'-----------------------------------------------------
Set oColumn = oTransformation.SourceColumns.New("Line1" , 1)
oColumn.Name = "Line1"
oColumn.Ordinal = 1
oColumn.Flags = 8
oColumn.Size = 50
oColumn.DataType = 129
oColumn.Precision = 0
oColumn.NumericScale = 0
oColumn.Nullable = False


'-----------------------------------------------------
' Add source column object to SourceColumns collection
'-----------------------------------------------------
oTransformation.SourceColumns.Add oColumn
Set oColumn = Nothing


'-------------------------------------------------------
' Create destination column object and set needed properties
'-------------------------------------------------------
Set oColumn = oTransformation.DestinationColumns.New("Line1" , 1)
oColumn.Name = "Line1"
oColumn.Ordinal = 1
oColumn.Flags = 104
oColumn.Size = 50
oColumn.DataType = 129
oColumn.Precision = 0
oColumn.NumericScale = 0
oColumn.Nullable = True


'-------------------------------------------------------
' Add destination column object to DestinationColumns collection
'-------------------------------------------------------
oTransformation.DestinationColumns.Add oColumn
Set oColumn = Nothing


'-------------------------------------------------------
```

**7. Data Transformation Services (DTS)**

```
' Add Address Line1 transformation to Transformations collection
'---------------------------------------------------------------
oCustomTask.Transformations.Add oTransformation
Set oTransformation = Nothing

End Sub
```

Because the Address **Line2** column also uses a simple copy transformation, the code for the **Transform_Line2** subroutine shown in Listing 7.14 is nearly identical to the code for the **Transform_Line1** subroutine. The main differences are the column names and the actual transformation name specified.

**Listing 7.14    Transform_Line2 subroutine.**

```
Public Sub Transform_Line2(ByVal oCustomTask As Object)
'----------------------------------------------
' Set up transformation for Address Line 2
'----------------------------------------------

    '----------------------------------------------
    ' Declare transformation and column objects
    '----------------------------------------------
Dim oTransformation As DTS.Transformation2
Dim oColumn As DTS.Column


    '------------------------------------------------------------
    ' Create transformation object and set needed propeties
    '------------------------------------------------------------
Set oTransformation = _
    oCustomTask.Transformations.New("DTS.DataPumpTransformCopy")
oTransformation.Name = "Address_Line2_Transformation"
oTransformation.TransformFlags = 63
oTransformation.ForceSourceBlobsBuffered = 0
oTransformation.ForceBlobsInMemory = False
oTransformation.InMemoryBlobSize = 1048576
oTransformation.TransformPhases = 4


    '------------------------------------------------------------
    ' Create source column object and set needed properties
    '------------------------------------------------------------
Set oColumn = oTransformation.SourceColumns.New("Line2" , 1)
oColumn.Name = "Line2"
oColumn.Ordinal = 1
oColumn.Flags = 104
oColumn.Size = 50
oColumn.DataType = 129
```

```
oColumn.Precision = 0
oColumn.NumericScale = 0
oColumn.Nullable = True


'-----------------------------------------------------
' Add source column object to SourceColumns collection
'-----------------------------------------------------
oTransformation.SourceColumns.Add oColumn
Set oColumn = Nothing


'-------------------------------------------------------------
' Create destination column object and set needed properties
'-------------------------------------------------------------
Set oColumn = oTransformation.DestinationColumns.New("Line2" , 1)
oColumn.Name = "Line2"
oColumn.Ordinal = 1
oColumn.Flags = 104
oColumn.Size = 50
oColumn.DataType = 129
oColumn.Precision = 0
oColumn.NumericScale = 0
oColumn.Nullable = True


'-------------------------------------------------------------
' Add destination column object to DestinationColumns collection
'-------------------------------------------------------------
oTransformation.DestinationColumns.Add oColumn
Set oColumn = Nothing


'-------------------------------------------------------------
' Add Address Line2 transformation to Transformations collection
'-------------------------------------------------------------
oCustomTask.Transformations.Add oTransformation
Set oTransformation = Nothing


End Sub
```

Because the **City** column also uses a simple copy transformation, the code for the **Transform_City** subroutine shown in Listing 7.15 is nearly identical to the code for the **Transform_Line1** subroutine. The main differences are the column names, column sizes, and the actual transformation name specified. One additional difference is the fact that the source and destination columns have different names. This is a minor detail, but an important difference if the routine is to function correctly.

### Listing 7.15 **Transform_City** subroutine.

```
Public Sub Transform_City(ByVal oCustomTask As Object)
'--------------------------------
' Set up transformation for City
'--------------------------------

    '-------------------------------------------
    ' Declare transformation and column objects
    '-------------------------------------------
    Dim oTransformation As DTS.Transformation2
    Dim oColumn As DTS.Column


    '----------------------------------------------------------
    ' Create transformation object and set needed propeties
    '----------------------------------------------------------
    Set oTransformation = _
        oCustomTask.Transformations.New("DTS.DataPumpTransformCopy")
    oTransformation.Name = "City_Transformation"
    oTransformation.TransformFlags = 63
    oTransformation.ForceSourceBlobsBuffered = 0
    oTransformation.ForceBlobsInMemory = False
    oTransformation.InMemoryBlobSize = 1048576
    oTransformation.TransformPhases = 4


    '----------------------------------------------------------
    ' Create source column object and set needed properties
    '----------------------------------------------------------
    Set oColumn = oTransformation.SourceColumns.New("Name" , 1)
    oColumn.Name = "Name"
    oColumn.Ordinal = 1
    oColumn.Flags = 8
    oColumn.Size = 50
    oColumn.DataType = 129
    oColumn.Precision = 0
    oColumn.NumericScale = 0
    oColumn.Nullable = False


    '----------------------------------------------------------
    ' Add source column object to SourceColumns collection
    '----------------------------------------------------------
    oTransformation.SourceColumns.Add oColumn
    Set oColumn = Nothing


    '----------------------------------------------------------
    ' Create destination column object and set needed properties
    '----------------------------------------------------------
```

```
Set oColumn = oTransformation.DestinationColumns.New("City" , 1)
oColumn.Name = "City"
oColumn.Ordinal = 1
oColumn.Flags = 104
oColumn.Size = 50
oColumn.DataType = 129
oColumn.Precision = 0
oColumn.NumericScale = 0
oColumn.Nullable = True


'-----------------------------------------------------------
' Add destination column object to DestinationColumns collection
'-----------------------------------------------------------

oTransformation.DestinationColumns.Add oColumn
Set oColumn = Nothing


'-----------------------------------------------------------
' Add City transformation to Transformations collection
'-----------------------------------------------------------

oCustomTask.Transformations.Add oTransformation
Set oTransformation = Nothing


End Sub
```

Because the **State** column also uses a simple copy transformation, the code for the **Transform_State** subroutine shown in Listing 7.16 is nearly identical to the code for the **Transform_Line1** subroutine. The main differences are the column names, column sizes, and the actual transformation name specified. As with the **City** column, the source and destination columns for the state information have different names as well.

**Listing 7.16    Transform_State subroutine.**

```
Public Sub Transform_State(ByVal oCustomTask As Object)
'--------------------------------
' Set up transformation for State
'--------------------------------
    '-------------------------------------------
    ' Declare transformation and column objects
    '-------------------------------------------
    Dim oTransformation As DTS.Transformation2
    Dim oColumn As DTS.Column


    '-----------------------------------------------------
    ' Create transformation object and set needed propeties
    '-----------------------------------------------------
```

```
Set oTransformation = _
    oCustomTask.Transformations.New("DTSPump.DataPumpTransformCopy")
oTransformation.Name = "State_Transformation"
oTransformation.TransformFlags = 63
oTransformation.ForceSourceBlobsBuffered = 0
oTransformation.ForceBlobsInMemory = False
oTransformation.InMemoryBlobSize = 1048576
oTransformation.TransformPhases = 4


'-----------------------------------------------------
' Create source column object and set needed properties
'-----------------------------------------------------
Set oColumn = oTransformation.SourceColumns.New("State_Code" , 1)
oColumn.Name = "State_Code"
oColumn.Ordinal = 1
oColumn.Flags = 24
oColumn.Size = 2
oColumn.DataType = 129
oColumn.Precision = 0
oColumn.NumericScale = 0
oColumn.Nullable = False


'--------------------------------------------------
' Add source column object to SourceColumns collection
'--------------------------------------------------
oTransformation.SourceColumns.Add oColumn
Set oColumn = Nothing


'-------------------------------------------------------------
' Create destination column object and set needed properties
'-------------------------------------------------------------
Set oColumn = oTransformation.DestinationColumns.New("State" , 1)
oColumn.Name = "State"
oColumn.Ordinal = 1
oColumn.Flags = 104
oColumn.Size = 30
oColumn.DataType = 129
oColumn.Precision = 0
oColumn.NumericScale = 0
oColumn.Nullable = True


'-------------------------------------------------------------
' Add destination column object to DestinationColumns collection
'-------------------------------------------------------------
oTransformation.DestinationColumns.Add oColumn
Set oColumn = Nothing
```

```
'-----------------------------------------------------------
' Add State transformation to Transformations collection
'-----------------------------------------------------------
oCustomTask.Transformations.Add oTransformation
Set oTransformation = Nothing

End Sub
```

Because the **Zip5** column also uses a simple copy transformation, the code for
the **Transform_Zip5** subroutine shown in Listing 7.17 is nearly identical to the
code for the **Transform_Line1** subroutine. The main differences are the column
names, column sizes, and the actual transformation name specified.

### Listing 7.17    **Transform_Zip5 subroutine.**

```
Public Sub Transform_Zip5(ByVal oCustomTask As Object)
'-------------------------------
' Set up transformation for Zip5
'-------------------------------

    '-----------------------------------------
    ' Declare transformation and column objects
    '-----------------------------------------
    Dim oTransformation As DTS.Transformation2
    Dim oColumn As DTS.Column


    '------------------------------------------------------
    ' Create transformation object and set needed propeties
    '------------------------------------------------------
    Set oTransformation = _
        oCustomTask.Transformations.New("DTS.DataPumpTransformCopy")
    oTransformation.Name = "Zip_Code_Transformation"
    oTransformation.TransformFlags = 63
    oTransformation.ForceSourceBlobsBuffered = 0
    oTransformation.ForceBlobsInMemory = False
    oTransformation.InMemoryBlobSize = 1048576
    oTransformation.TransformPhases = 4


    '------------------------------------------------------
    ' Create source column object and set needed properties
    '------------------------------------------------------
    Set oColumn = oTransformation.SourceColumns.New("Zip5" , 1)
    oColumn.Name = "Zip5"
    oColumn.Ordinal = 1
    oColumn.Flags = 24
    oColumn.Size = 5
    oColumn.DataType = 129
    oColumn.Precision = 0
```

```
        oColumn.NumericScale = 0
        oColumn.Nullable = False


        '-----------------------------------------------------------
        ' Add source column object to SourceColumns collection
        '-----------------------------------------------------------
        oTransformation.SourceColumns.Add oColumn
        Set oColumn = Nothing


        '-----------------------------------------------------------
        ' Create destination column object and set needed properties
        '-----------------------------------------------------------
        Set oColumn = oTransformation.DestinationColumns.New("Zip5" , 1)
        oColumn.Name = "Zip5"
        oColumn.Ordinal = 1
        oColumn.Flags = 120
        oColumn.Size = 5
        oColumn.DataType = 129
        oColumn.Precision = 0
        oColumn.NumericScale = 0
        oColumn.Nullable = True


        '-----------------------------------------------------------
        ' Add destination column object to DestinationColumns collection
        '-----------------------------------------------------------
        oTransformation.DestinationColumns.Add oColumn
        Set oColumn = Nothing


        '-----------------------------------------------------------
        ' Add Zip5 transformation to Transformations collection
        '-----------------------------------------------------------
        oCustomTask.Transformations.Add oTransformation
        Set oTransformation = Nothing

End Sub
```

Because the **Zip4** column also uses a simple copy transformation, the code for the **Transform_Zip4** subroutine shown in Listing 7.18 is nearly identical to the code for the **Transform_Line1** subroutine. The main differences are the column names, column sizes, and the actual transformation name specified.

### Listing 7.18    **Transform_Zip4** subroutine.

```
Public Sub Transform_Zip4(ByVal oCustomTask As Object)
'---------------------------------
' Set up transformation for Zip4
'---------------------------------
```

```
'---------------------------------------
' Declare transformation and column objects
'---------------------------------------
Dim oTransformation As DTS.Transformation2
Dim oColumn As DTS.Column


'----------------------------------------------------
' Create transformation object and set needed propeties
'----------------------------------------------------
Set oTransformation = _
    oCustomTask.Transformations.New("DTS.DataPumpTransformCopy")
oTransformation.Name = "Zip_Code_Extension_Transformation"
oTransformation.TransformFlags = 63
oTransformation.ForceSourceBlobsBuffered = 0
oTransformation.ForceBlobsInMemory = False
oTransformation.InMemoryBlobSize = 1048576
oTransformation.TransformPhases = 4


'----------------------------------------------------
' Create source column object and set needed properties
'----------------------------------------------------
Set oColumn = oTransformation.SourceColumns.New("Zip4" , 1)
oColumn.Name = "Zip4"
oColumn.Ordinal = 1
oColumn.Flags = 120
oColumn.Size = 4
oColumn.DataType = 129
oColumn.Precision = 0
oColumn.NumericScale = 0
oColumn.Nullable = True


'----------------------------------------------------
' Add source column object to SourceColumns collection
'----------------------------------------------------
oTransformation.SourceColumns.Add oColumn
Set oColumn = Nothing


'----------------------------------------------------
' Create destination column object and set needed properties
'----------------------------------------------------
Set oColumn = oTransformation.DestinationColumns.New("zip4" , 1)
oColumn.Name = "zip4"
oColumn.Ordinal = 1
oColumn.Flags = 120
oColumn.Size = 4
```

```
oColumn.DataType = 129
oColumn.Precision = 0
oColumn.NumericScale = 0
oColumn.Nullable = True


'-------------------------------------------------------------
' Add destination column object to DestinationColumns collection
'-------------------------------------------------------------
oTransformation.DestinationColumns.Add oColumn
Set oColumn = Nothing


'-------------------------------------------------------------
' Add Zip5 transformation to Transformations collection
'-------------------------------------------------------------
oCustomTask.Transformations.Add oTransformation
Set oTransformation = Nothing


End Sub
```

Once the package objects are all created and set up the way you want them, you can execute the package. The code shown in Listing 7.19 is taken from the end of the main procedure in this sample application. It shows how to call the **Execute** method of your package object and also provides the code needed to release the resources used by the package once execution is complete.

**Listing 7.19   Execute package and free package resources.**

```
'----------------
' Execute package
'----------------
goPackage.Execute


'------------------------
' Free package resources
'------------------------
goPackage.Uninitialize
set goPackage = Nothing
```

# Chapter 8

# Black Book Databases

# *In Depth*

Providing a sample database for a broad audience is no simple task. Therefore, a few different databases (other than those supplied by Microsoft) have been provided for you to use as a learning tool for *SQL Server 2000 Black Book*. The Pubs and Northwind databases will be referred to periodically, but the bulk of the work will be done within the databases discussed in this chapter.

The Employee, Address, Utility, and Inventory databases will be discussed in depth, and then you will be walked through the process of creating your own copies of these databases on your server in the "Immediate Solutions" section of this chapter. Data modeling will be covered in depth in Chapter 16, but a few of the basics will be covered in this chapter, so you can start using the proper terms and lingo associated with databases in the development world. Many of these terms are used incorrectly in organizations out of habit or lack of understanding. Making sure everyone is using the same term makes the text clearer and hopefully helps you to understand the why behind the term.

---

**NOTE:** *Refer to the Glossary at the back of the book for definitions or explanations of terms and how they are used in the context of this book.*

---

The databases used in this chapter illustrate some of the techniques that can be employed by developers to create enterprise level client/server applications. This chapter focuses on the developer's need to use the database in such a way that the database administrator's job for large systems does not become overwhelming.

## Entities

The entities created in any database are essentially the nouns or items that you describe when talking about a process. A person, place, or thing can be an entity in a data model. Entities are in essence tables in database design. Each table should have a unique identifier that allows for each record to be identified within a set of records returned when querying the table. You should limit the number of columns (attributes), so that you can keep the performance high across each entity you are querying. Also, avoid **NULL** values in your entities when possible. A **NULL** value can adversely impact query performance or return unexpected results in joins or aggregates.

## Relationships

Relationships are how entities relate to each other, so that records can be associated with each other in queries or view definitions. A relationship is similar to a parent and a child within a family. The parent entity has a key value (*primary key*) that uniquely identifies a record in one table with any other tables or entities that are considered children. The child table or entity has what is called a *foreign key*. This key is a column that holds the value of the parent entity, so that you can join the two entities during the query process.

## Attributes

Attributes (or columns) describe the entity. They contain the details of the entity and make each record unique in relation to other records stored in the same table. For example, the Employee entity can be described by attributes like first and last names. These columns allow you to "describe" the entity by supplying individual values that make up the employee record. Again, try to avoid **NULL** values when considering attributes.

---

**NOTE:** *Defining a default value for attributes can help you avoid **NULL** values for attributes.*

---

## Entity List

A description of each of the entities in their respective databases is presented in the following sections. The attributes of each entity and how they are used in this book are also explained. The details of how each attribute is used is described in various other chapters and code samples based upon the data structures described in this chapter. See the accompanying CD for scripts that can be loaded into the Query Analyzer and run to create these tables. (Optionally, you can walk through the "Immediate Solutions" section at the end of this chapter for detailed instructions on how to install these database tables and create entries in the model database, so that they can be automatically added to new databases.) Each entity is generic and may not exactly match your requirements. Take the time to understand the premise of each entity, and feel free to modify them to your needs.

Entities should be described in a few sentences, even when data modeling, so that you have a good description of what you are trying to accomplish in the table, columns, and data. This practice is especially helpful in writing technical specifications for applications that will use the database. Try to create generic entities to serve a broad range of needs.

## Clustered Indexes

Clustered indexes are a special type of index structure that should be used with care. Before creating a clustered index on a table, it is important to understand how the data in the table will be referenced as well as how a clustered index affects your data storage.

A clustered index imposes a physical order on the rows in the table. This means that as rows in the table are inserted, updated, and deleted, the table must be physically reordered to keep the key values in the correct order. You must be careful in creating clustered indexes to ensure that the performance gains allowed by this physical ordering are not negated by the overhead required to reorganize the data as modifications occur. You should create clustered indexes only when you will need to regularly retrieve a range of rows based on the column values in the index.

One other important consideration is the fact that you can have only one clustered index per table. This limitation is imposed by the nature of how clustered indexes work. It would not be possible to physically order the rows in the table in more than one way. Multiple physical orderings of the data would require multiple copies of the data to be maintained, which would definitely hinder performance.

Due to the nature of clustered indexes and how they are generally used, a primary key is usually not the best choice for a clustered index on a table; however, primary keys will generate a clustered index automatically unless otherwise specified. You should usually specify the **NONCLUSTERED** option when creating a primary key constraint on a table. For more complete information on creating and using clustered indexes, see Chapter 16.

### A Note on Primary and Foreign Keys

In this section you will notice that no primary or foreign keys are created for any of the tables. This chapter focuses on providing the table structures used in the examples in later chapters as well as introducing you to some of the basic terminology and concepts of table and database design. The relational integrity constraints for these tables will be introduced in Chapter 16, which goes into much greater detail on the concepts of data modeling and database design.

# Address Database

The Address database is provided to demonstrate the performance characteristics of a well-normalized database versus a denormalized database. Both the normalized and denormalized versions of the data are stored in this one database for ease of comparison. Addresses were chosen for this example because they are elements that virtually everyone has to include in a database and they provide some insight into how I/O and performance are affected by structure.

## Tbl_AddressDN

The **Tbl_AddressDN** entity contains the denormalized version of the address data. The population script will generate 100,000 addresses by deafult to provide enough data to do some meaningful benchmarking. All of the information associated with a single address is contained in this table. This structure should look familiar to many people who have started normalizing their data and have moved addresses into a separate entity to remove duplication elsewhere. Many systems begin with a variety of address information distributed across many different tables, and then create a similar structure to consolidate data and shrink the width of the tables. See Listing 8.1 for the SQL statement that creates the address denormalized table.

**Listing 8.1  Tbl_AddressDN.**

```
CREATE TABLE [tbl_addressDN] (
        [Address_ID]         [int] IDENTITY (1, 1)           NOT NULL,
        [Line1]              [varchar] (50)                  NULL,
        [Line2]              [varchar] (50)                  NULL,
        [City]               [varchar] (50)                  NULL,
        [State]              [varchar] (30)                  NULL,
        [Zip5]               [char] (5)                      NULL,
        [zip4]               [char] (4)                      NULL
) ON [PRIMARY]
GO
```

The attributes for the **AddressDN** table cover the majority of address storage needs. Specific applications may require additional information or segregation of the existing fields, but this is the form that is most commonly used. The **Address_ID** attribute is the **IDENTITY** column, which creates a unique number (integer) for each record when a new row is inserted into the table. This becomes the foreign key for any table that uses address entries. Using an integer for joins is preferable for performance reasons. The attributes for this table are provided and explained in Table 8.1.

The **AddressDN** table is normally used to store any address needed in the database. You might have employee, vendor, or customer addresses. All of these can be stored in this one table and referenced from any record that needed access to the address information. This table is a big improvement over storing the address information across numerous tables in the database and duplicating that information unnecessarily. It does tend to become very large and can be difficult to manage in very large databases.

**8. Black Book Databases**

**NOTE:** *The remaining tables in this section show how the **Tbl_AddressDN** structure can be improved upon and provide additional flexibility for queries that deal with addresses.*

**Table 8.1    Attribute list for Tbl_AddressDN.**

| Column Name | Data Type | Description |
| --- | --- | --- |
| **Address_ID** | **INT** | An auto-incremented identity value that represents a unique number for this address in any table that requires an address. This column will be used as the primary key and an index should be created to support relational lookups and joins. |
| **Line1** | **VARCHAR(50)** | This is the first line of the street address. It should be used for every address. |
| **Line2** | **VARCHAR(50)** | This is the second line of the street address. This attribute is normally not required, but does come into play in many systems. |
| **City** | **VARCHAR(50)** | The city name should be entered for every address. |
| **State** | **VARCHAR(30)** | The state field stores the full state name. The postal abbreviation can be substituted depending on your needs. |
| **Zip5** | **CHAR(5)** | This column stores the first five digits of the ZIP code, which should be present for every address. |
| **Zip4** | **CHAR(4)** | This additional column holds the last four digits of the extended ZIP code, which would be present if available. |

# Tbl_Address

The **Address** entity is part of the normalized address structure. This entity includes links to the **City** and **ZipCode** entities, instead of storing the data directly. The links provide a greater capability to eliminate duplicated information. These integer columns require less storage structure space, so the table is actually smaller in width and performs better. See Chapter 11 for more information on performance tuning and optimization. Listing 8.2 shows the address table structure.

**Listing 8.2    Tbl_Address.**

```
CREATETABLE [tbl_Address] (
        [Address_ID]      [int] IDENTITY (1, 1)    NOT NULL,
        [Line1]           [varchar] (50)           NOT NULL,
        [Line2]           [varchar] (50)           NULL,
        [Zip4]            [char] (4)               NULL,
        [City_ID]         [int]                    NOT NULL,
        [Zip_ID]          [int]                    NOT NULL) ON [PRIMARY]
GO
```

Address attributes are shown in Table 8.2. Each entry in this table provides the information and links to build a complete address without duplicating information unnecessarily. The additional keys at the bottom of Table 8.2 allow you to

Table 8.2   Attribute list for **Tbl_Address.**

| Column Name | Data Type | Description |
| --- | --- | --- |
| Address_ID | INT | An auto-incremented identity value that represents a unique number for this address in any table that requires an address. This column will be used as the primary key and an index should be created to support relational lookups and joins. |
| Line1 | VARCHAR(50) | This is the first line of the street address. It should be used for every address. |
| Line 2 | VARCHAR(50) | This is the second line of the street address. It is used for long addresses or a c/o line. |
| Zip4 | CHAR(4) | This is the last four digits of the extended ZIP code, which are present if available. |
| City_ID | INT | The ID of the city for this address. It allows for cities to be stored only one time no matter how many times they are used. |
| Zip_ID | INT | The ID of the ZIP code for this address. Same as the previous attribute, it allows for the removal of redundant data from this table. (The resulting ZIP code table provides for a fast way to search addresses by ZIP codes.) |

create very fast queries by city, state, and ZIP code against this structure. (Something you could do if the table was denormalized, but would be much slower.)

## Tbl_City

The **Tbl_City** entity contains the normalized city information for the addresses in the Address entity. Cities are normally replicated many times in a denormalized structure. Listing 8.3 shows how a city entity can be created to hold a single city row for relational joins in queries. This normalized structure results in lower storage requirements and reduces I/O, which translates to better query performance in most instances.

Listing 8.3   **Tbl_City.**

```
CREATE TABLE [tbl_City] (
        [City_ID]       [int] IDENTITY (1, 1)    NOT NULL,
        [Name]          [varchar] (50)           NOT NULL,
        [State_ID]      [tinyint]                NOT NULL) ON [PRIMARY]
GO
```

City attributes are shown in Table 8.3. This table contains the city name and an ID field for easy reference in any table that needs to store a city. The state ID allows for the duplication of cities within different states to generate a unique record for table join purposes. This entity also provides for fast city and state queries without having to read the entire address table.

**Table 8.3    Attribute list for Tbl_City.**

| Column Name | Data Type | Description |
|---|---|---|
| City_ID | INT | An auto-incremented identity value that represents a unique number for this city in any table that requires a city. This column will be used as the primary key, and an index should be created to support relational lookups and joins. |
| Name | VARCHAR(50) | Name of the city. |
| State_ID | TINYINT | The ID for the state record that goes with this city. |

# Tbl_State

The **TBL_State** entity contains the normalized state information for the addresses in the **Address** entity. In the normalized structure, shown in Listing 8.4, there should be a maximum of 50 state records regardless of the number of addresses being stored. This translates into significant savings in terms of storage and disk I/O.

**Listing 8.4    Tbl_State.**

```
CREATE TABLE [tbl_State] (
        [State_ID]      [tinyint] IDENTITY (1, 1)   NOT NULL,
        [Name]          [varchar] (30)              NOT NULL,
        [State_Code]    [char] (2)                  NOT NULL) ON [PRIMARY]
GO
```

State attributes are shown in Table 8.4. This is a very simple structure that is almost identical to the **City** entity. Once populated, this table becomes virtually read-only data. Business and application logic will dictate whether any change to this data would require a relational key update or the creation of a new record to support the new data.

# Tbl_ZipCode

The **Tbl_ZipCode** entity contains the normalized ZIP code information for the addresses in the **Address** entity. In the normalized structure, the duplicated ZIP

**Table 8.4    Attribute list for Tbl_State.**

| Column Name | Data Type | Description |
|---|---|---|
| State_ID | TINYINT | An auto-incremented identity value that represents a unique number for this state in any table that requires a state. This column will be used as the primary key, and an index should be created to support relational lookups and joins. |
| Name | VARCHAR(50) | This is the long name for the state. |
| State_Code | CHAR(2) | This is the standard postal abbreviation for the state. |

**Table 8.5  Attribute list for Tbl_ZipCode.**

| Column Name | Data Type | Description |
|---|---|---|
| Zip_ID | INT | An auto-incremented identity value that represents a unique number for this ZIP code in any table that requires a ZIP code. This column will be used as the primary key, and an index should be created to support relational lookups and joins. |
| Zip5 | CHAR(5) | This is the first five digits of the ZIP code, which should be present for every address. |
| State_ID | TINYINT | The ID for the state record that goes with this ZIP code. |

codes are eliminated to reduce storage and I/O requirements in the database. See Listing 8.5 for the ZIP code structure.

**Listing 8.5  Tbl_ZipCode.**

```
CREATE TABLE [tbl_ZipCode] (
        [Zip_ID]        [int] IDENTITY (1, 1)   NOT NULL,
        [Zip5]          [char] (5)              NOT NULL,
        [State_ID]      [tinyint]               NOT NULL) ON [PRIMARY]
GO
```

**Tbl_ZipCode** attributes are shown in Table 8.5. This is a very simple structure that is almost identical to the **City** entity. The **State_ID** provides a quick and easy means to pull a list of ZIP code values by state.

# Employee Database

The Employee database supplied with this book is intended to furnish sample data for queries written in various chapters. No real functionality is intended by these entities; they are just used as demonstration data. The combination of data from different databases and the stored procedures and views created by these entities provide a valuable lesson. Each system has its own particular needs, so it would be nearly impossible to create a generic enough database for all needs. Customize these tables or use portions of them in your systems where they fit best.

## Tbl_Employee

The **Tbl_Employee** entity represents the employee or person in the system. Some of this data can be further normalized if needed or placed in separate one-to-one relational tables to save query I/O. Remember to keep your tables organized into logical groupings and not query or return unneeded data. For more on the technique of splitting tables into smaller structures, see Chapter 16. See Listing 8.6 for the SQL that generates the employee table.

**Listing 8.6   Tbl_Employee.**

```
CREATE TABLE [dbo].[tbl_Employee] (
        [employee_id]       [int] IDENTITY (1, 1)   NOT NULL,
        [first_name]        [varchar] (30)          NOT NULL,
        [last_name]         [varchar] (30)          NOT NULL,
        [user_id]           [char] (10)             NULL,
        [manager_id]        [int]                   NULL,
        [title]             [int]                   NULL,
        [email]             [varchar] (255)         NULL,
        [extension]         [char] (10)             NULL,
        [phone]             [char] (10)             NULL,
        [notify_pref]       [int]                   NULL,
        [net_send]          [varchar] (255)         NULL,
        [page_string]       [varchar] (255)         NULL,
        [department]        [int]                   NULL,
        [date_hired]        [smalldatetime]         NOT NULL)
ON [PRIMARY]
GO
```

Employee attributes are listed in Table 8.6. There are a few attributes that de-serve mention. The **Manager_ID** is a self-referencing attribute. The value that is placed in this attribute would have to exist previously in the employee table, and a self-join would then be used to determine reporting structures. See Chapter 9 for more on join conditions. There are a few attributes that are defined as inte-gers, but are in fact references to the code table in the utility databases.

**Table 8.6   Attribute list for Tbl_Employee.**

| Column Name | Data Type | Description |
| --- | --- | --- |
| Employee_ID | INT | An auto-generated number to uniquely identify the employee in joins. |
| First_Name | VARCHAR(30) | The employee's first name would be stored here. |
| Last_Name | VARCHAR(30) | The employee's last name is held in this column. |
| User_ID | CHAR(10) | A user identification or login attribute that can be used for short, text-based references to an employee. |
| Manager_ID | INT | The employee's manager would have to exist in the employee table, and the resulting employee ID would be placed in this attribute. (A self-join would be used to find the manager's employees or vice versa.) |
| Title | INT | A code table lookup that stores the code ID for the employee's title. |
| Email | VARCHAR(255) | The email address for the employee is stored in this attribute. |

*(continued)*

**Table 8.6    Attribute list for Tbl_Employee *(continued)*.**

| Column Name | Data Type | Description |
|---|---|---|
| Extension | CHAR(10) | Telephone extension. |
| Phone | CHAR(10) | Phone number. |
| Notify_Pref | INT | A code table lookup that represents the employee's preferred method of contact, should that be required. |
| Net_Send | VARCHAR(255) | Net send string to be passed to Windows NT. |
| Page_String | VARCHAR(255) | String that is passed to a paging application. Typically phone number and modem string characters are stored in this attribute. |
| Department | INT | A code table lookup for the various departments in the system. |
| Date_Hired | SMALLDATETIME | The date the employee was hired. |

## Tbl_EmployeeRates

The **Tbl_EmployeeRates** entity holds the monetary rates for each employee. This entity has a one-to-one relationship with the employee entity. For the SQL to create the **EmployeeRates** entity, see Listing 8.7.

**Listing 8.7    Tbl_EmployeeRates.**

```
CREATE TABLE [dbo].[tbl_EmployeeRates] (
        [employee_id]           [int]              NOT NULL,
        [hourly_rate]           [smallmoney]       NOT NULL,
        [charge_rate]           [smallmoney]       NOT NULL,
        [annual_salary]         [money]            NOT NULL) ON [PRIMARY]
GO
```

Notice the use of small data types to reduce the amount of storage space for lesser amounts of data. The **SMALLMONEY** data type requires half the storage (4) of the **MONEY** data type. The limit of the size of the **SMALLMONEY** data type (+/- 214,748.3648) would be hard to exceed as an hourly rate, but could be exceeded for an annual salary. Therefore, the **MONEY** data type is used to allow for those *really* good salaries. See Table 8.7 for the attribute list for employee rates.

**Table 8.7    Attribute list for Tbl_EmployeeRates.**

| Column Name | Data Type | Description |
|---|---|---|
| Employee_ID | INT | The employee ID from the employee table. |
| Hourly_Rate | SMALLMONEY | The charge rate used for cost-based computations. |
| Charge_Rate | SMALLMONEY | The rate charged for this employee for client billing purposes. |
| Annual_Rate | MONEY | Annual salary for each employee. |

## Tbl_Meeting

The **Tbl_Meeting** entity is used to track meetings within an organization. Key pieces of information in this attribute describe the meeting details. Some additional data type tricks are used to handle range type queries when looking at date and time values. See Listing 8.8 for the SQL to create the **Meeting** entity.

**NOTE:** *The integer date and time attributes can be used to optimize queries of date values in an often-queried entity. Effective dating and range queries perform better using this technique. See Chapter 16 for more information on modeling techniques for speed.*

Listing 8.8   Tbl_Meeting.

```
CREATE TABLE [dbo].[tbl_Meeting] (
        [meeting_id]     [int] IDENTITY (1, 1)   NOT NULL,
        [subject]        [varchar] (50)          NOT NULL,
        [location]       [varchar] (50)          NULL,
        [fixed_costs]    [smallmoney]            NULL,
        [overhead]       [decimal] (8,4)         NULL,
        [start_date]     [int]                   NOT NULL,
        [start_time]     [int]                   NOT NULL,
        [end_date]       [int]                   NULL,
        [end_time]       [int]                   NULL,
        [total_cost]     [money]                 NULL) ON [PRIMARY]
GO
```

The columns in the meeting table are actually a good example of the specific nature that some attributes can describe in an entity. The details of a meeting are explained very well by simply reading the attribute list. Notice the data type selection for the attributes. Certain types have been used to save space, and others are used purely for performance reasons. See Table 8.8 for a complete list of the **Tbl_Meeting** entity attributes.

Table 8.8   Attribute list for Tbl_Meeting.

| Column Name | Data Type | Description |
| --- | --- | --- |
| Meeting_ID | INT | A unique, auto-generated ID for each meeting in the system. |
| Subject | VARCHAR(50) | A description of the subject matter of the meeting. |
| Location | VARCHAR(50) | The location of the meeting. (This could be a code table entry.) |
| Fixed_Costs | SMALLMONEY | Any amount of fixed costs to be used when calculating the total cost of a meeting. |

*(continued)*

**Table 8.8    Attribute list for Tbl_Meeting** *(continued).*

| Column Name | Data Type | Description |
|---|---|---|
| Overhead | DECIMAL(8,4) | Any overhead amount that should be taken into consideration when calculating the total cost of a meeting. |
| Start_Date | INT | Date the meeting starts. Format is YYYYMMDD. (20000624, 19990624, etc.) |
| Start_Time | INT | Time the meeting starts. Stored in 24-hour clock format: HHMM. |
| End_Date | INT | Date the meeting ends. Format is YYYYMMDD. (20000624, 19990624, etc.) |
| End_Time | INT | Time the meeting ends. Stored in 24-hour clock format: HHMM. |
| Total_Cost | MONEY | Calculated cost of the meeting. (Total for all employees' **Person_Cost** from the **Tbl_MeetingPeople** entity [see the next section], plus fixed cost and overhead.) |

## Tbl_MeetingPeople

**Tbl_MeetingPeople** is an historical cross-reference entity. Employee rates are pulled in when an employee is added to a meeting, and then, based upon the length of the meeting, a per-person cost is either calculated when a person leaves or the meeting is completed. Each time a new meeting is created, associated employee information is gathered and stored in this entity. For the SQL statement that creates this entity, see Listing 8.9.

**Listing 8.9    Tbl_MeetingPeople.**

```
CREATE TABLE [dbo].[tbl_MeetingPeople] (
        [meeting_id]            [varchar] (255) NOT NULL,
        [employee_id]           [varchar] (255) NOT NULL,
        [start_date]            [int]           NULL,
        [start_time]            [int]           NULL,
        [end_date]              [int]           NULL,
        [end_time]              [int]           NULL,
        [person_cost]           [money]         NULL) ON [PRIMARY]
GO
```

The attributes for each **MeetingPeople** record consist of the details for each employee including start dates and time, end dates and time, and the calculated cost of the employee attending the meeting. A stored procedure or trigger can calculate the cost attribute. See Table 8.9 for the attribute listing for the entity **Tbl_MeetingPeople**.

8. Black Book Databases

**Table 8.9   Attribute list for Tbl_MeetingPeople.**

| Column Name | Data Type | Description |
| --- | --- | --- |
| Meeting_ID | INT | The meeting ID for an employee's meeting. |
| Employee_ID | INT | The employee's ID. |
| Start_Date | INT | The date the meeting started in YYYYMMDD format as an integer. |
| Start_Time | INT | The time the meeting started in the 24-hour integer format of HHMM. |
| End_Date | INT | The date the meeting ended in YYYYMMDD format as an integer. |
| End_Time | INT | The time the meeting ended in the 24-hour integer format of HHMM. |
| Person_Cost | MONEY | The total cost of this employee based on the time in the meeting times the rate for the employee. |

## Tbl_EmployeeAddressXref

The **Tbl_EmployeeAddressXref** entity is used to associate an employee to one or more address entities. This technique allows for an unlimited number of addresses to be associated with an employee without wasting space. See Listing 8.10 for the structure of the employee address cross-reference table.

**Listing 8.10   Tbl_EmployeeAddressXref.**

```
CREATE TABLE [dbo].[tbl_EmployeeAddressXref] (
        [employee_id]           [int]   NOT NULL,
        [address_id]            [int]   NOT NULL,
        [address_type]          [int]   NOT NULL) ON [PRIMARY]
GO
```

One of the unique attributes introduced in this entity is the address type. The address type is a code table lookup that stores keys to the various types of addresses in the system. For a complete list of the attributes for the employee address cross-reference table, see Table 8.10

**Table 8.10   Attribute list for Tbl_EmployeeAddressXref.**

| Column Name | Data Type | Description |
| --- | --- | --- |
| Employee_ID | INT | The employee ID from the employee table. |
| Address_ID | INT | The Address ID from the address entity. |
| Address_Type | INT | A code table reference for identifying the type of address record this is for a particular employee. |

# Utility Database

The Utility database is perhaps the most portable database in this book. Many of the entities and eventual procedures supplied in the book can be used in almost any database environment. The features and functions that these objects provide can really improve any system that uses the techniques discussed.

## Tbl_Codes

**Tbl_Codes** is a general purpose entity in many systems and is used to create a centralized storage structure of codes used throughout an application. This centralized storage mechanism for codes can become the central point of your system. This table can reduce column width in some tables by providing a 4-byte key for otherwise wider data. It can also be used to populate drop-down list boxes and reports with descriptive data. See Listing 8.11 for the syntax used to create the **Tbl_Codes** entity.

**Listing 8.11    Tbl_Codes.**

```
CREATE TABLE [dbo].[tbl_Codes] (
        [Code_ID]               [int] IDENTITY (1,1)    NOT NULL,
        [Code]                  [varchar] (12)          NOT NULL,
        [Description]           [varchar] (100)         NULL,
        [Code_Group_ID]         [int]                   NULL) ON [PRIMARY]
GO
```

The attributes for the code table are actually very few and present a very broad functionality in many areas. The **Code_ID** attribute is the **IDENTITY** column, which creates a unique number (integer) for each record when a new row is inserted into the table. This becomes the foreign key in any table that uses code entries. Using an integer for joins is preferable for performance reasons. The code attribute holds up to 12 characters, which are the display characters or data entry characters within applications. The description is used for reports when the code must be fully expanded for more detail. The **Code_Group_ID** attribute actually allows you to group your codes by type, so that this structure can store codes for many different functions. See Table 8.11 for more detailed attribute listings.

The data in the codes table can be used in a number of ways. Let's look at how to account for a range of status values, for example. Suppose you had a drop-down combo box that needed to be populated with a set of values, like **Failed, Succeeded, Retry, Cancel,** and **InProgress**. These values are easy enough to hard code into an application, but if they need to be added to or customized, the client code would have to modify them and recompile the code. If you use a code table to store the values and retrieve them when you instantiate the object, you could

**Table 8.11    Attribute list for Tbl_Codes.**

| Column Name | Data Type | Description |
|---|---|---|
| Code_ID | INT | An auto-incremented identity value that represents a unique number for this code in any table that requires a code. This column will be used as the primary key column, and an index should be created to support relational lookups and joins. |
| Code | VARCHAR(12) | The code displayed in a combo box or on a report. |
| Description | VARCHAR(100) | The long description for the code, typically displayed in reports. |
| Code_Group_ID | INT | The grouping code foreign key that relates to the code group table. |

change the list at any time by adding a record to the codes table. See the "Immediate Solutions" section of this chapter for an example using the codes table.

**NOTE:** *In Chapter 14, stored procedures will be created that will rely on the code table structure.*

## Tbl_CodeGroup

The **Tbl_CodeGroup** entity is a grouping mechanism for codes. It can provide an easy-to-manage method of creating application and database specific codes for a number of reasons. This entity essentially consists of a name and description for a set of codes. See Listing 8.12 for the syntax used to create **Tbl_CodeGroup**.

**Listing 8.12    Tbl_CodeGroup.**

```
CREATE TABLE [dbo].[tbl_CodeGroup] (
        [Code_Group_ID]         [int] IDENTITY (1,1)    NOT NULL,
        [Name]                  [varchar] (30)          NOT NULL,
        [Description]           [varchar] (100)         NULL) ON [PRIMARY]
GO
```

The attributes for the **Tbl_CodeGroup** entity are very simple. See Table 8.12 for a listing and definition of the attributes. Some developers question the creation of a separate entity to hold this type of data, which in some limited situations may be a valid query. However, to create a fast and flexible code environment, this entity allows you the most flexibility.

## Tbl_Registry

The **Tbl_Registry** entity is perhaps one of the most useful entities in client/server development. In *Microsoft SQL Server Black Book*, published in 1997 by The Coriolis Group, some undocumented external procedures to read and write to the

**Table 8.12  Attribute list for Tbl_CodeGroup.**

| Column Name | Data Type | Description |
|---|---|---|
| Code_Group_ID | INT | An auto-incremented identity value that represents a unique number for this code group in the code table. This column will be used as the primary key, and an index should be created to support relational lookups and joins. |
| Name | VARCHAR(30) | The name of the group. The **VARCHAR** data type allows for less wasted space because most names will not be 30 characters in length. |
| Description | VARCHAR(100) | The long description for the group, typically displayed in reports. |

Windows NT Registry on the server were discussed. This table works and functions in essentially the same way except faster! After having benchmarked accessing the Windows NT Registry versus using a table structured in this way, it was found that this approach is much faster and even provides more functionality. Roaming profiles for users and applications can be stored in this table for ease of use. Listing 8.13 shows the syntax used to create the **Tbl_Registry** entity.

**Listing 8.13  Tbl_Registry.**

```
CREATE TABLE [dbo].[tbl_Registry] (
        [Reg_Key]                   [varchar] (255) NOT NULL,
        [Reg_Value]                 [varchar] (255) NOT NULL,
        [Date_Created]              [smalldatetime] NOT NULL,
        [Date_Modified]             [smalldatetime] NULL) ON [PRIMARY]
GO
```

The attributes for the **Tbl_Registry** entity are few, but are very useful. See Table 8.13 for a listing and definition of the attributes. This table should be thought of as a mirror of the operating system Registry with regard to how you create the keys. Use descriptive grouping of values and a common separator, so that lots of "nodes" can be stored in this structure.

## Tbl_ErrorDetail

The **Tbl_ErrorDetail** entity provides a storage mechanism for system-defined errors that a thorough error-handling routine would employ. See Chapter 12 for more details on a server-side error-handling methodology. This entity only stores the errors to be escalated or reported on by an error-handling system. See Listing 8.14 for the schema definition of the **ErrorDetail** entity.

**Table 8.13    Attribute list for Tbl_Registry.**

| Column Name | Data Type | Description |
|---|---|---|
| Reg_Key | VARCHAR(255) | This attribute is a string value that represents the node and key that you wish to store a data value in. (The 255 character width also provides backward compatibility to earlier versions of SQL Server.) |
| Reg_Value | VARCHAR(255) | This attribute stores the actual value to be associated with the key. The data type of this key is generic for storage and can be converted to any appropriate data type in stored procedures or client code. (The 255 character width also provides backward compatibility to earlier versions of SQL Server.) |
| Date_Created | SMALLDATETIME | This column is used mostly for informational reasons. There are times when the creation of a record will come into question. A default can be added to this column, and the stored procedure that populates the Registry can mask this data from the user and client code very easily. |
| Date_Modified | SMALLDATETIME | The modification of the data stored in this column may become important (see the **Date_Created** attribute for more details). A trigger is typically the best way to populate or maintain this kind of data. |

Listing 8.14    Tbl_ErrorDetail.

```
CREATE TABLE [dbo].[tbl_ErrorDetail] (
        [Error_Number]          [int]              NOT NULL,
        [Last_Occur]            [smalldatetime] NULL,
        [Occur_Count]           [int]              NULL,
        [Reset_Occur]           [smalldatetime] NULL,
        [Description]           [varchar] (100) NULL) ON [PRIMARY]
    GO
```

**ErrorDetail** attributes are shown in Table 8.14. An entry in this table would be the trigger to an error being added to the server-side error-handling routines.

## Tbl_ErrorLog

The **Tbl_ErrorLog** entity is at the center of an effective server-side error-handling scheme. This entity is the active repository for errors in client, server, and middle-tier processing. In Chapter 12, a great deal of time is spent discussing the uses and management of this data. Listing 8.15 shows the error log generation SQL.

**Table 8.14   Attribute list for Tbl_ErrorDetail.**

| Column Name | Data Type | Description |
| --- | --- | --- |
| Error_Number | INT | The value of this attribute can be any valid error defined on the server or in a client application. |
| Last_Occur | SMALLDATETIME | The date and time of the last occurrence of this particular error. |
| Occur_Count | INT | A number representing the total number of errors since the last time the reset action was taken on this record. |
| Reset_Occur | SMALLDATETIME | The date of the last reset action against this row typically executed through a stored procedure or client interface. |
| Description | VARCHAR(100) | The long description of the error. This value can be used in reports and email notifications. |

**Listing 8.15   Tbl_ErrorLog.**

```
CREATE TABLE [dbo].[tbl_ErrorLog] (
        [Error_DateTime]          [smalldatetime] NOT NULL,
        [Application]             [varchar] (50)  NULL,
        [Process]                 [varchar] (50)  NULL,
        [Error_Number]            [int]           NULL,
        [System_Error_Number]     [int]           NULL,
        [Description]             [varchar] (255) NULL) ON [PRIMARY]
GO
```

**Tbl_ErrorLog** attributes are usually modified to suit the needs of the error-handling system that is implemented on the server. Feel free to adjust them as required to suit your specific needs. Be sure to allow for the gathering of *all* useful information in this log. Some systems have even created a new entity that holds the error data for retry and troubleshooting when possible. Table 8.15 shows the attribute details for the **Tbl_ErrorLog** entity.

## Tbl_ErrorNotifyXref

The **Tbl_ErrorNotifyXref** table, shown in Listing 8.16, holds the relationship records that tie a particular error to an employee in the employee database. The employee record has the necessary attributes to handle contact information and notification preferences.

**Listing 8.16   Tbl_ErrorNotifyXref.**

```
CREATE TABLE [dbo].[tbl_ErrorNotifyXref] (
        [Error_Number]    [int]       NOT NULL,
        [Employee_ID]     [int]       NOT NULL) ON [PRIMARY]
GO
```

The **ErrorNotifyXref** attributes are simply entries for each notification association that the error escalation routine uses to contact people when errors of a specific type occur in the system. See Table 8.16 for a listing and definition of the attributes.

**Table 8.15    Attribute list for Tbl_ErrorLog.**

| Column Name | Data Type | Description |
| --- | --- | --- |
| Error_DateTime | SMALLDATETIME | The date and time the error occurs. This data can be supplied by the stored procedure or defaulted to the current date and time on the server. (Most people prefer to use the server date and time because it provides a common point of measurement instead of being at the mercy of many different system clocks.) |
| Application | VARCHAR(50) | The name of the application in which the error occurs. |
| Process | VARCHAR(50) | The actual process or subprocess in which the error occurs. |
| Error_Number | INT | The error number raised by the error-handling system. This number may not be the actual error number returned by the server or client application. An entry in the error list table would be a match for error escalation routines. This number can be especially useful for debugging client application issues that relate to server-side errors. |
| System_Error_Number | INT | The actual error number value from the system where the error occurs. This value can be a Delphi error code, a SQL error number (**@@ERROR**), or any other error that is environmentally generated. |
| Description | VARCHAR(255) | The description can be used to provide the detailed text of the error or store some descriptive data to point to where you should start troubleshooting the problem. The length of this description is 255 characters for backward compatibility only. (You can optionally change it to a larger number if your environment supports a larger size.) |

**Table 8.16    Attribute list for Tbl_ErrorNotifyXref.**

| Column Name | Data Type | Description |
| --- | --- | --- |
| Error_Number | INT | Error number from the **ErrorDetail** table. |
| Employee_ID | INT | Employee ID from the **Employee** entity. |

## Tbl_Process

The **Tbl_Process** entity is the master list for any process that will be monitored and logged in a system. The definition of the process and useful status information are stored in this table. One other key to this entity is that the enabled attribute allows you to selectively turn processes on or off based on your needs. This entity can be updated automatically via triggers on the MSDB database tables, so that you can consolidate automated scheduled tasks and server process information in a single location. Microsoft recommends against placing triggers on system tables (MSDB and Master should be regarded as containing only system tables), but in some situations it can be useful. You will always run the risk that your triggers will fail after an update due to structure changes in future releases of SQL Server. See Chapter 17 for more information on triggers and how this particular process entity update works. Listing 8.17 is a code snippet that creates the Process entity.

**Listing 8.17    Tbl_Process.**

```
CREATE TABLE [dbo].[tbl_process] (
        [process_id]            [int] IDENTITY (1, 1)    NOT NULL,
        [name]                  [varchar] (30)           NOT NULL,
        [enabled]               [tinyint]                NOT NULL,
        [description]           [varchar] (100)          NULL,
        [category]              [int]                    NULL,
        [run_duration]          [int]                    NULL,
        [run_outcome]           [int]                    NULL,
        [version_number]        [int]                    NOT NULL,
        [date_created]          [smalldatetime]          NOT NULL,
        [date_modified]         [smalldatetime]          NULL) ON [PRIMARY]
GO
```

This table acts as a collection and reporting master table, which holds the definition and recent execution information for a process that the system will monitor. See Table 8.17 for a listing and definition of the attributes for the **Tbl_Process** entity.

**Table 8.17    Attribute list for Tbl_Process.**

| Column Name | Data Type | Description |
| --- | --- | --- |
| **Process_ID** | **INT** | This is a unique integer that is automatically incremented each time a process is added to the table. It is the primary key column and is used as the parent value for process steps that are defined in the **ProcessSteps** entity. |
| **Name** | **VARCHAR(30)** | A descriptive name for the process; typically used in reports, email notification, or management screens. |

*(continued)*

**Table 8.17   Attribute list for Tbl_Process** *(continued).*

| Column Name | Data Type | Description |
|---|---|---|
| Enabled | TINYINT | A flag to determine if the process is active and enabled or disabled. The default value should be a 0 (disabled) and set to a 1 when enabled in the system. (Note the use of the **TINYINT** data type to save storage space.) |
| Description | VARCHAR(100) | A longer description of the process that can include more detail than the name. This data can also be used for reports and management screens. |
| Category | INT | A code table entry that allows the creation and management of processes by category. This is a grouping mechanism in most systems. |
| Run_Status | INT | A code table entry that provides status information for each process. See the code table earlier in this chapter for an example of the values for this status and the "Immediate Solutions" section for sample code data. |
| Run_Duration | INT | Duration in seconds of all the process steps combined. |
| Run_Outcome | INT | Error code or zero (0) for success. |
| Version_Number | INT | This attribute allows you to have versioned processes and potentially keep historical data for processes in the system. (A business rule could be written that would allow for only one version of a process to be enabled at any one time.) |
| Date_Created | SMALLDATETIME | This column is mostly used for informational reasons. There are times when the creation of a record will come into question. A default can be added to this column. |
| Date_Modified | SMALLDATETIME | The modification of the data stored in this column may become important (see the **Date_Created** attribute for more details). A trigger is typically the best way to populate or maintain this kind of data. |

## Tbl_ProcessLog

The **Tbl_ProcessLog** entity is the historically run information for processes on the server. The entries are relational in nature to the **Tbl_Process** entity and therefore do not store redundant information about the process definition, but rather store the instance or occurrence information. The **Tbl_ProcessLog** entity definition is shown in Listing 8.18.

### Listing 8.18   Tbl_ProcessLog.

```
CREATE TABLE [dbo].[tbl_ProcessLog] (
        [processlog_id]          [int] IDENTITY (1, 1)   NOT NULL,
```

```
        [process_id]          [int]                  NOT NULL,
        [run_datetime]        [smalldatetime]        NOT NULL,
        [run_status]          [int]                  NOT NULL,
        [run_duration]        [int]                  NULL,
        [run_outcome]         [int]                  NULL) ON [PRIMARY]
GO
```

Process log information is restricted to the actual execution of the process. The attributes are only required to provide instance or runtime information. Any detail information is pulled into a query through a join to the **Tbl_Process** entity. Table 8.18 shows the actual attributes and their definitions.

**Table 8.18   Attribute list for Tbl_ProcessLog.**

| Column Name | Data Type | Description |
| --- | --- | --- |
| **ProcessLog_ID** | **INT** | An auto-incrementing value that uniquely identifies this process with the process steps. |
| **Process_ID** | **INT** | The number generated from **Tbl_Process** each time a process is added to the table. This attribute can be used to join to the **ProcessStepsLog** entity. |
| **Run_DateTime** | **SMALLDATETIME** | The date and time the process is started. This data can be passed into a stored procedure or populated via a trigger. |
| **Run_Status** | **INT** | This column provides the current information for the process based on code table entries. This column can be updated during the process run to reflect current step status and eventual process exit or completion codes. |
| **Run_Duration** | **INT** | The number of seconds that the process takes. This column is a calculated value based on **Run_DateTime** and the system date/time of the final step or exit of the process. (This data could be orphaned if a step or process fails to log completion correctly.) |
| **Run_Outcome** | **INT** | Error number or zero (0) for success. |
| **Date_Created** | **SMALLDATETIME** | This column is mostly used for informational reasons. There are times when the creation of a record will come into question. A default can be added to this column. |
| **Date_Modified** | **SMALLDATETIME** | The modification of the data stored in this column may become important (see the **Date_Created** attribute for more details). A trigger is typically the best way to populate or maintain this kind of data. |

# Tbl_ProcessSteps

Processes can contain one or more steps. This entity stores the master definition of the steps defined for each process. Similar to the **Tbl_Process** entity, the details of the definition are stored in this entity. The SQL statement that creates the **Tbl_ProcessSteps** entity is shown in Listing 8.19.

**Listing 8.19   Tbl_ProcessSteps.**

```
CREATE TABLE [dbo].[tbl_ProcessSteps] (
        [process_id]          [int]              NOT NULL,
        [step_id]             [tinyint]          NOT NULL,
        [name]                [varchar] (30)     NOT NULL,
        [command]             [varchar] (3000)   NULL,
        [parameters]          [varchar] (3000)   NULL,
        [success_step]        [tinyint]          NULL,
        [fail_step]           [tinyint]          NULL,
        [run_status]          [int]              NULL,
        [run_duration]        [int]              NULL,
        [run_outcome]         [int]              NULL,
        [Date_Created]        [smalldatetime]    NOT NULL,
        [Date_Modified]       [smalldatetime]    NULL) ON [PRIMARY]
GO
```

See Table 8.19 for definitions of this entity's attributes. The key attributes for this entity are the **Command** and **Parameters** columns. They can optionally hold dynamic SQL or client code and named value-pairs for processes.

**Table 8.19   Attribute list for Tbl_ProcessSteps.**

| Column Name | Data Type | Description |
|---|---|---|
| Process_ID | INT | The number generated from **Tbl_Process** each time a process is added to the table. This attribute can be used to join to the **Tbl_ProcessStepsLog** entity. |
| Step_ID | TINYINT | Sequential number for each step in the process. |
| Name | VARCHAR(30) | The process step name. |
| Command | VARCHAR(3000) | The actual command that this step executes. This can be SQL or client code that is requested, and then parsed when executed. |
| Parameters | VARCHAR(3000) | Named value-pairs or a list of required parameters for the command when it is executed. These can be static or dynamic values. |

*(continued)*

**Table 8.19  Attribute list for Tbl_ProcessSteps** *(continued).*

| Column Name | Data Type | Description |
|---|---|---|
| **Success_Step** | **TINYINT** | This column can optionally be used to define the order of the step execution. It should hold the value of the next step to be executed upon successful completion of this step. |
| **Fail_Step** | **TINYINT** | The step that should be executed if this step fails is stored in this attribute. This allows for cleanup steps or error-handling steps to be defined for processes. |
| **Run_Status** | **INT** | This column provides the current information for the process step based on code table entries. |
| **Run_Duration** | **INT** | The number of seconds that the process step takes. This column is a calculated value based on **Run_DateTime** and the system date/time of the final step or exit of the process. (This data could be orphaned if a step or process fails to log completion correctly.) |
| **Run_Outcome** | **INT** | Error number or zero (0) for success. |
| **Date_Created** | **SMALLDATETIME** | This column is mostly used for informational reasons. There are times when the creation of a record will come into question. A default can be added to this column. |
| **Date_Modified** | **SMALLDATETIME** | The modification of the data stored in this column may become important (see the **Date_Created** attribute for more details). A trigger is typically the best way to populate or maintain this kind of data. |

## Tbl_ProcessStepsLog

This **Tbl_ProcessStepsLog** entity, shown in Listing 8.20, holds the actual step execution and runtime values for the process step. This data relates to the **Tbl_ProcessLog** entity. The **ProcessLog_ID** attribute is used to associate the step entry with the process log entry.

**Listing 8.20  Tbl_ProcessStepsLog.**

```
CREATE TABLE [dbo].[tbl_ProcessStepsLog] (
        [processlog_id] [int]            NOT NULL,
        [step_id]       [tinyint]        NOT NULL,
        [parameters]    [varchar] (3000) NULL,
        [run_datetime]  [smalldatetime]  NULL,
        [run_status]    [int]            NULL,
        [run_duration]  [int]            NULL,
        [run_outcome]   [int]            NULL,
        [date_created]  [smalldatetime]  NOT NULL,
        [date_modified] [smalldatetime]  NULL) ON [PRIMARY]
    GO
```

The **ProcessStepsLog** attributes are explained in Table 8.20. Actual process and step details can be referenced via joins back to the **Process** and **ProcessStep** entities.

**Table 8.20    Attribute list for Tbl_ProcessStepsLog.**

| Column Name | Data Type | Description |
| --- | --- | --- |
| ProcessLog_ID | INT | The number generated from **Tbl_ProcessLog** each time a process is added to the table. |
| Step_ID | TINYINT | Sequential number for each step in the process. (These steps should exist in the **ProcessSteps** entity.) |
| Parameters | VARCHAR(3000) | Named value-pairs or a list of required parameters for the command when it is executed. Normally, this data would be any runtime data that is used to execute the command. |
| Run_Status | INT | This column provides the current information for the process step based on code table entries. |
| Run_Duration | INT | The number of seconds that the process step takes. This column is a calculated value based on **Run_DateTime** and the system date/time of the final step or exit of the process. (This data could be orphaned if a step or process fails to log completion correctly.) |
| Run_Outcome | INT | Error number or zero (0) for success. |
| Date_Created | SMALLDATETIME | This column is mostly used for informational reasons. There are times when the creation of a record will come into question. A default can be added to this column. |
| Date_Modified | SMALLDATETIME | The modification of the data stored in this column may become important (see the **Date_Created** attribute for more details). A trigger is typically the best way to populate or maintain this kind of data. |

# *Immediate Solutions*

## Installing the Book Databases from Scripts

You can install the databases provided in a number of ways. Using scripts is probably the most portable method and allows you to see the syntax behind each structure. On the CD accompanying this book, you will find a directory called CODE. Each chapter has a subdirectory that contains all the listings in each chapter. Look in the Chapter 8 folder, and follow the steps in this section to install the book databases on a server.

---

**NOTE:** *The scripts should be read thoroughly before running them against your server. The directory the data and log files will be installed to should be modified to reflect your server. The path in the scripts reflects the default instance installation of Microsoft SQL Server.*

---

### Address

The following steps can be used to create the Address database, which is used in numerous examples throughout the remainder of this book:

**WARNING! If you already have an Address database installed on your server, do not run the script without first backing up the existing database, and then deleting it. The script assumes that no database called Address exists.**

1. Locate the address_all.sql file in the Chapter 8 directory.
2. Open the file in the Query Analyzer.
3. Read through the script before running it against your server.
4. Modify the script to reflect your installation of Microsoft SQL Server. (Place the data and log files on separate devices when possible for better performance.) See Listing 8.21 for the location of the data and log files in the script.
5. Run the entire script at one time.
6. Check the Enterprise Manager to make sure the database and tables were created successfully.

Listing 8.21 **Address_all.sql code sample.**

```
/* Create the Employee database              */
/* If your data and log are in a different location, */
```

```
/* change the paths for the filenames before running */
/* this script.                                       */
CREATE DATABASE [Address] ON (
  NAME        = N'Address_Data',
  FILENAME    = N'C:\Program Files\Microsoft SQL
Server\MSSQL\Data\Address_Data.MDF',
  SIZE        = 27,
  FILEGROWTH = 10%)
  LOG ON (
    NAME        = N'Address_Log',
    FILENAME    = N'C:\Program Files\Microsoft SQL
Server\MSSQL\Data\Address_Log.LDF',
    SIZE        = 1,
    FILEGROWTH = 10%)
GO
```

| Related solutions: | Found on page: |
| --- | --- |
| Installing MSSQL Server 2000 | 110 |
| Enterprise Manager | 178 |
| Query Analyzer | 193 |

## Employee

Follow the steps in this section to create the Employee database, which is used in various examples later in this book:

***WARNING!*** *If you already have an Employee database installed on your server, do not run the script without first backing up the database, and then deleting it. The script assumes that no database called Employee exists.*

1. Locate the employee_all.sql file in the Chapter 8 directory.

2. Open the file in the Query Analyzer.

3. Read through the script before running it against your server.

4. Modify the script to reflect your installation of Microsoft SQL Server. (Place the data and log files on separate devices when possible for better performance.) See Listing 8.22 for the location of the data and log files in the script.

5. Run the entire script at one time.

6. Check the Enterprise Manager to make sure the database and tables were created successfully.

Listing 8.22 **Employee_all.sql** code sample.

```
/* Create the Employee database               */
/* If your data and log are in a different location, */
/* change the paths for the filenames before running */
/* this script.                               */
CREATE DATABASE [Employee] ON (
  NAME       = N'Employee_Data',
  FILENAME   = N'C:\Program Files\Microsoft SQL
Server\MSSQL\Data\Employee_Data.MDF',
  SIZE       = 20,
  FILEGROWTH = 10%)
  LOG ON (
    NAME       = N'Employee_Log',
    FILENAME   = N'C:\Program Files\Microsoft SQL
Server\MSSQL\Data\Employee_Log.LDF',
    SIZE       = 5,
    FILEGROWTH = 10%)
GO
```

| Related solutions: | Found on page: |
|---|---|
| Installing MSSQL Server 2000 | 110 |
| Enterprise Manager | 178 |
| Query Analyzer | 193 |

## Utility

Follow these steps to create the Utility database, which will be required to run some of the examples presented later in this book:

**WARNING! If you already have a Utility database installed on your server, do not run the script without first backing up the database, and then deleting it. The script assumes that no database called Utility exists.**

1. Locate the utility_all.sql file in the Chapter 8 directory.

2. Open the file in the Query Analyzer.

3. Read through the script before running it against your server.

4. Modify the script to reflect your installation of Microsoft SQL Server. (Place the data and log files on separate devices when possible for better performance.) See Listing 8.22 for the location of the data and log files in the script.

5. Run the entire script at one time.

8. Black Book
Databases

6. Check the Enterprise Manager to make sure the database and tables were created successfully.

**Listing 8.23   Utility_all.sql code sample.**

```
/* Create the Employee database                          */
/* If your data and log are in a different location,  */
/* change the paths for the filenames before running */
/* this script.                                           */
CREATE DATABASE [Utility] ON (
  NAME        = N'Utility_Data',
  FILENAME    = N'C:\Program Files\Microsoft SQL
Server\MSSQL\Data\Utility_Data.MDF',
  SIZE        = 10,
  FILEGROWTH = 10%)
  LOG ON (
    NAME        = N'Utility_Log',
    FILENAME    = N'C:\Program Files\Microsoft SQL
Server\MSSQL\Data\Utility_Log.LDF',
    SIZE        = 1,
    FILEGROWTH = 10%)
GO
```

| Related solutions: | Found on page: |
| --- | --- |
| Installing MSSQL Server 2000 | 110 |
| Enterprise Manager | 178 |
| Query Analyzer | 193 |

# Refreshing the Book Databases from CD

In the event that you want to obtain a fresh copy of the databases that ship with the *SQL Black Book*, copies of the databases have been provided in a self-extracting archive on the CD. To copy them from the CD, follow these steps:

1. Double-click on the databases.exe in the chapter folder and databases subdirectory.

2. Extract to a folder on the target machine following the prompts from the extractor.

**NOTE:** *You can place the database file anywhere on the local machine or even on the network and use it with Microsoft SQL Server. Microsoft does not support network attached databases, however.*

## Detach

If you already have a copy of the required database on the server, you will first need to detach that copy of the database. Follow these steps to detach a database from Microsoft SQL Server:

---

**NOTE:** *The Address database is used in this example; however, the same procedure can be used for any database on the server.*

---

1. Right-click on the Address database in the Enterprise Manager.

2. Select All Tasks from the menu.

3. Select Detach Database as shown in Figure 8.1.

4. A confirmation dialog appears allowing you the option to update statistics prior to detaching the database. See Figure 8.2 for the detach database confirmation dialog.

---

**NOTE:** *Updating the statistics before detaching is only needed if you are going to reattach the database at a later time or on another server. For this example, it would be a waste of time.*

---

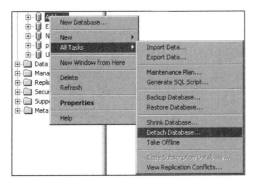

Figure 8.1    Detach Database menu selection.

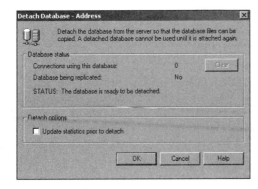

Figure 8.2    Detach database confirmation dialog.

5. Click on OK. The server detaches the database. This process only takes a few seconds depending on the server and size of the database.

6. When the process is completed, you should receive a dialog box like the one in Figure 8.3, stating the success of this task. Click on OK to close all the windows.

Once you have detached the database through the Enterprise Manager, you can delete or copy the files to a new server. This process is extremely useful for moving data between servers or migrating to new hardware. Repeat these steps as needed for each database you want to refresh on the server.

## Copy

The actual copy procedure used is the standard Windows drag-and-drop file copy, any command-line copy, or any other method of file transfer you may require or prefer. The files that Microsoft SQL Server uses are just files as far as the server is concerned. The real trick is to ensure you get both the MDF and LDF (data and log) files and move them to your target locations. You can also programmatically use the copy commands through **xp_cmdshell** calls to move data on a scheduled basis.

The default location for the self-extracting archive holding the databases is your Windows Temp directory. Simply move the files to your data and log locations, or extract them directly to the data folder once the database has been detached.

---

**NOTE:** *Be sure to copy only the files that you plan to replace. The files that are open (attached) will not allow you to overwrite them until they are detached.*

---

## Attach

Now that you have copied the new database files to the required locations, you need to reattach the databases so they will again be usable from SQL Server.

1. Right-click on the databases folder in the Enterprise Manager.

2. Select All Tasks.

3. Select Attach Database as shown in Figure 8.4.

**Figure 8.3    Completion dialog for detaching a database.**

Figure 8.4    Popup menu selections for attaching a database.

4. You are presented with a dialog asking you to select an MDF (data) file. You can type in the path of the MDF file, or select it by clicking on the ellipsis button next to the Verify button as shown in Figure 8.5.

5. For this exercise, click on the ellipsis button.

6. You are then presented with a browse window that uses the standard Windows directory tree and lists the available drives and folders on your server. Navigate through the directory tree until you find the target MDF file.

---

**NOTE:** *Files and folders are displayed in this dialog; the default installation of Microsoft SQL Server is assumed for this example.*

---

7. Select the MDF file for the database you want to attach. Because the Address database is being used in this example, select the address_ data.mdf file, and click on OK. See Figure 8.6 for the browse window presented for attaching your database.

8. The selected MDF file stores the LDF information as well as some other useful data. Once the MDF file is selected, all the information that was missing in Figure 8.5 is filled in. See Figure 8.7 for a complete attach database dialog.

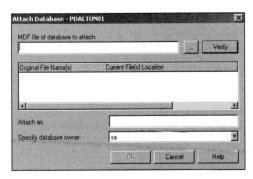

Figure 8.5    Select MDF file dialog.

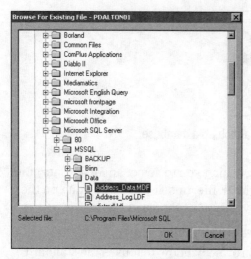

Figure 8.6   Browse window presented when searching for MDF files.

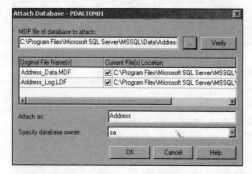

Figure 8.7   Attach database dialog with data ready to attach.

9.  Before you click on OK to start the attach process, verify the file locations, database name, and the owner of the database. If any of these selections are incorrect for your environment, change them before clicking on OK.

10. Once you have verified the selected information, click on OK.

11. The server processes the attach steps, which only takes a few seconds. You are then presented with an informational completion dialog. See Figure 8.8 for the completion dialog.

Figure 8.8   Attach database completion dialog.

12. Repeat the previous steps as needed to attach any other databases to your server.

| Related solutions: | Found on page: |
|---|---|
| Enterprise Manager | 178 |
| Creating a Maintenance Plan for the System Databases | 256 |
| Creating a Stored Procedure That Will Detach, Zip, Copy, and Attach the Inventory Database | 270 |

# Reverse-Engineering a Database Diagram

You can reverse-engineer a database model very easily in Microsoft SQL Server 2000. The diagram tool can actually become the structure maintenance utility for your database. To use this tool to its full advantage, you must first understand what it will and will not do for you. It will not perform all the tasks that some expensive third-party tools will, but it does a good job of graphically representing the tables and their respective relationships in a database.

When you installed the book databases, they did not create a diagram. So, let's walk through the steps to create one for the Address database. You can use the following technique to create a diagram for each of the other databases at your leisure:

1. In the Enterprise Manager, right-click on the diagram and select New Database Diagram from the menu.

2. The Create Database Diagram Wizard opens and asks you some questions to make the task easier. See Figure 8.9 for the opening screen of this wizard.

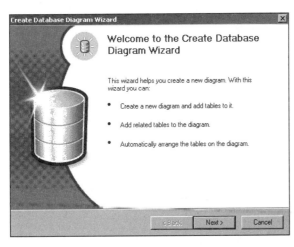

Figure 8.9  Create Database Diagram Wizard.

3. Click on Next.

4. You are presented with the page where you select the tables to add to the diagram.

5. Click on the Tbl_Address.

6. Hold down the Shift key, and click on the Tbl_ZipCode to select the entire list of tables.

7. Click on Add.

8. All the tables should now be in the pane on the right of the page. See Figure 8.10 to see what this screen should look like.

9. Click on Next.

10. You are ready to generate your diagram. Your screen should look like Figure 8.11 before you click on Finish.

---

**NOTE:** *If you perform this task on another database, the table names will be different, but the steps will be identical.*

---

At this stage, the new diagram will not have any relationships. (Relationships will be discussed in Chapter 16.) You can scale the drawing, move tables around to fit your thought process, and save your changes in the database. If you detach and attach a database, the diagram will move with it. This diagram provides a graphical way to manage your structures and define relationships in your model.

| *Related solutions:* | *Found on page:* |
|---|---|
| Enterprise Manager | 178 |
| Database Design Steps | 725 |

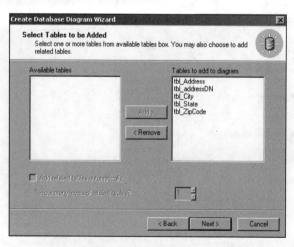

Figure 8.10    Selected tables for the diagram.

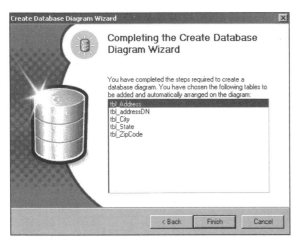

Figure 8.11    Final page of the Create Database Diagram Wizard.

# Populating Data with Scripts

Should the data become unusable or need to be restored to its installation state, you can run the population script on the CD to remove all records from the tables and replace them with the original records. You do not have to rebuild the database from scratch; these scripts perform the housecleaning needed to reset the data automatically.

On the CD accompanying this book, you will find a directory called CODE. Each chapter will have a subdirectory that contains all the listings in each chapter. Look in the Chapter 8 folder, and follow these steps to install the book databases on a server.

---

***NOTE:*** *The scripts should be read thoroughly before running them against your server.*

---

## Address

The following steps can be used to generate test data for the Address database:

1. Locate the populate_address.sql file in the Chapter 8 directory.

2. Open the file in the Query Analyzer.

3. Read through the script before running it against your server.

4. Modify the script to set the number of autogenerated addresses you want in the tables (100,000 rows is only the default value). See Listing 8.24 for the location of the data and log files in the script. Change the value of **@v_Max** to the number of addresses you want to generate.

---

**NOTE:** *This code exists roughly half-way down the file and has a listing reference just above it.*

---

**Listing 8.24   Section of the populate_address.sql file.**

```
PRINT 'Generating address data...'

DECLARE @i        INTEGER, -- Loop counter
        @n        INTEGER, -- House number
        @v_Max    INTEGER, -- Number of addresses to populate
        @v_Line1  VARCHAR(50),
        @v_Line2  VARCHAR(50),
        @v_Street VARCHAR(30),
        @v_CityID  INTEGER,
        @v_StateID INTEGER,
        @v_ZipID   INTEGER,
        @v_Str    VARCHAR(255)

SELECT @i         = 1,
       @n         = 100,
       @v_Max     = 100000, -- Target number of addresses
       @v_Street  = ' Main St.',
       @v_CityID  = 1, -- Pre-populated City
       @v_StateID = 1, -- Pre-populated State
       @v_ZipID   = 2  -- Pre-populated Zip

PRINT 'Adding new addresses...'
```

5. Run the entire script at one time.

6. You will see output similar to Listing 8.25 upon completion of the script. Any errors that may occur should be checked thoroughly. Make sure that you have the database selected and that there are no issues with the database before running the script.

**Listing 8.25   Output from populate_address.sql.**

```
Removing existing DATA...
Adding new zip codes...
Adding new states...
Adding new cities...
```

```
Checkpointing DB...
Generating address data...
Adding new addresses...
10000...
20000...
30000...
40000...
50000...
60000...
70000...
80000...
90000...
100000...
Creating denormalized dataset...
Done.
```

**NOTE:** *This script may take 5 to 10 minutes on some servers to generate a large number of rows. Be patient and let it run through completion. In previous tests, 100,000 rows averaged six minutes to generate. (It also creates an identical set of denormalized data with the same number of rows.) The net is two times the **@v_Max** value of records in the Address database.*

## Employee

The following steps will populate the Employee database with data to be used in various examples:

1. Locate the populate_employee.sql file in the Chapter 8 directory.

2. Open the file in the Query Analyzer.

3. Read through the script before running it against your server.

**NOTE:** *There is no real need to modify any data in this script unless you want to change names or other values in the insert statements to fit your environment.*

4. Run the entire script at one time.

5. You will see output similar to Listing 8.26 upon completion of the script. Any errors that may occur should be checked thoroughly. Make sure that you have the database selected and that there are no issues with the database before running the script.

**Listing 8.26  Output from populate_employee.sql.**

```
Removing existing DATA...
Adding Employees...
Adding address Xref records...
Adding employee rate records...
```

```
Checkpointing DB...
Done.
```

## Utility

Use the following steps to populate the Utility database with basic test data:

1. Locate the populate_utility.sql file in the Chapter 8 directory.

2. Open the file in the Query Analyzer.

3. Read through the script before running it against your server.

4. You will see output similar to Listing 8.27 upon completion of the script. Any errors that may occur should be checked thoroughly. Make sure that you have the database selected and that there are no issues with the database before running the script.

5. Run the entire script at one time.

**Listing 8.27   Output from populate_utility.sql.**

```
Removing existing DATA...
Adding code groups...
Adding new codes...
Adding new registry records...
Checkpointing DB...
Done.
```

| Related solutions: | Found on page: |
|---|---|
| Enterprise Manager | 178 |
| Query Analyzer | 193 |
| Using **INSERT/SELECT** | 435 |

# Scripting Database Objects

This example will walk you through the basic steps required to generate scripts for your database objects using the Enterprise Manager. These scripts can be an invaluable part of your system backup that will allow you to recreate your database structure quickly and easily.

1. Right-click on the Address database.

2. Select All Tasks.

3. Select Generate SQL Script as seen in Figure 8.12.

4. In the object selection dialog box, click on Show All. This enables the filtering checkboxes, so that you can select the objects you want to script.

5. Select the Script All Objects checkbox. See Figure 8.13 for an example of what the dialog box looks like at this point.

6. You can selectively add or remove items from the objects to be scripted list. For this example let's script all objects.

7. You can also preview the script without generating it by clicking on the Preview button.

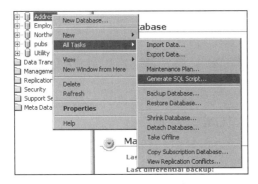

Figure 8.12   Generate SQL Script popup menu.

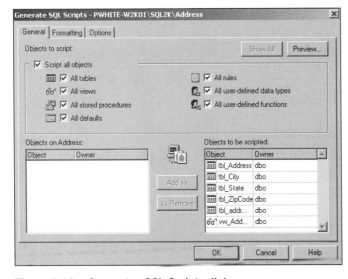

Figure 8.13   Generates SQL Scripts dialog.

8. Next, select the Formatting tab.

9. You can add formatting options to the script. For this exercise, let's leave the default values. See Figure 8.14 to view the Formatting tab.

10. Select the Options tab. This tab allows you to split the script into individual files or use one large file. Let's leave the single file default selected.

11. Change the file format to Windows text (ANSI).

12. Click on OK. You are presented with a standard Windows Save dialog box to provide a location and name for the script.

13. Type "test.sql", and save the file in your Temp directory.

14. A progress bar informs you of what objects have been generated and the percent of completion. You should then be presented with a success dialog box. Click on OK.

15. The scripting of the objects into a file is complete.

| Related solution: | Found on page: |
|---|---|
| Enterprise Manager | 178 |

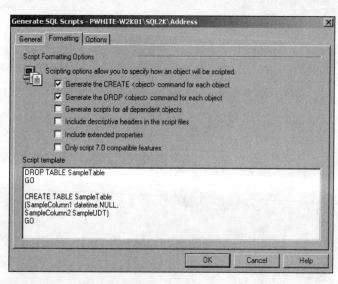

**Figure 8.14   Formatting tab.**

# Transferring Objects with Scripts

You can script and transfer objects between databases by generating text files and saving them (see previous section). You can then open a saved script and run it against another database or server to create an exact structure copy of the objects in the script. Let's assume that the test.sql file from the previous exercise exists. You can substitute any file you create in this exercise to achieve the same results.

1. Open the Query Analyzer.

2. Connect to the server you want to transfer objects to.

3. Select the database from the list of available databases.

4. Open the test.sql file in the Query Analyzer.

5. Run the script.

6. You can verify the new object's existence by looking in the Enterprise Manager (remember that you may have to refresh the display) or by selecting from sysobjects to see if there are entries in that table for the objects you created.

When you run a script on another server or database, ensure that you do not receive any object creation errors. These typically occur if you do not generate drop statements to match the create statements in the script.

---

**NOTE:** *Be sure not to lose any data when running scripts to drop and create objects in a foreign database. You should run a query against the sysobjects or check in the Enterprise Manager before you run your script.*

---

You can schedule the migration of objects via scripts through the scheduled jobs. This method works if you are only concerned about structures. If you need to migrate data, you should be considering Data Transformation Services (DTS) packages as a method of population.

| *Related solutions:* | *Found on page:* |
|---|---|
| Enterprise Manager | 178 |
| Query Analyzer | 193 |
| Creating a Maintenance Plan for the System Databases | 256 |
| Creating a Custom Package with the DTS Designer | 322 |

**8. Black Book Databases**

# Using a Codes Table

This solution will provide you with the basic steps necessary to start taking advantage of the flexibility provided by the Codes table in the Utility database.

1. Create a code group entry to create a grouping ID for the new code. See Listing 8.28 for an example of the syntax to insert a record into **Tbl_CodeGroup**. (This code is used in the populate_utility.sql file, but is formatted in this section for legibility.)

**Listing 8.28   Insert into Tbl_CodeGroup.**

```
INSERT INTO tbl_CodeGroup (
  Code_Group_ID,
  Name,
  Description)
VALUES (
  1,
  'Title',
  'Employee Title')
```

2. You can then add the codes that will be used to define the group. See Listing 8.29 for some example codes from populate_utility.sql. These statements insert an **IDENTITY** value in the script, so the **SET** statement is required as well as the column list. See the comment (—) that holds the SQL statement syntax that is used once the database is configured with the scripts.

**Listing 8.29   Code table insert example.**

```
SET IDENTITY_INSERT tbl_codes ON

-- Example (if not in this script)
-- INSERT INTO tbl_Codes VALUES ('DBArch', 'DB Architect',1)
INSERT INTO tbl_Codes (Code_ID, Code, Description,Code_Group_ID)
  VALUES (1, 'DBArch', 'DB Architect',1)
INSERT INTO tbl_Codes (Code_ID, Code, Description,Code_Group_ID)
  VALUES (2, 'DBA', 'DB Administrator',1)
INSERT INTO tbl_Codes (Code_ID, Code, Description,Code_Group_ID)
  VALUES (3, 'SQLProg', 'SQL Programmer',1)
INSERT INTO tbl_Codes (Code_ID, Code, Description,Code_Group_ID)
  VALUES (9, 'SRDBA', 'Senior DBA',1)
INSERT INTO tbl_Codes (Code_ID, Code, Description,Code_Group_ID)
  VALUES (10, 'NetTech', 'Network Technician',1)
INSERT INTO tbl_Codes (Code_ID, Code, Description,Code_Group_ID)
  VALUES (11, 'MISMgr', 'MIS Manager',1)
```

```
INSERT INTO tbl_Codes (Code_ID, Code, Description,Code_Group_ID)
  VALUES (12, 'QAMgr', 'QA Mananger',1)
INSERT INTO tbl_Codes (Code_ID, Code, Description,Code_Group_ID)
  VALUES (13, 'QATech', 'QA Technician',1)
INSERT INTO tbl_Codes (Code_ID, Code, Description,Code_Group_ID)
  VALUES (14, 'Admin', 'Admin Support',1)
INSERT INTO tbl_Codes (Code_ID, Code, Description,Code_Group_ID)
  VALUES (15, 'SrAdmin', 'Senior Administrator',1)
INSERT INTO tbl_Codes (Code_ID, Code, Description,Code_Group_ID)
  VALUES (16, 'CEO', 'Chief Operations Officer',1)
INSERT INTO tbl_Codes (Code_ID, Code, Description,Code_Group_ID)
  VALUES (17, 'CTO', 'Chief Technical Officer',1)

SET IDENTITY_INSERT tbl_codes OFF
```

---

**NOTE:** *The list has been edited to only show code group 1 statements*

---

3. When creating a table in a database, use an **INT** data type to store the code table ID for the code that is used to describe the entity.

4. Join back to the codes table or create a code lookup function that resolves the code or description when used in user queries.

| Related solutions: | Found on page: |
| --- | --- |
| Query Analyzer | 193 |
| Using **INSERT/SELECT** | 435 |
| Code Table Procedures | 651 |
| Database Design Steps | 725 |

# Using the Registry Table

This example will help you become familiar with the techniques needed to work with the Registry table in your own applications. You can use the power and flexibility provided by this structure to enhance your own application and processes.

1. Determine the Registry table key that will be used. Be sure to use as descriptive a key as possible, for example, <SYSTEM>\<PROCESS>\ <TITLE>. Be sure to enforce a common standard for your keys with all other programmers. This will ensure that you do not perform duplicated efforts or produce hard-to-follow data.

2. Insert a record into the Registry table with the key and value to be used later. See Listing 8.30 for an example Registry table entry from populate_utility.sql.

### Listing 8.30    Registry table **Insert** statement.

```
INSERT INTO tbl_Registry (Reg_Key, Reg_Value, Date_Created, Date_Modified)
   VALUES ('Company\Setup\Phone\AreaCode', '555', '07/20/2000', NULL)
```

**NOTE:** *Most systems use standard stored procedure interfaces to add, update, delete, and obtain this data in application development. This makes the use of the data very easy and masks the date created and modified data elements from the general user.*

3. Use the data for this key for setup, profile, application, or process parameters in your process engineering.

| Related solutions: | Found on page: |
|---|---|
| Query Analyzer | 193 |
| Using **INSERT/SELECT** | 435 |
| Registery Procedures | 646 |

# Chapter 9

# Structured Query Language (SQL)

# In Depth

There are as many ways to access data as there are ways to write programs. Each database has its own unique method of accessing the data stored on disk. Over time, a standard has evolved that has come to be known as the Structured Query Language (SQL).

This standard is still being defined today, but it is by far better than it was 20 years ago. When looking back at early forms of databases, especially in smaller systems, you will find that a proprietary language was the order of the day for most programmers. SQL was considered a second-class language compared with most programming languages available.

Even today, many true programmers look at SQL as a scripting language, believing that it is too simple to be as fast as code that is compiled and executed. Although SQL is not Pascal or C++, it is a very powerful language that takes data access to a higher level than either the Pascal or C++ programming languages.

This chapter introduces the core elements of the SQL language and its syntax. It is mainly intended for beginners, but more advanced users should probably at least skim the material provided to make sure they are familiar with all of the information presented.

## ANSI-Compliant SQL

SQL has been developed to provide a uniform method for accessing data stored in a database. Even the desktop and shared file applications, like Microsoft Access and Microsoft Visual Fox Pro, support SQL queries against their database files. In 1992, the American National Standards Institute (ANSI) published a set of standard SQL statements that should be supported by database applications. This standard was intended to provide functionality that could be depended on to run on many different platforms. Microsoft SQL Server, as well as other databases, support this standard (or at least most of it) as a core level of functionality and then provide extensions to it.

If you write your SQL code to follow the ANSI standard, your scripts and queries can be run against a broad range of databases without modification. This capability has thrust database development into the forefront of application development in today's businesses. Coupled with the development of ODBC, your client application can now take advantage of the features of many large database systems without your having to change client code.

Microsoft SQL Server can be configured to be ANSI-SQL 92-compliant and supports ANSI queries. In addition, extensions to this ANSI standard allow you more freedom in your code. These extensions, along with different syntax that can be used to write queries, are available on Microsoft SQL Server and may not be available on all systems you run your code against. Be careful when using non-ANSI standard queries in your code. You might have to modify your code slightly to run on other systems.

---

**NOTE:** *Because Microsoft SQL Server is the focus of this book, this chapter discusses its version of SQL (Transact-SQL). For the differences in syntax, refer to the Microsoft SQL Server Books Online.*

---

In addition, some very useful quick-reference guides for writing ANSI-compliant code are available, one of which is the *SQL Instant Reference* by Martin Gruber (Sybex, 2000). This manual is a desktop reference that every database administrator (DBA) should own. It illustrates the differences between ANSI 89 and 92 SQL and has very helpful code examples for writing almost any query you require.

Queries, ranging from the simplest to the most advanced, written against multiple tables with complex formatting and output are covered in this chapter. The Pubs database installed on your server is used as an example. You can run the queries given in this chapter against your own system to test them and determine if they are useful. Because most production systems will not have the Pubs database installed, run the queries against a development system for test purposes.

## Syntax

SQL is a very readable language once you get to know the different statements involved. You'll find the basics of SQL easy to memorize, but the more elaborate statements and functions require a quick lookup in Microsoft SQL Server Books Online.

## Comments

Do not fall into the trap of leaving comments out of your code. Comment your code in blocks, so that at a minimum you can look back on it in six months and remember what you were trying to do.

Comments are placed in your code in two ways: by using the forward slash and asterisk (/*) at the beginning of a comment and an asterisk and forward slash (*/) to close the comment out or by beginning and ending inline comments with a dash, dash (SQL code-comment). Whether you use the slashes or the dashes, you will be doing yourself a favor by having good notes in your code for future use.

---

***TIP:*** *Similar to other major programming languages, slashes comment out a single line of code or multiple lines of code. Dashes are used for inline comments. Use a style that makes sense to you and stick with it. Adopting a standard for comments in a production environment can save many hours of work.*

---

## Formatting

SQL statements ignore white space. Therefore, you can use spaces freely to make your code more legible. As you read through this chapter, notice that different sections of code have been aligned with other sections in the code. This is done for clarity—you do not have to follow this convention. However, in a multi-programmer shop, some kind of standard should be adopted for consistency and ease of understanding among the group. Additionally, when you want to see all the columns in a table, use an asterisk (*) in place of each column name. This technique makes it easy to obtain all columns backing a query. Keep in mind, however, that this method can also cause problems. If a client software package expects five columns to be returned from a query and the query uses the asterisk to get the columns, a schema change can break the client. As a rule, specify the names of the columns you want returned with your queries.

# Pubs Database

Let's start our tour of SQL with a quick look at the Pubs database. A few of the tables in the Pubs database are used to illustrate the data manipulation techniques you need to write effective queries. These tables are loaded automatically by the installation program and are placed inside the master device along with the master database. Microsoft has populated each table with sample data.

## Authors

Let's first look at the **Authors** table, which is shown in Table 9.1. This table has nine columns and two indexes. Like any other entity tracking table, the Author table holds address information. After installing SQL Server, 23 rows comprise this table.

## Sales

The **Sales** table is shown in Table 9.2. This table has six columns and two indexes. The Sales table holds sales information for each title sold for a particular store. After installing SQL Server, this table is comprised of 21 rows.

## Titleauthor

Of all the sample tables, the **Titleauthor** table is probably the most confusing. Shown in Table 9.3, this table has four columns and three indexes. There is one

Table 9.1    **Authors** table schema.

| Column | Data Type |
|--------|-----------|
| Au_id | VARCHAR(11) |
| Au_lname | VARCHAR(40) |
| Au_fname | VARCHAR(20) |
| Phone | CHAR(12) |
| Address | VARCHAR(40) |
| City | VARCHAR(20) |
| State | CHAR(2) |
| Zip | CHAR(5) |
| Contract | BIT |

*Indexes are on the **au_id** column and the **al_lname** and **au_fname** columns.*

Table 9.2    **Sales** table schema.

| Column | Data Type |
|--------|-----------|
| Store_id | CHAR(4) |
| Ord_Num | VARCHAR(20) |
| Ord_Date | DATETIME |
| Qty | SMALLINT |
| Payterms | VARCHAR(12) |
| Title_id | VARCHAR(6) |

*Indexes are on the **title_id** column and the **store_id**, **ord_num**, and **title_id** columns.*

Table 9.3    **Titleauthor** table schema.

| Column | Data Type |
|--------|-----------|
| au_id | VARCHAR(11) |
| title_id | VARCHAR(6) |
| au_ord | TINYINT |
| royaltyper | INT |

*Indexes are on the **au_id** and **title_id** columns and another index combines the two columns **au_id** and **title_id**.*

record for each title that each author has written. It does not hold a lot of meaningful data except that each book can have many authors, and each author is responsible for a percentage of each title's royalties. This table holds the ID values for each author and title. There are 25 rows in this table.

# SELECT Statements

**SELECT** statements do not modify the underlying data in any way. They are simply a method of looking at the data stored in a single table or in many related tables. **SELECT** statements also do not generate a transaction in Microsoft SQL Server. Let's use the **Authors** table to illustrate some **SELECT** statements. See Listing 9.1 for the syntax.

---

**NOTE:** *Spend a few minutes in Microsoft SQL Server Books Online to become familiar with all of the clauses in a* ***SELECT*** *statement. This up-front time can mean the difference between hours and minutes when you are trying to get a query to perform to meet the  user's needs.*

---

**Listing 9.1    SELECT statement syntax.**

```
SELECT [ ALL | DISTINCT ] select_list
 [ INTO new_table ]
[ FROM table_name | view_name ]
[ [ LEFT [ INNER | OUTER ] | RIGHT [ INNER | OUTER ] | CROSS ]
 JOIN table_name | view_name ON join_condition ]
[ WHERE search_condition ]
[ GROUP BY group_by_expression ]
[ HAVING search_condition ]
[ ORDER BY order_expression [ ASC | DESC ] ]
[ COMPUTE aggregate_functions ]
[ FOR { BROWSE | XML { RAW | AUTO | EXPLICIT }
            [ , XMLDATA ]
            [ , ELEMENTS ]
            [ , BINARY BASE64 ]
      } ]
```

There are three keywords to keep in mind when retrieving data through SQL: **SELECT, FROM,** and **WHERE**. The **SELECT** list is the list of columns that you want to return from the query. Depending on your query, these columns can be from one table or multiple tables. You can return all of the column values, manipulate the column to return a computed value, or you can combine column values to create something totally new (like building an ID number from various fields). The **FROM** statement specifies the table, tables, or views from which you want to retrieve the data. The **WHERE** clause specifies which rows to include or exclude for your query's output.

---

**NOTE:** *Omitting the* ***WHERE*** *clause returns or manipulates all rows in the table. Be careful to omit the* ***WHERE*** *clause only when you really intend to query the entire table or view. Omitting* ***WHERE*** *places an extra burden on the server, so in production queries, always use a* ***WHERE*** *clause.*

---

Listing 9.2 shows some basic queries. The first four example queries return the same columns and number of rows. As shown in Query 5, the order of the columns or which columns are included can be changed to affect what the query returns. It is preferable to use some formatting to help keep your SQL code clear and easy to change. With each column specified in the **SELECT** list, easy changes, such as column order or adding and removing columns can be achieved with little problem. Notice in Query 2 that the long line of code, even with this basic query, is harder to read than the stacked code in Query 4. Use formatting to clarify your code.

**Listing 9.2    Basic SQL queries.**

```
/* Query 1 */
SELECT * FROM authors

/* Query 2 */
SELECT au_id, au_lname, au_fname, address, city, state, zip, phone, contract
FROM authors

/* Query 3 (Formatted) */
SELECT *
  FROM authors

/* Query 4 (Formatted) */
SELECT au_id,
       au_lname,
       au_fname,
       address,
       city,
       state,
       zip,
       phone,
       contract
  FROM authors

/* Query 5 (Formatted) */
SELECT au_lname,
       au_fname,
       address,
       city,
       state,
       zip
  FROM authors
```

String functions can be used to manipulate the output to read exactly the way you need it to. For example, Listing 9.3 shows a basic query (Query 1) that returns the first name, last name, and phone number for each author. Let's apply some string functions and formatting to make this list a bit easier to read. For the sake of this example, let's assume that you want the list to show first initial, last name, and the area code of the phone number in parentheses.

Query 2 of Listing 9.3 shows the syntax. The **UPPER** function converts the text to uppercase, and the **LEFT** function returns text beginning with the first character of the first name and includes only one character. Notice that the period after the first initial is added by using the string concatenation operator "**+**". This allows for good formatting and user-friendly output. Only three columns worth of data are returned to the client.

**NOTE:** For more detailed explanations of these or any other functions, refer to Microsoft SQL Server Books Online.

### Listing 9.3    Phone list example.

```
/* Query 1 (name and phone number) */
SELECT au_fname,
       au_lname,
       phone
  FROM authors


/* Query 2 (first initial, last name, phone number) */
SELECT UPPER(LEFT(au_fname, 1)) + '.',
       au_lname,
       phone
  FROM authors


/* Query 3 (first initial, last name, formatted phone number) */
SELECT UPPER(LEFT(au_fname, 1)) + '.',
       au_lname,
       '(' + LEFT(phone, 3) + ') ' + RIGHT(phone, 8)
  FROM authors


/* Query 4 (finished output with formatting and titles) */
SELECT UPPER(LEFT(au_fname, 1)) + '. ' + au_lname AS "Name",
       '(' + LEFT(phone, 3) + ') ' + RIGHT(phone, 8) AS "Phone"
  FROM authors
```

Formatting the phone number is accomplished in the same way as the formatting of the first name except with a bit more string manipulation. Query 3 in Listing 9.3 shows the phone number formatting required. You need to tell SQL Server to combine the first two columns into one column, restrict the length to a reasonable value to limit wasted white space, and change the titles displayed for each column to a user-friendly title instead of the column name in the table. Functions and string manipulations are common in SQL code. These functions are very fast and make the output easy to read. See Listing 9.4 for the sample outputs for Queries 1 and 4 from Listing 9.3 to compare the reports. You can copy these queries and run them on your system to make sure the results match.

**Listing 9.4    Sample output.**

```
Query 1
au_fname              au_lname                                 phone
--------------------  ---------------------------------------  ------------

Johnson               White                                    408 496-7223
Marjorie              Green                                    415 986-7020
Cheryl                Carson                                   415 548-7723
Michael               O'Leary                                  408 286-2428
Dean                  Straight                                 415 834-2919


Query 4
Name                                             Phone
---------------------------------------------    --------------

J. White                                         (408) 496-7223
M. Green                                         (415) 986-7020
C. Carson                                        (415) 548-7723
M. O'Leary                                       (408) 286-2428
D. Straight                                      (415) 834-2919
M. Smith                                         (913) 843-0462
A. Bennet                                        (415) 658-9932
```

# WHERE Clause

Using the same sample data, let's look at restricting the number of rows returned by your queries. This horizontal partitioning is done with the **WHERE** clause. Let's assume, for the sake of this example, that you want to see only the authors that live in the 415 area code. As shown in Query 1 of Listing 9.5, you would add a **WHERE** clause to your query.

**Listing 9.5    Horizontal partitioning of data.**

```
/* Query 1 (only 415 area code) */
SELECT UPPER(SUBSTRING(au_fname, 1, 1)) + '. ' + au_lname AS "Name",
       '(' + LEFT(phone, 3) + ') ' + RIGHT(phone,8) AS "Phone"
   FROM authors
   WHERE LEFT(Phone, 3) = '415'

/* Query 2 (California authors) */
SELECT UPPER(SUBSTRING(au_fname, 1, 1)) + '. ' + au_lname AS "Name",
       '(' + LEFT(phone, 3) + ') ' + RIGHT(phone,8) AS "Phone"
   FROM authors
   WHERE State = 'CA'
```

**WHERE** clauses use comparison operators to check the value of a column against another value to determine if it should be avoided, because the Query Optimizer has a difficult time knowing if a record is *not* something. **NOT** is *not* optimizable! Most queries can be rewritten to take advantage of equalities rather than inequalities.

Notice the same **SUBSTRING** function is used, along with an equal sign and 415 in quotes. You could use a column name instead of the string function if you only wanted the authors in California. Or, you could use Query 2 in Listing 9.5 to return just those records where the author lives in California. Notice in Query 2 that the **WHERE** clause uses a column that does not exist in the **SELECT** list. Listing the column in the **SELECT** list is not always required in your queries. However, it is required when using aggregate functions; those functions are covered in the "Aggregates and Functions" section later in this chapter.

When you execute these queries, even though different records are returned, they are still formatted by the function in the **SELECT** list. These interchangeable **WHERE** clauses allow you to view the same data from a table while restricting the row-matching and shortening the list considerably. See Listing 9.6 for the results of these two queries.

**Listing 9.6    State and area code query sample output.**

```
Query 1
Name                                                Phone
------------------------------------------------    -------------
M. Green                                            (415) 986-7020
C. Carson                                           (415) 548-7723
D. Straight                                         (415) 834-2919
A. Bennet                                           (415) 658-9932
A. Dull                                             (415) 836-7128
C. Locksley                                         (415) 585-4620
A. Yokomoto                                         (415) 935-4228
D. Stringer                                         (415) 843-2991
S. MacFeather                                       (415) 354-7128
L. Karsen                                           (415) 534-9219
S. Hunter                                           (415) 836-7128

(11 row(s) affected)

Query 2
Name                                                Phone
------------------------------------------------    -------------
J. White                                            (408) 496-7223
M. Green                                            (415) 986-7020
```

```
C. Carson                                     (415) 548-7723
M. O'Leary                                    (408) 286-2428
D. Straight                                   (415) 834-2919
A. Bennet                                     (415) 658-9932
A. Dull                                       (415) 836-7128
B. Gringlesby                                 (707) 938-6445
C. Locksley                                   (415) 585-4620
A. Yokomoto                                   (415) 935-4228
D. Stringer                                   (415) 843-2991
S. MacFeather                                 (415) 354-7128
L. Karsen                                     (415) 534-9219
S. Hunter                                     (415) 836-7128
H. McBadden                                   (707) 448-4982

(15 row(s) affected)
```

With these simple queries, there are no real mysteries as to what should be indexed on the table. If you were selecting only certain states, you would want to place an index on the state column to get the fastest results. Indexing strategies are covered in more detail in Chapter 16. **WHERE** clauses are one of two critical areas for indexes. Depending on your **WHERE** clause, the Microsoft SQL Server Query Optimizer may decide that an indexed search for matching records is faster; if so, it would create a temporary table to support your query. Once your query is finished, Microsoft SQL Server drops the temporary table because it is no longer needed.

The second and most critical area for index placement with regard to **SELECT** statements is the **ORDER BY** clause.

# ORDER BY Clause

Now let's alphabetize the phone list. The output of Query 2 in Listing 9.5 can be rearranged to follow the last name in ascending or descending order by adding an **ORDER BY** clause. See Listing 9.7 for the new query using an **ORDER BY** clause and the resulting output.

**Listing 9.7    Phone list with an ORDER BY clause.**

```
/* Phone List in Alpha Order (CA) */
SELECT UPPER(SUBSTRING(au_fname, 1, 1)) + '. ' + au_lname AS "Name",
       '(' + LEFT(phone, 3) + ') ' + RIGHT(phone,8) AS "Phone"
  FROM authors
  WHERE State = 'CA'
  ORDER BY au_lname
```

**9. Structured Query Language (SQL)**

```
Output
Name                                              Phone
--------------------------------------------      --------------
A. Bennet                                         (415) 658-9932
C. Carson                                         (415) 548-7723
A. Dull                                           (415) 836-7128
M. Green                                          (415) 986-7020
B. Gringlesby                                     (707) 938-6445
S. Hunter                                         (415) 836-7128
L. Karsen                                         (415) 534-9219
C. Locksley                                       (415) 585-4620
S. MacFeather                                     (415) 354-7128
H. McBadden                                       (707) 448-4982
M. O'Leary                                        (408) 286-2428
D. Straight                                       (415) 834-2919
D. Stringer                                       (415) 843-2991
J. White                                          (408) 496-7223
A. Yokomoto                                       (415) 935-4228

(15 row(s) affected)
```

Notice that only the column name is used for the **ORDER BY** clause. You also could have used the area code substring to further sort the resulting list. Another, more cryptic option would be to list the number of the column in the **SELECT** list. This method is seldom used because of the hard-to-follow "**ORDER BY 2**" or "**ORDER BY 2,3**" in the SQL statement.

**ORDER BY** clauses are the first place to look for matching indexes. Anytime you write an ordered or sorted query, verify that a corresponding index exists on the table you are querying. A clustered index on the ordered column or columns helps ensure that the server will not create a worktable for this query. Keep in mind that you can have only one clustered index on each of your tables. Microsoft SQL Server almost always needs an index to perform an **ORDER BY** statement efficiently.

**NOTE:** You can use the Query Analyzer to examine the query plan to see whether or not the index you create is being used as you expect. In some cases, a statistics set on the column can be used in place of an index, especially if the table is small.

You can sort by as many as 16 columns with an **ORDER BY** statement, although for performance reasons, this is not recommended. Offline reporting and overnight processes are the only place that **ORDER BY** statements with a great number of columns are usually seen. On larger tables with queries that return large result sets, you can run out of space in TempDB very quickly. Remember that worktables are placed in TempDB while in use. Everyone shares this space for in-process query manipulation. If you place a large ordered worktable in TempDB, it cannot be allocated. This is not something you want to happen.

# GROUP BY Clause

Now let's group the data in the **Authors** table so that the authors are listed in alphabetical order. grouped by state. You'll first need to add the state column to the **SELECT** list and list the other displayed columns in the **GROUP BY** clause. See Listing 9.8 for this grouped query and its corresponding output. Note that there is no **ORDER BY** in this list, but that the names returned are in alphabetical order. The **GROUP BY** sorts in the desired order to group columns.

**Listing 9.8    Phone list grouped by state.**

```
/* Phone List grouped by state */
SELECT UPPER(SUBSTRING(au_fname, 1, 1)) + '. ' + au_lname AS "Name",
       '(' + LEFT(phone, 3) + ') ' + RIGHT(phone,8) AS "Phone"
  FROM authors
  GROUP BY state, au_lname, au_fname, phone
```

```
Output
Name                                               Phone
-------------------------------------------------- --------------
A. Bennet                                          (415) 658-9932
C. Carson                                          (415) 548-7723
A. Dull                                            (415) 836-7128
M. Green                                           (415) 986-7020
B. Gringlesby                                      (707) 938-6445
S. Hunter                                          (415) 836-7128
L. Karsen                                          (415) 534-9219
C. Locksley                                        (415) 585-4620
S. MacFeather                                      (415) 354-7128
H. McBadden                                        (707) 448-4982
M. O'Leary                                         (408) 286-2428
D. Straight                                        (415) 834-2919
D. Stringer                                        (415) 843-2991
J. White                                           (408) 496-7223
A. Yokomoto                                        (415) 935-4228
M. DeFrance                                        (219) 547-9982
M. Smith                                           (913) 843-0462
S. Panteley                                        (301) 946-8853
I. del Castillo                                    (615) 996-8275
R. Blotchet-Halls                                  (503) 745-6402
```

**9. Structured Query Language (SCL)**

```
M. Greene                                          (615) 297-2723
A. Ringer                                          (801) 826-0752
A. Ringer                                          (801) 826-0752
```

(23 row(s) affected)

**GROUP BY** can be used for much more than is illustrated in this example. Calculating summary data and reports with sectional summaries and grand totals can be accomplished as well. See Listing 9.9 for a sales grouping query from the **Sales** table. This query uses **GROUP BY** and **HAVING** clauses, which are frequently used together. The **HAVING** clause works like a **WHERE** clause, but is used to evaluate the aggregates returned using a **GROUP BY** clause.

**Listing 9.9   Sales report query.**

```
/* Query 1 Listing of sales with no grouping */
SELECT title_id,
       CONVERT(VARCHAR, ord_date, 100) as ord_date,
       qty
  FROM sales
  ORDER BY title_id


/* Query 2 Volume sales > 20 */
SELECT title_id AS "Title ID",
       CONVERT(VARCHAR, MAX(ord_date), 100) AS "Last Sale Date",
       SUM(qty) AS "Total Sales"
  FROM sales
  GROUP BY title_id
  HAVING SUM(qty) > 20
  ORDER BY SUM(qty) DESC


Output Query 1
title_id ord_date                              qty
-------- ------------------------------------- ------
BU1032   Sep 14 1994 12:00AM                   5
BU1032   Sep 14 1994 12:00AM                   10
BU1111   Mar 11 1993 12:00AM                   25
BU2075   Feb 21 1993 12:00AM                   35
BU7832   Oct 28 1993 12:00AM                   15
MC2222   Dec 12 1993 12:00AM                   10
MC3021   Sep 14 1994 12:00AM                   25
MC3021   Sep 14 1994 12:00AM                   15
PC1035   May 22 1993 12:00AM                   30
PC8888   May 24 1993 12:00AM                   50
PS1372   May 29 1993 12:00AM                   20
```

```
PS2091    Sep 13 1994 12:00AM            3
PS2091    Sep 13 1994 12:00AM            75
PS2091    Sep 14 1994 12:00AM            10
PS2091    Sep 14 1994 12:00AM            20
PS2106    May 29 1993 12:00AM            25
PS3333    May 29 1993 12:00AM            15
PS7777    May 29 1993 12:00AM            25
TC3218    Jun 15 1992 12:00AM            40
TC4203    Jun 15 1992 12:00AM            20
TC7777    Jun 15 1992 12:00AM            20

(21 row(s) affected)

Output Query 2
Title ID Last Sale Date                 Total Sales
-------- ------------------------------ -----------
PS2091    Sep 14 1994 12:00AM            108
PC8888    May 24 1993 12:00AM            50
MC3021    Sep 14 1994 12:00AM            40
TC3218    Jun 15 1992 12:00AM            40
BU2075    Feb 21 1993 12:00AM            35
PC1035    May 22 1993 12:00AM            30
BU1111    Mar 11 1993 12:00AM            25
PS2106    May 29 1993 12:00AM            25
PS7777    May 29 1993 12:00AM            25

(9 row(s) affected)
```

The aggregate functions **SUM( )** and **MAX( )** were used for the first time in Query 2 to add each sale together into one record in the result set and to display the last date of a sale for that title. Aggregate functions are discussed in the "Aggregates and Functions" section later in the chapter. For more information on **GROUP BY** statements and **HAVING** clauses, see the Books Online.

Some special conditions are associated with the **GROUP BY** and **HAVING** clauses:

- ANSI-SQL requires that every column (non-aggregate) in the **SELECT** list must be mentioned in your **GROUP BY** statement.
- Columns in a **HAVING** clause must have one and only one value. This requirement precludes subqueries that return more than one row.
- Any query with a **HAVING** clause must contain a **GROUP BY** clause.

These requirements are usually not hard to meet and should pose little problem to you as a programmer.

# JOIN Conditions

Now you'll need to put some information together from more than one table, so that the title ID can show the name and author for each sales report line or new report. You can use the same preceding basic query and add a join condition to it so that the server connects the data. See Listing 9.10 for the new query and the sample output.

Microsoft SQL server supports ANSI join syntax and Transact-SQL syntax (Microsoft SQL Server extended SQL). Use of inner, cross, and outer joins are supported fully on Microsoft SQL Server. The syntax for ANSI joins is slightly different than for Transact-SQL, so a trip to the Books Online would be prudent. Transact-SQL uses join operators instead of actual text to perform the join in a **WHERE** clause. In the following examples, ANSI join methods are used.

**Listing 9.10    Sales by author join example.**

```
/* Query 1 titleauthor table */
SELECT *
  FROM titleauthor


/* Query 2 Volume sales > 20 by author */
SELECT UPPER(LEFT(authors.au_fname, 1)) + '. ' +
        authors.au_lname AS "Name",
      SUM(sales.qty) AS "Total Sales"
  FROM sales
  INNER JOIN titleauthor ON sales.title_id = titleauthor.title_id
  INNER JOIN authors ON titleauthor.au_id = authors.au_id
  GROUP BY authors.au_fname, authors.au_lname
  HAVING SUM(qty) > 20
  ORDER BY SUM(qty) DESC


Output Query 1
au_id       title_id au_ord royaltyper
----------  -------- ------ ----------
172-32-1176 PS3333   1      100
213-46-8915 BU1032   2      40
213-46-8915 BU2075   1      100
238-95-7766 PC1035   1      100
267-41-2394 BU1111   2      40
267-41-2394 TC7777   2      30
274-80-9391 BU7832   1      100
409-56-7008 BU1032   1      60
427-17-2319 PC8888   1      50
472-27-2349 TC7777   3      30
486-29-1786 PC9999   1      100
```

```
486-29-1786 PS7777    1      100
648-92-1872 TC4203    1      100
672-71-3249 TC7777    1      40
712-45-1867 MC2222    1      100
722-51-5454 MC3021    1      75
724-80-9391 BU1111    1      60
724-80-9391 PS1372    2      25
756-30-7391 PS1372    1      75
807-91-6654 TC3218    1      100
846-92-7186 PC8888    2      50
899-46-2035 MC3021    2      25
899-46-2035 PS2091    2      50
998-72-3567 PS2091    1      50
998-72-3567 PS2106    1      100


(25 row(s) affected)


Output Query 2
Name                                         Total Sales
-------------------------------------------- ----------

A. Ringer                                    148
A. Ringer                                    133
A. Dull                                      50
M. Green                                     50
S. Hunter                                    50
S. MacFeather                                45
M. O'Leary                                   45
M. DeFrance                                  40
S. Panteley                                  40
C. Carson                                    30
C. Locksley                                  25

(11 row(s) affected)
```

Query 1 in Listing 9.10 displays what is in the **Titleauthor** table. This data is a collection of key values used to join related pieces of information. Not all databases need this type of table, but good relational database design will produce a similar table in most situations.

Query 2 joins the Sales, Titleauthor, and Author tables. You specify the tables in a comma-delimited list in the **FROM** clause. In the **SELECT** list, you use the table.column reference to specify each column independently of the others. This allows you to use data from many tables and present it to the user as if it was from one table.

**9. Structured Query Language (SQL)**

Hiding the complexity of the database structure is very important to your users. If a column name is unique to all tables involved in a query, such as qty in the **Sales** table, you can list the column without the table reference. The Optimizer will not be confused by it because it knows there is only one qty column in all three tables.

By using the table.column reference in all your join queries, you'll be able to keep yourself in check and track which columns come from which table.

**WARNING! If you use the Transact-SQL join syntax in your queries, you must include a join condition in the WHERE clause for each table in the JOIN. The formula N = T-1 should come to mind when joining tables using the Transact-SQL join syntax. T is the number of tables in your FROM clause, and N is the number of join conditions you should have. The wrong number of join conditions can return incorrect result sets to the user. The ANSI join syntax makes this relationship much clearer, and you are forced to specify either a join condition or the CROSS JOIN operator when using the ANSI join syntax. Refer to the Books Online for more information about joining tables using the Transact-SQL join syntax.**

# Aliases

In Query 3 of Listing 9.10, aliases have been introduced to each of the table names in the **FROM** clause. Although you do not have to do this, it prevents you from having to type the full table names over and over. In addition, aliases enhance readability of the code.

In Query 2, notice the long lines of code with the table reference repeated many times. Repeating the table name is not harmful; it's just costly in the amount of typing you must do. Queries 2 and 3 return the same results, yet Query 3 is about 55 characters shorter. This might seem insignificant, but when you have to pass queries over a network or modems many times during the running of an application, shorter queries can save time in the communications between the client and server. (Typically, you do not pass a query string from client to server; instead, you should use stored procedures to keep the requests as short as possible. See Chapter 14 for more information on stored procedures and their benefits.)

To use aliases, add a space after each of the tables in the **FROM** clause and then type the character or characters you want to refer or connect to each table. The Query Optimizer checks for the alias in the **FROM** clause first; then, it uses those aliases to parse the **SELECT** list and **WHERE** clauses, respectively.

# Aggregates and Functions

No system would function without a standard set of functions that can be used to simplify queries. The aggregates and functions in Microsoft SQL Server are no different than their counterparts in other, more refined programming languages.

Let's spend some time looking at some of the more useful aggregates and functions. You should also look up each one in Microsoft SQL Server Books Online to reinforce what is discussed in this section.

---

---

The functions included in the following sections support nesting and are data type-sensitive where needed. They can return values to a query or to a local variable for manipulation in other parts of a script or stored procedure. For the syntax of each function, refer to Microsoft SQL Server Books Online.

## SUM

The **SUM()** function returns the total of a column's values. In the previous examples, the **SUM()** function was used to add the quantity column for each title sold. Depending on how you use this function, it will work on an entire table or on a group of records.

Keep in mind that the columns must be numeric for this function to work properly. You can use the **CONVERT()** function to change numbers stored as text to the required numeric data type, which must also be specified in the function.

## MAX

The **MAX()** function returns the maximum value for a column in a table or set of rows returned in a query. In the previous examples, this function was used to return the greatest date value in the Sales table for each title listed. This was accomplished by grouping the rows by title and applying the aggregate function for each row. This function works with text as well as with dates and numbers.

## MIN

**MIN()** is the opposite of **MAX()** in every regard. The same rules and features of the **MAX()** function apply to the **MIN()** function. Remember that the lowest value returned for text depends on sort order and case sensitivity.

## AVG

Many reports depend on averages to keep track of trends over time. The **AVG()** function calculates the average value of a column in a table or in a set of rows, depending on how it is used. Only numeric values can be passed to the **AVG()** function. You can use the **CONVERT()** function nested inside of the **AVG()** function to return the numeric value of a number stored as text to get around the numeric restriction of this function.

## COUNT

**COUNT( )** is a very common function that returns the count of rows in the query that match a particular **WHERE** clause. The number of rows in a table can be returned to a variable for testing purposes very effectively. **COUNT( )** returns the number of non-**NULL** values indicated by the **WHERE** clause in any query. You can pass the asterisk to the **COUNT(*)** function to get a row count from a query. **COUNT( )** is useful in triggers and stored procedures for determining not only the existence of rows but the exact number of rows you are dealing with. The return value for this function is numeric.

## CONVERT

The **CONVERT( )** function is frequently used in SQL code to ensure that you have the correct data types to perform an operation This versatile function converts one data type to another, so that a number of operations can be performed. The first parameter of the function is the data type to which you wish the existing column or expression to be converted.

Microsoft SQL Server will attempt to convert like data types to the proper type automatically when it can if Microsoft SQL Server cannot process a function or query with the data passed to it. The server returns an error message that suggests the use of the **CONVERT( )** function to solve the problem. See the "Calculated Values" section later in this chapter for an example of the **CONVERT( )** function.

## GETDATE

The **GETDATE( )** function returns the current date and time from the server's system clock. This function can be used to automatically insert date values into columns or to find out the current date for comparisons in **WHERE** clauses. The **GETDATE( )** function is especially useful for audit trails and tracking tables, as is the **CURRENT_USER** function.

## DATEDIFF

You can use the **DATEDIFF( )** function to compare and return the difference between date items, such as days, weeks, minutes, and hours. When used in a **WHERE** clause, you can return records that meet a range of dates or that meet certain time-span intervals. Make sure you specify the arguments to this function in the correct order, or the value returned might be the opposite of what you expected.

# DATEPART

The **DATEPART( )** function returns a value equal to the part of a date that you specify. If, for instance, you need to know the day of the week of a particular date, you can use this function to quickly pull that data out of a column or variable.

# SOUNDEX

The **SOUNDEX( )** function converts a string to a four-digit code that represents the string. If two strings are very close to the same spelling, they will have the same **SOUNDEX( )** value returned. This function can be used to find a list of potential matches for a string in a set of rows.

You can think of this function as the "sounds like" function. If the strings sound alike, the number returned by this function will be the same. It can be useful for finding data when the user does not know the exact spelling. **SOUNDEX( )** is critical to creating a full-featured Find for database records.

# SUBSTRING

The **SUBSTRING( )** function is used many times throughout this book. Any string manipulation can be accomplished with this function in conjunction with a few string operators and some other basic string functions.

Another useful string function you should take a moment to look up in Microsoft SQL Server Books Online is the **STUFF( )** function. **STUFF( )** and **SUBSTRING( )** in combination are useful for building strings on the fly in your SQL code. See the "Calculated Values" section later in this chapter for more information on **SUBSTRING( )** and its uses.

# LEFT and RIGHT

The **LEFT( )** and **RIGHT( )** functions work similarly to the **SUBSTRING** function, but they are specially designed to work with the left or right end of the string you are manipulating. These functions return the specified number of characters from the appropriate end of the string. The **SUBSTRING** function can easily be used in place of the **LEFT** function, but returning data from the right end of a string is much more tricky to code without the **RIGHT** function.

# UPPER

**UPPER( )** converts the string passed to the function into all uppercase characters. You can use this function to maintain the data integrity of text columns in your tables without the user or client intervening. Some client software always assumes this function to be bound to a control with very little overhead, so it is seldom used for much more than making sure that uppercase characters are passed where needed.

## CHARINDEX

The **CHARINDEX( )** function can be used to search for a match for a string in a column. This function is used to return the starting position of one string within another string. If the "search string" is not located within the "target string," the function will return zero. If you use this function to search an entire table, it returns a result set with a nonzero value for each row that contains a string.

**CHARINDEX( )** does not allow wild-card characters. If you need to search for a string containing wild cards, use the **PATINDEX( )** function instead.

## RTRIM and LTRIM

**RTRIM( )** removes any trailing blanks from a string or column. In some situations, it helps to keep formatting and reporting working the way your applications expect. **RTRIM( )** is most useful in text reports generated from raw **SQL**. **LTRIM( )** works the same way as **RTRIM( )** except that it removes blanks from the beginning of a string instead of the end.

## LEN

The **LEN( )** function is used to return the number of characters (not bytes) of a given character string. It allows you to correctly determine the length of string in characters whether or not a Unicode string is being used.

## REPLICATE

The **REPLICATE( )** function returns a character string repeated a specified number of times. It can be useful for formatting output from a query. Instead of typing 50 dashes in a **PRINT** command to separate information in the output, this function allows you to replicate the dash 50 times with less typing.

## SPACE

The **SPACE( )** function returns the specified number of spaces. It is another function that is mainly useful for formatting.

## REPLACE

The **REPLACE( )** function takes three string parameters. All occurrences of the second string in the first string are replaced with the value of the third string. If this sounds a bit confusing, give it a try. It basically works like the find and re-place function in a word processing application.

## STR

The **STR( )** function converts a numeric value to character data. Unlike the **CON-VERT( )** function, the **STR( )** function allows you to specify the total length and number of decimal places to be included when it is converted to character data.

## CHAR

The **CHAR( )** function returns the character that corresponds to the ASCII code passed as an integer to the function. It can be useful for adding otherwise unus-able characters to your output. **CHAR(10)** returns a line feed, and **CHAR(13)** returns a carriage return. **CHAR(34)** is a double quote, which can be helpful in constructing an output string that would have confusingly nested quotation marks without the use of this function.

## ASCII

**ASCII( )** is the reciprocal function to the **CHAR( )** function. It returns the ASCII code as an integer of the left-most character in a string.

# System Functions

Similar to the functions covered thus far, system functions return server-based values or perform functions that would otherwise require a great deal of code. These functions are typically used to give your scripts and stored procedures more intelligence and functionality.

You could write SQL queries to return most of the values returned by these func-tions, because almost all the data returned by these functions exist in system tables on the server. However, using these functions is faster and more convenient.

For more information on these and other very useful system functions, look up System Functions in Microsoft SQL Server Books Online and choose Item 6 from the Results list.

## ISNULL

You can replace **NULL** values in your results sets dynamically with the **ISNULL( )** function. Specify what value you want to have returned if the corresponding col-umn contains a **NULL** value, and this function checks for you on the fly. It can be a very handy function in reports and daily run queries written to text files. See **NULLIF( )** for a reciprocal type of function to **ISNULL( )**.

## COALESCE

The **COALESCE()** function is similar to the **ISNULL()** function, but it allows for a list of values to replace the null. A variable length list of values is provided, and SQL Server chooses the first non-**NULL** item in the list. This function is actually a replacement for using the **ISNULL()** function in a **CASE** statement to find a non-**NULL** replacement in a list of values. You will find this function listed as part of the Help for **CASE** statements in the Books Online.

## USER_ID

The **USER_ID()** function takes a name string and returns the current database ID for that name. The **USER_ID()** function is useful when you are accessing the system tables and need to check names against group membership or permissions values.

## USER_NAME

**USER_NAME()** is the opposite of the **USER_ID()** function. You pass it as a valid database user ID, and it returns the name for that user. As with **USER_ID()**, this function is good for on-the-fly checks of permissions or memberships. It is also useful in error handling. When an error occurs, you can return more specific information from an error handling routine by getting the user's name and writing it to a log or to a procedure for error escalation.

## DATALENGTH

The **DATALENGTH()** function returns the length of the data stored in a variable or in a column. The **DATALENGTH()** function works on all text data types and is very handy for reporting and string manipulation routines. It works with text and image data types as well as with character data.

## COL_LENGTH

**COL_LENGTH()** returns the defined length of a column in a table. This function works well with most data types. With it, you can determine whether the data you want to insert into a column will fit.

## CONVERT

**CONVERT()** is used to convert columns from one data type to another. One typical use of this function is to specify the format of a date field when converting it to **CHAR** or **VARCHAR** from **DATETIME**. The Books Online provides a list of the data types and the implicit and explicit conversions that are allowed. Also provided is a table showing the possible formatting options for converting data fields to a readable character format.

# Calculated Values

Calculated values are created when you perform math functions on columns to generate an average or some other derived piece of data. These calculations can be created on the fly to avoid using up storage space in your databases, yet still be presented so they appear to be stored some place in a table. A lot of calculated values are needed for the day-to-day operation of any system. In the following sections, the focus will be on the methods to get these values to the user.

As a general rule, you should not store calculated values in a table when you can display the value to the user another way. Calculated values work best for items of data that are built from pieces of other data in a corresponding record. If you need to change data that is calculated, you must change the underlying data anyway, so why change it more than once?

To clarify this method, let's use the tables already defined to create a new, unique author ID. The existing ID is the author's Social Security number. If, for some reason, you cannot use the existing ID number, you would need to display some kind of unique key to identify each author in your system. See Listing 9.11 for the query that displays the new author ID from the stored values in the **Authors** table. For this example, part of the author's Social Security number and his or her initials, state of residence, and contract status are used.

Listing 9.11   New author ID key.

```
/* New Author ID query */
SELECT au_id AS "Old Author ID",
       UPPER(LEFT(au_fname, 1)) +
         UPPER(LEFT(au_lname, 1)) +
         '-' + LEFT(au_id, 3) +
         '-' + UPPER(state) +
         CONVERT(CHAR(1), contract) AS "New Author ID",
       UPPER(LEFT(au_fname, 1)) + '. ' +
         LEFT(au_lname, 15) AS "Name"
  FROM authors
  ORDER BY au_lname


Output
Old Author ID New Author ID  Name
------------  -------------  -------------------
409-56-7008   AB-409-CA1     A. Bennet
648-92-1872   RB-648-OR1     R. Blotchet-Halls
238-95-7766   CC-238-CA1     C. Carson
```

```
722-51-5454    MD-722-IN1    M. DeFrance
712-45-1867    ID-712-MI1    I. del Castillo
427-17-2319    AD-427-CA1    A. Dull
213-46-8915    MG-213-CA1    M. Green
527-72-3246    MG-527-TN0    M. Greene
472-27-2349    BG-472-CA1    B. Gringlesby
846-92-7186    SH-846-CA1    S. Hunter
756-30-7391    LK-756-CA1    L. Karsen
486-29-1786    CL-486-CA1    C. Locksley
724-80-9391    SM-724-CA1    S. MacFeather
893-72-1158    HM-893-CA0    H. McBadden
267-41-2394    MO-267-CA1    M. O'Leary
807-91-6654    SP-807-MD1    S. Panteley
998-72-3567    AR-998-UT1    A. Ringer
899-46-2035    AR-899-UT1    A. Ringer
341-22-1782    MS-341-KS0    M. Smith
274-80-9391    DS-274-CA1    D. Straight
724-08-9931    DS-724-CA0    D. Stringer
172-32-1176    JW-172-CA1    J. White
672-71-3249    AY-672-CA1    A. Yokomoto

(23 row(s) affected)
```

If the author ID were used to join tables in queries, you would naturally need to store this key value in a column. If it is used for display purposes only, as file or case numbers sometimes are, this type of query would display the number exactly the way it needs to be used without being stored in another column in the table. In the event you change the file numbering system or outgrow the existing ID scheme, you would simply modify the query; you wouldn't need to rebuild any underlying data. This technique is much more efficient than reworking the entire table structure to allow for a new numbering method.

In Listing 9.11, notice that the **UPPER()** functions are used to ensure that the text portions of the result set are formatted correctly, and the bit data type is converted to a single character. This way, the string operators can be used without error. This technique of displaying an expression as real data to the user saves disk space without affecting performance. Because this data appears to the user as a static piece of data that can be modified as business rules dictate, this method is very useful in production environments.

Some of you might be saying to yourselves, "What if the underlying data changes?" or "What about incomplete data?" You do have to be very careful when building this kind of data. However, tons of disk space can also be chewed up on data servers storing information that could have been displayed with this very technique with no problem. At the same time, there are other systems where this technique doesn't work as well. You have to use data that is stable and has some built-in integrity. Try this method only if you're sure the data is stable and none of the needed pieces of data are going to change.

# Optimizer Hints

You have the ability to tell Microsoft SQL Server that you want a certain action to be performed without the optimizer using its normal methods. This is good in some cases and a disaster in others. Use optimizer hints with great caution. Many years of programming have gone into the design and optimization of your queries in the built-in optimizer. Although no tool is perfect, the Query Optimizer checks many details each time a query is run. In most situations, the Query Optimizer chooses the correct plan based on the existing state of your tables and indexes.

You might want to use optimizer hints in two situations. The first is when you are reading data that is highly fluid. Use the **(NOLOCK)** option in your **SELECT** statements to be sure that you are not locking pages in your queries when someone else is trying to access that data or perform another function. See Listing 9.12 for an example of a query with the **NOLOCK** optimizer hint.

**Listing 9.12 Reading data without locking pages.**

```
/* Select ID and name without locking */
SELECT au_id AS "Author ID",
       UPPER(LEFT(au_fname, 1)) + '. ' +
         LEFT(au_lname, 15) AS "Name"
  FROM authors (NOLOCK)
  ORDER BY au_lname
```

The results are the same as they would have been without the hint, but the risk of creating a deadlock or wait state on the server has been avoided. At least every other day you will find a message in some of the Internet newsgroups about locking, hanging, or slow queries. In some of those situations, this hint would solve the problem.

The reason highly active data benefits from the **NOLOCK** hint is that a query will not attempt to place any shared locks on the pages SQL Server must access for the query. If a client does not read all the records it has requested from the server, Microsoft SQL Server holds those pages with a shared lock until the last record has been returned to the client. Shared locks can cause problems with very active data.

The second situation in which you might want to use optimizer hints is when you want to lock data sets or a table. Specify a table-level lock to reduce overhead and ensure that you have the whole table when you need it. See Table 9.4 for a list of optimizer hints and their uses in your queries.

**Table 9.4   Useful Optimizer hints and their uses.**

| Hint Type | Option | Description |
|---|---|---|
| Join | **LOOP I HASH I MERGE I REMOTE** | Specifies the strategy to use when joining the rows of two tables. |
| Query | **{ HASH I ORDER } GROUP** | Specifies whether hashing or ordering is used to compute **GROUP BY** and **COMPUTE** aggregations |
| Query | **{ MERGE I HASH I CONCAT } UNION** | Specifies the strategy used for all **UNION** operations specified in the query. |
| Query | **FORCE ORDER** | Performs joins in the order in which the tables appear in the query. |
| Query | **KEEP PLAN** | Instructs the Query Optimizer to keep an exiting query plan longer by relaxing the estimated recompile. |
| Query | **KEEPFIXED PLAN** | Instructs the Query Optimizer not to recompile a query due to changes in statistics or to the indexed column (update, delete, or insert). The query will not be recompiled when the estimated number of indexed column changes (update, delete, or insert) has been made to a table. |
| Table | **INDEX ( )** | Instructs SQL Server to use the specified index(es) for a table. |
| Table | **HOLDLOCK I REPEATABLEREAD I READCOMMITTED I NOLOCK** | Causes certain locks to be set (or not) for a table, and overrides the locks that would have been used to enforce the isolation level of the current transaction. |
| Table | **ROWLOCK I PAGLOCK I TABLOCK I TABLOCKX** | Specifies the size of the shared locks to be taken for this table. The **TABLOCKX** hint causes SQL Server to acquire an exclusive lock for the entire table, rather than a shared lock. |
| Table | **READPAST** | Skips locked rows altogether. This will prevent dirty reads but will not wait for locked rows to be released before proceeding. |
| Table | **UPDLOCK** | Takes update locks instead of shared locks. This ensures that you will be able to update these rows later in the transaction. |

# Subqueries

To improve the intelligence of your code, you can nest a query inside a query to return information to the outer query. Any place an expression is valid in a query, you can place another query to evaluate and return a value for use in your SQL code. **INSERT**, **UPDATE**, **DELETE**, and **SELECT** statements support expressions in many places. In many situations, a subquery can be rewritten as a join condition to return the same results. In some situations, a join condition can actually perform your query faster than a subquery. Triggers can be made more intelligent through subqueries as well.

You can write a lot of table-driven stored procedures that will run with only a few parameters but may query many user or system tables to actually perform the tasks internally. By reducing the amount of data required to perform a given task, the client code can be substantially simplified.

There are two types of subqueries: noncorrelated and correlated. An example of a noncorrelated subquery is one that runs before the outer query to return its result to the outer query for execution. This nesting is very similar to the execution of a function call in your code. A correlated subquery references the outer query internally and is executed one time for each of the matching rows in the **WHERE** clause of the outer query. This might sound confusing at first, but it makes sense if you think about what actually happens.

When the outer query executes, it might only have five rows of a thousand row table returned. If the inner query must be executed one time for each of the thousand rows checked, the process will be slow. By referencing the outer query's **WHERE** clause in the inner query, you are telling the optimizer to first filter out the thousand rows and perform the subquery five times instead of a thousand.

A subquery uses the same syntax as a regular query. You must, however, adhere to a few restrictions when using subqueries. A subquery is always enclosed in parentheses. It can only specify one column name of any data type except test and image. Any **DISTINCT** option will be maintained inside the subquery only. If you are testing for equality, you can only return a single item, If you are using a subquery in a **WHERE** clause and use the **IN** option for a list, the subquery can return more than one row. See Listing 9.13 for an example of a subquery and its syntax.

**Listing 9.13    Subquery example.**

```
/* Percentage of total sales by quantity */
SELECT title_id AS "Title ID",
       qty AS "Sales",
       CONVERT(NUMERIC(5, 2), (CONVERT(NUMERIC, qty) /
         (SELECT SUM(qty) FROM sales)) * 100) as "Percentage"
  FROM sales
  ORDER BY qty DESC

Output
Title ID Sales  Percentage
-------- ------ ----------
PS2091   75     19.21
PC8888   50     10.14
```

| | | |
|---|---|---|
| TC3218 | 40 | 8.11 |
| BU2075 | 35 | 7.10 |
| PC1035 | 30 | 6.09 |
| BU1111 | 25 | 9.07 |
| MC3021 | 25 | 9.07 |
| PS2106 | 25 | 9.07 |
| PS7777 | 25 | 9.07 |
| PS1372 | 20 | 4.06 |
| PS2091 | 20 | 4.06 |
| TC4203 | 20 | 4.06 |
| TC7777 | 20 | 4.06 |
| PS3333 | 15 | 3.04 |
| BU7832 | 15 | 3.04 |
| MC3021 | 15 | 3.04 |
| BU1032 | 10 | 2.03 |
| MC2222 | 10 | 2.03 |
| PS2091 | 10 | 2.03 |
| BU1032 | 5 | 1.01 |
| PS2091 | 3 | .61 |

(21 row(s) affected)

# UNION

You can use the **UNION** operator to combine two or more results sets into a single results set. This operation is used in many systems to provide for the combination of current and historical data. If your system archives data into a history table to keep the current working set of data smaller and more manageable, the **UNION** operator can be used to combine your current and historical data for statistical analysis and to archive lookup queries.

By default, the **UNION** operator removes any duplicate rows, which can be very useful when combining data from more than one source. An important issue with the **UNION** operator is that the **SELECT** lists for both queries must match exactly. Number of columns, data types, and order are very important in performing a union between two queries. If your query contains an **ORDER BY** statement, the entire final result set is sorted based on your **ORDER BY** statement.

The output result set pulls the column headings from the first query. If you want to replace the default column headers with legible English, you must modify the **SELECT** list of the first query. The **WHERE** clauses do not have to match in either query. You can also use placeholders for missing columns in the union to fill in any missing information in one table or another in your queries. For more information on the use of unions in your SQL code, see the Books Online.

# INSERT Statements

Up to this point, the focus has been on the retrieval of data. In a client/server environment, you have two real processes for which you must program: the presentation of data to the user and the modification or creation of data on the server. Presenting data to the client application does not typically modify data or create transaction log entries. Modifications of data places entries into the **Syslogs** table and generates transactions on your server.

The discussion of **INSERT** statements has been delayed until now because, as shown in Listing 9.14, much of its syntax is identical to that of the **SELECT** statement. You must specify the table into which you want to insert data and the columns for which you are passing data. You are not required to pass data for all columns. Any column for which you have a default value defined or that allows a **NULL** value can be omitted from the column list.

**Listing 9.14** **INSERT** statement syntax.

```
INSERT [ INTO]
    { table_name WITH ( < table_hint_limited > [ ...n ] )
        | view_name
        | rowset_function_limited
    }
    {    [ ( column_list ) ]
        { VALUES
            ( { DEFAULT | NULL | expression } [ ,...n] )
            | derived_table
            | execute_statement
        }
    }
    | DEFAULT VALUES
< table_hint_limited > ::=
    { FASTFIRSTROW
        | HOLDLOCK
        | PAGLOCK
        | READCOMMITTED
        | REPEATABLEREAD
        | ROWLOCK
        | SERIALIZABLE
        | TABLOCK
        | TABLOCKX
        | UPDLOCK
    }
```

Notice that you can use a **SELECT** statement to query for the values you want to insert into a table. In the "Immediate Solutions" section of this chapter, you will walk through an example using an **INSERT/SELECT** statement to populate a table with data from another source.

**INSERT** statements typically involve a single row (unless an **INSERT/SELECT** is used), and they will place the data you specify into the table and update any indexes with the appropriate values. This is important. The more indexes you have on the table, the longer an insert will take. If you are performing a nightly insert process of many rows with little activity on the table otherwise, you might consider dropping the indexes prior to the insert operation and rebuilding them when you are finished. This method would result in better performance and would increase the integrity of your indexes.

---

**NOTE:** *On occasion, Microsoft SQL Server generates some index/insert related error messages. By using **INSERT/SELECT** statements when inserting many records after dropping any indexes, you can reduce the possibility of this type of error.*

---

Listing 9.15 shows how to insert a row into a table. A record in the **Authors** table containing some sample information has been created as an example. This information is provided as an example only—it will not exist in your table unless you run this query on your table.

**Listing 9.15   Sample insert into the Authors table.**

```
/* Sample insert into Authors table (not formatted) */
INSERT INTO authors
  (au_id, au_lname, au_fname, phone, address, city, state, zip, contract)
  VALUES ('123-45-6789', 'Author', 'Some', '954 555-1234', '123 Main
Street',
        'Ft. Lauderdale', 'FL', '40165', 1)


/* Same query formatted in line */
INSERT
  INTO authors
    (au_id, au_lname, au_fname, phone, address, city, state, zip, contract)
  VALUES
    ('123-45-6788', 'Whitehead', 'Paul', '954 555-1235', '456 Main Street',
     'Ft. Lauderdale', 'FL', '33309', 1)


/* Formatted in column form */
INSERT
  INTO authors
  VALUES ( '123-45-6787',
          'Dalton',
          'Patrick',
          '954 555-1236',
```

```
'789 Main Street',
'Ft. Lauderdale',
'FL',
'33309',
1 )
```

Notice that the column list from the third query has been omitted. You can do this because you are supplying all the values in the exact order they are specified in the table schematic. You can reorder the columns any way you want as long as the column list and the values are the same. You can pass string or numeric literals, variables, or explicit **NULL** values in an **INSERT** statement. **INSERT** statements return the number of rows affected to the client and to the global variable **@@rowcount**. You must select the row again to see the data after it is inserted.

**INSERT** statements affect one table at a time and cannot be combined to add rows to multiple tables simultaneously. You must issue a separate **INSERT** statement for each table you want to modify.

## Identity Columns

In Microsoft SQL Server, the identity column generates a unique number for a record when that record is inserted into the table. This identity can be incremented or decremented by one or any other number and can be maintained automatically by Microsoft SQL Server. You do *not* supply a value for this column when you insert records. Should you want to override the automatic generation of the next number for an identity column, you can set the property for the table called "identity insert." See the Books Online for more information on the identity column and its uses.

## Stored Procedures

Stored procedures can be used to optimize SQL code execution and the methods of communication between client applications and Microsoft SQL Server. Stored procedures can have parameters with specific data types passed to them for execution of **SELECT**, **INSERT**, **UPDATE**, and **DELETE** statements. Return codes and output parameters are also useful in developing client interfaces to Microsoft SQL Server. To use a stored procedure in your scripts, use the **EXECUTE** statement prior to the stored procedure and parameter list. See Chapter 14 for more information on the use and syntax of stored procedures.

## Triggers

**INSERT** statements cause any defined insert trigger to be fired each time the **INSERT** statement is used. If you are using **INSERT/SELECT**, you will place multiple rows into the virtual table that is "inserted." The inserted table matches the structure of the target table exactly and will contain any records that are to be inserted into the target table containing a trigger. A trigger fires one time for each insert, not one time for each row.

# UPDATE Statements

**UPDATE** statements are only slightly different than **INSERT** statements. They are set-based and can affect the entire table. **UPDATE** statements use a **WHERE** clause with the same restrictions and functionality as a **SELECT** statement to determine which rows of the table to affect. See Listing 9.16 for a sample **UPDATE** statement.

In Listing 9.16, the **SET** statement involves one column. In **SET** statements involving multiple columns, the columns and values are delimited by commas. The **WHERE** clause determines what row or rows in the table will be changed by this query. If the **WHERE** clause evaluates to more than one row in the table, each matching row will be changed by the query.

**Listing 9.16   Sample update to the Authors table.**

```
/* Change my phone number in the Authors table */
UPDATE authors
   SET phone = '954 555-4321'
   WHERE au_id = '123-45-6788'
```

If you omit the **WHERE** clause from an **UPDATE** statement, the entire table will be updated on the columns specified. This feature can be useful. For example, if you want to place a price increase across the board for your product line, you would use an **UPDATE** statement with no **WHERE** clause on your inventory tables that contain a price column. However, be careful not to omit the **WHERE** clause unless you intend to modify every row.

**NOTE:** The only way to safeguard against accidental modification of your data is to use transactional processing (even from query tools), and then check that the modification was what you intended before committing the changes.

**UPDATE** statements support subqueries to return data for an update operation. Be careful to return one and only one value when using subqueries in an **UPDATE** statement. Multiple rows returned by a subquery will generate an error upon execution.

**UPDATE** statements utilize virtual tables when a trigger is applied to a table for updates to records: the same "inserted" table the **INSERT** statement used and the "deleted" table. Microsoft SQL Server places the record prior to the changes into the deleted table and the new record with the applied changes into the inserted table. Triggers can then use the original data and the changes when carrying out their functions. Beware of multiple row **UPDATE** statements in your triggers. You must cycle through each record in the inserted table and match it to a deleted record (typically with a cursor) in order to manipulate multiple rows inside the trigger.

The **UPDATE** statement is executed once for each table and affects a row one time during execution. The same row is never updated twice by a single **UPDATE** statement. You can use join conditions to optimize your **UPDATE** statements. Refer to the Books Online for more information on the **UPDATE** statement.

# DELETE Statements

The **DELETE** statement is probably the most dangerous statement in your SQL arsenal. You can remove a record from a table permanently with the **DELETE** statement. Like the **SELECT** and **UPDATE** statements, **DELETE** statements use the **WHERE** clause. Once a record has been deleted, it no longer exists in a recoverable state in any location other than a backup of either the transaction log or database. You should always use transactional processing when deleting records. If an error occurs in the execution of the command, you can roll back the deletion and restore your records.

If you omit the **WHERE** clause from your query, the entire table will be cleaned out; each and every record will be removed. This is a logged operation, so if your table has many rows, you will generate a lot of traffic in the transaction log. If you are trying to remove all the records in a table and no longer need to log the transactions, use the **TRUNCATE TABLE** statement instead of **DELETE**. **TRUNCATE TABLE** is not logged and gives you the same results much faster than **DELETE**. For more information on the **TRUNCATE TABLE** statement, see the Books Online.

Both statements leave the schema of a table intact and do not drop existing indexes from the target table. Use this feature with great caution. A common question asked is how to recover from a non-logged delete without affecting other tables and the relational integrity within a database. You *can* recover from it, but it takes time and disk space and requires a sound backup of your data. See Listing 9.17 for a sample **DELETE** statement.

Listing 9.17   Sample **DELETE** statement.

```
/* Remove myself from the Authors table */
DELETE FROM authors
  WHERE au_id = '123-45-6788'
```

# Batches

A *SQL Script* is a file that contains one or more batches of SQL code that you want to run against your server. SQL statements are inherently implied transactions and are executed one by one unless you specify otherwise. A *batch* is a section or grouping of SQL statements that you want to execute together and treat as a unit of execution. They are not transactions, although you can use transactional processing inside of batches to maintain the integrity of your data.

Up to this point, single statements executed one at a time have been used. If you want to insert, display, or modify data, you could create a text file with a batch in it and open the text file in the Query Analyzer to run when needed. You might want to create many of these for installation of systems, day-to-day reports, or troubleshooting.

A script can contain many batches. A batch is delimited by the word **GO** on a line by itself. See Listing 9.18 for a sample batch of SQL code. For clarity, queries that you have already seen are used in this example.

**Listing 9.18   Sample batch script.**

```
/* Sample batch to add remove and display authors */
/* Dated 08/26/2000                               */

/* Batch 1 - Insert */
BEGIN
  BEGIN TRANSACTION

  INSERT
    INTO authors
    VALUES ( '123-45-6789',
             'Author',
             'Some',
             '954 555-1234',
             '123 Main Street',
             'Ft. Lauderdale',
             'FL',
             '33309',
             1 )
  IF (@@error <> 0)
    BEGIN
      /* Place any additional error handling here */
      ROLLBACK
    END
    ELSE
```

```
    BEGIN
      COMMIT TRANSACTION
    END


  /* Display the Record to verify the insert */
  SELECT *
    FROM authors
    WHERE au_id = '123-45-6789'


END
GO

/* Batch 2 - Update new record */
BEGIN
  /* Declare any local variables */
  DECLARE @v_OldPhone CHAR(12),
          @v_NewPhone CHAR(12),
          @v_TempString CHAR(255)


  BEGIN TRANSACTION

  /* Set message string to default value */
  SELECT @v_TempString = 'Update Failed.'

  /* Get the current phone numer */
  SELECT @v_Oldphone = phone
    FROM authors
    WHERE au_id = '123-45-6789'

  /* Change the phone number and contract status */
  UPDATE authors
    SET phone = '502 555-1122',
        contract = 0
    WHERE au_id = '123-45-6789'

  IF (@@error <> 0)
    BEGIN
      /* Place any additional error handling here */
      ROLLBACK
    END
    ELSE
    BEGIN
      COMMIT TRANSACTION
```

```
        /* Retrieve updated phone number for verification */
        SELECT @v_NewPhone = phone
          FROM authors
          WHERE au_id = '123-45-6789'

        /* Build message string to display */
        SELECT @v_TempString = 'Old Number: ' + @v_OldPhone + CHAR(10) +
                                'New Number: ' + @v_NewPhone
    END

  /* Show old and new phone number for verification */
  PRINT @v_TempString
END
```

In this batch script, some control-of-flow statements with local and global variables have been introduced to help illustrate just what can be done with batches. Local variables are only available inside a single batch, so be careful not to use them across batches without reinitializing them and assigning new values to them. The **IF**, **BEGIN**, and **END** statements help define the conditional nature and flow of this code. You do not have to use the **BEGIN** and **END** statements in all areas, but you may want to make it a habit for improved readability. The only time you have to use **BEGIN** and **END** statements is after a conditional or looping statement that has more than one line of code.

Some string manipulation was used again to illustrate how to build a string inside your code. The **CHAR( )** function evaluates *10* to be the new line character, and places that character in the string. The use of the **global @@error** variable to check for an error state should be standard practice. An **@@error** holds the return value for the previous SQL statement only. A value of zero means successful execution with no warnings or errors.

The **GO** statement at the end of the batch tells the server that you are finished and want this section of your code to be executed as a group. Some transactional processing has been included in these batches to show how you can "undo" a modification or group of modifications in the event of an error on the server. For more information on batches, control-of-flow statements, and variables, see the Books Online.

# Cursors

Most SQL programmers master cursors last. Using cursors requires intimate knowledge of your table structures and the ability to visualize what is happening with your code on the server. Cursors are very powerful and provide a great deal of flexibility.

Cursors are very versatile. From overnight processes to table-driven procedures and queries, their usefulness covers many areas of a production environment. Cursors allow you to manipulate data on a row-by-row basis rather than with result set-based queries. This method of processing is in most cases slower than result set-based queries, and it typically takes up more memory on the server. Depending on your needs, you can implement cursors at the client or at the server. This section will focus on the server-side cursors because each client has different requirements.

Cursors require you to use local variables for each column value that you load into a cursor. They also require the definition and manipulation of the cursor as if it were a pointer definition. When you use cursors in your scripts or stored procedures, five keywords play important roles: **DECLARE**, **OPEN**, **FETCH**, **CLOSE**, and **DEALLOCATE**. See Table 9.5 for the purpose of each of these keywords.

On any system that places structures into memory, it is a good idea to properly dispose of those structures. The **CLOSE** and **DEALLOCATE** statements should be issued when you have completed the manipulation of data. Leaving them open holds those resources and limits others' ability to perform tasks on the server.

The Books Online contains a very good example of how to use a cursor to perform an update of the index statistics for all the tables in your database. See Listing 9.19 for the code from the Books Online. The code has been modified and formatted slightly in accordance with personal preferences. Previously, there was no **CLOSE** statement at the end of the run, just a **DEALLOCATE** statement.

**Table 9.5    Keywords for cursors.**

| Key Word | Use |
| --- | --- |
| **DECLARE** | Defines the cursor through a **SELECT** statement that shows the columns and defines the rows that will be included in this cursor. A standard **SELECT** statement is used after the cursor name and type is given. Must be supplied before an **OPEN** statement can be issued. |
| **OPEN** | Physically opens the cursor and gets the defined record set as it exists in the table at the time of the statement execution. |
| **FETCH** | Retrieves the specified record and places the column values for that row into local variables for further manipulation. |
| **CLOSE** | Closes the cursor and releases any locks that may have been placed automatically on any data pages due to the cursor definition. |
| **DEALLOCATE** | Removes the data structure from memory on the server. You may reopen a cursor after it has been closed, but not after deallocation. You must redefine the cursor once it has been released with this statement. |

*A cursor can also be created through SQL-passthrough and ODBC function calls. See the Books Online for more details.*

**9. Structured Query Language (SQL)**

Although the code will still run, it is against good programming practices to assume code will always work as advertised. Better safe than sorry.

In addition, a **SET** statement has been added to turn off the display of the number of rows affected by the query. This is strictly for personal preference and could be removed at no cost to the actual performance of the procedure.

Listing 9.19 introduces the syntax needed to create a stored procedure. Stored procedures are covered in detail in Chapter 14. This example illustrates that in some situations code in the Books Online can be both copied and pasted right into your server and be highly useful. If you would like to copy this procedure instead of the one in the online documentation, see the code listings for this chapter on the CD-ROM accompanying this book.

**Listing 9.19   Modified Books Online code illustrating cursor uses.**

```
CREATE PROCEDURE update_all_stats
AS
/* This procedure will run UPDATE STATISTICS against */
/* all user-defined tables within this database.    */

/* Turn off row count display */
SET NOCOUNT ON

/* Declare Local Variables */
DECLARE @v_tablename VARCHAR(30)

/* Declare the Cursor */
DECLARE c_tnames_cursor CURSOR FOR
  SELECT name
    FROM sysobjects (NOLOCK)
    WHERE type = 'U'

OPEN c_tnames_cursor

FETCH NEXT FROM c_tnames_cursor INTO @v_tablename

WHILE (@@FETCH_STATUS <> -1)
  BEGIN
    IF (@@FETCH_STATUS <> -2)
      BEGIN
        PRINT 'Updating: ' + UPPER(RTRIM(@v_tablename))
        EXEC('UPDATE STATISTICS ' + @v_tablename)
      END
    FETCH NEXT FROM c_tnames_cursor INTO @v_tablename
  END
```

```
PRINT ''
PRINT ''
PRINT '******************** NO MORE TABLES ********************'
PRINT ''
PRINT 'Statistics have been updated for all tables.'

CLOSE c_tnames_cursor
DEALLOCATE c_tnames_cursor
GO
```

The key to using cursors well is to understand the **FETCH** statement. You can fetch rows in any direction as well as rows in absolute positions into variables for manipulation. The global variable **@@fetch_status** tells you if there are no more rows to be returned and helps you control flow within the **WHILE** loop construct. Fetching **NEXT** or **PREVIOUS** inside of a loop allows you to move through the records one at a time and exit the loop when finished. Beware of missing the **FETCH** statement and variable check when writing your code. You can place yourself in a continuous loop with no exit point if you are careless and miss a logic check.

You can nest cursors inside other cursors to add to the feature and function of your code. Nesting cursors requires a bit of planning and some good naming conventions with regard to your local variables. Tackle nested cursors only after you have become comfortable with a standard cursor and can visualize what is being done on the server. You can add **PRINT** statements to your cursors to check the values of variables at different stages in the cursor.

---

**NOTE:** *The* **PRINT** *statement only allows character data types, so use the* **CONVERT** *function to change any noncharacter data to text before printing.*

---

# The Main Points

Many important features and functions have been presented throughout the previous sections. Let's review some of the basic principles before moving on:

- Comment your code clearly.
- Specify the name of the columns you want returned in your queries.
- Always use a **WHERE** clause in production-based queries.
- **NOT** is *not* optimizable!
- Use the **(NOLOCK)** optimizer hint on highly active data for read-only queries.

- Use transactional processing when modifying data for safety and recoverability.

- Do *not* omit the **WHERE** clause from a SQL statement unless you intend to affect an entire table.

- Use **PRINT** statements inside your cursors to help debug your code.

- Familiarize yourself with SQL and troubleshooting your queries using the Books Online. It is extremely useful—get in the habit of using it!

# Immediate Solutions

## Joining Tables

Joining tables is one of the most common functions that you will perform using SQL. Due to the nature of relational databases and their intended design and uses, very little of the work that you do in a database will involve a single table. For this example, we will write a query to return a complete address from the normalized address structure in the Address database provided with this book. Listing 9.20 provides the completed code to join the required tables and produce the desired information. You can refer to it while following the steps of this example to clear up any questions you might have about the query structure.

1. Start by examining the database structure to determine which tables will be needed to complete the query. To construct a complete address, it will be necessary to join the **tbl_Address**, **tbl_City**, **tbl_State**, and **tbl_ZipCode** tables.

2. To keep the code shorter and easier to read, create an alias for each table. For this example, the simplest aliasing strategy is to use the first letter of each table name (after the prefix) because there are no duplicates.

3. Establish the field list for the **SELECT** statement. The following is a list of fields for an address, prefixed by the appropriate table alias: **a.Line1**, **a.Line2**, **c.Name**, **s.State_Code**, **z.Zip5**, **a.Zip4**.

4. The starting point for the address relationships is the **tbl_Address** table. This should be the base table for the joins, so it should be referenced in the **FROM** clause.

---

**NOTE:** *Don't forget to add the table alias for each table, and it is a good idea to use **(NOLOCK)** hints to avoid unnecessary database concurrency issues.*

---

5. Next, add a **JOIN** clause for the **tbl_City** table. This table is joined on the **City_ID** columns in the **tbl_Address** and **tbl_City** tables. This is where the table aliases start to come in handy. Without providing the table alias, you would need to type the full table name as a prefix for the join columns because the column name is the same in both tables.

**9. Structured Query Language (SQL)**

6. Now add a second **JOIN** clause for the **tbl_State** table. This table is joined on the **State_ID** columns in the **tbl_City** and **tbl_State** tables. The **tbl_Address** table does not contain a reference to the **tbl_State** table, because the **tbl_State** table is referenced by both the **tbl_City** and **tbl_ZipCode** tables.

7. Finally, add the **JOIN** clause for the **tbl_ZipCode** table. This table is joined on the **Zip_ID** columns in the **tbl_Address** and **tbl_ZipCode** tables.

To make the address more readable, you can use a **CASE** statement to combine the **z.Zip5** and **a.Zip4** columns when the a.Zip4 is not **NULL**. The combined columns can then be aliased as "Zip Code". You can also alias the **s.State_Code** column as "State".

**Listing 9.20    Using joins to retrieve a complete address.**

```
/* Construct complete address information from normalized */
/* address structure                                     */
SELECT a.Line1,
       a.Line2,
       c.Name AS City,
       s.State_Code as "State",
       z.Zip5 + CASE WHEN a.Zip4 IS NOT NULL
                     THEN '-' + a.Zip4 ELSE '' END AS "Zip Code"
  FROM tbl_Address a (NOLOCK)
  JOIN tbl_City c (NOLOCK) ON a.City_ID = c.City_ID
  JOIN tbl_State s (NOLOCK) ON c.State_ID = s.State_ID
  JOIN tbl_ZipCode z (NOLOCK) ON a.Zip_ID = z.Zip_ID
```

| Related solutions: | Found on page: |
|---|---|
| Using **QUERYOUT** | 709 |
| Importing Data from a Denormalized Table to a Normalized Structure | 836 |

# Cross-Database Joins

This example looks at how to retrieve the information needed to generate an employee mailing list. This example will require joining several tables from separate databases to retrieve the needed information. The Employee and Address databases provided with this book will be used for this example. The completed code for this example is provided in Listing 9.21 as reference.

1. If you have not already done so, complete "Joining Tables" in the Immediate Solutions section of this chapter. It will be used as a basis for constructing the mailing list.

2. Because you will be dealing with more than one database in this query, it is a good idea to prefix all table references with the proper database name. For example, the **tbl_Address** would be referenced as **Address..tbl_Address**. Change all of the existing table references to include the database prefix.

3. Because this is an Employee mailing list, the **Employee..tbl_Employee** table will become the driving table for this query. It should be placed in the **FROM** clause, and the **Address..tbl_Address** table should be moved to a **JOIN** clause.

4. You will also need to add a **JOIN** clause for the **Employee..tbl_EmployeeAddressXRef** table, because it provides the link between the **Employee..tbl_Employee** table and the **Address..tbl_Address** table. It is joined to the **Employee..tbl_Employee** table on the **Employee_ID** columns in both tables.

   The **Address..tbl_Address** table now joins to the **Employee..tbl_EmployeeAddressXRef** on the **Address_ID** columns in the tables.

5. Add the employee name to the query field list. The name can be constructed by concatenating the first and last names separated by a space and aliasing the resulting column as "Employee".

6. Add an **ORDER BY** clause to order the addresses by ZIP Code, as this is the required order for processing bulk mail. Ordering by ZIP code requires specifying both the **z.Zip5** column and the **z.Zip4** column in the **ORDER BY** clause.

**Listing 9.21   Using cross-database joins to generate a mailing list.**

```
/* Generate an Employee Bulk Mailing List */
SELECT e.First_Name + ' ' + e.Last_Name AS "Employee",
       a.Line1,
       a.Line2,
       c.Name AS "City",
       s.State_Code,
       z.Zip5 + CASE WHEN a.Zip4 IS NOT NULL
                       THEN '-' + a.Zip4 ELSE '' END AS "Zip Code"
  FROM Employee..tbl_Employee e (NOLOCK)
  JOIN Employee..tbl_EmployeeAddressXRef ea (NOLOCK)
    ON e.Employee_ID = ea.Employee_ID
  JOIN Address..tbl_Address a (NOLOCK) ON ea.Address_ID = a.Address_ID
  JOIN Address..tbl_City c (NOLOCK) ON a.City_ID = c.City_ID
  JOIN Address..tbl_State s (NOLOCK) ON c.State_ID = s.State_ID
  JOIN Address..tbl_ZipCode z (NOLOCK) ON a.Zip_ID = z.Zip_ID
  ORDER BY z.Zip5, a.Zip4
```

**9. Structured Query Language (SQL)**

| *Related solution:* | *Found on page:* |
|---|---|
| Creating Triggers to Maintain Cross-Database Referential Data Integrity | 765 |

# Using **GROUP BY** and **HAVING**

Working with data groupings and aggregate functions is another common use of SQL. This example addresses the problem of locating authors who have written more than one book. To perform this operation, it is necessary to get a count of the number of books written by each author and then filter the list to retrieve only the authors who have written more than a single book. This example will use the **Authors** and **TitleAuthor** tables in the Pubs database.

1. Create the query that returns the number of books written for each author. Start by creating a select list that includes the author name and a **COUNT(*)** entry.

2. Next, add the **FROM** clause using the **Authors** table as the driving table for the query.

3. Add a **JOIN** clause to connect the **Authors** table to the **Titleauthor** table joining on the **au_id** columns in these tables. You do not actually need to join to the **Titles** table, because you only want a count of the titles, not information about the actual titles involved.

4. Add a **GROUP BY** clause that groups the count information by the author name.

5. Run this query to test that it returns the author names and the number of books they have written.

6. Add a **HAVING** clause that specifies that only entries having **COUNT(*) > 1** should be returned. The completed code for this example is shown in Listing 9.22.

### Listing 9.22    Using **GROUP BY** and **HAVING**.

```
/* Find Authors who have written more than one book */
SELECT a.au_fname + ' ' + a.au_lname AS "Author",
       COUNT(*) AS "Number of Books"
  FROM Authors a (NOLOCK)
  JOIN TitleAuthor ta (NOLOCK) ON a.au_id = ta.au_id
  GROUP BY a.au_fname + ' ' + a.au_lname
  HAVING COUNT(*) > 1
```

# Using **INSERT/SELECT**

In this example, the **INSERT/SELECT** syntax will be used to populate a table. The premise of this example is that you have been asked to provide a denormalized table to another organization or department. Using the **tbl_AddressDN** table in the Address database, you can write an **INSERT/SELECT** statement to populate the table with data from the normalized address tables. Listing 19.23 provides the completed code for this example.

1. Use the **TRUNCATE TABLE** command to remove any existing data from the **tbl_AddressDN** table.

2. Create an **INSERT** statement for the **tbl_AddressDN** table specifying the following fields: **Line1**, **Line2**, **City**, **State**, **Zip5**, and **Zip4**.

3. Create a **SELECT** statement to "feed" the insert from the normalized address tables. The required **SELECT** statement must retrieve each individual column in the same order and in the column list specified in the field list for the insert. As a basis, you can use the **SELECT** statement created in the "Joining Tables" section of the Immediate Solutions in this chapter.

4. Modify the **SELECT** statement to separate the **Zip5** and **Zip4** columns and remove the column aliases because they are not needed.

5. Execute the Query to populate the **tbl_AddressDN** table with the information from the normalized address structure.

**Listing 9.23   Populate tbl_AddressDN using INSERT/SELECT.**

```
/* Populate tbl_AddressDN from the normalized address tables */
INSERT INTO tbl_AddressDN
  (Line1,
   Line2,
   City,
   State,
   Zip5,
   Zip4)
  SELECT a.Line1,
         a.Line2,
         c.Name,
         s.State_Code,
         z.Zip5,
         a.Zip4
    FROM tbl_Address a (NOLOCK)
    JOIN tbl_City c (NOLOCK) ON a.City_ID = c.City_ID
    JOIN tbl_State s (NOLOCK) ON c.State_ID = s.State_ID
    JOIN tbl_ZipCode z (NOLOCK) ON a.Zip_ID = z.Zip_ID
```

9. Structured Query Language (SQL)

| Related solution: | Found on page: |
|---|---|
| Importing Data from a Denormalized Table to a Normalized Structure | 836 |

# Creating a Worktable Using SELECT INTO

This example will demonstrate the technique of using **SELECT INTO** to create a worktable in your queries. Creating a worktable is another commonly used technique in SQL programming. In this example, a temporary worktable is created that contains the title of each book in the **Titles** table and the total number of copies that have been sold. The completed source code for this example is provided in Listing 9.24. This example uses the **Titles** and **Sales** tables in the Pubs database.

1. Create a **SELECT** list that includes the title from the **Titles** table and the **SUM( )** of the quantities for each order from the **Sales** table.

2. Provide an alias for the sales quantity column.

3. Add a **FROM** clause using Titles as the driving table for the query.

4. Add a **JOIN** clause for the **Sales** table linking the tables on the **title_id** column in each table.

5. Add a **GROUP BY** clause to group the output by book title.

6. Run this query to verify that it produces the desired results.

7. Add an **INTO** clause between the **SELECT** list and the **FROM** clause to specify that the query results should be used to create a new table. The table name for this example should be **#tbl_TitleCount**.

**Listing 9.24  Create a temporary worktable using SELECT INTO.**

```
/* Create a worktable with the number of copies sold by title */
SELECT t.Title,
       SUM(Qty) AS "Number Sold"
  INTO #tbl_TitleCount
  FROM Titles t (NOLOCK)
  JOIN Sales s (NOLOCK) ON t.Title_ID = s.Title_ID
  GROUP BY t.Title
```

# Chapter 10

# New Features

# In Depth

Microsoft SQL Server 2000 has introduced some very impressive and much-awaited features. Database Administrators (DBAs) consistently ask the question, "Can SQL Server compete with Oracle?" Up until SQL 7.0, the reply has been humbling and negative. Ease of use and an intuitive interface are not always features people look for in a database product. They want speed, more speed, and really fast speed! Consumers want to be able to take a product's current design state, place it on the server, and have it run like a well-designed and -tuned system, which does not often happen. SQL Server performs many functions well, and will do even more if you follow the recommendations and suggestions for good database design. In the real world, it is not always possible to follow such recommendations, and you end up being disappointed or look to some other platform or vendor as a savior. There is no substitute for good design. Early versions of SQL server were not as industrial-strength as some of the more established products in the market. Microsoft gave consumers some hope with SQL 7.0 and started to offer some of the key features of database administration and performance in its product. It addressed the competition and took the proper design steps with SQL 7.0. The bigger issues addressed with SQL 7.0 were the design changes that you did not see. Microsoft placed the "hooks" in SQL 7.0 to make the delivery of SQL 2000 incredibly fast and feature-rich.

SQL 2000 offers a feature set that can compete and win in today's marketplace. Microsoft is by no means done innovating or improving, but it has made great strides in the performance of SQL 2000, catching (or surpassing) other database applications. Stability, speed, ease of use, speed, features, speed, and the capability to create scalable (fast) solutions are finally at your disposal with this product.

Many of the chapters in this book provide in-depth details of some of the new features, but are topic-centric. Entire chapters have been dedicated to some of the new features, such as English Query enhancements, Tools, and Meta Data. This chapter discusses a collection of the new features that apply to the relational engine and programming techniques. Some of the concepts introduced in this chapter may be difficult to follow at first. Take some time and work through the examples in the "Immediate Solutions" section to fully understand how these new features can be integrated into existing and new application development.

# Federated Servers

Federated servers are essentially servers that share the load of storage and processing transparently to the user or client application. The data is segmented programmatically into horizontal portions and stored on servers that hold a subset of the actual data. The segmentation is accomplished through a distributed partitioned view. This technique can really extend the scalability of an application, but requires that a few prerequisites be in place first. You must have an experienced DBA and some skilled SQL programmers to make this successful. You *must* also have a well-thought-out data model and well-constructed and designed tables. (See Chapter 16 for database design topics.) If you have or believe you have these requirements in place, there are essentially eight steps to creating a federated server environment:

1. Analyze the query load on your server to determine where segmentation of data can be accomplished. Based on your needs, determine whether entire sets of data or individual tables can be partitioned.

2. Determine the frequency of data modification in target tables. Highly modified data may require different approaches.

3. Create routing rules for business logic and view definitions. These rules will constitute the basis for placing the data where it will be used most. (Placement of related data on the member server allows for much better performance, but requires more programming.)

4. Create a duplicate image or structure of the database objects on each of the participating servers.

5. Define the member tables that will be horizontally partitioned. (Include all your constraints, and be sure that you have a good primary key.)

6. Create each server's linked server reference.

7. Define the distributed partitioned views in each of the member databases that will service user connections.

8. Migrate the data to the appropriate member server.

The view definition will contain a **UNION** operator that will join the data between each server into one logical grouping for query processing and data manipulation. You will have to create **INSTEAD OF** triggers, which are covered in Chapter 17, to handle the data updates on the view. You can segment your data by region or code or ID range, which will drive the rules to determine what data goes on which server. See Figure 10.1 for an example of federated address data.

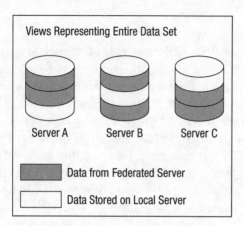

**Figure 10.1    Federated address data.**

## Partitioning a Database

The partitioning technique is very difficult and should be planned thoroughly. You may have to replicate copies of portions of data in a database to the local server, so that you are not creating a great deal of distributed query activity. A good rule of thumb is to keep 80 percent of the related data stored locally and allow the remaining 20 percent to reside on another server. This 80/20 rule is a guideline, and each situation may require different methods of synchronization. Some models require cross server triggered updates and others require snapshot or replicated data migration to support the queries run on the local server. Most systems cannot partition an entire database, but rather choose larger tables that have good segmentation and split them between one or more servers. As a result, you only have to manage those views and related data when scaling your application. This technique allows you to address speed issues and storage requirements on a more granular level than at the database level.

Database partitioning requires you to devise data routing rules that can be incorporated into the business services tier, so that applications can send each SQL statement to the member server that stores most of the data required by the statement. This is not always possible in existing applications that do not have a middle tier for implementing business logic. If you use a master and member server model, allowing users to connect to the master server only, you can reduce the amount of code that has to be written and provide a seamless distribution of the data to an application. The master/member model has some speed disadvantages, however. If the data you are requesting resides on another server, that data must be pulled and returned to the application through the master server, which must first retrieve the information from the member server and then forward it to the client application. This is inefficient and complicated, and usually means slow transmissions in the database world. If you can direct the connections of an application to the member servers that store the data you are looking for based on routing rules, your application will be *much* faster. This requires you to create views on each member server to pull remote data when needed and will add to the complexity of the management and SQL programming behind the application, but it allows you to scale to virtually unlimited sizes.

## Partitioning Data

Partitioning data is the most-likely path developers take in creating federated systems. The timing of completely reengineering an application and data model are seldom such that they are undertaken in one project. A phased approach is usually the method taken, although not always the best approach, to solve specific problems in the design of a system. Many of you will most likely start by partitioning portions of your data, and then move to the more complicated changes after you have solved your major problems and can devote more time and planning to fully partitioning the data and making the necessary changes in all aspects of your application. In order to build sets of federated data, you should horizontally partition the data in multiple servers and tables. Horizontally partitioning a table or multiple tables is defined as dividing them into many smaller tables or subsets of data on different servers that can be organized by specific rules that govern where the data must be routed to for storage and retrieval. These smaller tables must have identical data structures and store segments of the whole data set. These tables are referred to as member tables. SQL 7.0 supported this technique, but would not allow you to easily update the underlying data. With the new features in SQL 2000, you can create updateable views that act just like a table and mask the location from the application or user.

You can then create views using **UNION** operators to represent the data as a whole to client connections. In the following example, the **tbl_AddressDN** table has been partitioned across three servers (Server1, Server2, and Server3). The distributed partitioned view defined on Server1 is illustrated in Listing 10.1. Similar views would be defined on each of the other servers, so that each server would appear to hold a complete data set if needed.

**Listing 10.1   Example view definition.**

```
CREATE VIEW vw_AddressDN
AS
SELECT *
  FROM tbl_AddressDN (NOLOCK)
  UNION ALL
SELECT *
  FROM Server2.Address.dbo.tbl_AddressDN (NOLOCK)
  UNION ALL
```

```
SELECT *
  FROM Server3.Address.dbo.tbl_AddressDN (NOLOCK)
```

A view allows the actual location of the data to be transparent to an application or user. This transparency allows DBAs to repartition tables when needed without the expensive and time-consuming rework of the client code in applications.

---

**NOTE:** *You can use the same technique to create local partitioned views that reference member tables on the same server, but a different database. This allows you to simulate the partition logic and test it before distributing it across many servers or remote locations.*

---

Once you have created your view, you then have to write the logic to route the update, insert, or delete to the appropriate server through the **INSTEAD OF** trigger (covered in Chapter 17).

# User-Defined Functions

SQL Server database administrators have waited for years for the ability to write user-defined functions that can be used to enhance stored procedure and query logic. Finally, Microsoft has started implementing user-defined functions at a fundamental level; fundamental, because there are still a few restrictions syntactically that will drive some SQL programmers a bit crazy trying to find usable work-arounds.

---

**NOTE:** *The Books Online are confusing on the topic of user-defined functions, so read those topics carefully. There are statements that contradict each other between function topics.*

---

Some of the limitations to be aware of in user-defined functions are:

- Built-in nondeterministic functions are not allowed in user-defined functions. See the Books Online "Create Function" topic for a specific list of the built-in nondeterministic functions.

- Dynamic **EXECUTE** statements *cannot* be used within a user-defined function.

- Data in tables cannot be modified within a user-defined function, with the exception of the **TABLE** data type local variable.

- **UPDATE** statements are only allowed in user-defined functions when they are modifying a table variable.

There are three types of user-defined functions supported in SQL Server 2000. Each function is intended to return a specific type of data. It is important to understand when each function is called because writing each function requires different syntax and thought processes. See Table 10.1 for a list of each function type and its intended use.

**Table 10.1   Function types.**

| Type | Description |
|------|-------------|
| Scalar | Returns a single value defined in the **RETURN**. Scalar functions can contain control of flow statements and return derived or calculated values. |
| Inline table-valued | There is no body to this type of function. No controls of flow statements exist in the function. The table returned from this function is the result of a single **SELECT** statement with optional parameters. |
| Multi-statement table-valued | The body of this function is defined by a **BEGIN** and **END** statement. SQL statements manipulate the table variable returned by the function. SQL statements in this type of function cannot have side effects out of the scope of the function. |

Functions fall into two categories: deterministic or nondeterministic. A deterministic function always returns the same result and is called with a specific set of input values. A nondeterministic function can return different results each time it is called, even with the same input values. Nondeterministic functions can cause side effects in your code. Extended stored procedures are considered nondeterministic.

Each function has unique syntax requirements. See Listing 10.2 for the three different flavors of the **CREATE FUNCTION** statement.

**Listing 10.2   Function SQL syntax.**

```
-- Scalar Functions
CREATE FUNCTION [owner_name.]function_name
  ([{@parameter_name [AS] scalar_parameter_data_type [= default]}
  [,...n]])
RETURNS scalar_return_data_type
[WITH <function_option> [[,] ...n]]
[AS]
BEGIN
  function_body
  RETURN scalar_expression
END

-- Inline Table-valued Functions
CREATE FUNCTION [owner_name.] function_name
  ([{@parameter_name [AS] scalar_parameter_data_type [= default]}
  [,...n]])
RETURNS TABLE
[WITH <function_option> [[,] ...n]]
[AS]
RETURN [(] select statement [)]
```

```
-- Multi-statement Table-valued Functions
CREATE FUNCTION [owner_name.]function_name
  ([{@parameter_name [AS] scalar_parameter_data_type [= default]}
    [,...n]])
RETURNS @return_variable TABLE <table_type_definition>
[WITH <function_option> [[,] ...n]]
[AS]
BEGIN
  function_body assigning values to table @return_variable
  RETURN
END
```

# Indexed Views

Views have been a common entity for some time in the database community. They are essentially a stored query plan that is presented to the user or query engine as a table. Any query passed to a view will be parsed based upon the stored query plan for the view, and the underlying tables supply the data to the query through the view definition. Microsoft SQL Server versions prior to 8.0 (2000) did not persist the data that a view represented in the database. Oracle, for example, began using what are called "materialized views" a few years ago to improve performance, albeit at some cost. The database community took notice, and when Microsoft shipped SQL Server 2000, it supported an implementation of the materialization technique.

When you create a view in SQL Server 2000, you can now create a unique clustered index on the view, causing the data in the view to be stored in the view object. The data in the view is persisted in that state through updates to the underlying data. The cost for this added feature is in update performance and complexity. However, the price is fairly small when you take some of the features into account that materialized views provide.

The query optimizer can get the data from view queries directly from the view, saving the aggregation and join overhead associated with the old method. When a query is run against an underlying table, an index from a materialized view may be chosen in the query plan, even though the view itself was not involved in the query.

Indexed views perform best when they represent data that does not change a great deal. The cost of maintaining the additional data and indexes above the overhead of the underlying table data and indexes should be a consideration. See Table 10.2 for a comparison of the types of queries that best fit the materialized view concept.

**Table 10.2    Query performance considerations.**

| Poor Type | Good Candidate |
|-----------|----------------|
| OLTP with heavy write activity. | Joins and aggregations that process many rows. |
| Databases with many **UPDATE** operations. | Join conditions that are executed many times without change in join structure. (The indexed view could store the joined results to improve performance.) |
| Queries that do not involve aggregations or joins. | Decision support workloads. (Reporting) |
| Expanding joins where the resulting data is larger than the original data in the base tables. | |
| Views that hold a similar number of records and width to the underlying tables. Try to reduce the width and rows in a view to only hold the data required. | |

## Requirements

The requirements for creating an indexed view are rather rigid, and depending upon the design of your database, may be very hard to implement. Client connectivity, server settings, and locations of the underlying tables play an important role in the rules for creating a materialized view. One other expense in using materialized views is the fact that you must use the Enterprise Edition of SQL Server 2000 to take advantage of this feature.

---

**NOTE:** *The Developer Edition supports materialized views as well, but is not a production licensed system. The Developer Edition lets you create and code the views for deployment to a production system as long as the production system is running Enterprise Edition.*

---

The query optimizer will use an indexed view under specific conditions. See Table 10.3 for the optimizer conditions that allow the optimizer to choose indexes on views. These settings should be systemwide before attempting to create a materialized view. Managing the connections and creation of objects would become an administrative nightmare if you tried to enforce them on the fly or through a client application.

**WARNING! Some applications will operate and return different results if they were developed in environments that are not compatible with these settings. Test your application thoroughly before assuming that your SQL statements will behave as expected when these options are changed!**

**Table 10.3   Indexed view conditions.**

| Condition | Value |
|---|---|
| SET statements that must be ON | ANSI_NULLS |
| | ANSI_PADDING |
| | ANSI_WARNINGS |
| | ARITHABORT |
| | CONCAT_NULL_YIELDS_NULL |
| | QUOTED_IDENTIFIERS |
| SET statements that must be OFF | NUMERIC_ROUNDABORT |
| Optimizer conditions | Search condition predicates in a query WHERE clause. |
| | Join operations |
| | Aggregate functions. |
| | Cost estimate for index is lowest cost access consideration by the optimizer. |

*The optimizer conditions are essentially the same for table index selection.*

There are additional requirements that are placed on the underlying tables that make up the potential materialized view. The following list contains the table creation rules for creating an indexed view:

**NOTE:** *All of the SET statements from Table 10.3 must be in effect when creating each table used to make up the view.*

- The view cannot reference any other views. Base tables are the only candidates for materialization. (Normal views do not share this requirement.)

- All of the underlying tables in a materialized view must be in the same physical database as the view. (Cross database views are not candidates for this technique.)

- The potential view must be created with the **SCHEMABINDING** option.

- User-defined functions used in the view must be created with the **SCHEMABINDING** option. Only deterministic functions are allowed in this type of view.

- The tables must be referenced with two-part names (***owner.object reference***). Three- and four-part names are not allowed.

- The column list must be listed out by name. No asterisk (* or **table_name.***) column references are allowed.

- A column name cannot be used more than one time as a simple column reference. See Listing 10.3 for examples of the syntax for this rule. You can use a column more than once in the column list, but it must be part of a calculated expression.

**Listing 10.3  Column name examples for materialized views.**

```
/* Not Allowed */
SELECT columnA, columnB, ColumnA

/* Allowed */
SELECT ColumnA, ColumnB, ColumnA * 2 AS SomeColumnValue
SELECT ColumnA, SUM(ColumnB) AS SumOfB, ColumnB
```

- A derived table cannot be used as a source table for the view.
- Row set functions or **UNION** operators cannot be used in the view definition.
- Subqueries are not allowed in any portion of the view definition.
- Outer or self-joins are not allowed.
- **TOP** and **ORDER BY** clauses are not allowed.
- The **DISTINCT** keyword cannot be used in the view definition.
- Complex aggregate functions are not allowed in the view definition. You may, however, use simple aggregate functions to achieve similar results. See the SQL Server Books Online topic "Creating an Indexed View" for a detailed list of the complex aggregate functions that are not allowed in materialized view definitions.
- The **SUM( )** function cannot be used if it references a nullable expression.
- Full-text predicates like **CONTAINS** or **FREETEXT** are not allowed.
- **COMPUTE** and **COMPUTE BY** are also not allowed in the view definition.
- The owner of the view and all underlying tables and functions must be the same.
- The potential materialized view cannot contain text, ntext, or image columns.
- All the remaining normal view creation rules apply.

---

**NOTE:** *It may be advisable to ensure that all database connections use the settings in Table 10.3 across your enterprise to reduce errors when trying to use the new features of SQL Server.*

---

## Index Considerations

The index creation issues are fewer than the table and column restrictions, but there are a few to consider. The index view conditions in Table 10.3 apply for the index **CREATE** statement as well as the following items:

- The owner of the index must be the owner of the view.
- The column that contains a float value or will evaluate to a float value cannot be used as a key in an index.

- If the view definition uses a **GROUP BY** clause, the key of the unique clustered index can reference only the columns in that **GROUP BY** clause.

- All the normal index creation rules still apply.

## Final Notes on Materialized Views

Once you have created a materialized view by defining the view within the scope of the previous restrictions and creating a unique clustered index on it, you can, and probably should, consider additional indexes (nonclustered) for that view to supplement queries that will be performed against the view or any of the underlying tables.

Connections that try to manipulate data in the underlying tables involved in the materialized view *must* have the same option settings listed in Table 10.3. If an attempt is made to alter any data without those settings in place, an error is generated, and the transaction is rolled back.

You cannot drop the view or any table participating in a materialized view due to the **SCHEMABINDING** used to create it. **ALTER** statements are not allowed on table columns that are involved in the view as well. If you drop the unique clustered index on a materialized view, the stored data is lost, and the view is processed under the normal view operations.

# New Data Types

It is rare that you get a new data type in a version release of any software package, especially a database engine. It is one factor that makes this release of SQL Server so unique. You now have three new data types to consider. Let's take a look at each one individually to discuss the good, the bad, and the ugly of each new data type.

## BIGINT

The **BIGINT** data type is provided as a larger integer solution to numbers that would grow out of the range of an **INT**. Some database designs have actually been altered to use a data type other than integer because of the limitation presented by using a continuously incrementing number on large tables. (The only way the integer value would be reset was to truncate the table.) The **BIGINT** data type solves that design problem. See Table 10.4 for each integer family data type and their storage particulars.

## VARIANT

Many programming languages have had a **VARIANT** data type for some time. SQL Server has now added this data type for additional flexibility in manipulating data. However, it is not recommended that you use this data type without first

**Table 10.4   Integer family data types.**

| Data Type | Storage Requirements | Range |
|-----------|---------------------|-------|
| TINYINT | 1 byte | 0 to 255 |
| SMALLINT | 2 bytes | –32,768 to 32,768 |
| INT | 4 bytes | –2,147,483,648 to 2,147,483,648 |
| BIGINT | 8 bytes | –9,223,372,036,854,775,808 to 9,223,372,036,854,775,808 |

giving it a great deal of thought and planning. Many people feel that storing nontyped or poorly cast data in a database structure should not be done. If you must use variant data, use it sparingly and only in your processing code.

Variant data variables are able to store values in a general nature. You must set or CAST the data to manipulate it reliably or move it between systems. Variant data has additional storage overhead. Similar to Visual Basic, variant data requires additional processing overhead that rarely justifies the use of this data type.

The following rules apply to using variant data:

- Comparison operations of variant data will return different results than strongly cast data type comparisons.

- Depending upon the library a client application uses to connect to the server, variant data may be translated to a **VARCHAR** value.

- **CAST** operations on variant data must be performed before attempting addition or subtraction operations.

- You cannot use variant data type variables to hold **text**, **ntext**, **image**, **timestamp**, or other variant data.

*NOTE: See the Microsoft SQL Server Books Online topic "Using sql_variant Data" for more information on this data type.*

## TABLE

The **TABLE** data type is perhaps the biggest improvement in the relational engine. This new variable data type can impact stored procedures and concurrency a great deal. You can load a local variable scoped to the procedure it runs in and manipulate it just as you would a temporary table. Table variables carry less concurrency issues with the system catalog than temporary tables and can easily be passed between procedures as parameters.

*NOTE: Table variables are limited to the scope of the function, procedure, or batch in which they are declared and are automatically cleaned up when they fall out of scope.*

There are a few advantages and rules to table variables:

- **SELECT INTO** or **INSERT EXEC** statements cannot be used to populate a table variable. See Listing 10.4 for an example of this rule and how it can and cannot be used in a batch.

- Using table variables in your stored procedures will result in fewer recompilations of query plans due to temporary tables.

- Using local variables instead of temporary tables will create smaller query plans and increase the efficiency of the query optimizer.

- Manipulating data in table variables only impacts that variable for the duration of the operation and requires no locking, blocking, or potential deadlocks on shared database resources with other transactions (as long as no other real tables are used in a join or filtering condition). Less locking and logging activity occurs in the use of table variables.

- Joining normal tables and table variables will enhance your queries and reduce record sets.

- Creating an indexed table variable can be accomplished by using the declarative method during the variable definition. Joins to the table variable may then choose the index for better performance. (**CREATE INDEX** will not work with a table variable.)

*WARNING! Creation of an indexed table variable is not mentioned in the documentation for SQL Server 2000, therefore Microsoft may not support this capability (even though it can be done) in future releases. Test the use of this technique with each release or service pack to ensure that it is supported, should you decide to use it.*

**Listing 10.4 Example table variable script.**

```
IF EXISTS (SELECT name
             FROM sysobjects (NOLOCK)
            WHERE name = 'InsertTestProc'
              AND type = 'P')
BEGIN
  DROP PROC InsertTestProc
END
GO

CREATE PROC InsertTestProc
AS
SELECT id,
       name
  FROM sysobjects (NOLOCK)
 WHERE type = 'U'
GO
```

```
EXEC InsertTestProc

DECLARE @v_Table
        TABLE (TestID    INT,
               TestName sysname)

/* WILL NOT WORK */
-- INSERT INTO @v_Table EXEC InsertTestProc

INSERT INTO @v_Table
SELECT id,
       name
  FROM sysobjects (NOLOCK)
 WHERE type = 'U'

SELECT *
  FROM @v_Table
```

The table variable opens the door to a number of solutions that were not possible or practical before. The capability to create a temporary data set and pass it between processes to be updated, manipulated, or massaged just like a table can be very useful for many systems. Remember the scope of the variable and the fact that if your server shuts down you will lose the data. It is just a working set of data and is not intended to carry state information or become a permanent solution.

# Collations

Sort orders and code pages have been replaced by collations in SQL Server 2000. These collations can be applied at various levels from the instance all the way down to column granularity. Collations coupled with Unicode support allow a database to store character data in an open format that can be presented to client applications in different languages transparently to the storage engine.

Each collation has three properties:

- The sort order to be used for Unicode character data types (**NCHAR**, **NVARCHAR**, and **NTEXT**)
- The sort order to be used for non-Unicode character data (**CHAR**, **VARCHAR**, and **TEXT**)
- The code page used to store non-Unicode character data

The choice of which collation you should use depends on the type of application you are writing. For most English applications, use Latin1_General for the U.S. English character set (code page 1252). This allows the greatest flexibility for your applications.

**NOTE:** *If you are going to support multiple languages, be sure to use Unicode character column definitions and variable declarations so that your code will support any collation request presented to the server.*

# Full-Text Search Enhancements

Microsoft SQL Server full-text search has been enhanced to include change tracking and image filtering. The change tracking is now a logged operation that can be written to the full-text index by flushing the log manually as a background operation or on a schedule.

Image filtering provides the capability to index and query documents stored in image columns in your database. In order to use this feature, you must provide the document type of the file extension of the document (the file extension it would have had if it were stored as a file in the file system). The Microsoft Search Service will then know which document filter to use in order to search the document in response to a query.

The Microsoft Search Service provides basic character data search capabilities. You can search for matching, greater than, or less than constant values in a document or string pattern matches. This ability allows you to provide basic document search capabilities in most applications. If you are not using the full-text indexing features of SQL Server, you can disable the search service to save system resources.

The indexes generated to support the full-text search capabilities are not maintained inside the SQL Server database. They cannot be backed up or restored through SQL statements. The search service should not be confused with the Microsoft Index Service. The index service is used to search operating system files, whereas the search service allows searching within documents stored in a SQL Server database. The indexing service also provides an OLE DB provider, so that distributed queries of operating system files can be run via SQL Server.

# Indexes

A number of index enhancements have been introduced with SQL Server 2000. Indexes are the number one performance tool provided to speed queries on your server. Proper indexing choices can mean the difference between seconds and minutes for some applications.

Data grows by nature. The longer a database is in production or use, the more data will be collected. As the data in a table grows, the indexing becomes more and more important to performance. Small tables can be read very quickly by scanning the table and sorting the data in memory, but this only works for a short time. As the number of rows in a table increase, the distribution patterns of the data used in joins and search conditions changes.

---

**TIP:** *Periodic analysis of index strategies should be planned on any system to ensure that you have created the appropriate indexes for the user load on the database. Any application can benefit from periodic index analysis and tuning!*

---

New to SQL Server 2000 are a few enhancements that provide greater capabilities than ever before:

- Computed columns can now be indexed.

- Ascending or descending order of an index can now be specified.

- Index creation time can be reduced on multiple CPU systems due to parallelism enhancements.

- Tempdb can now be used for index creation space on optional performance increases (providing you have placed tempdb on a separate drive for better performance).

- An index can now be defragmented without taking it offline (see Chapter 6).

You may be able to migrate your enterprise application to SQL Server 2000 and modify your existing indexes using these new capabilities to increase the speed of your application without changing any code in the application. See the "Immediate Solutions" section of this chapter and the Microsoft SQL Server Books Online for more on how these enhancements work.

# Text in Row Data

For many years, DBAs have fought the battle of the dreaded memo. Users always wanted to type notes that exceeded the 255 character limit that made the most sense for storage. Many users could not understand why a DBA was so reluctant to use the memo field in early databases or the text field in some of the newer ones. The pros and cons of storage techniques and how the database engine worked were explained many times over. The fact that these seemingly easy-to-use utility columns chewed up more disk space than AutoCAD drawings and full-motion video in some systems seemed to be unnoticed or ignored by many developers.

In the past, text data in SQL Server was stored in a separate page structure from the actual data. The only item that was stored in the data row was a pointer to the page where the text was to be stored. Each record chewed up an entire page of storage whether 25 or 500 characters were stored in it (highly inefficient!). This storage method meant that to read a row of data, you would have to perform additional disk I/O operations to read the text data. Performance and storage considerations seldom outweighed the need to store this data; many of the battles not to use the memo field were lost and the sizes of the databases would continue to grow to accommodate the note storage.

---

**NOTE:** *You can use the query of a text column to find the average data length stored in the text column as well as the number of zero-length rows that exist, which will help you determine how much wasted space you have in your text columns.*

---

In response to this trend, many DBAs started using a text entity—a table designed to hold the text data and a unique key that could be used to join it back to the text table. At least then, only a page of storage would have to be used if a note was added for the data record. This saved a lot of room in the database.

SQL Server 7.0 introduced a new page size of 8KB versus the old 2KB. This change also increased the variable character size to 8KB as well. By providing for larger variable strings in a table, you could address some of the needs for memos in applications. You still needed to use text for strings in excess of 8KB, but the use of the text column was reduced by the increase.

Microsoft has now given the database designer and developer a new tool to fight the need for large text storage and provide higher performance. You can now specify placing the text data in the same row as the data row in the table. The new table option "text in row" allows for data that will fit in the data row to be stored with the data and any text that does not fit to be stored in a separate page. You can specify the size limit for text in row data when you specify the table option, providing there is enough room left after other column specifications.

---

**NOTE:** *See the topic "**sp_tableoption**" in the Microsoft Books Online for more information on this new option.*

---

# Functions

As with any release of a new version of software, there are a number of new functions to make the lives of developers and DBAs easier. Volumes could be written discussing each function available. Refer to the Books Online for a more complete reference and list of the functions available to you. The following functions are new and can provide a great deal of flexibility in writing your database applications.

## COUNT_BIG

**COUNT_BIG()** is the equivalent of the **COUNT()** function except that it returns its integer result as the **BIGINT** data type. You will get different results from **COUNT()** and **COUNT_BIG()** depending on how you use them. Take the time to check the column values you want to count or the method in which **NULL** values will be evaluated before relying on these aggregate functions.

Remember these rules when using **COUNT( )** and **COUNT_BIG( )**:

- If you supply an asterisk (*) to the function, all rows will be counted in the record set, including **NULL** values and duplicates.

- If you use the (**ALL** expression) keyword, you will get the number of non-**NULL** values in the record set.

- If you use the (**DISTINCT** expression) keyword, you will get the number of unique non-**NULL** values in the record set.

See Listing 10.5 for an example of how to use the **COUNT_BIG( )** function to count address data.

### Listing 10.5   **COUNT_BIG()** example.

```
SET NOCOUNT ON

SELECT COUNT_BIG(*) AS 'Big Count'
  FROM tbl_Address (NOLOCK)

SELECT COUNT_BIG(line2) AS 'Big Count'
  FROM tbl_Address (NOLOCK)

SELECT COUNT_BIG(ALL line2) AS 'Big Count'
  FROM tbl_Address (NOLOCK)

/* Results */
Big Count
-------------------
100000

Big Count
-------------------
33332

Warning: Null value is eliminated by an aggregate...
Big Count
-------------------
33332

Warning: Null value is eliminated by an aggregate...
```

**NOTE:** The **NULL** elimination warning is presented in the query output in order to let you know that the aggregate function found **NULL** values in the specified column and did not consider them in the function call.

# ROWCOUNT_BIG

**ROWCOUNT_BIG( )** returns the number of rows affected by the last SQL statement executed. (Similar to the **@@ROWCOUNT** global variable, both methods have the same overhead involved, but the global variable is a regular integer value and the function returns a **BIGINT** data type.) See Listing 10.6 for an example of how to use the **ROWCOUNT_BIG( )** function.

### Listing 10.6    ROWCOUNT_BIG() function example.

```
SET NOCOUNT ON

SELECT DISTINCT Code
  FROM tbl_Codes (NOLOCK)
 WHERE Code_Group_ID = 2

SELECT ROWCOUNT_BIG() AS 'Number of Rows'

SELECT DISTINCT Code
  FROM tbl_Codes (NOLOCK)
 WHERE Code_Group_ID = 2

SELECT @@ROWCOUNT AS 'Number of Rows'

SELECT ROWCOUNT_BIG() AS 'Number of Rows'

/* Results */
Code
------------
Email
NetSend
Page


Number of Rows
--------------------
3


Code
------------
Email
NetSend
Page


Number of Rows
--------------
3
```

```
Number of Rows
-------------------
1
```

The highlighted code shows how executing any statement will change both the **@@ROWCOUNT** global variable and the results from the **ROWCOUNT_BIG( )** functions.

## OBJECTPROPERTY

**OBJECTPROPERTY( )** allows you to interrogate database objects and determine their associated properties. Some applications must dynamically determine if an object is a table, index, or may have certain conditions associated with it like SCHEMABINDING or the object owner. See Listing 10.7 for an example of how to use the **OBJECTPROPERTY( )** function.

Listing 10.7   Example of the **OBJECTPROPERTY()** function.

```
SET NOCOUNT ON
DECLARE @v_Object sysname,
        @v_String VARCHAR(255)

SET @v_Object = 'tbl_Codes'

SELECT @v_String = 'The table: ' + @v_Object +
                   ' was created with ANSI NULLS '
IF OBJECTPROPERTY(OBJECT_ID(@v_Object),'ISANSINULLSON') = 1
BEGIN
  PRINT @v_String + 'ON.'
END
ELSE
BEGIN
  PRINT @v_String + 'OFF.'
END

/* Results */
The table: tbl_Codes was created with ANSI NULLS ON.
```

## SERVERPROPERTY

The **SERVERPROPERTY( )** function allows you to retrieve information about the current instance of SQL Server in your SQL statements and stored procedures. See Listing 10.8 for an example of how to use the **SERVERPROPERTY( )** function.

### Listing 10.8   **SERVERPROPERTY()** function example.

```
SET NOCOUNT ON

SELECT CONVERT(VARCHAR,
       SERVERPROPERTY('Edition'))        AS Edition,
       SERVERPROPERTY('ProductVersion') AS LicenseType

/* Results */
Edition                                 LicenseType
----------------------------            ----------------------------------
Developer Edition                       8.00.194
```

# CHECKSUM

The **CHECKSUM()** function creates a checksum value over an expression, column list, or an entire row in a table. Its primary use is to create a computed column in a table that is used as a hash index column providing state change comparisons or hash index joins between tables with computed hash value columns.

If you have a complicated key structure that you would consistently join on, you could create a hash column in each table to hold a value that represented the key's hash value to help speed joins between the tables. Care should be taken using this technique because all **CHECKSUM()** functions are not guaranteed to return unique values. See Listing 10.9 for an example of how to use the **CHECKSUM()** function.

---

**NOTE: CHECKSUM** and **BINARY_CHECKSUM()** should not be compared against each other for equality. Collation and locale settings can impact the results of **CHECKSUM** functions.

---

### Listing 10.9   **CHECKSUM()** function example.

```
SET NOCOUNT ON

SELECT CHECKSUM('Dalton',1234,'Patrick',01/01/2001)
SELECT CHECKSUM('Dalton',1235,'Patrick',01/01/2001)

/* Results */
----------
654809872
----------
654809616
```

## BINARY_CHECKSUM

The **BINARY_CHECKSUM()** function is intended to provide a method of detecting changes in a row of data or to provide input to the **CHECKSUM_AGG()** function. (It is used to determine if a set of rows has changed.) See Listing 10.10 for an example of how to use the **BINARY_CHECKSUM()** function.

Listing 10.10    **BINARY_CHECKSUM()** function example.

```
SET NOCOUNT ON

SELECT BINARY_CHECKSUM('Dalton',1234,'Patrick',01/01/2001)
SELECT BINARY_CHECKSUM('Dalton',1235,'Patrick',01/01/2001)

/* Results */
----------
488228855
----------
488228599
```

## CHECKSUM_AGG

The **CHECKSUM_AGG()** function is used to determine if an aggregate of rows or column values have changed. This function can be used to determine if a table or a subset of a table has changed. See Listing 10.11 for an example of how to use the **CHECKSUM_AGG()** function.

Listing 10.11    **CHECKSUM_AGG()** function example.

```
SET NOCOUNT ON

SELECT CHECKSUM_AGG(BINARY_CHECKSUM(name))
  FROM tbl_codegroup (NOLOCK)

INSERT INTO tbl_CodeGroup (
  Name,
  Description)
VALUES (
  'Team',
  'Team')

SELECT CHECKSUM_AGG(BINARY_CHECKSUM(name))
  FROM tbl_codegroup (NOLOCK)

/* Result */
```

```
793690717
----------
793501984
```

# DATABASEPROPERTYEX

The **DATABASEPROPERTYEX( )** function returns the current setting of the specified database property. This function replaces the **DATABASEPROPERTY( )** function, which is still available, but is only included for backward compatibility. See Listing 10.12 for an example of how to use the **DATABASEPROPERTYEX( )** function.

**Listing 10.12   DATABASEPROPERTYEX() function example.**

```
SET NOCOUNT ON

SELECT CASE DATABASEPROPERTYEX('Utility','IsAnsiPaddingEnabled')
       WHEN 1 THEN
         'ON'
       ELSE
         'OFF'
       END AS 'ANSI Padding',
       CASE DATABASEPROPERTYEX('Utility','IsNullConcats')
       WHEN 1 THEN
         'ON'
       ELSE
         'OFF'
       END AS 'Concat NULL'

/* Results */
ANSI Padding Concat NULL
------------ ----------
OFF          OFF
```

# *Immediate Solutions*

## Creating Federated Data

In order to take advantage of federated data features in SQL Server 2000, your data must support a clear and concise horizontal partitioning. You must be able to create a cross-section of data that can clearly be managed by **INSTEAD OF** triggers. Not all database designs will lend themselves to federation. You may need to redesign some tables in order to use federation.

Each step in this process needs to be repeated for each table or view participating in the federation. To create federated data, follow these steps:

1. Determine if the data is designed well enough to participate in federation.

2. Create or update a routing rules table that will provide the business logic tier of your application with information about the data distribution across servers (providing your application has a processing logic tier).

3. Determine which view modifications will be required. For example, will each server participating in the federation require a view to represent the entire data set?

4. Migrate the data from the source server to each server participating in the federation based on the key value ranges from the routing rules table.

5. Modify the view definitions to reflect the new federation.

6. Test queries of all types against the new model. **INSERT**, **UPDATE**, and **DELETE** statements that will affect *each* server participating in the federation should be tested.

| Related solutions: | Found on page: |
|---|---|
| Installing the Book Databases from Scripts | 369 |
| Steps | 725 |
| Creating **INSTEAD OF** Triggers for Inserts and Updates to a View | 780 |

# Creating Indexed Views

Remembering that there is a list of ANSI settings that must be present when you create a view that will be indexed, see Listing 10.13 for an example of creating an indexed view. The view exists in the Address database already, so it has to be dropped before a new view is created with the **SCHEMABINDING** option.

**NOTE:** *Ensure that all database connections across your enterprise use the settings in Table 10.3 to reduce errors trying to use the new features of SQL Server.*

**Listing 10.13    Creating an indexed view example.**

```
IF EXISTS (SELECT name
             FROM sysobjects (NOLOCK)
            WHERE name = 'vw_Address'
              AND type = 'v')
BEGIN
   DROP VIEW vw_Address
END
GO


/* Environment SET statements */
SET ANSI_NULLS ON
SET ANSI_PADDING ON
SET ANSI_WARNINGS ON
SET ARITHABORT ON
SET CONCAT_NULL_YIELDS_NULL ON
SET QUOTED_IDENTIFIER ON
SET NUMERIC_ROUNDABORT OFF
GO


CREATE VIEW [dbo].[vw_Address]
WITH  SCHEMABINDING
AS
SELECT dbo.tbl_Address.Address_ID,
       dbo.tbl_Address.Line1,
       dbo.tbl_Address.Line2,
       dbo.tbl_City.Name        AS City,
       dbo.tbl_State.State_Code AS State,
       dbo.tbl_ZipCode.Zip5,
       dbo.tbl_ZipCode.Zip4
  FROM dbo.tbl_Address
INNER JOIN dbo.tbl_City
   ON dbo.tbl_Address.City_ID  = dbo.tbl_City.City_ID
```

```
INNER JOIN dbo.tbl_State
    ON dbo.tbl_Address.State_ID = dbo.tbl_State.State_ID
INNER JOIN dbo.tbl_ZipCode
    ON dbo.tbl_Address.Zip_ID   = dbo.tbl_ZipCode.Zip_ID

GO
CREATE UNIQUE CLUSTERED INDEX CIDX_vw_Address
    ON vw_address(Address_ID)
GO
CREATE INDEX IDX_vw_Address
    ON vw_Address(zip5)
GO
```

| Related solutions: | Found on page: |
|---|---|
| Database Design Steps | 369 |
| Creating **INSTEAD OF** Triggers for Inserts and Updates to a View | 780 |

# Using the **TABLE** Data Type

You can now create a variable of the **TABLE** data type that can be manipulated with SQL statements in the same way as a permanent or temporary table. See Listing 10.14 for an example of creating and using a table variable.

## Listing 10.14    Table variable example.

```
SET NOCOUNT ON

DECLARE @v_TitleCodes TABLE (
  Code_ID     INTEGER,
  Code        VARCHAR(12),
  Description VARCHAR(100))

INSERT INTO @v_TitleCodes
SELECT Code_ID,
       Code,
       Description
  FROM tbl_Codes
 WHERE Code_Group_ID = 1

SELECT Code,
       Description
  FROM @v_TitleCodes
```

```
/* Results */
Code           Description
------------   ----------------------------------------------------------
DBArch         DB Architect
DBA            DB Administrator
SQLProg        SQL Programmer
SRDBA          Senior DBA
NetTech        Network Technician
MISMgr         MIS Manager
QAMgr          QA Manager
QATech         QA Technician
Admin          Admin Support
SrAdmin        Senior Administrator
CEO            Chief Operations Officer
CTO            Chief Technical Officer
```

| Related solutions: | Found on page: |
|---|---|
| Using a Codes Table | 385 |
| Running Traces for Optimization | 518 |

# Creating an Inline User-Defined Function

An inline function is one that has no control-of-flow logic in the body of the function. The only variable in the code is the parameter(s) that is passed in to filter the **SELECT** statement in the code. The **SELECT** statement determines the column names of the table variable returned. See Listing 10.15 for an example of an inline function.

**Listing 10.15   Inline user-defined function example.**

```
SET NOCOUNT ON

IF EXISTS (SELECT name
           FROM sysobjects (NOLOCK)
           WHERE name = 'fn_GetCodeList'
           AND type = 'fn')
BEGIN
  DROP FUNCTION fn_GetCodeList
END
GO
```

```
CREATE FUNCTION fn_GetCodeList (
  @p_CodeGroupID INTEGER)
RETURNS table
AS
RETURN (
  SELECT Code_ID,
         Code,
         Description
    FROM tbl_Codes (NOLOCK)
   WHERE Code_Group_ID = @p_CodeGroupID
)
GO


/* Example of calling the function */
SELECT *
  FROM fn_GetCodeList(1)
GO
```

| Related solutions: | Found on page: |
|---|---|
| Using a Codes Table | 385 |
| Running Traces for Optimization | 518 |

# Creating a Scalar User-Defined Function

Scalar functions operate on a single set of values and return a specific single value of the data type in the **RETURNS** portion of the **CREATE** statement. You can perform math, string, and data manipulation routines on parameters passed in as a user-defined scalar function. See Listing 10.16 for an example of a scalar function example.

### Listing 10.16   Scalar function example.

```
SET NOCOUNT ON

IF EXISTS (SELECT name, type
             FROM sysobjects (NOLOCK)
            WHERE name = 'fn_AddDays'
              AND type = 'fn')
BEGIN
  DROP FUNCTION fn_AddDays
END
```

```
GO

CREATE FUNCTION fn_AddDays (
  @p_Date DATETIME,
  @p_Days  INTEGER)
RETURNS VARCHAR(10)
AS
BEGIN
  RETURN (CONVERT(VARCHAR(10),DATEADD(DD,@p_Days,@p_Date),110))
END
GO

/* Example of calling the function */
SELECT dbo.fn_AddDays('01/01/2000',5) AS NewDate
GO
```

## Creating a Multi-Statement Function

A multi-statement function has a **BEGIN** and **END** block that can contain multiple statements. The control-of-flow statements and manipulation of the table variable to be returned must be between the **BEGIN** and **END** blocking of the function. As with the inline function, the multi-statement function returns a table variable to the calling process. Both types of functions can be used in **JOIN** statements with user tables or views. See Listing 10.17 for a multi-statement function example.

**Listing 10.17   Multi-statement function example.**

```
SET NOCOUNT ON

IF EXISTS (SELECT name
             FROM sysobjects (NOLOCK)
            WHERE name = 'fn_GetCodeListLong'
              AND type = 'fn')
BEGIN
  DROP FUNCTION fn_GetCodeListLong
END
GO

CREATE FUNCTION fn_GetCodeListLong (
  @p_CodeGroupID INTEGER)
```

```
RETURNS @v_Table TABLE (
  Code_ID     INTEGER,
  Code        VARCHAR(12),
  CodeGroup   VARCHAR(30),
  Description VARCHAR(100))
AS
BEGIN
  INSERT INTO @v_Table
  SELECT c.Code_ID,
         c.Code,
         g.Name,
         c.Description
    FROM tbl_Codes      c (NOLOCK)
    JOIN tbl_CodeGroup g (NOLOCK)
      ON c.Code_Group_ID = g.Code_Group_ID
   WHERE g.Code_Group_ID = @p_CodeGroupID
  RETURN
END
GO

/* Example of calling the function */
SELECT *
  FROM fn_GetCodeListLong(1)
GO
```

| Related solutions: | Found on page: |
|---|---|
| Using a Codes Table | 385 |
| Running Traces for Optimization | 518 |

# Letting the Server Suggest Indexes for You

SQL Server has an interesting, little-known internal feature that can be used to tell you when you need to address the indexing of a table. If you have selected the autocreate statistics option on a database, the query optimizer will create statistic sets to satisfy data distribution questions for any queries run in that database. You can then query the **sysindexes** table for these statistics to determine where you may need to create permanent indexes to increase performance. You can run a query similar to the one in Listing 10.18 to get a list of the tables and the statistic sets.

**Listing 10.18    Sysindexes query example.**

```
SELECT CONVERT(VARCHAR,obj.name) AS 'Table Name',
       idx.name                  AS 'Stats Name'
  FROM sysindexes idx (NOLOCK)
  JOIN sysobjects obj (NOLOCK)
    ON idx.ID = obj.ID
 WHERE idx.name LIKE '_WA_%'

/* Results */
Table Name                        Stats Name
-------------------------------   -------------------------------
tbl_Codes                         _WA_Sys_Code_Group_ID_75D7831F
tbl_Codes                         _WA_Sys_Code_ID_75D7831F
tbl_Codes                         _WA_Sys_Code_75D7831F
tbl_CodeGroup                     _WA_Sys_Code_Group_ID_76CBA758
```

Each statistic set will have an autogenerated name that contains the column reference that required an index. Interrogating the list of statistics in this example suggests that **tbl_CodeGroup** needs an index on the **Code_Group_ID** column, and **tbl_Codes** would respond better to queries if it had indexes on each of the **Code**, **Code_ID**, and **Code_Group_ID** columns.

You should test each index to determine if it actually does increase performance or not. In some cases, just having statistics is enough to satisfy the query optimizer. Test each index individually for performance impact. Indexes do take up space in your database, and too many indexes could slow SQL statements that affect those indexes.

| Related solutions: | Found on page: |
| --- | --- |
| Using a Codes Table | 385 |
| Running Traces for Optimization | 518 |

# Indexing Computed Columns

In order to create an index on a computed value, you must ensure that the following settings are in place. The computed column value must be deterministic and precise. (Float data types are not allowed due to their inherent precision problem.)

You must have the following **SET** statements on:

• **ANSI_NULLS**

• **ANSI_PADDING**

- **ANSI_WARNINGS**
- **ARITHABORT**
- **CONCAT_NULL_YIELDS_NULL**
- **QUOTED_IDENTIFIER**
- **NUMERIC_ROUNDABORT** should be **SET OFF**

# Ascending or Descending Indexes

If your applications running against SQL Server pass queries that use **ORDER BY** clauses, you may want to consider the appropriate use of additional ascending or descending indexes to increase performance. If you are consistently ordering data in a specific manner, having an index that already contains the key values sorted in the proper order can save disk I/O and tempdb use. When a multiple column **ORDER BY** requires that columns be sorted in a different order from each other (one ascending and another descending), you can create a specific index to match that statement to increase performance. See Listing 10.19 for the **CREATE INDEX** syntax with the new keywords to support ascending and descending data in the same index.

**Listing 10.19   CREATE INDEX syntax.**

```
CREATE [UNIQUE] [CLUSTERED | NONCLUSTERED] INDEX index_name
    ON {table | view} (column [ASC | DESC] [,...n] )
[WITH <index_option> [,...n]]
[ON filegroup]
<index_option> :: =
    {PAD_INDEX |
     FILLFACTOR = fillfactor |
     IGNORE_DUP_KEY |
     DROP_EXISTING |
     STATISTICS_NORECOMPUTE |
     SORT_IN_TEMPDB}
```

You can specify the sort order for each column in the index. Be careful not to create too many indexes on a table. The number of indexes that make sense depends upon the number of columns and rows that will be indexed and the performance trade-off that an index provides. Indexes increase performance of read and join operations, but can slow **INSERT**, **UPDATE**, and **DELETE** statements because of the index key maintenance involved.

# Using the **SORT_IN_TEMPDB** Option

You can distribute the creation of indexes by adding the index option **SORT_IN_TEMPDB** to the **CREATE** statement. See Listing 10.19 for an example of the **CREATE INDEX** statement. The advantages of using this index option are generally not realized unless you have placed tempdb on a different drive from the data.

---

**NOTE:** *Using this option does increase the space required to create an index.*

---

# Creating a Text in Row Table

SQL Server 2000 now allows you to place small **TEXT**, **NTEXT**, and **IMAGE** data in the same row as the rest of the data in a table. This reduces the amount of disk I/O needed to perform queries and speeds operations against **TEXT** and **IMAGE** data. You should not rely on this option to save disk space unless you know the size of your text and data.

The text in row data option is best suited for tables that use text columns to store notes that vary in size but can be stored in between 24 and 7000 bytes. You could use a query like the one in Listing 10.20 to determine if a text column is under the 7000 byte limit or not. The query in Listing 10.20 uses the Northwind database to test the **NTEXT** column description for its maximum and average values to make sure it is a good candidate for text in row data.

**Listing 10.20    Text column length test.**

```
SELECT MAX(DATALENGTH(Description)) AS 'Max Length',
       AVG(DATALENGTH(Description)) AS 'Average Length'
  FROM Categories (NOLOCK)

/* Results */
Max Length  Average Length
----------  --------------
116         58
```

Because the column length test results are far below the 7000 byte limit for text in row data, this table would be a prime candidate for using the text in row data option. See Listing 10.21 for the stored procedure call to change this table option. You can also specify a maximum size for the **TEXT** or **IMAGE** data to consume before it is allocated in a separate page structure.

### Listing 10.21   Procedure for setting the text in row data option for a table.

```
/* Set text in row on */
EXEC sp_tableoption N'Categories', 'text in row', 'ON'

/* Set text in row to a 500 byte limit */
EXEC sp_tableoption N'Categories', 'text in row', 500

/* Disable the text in row option */
EXEC sp_tableoption N'Categories', 'text in row', 'OFF'
```

| *Related solution:* | *Found on page:* |
| --- | --- |
| Running Traces for Optimization | 518 |

# Chapter 11

# Performance, Tuning, and Optimization

# In Depth

Writing efficient SQL code is a necessity in almost every environment. The larger and more complex your database becomes, the more important code efficiency becomes for maintaining system performance at acceptable levels. The techniques and environmental considerations presented in this chapter will not only help you optimize your existing SQL code, but will also provide you with an understanding of the factors that influence the way in which the queries you write are processed by the server. This chapter will enable you to write much more efficient code as you continue to work with SQL Server.

There are too many factors that can influence the performance of your queries for any one reference to be able to give you the "best" method to optimize the queries in your environment. Therefore, there is no absolute source of information when it comes to optimization. This chapter presents ideas and techniques that work well in many situations, but it is up to you to test these techniques to determine what works best in your environment. It is impossible to cover every possible technique and consideration in the scope of a single chapter. Consequently, this chapter is intended to provide enough information to help get you started and to open your mind to the possibilities that exist in SQL Server. There are always alternatives to any given approach when writing queries, and some of them will perform better than others, depending on the data and the environment in which they are run. The only way to determine what works best for you is by experimenting with different techniques and testing the results.

Sometimes, the only way to find a more efficient approach to a problem is to completely rethink the entire approach. As you look at a problem, you should consider whether or not there are alternatives to not only the individual queries in the process, but to the process as a whole. It may be possible to achieve significantly better performance by performing the steps in a different order or grouping certain steps differently. There is something of an art to the process of finding the most efficient way to write your code, and it takes experience and experimentation to become good at it. This chapter helps guide you down the path to becoming proficient at the optimization process as well as writing better and more efficient SQL code at the outset.

## Optimization Considerations

There are many factors to consider when beginning the process of optimizing your database. Issues like performance expectations and concurrency needs should be addressed and documented to provide you with a tangible goal before you begin the design or optimization process. You need to consider the type of processing that will be performed against the server and what resources you have available. This section provides some detailed information about a number of factors that influences database performance.

## Server Optimization

The first component that should be addressed is the server. Even if the database design is perfect and the SQL code is fully optimized, a poorly configured or underpowered server can lead to inferior performance. Alternatively, a strong server that is well tuned can make even a poorly constructed system run at an acceptable level. Recall that the first three chapters of this book dealt with hardware selection and tuning the Windows NT operating system. Both hardware and OS tuning issues should be addressed prior to starting the SQL Server tuning process. The two main considerations that will affect server performance from a hardware standpoint are RAM and the disk subsystem. You should make every effort to ensure that both of these areas are given as many resources as possible to improve overall system performance.

Once you have configured the hardware and operating system, you need to make sure that SQL Server is configured properly. Refer to "Modifying SQL Server Properties" in the "Immediate Solutions" section of Chapter 5 for step-by-step instructions on setting the SQL Server configuration options. One detail to keep in mind when configuring the server is that all resources incur a cost. It is important not to enable options that will not be needed or used, so that system resources are conserved.

## Speed Vs. Concurrency

One key factor in optimizing the performance of your database is to identify the speed and concurrency needs of your environment. Although these two factors are not mutually exclusive, you may encounter situations where you are forced to sacrifice one for the other. If you must have the capability of 1,000 simultaneous user connections in a heavy online transaction processing (OLTP) environment, take this into consideration during the optimization process to avoid introducing "hot spots" that will cause problems in this environment. Both of these issues play a role in determining the best options to take in various situations. These issues should be carefully considered and documented at the beginning of the system design or optimization process.

## Database Design

The optimization process can be made more or less difficult by the way the database has been designed. If you are in the early stages of a project, it may be possible to redesign the database to eliminate performance problems caused by the initial design. If your database is already in production, it will likely be difficult to make major design modifications without having to rework your application code. This can prove to be an extremely difficult task on an existing system. The following sections provide some insight into the types of design issues that can cause difficulties in the optimization process if they are not considered up front. Issues that are discussed should be looked at as part of the optimization process. More detailed information on most of these topics is available in Chapter 16.

### Referential Integrity

Referential integrity can play a key role in the optimization process. If you have established foreign key constraints for all related tables, it is much easier to code the joins without the need to worry about whether or not the data will be present in the linked table. Without these constraints on the database, it can be extremely time-consuming to identify where problems exist when debugging your code. It is much more likely that you will find data that does not conform to your expectations that causes your queries to either fail or behave erratically. This is an area that you may be able to address on an existing system, but you will have to resolve any existing data problems before implementing the integrity checking.

Performance-minded developers may disagree with enforcing referential integrity at the database level. In practice, a poorly implemented referential integrity model will cause a developer to write more complicated **JOIN** and **WHERE** clause logic. Knowing that key pieces of data will exist in an expected and reliable format allows the index utilization by the query optimizer to be more reliable. Enforcing the relational integrity of the data will also make the output of the queries against the data more reliable without the need to resort to extraneous use of functions and conversions in joins and **WHERE** clauses to make the data match properly.

**NOTE:** *There is much less overhead required to manage the referential integrity using the standard constraints provided by SQL Server rather than making multiple checks on the data from the client. Performing these checks in client code will most likely result in the need for multiple round trips to the server or more data than necessary being passed between the client and server.*

### Nullability

Allowing **NULL**s in columns can be useful, but it should be carefully considered. This can be especially problematic if the column is used in an index. Allowing **NULL**s in an indexed column can cause the query optimizer to make bad decisions about whether or not to use the index. It can also put you in the situation of having to coalesce the column in order to use it in your query, which definitely hinders the usability of the column in the index. Additionally, NULLs can cause problems in aggregate functions if you do not take them into account from the start. One key issue to note with **NULL** columns is the fact that any Boolean comparison with a **NULL** yields a result of **UNKNOWN** when **ANSI_NULLS** is enabled for the connection. Because **UNKNOWN** is not true, the net effect works as if the response is **FALSE**. Both "= NULL" and "<> NULL" effectively evaluate as **FALSE** in your queries. In order to check for **NULL** values directly, you can check for "**IS NULL**" or "**IS NOT NULL**", which will evaluate correctly when comparing against **NULL** values in a column. These issues can cause problems in the query functionality as well as in the optimization process. It is a good idea to get in the habit of using the "**IS NULL**" and "**IS NOT NULL**" method to check for **NULL** values becaue this method will work regardless of the **ANSI_NULLS** setting for the connection.

### Indexes and Statistics

Indexes and statistics play an important role in database optimization. Too many indexes can make your update and insert performance prohibitively slow. You will have to be careful, especially in an OLTP environment, to keep the number of indexes to a minimum so that the performance of **UPDATE**, **INSERT**, and **DELETE** operations remains at an acceptable level. Data retrieval, on the other hand, relies on good index and statistic information for optimum performance. Several indexing considerations should be kept in mind for optimizing your query performance.

A covering index is one that contains all the columns for a particular table that are referenced by a query. In this case, SQL Server has the capability to use the index to satisfy the query without having to read the data pages associated with the index. This type of index can be extremely useful in improving the performance of a query, but adding too many columns to an index can result in poor performance in other areas. Beginning with SQL Server 7.0, the query optimizer has the capability to aggregate multiple indexes together to create a covering index for a query. This can make it possible to produce several indexes that can be used to create covering indexes for a variety of queries.

Another indexing option that should be used carefully is a clustered index. A clustered index forces the physical order of the data to match the indexed column(s). These indexes should be created with care because they can play a large role in query speed. However, you can only have one of them per table. These indexes are often implemented poorly on a database. It is generally not the best idea to make the primary key a clustered index. This type of index is mainly useful when you are accessing a large number of rows that need to be ordered by the column(s) contained in the clustered index or data that is normally searched sequentially on ranges of values. This normally occurs in a reporting function or some other similar activity. If you look at the **tbl_AddressDN** table in the address database, you will notice that the table contains an identity column, which should probably be used for the primary key for this table. Under normal circumstances, this is probably a poor choice for a clustered index because you generally use this index for single record or small record set lookups from this table. A good choice for a clustered index on this table might be the ZIP code and/or state columns because it is far more likely that you would want to access all records from this table ordered by one or a combination of these two fields for mass mailing purposes. The primary key in this case would basically result in a random ordering of the data because it would indicate the order in which the records were entered and not any geographically significant order.

Clustered indexes can also impact the performance of **UPDATE**, **INSERT**, and **DELETE** operations. If you have a clustered index on a table, the physical ordering of the rows must be maintained when these operations are executed. This can cause a significant negative impact on the speed of these operations. Beginning with SQL Server 7.0, the management of unused space in the database was enhanced to allow inserts to be placed in any available space in the table. This removed the need for creating a clustered index for managing space created by deleted records. This enhancement also helped to eliminate the problems associated with "hot spots" on inserts by changing the need to always insert the records at the end of the table. With this information in mind, consider whether or not a particular table might benefit from the addition of a clustered index enough to outweigh the impact on these operations.

The type of data used in an index can also make a significant difference in the performance of your queries. When possible, you should attempt to use integer or other binary data types for indexes that will be used in JOIN operations. These indexes not only provide faster performance, but also eliminate potential problems with issues like padding. Using an identity column as the primary key for a table provides fast and easy access to the specific record you are trying to retrieve. Integer columns may not provide humanly understandable links between the tables, but the server will utilize these columns much more efficiently than **CHAR** or **VARCAR** columns for lookup and **JOIN** operations. Every table should have at least one unique index to provide access to the specific record for updating and lookups. This index should ideally be created on an integer column for best performance.

Statistics can be created on a column that does not have an index to help the query optimizer more effectively determine the data distribution when calculating the query plan. These statistic sets have much lower overhead than an index. The main difference is that an index provides a link to the actual record that can be used when the query is executed, whereas the statistic set only provides distribution information about a particular column. Statistics seem to work much better for ad hoc queries than they do for stored procedures. You will need to test the addition or removal of these sets to determine whether or not they are beneficial in your environment. It can also be useful to experiment with changing statistic sets into indexes and vice versa to see which provides the best overall performance in your environment. Creating statistic sets for all columns in multicolumn indexes can make a significant difference in your query performance. By default, SQL Server only maintains distribution statistics for the first column in a multicolumn index. However, there is a stored procedure that can make this task simpler. Executing **sp_createstats** with the **INDEX ONLY** parameter causes SQL Server to create statistics for all columns contained in any index in the database that do not currently have statistics generated for them. The query optimizer makes use of these additional statistics when determining the best query plan. These statistics seem to work equally for ad hoc queries and stored procedures. It is recommended that two options be turned on for all databases: Auto Create Statistics and Auto Update Statistics. These options cause the index statistics and statistic set information to be maintained automatically by SQL Server.

### ANSI Defaults

ANSI Defaults can cause serious problems in your database if you do not choose the defaults you want to work with and keep them consistent throughout your data. You can run into problems with data padding that cause joins and compares to fail on **CHAR** and **VARCHAR** fields if these options are changed during the course of using the database. Inconsistent nullability between related columns can also cause severe problems when trying to relate the data at a later time. The Books Online provides detailed information about these options and the effects of enabling and disabling each one. These settings should be studied carefully and decided on in the early design stages. If you find that you must change these settings once the system is in production, be prepared for some unpredictable side effects to crop up in your system. Keep in mind when making these choices that as Microsoft moves forward with SQL Server, it is moving closer and closer to the ANSI standards in almost every area. With this in mind, it is probably best to choose the ANSI standard options for your database to avoid problems in future upgrades of SQL Server. This can also help keep both your data and your code more portable if you ever decide to change database platforms.

### Triggers

Triggers play an important role in many databases. They are used for enforcing referential integrity and other business rules in the database. They are also used for cascading deletes and updates to related tables in the database. Triggers must be used with care because they can create problems in both speed and concurrency if they are not coded with extreme care. Remember to consider the impact on other processes when a trigger is executed, and be sure that the impact on system performance will not be more severe than the benefit of using the trigger.

Actions performed by triggers should be kept small and fast to minimize their impact on the system. You also need to consider whether or not the action performed by the trigger will activate triggers on the affected tables as well as how those triggers will impact the overall performance of the operation. Triggers are an important asset in database management and design, but like any other tool, if they are not used properly, serious problems can arise.

### Views

Views are useful tools for presenting a data snapshot in a way other than the way it is stored in the physical tables. Views can be referenced like tables in a query and can be used to provide access to a subset of the available information or to provide the data in a denormalized form for easier use. With SQL Server 2000, you also have the ability to create Indexed Views, which can provide greatly enhanced lookup performance over traditional views. Indexed Views are covered in more detail in Chapter 10 as well as in the Books Online. You can use views to simplify the **JOIN** conditions for a query by joining several views instead of a large number of tables. This should be tested, however, to make sure that the performance of the join is better using the views than using individual tables. Performance may vary depending on the specific structures and data involved.

## Legacy Systems

Working with legacy systems can provide the greatest challenge to optimization that you will encounter. The size and complexity of the legacy code determines the level of changes that you can make to the underlying data structure to affect performance changes. The larger the system, the harder it is to absorb structure changes when attempting to optimize your queries. If you have a large system with poorly designed tables, you may be forced to work around the design problems instead of fixing them. This is an area where realistic expectations can be extremely important.

### SQL Server Versions

In some cases, you will have to deal with code running on multiple versions of SQL Server. This can be especially true for software development companies who have clients running on various versions. In any event, it may not be possible to get all of the servers that will be running your code on the same version of SQL Server. In this case, optimization becomes extremely difficult. You will have to focus on finding the best method to provide reasonable execution time on each platform where the query will be run. You have the option of creating version-specific code, but if you are managing a large code base, this choice can quickly become unmanageable. However, you may be able to manage the indexing strategy used on the various versions of the server differently. This can make a big difference in query performance because SQL Server 6.x used a very different query optimization scheme than SQL Server 7.0 and later. What works well for one version may work extremely poorly (or not at all) for another version of SQL Server. This is an area where you will have to experiment with the techniques presented in this chapter to see what works well in your environment. One of the major issues that has been raised in cross-version support is that later versions of SQL Server seem to be less forgiving of poorly normalized database designs. The performance of these databases on newer servers is much harder to maintain at an acceptable level.

### Existing Database Design

If you have a database with a large number of wide tables that all have high row counts, you will not be able to achieve the same performance that would be possible if you could redesign the system with better normalization. Character indexes used as join fields are another issue that you may have to deal with in this type of situation. When faced with a poor design that you cannot change, you have to make the best of it and apply a little slight of hand to achieve the best possible performance for the data you have to work with.

Two issues that you may be able to change in an existing database are enforcing referential integrity and making sure you have a good indexing strategy in place. Both of these issues can normally be addressed without major changes to the existing code base. Before you apply referential integrity constraints to your database, you will need to "scrub" the data to ensure that the existing data conforms to the constraints you are adding. You will also probably find it necessary to add some additional error checking code to your client application to manage attempts to perform data manipulations that violate these constraints. See Chapter 19 for more information on data analysis and coding techniques. Enforcing referential integrity allows you to make assumptions about the state of the data used in joins and avoid erroneous results caused by orphaned or missing records. Indexing is always an issue that should be addressed with forethought and care to ensure that query performance is as high as possible. Keep in mind when changing the indexing strategy of a legacy system that there may be code in place using index hints for existing indexes. If that is the case, then removing an index that you do not feel is useful can have a negative impact on the current code. You will need to determine the impact of changing the code versus leaving the existing index in place. See Chapter 16 for more information on designing referential integrity.

## Test, Test, Test!

When it comes to tuning database performance, there is no substitute for testing and documentation. Once you have determined the performance requirements, you are ready to start tuning the system. You should first test and document the performance of the database in its current condition, and then save this information as a baseline for comparing future test results. This is the only way to provide an accurate comparison of the optimized performance to the original when you are finished with the optimization process. This initial testing also provides the information you need to determine which areas of the query need to be addressed first. You should always apply changes one at a time and test the effect of each individual change. If you make numerous changes before retesting the performance, it may be extremely difficult to know which changes in the code were responsible for the performance differences. It is also possible that some changes may have negated one another and one or more of them would produce better results if the others had not been made.

### Documenting Test Results

You should always document the results of your testing at each step. This can provide a clear picture of how the database performance changes during the course of your efforts. You need to pay special attention to query time and IO for the various parts of the queries you are monitoring. You should document these statistics individually for each piece of the query. As you make changes to the query, this documentation will allow you to determine whether or not each change has the desired effect. This documentation can also help you to determine which changes had the most impact at a later time. You should examine the test results carefully after each successful change to identify the best area to address next in the process. If you have a query that is running in 50 milliseconds and the overall process takes 20 seconds, you probably don't need to address this particular query in your optimization process. Try to find the longest-running query, and work on it first. Once the performance of the longest query is shorter than other longer-running queries or once you have determined that there isn't any additional improvement to be gained, move on to the next-longest query and start again. This granular approach can make the optimization process much easier to manage.

### Watching for Side Effects

You may need to monitor more than one piece of the process to accurately assess the impact of the change. In some cases, a change to one query can have an effect on the performance of another query in the batch. As you change the query plan, the data that is stored in the cache changes, and this can affect how other queries perform. You need to keep a close eye on all the components of the batch that you are changing to be sure that you are not improving one piece while offsetting or producing inferior performance changes in another piece.

### Testing to Ensure Script Integrity

When performing optimization, it is often easy to forget about testing the script integrity. You need to develop a plan for regression testing the system before you start the optimization process. Make sure you have adequate test scenarios as well as their expected results to verify that you have not changed the output of any of the various queries that you optimize in the course of this process. It is sometimes necessary to make substantial structural changes to the queries in order to obtain the performance level you need. It is easy to inadvertently change the results of a query in this situation. You need to provide a mechanism for verifying that the system integrity is maintained when you are done with the optimization process. If possible, an automated test should be used to eliminate the possibility of erroneous changes in the results that may have been produced by the "human equation." It is also important to keep a backup of the data so that you can be absolutely certain that the test is being conducted on the same data and that only the code has changed. You should probably choose milestones in the project where you run this test so that you do not find yourself weeks into the project and suddenly realize that a mistake was made at the beginning, which leaves your changes useless.

### Timing Scripts

With the current set of tools shipped with SQL Server, the need for internal script timing has diminished. Now that the Profiler is available to assist you in tracking the performance of each command in a batch, it is no longer necessary to implement logic in the script itself to perform incremental timing. It can be useful, however, to perform this type of timing within your scripts for the purposes of logging and tracking specific runtimes over a period of time for trend analysis. With this thought in mind, Listing 11.1 provides the basic components for timing command execution within a script with millisecond precision. This example outputs the elapsed running time with the **PRINT** command, but it would also be easy to take this elapsed time and store it in a table along with the beginning datetime information and a step description for reporting purposes. If all you actually want to do is print the elapsed time for each query in the batch, using the **SET STATISTICS TIME ON** command is easier and will provide more detailed information.

Listing 11.1 Internal script timing example.

```
/* SET CONTEXT TO ADDRESS DATABASE */
USE Address

/* DECLARE TIMING VARIABLES */
DECLARE @v_Begin DATETIME,
        @v_elapsed INT

/* SET BEGIN TIME */
SELECT @v_begin = GETDATE()

/* ACTUAL WORK TO BE TIMED */
SELECT a.Line1,
       c.Name,
       s.State_Code,
       z.Zip5
```

```
        FROM tbl_Address a (NOLOCK)
        JOIN tbl_City c (NOLOCK) ON a.City_ID = c.City_ID
        JOIN tbl_State s (NOLOCK) on a.State_ID = s.State_ID
        JOIN tbl_ZipCode z (NOLOCK) on a.Zip_ID = z.Zip_ID

    /* GET ELAPSED TIME */
    SELECT @v_elapsed = DATEDIFF(ms, @v_begin, GETDATE())

    /* SHOW ELAPSED TIME */
    PRINT 'Elapsed Time: ' + CONVERT(VARCHAR(5), @v_elapsed) + ' milliseconds'
```

### Realistic Test Scenarios

"It works on my machine!" has become the mantra for many software developers in a testing situation. In many cases, the developer's inability to duplicate a problem is caused by severely inadequate test data. If testing is not done using realistic data, many problems that arise in a production environment are missed. The same is true for the optimization process. If you do not have a realistic representation of the production data that the SQL code will be run against, there is no way to accurately gauge the true performance characteristics of the code.

It is important to understand that true optimization is data-dependent. This means that you may not have the same performance on your production system if you do not use realistic (preferably "live") data in your testing. It may be prohibitively time-consuming to run the queries you are testing against your entire production database for every step of the optimization process, but you will need to run these queries against the "live" data at some point to get a true measure of the system performance. If you are optimizing a database for a system that is resold to your clients and used in various environments, it is important to try to get a good cross section of actual client data to test. This will ensure that you arrive at a happy medium that does not improve performance for one client at the expense of the others. Accurate performance measurement can be a tricky issue, but adequate testing and experimentation usually prove beneficial.

## Team Optimization

As with many other topics in software development, a single point of view is limiting when working on optimizing a database. It is always better to have at least two opinions and points of view to work with. However, there is a limit to the size of a team that can work on a project effectively, but having at least two people is strongly recommended. An extra set of eyes can often help spot problems and errors in the code before the process gets too far. If you significantly restructure a query, you should always have someone else look at the code to make sure that it produces the same results as the original code.

One major issue that can play an important role in a team environment is keeping the code readable for the entire group. Chapter 9 presented some blocking suggestions that helped make your code more readable, but any consistent formatting method agreed on by the team should work well. Commenting on the code is also helpful when someone else is reviewing it. Both commenting and consistent formatting make it easier to maintain the code in the future. It may take some time up front to format the code for readability, but the time saved later is generally worth the effort. Consistently formatted code is also less likely to be misinterpreted in the rewrite process, which will help prevent errors from being introduced in the new code.

It is also a good idea to establish coding standards for such items as join syntax and column aliasing. Any optional command syntax of this nature should be decided on and enforced by the entire group. Any existing code should be reformatted and made to conform to these standards before beginning the optimization process. This will ensure that all code is clear and reduce the potential for mistakes. The ANSI join syntax is generally easier to read and is less ambiguous in terms of the columns used to join the tables. It is probably a good idea to stick with that syntax for joins. It will also eliminate unintentional cross-joins in your queries.

# Optimization Tools

Microsoft SQL Server 2000 ships with several tools that help you in the process of optimizing your database and server performance. These tools include the Query Analyzer, the Profiler, the Performance Monitor, and the Index Tuning Wizard. Each of these tools has special functionality to help you with specific parts of the optimization process. The Query Analyzer, the Profiler, and the Index Tuning Wizard are discussed in Chapter 5.

## Query Analyzer

The Query Analyzer is probably the first tool you will use to start optimizing a query. This tool provides the basic functionality that allows you to examine the query plan and view the statistics generated for time and IO produced by running the query. The Query Analyzer provides an easy environment in which to make modifications and perform the initial debugging of the queries you are changing. Features like syntax highlighting make this tool an ideal environment for creating and modifying SQL code.

### Examining the Query Plan

Once you have entered a query in the Query Analyzer, you can examine the query plan by selecting Display Estimated Execution Plan from the Query menu or by pressing the corresponding button on the toolbar. This feature is also available by pressing Ctrl+L from the query window. Refer to "Adding an Entry to Favorites" in the "Immediate Solutions" section of Chapter 5 to learn how to find the legend for the icons used in the graphical query plan. These icons are used to present an easy-to-understand execution plan that can be used to determine the efficiency of the query. Holding the mouse cursor over each icon displays detailed information about that step and the cost associated with it. Looking at the cost of each step can help you determine which parts of the query are consuming the most resources and need to be examined. If you have a three-table join in your query, you will be able to determine the amount of resources in the query that are used to retrieve information from each table. This can help you identify which tables might need an additional index or statistics to improve the query performance.

### Statistics IO

The statistics IO option is enabled in the Current Connection Properties dialog, which can be accessed by selecting Current Connection Properties from the Query menu. In the top section of the dialog, select the Set Statistics IO option, and the statistics will be included when the query is executed. The IO statistics are presented on the Messages tab if the results are displayed to a grid or saved to a file. If the results are displayed as text, the IO statistics appear on the Results tab immediately following the query results. There are four pieces of information returned for each table used in the query:

• Scan Count

• Logical Reads

• Physical Reads

• Read-Ahead Reads

These statistics include the reads for both data and index pages. They can help you determine the effectiveness of your indexes. If the read count is higher than you estimated, you should evaluate the possibility of adding or modifying indexes on the table. For example, if the number of reads to retrieve a small number of rows from a table is equal to (or close to) the number of data pages in the table, this table is probably a good candidate for an index.

### Statistics Time

The statistics time option is enabled in the Current Connection Properties dialog, which can be accessed by selecting Current Connection Properties from the Query menu. In the top section of the dialog, select the Set Statistics Time option, and the statistics will be included when the query is executed. The timing statistics are presented on the Messages tab if the results are displayed to a grid or saved to a file. If the results are displayed as text, the timing statistics appear on the Results tab immediately following the query results. The timing statistics are shown as two sections: SQL Server Execution Times and SQL Server Parse And Compile

Time. The execution times are given as the CPU Time and the Elapsed Time for the query. The execution times represent the actual time required for the server to execute the query in milliseconds. The parse and compile time is the CPU and elapsed time required to create the execution plans for all queries in the batch. This statistic is actually presented at the top and bottom of the list, but only the one at the top of the list represents the actual time statistics for the batch. The execution times are shown at the top and after each query in the batch, but the statistics shown in the top one do not relate to any of the queries in the batch; this top entry provides accurate information only for the parse and compile time.

# Profiler

The Profiler is an extremely useful tool for optimizing system performance. It allows you to monitor query traffic running against the server and record the query time and IO statistics for this traffic. Using the Profiler is one of the best ways to start the testing and documentation process. You can start by tracing the system under relatively normal conditions, and then examine the trace to find the slow-running queries that need to be addressed. These queries can be experimented with individually in the Query Analyzer, and then merged back into the system to see how the new version affects system performance. It is a good idea to save the trace files that you capture during this process to allow you to do point-in-time analysis on your progress. This can be extremely valuable documentation as you move from step to step.

### Tracing Script Performance

An example that helps you set up a good template for tracing script performance can be found in "Creating a Trace Template for Optimization" in the "Immediate Solutions" section in Chapter 5. This template allows you to see the various steps executed by your application(s) as well as the performance characteristics of each. The template can also be used for debugging stored procedures, but you might find that you do not need some of the performance information when your main focus is debugging. The performance template does include the success or failure information for each step, because a failed step can report an erroneously short execution time that is misleading. The template also captures deadlocking information to allow you to monitor for concurrency problems at the same time.

### Interpreting Trace Results

Once you have run a trace and have captured the results, you will need to examine and interpret the trace results to determine where to concentrate your optimization efforts. There are several columns in the optimization template that provide the key information that you need to help you decide where to begin. The duration, reads, and writes columns display the time and IO required for each step captured by the Profiler. It is generally best to keep these columns near the top of the list (which will be the beginning of the display grid in the Profiler) to make it easier to see the events that use the most resources. When you highlight the event, the command text (if any) is displayed in the bottom pane, which allows you to see the actual query that is taking a long time to run. The template that was created in Chapter 5 also includes the execution plan for each query, which provides the plan text for you to determine how the server is executing the query. In some cases, this can allow you to spot and correct a problem with table indexes without having to run the query individually. Once the results are saved to a file, you can open the file and modify the filters, events, and data columns to refine the information you are viewing at any particular time. It is possible to add filters and remove columns and events from the display that are not currently useful to you. You cannot, however, add columns and events that were not originally captured or view any events eliminated by existing filters when the file was captured. For this reason, it is best to capture as much information as possible to have available later, and then eliminate any details you don't want to see when you are reviewing the captured information. It is generally better to start with too much information than not enough.

## Index Tuning Wizard

The Index Tuning Wizard can be used to assist you in determining the best indexing strategy for your database. You can use the Profiler to create a workload file that the Index Tuning Wizard can use to recommend the optimal set of indexes for your database. You can use the Sample 1 TSQL template in the Profiler to capture an appropriate workload for the wizard. You should capture a workload file of actual system activity processed during normal working conditions. The wizard can only provide a realistic set of indexing recommendations if it is given an accurate sample of work to examine. As with any tool, you should always test the recommendations provided by the wizard before accepting that these recommendations will actually provide the best performance in your environment. This tool seems to provide the most accurate results when the database is well normalized and the queries are not overly complex. Even when the results work well, it may be possible to improve performance further by additional testing and modification of the indexing strategy. Never assume that the indexing recommendations provided by this or any other tool should be used without question.

## Performance Monitor

The Performance Monitor is used to monitor the performance of the operating system as well as SQL Server. It can provide insight into issues such as insufficient memory or processing power for the workload on the server. It is a good idea to use this tool to monitor the system performance periodically to check for bottlenecks. If you are consistently running low on available memory and the server is resorting to paging, you should consider upgrading the system memory to improve performance. You should also watch the processor utilization during normal system activity. It is okay for the processor usage to spike up to or near 100 percent occasionally, but if it stays at high levels for long periods of time, you may need to consider adding additional processors or upgrading the server. The Performance Monitor provides the capability to monitor a large number of statistics including network traffic and errors in addition to memory and processor statistics. It can also prove to be an extremely useful tool for detecting system level problems. Additionally, this tool provides the capability to save the monitoring information to a file, so that you can compare the results with previous sessions to track system trends.

## Third-Party Tools

There are numerous tools available that claim to assist in the process of optimizing SQL code. Most of them are useful to some degree. You should carefully evaluate any tool before making a decision to purchase it. Some of these tools can provide you with equivalent alternative queries for the code you are trying to optimize, which can help you determine alternative ways to write a particular query. These tools may even provide the capability to perform speed tests on these alternatives to find the one(s) with the fastest execution times. Keep in mind that you should never accept these results without testing them yourself in a more realistic environment. One benefit to working with a tool that provides alternatives to your query structure is that you will become more familiar with the various ways in which you can perform the same task. A key ingredient to successful query optimization is to be aware of the alternatives.

Another benefit that some tools provide is an automated process for testing various hint combinations on a particular query. This is a process that can be very tedious and time-consuming to perform manually. A tool that does a good job of testing these combinations can be extremely helpful. You will still need to manually test the recommended query changes to make sure that they produce the results claimed by the tool, but it can save you hours of manual testing that might be required to test all of the possible combinations yourself. It is best to find a tool that provides you with a number of possible queries and ranks them by performance. You may find that the query the tool selects is not as good as a close alternative.

Keep in mind when working with any tool that the tool cannot *understand* your data. It knows what the tables, fields, indexes, and declared relationships are, but it does not understand your data. There is no substitute for the human component in the optimization process. Tools of this nature should be evaluated on the basis of their capability to assist the developer or database administrator (DBA) to evaluate various options, but not be a replacement for them. A skilled, experienced SQL programmer or DBA will be able to come up with solutions that no tool would even be able to consider. These tools operate within some finite set of rules and consider only the query that they are fed and the data that they are run against. A thorough understanding of the data and the process enables you to see alternatives to the method being employed, which may bear no resemblance to the query that you may be trying to optimize. As you become more familiar with the process being optimized and the data involved, you will be able to intuitively find alternatives to queries that involve a completely different approach to the one originally taken. These intuitive leaps often provide the most striking performance increases. Never underestimate the power of a good guess!

# Optimizing for Speed

Optimizing for speed is the most common goal of optimization efforts. In many cases, it can also help with concurrency issues because the faster a transaction completes, the less likely it is to run into another operation. Reducing query runtimes will also generally result in a lighter load on the server overall, which in turn will increase general system performance. It is definitely true that a single poorly written query can impact the performance of the entire system by making the server too busy to handle other requests in a timely fashion. It is even possible to overburden the server to the point that it stops responding or even crashes in some cases. You need to be careful when you are optimizing one portion of your system for speed so that you do not negatively impact other areas and offset or worsen overall performance.

## Indexes and Statistic Sets

Indexes and statistic sets play a vital role in optimizing your database. A good indexing strategy can make the difference between queries that run for hours and queries that run for seconds or minutes. Indexing strategies will vary based on the workload run against your system. **INSERT**, **UPDATE**, and **DELETE** operations will incur overhead to manage the indexes created on the tables affected by them. An index that allows an **UPDATE** or **DELETE** operation to locate the affected row more quickly generally yields more of a performance gain than overhead to maintain the index. The overhead required to maintain indexes is mainly a problem when tables become overburdened by indexes for lookup and reporting queries that do not benefit the **UPDATE**, **INSERT**, or **DELETE** operations. In the case of reporting and some batch processing operations, it may be beneficial to create an index on the fly for the report, and then drop the index when you are done. You will need to determine if the overhead of creating the index is offset by the performance gain associated with having it in place for these operations. Be careful not to overuse this strategy, because it can place a burden on the server to create and drop indexes frequently in this manner.

Statistic sets enable the query optimizer to develop execution plans with greater accuracy based on the data distribution. These statistics are even more useful when they are created for the additional columns in an aggregate index. Because SQL Server only keeps statistics for the first column in an index by default, generating statistics on the additional columns can greatly increase the usability on an aggregate index. Don't forget to run **sp_createstats** with the **INDEX ONLY** parameter to create statistics for all columns contained in any index in the database. You can also create statistic sets for columns that do not contain an index to assist the query optimizer in determining the data distribution for processing **WHERE** clause conditions that do not make use of an indexed column. These statistic sets also require significantly less storage and maintenance than indexes. The performance benefits of statistics are not generally as good as an index, but the offsetting maintenance of an index may outweigh the other performance benefits.

As noted previously, the statistic sets are more beneficial to ad hoc queries than they are to stored procedures. Statistic sets that are not created on index columns seem to become outdated, and query performance drops in stored procedures after a short time. One possible solution to this problem is to schedule a task to update the statistics periodically. However, you will need to experiment with this process to ensure that you can incur this overhead while maintaining acceptable performance levels.

## Autogenerated Statistics

The query optimizer creates autogenerated statistics when it determines that statistics are needed to effectively run a query. These statistic sets are especially useful for ad hoc queries, but do not appear to be considered by stored procedures. They can be identified by their naming convention, which is prefixed by _WA_Sys_. Listing 11.2 provides a script that can be used to identify and remove the automatically created statistics from your tables. This script can be useful if you are adding indexes to cover these columns and do not want to retain these statistic sets.

**Listing 11.2   Drop autogenerated statistics.**

```
DECLARE @v_AutoGen VARCHAR(100)
/* Create Cursor to Locate Auto-Generated Statistic Sets*/
DECLARE c_Cursor CURSOR FOR
  SELECT SO.Name + '.' + SI.Name
    FROM sysindexes SI (NOLOCK)
    JOIN sysobjects SO (NOLOCK) ON SI.ID = SO.ID
    WHERE SI.Name LIKE '[_]WA[_]Sys[_]%'
```

```
/* Open Cursor */
OPEN c_Cursor
FETCH NEXT FROM c_Cursor INTO @v_AutoGen

/* Loop Through Statistic Sets and Generate Drop Code */
WHILE @@Fetch_Status <> -1
  BEGIN
  IF @@Fetch_Status <> -2
    BEGIN
    PRINT 'DROP STATISTICS ' + @v_AutoGen
    EXEC('DROP STATISTICS ' + @v_AutoGen)
    END
  FETCH NEXT FROM c_Cursor INTO @v_AutoGen
  END

/* Close and Deallocate the Cursor */
CLOSE c_Cursor
DEALLOCATE c_Cursor
```

This script can also be useful to drop these statistic sets and create single-column
indexes in their place. Listing 11.3 shows an expanded version of the script that
automates the single-column index creation as well as drops the statistic sets.
You will need to determine whether it is more beneficial to create single-column
indexes, leave the statistic sets, or group some or all of the columns into aggregate indexes.

**Listing 11.3    Drop autogenerated statistics and create single-column indexes.**

```
DECLARE @v_Tbl VARCHAR(50),
        @v_Stat VARCHAR(50),
        @v_Fld VARCHAR(50)
/* Create Cursor to Locate Auto-Generated Statistic Sets*/
DECLARE c_Cursor CURSOR FOR
  SELECT SO.Name, SI.Name
    FROM sysindexes SI (NOLOCK)
    JOIN sysobjects SO (NOLOCK) ON SI.ID = SO.ID
    WHERE SI.Name LIKE '[_]WA[_]Sys[_]%'

/* Open Cursor */
OPEN c_Cursor
FETCH NEXT FROM c_Cursor INTO @v_Tbl, @v_Stat

WHILE @@Fetch_Status <> -1
  BEGIN
  IF @@Fetch_Status <> -2
    BEGIN
    SELECT @v_Fld = SubString(@v_Stat, 9, DATALENGTH(@v_Stat) - 17)
```

```
      /* Generate Drop Code */
      PRINT 'DROP STATISTICS ' + @v_Tbl + '.' + @v_Stat
      EXEC('DROP STATISTICS ' + @v_Tbl + '.' + @v_Stat)

      /* Generate Create Index Code */
      PRINT 'CREATE INDEX IDX_AUTO_' + @v_FLD + ' ON ' + @v_Tbl +
          ' (' + @v_Fld + ')'
      EXEC('CREATE INDEX IDX_AUTO_' + @v_FLD + ' ON ' + @v_Tbl +
          ' (' + @v_Fld + ')')
      END
  FETCH NEXT FROM c_Cursor INTO @v_Tbl, @v_Stat
  END

/* Close and Deallocate the Cursor */
CLOSE c_Cursor
DEALLOCATE c_Cursor
```

## Covering Indexes

Covering indexes can be used to speed up the performance of a lookup query. A covering index includes every column referenced for a particular table in a query. It contains all columns referenced in **JOIN** conditions, the **WHERE** clause, and the select list of the query. If all columns in the query are contained in a single index, the index becomes a covering index for the query. This type of index allows SQL Server to retrieve all needed information from the index without having to read the data pages. The savings in IO can be significant, especially for wide tables. In Listing 11.4, the following columns would need to be included in an index to create a covering index on the **tbl_address** table for the query: **Line1**, **City_ID**, and **State_ID**. The index is created at the top of the code sample, and the query is executed thereafter. The index creation is separated from the query by a GO command, which separates these two commands into distinct batches that allow the query to be optimized after the index is created. If the **GO** command is removed, the query will not be optimized to make use of the index because it will not be created when the execution plan is determined for the batch. This also applies to indexes that you create on temporary tables in your scripts. You must either separate the batches or use an **EXEC** statement to force the code to be optimized after the index is created.

### Listing 11.4 Covering index sample query.

```
/* Create the Covering Index */
CREATE INDEX IDX_COVER_EXAMPLE ON tbl_address (Line1, City_ID, State_ID)
GO

/* Query Covered by IDX_COVER_EXAMPLE Index Created Above */
SELECT a.Line1, c.name, s.State_Code
```

```
FROM tbl_address a (NOLOCK)
JOIN tbl_city c (NOLOCK) ON a.City_ID = c.City_ID
JOIN tbl_state s (NOLOCK) ON a.State_ID = s.State_ID
```

Covering indexes should definitely be created with extreme care because they often have a high maintenance cost associated with maintaining them for **INSERT**, **UPDATE**, and **DELETE** operations. This technique is best used on data that changes infrequently or not at all. It requires ample testing to verify that the benefits of this type of index outweigh the cost. The more columns that you must include to create a covering index, the less likely it is to have an overall positive impact on system performance.

## Inequality

Beginning with SQL Server 7, the query optimizer handles inequalities in the form of *Field <> Value* **OR** *Field != Value* by automatically converting the inequality check to the equivalent syntax of *Field < Value* **OR** *Field > Value* internally. This allows the optimizer to correctly determine whether or not an index is usable for the field(s) being referenced. This works correctly in most cases, but you may find situations where making this change manually will have a positive effect on the query plan. This seems to become more likely as the query becomes more complex.

Try to avoid the use of **NOT** in the search conditions wherever possible. There will be times when you have no other alternative, but you should always try to think of a way to restate the search condition to eliminate the need for the **NOT** operator. The **NOT** operator will prevent the query optimizer from being able to correctly utilize indexes for the fields referenced after this operator. This problem exists in search conditions specified in the **WHERE** clause as well as in the **ON** clause of a **JOIN** condition. There is one exception to this: the use of **IS NOT NULL** does not seem to suffer from this problem.

## Optimizer Hints

Optimizer hints are used to override the default behavior of the query optimizer. Some of these hints, like the locking hints, are useful for controlling certain behaviors of SQL Server. These hints can be used to specify the locking granularity and retention of specific queries in a batch or transaction to provide the transaction isolation level required by your application. These hints can also play an important role in eliminating unnecessary concurrency problems by eliminating locks when they are not actually needed. You should become familiar with the available optimizer hints so that you will be able to more effectively control the locking behavior in various parts of the system.

Table 11.1 contains a number of optimizer hints that can be used to change the default behavior of the query optimizer. Because the query optimizer has access to information that is normally not readily apparent to the SQL developer, most of these hints should only be used with extreme care by an experienced DBA. Table 11.1 shows the hints, their scope, and the default behavior if no hint is specified. Depending on your environment, you may get a performance increase from the **KEEP PLAN** or **KEEPFIXED PLAN** hints. You may want to do some experimentation and testing with various hints to see how they impact performance in your environment.

**Table 11.1   Optimizer hints.**

| Hint Type | Option | Description | Default Setting |
|---|---|---|---|
| Join | **LOOP I HASH I MERGE I REMOTE** | Specifies the strategy to use when joining the rows of two tables. | Chosen by SQL Server. |
| Query | **{ HASH I ORDER } GROUP** | Specifies whether hashing or ordering is used to compute **GROUP BY** and **COMPUTE** aggregations. | Chosen by SQL Server. |
| Query | **{ MERGE I HASH I CONCAT } UNION** | Specifies the strategy used for all **UNION** operations within the query. | Chosen by SQL Server. |
| Query | **FAST *integer*** | Optimizes the query for retrieval of the specified number of rows. | No such optimization. |
| Query | **FORCE ORDER** | Performs joins in the order in which the tables appear in the query. | Chosen by SQL Server. |
| Query | **ROBUST PLAN** | Forces the query optimizer to attempt a plan that works for the maximum potential row size, possibly at the expense of performance. | Chosen by SQL Server. |
| Query | **KEEP PLAN** | Forces the query optimizer to relax the estimated recompile threshold for a query. | Query will be recompiled more frequently. |
| Query | **KEEPFIXED PLAN** | Forces the query optimizer not to recompile a query due to changes in statistics or to the indexed column (**UPDATE**, **DELETE**, or **INSERT**). | Query will be recompiled when the estimated number of indexed column changes (**UPDATE**, **DELETE**, or **INSERT**) have been made to a table |

*(continued)*

**Table 11.1 Optimizer hints** *(continued)*.

| Hint Type | Option | Description | Default Setting |
|---|---|---|---|
| Query | **MAXDOP** *integer* | Overrides the Max Degree of Parallelism configuration option (of **sp_configure**) only for the query specifying this option. | The Max Degree of Parallelism option is used to make this determination. |
| Table | **FASTFIRSTROW** | Has the same effect as specifying the **FAST 1** query hint. | No such optimization |
| Table | **INDEX =** | Instructs SQL Server to use the specified index(es) for a table. | Chosen by SQL Server. |
| Table | **HOLDLOCK I SERIALIZABLE I REPEATABLEREAD I READCOMMITTED I READUNCOMMITTED I NOLOCK** | Causes certain locks to be set (or not) for a table, and overrides the locks that would have been used to enforce the isolation level of the current transaction. | The locks required by the current transaction. |
| Table | **ROWLOCK I PAGLOCK I TABLOCK I TABLOCKX** | Specifies the size of the shared locks to be taken for this table. | Chosen by SQL Server. |
| Table | **READPAST** | Skips locked rows altogether. | Wait for locked rows. |
| Table | **UPDLOCK** | Takes update locks instead of shared locks. | Take shared locks. |

Two sets of hints that can prove extremely worthwhile to experiment with deal with the strategy used for joins and unions. It is possible to achieve significantly better query times by experimenting with the various options in your queries. It will take some time to test all possible combinations, but if you have a long running query, which you cannot find a better way to optimize, hinting the join or union strategy can be an effective technique.

## Dealing with NULLs

Use caution when dealing with **NULLs** in your queries. Ideally, you should not have joins on columns that allow **NULLs**. Allowing **NULLs** in an index lowers the chances of that index being selected as useful by the query optimizer. If there are a large number of **NULL** values in an indexed column, the index selectivity rating will be lowered. **NULLs** can also affect other operations like aggregate functions. In most cases, it is better to remove **NULLs** from aggregates. Depending on your server and connection settings, **NULL** values in an aggregate can cause the result to return zero regardless of the other values included. **NULL** values can also result in a warning message being generated when the query is run, which can cause problems in some client applications. If there is only one column being used in an aggregate function in the query, it may be more efficient to specify **WHERE** *Field* **IS NOT NULL** as part of the **WHERE** clause for the query. In many cases, this is not practical because the query will contain two or more fields used in aggregate functions. In either case, it is easy to eliminate the **NULL** values by using the **COALESCE** function to specify an alternate value for any **NULLs** encountered. You can specify a fixed value (like 0) or use a variable or other column for the alternative value depending on the situation. The **COALESCE** function supports chaining multiple alternatives, so that the first non-**NULL** value will be selected. Remember to use **IS NULL** and **IS NOT NULL** to check for **NULL** values in your selection criteria. SQL Server may not evaluate standard comparison operators (**<, >, <=, >=, <>, !=, & =**) correctly when they are used in **NULL** value comparisons.

## Psuedonormalization and Temporary Denormalization

In some cases, it is necessary to temporarily change the normalization level of your data to improve query performance. This is generally only effective when the data that you are modifying will be accessed multiple times in the batch or process you are working with. One example of this is when you have a wide table with a few fields that are used in the selection criteria of several queries. In some cases, it can be difficult to find an indexing strategy that works well for these queries. One method that may work is to pull these fields into a temporary table so that the row size is considerably smaller than the original table and the rows-per-page is high. This table can be used to satisfy the selection criteria in your **WHERE** clause and join to the original table on a unique key for faster retrieval. This smaller table may also benefit from the creation of one or more covering indexes for your queries to improve performance even further. In this case, the number of columns required to create a covering index would likely be much smaller than including every referenced column from the original table.

You might also find it beneficial to create a denormalized data set for reporting or certain batch processing operations if the data is referenced several times in your process. These approaches would eliminate the need to perform a complex join repeatedly to retrieve the needed information. This denormalized table would only need to include the columns referenced in your process and might therefore be smaller than a fully denormalized table.

This type of data manipulation can be used to completely alter the performance characteristics of a complex system. These techniques used in conjunction with your indexing strategy can make a tremendous difference in server load and responsiveness. Practice and experimentation is the key to making this type of change successful, but the rewards can easily be worth the effort.

# Changing the Query Plan

Changing the query plan can be an extremely difficult task. The query optimizer will do its best to find the best join order and the most efficient way to perform the query. It has the capability to rearrange the joined tables in an attempt to find the most efficient order, but there will be cases when it does not make the best selection. This becomes significantly more likely as the query and data structures become more complex. Be sure to examine the table structures to see if there is more than one way to join the tables you are working with. The query optimizer is most effective in rearranging the joins if they are done on the same columns in multiple tables. It does not have as many options if the columns used to join the tables are unique for each join condition. If you have a number of tables that join on the same columns, consider joining all of the child tables back to the columns of a single master table instead of chaining them one after another. This can also give the query optimizer a clearer picture of which tables it should try to rearrange.

Adding, removing, or hinting indexes on a table in the join can cause the query optimizer to select a radically different query plan. You can also try a clever technique by pulling the search fields into a temporary table with a covering index to allow a quick method of filtering the records of a larger complex table. The wider the table is and the more rows it contains, the better this technique works for shortening the data retrieval time. However, you will probably only see an overall benefit to this method if you need the temporary table for more than one join.

An additional method for changing the query plan is to break a complex join into multiple queries that generate temporary result sets, and then join these sets in an additional query. You will have to experiment to find out which grouping produces the best results for you, but this can often lead to a marked speed increase in the overall query.

# Stored Procedures Vs. Dynamic SQL

Stored procedures provide some definite advantages over dynamic SQL. One advantage is the fact that the code resides on the server. If you need to modify the code, you only have one place to update. This can simplify sending an update to all clients because the actual client machines are not affected. The fact that stored procedures are optimized when they are created and do not need to be fully reoptimized each time they are run can be a definite advantage in system performance. Unlike SQL Server 6.5, the newer versions of SQL Server reoptimize based on changes in the distribution statistics in the tables, which can help maintain performance as your data evolves. Stored procedures won't consider an index that was not present when the stored procedure's execution plan was determined, so it is a good idea to issue the **sp_recompile** command for any table that you add or change indexes on. The **sp_recompile** command marks any stored procedures that reference the table to be recompiled the next time they are run. The script in Listing 11.5 shows a method for issuing this command for every table in a database, which might be beneficial to schedule once a month depending on the volatility of your data.

**Listing 11.5    Issuing sp_recompile for all tables.**

```
DECLARE @v_Tbl VARCHAR(50)
/* Create Cursor to Find ALL User Tables */
DECLARE c_MyCursor Cursor FOR
  SELECT Name
    FROM sysobjects (NOLOCK)
    WHERE Type='U'

/* Open Cursor */
OPEN c_MyCursor
FETCH NEXT FROM MyCursor INTO @v_Tbl

/* Loop Through ALL User Tables and Issue sp_recompile Command for Each */
WHILE @@FETCH_STATUS<>-1
  BEGIN
  IF @@FETCH_STATUS<>-2
    BEGIN
    print 'EXEC sp_recompile ' + @v_Tbl
    EXEC('sp_recompile ' + @v_Tbl)
    END
  FETCH NEXT FROM c_MyCursor INTO @v_Tbl
  END

/* Close and Deallocate Cursor */
CLOSE c_MyCursor
DEALLOCATE c_MyCursor
```

Another advantage to using stored procedures is the reduction in network traffic. Because the code contained in the stored procedure does not have to be passed from the client to the server, a significant amount of traffic can be eliminated. If you have a 2KB query that is used on the average of 100 times a day, you can eliminate almost 200KB of network traffic by creating a stored procedure. This may not seem significant until you consider numerous similar queries being used in an application by hundreds of users on a daily basis. This reduction in network traffic combined with the reduced load on the server to prepare the queries for execution can produce a large net gain in performance. Using a stored procedure to move image data back and forth to the server can have a tremendous effect on network traffic and performance. With dynamic SQL, passing image data to or from the server requires converting the image into character data and then into a character string, which doubles its size. This doubled data is then sent across the network and has to be converted back to a binary format on the other side. This process represents a significant amount of network traffic as well as processing overhead for the server and client. Using a stored procedure that has a parameter of the image data type allows the image data to be sent to and from the server in the original binary format. This eliminates the additional network traffic and the processing overhead required to make the conversion to and from character format.

Dynamic SQL, on the other hand, has the advantage of being able to take into account the current structure of all tables and indexes as well as making better use of the autogenerated statistic sets created by the query optimizer. There can also be advantages in creating and executing dynamic SQL from your stored procedures in some cases. If you create temporary tables with indexes in the stored procedure, the only way to get the query optimizer to consider these indexes is to execute the SQL dynamically after the table and index has been created. You can also use dynamic SQL to replace variables with constant expressions to allow the optimizer to have a clearer picture of the data being accessed by the query. This can result in faster execution time because the optimizer is able to accurately assess the data distribution when creating the execution plan.

## Manual Checkpoints

Checkpoints can play a large role in some batch situations. You may find it necessary to manually initiate a checkpoint in the script to control where and when they happen. If an operation is running, which is log-intensive, and SQL Server initiates a checkpoint, the two operations seem to block each other and a subsecond query can become a 20 second query for no apparent reason. The most likely place that you will run into problems with checkpoints is with multiple updates in a batch or when creating intermediate worktables to speed or simplify later processing steps. You may find that you need to add a manual checkpoint to the script following these types of operations to keep performance at a reasonable level. Also, keep in mind that the problem will become more likely for these operations as the dataset that you are working with becomes larger.

## Temporary Tables Vs. Permanent Tables

Creating permanent worktables can be especially beneficial when you are working with stored procedures. If you use temporary tables, you will need to execute dynamic SQL in order to gain any benefit from the indexes you create on the worktables. If the worktables are permanent, the tables and indexes should exist when the stored procedures are created. This allows the optimizer to consider the indexes on these tables when developing the execution plan for the procedure. The one drawback is that your worktables are normally empty when the stored procedure is created, so the indexes will have no statistics. There are several ways to deal with this problem. One way is to use index hints for these tables, although this has some drawbacks that were noted earlier in the chapter. Another way is to use a clustered index or primary key on the table. These two types of indexes seem to be selected by the optimizer where appropriate regardless of the data distribution. Another option is to use the new **SORT_IN_TEMPDB** setting, which is covered in Chapter 10.

In many cases, you will obtain better performance working with permanent tables in general. There are also some concurrency issues associated with temporary tables that can be avoided by using permanent tables. TempDB is used by SQL Server to perform intermediate work during query processing, so it is best to let SQL Server have exclusive use of it wherever possible. SQL Server does not manage TempDB under the same rules that apply to other databases. One noticeable difference is the fact that SQL Server seems to allow rows from multiple tables in TempDB to occupy the same page. This can cause serious concurrency problems when a query acquires (or escalates to) a page lock and inadvertently locks rows in use by another user.

## Joins

Good join techniques can make or break your system performance. Wherever possible, you should always attempt to join tables on unique keys. The simpler the key, the better the performance. You will get much better performance joining two tables on a unique RecID key that contains a single integer field than on an aggregate key containing several **CHAR** or **VARCHAR** fields. As a general rule, the binary data types (integers in particular) will yield a minimum of 15 percent to 20 percent better performance on **JOIN** operations than on other field types. Aggregate keys should be used as a last resort because additional processing is required for each field in the **JOIN** condition.

When performing joins using **CHAR** and **VARCHAR** columns, it is a good idea to keep the column definitions identical between the tables. The type, data length, and nullability of the columns should be kept the same to maximize the effectiveness of any indexes used to join the tables. One technique that can prove helpful in cases where the column nullability is different between the tables is to add an empty string to the column that allows **NULLs**. Turning off the **concat_null_yields_null** option for the connection is required for this to be effective. Because one table will not have **NULL** values in the joined column, this concatenation can be used to force the column from the second table to have non-**NULL** values for all rows as well. This can actually improve the index performance in many cases. The code snippet in Listing 11.6 shows a **JOIN** condition using this method. **Column1** in **Table1** allows **NULLs**, but **Column1** in **Table2** does not. Other than the nullability setting, the columns are identical. This method can also be used on numeric fields by adding zero instead of an empty string to the nullable field. You must accurately understand the data involved in the query to make sure that eliminating the NULL values to boost performance doesn't inadvertently change your query result.

**Listing 11.6   Example of using concatenation to eliminate NULLs in a JOIN condition.**

```
FROM Table1 T1
JOIN Table2 T2 ON T1.Column1 + '' = T2.Column1
```

The ANSI Join syntax is the preferred method for joining tables for several reasons. There are some functional differences in the outer joins between the ANSI Join and Transact-SQL Join syntax in a few cases. In these cases, the ANSI Join syntax produces a more accurate result set. Another advantage to the ANSI Join syntax is that it does not allow you to inadvertently cross-join two tables. In order to perform a cross-join using the ANSI Join syntax, you must specify the **CROSS JOIN** operator explicitly in the **JOIN** clause. This can help you avoid costly mistakes in terms of retrieval time and unexpectedly large result sets. The ANSI Join syntax also provides a clearer picture of the conditions being used to join two tables because the **JOIN** conditions must be included with the join instead of jumbled in the **WHERE** clause.

In terms of performance, inner-joins are generally the fastest, followed by outer-joins, and then cross-joins. Although cross-joins can be useful, they should always be used with extreme care because the result set produced can be exceptionally large. Another type of join is the self-join, which can actually be any of the other three types of joins, but involves joining a table back to itself. One use for a self-join might be to look up a manager or list of employees in an employee table. Assuming that all employees are in the table and the manager ID is just a pointer to the correct employee record, a self-join could be used to extract either of these result sets. There are a number of cases where this can be extremely helpful, and it eliminates the need to perform this type of operation in multiple steps using worktables, which can provide a performance boost to your query.

## Cross Database/Cross Server Joins

In almost any environment, joining two tables in the local database is faster than making joins outside the local database. With SQL Server 2000, it is possible to join tables in other databases on the server, other data sources outside SQL Server, and other databases on remote SQL Servers. Although this functionality definitely has the potential to make your life easier, it may not make your system performance better. You should use these capabilities with care and with the knowledge that you will probably be negatively impacting the speed of your queries to access data sources outside the local database.

This is an issue that requires experimentation to determine whether there is a better alternative in your environment. Of these three options, cross database joins on the same server provide the least impact on performance. You may find that a scheduled task to bring external data into your local server (either the local database or another database on the server) may be worthwhile in terms of performance. This may or may not be feasible depending on the data and the time sensitivity of keeping required data up-to-date. The key to handling these issues successfully is to know your options and understand the cost associated with each of them. You may find that in your environment you do not have a choice as to how to access a particular piece of information, but you will need to consider this in establishing a realistic expectation for the performance of any queries involved in gathering outside data.

## UNION Vs. UNION ALL

The **UNION** operator can be used to combine the results of two or more queries into a single result set. It can be an extremely handy tool for consolidating information to return to the client application. This operator also removes any duplicate rows from the result set before returning it. If you know the result set will not have duplicates or if you do not need this filtering performed, there is a huge speed benefit to using the **UNION ALL** operator instead. It still combines the results into a single result set, but it will not scan all of the rows for duplicates. The time involved to perform this task increases significantly as the size of the result set increases. The process of removing duplicates involves scanning each row that has been added to the result set previously to make sure it does not duplicate the current row before the current row is added to the result set. When you are returning 1,000 rows, this results in a lot of scanning for duplicates. You may find it beneficial to apply filtering to the data that you are planning to combine with the **UNION** operator to remove duplicate rows up front and eliminate the need for this costly procedure on the backend.

## IN Vs. EXISTS Vs. JOIN

The three commands, **IN**, **EXISTS**, and **JOIN**, can be used to perform the same function in a query. Listing 11.7 shows three equivalent queries that produce the same results along with the output and statistics for each query. In this case, the **JOIN** results in lower IO than either of the other two methods. This is not always the case, however. You should experiment with these three methods to see which one produces the best results in each situation. Notice the use of **DISTINCT** in the **JOIN** query. This is needed to keep the result set consistent with the original two queries. You should examine the data structures to determine whether or not the **JOIN** produces duplicate rows. In some cases, this option will not be practical due to other considerations. If duplicate rows are produced that cannot practically be eliminated using **DISTINCT**, you should determine which of the other two options is best in your situation. This is another situation in which larger data sets and more complex queries seem to produce greater differences in the performance of these three methods.

### Listing 11.7   IN versus EXISTS versus JOIN query examples.

```
/* Get a list of managers from the Employee table using IN */
SELECT First_Name + ' ' + Last_Name AS Managers
  FROM tbl_Employee (NOLOCK)
  WHERE Employee_ID IN (SELECT Manager_ID
                          FROM tbl_Employee (NOLOCK))
```

```
OUTPUT:


Managers
---------------------------------------------------------------

Patrick Dalton
Jeff Jones
Paul Whitehead
Chris Maddux
Heidi Michelle


(5 row(s) affected)


Table 'tbl_Employee'. Scan count 11, logical reads 11, physical reads 0,
read-ahead reads 0.


SQL Server Execution Times:
 CPU time = 0 ms, elapsed time = 3 ms.
```

```
/* Get a list of managers from the Employee table using EXISTS */
SELECT First_Name + ' ' + Last_Name AS Managers
  FROM tbl_Employee a (NOLOCK)
  WHERE EXISTS (SELECT *
                  FROM tbl_Employee b (NOLOCK)
                  WHERE a.Employee_ID = b.Manager_ID)
```

```
OUTPUT:


Managers
---------------------------------------------------------------

Patrick Dalton
Jeff Jones
Paul Whitehead
Chris Maddux
Heidi Michelle
```

```
(5 row(s) affected)

Table 'tbl_Employee'. Scan count 11, logical reads 11, physical reads 0,
read-ahead reads 0.

SQL Server Execution Times:
 CPU time = 0 ms, elapsed time = 2 ms.

/* Get a list of managers from the Employee table using JOIN */
SELECT DISTINCT a.First_Name + ' ' + a.Last_Name AS Managers
  FROM tbl_Employee a (NOLOCK)
  JOIN tbl_Employee b (NOLOCK) ON a.Employee_ID = b.Manager_ID

OUTPUT:

Managers
------------------------------------------------------------
Chris Maddux
Heidi Michelle
Jeff Jones
Patrick Dalton
Paul Whitehead

(5 row(s) affected)

Table 'tbl_Employee'. Scan count 2, logical reads 2, physical reads 0, read-
ahead reads 0.

SQL Server Execution Times:
 CPU time = 0 ms, elapsed time = 5 ms.
```

## NOT IN Vs. NOT EXISTS Vs. LEFT JOIN

As with the previous section, the three commands, **NOT IN**, **NOT EXISTS**, and **LEFT JOIN**, can be used to perform the same function in a query. Listing 11.8 shows three equivalent queries that produce the same results, along with the output and statistics for each query. Unlike the **IN** versus **JOIN** scenario, the **LEFT JOIN** used in this example does not produce duplicate rows. In this case, all three methods produce essentially the same IO and timing statistics. This is not always the case, however. You should experiment with these three methods to see which one produces the best results in each situation. Note the **WHERE** clause used in the subquery for the **NOT IN** example. If the row(s) with **NULL Manager_IDs** are not removed, the **NOT IN** will fail to return any results. This can cause an otherwise simple query to fail to produce the expected results.

### Listing 11.8    NOT IN versus NOT EXISTS versus LEFT JOIN query examples.

```
/* Get a list of non-managers from the Employee table using NOT IN */
SELECT First_Name + ' ' + Last_Name AS "Non-Managers"
  FROM tbl_Employee (NOLOCK)
  WHERE Employee_ID NOT IN (SELECT Manager_ID
                              FROM tbl_Employee (NOLOCK)
                              WHERE Manager_ID IS NOT NULL)


OUTPUT:

Non-Managers
-------------------------------------------------------------
Jared Kirkpatrick
Steve Smith
Fred Couples
David Woods
Cathy David

(5 row(s) affected)

Table 'tbl_Employee'. Scan count 11, logical reads 11, physical reads 0,
read-ahead reads 0.

SQL Server Execution Times:
  CPU time = 0 ms, elapsed time = 3 ms.

/* Get a list of non-managers from the Employee table using NOT EXISTS */
SELECT First_Name + ' ' + Last_Name AS "Non-Managers"
  FROM tbl_Employee a (NOLOCK)
  WHERE NOT EXISTS (SELECT *
                      FROM tbl_Employee b (NOLOCK)
                      WHERE a.Employee_ID = b.Manager_ID)


OUTPUT:

Non-Managers
-------------------------------------------------------------
Jared Kirkpatrick
Steve Smith
Fred Couples
David Woods
Cathy David

(5 row(s) affected)

Table 'tbl_Employee'. Scan count 11, logical reads 11, physical reads 0,
read-ahead reads 0.
```

```
SQL Server Execution Times:
 CPU time = 0 ms, elapsed time = 2 ms.

/* Get a list of non-managers from the Employee table using LEFT JOIN */
SELECT a.First_Name + ' ' + a.Last_Name AS "Non-Managers"
  FROM tbl_Employee a (NOLOCK)
  LEFT JOIN tbl_Employee b (NOLOCK) ON a.Employee_ID = b.Manager_ID
  WHERE b.Manager_ID IS NULL

OUTPUT:

Non-Managers
-----------------------------------------------------------------
Jared Kirkpatrick
Steve Smith
Fred Couples
David Woods
Cathy David

(5 row(s) affected)

Table 'tbl_Employee'. Scan count 11, logical reads 11, physical reads 0,
read-ahead reads 0.

SQL Server Execution Times:
 CPU time = 0 ms, elapsed time = 3 ms.
```

### BETWEEN

**BETWEEN** is another command that is automatically rearranged by the query optimizer into a simpler form that allows the use of indexes. When you specify a search condition in the form of *Field* **BETWEEN** *Value1* **AND** *Value2* the query optimizer will restate the search condition as *Field* **>=** *Value1* **AND** *Field* **<=** *Value2*. This alternate arrangement allows the query processor to make proper use of indexes for the field(s) in the specified search condition. As with some other "automatic" changes to the query performed by the optimizer, this one does not always seem to occur as expected. In more complex queries, you may find that the query optimizer will generate a better query plan if you manually rearrange the search condition to eliminate the **BETWEEN** keyword.

## Cursors

Although cursors provide functionality that may not otherwise be available in your SQL code, they should be avoided whenever possible. Cursors are slow compared to other processing options. In many cases, queries written using cursors can be rewritten using other elements of Transact-SQL, which provide faster processing with less concurrency issues. If you do find it necessary to use a cursor in your processing, it is best to keep the processing within the cursor as small and fast as possible to minimize the impact on performance.

## Functions

The use of functions, like **RTRIM( )** or **COALESCE( )**, in the **WHERE** clause may cause the Query Analyzer to be unable to use an index to satisfy the search condition. This results in slower processing of the query. When these functions are necessary to complete the query successfully, you may want to consider using the techniques discussed in the "Psuedonormalization and Temporary Denormalization" section of this chapter. You can preprocess the data to make it conform to the conditions created by the use of functions, and then perform the join normally against the temporary data set.

## GROUP BY and ORDER BY Operations

The **GROUP BY** and **ORDER BY** operations can require the creation of temporary worktables during query processing. Ordering a query by an indexed column does not generally require the creation of a temporary worktable, but a **GROUP BY** operation always needs to create a temporary worktable to perform the aggregation before returning a result set. In any case, these operations add more overhead to a query and should be avoided when they are not necessary. Using an **ORDER BY** clause to populate an intermediate worktable is generally not necessary and not beneficial to the process. You should also consider using the **DISTINCT** operator instead of **GROUP BY** when you are eliminating duplicates but do not need to create any aggregate results.

## INSERT, UPDATE, and DELETE Operations

The **INSERT**, **UPDATE**, and **DELETE** operations are affected by some of the same factors that affect other queries. If you are using a query to perform an **INSERT** operation, then the execution time of the query will partially determine the execution time of the **INSERT** operation. Another factor that will affect your **INSERT** operations is indexing. The more indexes in place on the table, the more work that must be performed by SQL Server when inserting the data. Too many indexes can create a serious problem for heavy **INSERT** operations. If your inserts are done as batch processes, it may be possible to drop the indexes before a large **INSERT** operation and re-create them afterward. You need to examine the dynamics of your system to determine whether or not this would be allowable in your environment. If this is an option, you need to thoroughly test this scenario to determine whether or not the time required to rebuild the indexes is offset by the time saved in the **INSERT** operations. This option would normally only be reasonable for very large batch inserting done outside of normal business hours.

UPDATE and DELETE operations that use a WHERE clause often benefit more from indexing despite the overhead required to maintain the indexes because a large portion of the time used for these operations is generally spent locating the affected records. These operations can be negatively affected by too many indexes, but the threshold is generally much higher than that of INSERT operations. You do need to pay special attention to the search conditions used in these operations to make sure that they are kept as efficient as possible to improve performance.

## COALESCE

The COALESCE function can be used in JOIN conditions and in the WHERE clause to alter the query plan, which often improves performance if your query needs to check for NULL values. Consider the code snippet from a WHERE clause in Listing 11.9, which deals with checking effective dates to return a record.

Listing 11.9   Example of effective date check using IS NULL.

```
AND (StopDate IS NULL
     OR StopDate <= @v_SearchDate)
```

This is common syntax used to test whether or not a dated row should be included in processing. Common applications of date-sensitive material are rates used in insurance and payroll calculations. Eliminating the additional NULL check by using COALESCE can be especially important when you are working with a system that contains rates or other information that covers a range of effective dates and only a particular record has the information you need. The most current record often does not have a stop date associated with it because it is in effect until the rate changes. In this situation, a selection similar to the preceding example would be employed. An alternative method, which often yields better performance is to use the COALESCE function to eliminate NULL values for the comparison. The code in Listing 11.10 shows the same effective date check rewritten to make use of the COALESCE function instead of the two-part check to handle the NULL records.

Listing 11.10   Example of effective date check using COALESCE.

```
AND COALESCE(StopDate, @v_SearchDate) <= @v_SearchDate
```

This code handles the NULL condition properly without interjecting the OR logic evaluation in the query. It produces an altered query plan and often results in better query performance.

## Text in Row Option

If you are using TEXT, NTEXT, or IMAGE columns in a table in which these columns are normally read or written in one unit by most of the statements that reference the table, you should consider using the Text in Row option for the table. Unless this option is enabled, these columns are stored in separate 8KB pages from the data rows of your table. Consequently, these additional pages must be accessed when these fields are read or updated, which can result in a significant amount of additional page IO. When the Text in Row option is enabled and the data in a text or image column is longer than what will fit in the row, the pointers that would otherwise be stored in the root node of the pointer tree are stored in the row instead. This can eliminate an additional 8KB page read that would otherwise be required to retrieve these pointers.

If the Text in Row option is specified, you can define a Text in Row option limit. This limit determines the maximum amount of text and image data that can be stored in the data row before the data must be moved to external 8KB pages. With the Text in Row option limit, you can specify a size from 24 to 7,000 bytes. You should never set this limit to a number lower than 72 unless you are sure that all strings that will be stored in the rows will be short or in excess of 3MB in length. If a text or image field is inserted in a row that exceeds the Text in Row option limit, SQL Server only uses enough space in the row to store the pointers, and not the full allowable space. If multiple text fields are stored in the same row and three of them fit in the defined limit, but the fourth one exceeds the remaining space, SQL Server stores the pointer to the data for the fourth field in the row along with the actual data for the first three fields. The order in which SQL Server attempts to store these columns in the row is sequentially based on the column ID.

The syntax for enabling this option is shown in Listing 11.11. If you specify **ON** instead of an option limit, the default of 256 is used. This default is large enough to allow large strings and the root pointers to be stored in the table, but not large enough to cause the rows per page to decrease sufficiently to affect performance.

**Listing 11.11   Set Text in Row option example.**

```
sp_tableoption N'MyTable', 'text in row', 'ON'
      -- OR --
sp_tableoption N'MyTable', 'text in row', '1000'
```

# Optimizing for Concurrency

Optimizing for concurrency is necessary in many environments. It may not be possible to completely eliminate blocking or deadlocking from your processing, but you should strive to make these conditions occur as infrequently as possible. It is therefore necessary to write your client applications and server-side code in such a manner that these conditions are trapped and handled in a nondestructive and graceful manner. In many cases, these situations can be handled by simple retry logic that is transparent to the user. In these cases, users may experience a short delay in processing, but no error needs to be reported and no additional actions are required on their part. In order to optimize for concurrency, you should become familiar with the various types of locking used by SQL Server as well as the ways in which you can influence this behavior. The following sections provide the basic information you need to begin lowering or eliminating the concurrency issues in your code.

## Types of Locks

SQL Server uses several different types of locks to manage database concurrency. These locks are selected based on the task being performed. SQL Server makes every effort to manage resource locking in an intelligent and efficient manner. There are times when you will need to intervene in this process to prevent SQL Server from taking locks when they are not needed. Each of these types of locks has several levels of granularity to help limit the effect of the locks on system concurrency. The types of locks are:

- *Shared Locks*—Shared locks allow a resource to be read by multiple concurrent transactions, but do not allow data to be modified while the shared lock exists on the resource.

- *Update Locks*—Update locks are used to eliminate a common deadlock scenario. If two transactions acquire a shared lock on the data and later attempt to acquire an exclusive lock for the purpose of updating the data, a deadlock occurs. With an update lock, only one transaction at a time can obtain an update lock on a resource, which eliminates this deadlock condition. When the actual update occurs, the update lock is converted to an exclusive lock.

- *Exclusive Locks*—Exclusive locks prevent concurrent access to a resource by multiple transactions. Only the transaction with the exclusive lock can read or modify the data. This type of lock is used when modifying data during an **UPDATE** operation.

- *Intent Locks*—Intent locks are used by SQL Server to indicate that a lock is being acquired for some resources further down in the hierarchy. A shared intent lock on a table indicates that a transaction plans to acquire a shared lock on rows or pages within the table. This prevents another transaction from placing an exclusive lock on the table containing the page or row locks. Intent locks allow a much more efficient scheme for determining whether or not a transaction can acquire a lock on the table because it can examine the intent locks on the table rather than looking for locks on every page and row in the table.

- *Schema Locks*—Schema locks are used to control concurrency for table and database alterations. Locks are established for data definition language (DDL) commands, like adding a column. These are Sch-M locks. There are also Sch-S locks, which are used for operations such as compiling a query. The Sch-S locks do not affect any of the standard transaction locking, but rather, they prevent schema changes from being made during this type of operation.

- *Bulk Update Locks*—The bulk update lock is used to allow multiple processes to bulk copy data into a table concurrently while preventing access to the table by any process that is not bulk copying data into it. This lock is used when you employ the **TABLOCK** hint for bulk copy operations or when you set the "table lock on bulk load" option with the **sp_tableoption** stored procedure.

## Lock Escalation

SQL Server uses lock escalation to balance concurrency and system overhead. When the number of fine-grained locks on a resource exceeds the escalation threshold, the locks are escalated to coarse-grained locks, which provide less concurrency but require less system overhead. This process is important to understand because it can greatly affect the concurrency of your system. As locks are escalated, their associated concurrency issues generally escalate along with them. Once you understand how the server handles this process, you will be better able to control how and when this happens. Unfortunately, there are certain aspects of the process that cannot be modified. Lock escalation thresholds that are automatically determined by SQL Server cannot be configured. You can, however, use the locking hints in your queries to change locking behavior. Table 11.2 shows the lock granularity levels utilized by SQL Server 2000.

## Optimizer Hints

Controlling the locking behavior at the query level instead of at the transaction or connection level allows you a far greater level of control over common system bottlenecks. Locking can be controlled by a number of optimizer hints, which are listed in Table 11.3. Not only does locking impact concurrency, but the locks also require system resources, which can be preserved by specifying the **NOLOCK** hint when locking is not required. Because SQL Server obtains a shared lock by

**Table 11.2   Lock granularity levels.**

| Resource | Description |
| --- | --- |
| RID | Row identifier. Used to enforce row level locking. |
| Key | A row lock within an index. |
| Page | 8KB data or index page. (This is the default page size.) |
| Extent | Contiguous group of 8 data pages or index pages. (This is the only guaranteed contiguous or sequential data structure in the database storage structure.) |
| Table | Entire table including all data and index pages. |
| DB | Entire Database. |

**Table 11.3** **Useful Locking hints**

| Locking Hint | Description |
|---|---|
| HOLDLOCK | A shared lock will be held until the transaction is complete instead of releasing the lock as soon as the data is no longer needed. This option is equivalent to issuing the **SEARIALIZABLE** hint. |
| NOLOCK | No locks will be created for the data that is read by the **SELECT** statement. This option will also cause the **SELECT** statement to ignore the locks generated by other transactions (potentially dirty reads). This hint can be used only for the **SELECT** statement. |
| READCOMMITTED | This is the default transaction isolation level enforced by SQL Server. This hint can be used to revert to this behavior when another transaction isolation level has been specified for the connection. |
| READPAST | Locked rows will be skipped by a **SELECT** statement using this hint. This hint applies only to transactions operating in the default isolation level. |
| ROWLOCK | Allows issuing row-level locks instead of page and table level locks for the rows affected by the query. |
| TABLOCK | This hint allows you to put a lock on the entire table to improve performance if the locks will eventually be escalated to this level by the operation being performed. This saves the overhead of obtaining the page locks initially and escalating the lock when needed. |
| TABLOCKX | Same as above option, but places an exclusive lock on the table rather than a shared lock. |
| UPDLOCK | Can be used to place a lock on the data when it is read to ensure its availability for update at a later point in the transaction. This lock will not block other read operations. |

default for any data read during a transaction and holds this lock until the transaction completes, the **NOLOCK** hint should be used any time you are not updating the rows being read to help prevent concurrency problems. This can be especially useful in the case of reporting, which tends to retrieve a large number of rows without needing to update any of them.

## Transactions

It is important to understand that locks are held for the duration of the transaction in which they are acquired. Every query is contained within either an explicit or implicit transaction. In order to minimize concurrency, it is important to keep transaction times as short as possible to allow the locks to be released before another transaction needs the data. This is where optimizing your queries for speed can play an important role in reducing concurrency problems. If you have a transaction that takes 300 seconds (5 minutes) to complete, you will likely run into some concurrency problems during the time it takes to complete the transaction. If you can find a way to cut the time of the query down to 150 seconds, the number of concurrency problems you encounter will be drastically reduced. If you can reduce the time to 3 seconds, you might actually see your concurrency problems virtually disappear. Speed may not cure all of your concurrency problems, but it can be the easiest way to eliminate the majority of them.

Any single SQL statement that reads or writes a data page(s) that is not wrapped in transactional code is considered an implied transaction unto itself. A long-running query issued by a client or through the Query Analyzer can therefore present a potential concurrency problem.

## Temporary Tables Vs. Permanent Tables

Temporary tables are used in a number of applications to manipulate data and store intermediate results for processing, which can lead to concurrency problems in your queries. The more temporary tables are used in your system, the more likely you are to run into problems with them at some point. SQL Server does not manage the TempDB database in the same manner as other databases. It is possible for multiple tables to have rows located on the same page in TempDB. When this happens, a page lock acquired by a query on a temporary table locks data for more than just that one table. The net result yields seemingly unrelated queries that run into concurrency issues with one another when the data they are accessing is not related. The most effective cure for this is to create permanent worktables wherever possible. This also allows you to create indexes on the worktables that will be used by your queries without resorting to dynamic execution and batch separation techniques. In addition, these tables can be used much more efficiently by stored procedures.

## Replication for Offline Reporting

One of the biggest problems for concurrency in some systems is reporting. Depending on the complexity of the queries involved in producing the report(s), they may place a huge burden on the server, which impacts performance across the system. There are several options that should be explored to help eliminate performance problems. Utilizing replication to another server for offline reporting is one such option. If your reporting load is heavy, this option can be advantageous to help maintain acceptable performance for your production system. You will have to assess the time sensitivity of your reporting to ensure that replication can meet your needs and that it is properly configured to do so. You should also be extremely careful to specify the appropriate locking hints on your reporting queries to eliminate unnecessary resource contention when you are not modifying the data. There are several lock hint options that allow you to eliminate locking for reporting and still maintain the integrity level you need for the reports.

# Using Data-Bound Controls in Client Applications

Data-bound controls can be a source of locking contention in your system. These controls often do not allow the same level of control that is inherently available in SQL Server. In many cases, it is required that you establish a lock on the row or page in order to allow editing of the data in these controls. Some of these controls also do not handle making granular updates to records. They will send the entire record back to the server when only one or a few of the fields are actually being changed. This creates more network traffic and slows the update process unnecessarily.

In many cases, it is better to develop your own controls that do not impose these limitations or create a library of routines for working with the standard controls. In this type of setup, you can make use of a timestamp field to handle concurrent editing concerns. By tracking the timestamp and including verification as part of the update, you can detect when another user has modified the record you are trying to change. It is also possible to implement change tracking to a level that allows concurrent editing of a record as long as the two users do not change the same fields. Once you detect a timestamp conflict, you can reread the record and compare it to the original to find out if any of the fields edited in the current session were affected by the update that has occurred. If there is no conflict, the update can be allowed to proceed. If there is a conflict, you can either stop the update or make the user decide whether to keep or drop the updates to the conflicting fields.

This type of implementation is generally more complex and involved than using the standard data-bound controls provided by languages like Visual Basic and Delphi, but the benefits can be worth the effort. You may also find that as you learn to exert more control over the processes affecting database access, you will be able to improve the performance of the client application and the database system as a whole.

# Immediate Solutions

## Examining an Execution Plan in the Query Analyzer

The following steps demonstrate how you can use the Estimated Execution Plan in the Query Analyzer to examine and understand the query plan generated for your query by the query optimizer:

1. Open the Query Analyzer.

2. Enter the query shown in Listing 11.12 in the query window.

3. Press Ctrl+L to display the estimated execution plan for the query.

4. Scroll to the far right of the Results pane.

   Two icons labeled "Table Scan" are located on the far right, one directly above the other. These icons indicate the fact that both of these tables are being accessed by using a table scan.

5. Place the mouse cursor directly over the top icon on the right. A pop-up dialog appears, which provides more detailed information about the operation being performed, including the name of the table being accessed.

6. Right-click on the lower of the two icons on the right.

7. Select Manage Indexes from the context menu that pops up.

8. In the Manage Indexes dialog, click on New at the bottom.

9. Enter "IDX_CodeID" in the Index Name edit box.

10. Select the **Code_ID** column checkbox. The checkbox is located to the left of the field name.

11. Under Index options, select the Unique Values checkbox.

12. Click on OK at the bottom of the dialog.

13. Press Ctrl+L to display the new estimated execution plan for the query.

14. Scroll to the far right of the results pane.

Notice that the top icon on the right is still a Table Scan, but the lower icon now shows a table and index name in dot notation. This indicates that the **tbl_codes** table is now being accessed using an index. Also notice that the cost percentages have changed to indicate that this table now represents a much smaller percentage of the overall query cost.

Because you are joining to the codes table twice in this query on the **Code_ID**, the second reference to this table has also changed to use the index instead of resorting to a table scan to retrieve the information.

The two icons on the right are connected with arrows to another icon. The processing flow is depicted from right to left with the first operation appearing at the far right of the diagram. This icon represents the operation used to join the results retrieved from the two tables. In this case, the method used for the join is a Nested Loop. This method performs a search on the inner table for each row of the outer table. The search will typically be performed using an index.

The next icon connected by an arrow to the left of the Nested Loop is a Bookmark Lookup operation. This icon indicates that a row ID or clustering key (a row ID in this case) is being used to locate the needed rows in the indicated table. Below the Bookmark Lookup icon is another reference to the codes table using the index you created earlier. This time the field being joined on is the department.

The next two steps in the diagram illustrate another Nested Loop join operation and another Bookmark Lookup operation. Below the second Bookmark Lookup icon is another Table Scan icon. This represents the lookup on the **Manager_ID** to retrieve the employee's manager in the query. Next is a final Nested Loop join operation.

The next step in the execution plan is a Compute Scalar operation, which evaluates the **CONVERT** and **COALESCE** functions used to build the employee and manager names for the query. It also evaluates the transformation of the phone number field.

The final step to be performed before the result set is returned is a Sort operation to satisfy the **ORDER BY** clause in the query.

Refer to "Adding an Entry to Favorites" in the "Immediate Solutions" section of Chapter 5 to locate the icon legend for the execution plan. This legend provides information on the meaning of every icon that appears in an estimated execution plan.

**Listing 11.12   Sample query for execution plan analysis.**

```
/* Select Basic Employee Information */
SELECT CONVERT(VARCHAR(30), e.First_Name + ' ' + e.Last_Name) AS Employee,
       SUBSTRING(e.Phone, 1, 3) + '-' + SUBSTRING(e.Phone, 4, 4) as Phone,
       t.Code as Title,
       COALESCE(CONVERT(VARCHAR(30),
                   m.First_Name + ' ' + m.Last_Name), '') AS Manager,
       d.Code AS Department
  FROM Employee..tbl_Employee e (NOLOCK)
```

```
LEFT JOIN Employee..tbl_Employee m (NOLOCK) ON e.Manager_ID =
                                             m.Employee_ID
JOIN Utility..tbl_Codes t (NOLOCK) on e.Title = t.Code_ID
JOIN Utility..tbl_Codes d (NOLOCK) on e.Department = d.Code_ID
ORDER BY m.Last_Name, m.First_Name
```

| Related solution: | Found on page: |
|---|---|
| Displaying and Examining a Query Plan | 197 |

# Running Traces for Optimization

The following steps walk you through the process of configuring and running a trace with the Profiler for the purpose of optimizing your code. This example will help you understand the information provided by a trace and how to interpret the various events.

1. Open the Query Analyzer.

2. Enter the query in Listing 11.13 into the query window.

3. Open the Profiler.

4. If you have not already done so, follow the instructions in "Creating a Trace Template for Optimization" in the "Immediate Solutions" section in Chapter 5.

5. Select File|New|Trace.

6. Select the server to connect to and provide the required login information.

7. In the Trace Properties dialog, enter "Test1" in the Trace Name edit box.

8. Using the drop-down list, select the template that you created in "Creating a Trace Template for Optimization" in the "Immediate Solutions" section in Chapter 5.

9. Select the Save To File checkbox.

10. Choose a file name and location for the trace file. Be sure the location contains enough room for the trace file. These files can become quite large in a hurry. Even a short trace can take up several megabytes of disk space.

11. The Events, Data Columns, and Filters tabs will be filled out correctly by the template.

12. Click on Run at the bottom of the Trace Properties dialog to start the trace.

13. If you do not have Named Pipes or Multi-Protocol enabled for the client and the server, the Profiler will return an error, and you will need to

configure one of these options in both places before attempting to run a trace.

14. Switch to the Query Analyzer, and execute the query.

15. When the query has finished running, switch back to the Profiler, and pause the trace.

16. The last line in the trace is highlighted. This is the Trace Stop event generated by pausing the trace.

17. Scroll to the top of the trace.

18. Locate the SQL:Batch Starting event, which will give you the start time for the batch execution.

19. Below this event is a SQL:StmtStatring event, which marks the beginning of execution for the first **SELECT** statement in the batch. Highlight this event to see the test for the statement in the bottom pane of the display.

20. Locate the Execution Plan event for this statement. Highlight this event to see the query plan in text format. This is the execution plan that was selected for the query by the query optimizer for this statement. The text execution plan is equivalent to the graphical plans shown in the Query Analyzer.

The next event is the SQL:StmtCompleted event. This event provides the execution time for this command in the duration column. The time is listed in milliseconds. This event also provides statistics on the number of reads and writes required to complete the command. If you see writes used for a command that is not updating data, it indicates that SQL Server needed to create a worktable to process the command. You will see these same events for each command in the batch.

For this batch, it is easy to see that the final command occupies the majority of execution time for the query. If you were trying to optimize this batch, this would be the first place you should look for opportunities to improve performance. This command would definitely be the bottleneck for this particular batch.

**Listing 11.13   Sample query for Profiler example.**

```
/* Select Employee Address Information */
SELECT First_Name,
       Last_Name,
       Line1 AS Address,
       c.Name AS City,
       State_Code AS State,
       Zip5 AS "Zip Code",
       Code AS "Address Type"
  FROM Employee..tbl_Employee e (NOLOCK)
```

```
        JOIN Employee..tbl_EmployeeAddressXref ea (NOLOCK) ON e.Employee_ID =
    ea.Employee_ID
        JOIN Address..tbl_Address a (NOLOCK) ON ea.Address_ID = a.Address_ID
        JOIN Address..tbl_City c (NOLOCK) on a.City_ID = c.City_ID
        JOIN Address..tbl_State s (NOLOCK) on a.State_ID = s.State_ID
        JOIN Address..tbl_ZipCode z (NOLOCK) on a.Zip_ID = z.Zip_ID
        JOIN Utility..tbl_Codes (NOLOCK) on Address_Type = Code_ID

    /* Select Employee Manager Information */
    SELECT CONVERT(VARCHAR(30), e.First_Name + ' ' + e.Last_Name) AS Employee,
            SUBSTRING(e.Phone, 1, 3) + '-' + SUBSTRING(e.Phone, 4, 4) as Phone,
            t.Code as Title,
            COALESCE(CONVERT(VARCHAR(30),
            m.First_Name + ' ' + m.Last_Name), '') AS Manager,
            d.Code AS Department
        FROM Employee..tbl_Employee e (NOLOCK)
        LEFT JOIN Employee..tbl_Employee m (NOLOCK) ON e.Manager_ID =
                                                  m.Employee_ID
        JOIN Utility..tbl_Codes t (NOLOCK) on e.Title = t.Code_ID
        JOIN Utility..tbl_Codes d (NOLOCK) on e.Department = d.Code_ID
        ORDER BY m.Last_Name, m.First_Name

    /* Get a List of All Managers From the Employee Table */
    SELECT DISTINCT a.First_Name + ' ' + a.Last_Name AS Managers
        FROM Employee..tbl_Employee a (NOLOCK)
        JOIN Employee..tbl_Employee b (NOLOCK) ON a.Employee_ID = b.Manager_ID

    /* Get a List of Non-Managers From the Employee Table */
    SELECT a.First_Name + ' ' + a.Last_Name AS "Non-Managers"
        FROM Employee..tbl_Employee a (NOLOCK)
        LEFT JOIN Employee..tbl_Employee b (NOLOCK) ON a.Employee_ID =
                                                  b.Manager_ID
        WHERE b.Manager_ID IS NULL

    /* Select All Information From Denormalized Address Table */
    SELECT *
        FROM Address..tbl_AddressDN (NOLOCK)
```

| Related solution: | Found on page: |
|---|---|
| Creating a Trace Template for Optimization | 198 |

# Using Optimizer Hints to Control Locking Behavior

The following example demonstrates the use of optimizer hints that affect how SQL Server locks the data read by your queries. These steps walk you through running a query once without the hints and once with the hints to see the difference in the lock events generated by the query.

1. Open the Query Analyzer.

2. Enter the query in Listing 11.14 into the query window. Because there are no locking hints on this query, a page lock will be obtained on each data and index page read to satisfy the query.

3. Open the Profiler.

4. Select File|New|Trace.

5. In the Trace Properties dialog, enter "Test2" in the Trace Name edit box.

6. Using the drop-down list, select the template that you created in "Creating a Trace Template for Optimization" in the "Immediate Solutions" section in Chapter 5.

7. Select the Save To File checkbox.

8. Choose a file name and location for the trace file. Be sure the location contains enough room for the trace file. These files can become quite large in a hurry. Even a short trace can take up several megabytes of disk space.

9. The Events, Data Columns, and Filters tabs will be filled to match the template.

10. Click on Run at the bottom of the Trace Properties dialog to start the trace.

11. If you do not have Named Pipes or Multi-Protocol enabled for the client and the server, the Profiler will return an error, and you will need to configure one of these options in both places before attempting to run a trace.

12. Click on Stop Selected Trace on the toolbar.

13. The second line in the trace should be an ExistingConnection event.

14. Locate the SPID column by scrolling the trace window to the right.

15. Click on Properties on the toolbar.

16. Switch to the Filters tab.

17. Expand SPID in the tree.

18. Expand the Equals entry under SPID in the tree.

19. Enter the SPID for your existing connection in the new entry created in the tree.

20. Switch to the Events tab.

21. Double-click on the Locks node in the tree to move it to the Selected Event Classes pane.

22. Click on OK at the bottom of the Trace Properties dialog.

23. Click on Start Selected Trace on the toolbar to restart the trace.

24. Switch to the Query Analyzer, and execute the query.

25. When the query has finished running, switch back to the Profiler, and stop the trace by clicking on the Stop Selected Trace button.

26. You will notice a large number of Lock:Acquired and Lock:Released events in the trace. The query optimizer generates many of these events when it is determining the best query plan for the query.

    There will be numerous sets of Lock:Acquired and Lock:Released events in the trace after the Execution Plan event. These events are the page locks placed on the data pages that are read to satisfy this query.

27. Restart the trace by clicking on Start Selected Trace.

28. Switch back to the Query Analyzer.

29. Uncomment the **(NOLOCK)** hint on the **tbl_Employee** table.

30. Run the query with the **(NOLOCK)** hint on the table.

31. When the query has finished running, switch back to the Profiler, and stop the trace by clicking on Stop Selected Trace.

32. This time you will notice that there are no Lock:Acquired or Lock:Released events in the trace after the Execution Plan event. This is due to the fact that the page locks for the data pages read by the query are not created when you use the **(NOLOCK)** hint.

33. Restart the trace by clicking on Start Selected Trace.

34. Switch back to the Query Analyzer.

35. Change the **(NOLOCK)** hint to a **(TABLOCKX)** hint for the table.

36. Run the query a final time with the **(TABLOCKX)** hint on the table.

37. When the query has finished running, switch back to the Profiler, and stop the trace by clicking on Stop Selected Trace.

38. This time there is an extra Lock:Released event after the Execution Plan event. The Lock:Released event shows when the exclusive lock obtained on the table is released prior to actually executing the query.

**Listing 11.14   Sample query for lock hint example.**

```
/* Select Employee Address Information */
SELECT Address_ID
  FROM Address..tbl_AddressDN --(NOLOCK)
```

# Improving Query Performance Using a Covering Index

In the following example, you will create a covering index to improve the performance of a query. These steps walk you through running the query without the index and examining the performance. You will then create the covering index and rerun the query to observe the difference.

In this example, the table is not particularly wide and most of the columns are included in the covering index. Depending on the structure of your data and the number of columns you need to include for a covering index, much greater differences in performance are possible when this type of index is used.

1. Open the Query Analyzer.
2. Enter the query in Listing 11.15 into the query window.
3. Execute the query. This caches the records to make the comparisons more accurate.
4. When the query has finished running, click on Current Connection Properties on the toolbar.
5. Select the Set Statistics Time checkbox.
6. Select the Set Statistics IO checkbox.
7. Click on Apply at the bottom of the Current Connection Properties dialog.
8. Click on OK at the bottom of the Current Connection Properties dialog.
9. Execute the query again.
10. When the query has finished running, scroll to the bottom of the results pane, and examine the statistics.
11. Notice the logical read count on the address table. If the table is populated with 100,000 rows, the count should be 813.
12. Open the Enterprise Manager.
13. Expand your Server Group in the tree view.
14. Expand your Server in the tree view.
15. Expand the Databases node under your Server in the tree view.
16. Expand the Address database in the tree view.
17. Click on the Tables node in the tree view.
18. Right-click on the **tbl_AddressDN** table in the tree view.
19. Select All Tasks|Manage Indexes from the menu.
20. Click on New at the bottom of the Manage Indexes dialog.
21. Enter "IDX_Cover1" in the Index Name edit box.

22. Select the **Zip5**, **Line1**, **City**, and **State** fields in the list box.

23. Use the Up button to move **Zip5** to the top of the list.

24. Click on OK at the bottom of the Create New Index dialog.

25. Click on Close at the bottom of the Manage Indexes dialog.

26. Switch back to the Query Analyzer, and execute the query again.

27. Notice that the query begins displaying results much more quickly this time. This is due to the fact that you just created a covering index for the query, and the index is already in the correct order for the **ORDER BY** clause in the query.

28. When the query is finished running, scroll to the bottom of the results pane, and examine the statistics again.

29. Notice that the logical read count for the address table has dropped. In the case of a 100,000 row table, the new number should be 669. Notice that the elapsed time is also about 15 percent less than the original execution.

**Listing 11.15   Sample query for covering index example.**

```
/* SET CONTEXT TO THE ADDRESS DATABASE */
USE Address


/* SELECT ALL ADDRESSES BY ZIPCODE FOR MAILING LIST */
SELECT Line1 AS Address,
       City,
       State,
       Zip5 AS ZipCode
  FROM tbl_AddressDN (NOLOCK)
  ORDER BY Zip5
```

# Changing the Execution Plan of a Query

The following example illustrates one way that the execution plan of a query can be changed. These steps walk you through generating the query plan for a query, making a change, and observing the difference in the new query plan:

1. Open the Query Analyzer.

2. Enter the query in Listing 11.16 into the query window.

3. Execute the query. This caches the records to make the comparisons more accurate.

4. Click on Display Estimated Execution Plan on the toolbar.

5. Notice that all of the tables are read using a Table Scan. Also notice that the table scan for the address table represents 47 percent of the total query time.

6. When the query has finished running, click on Current Connection Properties on the toolbar.

7. Select the Set Statistics Time checkbox.

8. Select the Set Statistics IO checkbox.

9. Click on Apply at the bottom of the Current Connection Properties dialog.

10. Click on OK at the bottom of the Current Connection Properties dialog.

11. Execute the query again.

12. When the query has finished running, scroll to the bottom of the results pane, and examine the statistics.

13. Notice the logical read count on the address table. If the address table is populated with 100,000 rows, the count should be 644.

14. Click on Display Estimated Execution Plan on the toolbar again.

15. Right-click on the Table Scan icon for the **tbl_Address** table.

16. Select Manage Indexes from the menu.

17. Click on New at the bottom of the Manage Indexes dialog.

18. Enter "IDX_AddressID" in the Index Name edit box.

19. Select the **Address_ID** field in the list box.

20. Click on OK at the bottom of the Create New Index dialog.

21. Click on Close at the bottom of the Manage Indexes dialog.

22. Click on Display Estimated Execution Plan on the toolbar.

23. Notice that the icon for the address table shows an Index Seek operation instead of a table scan, and the address table now only represents 3 percent of the total query time.

24. Execute the query again.

25. When the query has finished running, scroll to the bottom of the results pane, and examine the statistics.

26. Notice that the logical read count for the address table has now dropped to 30.

**Listing 11.16   Sample query for changing execution plan example.**

```
/* SET CONTEXT TO THE ADDRESS DATABASE */
USE Address
```

```
/* SELECT ALL EMPLOYEE HOME ADDRESSES BY ZIPCODE FOR MAILING LIST */
SELECT a.Line1 AS Address,
       c.Name AS City,
       s.State_Code AS State,
       z.Zip5 as ZipCode
  FROM tbl_Address a (NOLOCK)
  JOIN tbl_City c (NOLOCK) ON a.City_ID = c.City_ID
  JOIN tbl_State s (NOLOCK) on a.State_ID = s.State_ID
  JOIN tbl_ZipCode z (NOLOCK) on a.Zip_ID = z.Zip_ID
  JOIN Employee..tbl_EmployeeAddressXref ea (NOLOCK) ON a.Address_ID =
ea.Address_ID
  JOIN Utility..tbl_Codes co (NOLOCK) ON ea.Address_Type = co.Code_ID
  WHERE co.Code = 'Home'
  ORDER BY Zip5
```

# Documenting Test Results

Documentation is perhaps the most important part of the optimization process. Without proper documentation, it is impossible to determine the true effect of the changes that you make to the various queries in your system. This example walks you through creating simple documentation that allows you to compare multiple executions of the same query after each change is made. This type of comparative documentation is invaluable in determining which changes to keep and which ones to discard.

Compare the differences in the three sets of results to see the alterations made by each successive change in the conditions of the test. This type of documentation can be extremely helpful in your optimization efforts to see which changes had the most impact on performance. Use the following steps to create test results with different combinations of proposed changes to help in your evaluation of selecting those changes to permanently include in your system:

1. Launch the Service Manager for SQL Server 2000.
2. Select your server (or instance) from the Server drop-down box.
3. Select SQL Server in the Services drop-down box.
4. Click on Stop to stop the service.
5. Once the service has stopped, click on Start/Continue to restart the service. This restarts the service with an empty cache.
6. Once the service has started, close the Service Manager.
7. Open the Query Analyzer.

8. Enter the query in Listing 11.17 into the query window.

9. Click on Current Connection Properties on the toolbar.

10. Select the Set Statistics Time checkbox.

11. Select the Set Statistics IO checkbox.

12. Click on Apply at the bottom of the Current Connection Properties dialog.

13. Click on OK at the bottom of the Current Connection Properties dialog.

14. Execute the query.

15. When the query has finished running, scroll to the bottom of the results pane, and examine the statistics.

16. Open either Notepad or a spreadsheet to record the query results. If you use Notepad, be sure to select a nonproportional font to prevent column alignment problems.

17. Create a row named "Test Run 1 No Cache".

18. Create a row for each query with a brief description of the query's purpose.

19. Create a row beneath the query row for each table used in the query. Indent the table rows to make it clear that they are subentries for the query.

20. Create columns named "Scan Count", "Logical Reads", "Physical Reads", "Read-ahead Reads", and "Elapsed Time".

21. Enter the read information for each table and the elapsed time for each query in that table.

22. Switch back to the Query Analyzer.

23. Execute the query again.

24. When the query has finished running, scroll to the bottom of the results pane, and examine the statistics.

25. In most cases, you will see at least some differences from the original run now that the data has been cached.

26. Switch back to the tool you are using for your documentation.

27. Below your original entries, create a row named "Test Run 2 Cache".

28. Create the same entries as you did for the first run, and record the new read and elapsed time information.

29. Open the Enterprise Manager.

30. Expand your Server Group in the tree view.

31. Expand your Server in the tree view.

32. Expand the Databases node under your Server in the tree view.

33. Expand the Address database in the tree view.

34. Click on the Tables node in the tree view.

35. Right-click on the **tbl_Address** table in the tree view.

36. Select All Tasks|Manage Indexes from the menu.

37. If there is an index on the **Address_ID** column in the table, highlight this entry, click on Delete at the bottom of the Manage Indexes dialog, and skip the next four steps. (Skip to step 42.)

38. Click on New at the bottom of the Manage Indexes dialog.

39. Enter "IDX_AddressID" in the Index Name edit box.

40. Select the **Address_ID** field in the list box.

41. Click on OK at the bottom of the Create New Index dialog.

42. Click on Close at the bottom of the Manage Indexes dialog.

43. Switch back to the Query Analyzer, and execute the query again.

44. When the query has finished running, scroll to the bottom of the results pane, and examine the statistics.

45. Adding or removing the index on the **Address_ID** column causes differences in the read statistics for the **tbl_Address** table and most likely in the elapsed time for the query as well.

46. Switch back to the tool you are using for your documentation.

47. Below your original entries, create a row named "Test Run 3 Added (or Removed) Index for Address_ID".

48. Create the same entries as you did for the previous tests, and record the new read and elapsed time information.

**Listing 11.17    Sample query for documentation example.**

```
/* Select Employee Address Information */
SELECT First_Name,
       Last_Name,
       Line1 AS Address,
       c.Name AS City,
       State_Code AS State,
       Zip5 AS "Zip Code",
       Code AS "Address Type"
  FROM Employee..tbl_Employee e (NOLOCK)
  JOIN Employee..tbl_EmployeeAddressXref ea (NOLOCK) ON e.Employee_ID =
ea.Employee_ID
  JOIN Address..tbl_Address a (NOLOCK) ON ea.Address_ID = a.Address_ID
  JOIN Address..tbl_City c (NOLOCK) on a.City_ID = c.City_ID
  JOIN Address..tbl_State s (NOLOCK) on a.State_ID = s.State_ID
```

```
      JOIN Address..tbl_ZipCode z (NOLOCK) on a.Zip_ID = z.Zip_ID
      JOIN Utility..tbl_Codes (NOLOCK) on Address_Type = Code_ID

/* Select Employee Manager Information */
SELECT CONVERT(VARCHAR(30), e.First_Name + ' ' + e.Last_Name) AS Employee,
       SUBSTRING(e.Phone, 1, 3) + '-' + SUBSTRING(e.Phone, 4, 4) as Phone,
       t.Code as Title,
       COALESCE(CONVERT(VARCHAR(30),
       m.First_Name + ' ' + m.Last_Name), '') AS Manager,
       d.Code AS Department
   FROM Employee..tbl_Employee e (NOLOCK)
   LEFT JOIN Employee..tbl_Employee m (NOLOCK) ON e.Manager_ID =
m.Employee_ID
   JOIN Utility..tbl_Codes t (NOLOCK) on e.Title = t.Code_ID
   JOIN Utility..tbl_Codes d (NOLOCK) on e.Department = d.Code_ID
   ORDER BY m.Last_Name, m.First_Name
```

11. Performance, Tuning, and Optimization

# Chapter 12

# Error Handling

# *In Depth*

Developing a coherent error handling approach for an enterprise-level application should not be undertaken without some prior planning. Careful analysis of the applications that currently run against the system as well as future development can influence the design of your error handling solution.

There are specific types of errors that you should anticipate in a client/server application. Process logic, incorrect results, or unexpected environment conditions can all create an error that will frustrate users and ultimately render the application too difficult to use or maintain. The maintenance of the application bears mention, because if you do not create a thorough error handling solution, you will find yourself, as a developer or database administrator, having to write a great deal of clean-up code in a reactive rather than proactive mode.

Many database developers write their SQL code in client applications or stored procedures assuming the SQL statement(s) will run every time without error. When they (SQL statements) do not, the data can become corrupt or useless to the user.

---

**TIP:** *It is the database administrator that will be blamed more often than not when the data becomes corrupt or error-ridden. Push for a solid error handling policy at the beginning of a project, and you will be far less stressed later when you have to troubleshoot problems.*

---

The goals of any error handling system should be to present useful error messages and provide the troubleshooting data necessary to speed the analysis and correction of problems in the system.

## Error Handling Approach

The approach you choose can be simple and effective. The more complicated the approach, the less likely developers will be to follow the guidelines of the error handling routines you have developed. You should provide to client and SQL developers an easy-to-use interface that is well documented, so there are no questions as to how they should be handling their code. In this chapter, a few options are discussed that will make your job of troubleshooting and error handling easier.

Internally, SQL Server has a global variable called **@@ERROR**, which holds the recent SQL statement execution results. This variable is updated for your connection each time a SQL statement is executed. Any nonzero value is an error value. In the simplest form of error handling, you would check this variable any time you manipulate data and code a reaction to any error based on a nonzero value.

---

**NOTE:** *The global variable is updated with any statement, so you should check this value immediately following a data modification statement, or the error value will be lost.*

---

A more complete solution includes logging the errors so that they can be analyzed to determine problem areas in processing logic. Many current client/server applications do *not* save error information to a log for analysis. The application is presumed to be running well (because users do not report all the errors) until a major problem is brought up and fixed. Trapping *all* errors, saving them to a log and looking for patterns and trends that point to problem areas in client or SQL code can uncover many errors in processing logic.

The best solution is to use the error logging methodology in concert with an error escalation routine. The escalation process looks for occurrences of errors of a certain type and generates a new error that can be handled based upon a predefined set of rules. The predefined set of rules includes logic for emailing or paging database administrators when a problem occurs.

## Using Alerts and Operators

You can create alerts on the server that keep track of errors in your system. Alerts can also trigger jobs or notifications of users on the network. Alerts track occurrence and date information, so that you can view the historical information and determine the number of times an error has occurred.

Operators are defined on a server and are available to be used by alerts for notification purposes. An operator can be notified via email, pager, or **NET SEND** commands. An operator is managed through the Enterprise Manager under the SQL Agent node of the server.

The add alert example in Listing 12.1 adds an alert that tracks any 50001 error in all databases on the server. This listing assumes that the error message has been defined and writes an event to the Windows NT Event Log. The notification is then added, so that the operator, "Patrick," is sent a **NET SEND** message that an error has occurred on the server. (The Patrick user would have to have been configured before running the example.)

**Listing 12.1    Add alert example.**

```
USE msdb
GO
```

```
EXEC sp_add_alert
  @name = 'Test Alert',
  @message_id = 50001,
  @severity = 0,
  @notification_message = 'Error 50001 has occurred.'

EXEC sp_add_notification 'Test Alert', 'Patrick', 4

RAISERROR(50001,16,1,'Foo')
```

If you are in a multiple server environment, you can create a forwarding server that is the central alert management server in your system. If you do not use SQL Mail, you should at least use alerts and **NET SEND** notifications to help manage your SQL Server proactively.

---

*Note: In order to use **NET SEND**, you must have the messenger service enabled and running.*

---

# User-Defined Error Numbers

You have the ability to define your own error numbers for use by your process code on your SQL Server. Any value over 50000 is valid; you can choose to define a range of values with specific messages for each of the anticipated problems. You can create a generic error message and pass a parameter to the message so that it is descriptive and more complete than a plain text generic error. See Listing 12.2 for an example of adding a user-defined error message programmatically to your server.

---

**NOTE:** *If you use an error message in conjunction with an alert, you must set the **WITH LOG** option to true. If the error does not write to the Windows NT Error Log, the alert engine will not be fired on the error.*

---

**Listing 12.2   Adding a user-defined error message example.**

```
EXEC sp_addmessage
  @msgnum   = 50001, @severity = 16,
  @msgtext  = N'Procedure: %s failed to %s.',
  @lang     = 'us_english',
  @with_log = true

RAISERROR(50001,16,1,'Foo','Execute')
```

Some third-party applications use user-defined error numbers in different ranges. Any valid, unused number can be added to the server. Try to choose a range of numbers that make sense and document each one.

# Error Handling Stored Procedure

In order to create a centrally managed error handling procedure, you should consider the minimum information that you want to log. Error numbers alone typically are not enough to provide any useful information for troubleshooting. Listing 12.3 shows the source SQL for **usp_ErrorLog**. This error log procedure is an example of capturing the basic list of information to a table in the Utility database. You can find the source file for this listing on the CD-ROM accompanying this book in the file named usp_ErrorLog.sql.

**Listing 12.3  usp_ErrorLog source SQL.**

```
CREATE PROC usp_ErrorLog
  @p_SystemErrorNumber INTEGER,
  @p_Process           VARCHAR(50),
  @p_Application       VARCHAR(50),
  @p_ErrorNumber       INTEGER,
  @p_Description       VARCHAR(255),
  @p_ErrorDateTime     SMALLDATETIME
AS
SET NOCOUNT ON
/* Fill in defaults */
/* Error_DateTime   */
IF (@p_ErrorDateTime IS NULL)
BEGIN
  SELECT @p_ErrorDateTime = GETDATE()
END -- ErrorDataTime

INSERT INTO tbl_ErrorLog (
  System_Error_Number,
  Process,
  Application,
  Error_Number,
  Description,
  Error_DateTime)
VALUES(
  @p_SystemErrorNumber,
  @p_Process,
  @p_Application,
  @p_ErrorNumber,
  @p_Description,
  @p_ErrorDateTime)

/* If @p_ErrorNumber <> NULL RAISERROR */
IF (@p_ErrorNumber IS NOT NULL)
```

```
BEGIN
  RAISERROR(@p_ErrorNumber,16,1)
END -- ErrorNumber so hit RAISERROR
GO

/* Test Procedure */
EXEC usp_ErrorLog
  1,                  -- INTEGER
  'Test',             -- VARCHAR(50)
  'MyAppliction',     -- VARCHAR(50)
  NULL,               -- INTEGER
  'Test Error',       -- VARCHAR(255)
  '01/03/2000'        -- SMALLDATETIME

SELECT *
  FROM tbl_ErrorLog (NOLOCK)
```

The parameters used by this procedure are listed in Table 12.1. Some parameters are optional and some may need to be added for your environment. If you need to track additional information, you should add the columns to the table **tbl_ ErrorLog** and add parameters to this procedure.

**Table 12.1    usp_ErrorLog parameters.**

| Parameter | Data Type | Description |
| --- | --- | --- |
| @p_SystemErrorNumber | INT | The actual error number value from the system where the error occurs. This value can be a Delphi error code, a SQL error number (**@@ERROR**), or any other error that is environmentally generated. |
| @p_Process | VARCHAR(50) | The actual process or subprocess in which the error occurs. |
| @p_Application | VARCHAR(50) | The name of the application in which the error occurs. |
| @p_ErrorNumber | INT | The error number raised by the error handling system. This number may not be the actual error number returned by the server or client application. An entry in the error list table would be a match for error escalation routines. This number can be especially useful for debugging client application issues that relate to server-side errors. |

*(continued)*

**Table 12.1   usp_ErrorLog** parameters *(continued)*.

| Parameter | Data Type | Description |
|---|---|---|
| @p_Description | VARCHAR(255) | The description can be used to provide the detailed text of the error or store some descriptive data to point to where you should start troubleshooting the problem. (You can optionally change the size of this parameter and the corresponding column in the error log table to a larger value if your needs dictate.) |
| @p_ErrorDateTime | SMALLDATETIME | The date and time the error occurs. This data can be supplied by the stored procedure or defaulted to the current date and time on the server. (Most people prefer to use the server date and time because it provides a common point of measurement instead of being at the mercy of many different system clocks.) |

The error handling procedure can be called to log process, client-side, or server-side errors. You will begin to see trends in processes and potentially uncover logic errors in your application design by periodically checking for errors in the error log table. You can log security information, key values of data being manipulated at the time of an error, or user interface errors. By capturing this information, your application will improve dramatically, because you will have the information you need to improve it gathered in one place.

You should not create an error log without having a plan for managing the log data, so it does not grow to an unmanageable size. You will need to create some sort of purge routine that keeps the error log table small and fast. It is recommended that you not delete records directly from the table because you may need that information for troubleshooting in the future. Instead, you can create a purge procedure that will BCP the data out before deleting the records. See Listing 12.4 for a sample purge procedure. See usp_PurgeErrorLog.sql for the source SQL needed to add this procedure to your server.

---

**NOTE:** *The usp_PurgeErrorLog.sql file also includes the code to add the* **usp_GetKeyOut** *stored procedure that is required by this procedure.*

---

**Listing 12.4   usp_PurgeErrorLog** example.

```
IF EXISTS (SELECT name
            FROM sysobjects (NOLOCK)
           WHERE name = 'usp_PurgeErrorLog'
             AND type = 'P')
```

```
BEGIN
  DROP PROC usp_PurgeErrorLog
END
GO

CREATE PROC usp_PurgeErrorLog
AS
SET NOCOUNT ON

DECLARE @v_PurgeDays VARCHAR(255),
        @v_PurgeLoc  VARCHAR(255),
        @v_PurgeFile VARCHAR(255),
        @v_SQL       VARCHAR(255)

/***       Purge Error Log          ***/
/* Get purge keys from tbl_Registry */
EXEC usp_GetKeyOut
  'System\ErrorHandling\PurgeDays',
  @v_PurgeDays OUTPUT

EXEC usp_GetKeyOut
  'System\ErrorHandling\PurgeLocation',
  @v_PurgeLoc OUTPUT

EXEC usp_GetKeyOut
  'System\ErrorHandling\PurgeFile',
  @v_PurgeFile OUTPUT

/* Build BCP Cmd                    */
SELECT @v_SQL =
  'EXEC master..xp_cmdshell ''BCP ' +
  '"SELECT * ' +
  'FROM Utility..tbl_ErrorLog (NOLOCK) ' +
  'WHERE Error_DateTime <= DATEADD(DD,-CONVERT(INT,''''' +
  @v_PurgeDays +'''''),GETDATE())" queryout ' +
  @v_PurgeLoc +
  @v_PurgeFile + CONVERT(VARCHAR(10),GETDATE(),110) + '.txt /Spdalton01' +
  ' /Usa /P /c /t, /b5000 /E'', no_output'

/* Create comma delimited text file */
EXEC (@v_SQL)

/* Remove records                   */
DELETE FROM tbl_ErrorLog
```

```
    WHERE Error_DateTime <=
          DATEADD(DD,-CONVERT(INT,@v_PurgeDays),GETDATE())

GO

EXEC usp_PurgeErrorLog
```

The error log purge routine looks in the Registry table (**tbl_Registry**) for key values that will drive the process: the number of days that will be kept in the error log, the error log directory, and the base error log file name base. Each of these values must exist before this process will run correctly. (See the "Immediate Solutions" section of this chapter for more information on creating and managing these keys.)

The dynamic string that is built to BCP the data out of the table **tbl_ErrorLog** is a query out BCP. See Chapter 15 for more on BCP and the different uses of BCP in a database environment. It runs the query to obtain the same data that the **DE-LETE** statement removes from the table. The purge file name is built from the base file name stored in the Registry table and the current date. The export file is a comma-delimited text file that holds any rows that the **DELETE** statement removes.

*WARNING! If you run this routine on the same day without modifying the code, it overwrites the output file without any warning. The schedule of the procedure is rarely daily, so this should not cause a problem. If you require a tighter schedule than a daily timetable, you can change the name to include the time.*

# Error Escalation

Once you have created a method of tracking errors in a table, you can create an even more flexible error handling routine that periodically searches the error data and looks for patterns or occurrences that a user may not have reported and defines a new error to be raised that notifies someone of the problem or the potential for a problem. If too many errors of a certain type occur within a range of time or during a specific time frame, this escalation routine finds them by querying the data and raises a newly defined error that has administrative action associated with it.

An escalation process needs to be flexible and is typically data-driven. Some rules are clearly defined and do not require any parameters, but for those that do, the Registry table is the perfect place to store any variable escalation data. For an example of an escalation procedure see Listing 12.5. You can find this procedure in the usp_ErrorEscalate.sql file on the CD-ROM. Run the usp_ErrorEscalate.sql file on your server to install **usp_ErrorEscalate** on your server.

### Listing 12.5    **usp_ErrorEscalate** example.

```
CREATE PROC usp_ErrorEscalate
AS
/*** Perform MAX Error Count ***/
DECLARE @v_MaxErrors VARCHAR(10)

EXEC usp_GetKeyOut
  'System\ErrorHandling\MaxErrors',
  @v_MaxErrors OUTPUT

IF (SELECT COUNT(*)
      FROM tbl_ErrorLog (NOLOCK)) > CONVERT(INT,@v_MaxErrors)
BEGIN
  EXEC usp_ErrorLog
    NULL,
    'Escalation',
    'Error Handling',
    60000,
    'Max Errors Exceeded!'
END -- Max Error Count
GO
```

You should comment each check carefully and ensure that you can revisit the code at a later time to understand what error checks you are performing and why. Any Registry table entries that you require should exist before running this procedure, so the results are what you expect. The escalation procedure can be a scheduled job that runs every 10 to 15 minutes or once per hour to check for errors.

Before attempting to create an error escalation routine, you may want to create a simple hierarchy of the errors that will cause other predefined errors to be triggered. A simple error escalation rule, for example, would be to write a test that counted the total number of errors in the table. And if the count of errors exceeded a value in the Registry, an additional error would be logged (60000 in the example in Listing 12.7).

Additional rules could be written for failed login attempts or invalid object references. The number of tests that you can write are limited only by your imagination and the amount of error handling in your system.

# Centralized Error Management

Alerts can be forwarded between servers for centralized management. Error processing can be centralized as well. Alerts use a forwarding server that is the collection point for errors in a multiple server environment. You can also use the same principle for error handling.

If you use linked servers and run distributed error checks between servers, you can create a master error log table that is populated either directly or through scheduled server polling, and then run your escalation checks against a single error log. This technique can simplify the error management, but can increase the time it takes for the notifications and error routines to respond to clients. Plan your error handling with care, because it can turn your errors into a positive rather than a negative.

One caveat with this centralized approach is that your error handling must include the server where the error occurred as an additional data element.

# *Immediate Solutions*

## Creating User-Defined Error Numbers

User-defined error messages are a little-used feature of SQL Server. However, they are incredibly powerful when integrated with a client/server application. You should plan the range of numbers you will use on the server. Determine what messages you want to save along with any macro substitution for the messages that will make one general error fit many uses.

For example, you could create a user-defined error message that allows for **INSERT**, **UPDATE**, and **DELETE** failures. See Table 12.2 for a list of sample messages. The 50000 series numbers show three different messages, whereas the 60000 message can be used to produce the same error message as the three preceding it. In fact, it provides more detail and a clearer message to a log or user through the use of the %s macro substitution in the message. Actually, macro substitution is not really occurring; instead, parameterized messages are being created and are passing values to the message, so that the message can be built at runtime.

There are a number of different parameter options for your messages. Each is intended to be data type-specific and is intended for use in building a coherent message to the client application, log, and user. See Table 12.3 for a list of message parameters. The format for the message string contains format characters similar to the C programming language PRINTF function. See Listing 12.6 for an example of the possible placeholder structures used in message strings.

---

**NOTE:** *See the Microsoft SQL Server Books Online topic, user-defined error messages, for more information on message string structures and placeholder values.*

---

### Listing 12.6   Placeholder structure.

```
% [[flag][width][precision][{h|I}]] type
```

### Table 12.2   Sample error messages.

| Error Number | Message Text |
|---|---|
| 50001 | Failed to **INSERT** row(s) in table |
| 50002 | Failed to **UPDATE** row(s) in table |
| 50003 | Failed to **DELETE** row(s) in table |
| 60000 | Failed to **%s** row(s) in table **%s** |

**Table 12.3   Message parameter list.**

| Placeholder | Use |
| --- | --- |
| %d | Signed integer value |
| %l | Signed integer value |
| %o | Unsigned octal |
| %p | Pointer |
| %s | String data value |
| %u | Unsigned integer value |
| %x | Unsigned hexadecimal value |

To create a general purpose error message in the Enterprise Manager, like the 60000 example in Table 12.2, follow these steps:

1. Right-click on the server name in the Enterprise Manager.
2. Under the menu item All Tasks, select Manage SQL Server Messages.
3. Select the Messages tab at the top of the dialog that appears.
4. Click on New.
5. In the New SQL Server Message dialog, fill in the error number that you want to use. For this example, type "60000" in the error number box.
6. In the Message text box, remove the existing text, and replace it with "Failed to %s row(s) in table %s".
7. Select the Always Write To The Windows Event Log checkbox (used for alert management).
8. Click on OK. You have now created a general purpose error message that can be used for any statement failing to perform the requested operation against a table. See Listing 12.7 for examples of how to test your new message.

**Listing 12.7   Sample tests of the new error message.**

```
RAISERROR(60000,16,1,'INSERT','tbl_address')
RAISERROR(60000,16,1,'UPDATE','tbl_address')
RAISERROR(60000,16,1,'DELETE','tbl_address')

/* Results */
Server: Msg 60000, Level 16, State 1, Line 1
Failed to INSERT Row(s) in table tbl_address.
Server: Msg 60000, Level 16, State 1, Line 2
Failed to UPDATE Row(s) in table tbl_address.
Server: Msg 60000, Level 16, State 1, Line 3
Failed to DELETE Row(s) in table tbl_address.
```

# Creating an Operator

Operators are used for event notification purposes in jobs and alerts for SQL Server. This exercise creates an operator "PatrickD" on a server for use in other error handling and process notification routines.

1. In the Enterprise Manager, open the navigation tree, find the node for SQL Server Agent, and open that node.

2. You should see three nodes: Alerts, Operators, and Jobs. Right-click on Operators, and select New Operator.

3. In the New Operator Properties dialog, enter "PatrickD". (You can substitute any operator name.)

4. Supply an email address for this operator (providing you have SQL Mail running). For this example, use the **NET SEND** option. Type a machine name for the **NET SEND** operation in the **NET SEND** address box. (Let's use pdalton01 for this example.)

5. Remember: In order to use the **NET SEND** method, you must have the messenger service running!

6. Once you have typed in an address, the test button will be enabled. Click on Test to make sure the operation of sending a message to the operator will succeed. You are then prompted with a message box that informs you that a pop-up message will be sent and asks if it is okay to send that message. Click on OK.

7. The machine you sent the message to should receive a pop-up dialog with a Please Ignore message referring to the test. This ensures that everything works and that this operator can be used for event notification. Click on OK to create the operator.

# Creating an Alert

An alert is an integral part of the SQL Server event processing architecture. You can define alerts to react to environmental conditions and process completions or failures, and to help manage error handling in your enterprise.

The question to ask when a problem occurs is, "What condition caused the problem?" If the answer can be articulated, chances are that a test procedure can be developed for the problem and an appropriate alert created to either notify someone as soon as the situation occurs or proactively attempt to correct the problem.

SQL Server ships with some general alerts that react to log files filling up and common errors that you may see on a server. You can and should create alerts to match your own particular needs, so that you can take control of the server environment rather than react to it. The following steps create an alert that is triggered by a SQL statement referring to an object that does not exist in the database context where the statement is executed.

1. In the Enterprise Manager, open the Management folder, and expand the SQL Server Agent node.

2. Right-click on the Alerts object, and select New Alert.

3. In the Name text box, type "Invalid Object Reference".

4. In the Event Alert Definition group box, select the Error Number radio button.

5. Type the number "208" in the text box next to the radio button.

6. Leave the database context set to All Databases, so that this alert will apply to any database on the server rather than to a specific database.

7. Click on OK to close the New Alert Properties dialog.

8. You are presented with a dialog, which states that occurrences of the 208 error will not invoke an alert by default because this error is not written to the event log. (Only errors that are logged can raise an alert.) Click on Yes to set the 208 error to be written to the log.

---

**NOTE:** *Optionally, you can have this alert send an email or some other notification when it occurs.*

---

You will now have a log entry for any corresponding 208 error that occurs on your server. You can and should always test new alerts by running some test SQL to make sure they work as expected. See Listing 12.8 for an example of testing the invalid object reference alert.

**Listing 12.8   Invalid reference alert test.**

```
SELECT * FROM foo

/* Results */
Server: Msg 208, Level 16, State 1, Line 1
Invalid object name 'foo'.
```

Once you have generated an error 208 in a database, you can check the Windows NT event log for an entry in the application log showing the error 208 reference.

**12. Error Handling**

See Figure 12.1 for an example of the event log entry. (You are limited to 440 bytes of data in the Windows NT event log.)

The alert in the Enterprise Manager interface is updated with a last occurrence and count increase to reflect the error as well. See Figure 12.2 for an example of the alert properties box with the error data displayed.

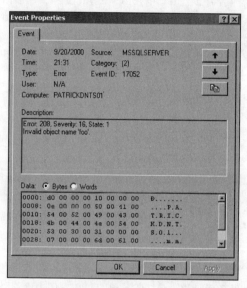

Figure 12.1    Windows NT event log entry.

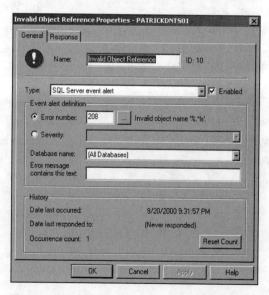

Figure 12.2    Alert properties dialog after generating a 208 error.

| Related solutions: | Found on page: |
| --- | --- |
| Useful Server Administration SQL | 236 |
| **usp_UPDKey** | 648 |
| Building and Executing Dynamic SQL | 834 |

# Using **RAISERROR**

**RAISERROR** allows you to either raise an error on-the-fly in your SQL code or call a predefined error based on conditions in your processing logic. The syntax for **RAISERROR** is shown in Listing 12.9.

> **NOTE:** *This example assumes that you completed the "Creating User-Defined Error Numbers" in this chapter to add the user-defined error numbers.*

### Listing 12.9 **RAISERROR** syntax.

```
RAISERROR ({msg_id | msg_str}{, severity , state}
          [, argument [,...n ]])
          [ WITH option [,...n ]]


Example:
RAISERROR (50001,16,1)
RAISERROR (60000,16,1,'INSERT','tbl_Address')
RAISERROR ('An error occurred',16,1)
```

Even a simple error number reference should provide a severity and state so that the server knows how to react to the error. If a severity level of 20 to 25 is provided and the **WITH LOG** option is used, the connection to the server will be terminated. Severity levels 0 through 18 can be used by any user and will not cause the connection to be lost. State is an arbitrary number and is usually 1.

> **NOTE:** *See the Microsoft SQL Server Books Online for more information on **RAISERROR** and error handling examples.*

| Related solutions: | Found on page: |
| --- | --- |
| Using **INSERT/SELECT** | 435 |
| **usp_UPDKey** | 648 |
| Building and Executing Dynamic SQL | 834 |

# Writing Error Information to the Windows NT Event Log

Some error handling routines want to control the activity written to the Windows NT event log, so they do not use alerts that write to the log by default, but rather use an external procedure, **xp_logevent**, to write to the log only when needed. Some server-side processing can take advantage of the capability to write to the log directly via the **xp_logevent** procedure as well. See Listing 12.10 for the syntax and an example of the use of **xp_logevent**.

**Listing 12.10   xp_logevent syntax.**

```
xp_logevent {error_number, 'message'} [, 'severity']


Example:
EXEC master..xp_logevent 60000,'Test message'
```

You must supply an error number greater than 50000 to use the stored procedure in your code. The error number supplied does not have to coincide with a predefined SQL Server error number. Another option for getting data into the Windows NT event log is to use **RAISERROR** and the **WITH LOG** option as shown in Listing 12.11.

**Listing 12.11   RAISERROR using WITH LOG option.**

```
RAISERROR (60000,16,1,'INSERT','tbl_Address') WITH LOG
RAISERROR ('An error occurred',16,1) WITH LOG
```

# Creating an Error Handling Stored Procedure

An error handling stored procedure should gather the information that you believe to be complete enough to troubleshoot a problem should it occur on your server. Each environment is different, and you may have valid reasons for needing or not needing certain pieces of information. Earlier in this chapter, a simple error handling procedure was created that gathered information and placed it in the error log table. Let's enhance that procedure to gather a bit more information and handle transactions more effectively.

You can use the base code from **usp_ErrorLog** and make a few additions. Add the user id of the connection that has an error to your process. You also need to add a column to the error log table with the proper data type for the user id, and add the **user_id( )** function to your **INSERT** statement. See Listing 12.12 for the **ALTER TABLE** code to add a new column to **tbl_ErrorLog**.

### Listing 12.12 **ALTER TABLE** statement.

```
ALTER TABLE tbl_errorlog
  ADD ErrorUserID INT NULL
```

The stored procedure code should then be modified to get the user id from the system to populate the new column. Notice the selected lines of code that were changed in the **INSERT** statement to allow for the user id to be added to the error table without being passed into the procedure. (No other modifications are needed to the base procedure to facilitate this change.) See Listing 12.13 for a section of the **usp_ErrorLog** procedure where you must make a code change to support the new structure.

### Listing 12.13 Changed **INSERT** statement to allow for user id.

```
INSERT INTO tbl_ErrorLog (
  System_Error_Number,
  Process,
  Application,
  Error_Number,
  Description,
  Error_DateTime,
  ErrorUserID)
VALUES(
  @p_SystemErrorNumber,
  @p_Process,
  @p_Application,
  @p_ErrorNumber,
  @p_Description,
  @p_ErrorDateTime,
  USER_ID())
```

For the additional code in the **usp_ErrorLog** procedure, see Listing 12.3 in the "In Depth" section of this chapter. Feel free to modify this code as needed to handle any other situations that your environment may require. Typical modifications include transaction rollback logic, additional data elements, or process logging operations.

| Related solutions: | Found on page: |
| --- | --- |
| Using **INSERT/SELECT** | 435 |
| **usp_UPDKey** | 648 |
| Building and Executing Dynamic SQL | 834 |

# Load the Registry Table with Error Handling Key Values

The error handling procedures described in this chapter require four entries to be created in the **tbl_Registry** table in the Utility database. The four entries required are MaxErrors, PurgeDays, PurgeFile, and PurgeLocation. The MaxErrors entry provides a threshold number of errors in the table that generates another error to notify the administrator that a problem exists. PurgeDays specifies the number of days an error should remain in the error table before being purged to an archive file. The base file name for error archive files is stored in the PurgeFile key. The final value, PurgeLocation, specifies the path where the error archive files should be created. Listing 12.14 provides a script that adds the needed keys and sets default values for them. You should modify these values to suit your environment.

**Listing 12.14    Insert error handling Registry values.**

```
/* Switch Context to Utility Database */
USE Utility


/* Insert Registry Key Values */
INSERT INTO tbl_Registry
  ( Reg_Key, Reg_Value, date_created, date_modified )
  VALUES( 'System\ErrorHandling\MaxErrors',
          '100', GETDATE(), GETDATE() )
INSERT INTO tbl_Registry
  ( Reg_Key, Reg_Value, date_created, date_modified )
  VALUES( 'System\ErrorHandling\PurgeDays',
          '30', GETDATE(), GETDATE() )
INSERT INTO tbl_Registry
  ( Reg_Key, Reg_Value, date_created, date_modified )
  VALUES( 'System\ErrorHandling\PurgeFile',
          'ErrorLog_', GETDATE(), GETDATE() )
INSERT INTO tbl_Registry
  ( Reg_Key, Reg_Value, date_created, date_modified )
  VALUES( 'System\ErrorHandling\PurgeLocation',
          'c:\temp\', GETDATE(), GETDATE() )

/* Verify insertion */
SELECT *
  FROM tbl_Registry (NOLOCK)
  WHERE reg_key like 'System\ErrorHandling\%'
```

| Related solutions: | Found on page: |
|---|---|
| **usp_UPDKey** | 648 |
| Using the Registry Table | 387 |
| Building and Executing Dynamic SQL | 834 |

# Creating an Error Processing Stored Procedure

Paging the error log table to keep the number of rows to a minimum may not always be a good idea. Many people think that letting the table grow to a large size over time allows for improved trend analysis or better historical records. This may be true, but too much data in the error log can slow down performance of the actual logging operation.

To address this, a stored procedure can be created that becomes a scheduled job on the server to check the age of the rows in the error log table and write them out to a text file. The age is determined by an entry in the Registry table and is fully tunable by changing the value stored in **tbl_Registry**. The procedure in Listing 12.4 obtains the number of days to purge based on a comparison with the current date on the server. Any errors in the error log table that are older than the newly calculated date are written to a text file with a specific name and the date of the purge. Writing the data to a text file before deleting the rows allows you to manage the size of the log and not lose any data. To configure this stored procedure to run as a scheduled job on your server, follow these steps:

1. Create the procedure on your server in the Utility database by running the script named **usp_PurgeErrorLog**, which is located in the Chapter 12 directory on the CD-ROM.

2. In the Enterprise Manager, open the Management node, and expand the SQL Server Agent node.

3. Right-click on the Jobs object, and select New Job.

4. In the Name text box, type "Purge Error Log".

5. Select the Steps tab.

6. Click on New.

7. In the New Job Step dialog, add a step name of "Purge Log".

8. Change Database Context to Utility.

9. In the Command box, type "EXEC usp_PurgeErrorLog".

10. Click on the Schedule tab.

11. Click on New Schedule.

12. Type the name of the schedule for this job, "Purge Schedule".

13. Click on Change to adjust the schedule this job will use.

14. Select the Daily radio button, and click on OK to close the Schedule Properties dialog.

15. Click on OK to close the New Job Schedule dialog.

16. Click on OK to save this job.

# Implementing Error Handling in Stored Procedures and Triggers

Once you have created an error handling environment, the next challenge is to get a uniform error handling code technique in place. From the server's perspective, all stored procedures can implement error handling regardless of the client code being run against the database.

Your stored procedures and triggers should have some sort of error handling routine in place to check and validate each data operation to ensure that it performs functions as expected. You can use a standard piece of code in your SQL statements to call the **usp_ErrorLog** procedure. See Listing 12.15 for some code snippets that can be used to integrate error handling in your code. The source for this listing is located in the ErrorTemplate.sql file on the CD-ROM.

**NOTE:** *The placement of the **@@ERROR** value into a local variable immediately after a data modification command is important. If any other statement is evaluated, the value of **@@ERROR** is replaced with that statement's result and not the one that caused the error. This is the safest method to use to ensure that you can check and pass the error number to another procedure without losing the value.*

### Listing 12.15    Error handling snippets.

```
/* Add to variable declarations */
DECLARE @v_Error INTEGER

/* For each statement in process */
/* perform data modification    */
/* INSERT, UPDATE, DELETE or     */
/* Check condidtion failure      */
SELECT @v_Error = @@ERROR
```

```
IF (@v_Error <> 0)
BEGIN
  EXEC usp_ErrorLog
    @v_Error,             -- Internal error number
    '<Process>',          -- VARCHAR(50)
    '<Application>',      -- VARCHAR(50)
    NULL,                 -- Add RAISERROR # Here if used
    '<Error Message>'     -- Be descriptive

/* Stored Procedure */
--  RETURN -1
  RETURN
END -- Error Check

/* Example - Insert your SQL code in place of the line below*/
INSERT <...>
SELECT @v_Error = @@ERROR

IF (@v_Error <> 0)
BEGIN
  EXEC usp_ErrorLog
    @v_Error,             -- Internal error number
    'Insert Record',      -- VARCHAR(50)
    'Data Import',        -- VARCHAR(50)
    NULL,                 -- Add RAISERROR # Here if used
    'Failed to add a row during import' -- Be descriptive

  RETURN -1
END -- Error Check
```

The selected code in Listing 12.15 shows how a data import stored procedure would log an error inserting a row into a table. You would place the error handling code directly after the **INSERT** statement, and then update the process, application, and message parameters in the call to **usp_ErrorLog**. Thereafter, you would be done testing that condition of failure. You would then repeat this process for any **UPDATE**, **DELETE**, or data integrity check statements in the procedure or trigger to complete the integration.

---

**NOTE:** *Trigger error handling is implemented in the same way except that the transactional rollback must be taken into account in the trigger as well.*

---

The one piece to this puzzle that truly makes a systemwide impact is to get the client code to integrate a call to **usp_ErrorLog** on any error condition. As long as the client still has a connection to the database, you can send a logging command to **usp_ErrorLog** to get front-end errors logged and potentially taken into account for troubleshooting purposes. Each language has its own syntax for calling stored procedures, so examples of each are not listed. Use the appropriate syntax to call stored procedures for your development language to make the code changes in the client applications and fill in the parameters as completely as possible.

| *Related solutions:* | *Found on page:* |
| --- | --- |
| Using **INSERT/SELECT** | 435 |
| **usp_UPDKey** | 648 |
| Building and Executing Dynamic SQL | 834 |

# Chapter 13

# Cursors

# *In Depth*

With the introduction of relational databases, data access at the server has become set oriented rather than row oriented. This is a fundamental shift in the way data is managed and processed from the older row-based data access methodologies. Most client applications still tend to present and work with data in a more row-oriented manner. For instance, you might look at the information for an employee and drill down into more detailed information such as pay history and address information, and then step to the next employee in the list and perform the same or similar actions. To allow the client application to work with the data in a way that is more row oriented, a bridging technology had to be developed.

The technology used to bridge the two access methods is called a *cursor*. Cursors are used to provide a pointer to a particular row in a result set. Cursors can be either client-side or server-side depending on the platform and development environment being used. Many development environments provide a client-side cursor that works on the result set retrieved from the server in some temporary storage medium either in memory or on disk. This allows the client to retrieve a set of records using the set-oriented access methods required by the server, and then use the results in a row-oriented fashion.

Many of the Application Programming Interfaces (APIs) that provide access to SQL Server also provide some implementation of server-side cursors to allow row-oriented processing of data in a result set. The types of cursors supported will vary based on the version of SQL Server you are using, as well as the specific API being used to access the data.

Transact-SQL also provides functionality for using cursors directly on the server as part of your queries or stored procedures. This functionality allows you to write row-based operations directly in the Transact-SQL programming language without needing to involve a client application in the processing. The primary focus of this chapter is the cursors implemented by Transact-SQL. Some general information is also provided to help you become more familiar with the concepts of cursors and how they are implemented in various applications and APIs.

## Cursor Basics

This section provides some insight into why cursors exist and the dangers of working with them. From the seeds of necessity, a convenience has grown into what is now called a cursor. You must exercise extreme care not to confuse this convenient tool with the solution to all your database needs. You will see that although cursors were a necessary invention, they can easily be misused to the extreme detriment of performance.

## A Look at the Past

Sometimes, in order to understand where you are or where you are going, it is necessary to take a step back and look at where you have been. Until a relatively short time ago, most of the personal computer (PC) world (not mainframe or Unix) was constrained to use flat-file, row-based database systems. Indexed Sequential Access Method (ISAM) database management was the norm.

Database engines, like dBASE IV, FoxPro, BTrieve, and Access, were the primary tools that most developers used to provide database functionality in their applications. Using these database engines, data was accessed by locating and retrieving the record in the database that you wanted to perform an operation against. Using the information in this record, detailed records from related tables could also be located and retrieved in a similar fashion. Each of these operations had to be coded directly by the developer, and the relationship between these tables was generally known only to the application. The database engine neither knew nor cared about the actual data in the various tables (files) and the relationships that existed between them.

This type of access required you to position the record pointer for a particular table to the row you wanted to modify. As a result, updates and deletes required two separate operations. The first operation would locate the record to be updated or deleted and position the record pointer on the row. The second operation would actually perform the work of updating or deleting the "current" record. This is referred to as *positioned updating*.

Although this method of database access is cumbersome and somewhat inefficient, it remains the most familiar way of dealing with data for a large number of developers. Millions of lines of source code in a variety of languages have been written to use this model to manipulate and manage data, and most users are more familiar with this approach to data presentation as well.

## Enter the Relational Database

In the late 1980s and early 1990s, relational database technology snuck quietly into the PC world by way of OS/2, and then Windows 3.0. Although this technology had been widely used in the mainframe world for years, it had not previously been available in the PC environment. This technology slowly gained popularity and eventually jumped into the mainstream of business processing on PC networks. This server-based database technology was a huge change for many developers who were accustomed to working with the more traditional flat-file database structures available in the PC market. The only language that could access the early versions of these servers was C, which kept a large number of developers from moving in this direction in the beginning.

The relational database model is designed to work with set-based operations, which is a concept that many PC developers still don't fully grasp. Instead of dealing with a single record, this technology is designed to work with a record set. This requires a fundamental shift in the thought patterns applied to managing data.

There were numerous attempts to port existing applications to this new technology, which failed miserably because developers were unable to access the data in a manner that resembled what they were used to. Even when methods were devised to retrieve and update the data in a row-based fashion from these servers, the performance was extremely poor due to the overhead required to force this type of access.

This fundamental difference in the methods used to manipulate data caused may developers to abandon the relational database model in the early years. In an attempt to boost sales, the relational database platform developers realized that they needed to devise a way for the flat-file developers to access data in a way that was easier for them to relate to.

## Meeting in the Middle

The efforts to bridge the gap between flat-file developers and relational database server technology eventually resulted in what is now known as cursors. Cursors provide a mechanism for referring to a record set in a row-based manner. This was a necessary step in the evolution of the technology if relational databases were to become truly popular in the PC world.

Cursors have been implemented in a couple of different ways, which complement each other to produce a variety of ways to make use of this bridging technology. Client-side cursors allow the client to retrieve a record set to the local machine, and then access the data either in memory or on disk in a row-by-row manner. This can be a simple and easy-to-use option, but it can be a real problem for large record sets being managed over low-speed wide area network (WAN) connections. Fortunately, there are server-side cursors available to help eliminate some of this problem. Server-side cursors can consume more resources on the server, but they allow more restricted network traffic for the client to get the information it needs.

Server-side cursors are implemented through various APIs intended for use with relational database servers. In Microsoft SQL Server, server-side cursors are also implemented in the Transact-SQL programming language. Client-side cursors are generally implemented by the development language or tools used to access the server.

Although cursors have provided a necessary bridge between the worlds of flat file and relational data access, extreme care must be exercised to ensure that you do not use this tool to cripple the advantages of a relational database. The server is still designed for set-based access, and the inappropriate use of cursors can quickly reduce the performance of your server to unusable levels. Every effort must be made to learn the skills needed to make effective use of the power and flexibility of relational databases before you begin writing applications that use SQL Server.

## Writing ISAM Style Applications for SQL Server

Many developers, accustomed to the previous database management tools available in PC development environments, have a tendency to continue writing ISAM style applications when they move to SQL Server. These developers tend to voice constant complaints about the speed and stability of SQL Server. Developing ISAM style applications for SQL Server is like purchasing a $100 professional framing hammer and trying to pound nails by gripping the head of the hammer and pounding the nails with the handle. A tool can only perform well if it is used properly. There are a number of problems created by developing ISAM style applications for SQL Server.

Using cursors to manage data in the client application results in excessive requests to the SQL Server. This also produces a huge increase in network activity over set-based requests for the same data. An operation that could be performed by a simple join using set-based logic might require hundreds or even thousands of operations to retrieve the same data using row-based access methods. This overhead significantly lowers the performance of the server and database application.

Cursors are almost always less efficient than the equivalent set-based logic. For example, if you use a row-based updating scheme, each update requires positioning the cursor to the row to be updated, and then performing a second operation to update the row. This results in numerous operations to perform even a limited number of updates. Using the set-based update techniques provided in Transact-SQL, updates that affect multiple rows can be performed in a single operation. This reduces the overhead for both the server and the client application. Performing a large number of positional updates also lengthens the time that locks must be maintained for transactional integrity, which leads to increased concurrency problems.

# Understanding the Cursor Models

Probably the main difficulty that many developers and database administrators (DBAs) face when trying to understand cursors is the fact that there are three distinct models of cursors available. Each of these models has its own niche in terms of developing applications to work with SQL Server. This section provides some details about each of these models to help you better understand the role intended for them.

## API Cursors

Each of the three major APIs provided for client access to SQL Server (OLE DB, Open Database Connectivity [ODBC], and DB-Library) offers special cursor functions that are optimized for cursor operations and network use between the client application and SQL Server. Limiting the communication between the client application and the server is essential for developing high-performance applications. The best way to achieve a high level of performance is for the client to issue a single, brief command, and then have the server respond with the needed data. If each row returned by the cursor had to be individually requested by the client, the performance would be intolerable.

API cursors implement a more efficient communication between the client application and the server. The main feature that makes this interface more efficient is the capability to specify a "wide" cursor. Instead of the cursor pointing to a single row, it actually points to a set of rows. For example, the cursor might perform fetches in blocks of 25 rows rather than one row at a time. This might still be less efficient than a set-based operation, but it is much more efficient than requesting the data a single row at a time.

This capability is provided by the functions exposed in the API. For ODBC, the function is **SQLFetchScroll**, and for OLE DB, the function is **IRowSet::GetNextRows**. These functions are used instead of **DECLARE CURSOR** and **FETCH** when accessing the server from a programming language like Visual Basic (VB) or Delphi. The APIs also provide functions that offer options and capabilities not supported in Transact-SQL, such as defining the "width" (number of rows) of the cursor.

In addition, API cursors optimize the client/server interaction by only sending meta data information once for the cursor instead of sending it with each fetch operation. API cursors provide other functionality that is not supported by Transact-SQL, like the capability to declare a cursor on a stored procedure as long as the procedure returns only a single result set. The implementation of API cursors allows you to write more efficient and flexible applications with SQL Server than would be possible with only client-side and Transact-SQL cursors.

## Client-Side Cursors

The main purpose of a cursor is to maintain a data pointer within a set of records, which obviously makes it possible for this job to be performed at the client rather than the server. Because SQL Server did not originally ship with cursor support, many software designers wrote client-side cursor libraries to implement this functionality in their applications. These cursors had to be implemented in one of two ways.

One method of implementing a client-side cursor was to have the application retrieve a set of data from the server (sometimes an entire table) and store it in memory or on disk. The cursor libraries would allow this local set of data to be manipulated in an ISAM fashion, and the records would be updated back to the server. This was often done for all records without regard to which rows were actually changed. This method did not work particularly well in a multiuser environment because it was likely that more than one user needed the same data, and changes were likely to be lost without rigorous checking of the data being updated to prevent overwriting another user's changes.

More often, client-side cursors would request and work with a single row at a time from SQL Server. This meant requesting the needed row, making changes, and then putting the modified data back into SQL Server. This method was extremely inefficient for large data sets, but was somewhat better than the first method in a multiuser environment.

Both of these implementations suffered greatly on large data sets, especially when the tables were arranged with master detail relationships. For a master detail table arrangement, the row from the master table would be retrieved, and then each needed detail row would also need to be retrieved. Just imagine the amount of network and server traffic required to deal with a large database that contained multiple levels of master detail relationships.

Some developers consider client-side cursors obsolete with the API and Transact-SQL cursors that are currently available in SQL Server. In fact, client-side cursors can be the best option in some circumstances if used properly. If you need to present the user with a list of records and provide forward and backward scrolling capability, it may be more efficient to retrieve the entire set and provide the scrolling capability via client-side cursors on local storage. The need for "stateless" data management for the Internet and other multitier applications may also present situations where client-side cursors need to be implemented to provide the desired functionality to the client application. It is important to be extremely careful to avoid database locking and concurrency issues when working with stateless objects.

## Transact-SQL Cursors

SQL 2000 provides a fairly rich set of cursor functionality that can be used in stored procedures and other queries to perform row-by-row processing. Both ANSI SQL-92 cursors and the much more flexible Transact-SQL cursors are supported by SQL Server 2000. The basic syntax for both versions involves only a few simple commands: **DECLARE CURSOR**, **OPEN**, **FETCH**, **CLOSE**, and **DEALLOCATE**. These statements are used to create and work with cursors within your SQL code.

# Cursor Types

There are several types of cursors available in Transact-SQL. The type of cursor that is created is based on the options supplied in the **DECLARE CURSOR** command and the contents of the select statement specified to define the cursor. It is important to understand the types of cursors available as well as the benefits and limitations of each option. This section provides some insight into the various types of cursors and some factors that influence which one is generated based on how you define the cursor.

## Static Cursors

A static cursor creates a "snapshot" of the data defined by the select statement and stores it in tempdb. This type of cursor does not allow modifications to the underlying data in the cursor. One important detail to understand about a static cursor is the fact that modifications to the rows contained in the cursor by other users after the static row-set is established are not visible to the cursor. Rows that are inserted or deleted by other users also do not change the contents of the static row-set once it is created.

If you are using a static cursor, you should probably take time to consider whether a cursor is really appropriate to your situation. If you are working with a static, read-only copy of the data, it may be more appropriate to retrieve the entire record set and handle the processing with a client-side cursor. If the record set is too large to manage on the client, you may find that building and keeping it in tempdb presents some serious performance problems for the server.

Static cursors can be either scrollable or forward-only depending on how they are defined. Table 13.1 provides the keywords used in the **DECLARE CURSOR** command that generates a static cursor. The table also indicates whether the syntax is ANSI or Transact-SQL.

**Table 13.1   Static cursor declaration options.**

| Option | Syntax | Description |
|---|---|---|
| **INSENSITIVE** | ANSI | Defines a forward-only static cursor. You can add the **SCROLL** option to create a scrollable static cursor with the ANSI syntax. |
| **STATIC** | Transact-SQL | Defines a static cursor. Other options can be specified to establish whether or not the cursor is scrollable. |

## Keyset-Driven Cursors

A keyset-driven cursor uses a set of unique key values for every row that is qualified by the **SELECT** statement used to define the query. These key values are stored in tempdb. A keyset-driven cursor allows you to see the changes made to the rows that qualify for the **SELECT** statement when the cursor is opened, but rows that are added are not visible. If a row in the keyset is deleted, an attempt to access this row returns a **@@Fetch_Status** of **-2**. If you are using a keyset-driven cursor, this value is important to check to prevent erroneous results in cursor processing. It is also important to understand that a row still appears in the cursor even if subsequent changes to the data would no longer make it valid for the specified **SELECT** statement. Keyset-driven cursors also retain the original order in which the **SELECT** statement returns rows when the cursor is created. Subsequent changes to fields specified in the **ORDER BY** for the **SELECT** statement used to define the cursor will not change the order of the rows in the cursor.

If you create a keyset-driven cursor on a table that does not have a unique index, the cursor is automatically converted to a static cursor. A unique index is required to provide the set of keys used to retrieve the rows included in the cursor.

## Dynamic Cursors

Dynamic cursors allow you to see the changes made to underlying rows in the data set defined for the cursor. These changes can include inserted and deleted rows as well as changes to key fields that alter the order in which the rows are accessed by the cursor. Because the order of the underlying data can change for each **FETCH** statement, the use of the **ABSOLUTE** keyword is not supported for **FETCH** operations on dynamic cursors. This type of cursor must reapply the **SELECT** statement for each fetch operation to determine the current set of rows that qualify for the cursor's definition.

If an **ORDER BY** is specified for a dynamic cursor, the fields in the **ORDER BY** must be contained in an index. If the fields are not contained in an index, the cursor is automatically converted to either a keyset-driven cursor or a static cursor. Because a keyset-driven cursor requires a unique index to exist on the table, if a unique index is not present, the cursor is converted to a static cursor. If a unique index is present on the table, then the dynamic cursor is converted to a keyset-driven cursor when the **ORDER BY** fields are not contained in an index.

## FORWARD_ONLY Cursors

FORWARD_ONLY cursors are actually dynamic cursors that only support forward scrolling. This scrolling option is the recommended method for using Transact-SQL for row-by-row operations. The only **FETCH** option that is allowed for a

**FORWARD_ONLY** cursor is **NEXT**, which is specified to retrieve the next row in the cursor. These cursors require less overhead and resources due to the removal of the other scrolling and positioning options.

The forward-only method of accessing rows will probably cover 90 percent or more of the situations where you need to use Transact-SQL cursors in your batches and stored procedures. **FORWARD_ONLY** is the default type of cursor created when the **STATIC**, **DYNAMIC**, or **KEYSET** keywords are not specified in the **DECLARE CURSOR** statement. A **FORWARD_ONLY** cursor can be explicitly specified using the **FORWARD_ONLY** option in the **DECLARE CURSOR** statement.

There is a special type of **FORWARD_ONLY** cursor called a **FAST_FORWARD_ ONLY** cursor. This type of cursor is read-only in addition to being **FORWARD_ ONLY**. It eliminates even more overhead in the cursor processing and improves the performance of the cursor if you will not be making changes to the underlying data. It is still a dynamic cursor, so the changes to the underlying data made by other users is visible as you step through the result set. **FAST_FORWARD_ ONLY** cursors are specified by using the **FAST_FORWARD** option in the **DELCARE CURSOR** statement.

The same implicit conversions apply to **FORWARD_ONLY** and **FAST_FOR- WARD_ONLY** cursors as were mentioned in the section on dynamic cursors because these cursors are actually dynamic cursors with limited scrollability by default. You can also explicitly convert them to keyset-driven or static cursors by specifying the **KEYSET** or **STATIC** argument in the **DECLARE CURSOR** statement.

There are some additional conditions that cause a **FAST_FORWARD_ONLY** cursor to be implicitly converted to another type. If the select statement joins one or more tables with triggers to one or more tables without triggers, a static cursor is created instead of a **FAST_FORWARD_ONLY** cursor. If the **FOR UPDATE** option is used in the definition of a **FAST_FORWARD_ONLY** cursor, it is converted to a dynamic cursor. If a distributed query that references one or more remote tables is used in the **SELECT** statement that defines the cursor, the **FAST_ FORWARD_ONLY** cursor is converted to a keyset-driven cursor.

## Implicit Type Conversion Warnings

Because implicit type conversion is possible on a cursor, it is a good idea to take this into account when writing the code for your cursor. Unless you are specifying a static cursor or using the **TYPE_WARNING** option to generate a warning message when the cursor is created, you may find that the cursor is not behaving as you expected. The **TYPE_WARNING** option does not prevent the cursor from being created, but it at least provides feedback that alerts you to the change in functionality imposed by an implicit conversion to an alternate cursor type.

A special consideration needs to be made for keyset-driven cursors. When you are working with a keyset-driven cursor, it is possible to receive a **@@Fetch_Status** of **-2** when a row is encountered in the keyset that has been deleted since the cursor was deleted. Listing 13.1 shows a very simple example of a cursor that performs the needed checking on **@@Fetch_Status** to handle this condition. You should pay special attention to the highlighted line of code, which is handling the check for **@@Fetch_Status <> -2** before attempting to process the row. The **IF** statement used to check this value skips processing rows that have been deleted, but notice that the **FETCH NEXT** for the **WHILE** loop is placed outside the **IF** so that the next row in the record set will be fetched regardless of the existence of the current row. If you place the **FETCH NEXT** inside the **WHILE**, you end up with an endless loop when you encounter a record that has been deleted.

**Listing 13.1   Kcyset-driven cursor example.**

```
DECLARE c_TestCursor CURSOR
  LOCAL FORWARD_ONLY KEYSET
  FOR SELECT au_fname + ' ' + au_lname
        FROM pubs.dbo.authors
        ORDER BY au_lname, au_fname


DECLARE @v_name varchar(50)


OPEN c_TestCursor
FETCH NEXT FROM c_TestCursor INTO @v_name


WHILE (@@Fetch_Status <> -1)
  BEGIN
    /* Check for deleted row */
    IF (@@Fetch_Status <> -2)
      BEGIN
      /* Display who we are processing */
      PRINT 'Processing: ' + @v_name

      /* Perform some processing Task Here */
      END
  FETCH NEXT FROM c_TestCursor INTO @v_name
  END

/* Even though it is a local cursor, it is good practice to */
/* close and deallocate any cursors you create.            */
CLOSE c_TestCursor
DEALLOCATE c_TestCursor
GO
```

Performing the checks in a manner that is safe for keyset-driven cursors is a good idea in any situation where an implicit conversion to a keyset-driven cursor is possible. The examples provided by most books and all but one or two examples in the Books Online indicate checking for **@@Fetch_Status = 0** for the **WHILE** loop and no checking of the **@@Fetch_Status** inside the loop at all. Because the additional checking required for keyset-driven cursors is minimal and will work correctly for any type of cursor, it might be a good idea to get in the habit of using the additional check in all of your cursors. If you always use this syntax for your cursors, then you can be sure that you will not receive erroneous results when an implicit conversion to a keyset-driven cursor occurs.

# Local and Global Cursors

Transact-SQL provides two keywords, local and global, which can be used to set the scope of a cursor when it is created. Specifying a local cursor means that it can only be seen and referenced within the batch, trigger, or stored procedure in which it was created. A local cursor is implicitly deallocated at the end of the batch or procedure in which it was created, or when the connection is terminated. The only exception is if the cursor is returned from the procedure as an **OUTPUT** parameter. If the cursor is returned from a stored procedure as an **OUTPUT** parameter, it is implicitly deallocated when the last variable referencing it goes out of scope or gets deallocated.

Global cursors are available for the life of the connection. They can be referenced by any batch or stored procedure executed in the connection. A global cursor must be explicitly deallocated before attempting to redeclare it for the same connection. Global cursors are implicitly deallocated only when the connection is terminated.

Even though a cursor will be implicitly deallocated either at the end of the procedure or when the connection terminates, it is considered poor programming form to skip the **CLOSE** and **DEALLOCATE** commands for a cursor. Regardless of the scope of a cursor, you should always **CLOSE** and **DEALLOCATE** a cursor when you are finished with it to release the resources back to SQL Server as soon as possible.

If neither of these keywords is used to declare the scope of the cursor in the **DECLARE CURSOR** statement, the **CURSOR_DEFAULT** database option determines whether the cursor is created as a local or global cursor. The **CURSOR_DEFAULT** option is discussed in the "Cursor Related Database Options" section later in this chapter. It is actually best to specify whether you want a local or global cursor in the **DECLARE CURSOR** statement to avoid scope issues later if the database option is changed. If you declare a cursor using the ANSI SQL-92 syntax, the cursor will exist within the default scope specified by the **CURSOR_DEFAULT** database option.

# Transact-SQL Syntax

The remainder of this chapter focuses on the syntax and uses of Transact-SQL cursors. Where appropriate, the ANSI cursor syntax is provided as a reference, but the feature set that is provided by the extended Transact-SQL syntax renders the ANSI implementation pale by comparison. The use of cursors is definitely one area where making use of the product-specific functionality enhancements is a must for optimizing your applications.

The following sections cover the syntax needed to work with cursors in Transact-SQL. Each of the major commands is presented along with the various options and arguments available. You are also provided with the basic knowledge necessary to begin using cursors in your Transact-SQL scripts.

## DECLARE CURSOR

In order to use a cursor in Transact-SQL, you must first declare the cursor. This provides a definition of the record set that the cursor will be used against as well as defines the characteristics of the cursor. There are two syntax variations supported by SQL Server 2000 for declaring cursors. Both the ANSI SQL-92 syntax and the Transact-SQL syntax are covered in the following sections, and the applicable arguments for each are described.

Once the cursor has been declared, the remaining cursor commands apply to both the ANSI SQL-92 syntax and the Transact-SQL syntax.

### ANSI SQL-92 Syntax

This chapter focuses mainly on the Transact-SQL cursor syntax because it provides a much more robust feature set than the ANSI SQL-92 syntax. However, because the ANSI SQL-92 syntax is supported by SQL Server 2000, the syntax is provided in this section. Listing 13.2 provides the syntax for creating a cursor using the ANSI SQL-92 compliant syntax.

Listing 13.2   ANSI SQL-92 **DECLARE CURSOR** syntax.

```
DECLARE cursor_name [ INSENSITIVE ] [ SCROLL ] CURSOR
  FOR select_statement
  [ FOR { READ ONLY | UPDATE [ OF column_name [ ,...n ] ] } ]
```

The arguments used to declare a cursor using the ANSI SQL-92 syntax are explained in the following list. The list is fairly short due to the limited cursor functionality that is supported by the ANSI SQL-92 standard.

- *cursor_name*—Is the name of the Transact-SQL server cursor being defined. *cursor_name* must conform to the rules for identifiers.

- **INSENSITIVE**—Is used to define a cursor that makes a temporary copy of the data to be used by the cursor. All requests to the cursor are answered from this temporary table in tempdb. Any modifications made to base tables are not reflected in the data returned by fetches made against this cursor. This type of cursor does not allow modifications to the underlying data in the cursor. **INSENSITIVE** can be omitted to have committed deletes and updates made to the underlying tables (by any user) reflected in subsequent fetches.

- **SCROLL**—Specifies that all fetch options (**FIRST**, **LAST**, **PRIOR**, **NEXT**, **RELATIVE**, **ABSOLUTE**) are available. If **SCROLL** is not specified, **NEXT** is the only fetch option supported.

- *select_statement*—Is a standard **SELECT** statement that defines the result set of the cursor. The keywords **COMPUTE**, **COMPUTE BY**, **FOR BROWSE**, and **INTO** are not allowed within the **SELECT** statement of a cursor declaration. (SQL Server implicitly converts the cursor to another type if clauses in *select_statement* conflict with the functionality of the requested cursor type.)

- **READ ONLY**—Prevents updates from being made through this cursor. The cursor cannot be referenced in a **WHERE CURRENT OF** clause in an **UPDATE** or **DELETE** statement. By default, cursors have the capability to be updated.

- **UPDATE [OF *column_name* [,...*n*]]**—Defines the updatable columns within the cursor. If **OF *column_name* [,...*n*]** is specified, only the columns listed will allow modifications. Specify **UPDATE** without a column list to allow all columns to be updated.

### Transact-SQL Extended Syntax

Transact-SQL provides a number of extensions to the ANSI SQL-92 standard. The syntax for declaring a cursor using this extended syntax is provided in Listing 13.3. The syntax may look more complex than the ANSI SQL-92 syntax, but a simple cursor is still declared almost identically. The additional options are used to extend (or limit) the functionality of a Transact-SQL cursor.

**Listing 13.3    Transact-SQL extended DECLARE CURSOR syntax.**

```
DECLARE cursor_name CURSOR [ LOCAL | GLOBAL ]
  [ FORWARD_ONLY | SCROLL ]
  [ STATIC | KEYSET | DYNAMIC | FAST_FORWARD ]
  [ READ_ONLY | SCROLL_LOCKS | OPTIMISTIC ]
  [ TYPE_WARNING ]
  FOR select_statement
  [ FOR UPDATE [ OF column_name [ ,...n ] ] ]
```

The arguments used to declare a cursor with the extended syntax are explained in the following list. Some of these arguments are similar to the ANSI SQL-92 syntax, and others provide the Transact-SQL cursors with a wider range of functionality options.

- *cursor_name*—Is the name of the Transact-SQL server cursor being defined. *cursor_name* must conform to the rules for identifiers.

- **LOCAL**—Specifies that the scope of the cursor is local to the batch, stored procedure, or trigger in which the cursor was created. The cursor name is valid only within this scope. The cursor can be referenced by local cursor variables in the batch, stored procedure, trigger, or a stored procedure **OUTPUT** parameter, which is used to pass the local cursor back to the calling batch, stored procedure, or trigger. The calling procedure can then assign the parameter to a cursor variable to reference the cursor after the stored procedure terminates. The cursor is implicitly deallocated when the batch, stored procedure, or trigger terminates, unless the cursor was passed back in an **OUTPUT** parameter, in which case, the cursor is deallocated when the last variable referencing it is deallocated or goes out of scope.

- **GLOBAL**—Specifies that the scope of the cursor is global to the connection. The cursor name can be referenced in any stored procedure or batch executed by the connection. The only time the cursor is implicitly disconnected is when the connection is closed.

  If neither **GLOBAL** nor **LOCAL** is specified, the default is controlled by setting it to local cursor database option. Previous versions of SQL Server supported only **GLOBAL** cursors, so you can set this as the default to preserve this behavior for legacy systems.

- **FORWARD_ONLY**—Specifies that the cursor can only be scrolled from one record to the next in a forward direction. The only supported fetch option for this type of cursor is **FETCH NEXT**. If **FORWARD_ONLY** is specified without the **STATIC**, **KEYSET**, or **DYNAMIC** keywords, the cursor operates as a **DYNAMIC** cursor. When neither **FORWARD_ONLY** nor **SCROLL** is specified, **FORWARD_ONLY** is generally the default. **STATIC**, **KEYSET**, and **DYNAMIC** cursors default to **SCROLL**. Unlike database APIs, such as ODBC and ActiveX Data Objects (ADO), **FORWARD_ONLY** is supported with **STATIC**, **KEYSET**, and **DYNAMIC** Transact-SQL cursors. You cannot specify both **FAST_FORWARD** and **FORWARD_ONLY** for the same cursor.

- **STATIC**—Defines a cursor that makes a temporary copy of the data to be used by the cursor. All requests to the cursor are answered from this temporary table in tempdb. Modifications made to base tables are not reflected in the data returned by fetches made to this cursor, and this cursor does not allow modifications.

- **KEYSET**—The membership and order of rows in the cursor are fixed at the time the cursor is opened. The table is created in tempdb to hold the set of keys that uniquely identify the rows. This table is known as the *keyset*. Changes to non-key values in the underlying tables, whether made by the cursor owner or committed by other users, are visible as the owner scrolls through the cursor. Newly inserted rows from any source are not visible. If a row is deleted, an attempt to fetch the row returns a **@@Fetch_Status** of **-2**. Updates of key values from outside the cursor resemble a delete of the old row followed by an insert of the new row. The row with the new values is not visible, and attempts to fetch the row with the old values return a **@@Fetch_ Status** of **-2**. The new values are visible if the update is done through the cursor by specifying the **WHERE CURRENT OF** clause.

- **DYNAMIC**—Defines a cursor that reflects all data changes made to the rows in its result set as you scroll through the cursor. The data values, order, and membership of the rows can change on each fetch. Dynamic cursors do not support the **ABSOLUTE** fetch option.

- **FAST_FORWARD**—Specifies a **FORWARD_ONLY**, **READ_ONLY** cursor with performance optimizations enabled. **FAST_FORWARD** cannot be specified in conjunction with the **SCROLL** or **FOR_UPDATE** options. You cannot specify both **FAST_FORWARD** and **FORWARD_ONLY** for the same cursor.

- **READ ONLY**—Prevents updates from being made through this cursor. The cursor cannot be referenced in a **WHERE CURRENT OF** clause in an **UPDATE** or **DELETE** statement. By default, cursors have the capability to be updated.

- **SCROLL_LOCKS**—Specifies that positioned updates or deletes made through the cursor are guaranteed to succeed. SQL Server locks the rows as they are read into the cursor to ensure their availability for modification. **SCROLL_LOCKS** cannot be specified in conjunction with the **FAST_FORWARD** option.

- **OPTIMISTIC**—Specifies that positioned updates or deletes made through the cursor should not succeed if the row has been updated since it was read into the cursor. SQL Server does not lock the rows as they are read into the cursor. Instead, it uses comparisons of timestamp column values, or a checksum value if no timestamp column is available, to determine whether the row was modified after it was read into the cursor. If the row has been modified, the attempted positioned update or delete will fail. **OPTIMISTIC** cannot be specified in conjunction with the **FAST_FORWARD** option.

- **TYPE_WARNING**—Is a warning message that is sent to the client if the cursor is implicitly converted from the requested type to another.

- *select_statement*—Is a standard **SELECT** statement that defines the result set of the cursor. The keywords **COMPUTE**, **COMPUTE BY**, **FOR BROWSE**, and **INTO** are not allowed within the **SELECT** statement of a cursor declaration.

(SQL Server implicitly converts the cursor to another type if clauses in **select_statement** conflict with the functionality of the requested cursor type.)

- **UPDATE [OF *column_name* [,...n]]**—Defines the updatable columns within the cursor. If **OF *column_name* [,...n]** is specified, only the columns listed will allow modifications. Specify **UPDATE** without a column list to allow all columns to be updated.

## OPEN

Once a cursor has been declared using either the Transact-SQL syntax or the ANSI SQL-92 syntax, it must be opened before it can be used in your procedure or batch code. The syntax **OPEN** command is provided in Listing 13.4. This command actually executes the **SELECT** statement specified in the cursor declaration to populate the cursor.

**Listing 13.4   OPEN cursor syntax.**

```
OPEN { { [ GLOBAL ] cursor_name } | cursor_variable_name }
```

The **OPEN** command has a very simple syntax with very few arguments. The arguments supported by the **OPEN** statement are explained in the following list.

- **GLOBAL**—Specifies that *cursor_name* refers to a global cursor.

- *cursor_name*—Is the name of a declared cursor. If both a global and a local cursor exist with *cursor_name* as their name, *cursor_name* refers to the global cursor if **GLOBAL** is specified; otherwise, *cursor_name* refers to the local cursor.

- *cursor_variable_name*—Is the name of a cursor variable that references a cursor.

## FETCH

The **FETCH** command is used to retrieve data from the cursor once it has been declared and opened. Once again, the **FETCH** command syntax is the same whether the cursor was declared using the ANSI SQL-92 or Transact-SQL syntax. The **FETCH** command has a number of arguments that allow you to control which row should be retrieved from the cursor when the command is issued. Listing 13.5 shows the syntax for the **FETCH** command. Some arguments are only available for specific cursor types.

**Listing 13.5   FETCH syntax.**

```
FETCH [ [ NEXT | PRIOR | FIRST | LAST

            | ABSOLUTE { n | @nvar }
            | RELATIVE { n | @nvar }
      ] FROM ]
```

```
{ { [ GLOBAL ] cursor_name } | @cursor_variable_name }
[ INTO @variable_name [ ,...n ] ]
```

The following list provides a description of the arguments that can be used with the **FETCH** command. The description for each argument also indicates any compatibility issues with regard to the type of cursor being used. These limitations are important to understand because they can present problems when an implicit conversion occurs in the type of cursor you are using. An implicit conversion can cause **FETCH** options that are perfectly valid for the cursor type you specified to generate an error indicating that the specified action is not valid for the type of cursor you are using.

- **NEXT**—Returns the result row immediately following the current row in the cursor. The row pointer is advanced to the row returned. If **FETCH NEXT** is the first fetch against a cursor, it returns the first row in the result set. **FETCH NEXT** is the default cursor fetch option.

- **PRIOR**—Returns the result row immediately preceding the current row in the cursor. The row pointer is decremented to the row returned. If **FETCH PRIOR** is the first fetch against a cursor, no row is returned, and the cursor is left positioned before the first row. This option is not allowed for **FORWARD_ONLY** and **FAST_FORWARD** cursors.

- **FIRST**—Returns the first row in the cursor and makes it the current row. This option is not allowed for **FORWARD_ONLY** and **FAST_FORWARD** cursors.

- **LAST**—Returns the last row in the cursor and makes it the current row. This option is not allowed for **FORWARD_ONLY** and **FAST_FORWARD** cursors.

- **ABSOLUTE {*n* | *@nvar*}**—If *n* or *@nvar* is positive, the row *n* position from the top of the row set defined in the cursor is returned and the returned row becomes the new current row. If *n* or *@nvar* is negative, the row *n* position from the bottom of the row set defined in the cursor is returned and the returned row becomes the new current row. If *n* or *@nvar* is **0**, no row is returned. *n* must be an integer constant and *@nvar* must be of type smallint, tinyint, or int.

- **RELATIVE {*n* | *@nvar*}**—If *n* or *@nvar* is positive, the row *n* position below the current row is returned and the returned row becomes the new current row. If *n* or *@nvar* is negative, the row *n* position above the current row is returned and the returned row becomes the new current row. If *n* or *@nvar* is **0**, the current row is returned. If **FETCH RELATIVE** is specified with *n* or *@nvar* set to negative numbers or **0** on the first fetch done against a cursor, no rows are returned. *n* must be an integer constant and *@nvar* must be of type smallint, tinyint, or int.

- **GLOBAL**—Specifies that *cursor_name* refers to a global cursor.

- ***cursor_name***—Is the name of an open cursor from which the fetch should be made. If both a global and a local cursor exist with ***cursor_name*** as their name, the inclusion or exclusion of the **GLOBAL** argument determines which cursor is being referred to by the **FETCH** command.

- ***@cursor_variable_name***—Is the name of a cursor variable referencing the open cursor from which the fetch should be made.

- **INTO** ***@variable_name[,...n]***—Allows data from the columns of a fetch to be placed into local variables. Each variable in the list, from left to right, is associated with the corresponding column in the cursor result set. The data type of each variable must either match exactly or support an implicit conversion from the data type of the corresponding result-set column. The number and order of variables must exactly match the columns in the cursor select list.

## CLOSE

The **CLOSE** command releases the current result set and frees any locks held by the cursor. Although it is true that deallocating the cursor (whether implicitly or explicitly) closes the cursor, it is considered poor programming practice to skip this step. You should issue a **CLOSE** command for every cursor before deallocating it. Listing 13.6 provides the syntax for the **CLOSE** command.

**Listing 13.6  CLOSE syntax.**

```
CLOSE { { [ GLOBAL ] cursor_name } | cursor_variable_name }
```

Like the **OPEN** statement, the **CLOSE** statement has very few parameters. The arguments that are available for the **CLOSE** command are explained in the following list. One important detail to remember is that a cursor can be closed and reopened as many times as you desire until it is deallocated. You cannot redeclare a cursor, however, until it has been deallocated.

- **GLOBAL**—Specifies that ***cursor_name*** refers to a global cursor.

- ***cursor_name***—Is the name of a declared cursor. If both a global and a local cursor exist with ***cursor_name*** as their name, ***cursor_name*** refers to the global cursor if **GLOBAL** is specified; otherwise, ***cursor_name*** refers to the local cursor.

- ***cursor_variable_name***—Is the name of a cursor variable that references a cursor.

## DEALLOCATE

A cursor is referenced by either a cursor name or a cursor variable. The **DEALLOCATE** command is used to remove this reference. When the last reference to a cursor has been deallocated, the data structures comprising the cursor and any resources it is using are freed. If the cursor has not yet been closed, the close is performed implicitly when the cursor is deallocated.

Listing 13.7 provides the syntax for the **DEALLOCATE** command. This command should be issued for every cursor reference in your batch, trigger, or stored procedure. Even though the cursor is implicitly deallocated when it goes out of scope, it is considered poor programming practice to skip this step. A cursor must be deallocated before it can be redeclared.

**Listing 13.7    DEALLOCATE syntax.**

```
DEALLOCATE { { [ GLOBAL ] cursor_name } | @cursor_variable_name }
```

There are only a few arguments that can be used with the **DEALLOCATE** command. These arguments are explained in the following list:

- **GLOBAL**—Specifies that *cursor_name* refers to a global cursor.

- *cursor_name*—Is the name of a declared cursor. If both a global and a local cursor exist with *cursor_name* as their name, *cursor_name* refers to the global cursor if **GLOBAL** is specified; otherwise, *cursor_name* refers to the local cursor.

- *@cursor_variable_name*—Is the name of a cursor variable that references a cursor.

# System Functions That Support Cursors

Along with the cursor functionality that is provided by the Transact-SQL and ANSI SQL-92 cursor syntax, SQL Server also provides a function and two global system variables that provide information to assist you in working with cursors. The following sections provide details on how to use the information provided by these functions and variables.

## CURSOR_STATUS

The **CURSOR_STATUS( )** function allows you to determine the current status of a cursor or cursor variable. This function is valid with both local and global cursors as well as cursor variables. The syntax for using the **CURSOR_STATUS( )** function is provided in Listing 13.8.

**Listing 13.8    CURSOR_STATUS syntax.**

```
CURSOR_STATUS
    (
        { 'local' , 'cursor_name' }
        | { 'global' , 'cursor_name' }
        | { 'variable' , 'cursor_variable' }
    )
```

The following arguments can be passed to the function:

- **LOCAL**—Indicates the cursor is a local cursor name.
- **GLOBAL**—Indicates the cursor is a global cursor name.
- *cursor_name*—Is the name of the cursor.
- **variable**—Indicates the cursor is a local variable.
- *cursor_variable*—Is the name of the cursor variable.

This function returns a **TINYINT** value that indicates the status of the cursor that was specified in the function arguments. The return values from this function are explained in Table 13.2. This function can be a useful debugging tool when working with cursors and can provide a way to check the status of a cursor parameter returned from a stored procedure before attempting to access it.

## @@Cursor_Rows

The **@@Cursor_Rows** variable contains the number of rows qualified by the **SELECT** statement used to define the most recently opened cursor on the connection. Depending on the type of cursor opened, the result of this variable will not necessarily be a positive row count. Table 13.3 provides the possible return values from this variable and how they should be interpreted.

## @@Fetch_Status

**@@Fetch_Status** returns the status of the last **FETCH** command issued for the connection. The **@@fetch_status** is global to all cursors on a connection, so care must be exercised to ensure that the value is meaningful when it is checked. It is

**Table 13.2  CURSOR_STATUS return values.**

| Return Value | Cursor Argument | Description |
|---|---|---|
| 1 | cursor name or cursor variable | The cursor is open. For static, insensitive, and keyset cursors, the cursor result set contains at least one row. |
| 0 | cursor name or cursor variable | The result set for the cursor is empty. This status code does not apply to dynamic cursors, which will return a 1 instead. |
| -1 | cursor name or cursor variable | The cursor is closed. |
| -2 | cursor variable | No cursor is assigned to the variable, or the cursor that was assigned to the OUTPUT parameter of a stored procedure was closed at the end of the procedure and has therefore been deallocated. |
| -3 | cursor name or cursor variable | The cursor name or cursor variable does not exist. If the cursor variable does exist, it has not had a cursor assigned to it. |

**Table 13.3   @@Cursor_Rows return values.**

| Return Value | Description |
| --- | --- |
| -n | If the cursor is populated asynchronously, the number reflects the number of rows currently in the keyset. **ABS**(-n) will yield the actual row count. |
| -1 | This value indicates that the cursor is dynamic. Because a dynamic cursor reflects all changes in the underlying data including inserts and deletions, the number of qualifying rows in the result set is not guaranteed to be the same from one **FETCH** command to the next. |
| 0 | No cursors have been opened, no rows qualified for the last cursor opened, or the last opened cursor has been closed. |
| n | The cursor is fully populated, and n indicates the total number of qualifying rows in the cursor result set. |

a good idea to check the **@@fetch_status** immediately after the **FETCH** command to avoid erroneous results. This variable can return three possible values, which are explained in Table 13.4.

Checking **@@Fetch_Status** must be done carefully to ensure proper and consistent cursor processing. If you are using an explicit or implicit keyset-driven cursor, you must check for the **-2** return value before attempting to process the row returned by the **FETCH** operation. You also do not want to exit the cursor in the event that the current row is missing from the result set. Listing 13.9 provides code snippets of a bad example of checking the **@@Fetch_Status** for a cursor, along with a good example of the same check. In the bad example, the **@@Fetch_Status** must be **0** for the **WHILE** loop to continue. (These are not complete listings and they cannot be executed without declaring an appropriate cursor.) If a missing row is encountered, the loop will terminate and any remaining rows will be skipped as well. The code in the good example takes the missing row possibility into account by checking for a value of **-1** to terminate the **WHILE** loop and skipping processing for any row where a **-2** is returned indicating that the row is missing.

Although the **-2** return value is only applicable to keyset-driven cursors, it does not hurt to perform this check for any cursor that you use. It is a good habit to check for both return values, so that any implicit cursor conversion that results in a keyset-driven cursor will not cause the cursor processing logic to fail or behave erratically.

**Table 13.4   @@Fetch_Status return values.**

| Return Value | Description |
| --- | --- |
| 0 | The **FETCH** operation was successful. |
| -1 | The **FETCH** operation failed or the requested row was beyond the result set. |
| -2 | The requested row was missing. This only applies to keyset-driven cursors. |

**Listing 13.9  Checking the result of FETCH commands using @@Fetch_Status.**

```
--Bad Example:
/* Get first row */
FETCH NEXT FROM @v_Cursor INTO @v_SomeVar

/* Loop through cursor rows */
WHILE (@@Fetch_Status = 0)
  BEGIN
  /* Perform processing here */

  /* Get next row */
  FETCH NEXT FROM @v_Cursor INTO @v_SomeVar
  END

--Good Example:
/* Get first row */
FETCH NEXT FROM @v_Cursor INTO @v_SomeVar

/* Loop through cursor rows */
WHILE (@@Fetch_Status <> -1)
  BEGIN
  /* If the row has not been deleted */
  IF (@@Fetch_Status <> -2)
    BEGIN
    /* Perform processing here */
    END

  /* Get next row */
  FETCH NEXT FROM @v_Cursor INTO @v_SomeVar
  END
```

# System Stored Procedures That Support Cursors

SQL Server 2000 provides some system stored procedures that can be used to return information about cursors defined within the scope of the current connection. Each of these stored procedures returns a cursor variable instead of a result set to allow your SQL code to work with the information one row at a time.

## sp_cursor_list

The **sp_cursor_list** stored procedure is used to return a list of the cursors open in the current connection. Only two parameters are required for this procedure, which are shown in Listing 13.10. The first parameter is a cursor variable to hold the cursor returned by the procedure. The second parameter is the cursor scope to return the list for. You have three scope options: 1—local cursors, 2—global cursors, and 3—both local and global cursors.

### Listing 13.10   **sp_cursor_list** syntax.

```
sp_cursor_list [ @cursor_return = ] cursor_variable_name OUTPUT,
                    [ @cursor_scope = ] cursor_scope
```

The cursor returned by **sp_cursor_list** describes each cursor and provides information about the current status of each cursor. The code in Listing 13.11 can be used to output this information in a readable form that can be used in the Query Analyzer to examine the information about the cursors you have used on the current connection for debugging purposes. This code is also provided as an example of how to process and interpret the information returned in the cursor variable. Refer to Chapter 19 for information about some of the techniques used to make this report more readable.

### Listing 13.11   Process and display information from **sp_cursor_list**.

```
/* Create test cursor */
USE Address
GO

DECLARE c_TestCursor CURSOR
  GLOBAL
  FOR SELECT a.Line1,
            c.Name AS City,
            s.State_Code AS State,
            z.Zip5 AS ZIP
        FROM tbl_Address a (NOLOCK)
        JOIN tbl_City c (NOLOCK) ON c.City_ID = a.City_ID
        JOIN tbl_State s (NOLOCK) ON s.State_ID = c.State_ID
        JOIN tbl_ZipCode z (NOLOCK) ON z.Zip_ID = a.Zip_ID


OPEN c_TestCursor

/* Declare Cursor variable and variables for each cursor column */
DECLARE @v_Cursor CURSOR,
        @v_ReferenceName SYSNAME,
        @v_CursorName SYSNAME,
        @v_CursorScope SMALLINT,
        @v_Status SMALLINT,
        @v_Model SMALLINT,
        @v_Concurrency SMALLINT,
        @v_Scrollable SMALLINT,
        @v_OpenStatus SMALLINT,
        @v_CursorRows INT,
```

```
            @v_FetchStatus SMALLINT,
            @v_ColumnCount SMALLINT,
            @v_RowCount SMALLINT,
            @v_LastOperation SMALLINT,
            @v_CursorHandle INT

/* Get list of cursors */
EXEC sp_cursor_list @v_Cursor OUTPUT, 3

/* Get first cursor row */
FETCH NEXT FROM @v_Cursor INTO @v_ReferenceName,
                              @v_CursorName,
                              @v_CursorScope,
                              @v_Status,
                              @v_Model,
                              @v_Concurrency,
                              @v_Scrollable,
                              @v_OpenStatus,
                              @v_CursorRows,
                              @v_FetchStatus,
                              @v_ColumnCount,
                              @v_RowCount,
                              @v_LastOperation,
                              @v_CursorHandle

/* Print Headings */
PRINT 'Reference Name             Cursor Name                  Scope   '+
      'Status Model            Concurrency  Scrollable   Open Status '+
      'Cursor Rows Fetch Status Column Count Row Count Last Operation '+
      'Handle'
PRINT '------------------------ ------------------------- ------ '+
      '------ ---------------- ------------ ------------ ---------- '+
      '---------- ------------ ------------ -------- -------------- '+
      '----------'

/* Loop through cursor rows */
WHILE (@@Fetch_Status <> -1)
  BEGIN
  /* If the row has not been deleted */
  IF (@@Fetch_Status <> -2)
    BEGIN
    /* Print the cursor information */
    PRINT CONVERT(CHAR(25), @v_ReferenceName) + ' ' +
          CONVERT(CHAR(25), @v_CursorName) + ' ' +
          /* Output Scope in readable form */
```

```
            CASE @v_CursorScope WHEN 1 THEN 'LOCAL   '
                                WHEN 2 THEN 'GLOBAL  '
                                ELSE 'UNKNOWN' END + ' ' +
      CONVERT(CHAR(6), @v_Status) + ' ' +
      /* Output Model in readable form */
      CASE @v_Model WHEN 1 THEN 'Static           '
                    WHEN 2 THEN 'Keyset-Driven    '
                    WHEN 3 THEN 'Dynamic          '
                    WHEN 4 THEN 'Fast Forward-Only'
                    ELSE 'UNKNOWN          ' END + ' ' +
      /* Output Concurrency in readable form */
      CASE @v_Concurrency WHEN 1 THEN 'Read-Only   '
                          WHEN 2 THEN 'Scroll Locks'
                          WHEN 3 THEN 'Optimistic  '
                          ELSE 'UNKNOWN     ' END + ' ' +
      /* Output Scrollable in readable form */
      CASE @v_Scrollable WHEN 0 THEN 'Forward-Only'
                         WHEN 1 THEN 'Scrollable  '
                         ELSE 'UNKNOWN     ' END + ' ' +
      /* Output Open Status in readable form */
      CASE @v_OpenStatus WHEN 0 THEN 'Closed      '
                         WHEN 1 THEN 'Open        '
                         ELSE 'UNKNOWN     ' END + ' ' +
      CONVERT(CHAR(11), @v_CursorRows) + ' ' +
      /* Output Fetch Status in readable form */
      CASE @v_FetchStatus WHEN  0 THEN 'Succeded    '
                          WHEN -1 THEN 'Failed      '
                          WHEN -2 THEN 'Missing Row '
                          WHEN -9 THEN 'N/A         '
                          ELSE 'UNKNOWN     ' END + ' ' +
      CONVERT(CHAR(12), @v_ColumnCount) + ' ' +
      CONVERT(CHAR(9), @v_RowCount) + ' ' +
      /* Output Last Operation in readable form */
      CASE @v_LastOperation WHEN 0 THEN 'N/A        '
                            WHEN 1 THEN 'Open       '
                            WHEN 2 THEN 'Fetch      '
                            WHEN 3 THEN 'Insert     '
                            WHEN 4 THEN 'Update     '
                            WHEN 5 THEN 'Delete     '
                            WHEN 6 THEN 'Close      '
                            WHEN 7 THEN 'Deallocate '
                            ELSE 'UNKNOWN    ' END + ' ' +
      CONVERT(CHAR(11), @v_CursorHandle)
END
```

```
        /* Get next cursor row */
        FETCH NEXT FROM @v_Cursor INTO @v_ReferenceName,
                                      @v_CursorName,
                                      @v_CursorScope,
                                      @v_Status,
                                      @v_Model,
                                      @v_Concurrency,
                                      @v_Scrollable,
                                      @v_OpenStatus,
                                      @v_CursorRows,
                                      @v_FetchStatus,
                                      @v_ColumnCount,
                                      @v_RowCount,
                                      @v_LastOperation,
                                      @v_CursorHandle
    END

/* Close and deallocate cursor when we're done with it */
CLOSE @v_Cursor
DEALLOCATE @v_Cursor

/* Close and deallocate cursor when we're done with it */
CLOSE @aCursor
DEALLOCATE @aCursor
```

Another possible use for the code in Listing 13.11 would be to create a stored procedure that you could use to produce this output for debugging purposes without having to load and execute this rather large section of code directly. For more information about creating and working with stored procedures, refer to Chapter 14.

The columns returned by **sp_cursor_list** provide information about how the cursor was created and details about the current status of the cursor. These columns are described in Table 13.5. This information helps you to interpret each row returned by the cursor.

**Table 13.5  Sp_cursor_list output columns.**

| Column | Data Type | Description |
|---|---|---|
| reference_name | SYSNAME | This is the name of the cursor given in the **DECLARE CURSOR** command or the name of the cursor variable that has a reference to the cursor. |
| cursor_name | SYSNAME | This is the name of the cursor given in the **DECLARE CURSOR** command or a system generated name if the cursor was created by assigning a cursor variable to a cursor. |

*(continued)*

13. Cursors

**Table 13.5    Sp_cursor_list** output columns *(continued)*.

| Column | Data Type | Description |
| --- | --- | --- |
| cursor_scope | SMALLINT | 1 = LOCAL and 2 = GLOBAL |
| status | SMALLINT | This is the value that would be reported by the **CURSOR_STATUS** system functions for the cursor. 1 = The cursor is open. For insensitive, static and keyset-driven cursors, this status indicates that the cursor has at least one row. 0 = The cursor is open but has no rows. This status is never returned for a dynamic cursor. -1 = The cursor is closed. -2 = There is no cursor assigned to the variable. This status applies only to cursor variables. -3 = The referenced cursor does not exist. |
| model | SMALLINT | 1 = Static (or insensitive), 2 = Keyset-driven, 3 = Dynamic, 4 = Fast forward-only |
| concurrency | SMALLINT | 1 = Read-only, 2 = Scroll locks, 3 = Optimistic |
| scrollable | SMALLINT | 1 = Forward-only, 2 = Scrollable |
| open_status | SMALLINT | 0 = Closed, 1 = Open |
| cursor_rows | INT | The number of qualifying rows in the result set defined by the **SELECT** statement specified in the cursor definition. |
| Fetch_Status | SMALLINT | 0 = Success, -1 = The fetch failed or is beyond the bounds of the cursor result set, -2 = The requested row has been deleted, -9 = No fetch operation has been performed on the cursor |
| column_count | SMALLINT | The number of columns in the cursor result set. |
| row_count | SMALLINT | The number of rows affected by the last cursor operation. This is the same information that is returned by the **@@rowcount** system variable immediately after the operation completes. |
| last_operation | SMALLINT | 0 = No operations have been performed on the cursor, 1= Open, 2 = Fetch, 3 = Insert, 4 = Update, 5 = Delete, 6 = Close, 7 = Deallocate |
| cursor_handle | INT | A unique value within the server used internally to identify the cursor. |

## sp_describe_cursor

The **sp_describe_cursor** stored procedure is used to return a description of a specified cursor for the current connection. Listing 13.12 provides the syntax that is used to call this procedure.

**Listing 13.12    sp_describe_cursor** syntax.

```
sp_describe_cursor [ @cursor_return = ] output_cursor_variable OUTPUT
                { [ , [ @cursor_source = ] N'local'
                , [ @cursor_identity = ] N'local_cursor_name' ]
                | [ , [ @cursor_source = ] N'global'
                , [ @cursor_identity = ] N'global_cursor_name' ]
```

```
      | [ , [ @cursor_source = ] N'variable'
          , [ @cursor_identity = ] N'input_cursor_variable' ]
      }
```

The cursor returned by **sp_describe_cursor** provides exactly the same information as the cursor returned by **sp_cursor_list** except that it is limited to the specified cursor. The arguments that can be passed to **sp_describe_cursor** are
explained in Table 13.6.

## sp_describe_cursor_columns

A list of the columns and their attributes in a cursor result set can be returned
using **sp_describe_cursor_columns**. The output of this procedure is a cursor
that allows you to process the result set one row at a time. The syntax used to call
this procedure is shown in Listing 13.13.

**Listing 13.13   sp_describe_cursor_columns syntax.**

```
sp_describe_cursor_columns
    [ @cursor_return = ] output_cursor_variable OUTPUT
    { [ , [ @cursor_source = ] N'local'
        , [ @cursor_identity = ] N'local_cursor_name' ]
          | [ , [ @cursor_source = ] N'global'
        , [ @cursor_identity = ] N'global_cursor_name' ]
          | [ , [ @cursor_source = ] N'variable'
        , [ @cursor_identity = ] N'input_cursor_variable' ]
```

The arguments passed to this procedure are identical to the arguments passed to
**sp_describe_cursor**. The code in Listing 13.14 can be used to output this information in a readable form that can be used for debugging purposes in the Query

**Table 13.6   Arguments for sp_describe_cursor.**

| Argument | Description |
| --- | --- |
| **[@cursor_return =]** *output_ cursor_variable* **OUTPUT** | The name of a declared cursor variable that will receive the output cursor from the procedure. The cursor that is returned is a scrollable, dynamic, read-only cursor. |
| **[@cursor_source =] { N'local' I N'global' I N'variable'** | This argument indicates whether the cursor being specified is a local cursor, global cursor, or cursor variable. |
| **[@cursor_identity =] N'***local_ cursor_name'***]** | The name that was specified in the **DECLARE CURSOR** statement for the local cursor. |
| **[@cursor_identity =] N'***global_ cursor_name'***]** | The name that was specified in the **DECLARE CURSOR** statement for the global cursor. |
| **[@cursor_identity =] N'***input_ cursor_variable'***]** | The name of a cursor variable that is associated with an open cursor. |

*13. Cursors*

Analyzer to examine the information about the cursors you have used on the current connection. This code is also provided as an example of how to process and interpret the information returned in the cursor variable. Refer to Chapter 19 for information about some of the techniques used to make this report more readable.

**Listing 13.14    Process and display information from sp_describe_cursor_columns.**

```
/* Create test cursor */
USE Address
GO

DECLARE c_TestCursor CURSOR
  GLOBAL
  FOR SELECT a.Line1,
            c.Name AS City,
            s.State_Code AS State,
            z.Zip5 AS ZIP
        FROM tbl_Address a (NOLOCK)
        JOIN tbl_City c (NOLOCK) ON c.City_ID = a.City_ID
        JOIN tbl_State S (NOLOCK) ON s.State_ID = c.State_ID
        JOIN tbl_ZipCode z (NOLOCK) ON z.Zip_ID = a.Zip_ID

OPEN c_TestCursor

/* Turn off row count messages */
SET NOCOUNT ON

/* Declare Cursor variable and variables for each cursor column */
DECLARE @v_Cursor CURSOR,
        @v_ColumnName SYSNAME,
        @v_OrdinalPosition INT,
        @v_ColumnFlags INT,
        @v_ColumnSize INT,
        @v_SQLDataType SMALLINT,
        @v_Precision TINYINT,
        @v_Scale TINYINT,
        @v_OrderPosition INT,
        @v_OrderDirection VARCHAR(1),
        @v_Hidden SMALLINT,
        @v_ColumnID INT,
        @v_ObjectID INT,
        @v_DBID INT,
        @v_DBName SYSNAME,
        @v_DataType CHAR(15),
        @v_ColSource CHAR(55),
        @v_SQL varchar(1000)
```

```
/* Create temporary table to use for column source information */
CREATE TABLE #tbl_TmpTbl (Source CHAR(55))

/* Get list of columns */
EXEC sp_describe_cursor_columns @v_Cursor OUTPUT, 'global', 'c_TestCursor'

/* Get first cursor row */
FETCH NEXT FROM @v_Cursor INTO @v_ColumnName,
                              @v_OrdinalPosition,
                              @v_ColumnFlags,
                              @v_ColumnSize,
                              @v_SQLDataType,
                              @v_Precision,
                              @v_Scale,
                              @v_OrderPosition,
                              @v_OrderDirection,
                              @v_Hidden,
                              @v_ColumnID,
                              @v_ObjectID,
                              @v_DBID,
                              @v_DBName

/* Print Headings */
PRINT 'Column Name                         Ordinal Characteristics Size  '+
      'Data Type       Precision Scale Order Position Direction   '+
      'Hidden  Column Source'
PRINT '---------------------------- ------ --------------- ---- '+
      '--------------- -------- ---- --------------- ---------- '+
      '------ ---------------------------------------------------'

/* Loop through cursor rows */
WHILE (@@Fetch_Status <> -1)
  BEGIN
  /* If the row has not been deleted */
  IF (@@Fetch_Status <> -2)
    BEGIN
    /* Lookup data type from systypes system table */
    SELECT @v_DataType = name
      FROM systypes (NOLOCK)
      WHERE xType = @v_SQLDataType

    /* Get Column Source (database, table, & column name) */
    IF (@v_ColumnID = -1)
      SELECT @v_ColSource = 'EXPRESSION'
      ELSE
      BEGIN
```

```
          /* Clear the temp table (this may not be the first column) */
          TRUNCATE TABLE #tbl_TmpTbl

          /* Build SQL to retrieve column source information */
          SELECT @v_SQL =
                  'SELECT ''' + @v_DBName +
                          ''' + ''..'' + so.name ' +
                          '+ ''.'' + sc.name '+
                  'FROM ' + @v_DBName + '..sysobjects so (NOLOCK) ' +
                  'JOIN ' + @v_DBName + '..syscolumns sc (NOLOCK) ON ' +
                          'sc.colID = ' +
                                  CONVERT(VARCHAR, @v_ColumnID) +
                          ' AND so.ID = sc.ID ' +
                  'WHERE so.ID = ' + CONVERT(VARCHAR, @v_ObjectID)

          /* Insert column source information into temp table */
          INSERT INTO #tbl_TmpTbl
            EXEC(@v_SQL)

          /* Put column source information into a variable */
          SELECT @v_ColSource = Source
            FROM #tbl_TmpTbl (NOLOCK)
          END

     /* Print the column information */
     PRINT CONVERT(CHAR(30),
              COALESCE(@v_ColumnName, '** NOT SPECIFIED **')) + ' ' +
          CONVERT(CHAR(7), @v_OrdinalPosition) + ' ' +
          /* Convert column flags to a readable form */
          CASE @v_ColumnFlags WHEN  1 THEN 'Bookmark       '
                              WHEN  2 THEN 'Fixed Length   '
                              WHEN  4 THEN 'Nullable       '
                              WHEN  8 THEN 'Row Versioning '
                              WHEN 16 THEN 'Updatable      '
                              ELSE 'NONE              ' END + ' ' +
          CONVERT(CHAR(5), @v_ColumnSize) + ' ' +
          @v_DataType + ' ' +
          CONVERT(CHAR(9), @v_Precision) + ' ' +
          CONVERT(CHAR(5), @v_Scale) + ' ' +
          CONVERT(CHAR(14), @v_OrderPosition) + ' ' +
          /* Convert Order Direction to a readable form */
          CASE @v_OrderDirection WHEN 'A' THEN 'Ascending '
                                 WHEN 'D' THEN 'Descending'
                                 ELSE 'N/A       ' END + ' ' +
          /* Convert Hidden attribute to a readable form */
```

```
            CASE @v_Hidden WHEN 0 THEN 'FALSE   '
                           WHEN 1 THEN 'TRUE    '
                           ELSE 'UNKNOWN' END + ' ' +
          @v_ColSource
    END

  /* Get next cursor row */
  FETCH NEXT FROM @v_Cursor INTO @v_ColumnName,
                                 @v_OrdinalPosition,
                                 @v_ColumnFlags,
                                 @v_ColumnSize,
                                 @v_SQLDataType,
                                 @v_Precision,
                                 @v_Scale,
                                 @v_OrderPosition,
                                 @v_OrderDirection,
                                 @v_Hidden,
                                 @v_ColumnID,
                                 @v_ObjectID,
                                 @v_DBID,
                                 @v_DBName
  END

/* Get rid of the temp table */
DROP TABLE #tbl_TmpTbl

/* Close and deallocate cursor when we're done with it */
CLOSE @v_Cursor
DEALLOCATE @v_Cursor

/* Close and deallocate the test cursor */
CLOSE c_TestCursor
DEALLOCATE c_TestCursor
```

The code in Listing 13.14 can also be used to create a stored procedure to use in the Query Analyzer to produce this output for debugging purposes without having to load and execute this rather large section of code directly. For more information about creating and working with stored procedures, refer to Chapter 14.

The columns returned by **sp_describe_cursor_columns** provide details about the column attributes of the result set defined by the **SELECT** statement specified in the **DECLARE CURSOR** command. The columns returned by the **OUTPUT** cursor are described in Table 13.7. This information helps you to interpret each row returned by the cursor.

**Table 13.7    Sp_describe_cursor_columns output columns.**

| Column | Data Type | Description |
| --- | --- | --- |
| column_name | SYSNAME nullable | The name assigned to the column in the result set. If the result set column is an expression and no column name was assigned, the **column_name** is **NULL**. |
| ordinal_position | INT | The position from left to right of the column in the result set beginning with 1 for the first column. Hidden columns have a **0** for the **ordinal_position**. |
| column_ characteristics_ flags | INT | A bitmask containing the information stored in DBCOLUMNFLAGS in OLE DB (1 = Bookmark, 2 = Fixed Length, 4 = Nullable, 8 = Row Versioning, 16 = Updatable Column). |
| column_size | INT | Maximum allowable size for a value in this column. |
| data_type_sql | SMALLINT | Returns a number than can be used to look up the SQL Server data type. This number can be found in the **xType** column of the systypes table. |
| column_precision | TINYINT | The maximum precision of the column. |
| column_scale | TINYINT | The number of digits to the right of the decimal point for decimal and numeric data types. |
| order_position | INT | The column's position from left to right in the **ORDER BY** clause specified for the result set. The first column in the **ORDER BY** clause is **1**, and any column not included in the **ORDER BY** clause has a **0** for the **order_position**. |
| order_direction | VARCHAR(1) nullable | If the column is contained in the **ORDER BY** clause, **order_ direction** contains an **A** for ascending or a **D** for descending sort ordering. If the column is not contained in the **ORDER BY** clause, **order_direction** is **NULL**. |
| hidden_column | SMALLINT | A value of **0** indicates that the column appears in the result set, a value of **1** indicates that the column is reserved for future use (hidden). |
| columnid | INT | The column ID of the source column. **columnid** contains a **-1** if the column source is an expression. |
| objectid | INT | The object ID of the source table. **objectid** contains a **-1** if the column source is an expression. |
| dbid | INT | The database ID of the source database. **dbid** contains a **-1** if the column source is an expression. |
| dbname | SYSNAME nullable | The database name of the source database. **dbname** is **NULL** if the column source is an expression. |

## sp_describe_cursor_tables

A list of the base tables and their attributes for a cursor result set can be returned using **sp_describe_cursor_tables**. The output of this procedure is a cursor that allows you to process the result set one row at a time. The syntax used to call this procedure is shown in Listing 13.15.

**Listing 13.15  sp_describe_cursor_tables syntax.**

```
sp_describe_cursor_tables
    [ @cursor_return = ] output_cursor_variable OUTPUT
    { [ , [ @cursor_source = ] N'local'
        , [ @cursor_identity = ] N'local_cursor_name' ]
          | [ , [ @cursor_source = ] N'global'
        , [ @cursor_identity = ] N'global_cursor_name' ]
          | [ , [ @cursor_source = ] N'variable'
        , [ @cursor_identity = ] N'input_cursor_variable' ]
```

The arguments passed to this procedure are identical to the arguments passed to **sp_describe_cursor**. The code in Listing 13.16 can be used to output this information in a readable form that can be used in the Query Analyzer for debugging purposes to examine the information about the cursors you have used on the current connection. This code is also provided as an example of how to process and interpret the information returned in the cursor variable. Refer to Chapter 19 for information about some of the techniques used to make this report more readable.

**Listing 13.16  Process and display information from sp_describe_cursor_tables.**

```
/* Create test cursor */
USE Address
GO

DECLARE c_TestCursor CURSOR
  GLOBAL
  FOR SELECT a.Line1,
             c.Name AS City,
             s.State_Code AS State,
             z.Zip5 AS ZIP
        FROM tbl_Address a (NOLOCK)
        JOIN tbl_City c (NOLOCK) ON c.City_ID = a.City_ID
        JOIN tbl_State S (NOLOCK) ON s.State_ID = c.State_ID
        JOIN tbl_ZipCode z (NOLOCK) ON z.Zip_ID = a.Zip_ID

OPEN c_TestCursor

/* Declare Cursor variable and variables for each cursor column */
DECLARE @v_Cursor CURSOR,
```

```
                    @v_Owner SYSNAME,
                    @v_TableName SYSNAME,
                    @v_Hints SMALLINT,
                    @v_LockType SMALLINT,
                    @v_ServerName SYSNAME,
                    @v_ObjectID INT,
                    @v_DBID INT,
                    @v_DBName SYSNAME

    /* Get list of columns */
    EXEC sp_describe_cursor_tables @v_Cursor OUTPUT, 'global', 'c_TestCursor'

    /* Get first cursor row */
    FETCH NEXT FROM @v_Cursor INTO @v_Owner,
                                   @v_TableName,
                                   @v_Hints,
                                   @v_LockType,
                                   @v_ServerName,
                                   @v_ObjectID,
                                   @v_DBID,
                                   @v_DBName

    /* Print Headings */
    PRINT 'Owner                          Table Name                   '+
          'Hint(s)                                                     '+
          '           Lock Type Server                      '+
          'Database'
    PRINT '------------------------------ ------------------------------ '+
          '------------------------------------------------------------'+
          '--------- -------- ------------------------------ '+
          '------------------------------'

    /* Loop through cursor rows */
    WHILE (@@Fetch_Status <> -1)
      BEGIN
      /* If the row has not been deleted */
      IF (@@Fetch_Status <> -2)
        BEGIN
        /* Print the table information */
        PRINT CONVERT(CHAR(30), COALESCE(@v_Owner, '')) + ' ' +
              CONVERT(CHAR(30), COALESCE(@v_TableName, '')) + ' ' +
              /* Create list of applied hints */
              CONVERT(CHAR(70),
                  CASE WHEN (@v_Hints &    1) =    1 THEN 'ROWLOCK '
                       ELSE '' END +
                  CASE WHEN (@v_Hints &    4) =    4 THEN 'PAGLOCK '
```

```
                                 ELSE '' END +
                 CASE WHEN (@v_Hints &    8) =    8 THEN 'TABLOCK '
                      ELSE '' END +
                 CASE WHEN (@v_Hints &   16) =   16 THEN 'TABLOCKX '
                      ELSE '' END +
                 CASE WHEN (@v_Hints &   32) =   32 THEN 'UPDLOCK '
                      ELSE '' END +
                 CASE WHEN (@v_Hints &   64) =   64 THEN 'NOLOCK '
                      ELSE '' END +
                 CASE WHEN (@v_Hints &  128) =  128 THEN 'FASTFIRSTROW '
                      ELSE '' END +
                 CASE WHEN (@v_Hints & 4096) = 4096 THEN 'HOLDLOCK '
                      ELSE '' END ) + ' ' +
         /* Convert Lock type to readable form */
         CASE @v_LockType WHEN 0 THEN 'None      '
                          WHEN 1 THEN 'Shared    '
                          WHEN 3 THEN 'Update    '
                          ELSE 'UNKNOWN   ' END + ' ' +
         CONVERT(CHAR(30), COALESCE(@v_ServerName, '')) + ' ' +
         CONVERT(CHAR(30), COALESCE(@v_DBName, ''))
    END

  /* Get next cursor row */
  FETCH NEXT FROM @v_Cursor INTO @v_Owner,
                                 @v_TableName,
                                 @v_Hints,
                                 @v_LockType,
                                 @v_ServerName,
                                 @v_ObjectID,
                                 @v_DBID,
                                 @v_DBName

  END

/* Close and deallocate cursor when we're done with it */
CLOSE @v_Cursor
DEALLOCATE @v_Cursor

/* Close and deallocate the test cursor */
CLOSE c_TestCursor
DEALLOCATE c_TestCursor
```

The code in Listing 13.16 can also be used to create a stored procedure to use in the Query Analyzer to produce this output for debugging purposes without having to load and execute this rather large section of code directly. For more information about creating and working with stored procedures, refer to Chapter 14.

The columns returned by **sp_describe_cursor_tables** provide details about the table attributes of base tables used in the **SELECT** statement specified in the **DECLARE CURSOR** command. The columns returned by the **OUTPUT** cursor are described in Table 13.8. This information helps you to interpret each row returned by the cursor.

# Cursor Related Database Options

There are two database options specifically related to cursors that you should be aware of. Both of these options can alter the default behavior of cursors, which may present a problem for the unwary. It is a good idea to become familiar with these defaults and make every effort to ensure that you fully understand the consequences to any code running against your database before changing them. The following sections provide some details on the two options and the behaviors affected by each.

## SET CURSOR_CLOSE_ON_COMMIT

When the **CURSOR_CLOSE_ON_COMMIT** database option is set to **ON**, any open cursors are closed automatically when a transaction is committed. This is the behavior specified by the ANSI SQL-92 standard. By default, this setting is **OFF,** which means that cursors remain open across transaction boundaries. A cursor is closed only when it is explicitly closed or when it is implicitly closed based on the rules for **LOCAL** and **GLOBAL** cursors. You can use the **SET** state-

**Table 13.8 sp_describe_cursor_tables output columns.**

| Column | Data Type | Description |
|---|---|---|
| table_owner | SYSNAME | The user ID of the table owner. |
| table_name | SYSNAME | The name of the base table. |
| optimizer_hints | SMALLINT | A bitmap consisting of one or more table hints (1 = Row-level locking, 4 = Page-level locking, 8 = Table lock, 16 = Exclusive table lock, 32 = Update lock, 64 = No lock, 128 = Fast first-row, 4096 = Hold lock). |
| lock_type | SMALLINT | The scroll-lock type requested (either explicitly or implicitly) for the base table (0 = None, 1 = Shared, 3 = Update). |
| server_name | SYSNAME nullable | The name of the linked server on which the base table resides. |
| objectid | INT | The object ID of the base table. |
| dbid | INT | The database ID of the database where the base table resides. |
| dbname | SYSNAME nullable | The database name of the database where the base table resides. |

ment to establish connection-level settings that override the default database setting for **CURSOR_CLOSE_ON_COMMIT**.

---

**NOTE:** *We have seen some strange behavior using this option. When an implicit transaction is used in the **WHILE** loop for the cursor, the cursor is closed after the first iteration of the loop when the implicit transaction is committed. This can be difficult to debug and extremely annoying, so this option should be used with extreme care.*

---

## SET CURSOR_DEFAULT LOCAL/GLOBAL

When **CURSOR_DEFAULT LOCAL** is set and a cursor is not specifically defined as **GLOBAL** in the **DECLARE CURSOR** statement, the scope of the cursor is local to the batch, trigger, or stored procedure in which it was created. The local cursor name is valid only within the scope of that batch or procedure. Local cursors can be referenced by local cursor variables in the batch, trigger, or stored procedure, or as a stored procedure **OUTPUT** parameter. A local cursor is implicitly deallocated upon termination of the batch, or procedure in which is was created, unless it was passed back in an **OUTPUT** parameter. If it is passed back in an **OUTPUT** parameter, the local cursor is deallocated when the last variable referencing it is deallocated or goes out of scope.

When **CURSOR_DEFAULT GLOBAL** is set and a cursor is not specifically defined as **LOCAL** in the **DECLARE CURSOR** statement, the scope of the cursor is global to the connection. A global cursor name can be referenced in any stored procedure or batch executed by the connection that created it. Global cursors are not implicitly deallocated until the connection is closed. **CURSOR_DEFAULT GLOBAL** is the default setting for a new database.

It is actually a good idea to specify either **GLOBAL** or **LOCAL** in the **DECLARE CURSOR** statement to prevent later changes in the **CURSOR_DEFAULT** database option from creating problems in your code. If the default is changed and you are counting on the current setting, you may find triggers and stored procedures that are broken unless you specify the appropriate option when the cursor is created.

# Concurrency and Locking

SQL Server 2000 supports four concurrency options for server-side cursors. These options can be specified for Transact-SQL cursors using the **READ_ONLY**, **OPTIMISTIC**, and **SCROLL_LOCK** keywords in the **DECLARE CURSOR** statement. The **OPTIMISTIC** keyword actually generates one of two behaviors depending on the structure of the underlying tables. The following sections provide some details about the behavior generated by each of these four options and any other factors that influence which option is applied to a cursor.

# READ_ONLY

Positioned updates through a **READ_ONLY** cursor are not allowed. No locks are held on the rows that make up the result set of the cursor.

# OPTIMISTIC WITH VALUES

Optimistic concurrency control is used in situations when there is a very slight chance that another user may update a row in the interval between when a cursor is opened and when the row is updated. The **OPTIMISTIC WITH VALUES** concurrency option is also best applied only when minimal updating is expected from the cursor as well. When a cursor is created with this option, no locks are held on the underlying rows. Although this helps maximize throughput, it requires that the current values in the row be compared to the values retrieved when the row was fetched before allowing the user to perform an update. If any of the values have been changed, the server returns an error indicating that someone else has already updated the row. If the values are the same, the server allows the modification to be completed.

Selecting this concurrency option forces the user or programmer to deal with the occasional error when another user has modified the row. An application would typically need to refresh the cursor with the new values, present the new values to the user, and then let the user decide whether to perform the modifications again on the new values. It is important to note that SQL Server 2000 compares **text**, **ntext**, and **image** columns as part of this concurrency check.

If a large number of updates will be performed with the cursor, the overhead of checking all the values in the row can create a severe performance bottleneck. If you want to use optimistic locking and perform a larger number of updates, refer to the "OPTIMISTIC WITH ROW VERSIONING" section to see how you can eliminate a large part of this burden.

# OPTIMISTIC WITH ROW VERSIONING

The **OPTIMISTIC WITH ROW VERSIONING** concurrency option is based on row versioning. In order to make use of row versioning, the underlying table must have some type of version identifier that the server can use to determine whether the row has been changed after it was read into the cursor. SQL Server implements row versioning by the use of the **TIMESTAMP** data type, which is a binary number that indicates the relative sequence of modifications in a database. Each database has a global current **TIMESTAMP** value, which can be read using the **@@DBTS** global system variable. Each time a row with a **TIMESTAMP** column is modified, SQL Server stores the current **@@DBTS** value in the **TIMESTAMP** column and then increments **@@DBTS**. If you include a **TIMESTAMP** column in your tables, SQL Server has the capability to compare the current **TIMESTAMP** value of a row rather than all values in the row to determine if the row has been updated. This can eliminate a huge amount of overhead in terms of making this comparison. Because the **TIMESTAMP** is a binary column, the comparison of this value is extremely fast. If you specify optimistic concurrency when you create a cursor on a table that does not have a **TIMESTAMP** column, the cursor defaults to values-based optimistic concurrency control.

### SCROLL LOCKS

The **SCROLL LOCKS** option implements pessimistic concurrency control. SQL Server attempts to place an update lock on the underlying database rows at the time they are read into the cursor result set. If the cursor is opened within a transaction, the transaction update lock is held until the transaction is either committed or rolled back, but the cursor lock is dropped when the next row is fetched. If the cursor has been opened outside a transaction, the lock is dropped when the next row is fetched. A cursor should be opened in a transaction if you need full pessimistic concurrency control. An update lock prevents any other task from acquiring an update or exclusive lock on the row, which prevents any other task from updating the row. Update locks do not block shared locks on the rows, so they do not prevent another task from reading the rows unless the second task is also requesting a read with an update lock.

# Positional Updates and Deletes

Transact-SQL provides a **WHERE CURRENT OF** clause for updates and deletes to allow modifications to the current row of the specified cursor. This functionality can be very beneficial when performing data modifications using a cursor. The capability to perform these tasks on the current row eliminates the need to use a set-based operation with a standard **WHERE** clause that must then relocate the row before performing the operation.

Be careful to use this functionality appropriately. Performing updates using set-based logic is almost always faster and more efficient than using the positional method with a cursor. Positional updates and deletes should be used only in situations where there is no clear way to achieve the same result using set-based logic.

# Cursor Threshold Option

Use the cursor threshold server option to specify the minimum number of rows in a cursor result set that will cause cursor keysets to be generated asynchronously instead of synchronously. Setting the cursor threshold option to -1 causes all keysets to be generated synchronously. Synchronous generation benefits small cursor sets. Setting the cursor threshold to 0 causes all cursor keysets to be generated asynchronously, which can slow the performance of small cursor sets. With other values, the query optimizer determines whether to build the keyset asynchronously by comparing the number of expected rows in the cursor set by the specified cursor threshold value. Asynchronous generation occurs if the expected number of rows exceeds the cursor threshold value. Be careful not to set the cursor threshold value too low, because small result sets should be built synchronously to improve performance.

The query optimizer uses the statistics for each of the tables in the **SELECT** statement to estimate the row count. The accuracy of this estimate depends on the currency of the statistics for each table. Because this concurrency is also a determining factor in the accuracy of index selections and other query plan estimates, it is a good idea to update the statistics for all tables in your database as part of your regular maintenance plan. See Chapter 6 for more information about setting up maintenance plans for your databases.

Cursor threshold is an advanced option, so if you are using **sp_configure** to change the setting, you must set the Show Advanced Options option to 1 before you can change the value of the cursor threshold. The setting takes effect immediately and does not require the server to be stopped and restarted.

# Cursor Transaction Isolation Levels

The transaction locking behavior of a specific cursor is determined by combining the locking behaviors of the cursor concurrency setting, the locking hints specified in the cursor **SELECT** statement, and the transaction isolation level option in effect for the current connection. SQL Server 2000 supports three transaction isolation levels for cursors.

## Read Committed

The Read Committed isolation level causes a shared lock to be acquired while reading each row into a cursor, but frees the lock immediately after the row is read. Because shared lock requests are blocked by an exclusive lock, the cursor is prevented from reading a row if another task has updated the row but has not yet committed the changes. Read Committed is the default isolation level for SQL Server.

## Read Uncommitted

If you specify the Read Uncommitted isolation level, no locks are requested when reading a row into a cursor, which means that exclusive locks are ignored when reading the rows (dirty reads). The rows in the cursor result set may contain updated values, but the changes have not yet been committed. Read Uncommitted allows you to bypass all of the locking transaction control mechanisms in SQL Server.

### Repeatable Read or Serializable

For the Repeatable Read or Serializable isolation level, SQL Server requests a shared lock on each row as it is read into the cursor. This is the same as Read Committed, but if the cursor is opened within a transaction, the shared locks are held until the end of the transaction instead of being freed after the row is read. This isolation level has the same effect as specifying **HOLDLOCK** on a **SELECT** statement.

# Templates

You should check out the new templates in the Query Analyzer, especially if you are not fully familiar with the **CREATE CURSOR** syntax. This is a new feature in the Query Analyzer for SQL Server 2000. The Query Analyzer provides several templates that will assist you in creating triggers for use in your batches and procedures. The following is a list of the templates provided that relate to cursors:

- Declare and Use **KEYSET** Cursor
- Declare and Use **READ_ONLY** Cursor
- Declare and Use **SCROLL** Cursor with Various **FETCH** Options
- Declare and Use **UPDATE** Cursor

These templates provide a basic framework for creating cursors and make it easier to get started working with them. For more information about the Query Analyzer and the new templates, refer to Chapter 5.

**13. Cursors**

# Immediate Solutions

## Updating Index Statistics on Multiple Tables

Although SQL Server 2000 provides the **sp_updatestats** system stored procedure to update the statistics for all tables in the current database, it is sometimes
desirable to perform this action on a subset of the tables. This section provides
you with step-by-step instructions for producing the code necessary to accomplish this task. This example updates statistics for all tables in the Employee
database that have a name that begins with **tbl_Emp**.

1. Open the Query Analyzer.

2. Select Edit|Insert Template.

*NOTE: The Insert Template option is only available when the query pane has focus, so if the option is grayed out, you
need to click in the query pane to give it focus, and then go back to the Edit menu and select Insert Template from
the menu.*

3. Open the Using Cursor folder.

4. Select Declare and Use READ_ONLY Cursor.tql. This pastes the template
text into the query window.

5. Select Edit|Replace Template Parameters.

6. Enter "csrTableList" for the **cursor_name** parameter.

7. You only want to update statistics for tables that begin with **tbl_Emp**, so
enter the following code for the **select_statement** parameter:

```
SELECT so.Name
  FROM sysobjects so (NOLOCK)
  WHERE so.Name LIKE 'tbl_Emp%'
  ORDER BY so.Name
```

8. Click on OK to close the dialog and replace the template parameters with
the specified values.

9. Apply any formatting changes to the template generated code that will
make it more readable for you.

10. There is no template for a **FAST_FORWARD_ONLY** template, but it is
easy to modify this code to use a **FAST_FORWARD_ONLY** cursor instead

of a **READ_ONLY** cursor. In the query pane, change the **READ_ONLY** option in the **DECLARE CURSOR** statement to **FAST_FORWARD**.

11. Remove the processing code generated by the template. It is located between the **BEGIN** and **END** statements after **IF (@@Fetch_Status <> -2)**.

12. Change all of the **@v_name** variable references to **@v_TblName**. This provides a more descriptive variable name and will make the code easier to read and understand in the future.

13. At this point, you need to insert code to display the processing actions you intend the cursor to take. This is a simple debugging step to make sure that the code is going to perform as you expect. Add the following line of code in the place where you removed the template generated processing code:

```
PRINT 'UPDATE STATISTICS ' + @v_TblName
```

14. Once you have inserted the code to display the action to be performed, execute the cursor to verify that it is producing the results you expect. Listing 13.17 displays the expected output from this cursor.

**Listing 13.17   Expected output for UPDATE STATISTICS cursor.**
```
UPDATE STATISTICS tbl_Employee
UPDATE STATISTICS tbl_EmployeeAddressXref
UPDATE STATISTICS tbl_EmployeeRates
```

15. If you do not receive the preceding output, the most likely problem is that your database context is not the Employee database. To eliminate the need to remember to switch the database in the drop-down menu before running this script, add the following code to the top of the script. These two lines should come before any other code in the batch. They will ensure that the code is executed against the Employee database regardless of what was originally selected in the database drop-down menu.

```
USE Employee
GO
```

16. The output from the cursor can actually be copied as-is into a query window and executed to update the table statistics. You can automate this process to eliminate the need to perform this additional step. Insert the following lines of code immediately after the **PRINT** statement to automatically execute the code to update the table statistics.

```
EXEC('UPDATE STATISTICS ' + @v_TblName)
```

17. Execute the cursor again to update the table statistics. This is very fast and does not provide any feedback other than the output from the **PRINT** statement you added earlier.

18. Add a few comments so that you can understand in the future what the code is supposed to be doing. You can then save the script. Listing 13.18 provides a completed script that is formatted and contains comments.

**Listing 13.18   Update statistics for specific list of tables.**

```
/***********************************************************/
/* Update table statistics for all tables in the Employee */
/* database that begin tbl_Emp.                            */
/***********************************************************/

/* Set context to the Employee Database */
USE Employee
GO

/* Declare a cursor to get a list of tables */
DECLARE csrTableList CURSOR FAST_FORWARD FOR
  SELECT so.Name
    FROM sysobjects so (NOLOCK)
    WHERE so.Name LIKE 'tbl_Emp%'
    ORDER BY so.Name

/* Declare a variable to hold the table names */
DECLARE @TblName VARCHAR(40)

/* Open the cursor */
OPEN csrTableList

/* Get the first table name */
FETCH NEXT FROM csrTableList INTO @TblName

/* Loop through the tables */
WHILE (@@Fetch_Status <> -1)
  BEGIN
  /* Skip deleted rows if needed */
  IF (@@Fetch_Status <> -2)
    BEGIN
    /* Display the operation that is being performed */
    PRINT 'UPDATE STATISTICS ' + @TblName

    /* Update the statistics for each table */
    EXEC('UPDATE STATISTICS ' + @TblName)
    END
```

```
/* Get the next table name from the cursor */
FETCH NEXT FROM csrTableList INTO @TblName
END

/* Close and deallocate the cursor */
CLOSE csrTableList
DEALLOCATE csrTableList
GO
```

| Related solution: | Found on page: |
|---|---|
| Create a Maintenance Plan for the System Databases | 256 |

## Performing Maintenance Tasks on Multiple Databases

The previous solution provided an example of performing a maintenance task on a list of tables in a database. The example in this section shows you how to use a cursor to perform a maintenance task on multiple databases. This can be extremely handy when you want to execute a specific set of tasks for several databases. Instead of creating a script for each database or a long script with the tasks repeated for each database and the appropriate context switch in between, you can use a cursor to loop through the databases to perform the tasks. In this example, you perform a **DBCC CHECKALLOC** for all databases on the server.

1. Open the Query Analyzer.

2. Select Edit|Insert Template.

3. Open the Using Cursor folder.

4. Select Declare and Use READ_ONLY Cursor.tql. This pastes the template text into the query window.

5. Select Edit|Replace Template Parameters.

6. Enter "csrDBList" for the **cursor_name** parameter.

7. You need to get a list of databases from the **sysdatabases** table in the master database, so enter the following code for the **select_statement** parameter:

```
SELECT sd.Name
  FROM master..sysdatabases sd (NOLOCK)
  ORDER BY sd.Name
```

8. Click on OK to close the dialog and replace the template parameters with the specified values.

9. Apply any formatting changes to the template generated code that will make it more readable for you.

10. There is no template for a **FAST_FORWARD_ONLY** template, but it is easy to modify this code to use a **FAST_FORWARD_ONLY** cursor instead of a **READ_ONLY** cursor. In the query pane, change the **READ_ONLY** option in the **DECLARE CURSOR** statement to **FAST_FORWARD**.

11. Remove the processing code generated by the template. It is located between the **BEGIN** and **END** statements after **IF** (**@@Fetch_Status** <> -2).

12. Change all of the **@v_name** variable references to **@v_DBName**. This provides a more descriptive variable name and will make the code easier to read and understand in the future.

13. At this point, you need to insert code to display the processing actions you intend the cursor to take. This is a simple debugging step to make sure that the code is going to perform as you expect. Add the following line of code in the place where you removed the template generated processing code:

```
PRINT 'DBCC CHECKALLOC (' + @v_DBName + ')'
```

14. Once you have inserted the code to display the action to be performed, execute the cursor to verify that it is producing the results you expect. Listing 13.19 displays the expected output from this cursor.

---

**NOTE:** *Your list may be different if you have additional databases on your server, if you have not created the book databases, or if you have removed the Pubs or Northwind databases from your system.*

---

**Listing 13.19   Expected output for DBCC CHECKALLOC cursor.**

```
DBCC CHECKALLOC (Address)
DBCC CHECKALLOC (Employee)
DBCC CHECKALLOC (Inventory)
DBCC CHECKALLOC (master)
DBCC CHECKALLOC (model)
DBCC CHECKALLOC (msdb)
DBCC CHECKALLOC (Northwind)
DBCC CHECKALLOC (pubs)
DBCC CHECKALLOC (tempdb)
DBCC CHECKALLOC (Utility)
```

15. The output from the cursor as it is can actually be copied into a query window and executed to update the table statistics. You can automate this process to eliminate the need to perform this additional step. Insert the

following lines of code immediately after the **PRINT** statement to automatically execute the code to update the table statistics.

```
EXEC('DBCC CHECKALLOC (' + @v_DBName + ')')
```

16. Due to the amount of information that is returned by this command, you need to add a few blank lines in the output to make it easier to locate the separations between the output for each database. Add three **PRINT** '' statements after the **EXEC** command to provide this separation.

17. Execute the cursor again to update the table statistics. This does not take long if you have only the system and book supplied databases. This may take a while if you have a large database of your own on the server.

**WARNING!** *It is not recommended that you run this script against a production server during normal business hours because it is an extremely server-intensive process and can negatively affect the performance of other running applications.*

18. Add a few comments to help you understand in the future what the code is supposed to be doing. You are now ready to save the script. Listing 13.20 provides a completed script that is formatted and contains comments.

**Listing 13.20   Execute DBBC CHECKALLOC for all databases.**

```
/************************************************************/
/* Execute DBCC CHECKALLOC for all databases on the server */
/************************************************************/

/* Declare a cursor to get a list of database */
DECLARE c_DBList CURSOR FAST_FORWARD FOR
  SELECT sd.Name
    FROM master..sysdatabases sd (NOLOCK)
    ORDER BY sd.Name

/* Declare a variable to hold the database names */
DECLARE @v_DBName VARCHAR(40)

/* Open the cursor */
OPEN c_DBList

/* Get the first database name */
FETCH NEXT FROM c_DBList INTO @v_DBName

/* Loop through the databases */
WHILE (@@Fetch_Status <> -1)
  BEGIN
  /* Skip deleted rows if needed */
```

```
    IF (@@Fetch_Status <> -2)
      BEGIN
      /* Display the operation that is being performed */
      PRINT 'DBCC CHECKALLOC (' + @v_DBName + ')'

      /* Update the statistics for each table */
      EXEC('DBCC CHECKALLOC (' + @v_DBName + ')')

      /* Print blank lines to provide separation */
      /* between the databases                   */
      PRINT ''
      PRINT ''
      PRINT ''
      END

    /* Get the next database name from the cursor */
    FETCH NEXT FROM c_DBList INTO @v_DBName
    END

/* Close and deallocate the cursor */
CLOSE c_DBList
DEALLOCATE c_DBList
GO
```

| Related solution: | Found on page: |
|---|---|
| **DBCC CHECKALLOC** | 246 |
| Create a Maintenance Plan for the System Databases | 256 |

# Identifying Autogenerated Statistics on All User Tables

When you are optimizing database performance, identifying the autogenerated statistics on your tables to locate places where an index might be helpful can be a useful strategy. The following example uses two cursors that are nested to find these statistics for all tables in all databases in one pass. The output indicates the database being scanned and the autogenerated statistics for each table.

1. The first step in this process is to create a cursor to loop through the databases. This was previously done in "Performing Maintenance Tasks on Multiple Databases" in the "Immediate Solutions" section of this chapter.

2. Next, you need to build the SQL code that outputs the list of statistic sets for each table in the database. This may seem like a complicated process, but it is actually fairly simple. The cursor that will perform the tasks

desired was provided as an example in the "Autogenerated Statistics" section of Chapter 11.

3. Take the code from Listing 11.2 and substitute it for the processing code in Listing 13.20.

4. Add an **ORDER BY** clause to the cursor from Listing 11.2 to order the cursor by **so.Name** and then **si.Name**.

5. Add a filter to the cursor from Listing 11.2 to look only at user tables. This can be accomplished by adding **so.xType = 'U'** to the **WHERE** clause.

6. Change the code that prints the **DROP STATISTICS** commands to simply print the **@v_AutoGen variable**.

7. Remove the code to **EXEC** the **DROP STATISTICS** commands.

8. Create an additional column in the cursor that loops through the auto-generated statistics. Use the following code to create a new column that shows the column name qualified by the table name for each statistic set:

```
so.Name + '.' + SUBSTRING(si.Name, 9,
                        DATALENGTH(CONVERT(VARCHAR, si.Name)) - 17)
```

9. Add a declaration for a variable of **CHAR(40)** to hold this new column value, and add it to the **FETCH** commands for the statistics cursor.

10. Change the output of the cursor to print the new variable in addition to the **@v_AutoGen** variable.

11. Add a filter to the database cursor to exclude the following databases: master, msdb, model, and tempdb.

12. At this point, you should execute the script to make sure that both cursors are functioning properly. You will notice in the output that all databases seem to have the tables with the same statistics.

13. Next, declare a variable called **@v_SQL** as **VARCHAR(8000)**, and assign all of the code for the statistics cursor to it so that it can be used in an **EXEC** statement.

---

**NOTE:** *Refer to Chapter 19 for details on how to build and execute dynamic SQL in your queries.*

---

14. Preface the system table names with **@v_DBName + '..'** in the **SELECT STATEMENT** for the statistics cursor that is now contained in the **@v_SQL** variable. This allows the cursor to get statistic set names for the specified database.

15. Add an **EXEC** statement to execute the contents of the **@v_SQL** variable.

16. Run the query again. If you have constructed the **@v_SQL** variable correctly, the output should now reflect the proper tables for the database that is being scanned. The entire listing for this script is provided in Listing 13.21, so that you can see how to construct the **@v_SQL** variable properly.

**Listing 13.21   Locate statistic sets on all user tables.**

```
/********************************************************************/
/* Locate all auto-generated statistic sets on user created tables */
/********************************************************************/

/* Declare a cursor to get a list of databases */
DECLARE c_DBList CURSOR FAST_FORWARD FOR
  SELECT sd.Name
    FROM master..sysdatabases sd (NOLOCK)
    WHERE sd.Name NOT IN ('master', 'msdb', 'model', 'tempdb')
    ORDER BY sd.Name

/* Declare a variable to hold the database names */
DECLARE @v_DBName VARCHAR(40),
        @v_SQL VARCHAR(8000)

/* Open the cursor */
OPEN c_DBList

/* Get the first database name */
FETCH NEXT FROM c_DBList INTO @v_DBName

/* Loop through the databases */
WHILE (@@Fetch_Status <> -1)
  BEGIN
  /* Skip deleted rows if needed */
  IF (@@Fetch_Status <> -2)
    BEGIN
    /* Build a SQL string to create and loop through a */
    /* cursor to locate auto-generated statistic sets  */
    SELECT @v_SQL = /* Create Cursor to Locate Auto-Generated */
                    /* Statistic Sets                         */
                    'DECLARE c_Stats CURSOR FAST_FORWARD FOR ' +
                    ' SELECT so.Name + ''.'' + si.Name, ' +
                    '        so.Name + ''.'' + SUBSTRING(si.Name, 9, '+
                    '            DATALENGTH(CONVERT(VARCHAR, '+
                    '               si.Name)) - 17) ' +
                    '   FROM ' + @v_DBName + '..sysindexes si (NOLOCK) ' +
                    '   JOIN ' + @v_DBName + '..sysobjects so (NOLOCK) ' +
                    '     ON si.ID = so.ID ' +
                    '  WHERE si.Name LIKE ''[_]WA[_]Sys[_]%'' ' +
```

```
'          AND so.xType = ''U'' ' +
'      ORDER BY so.Name, si.Name '+

/* Declare Variables */
'DECLARE @v_AutoGen VARCHAR(100), ' +
'          @v_ColName CHAR(40) ' +

/* Open Cursor */
'OPEN c_Stats ' +

/* Display the database being scanned */
'PRINT ''Scanning ' + @v_DBName + ''' ' +
'PRINT ''================================='' ' +

/* Fetch first statistic set */
'FETCH NEXT FROM c_Stats INTO @v_AutoGen, ' +
'                              @v_ColName '+

/* Loop Through Statistic Sets and Generate Drop Code */
'WHILE @@Fetch_Status <> -1 ' +
'  BEGIN ' +
'  IF @@Fetch_Status <> -2 ' +
'    BEGIN ' +
'    PRINT @v_ColName + '' *** '' + @v_AutoGen ' +
'    END ' +
'  FETCH NEXT FROM c_Stats INTO @v_AutoGen, ' +
'                              @v_ColName '+
'  END ' +

/* Close and Deallocate the Cursor */
'CLOSE c_Stats ' +
'DEALLOCATE c_Stats '

/* Execute the cursor to locate statistics */
EXEC(@v_SQL)

/* Add blank lines to separate result sets */
/* between databases                       */
PRINT ''
PRINT ''
END

/* Get the next database name from the cursor */
FETCH NEXT FROM c_DBList INTO @v_DBName
END
```

```
/* Close and deallocate the cursor */
CLOSE c_DBList
DEALLOCATE c_DBList
GO
```

| Related solutions: | Found on page: |
|---|---|
| Examining an Execution Plan in the Query Analyzer | 516 |
| Building and Executing Dynamic SQL | 834 |

# Performing Positioned Updates

In this example, let's assume that a publishing house has just been bought out and the new management wants to make some changes. After reviewing the books, the new management has concluded that no matter how many books are sold at a loss, the company can't make it up in volume. With that in mind, some serious price increases are called for to get the publishing house back to a profit-making level. After some deliberation, a calculation is created to raise the price of each title in the Pubs database. The calculation consists of taking the year-to-date sales of each book and dividing by the total year-to-date sales for all books. The result is the sales percentage for the current book. A smaller markup is applied to the better selling books by taking the books' sales percentage and subtracting it from 100 to find the markup percentage. Then, by converting the percentage to a decimal value and adding 1, a new price is calculated. The following code shows the actual calculation for the markup multiplier (both variables are of type **MONEY**).

```
(1 - (@v_YTD / @v_TotYTD)) + 1
```

This example demonstrates the technique of performing a Positioned Update. Although this update can actually be coded to use set-based logic and would likely perform more efficiently, it will serve as an example of how to use a cursor to perform a Positioned Update.

1. You first need to declare a cursor to loop through the titles table. Three fields are needed in order to perform this operation: **title**, **price**, and **ytd_sales**.

2. Next, you need to declare variables for the title, old price, year-to-date sales, total year-to-date sales, new price, and markup rate.

3. Because it is part of this calculation, you need to get the total year-to-date sales amount for all titles. This should be done before you begin processing the cursor.

4. Once you have everything set up, it's time to open and loop through the cursor. Don't forget to check for deleted records and skip them in your processing.

5. The processing code for the cursor first needs to use the calculation provided previously to find the markup rate.

6. After you find the markup rate, you can calculate a new price for the title.

7. Before you do anything else, you should add some display code to the loop to show the title, old price, and new price. Once this display code is in place, you can test the cursor and make sure that your calculation is working properly.

8. When the debugging output looks like it is working correctly, you are ready to perform the actual Positioned Update. The new price is assigned to the current title using a **WHERE CURRENT OF** clause on the update statement in the cursor processing code.

9. Run the query one last time to actually update the prices in the **titles** table. The entire listing for this script is provided in Listing 13.22 to assist you in setting up this example.

---

**NOTE:** *This code permanently modifies the price column in the titles table. You should take a backup before executing this example, so that you can restore the original values.*

---

### Listing 13.22    Positioned update example.

```
/*********************/
/* Markup All Titles */
/*********************/

/* Switch database context */
USE pubs

/* Turn off query row count displays */
SET NOCOUNT ON

/* Declare a cursor to get a list of titles */
DECLARE c_Titles CURSOR FORWARD_ONLY KEYSET
  FOR SELECT title,
             price,
             ytd_sales
        FROM titles
        WHERE price IS NOT NULL

/* Declare variables to hold the price information */
DECLARE @v_Title VARCHAR(80),
```

13. Cursors

```
                  @v_Price Money,
                  @v_YTD MONEY,
                  @v_TotYTD MONEY,
                  @v_NewPrice MONEY,
                  @v_MURate DECIMAL(16,6)

/* Get Total YTD Sales */
SELECT @v_TotYTD = SUM(COALESCE(ytd_sales,0))
  FROM pubs..titles (NOLOCK)

/* Open the cursor */
OPEN c_Titles

/* Get the first title name */
FETCH NEXT FROM c_Titles INTO @v_Title,
                              @v_Price,
                              @v_YTD

/* Loop through the titles */
WHILE (@@Fetch_Status <> -1)
  BEGIN
    /* Check for deleted row */
    IF (@@Fetch_Status <> -2)
      BEGIN
      /* Get percentage of total sales */
      SELECT @v_MURate = (1 - (@v_YTD / @v_TotYTD)) + 1

      /* Calculate New Price */
      SELECT @v_NewPrice = (@v_MURate * @v_Price)

      /* Display the markup being performed */
      PRINT 'Maring up: ' + @v_Title
      PRINT 'Old Price: ' + CONVERT(VARCHAR,@v_Price)
      PRINT 'New Price: ' + CONVERT(VARCHAR,@v_NewPrice)
      PRINT ''
      PRINT ''

      /* Perform the update */
      UPDATE pubs.dbo.titles
        SET price = @v_NewPrice
        WHERE CURRENT OF c_Titles
      END

  /* Get the next title from the cursor */
  FETCH NEXT FROM c_Titles INTO @v_Title,
                                @v_Price,
                                @v_YTD
```

```
        END

/* Close and deallocate the cursor */
CLOSE c_Titles
DEALLOCATE c_Titles
GO
```

# Performing Positioned Deletes

In performing some routine maintenance on the Pubs database, you notice that there are some duplicate rows in the **authors** table. Because you should only have one row per author, it is determined that the duplicate rows should be removed. In order to accomplish this task, you decide to implement a cursor that removes duplicate rows via a Positioned Delete.

There are no duplicate entries in the **authors** table that ships with SQL Server 2000, but it is a simple matter to create duplicate rows to test this cursor. Listing 13.23 provides a simple script that clones the current entries in the **authors** table to create duplicate entries.

### Listing 13.23    Clone **authors**.

```
/* Switch database context */
USE pubs

/* Clone author records to create duplicate entries */
INSERT INTO authors ( au_id,
                      au_lname,
                      au_fname,
                      phone,
                      address,
                      city,
                      state,
                      zip,
                      contract )
    SELECT '0' + SUBSTRING(au_id, 2, 10),
           au_lname,
           au_fname,
           phone,
           address,
           city,
           state,
           zip,
           contract
```

```
FROM authors (NOLOCK)
WHERE substring(au_id,1,1)<>'0'
```

1. You first need to run the cloning script to add duplicate rows to the **authors** table.

2. Next, you need to create a cursor to loop through the **authors** table and find duplicates. It is important to order the selected authors by **au_lname** and **au_fname** to make it easier to find the duplicate rows.

3. You need to declare two variables, one to hold the name and one to hold the name from the previous record.

4. The processing code should compare the old name with the current name to determine if the row is a duplicate that should be deleted.

5. Add code to display information about the row that will be removed if the row is a duplicate.

6. After checking to see if the old name and current name are the same, assign the current name to the old name before fetching the next row.

7. Once the display code is in place, it is a good idea to execute the cursor to make sure that the logic appears to be working correctly.

8. When the debugging process is complete, it is time to add the Positioned Delete. This is accomplished by adding a **DELETE** statement with a **WHERE CURRENT OF** clause to the processing code in the cursor.

9. Execute the cursor to remove the duplicates.

10. You will most likely receive one or more of the errors shown in Listing 13.24. This is because the order in which the rows are being processed is causing your code to attempt to delete the original row, which is referenced in another table.

**Listing 13.24   Error deleting duplicates.**

```
Server: Msg 547, Level 16, State 1, Line 28
DELETE statement conflicted with COLUMN REFERENCE constraint
'FK__titleauth__au_id__0519C6AF'. The conflict occurred in
database 'pubs', table 'titleauthor', column 'au_id'.
The statement has been terminated.
```

11. This error is annoying and would take some time to eliminate from the code. A simpler solution in the interest of time is to reverse the sort order on the cursor to get the remaining duplicate rows deleted. This can be accomplished very simply by adding the **DESC** argument after each field in the **ORDER BY** clause.

12. Once this change is made, you can execute the query again to remove the remainder of the duplicate rows. Because this is not a process that you will be performing regularly, the extra step required to remove the remaining duplicates is probably acceptable.

13. Add a few comments to help you understand what the code is doing when you go back to it later. You are now ready to save the script. Listing 13.25 provides a completed script that is formatted and contains comments. It also contains a commented line for the **ORDER BY** to make switching the direction of the query a simple matter of changing which **ORDER BY** is commented.

### Listing 13.25    Positioned delete example.

```
/*****************************/
/* Remove Duplicate Authors */
/*****************************/

/* Switch database context */
USE pubs

/* Turn off query row count displays */
SET NOCOUNT ON

/* Declare a cursor to get a list of authors */
DECLARE c_Authors CURSOR FORWARD_ONLY KEYSET
  FOR SELECT au_fname + ' ' + au_lname
        FROM authors
        ORDER BY au_lname, au_fname
--        ORDER BY au_lname DESC, au_fname DESC

/* Declare variables to hold the current and previous author names */
DECLARE @v_name varchar(50),
        @v_oldname varchar(50)

/* Open the cursor */
OPEN c_Authors

/* Get the first author name */
FETCH NEXT FROM c_Authors INTO @v_name

/* Loop through the authors */
WHILE (@@Fetch_Status <> -1)
  BEGIN
    /* Check for deleted row */
    IF (@@Fetch_Status <> -2)
      BEGIN
```

13. Cursors

```
                /* Remove duplicate entries */
                IF (@v_oldname = @v_name)
                  BEGIN
                  /* Remove duplicate row */
                  DELETE FROM pubs.dbo.authors
                    WHERE CURRENT OF c_Authors

                  /* Show records removed */
                  PRINT @v_name + ' (Duplicate Removed)'
                  END

                /* Save name to check for duplicate entries */
                SELECT @v_oldname = @v_name
                END

          /* Get the next author name from the cursor */
          FETCH NEXT FROM c_Authors INTO @v_name
          END

    /* Close and deallocate the cursor */
    CLOSE c_Authors
    DEALLOCATE c_Authors
    GO
```

# Selecting a Random Employee

In this example, let's assume that the HR director of your company has decided that for morale reasons the company needs to have a random drawing once a month and award an extra vacation day to the lucky winner. Because the process of selecting the winning employee is tedious to perform manually and the director wants to make sure the selection is fair, it's been decided that a script be created to make the selection.

There are a number of ways that this can be done, but for this example let's construct a cursor script to perform this task. Although this is something of a gimmicky script, it does illustrate a couple of useful techniques.

1. Open the Query Analyzer.
2. Select Edit|Insert Template.
3. Open the Using Cursor folder.
4. Select Declare and Use READ_ONLY Cursor.tql. This pastes the template text into the query window.
5. Select Edit|Replace Template Parameters.

6. Enter "csrRandomEmployee" for the **cursor_name** parameter.

7. You need to get a list of employees from the **tbl_Employee** table in the Employee database, so enter the following code for the **select_statement** parameter:

```
SELECT Employee_ID,
       First_Name + ' ' + Last_Name AS EmpName
 FROM tbl_Employee (NOLOCK)
```

8. Click on OK to close the dialog and replace the template parameters with the specified values.

9. Apply any formatting changes to the template generated code that will make it more readable for you.

10. Add the **SCROLL** keyword to the **DECLARE CURSOR** statement because a standard **READ_ONLY** cursor does not support the **FETCH ABSOLUTE** command. This command is needed for your code to work properly.

11. Add the **STATIC** keyword to the **DECLARE CURSOR** statement, so that you can be sure that the result set will not change in any way during your processing.

12. Remove the processing code generated by the template, including the entire **WHILE** loop.

13. The following code shows the variables that you need to declare for this script, which should replace the template code used to declare **@name**:

```
DECLARE @v_EmpID INT,
        @v_EmpName varchar(40),
        @v_EmpCount INT,
        @v_WinnerRow INT,
        @v_MailMsg VARCHAR(1000)
```

14. Immediately after the **OPEN** command, you need to save the number of rows that are qualified by the **SELECT** statement in the cursor definition. This count can be obtained from the **@@CURSOR_ROWS** global system variable. The following code saves this value in the **@EmpCount** variable:

```
SELECT @v_EmpCount = @@CURSOR_ROWS
```

15. Once you have obtained the employee count, you are ready to start the processing logic. You first need to make sure that you have at least one employee. The following code performs this check and should be inserted after the assignment for **@EmpCount**:

```
IF (@v_EmpCount <> 0)
  BEGIN
  END
```

16. The actual processing occurs between the **BEGIN** and **END** statements for the **IF** check. The first step is to select the winning employee. Transact-SQL provides a function that generates a random number between 0 and 1. Using this function, you can create a calculation to select one of your employees as the winner. The following code shows the calculation needed to select the winner:

```
SELECT @v_WinnerRow = CONVERT(INT,RAND() * @v_EmpCount) + 1
```

17. Once you have picked the winning row, you need to perform a fetch to find out who the winning employee actually is. This is accomplished by using the **FETCH ABSOLUTE** command as shown in the following code:

```
FETCH ABSOLUTE @v_WinnerRow FROM c_RandomEmployee INTO @v_EmpID,
                                                       @v_EmpName
```

18. Once you have retrieved the winning employee, you now need to notify the HR director of the winner, so that the extra day off can be processed and the winner can be notified. The following code constructs the body of a simple mail message that you can send to the HR director:

```
SELECT @v_MailMsg = 'The lucky winner for ' +
                CONVERT(VARCHAR, GETDATE(), 107) +
                ' is ' + @v_EmpName + ' Employee # ' +
                CONVERT(VARCHAR, @v_EmpID)
```

19. You can also add a **PRINT** statement that allows you to debug the output of the cursor. The following line displays the message so that you can make sure the formatting is okay and the random employee selection is working correctly.

```
PRINT @_MailMsg
```

20. Once you have added the **PRINT** statement, execute the query a few times to be sure that different employees are being selected. You may get some duplicates, but the random selection should be obvious.

21. As soon as the debug session determines that the code is functioning properly and the message is formatted in a readable fashion, you are ready

to actually send the email. The following code uses the **xp_sendmail** extended stored procedure to send the message to the HR director:

```
EXEC master..xp_sendmail @Recipients = 'HRDirector',
                         @Message = @v_MailMsg,
                         @Subject = 'PTO Winner'
```

22. During the testing phase for this script, you should change the **@Recipients** parameter to send the email to your address instead of the HR director to make sure the email is working correctly. Once you have verified that the mail is sending properly, you can make arrangements to send one test mail to the HR director to ensure that the address information is entered correctly.

23. Add a few comments to help you understand in the future what the code is supposed to be doing. You are now ready to save the script. Listing 13.26 provides a completed script that is formatted and contains comments.

24. This script can easily be used as a processing step in a scheduled job that executes at some desired interval. For more information on scheduling jobs in SQL Server, refer to Chapter 6.

### Listing 13.26   Select random winner.

```
/**********************************************************/
/* Select a random employee to receive an extra day off */
/**********************************************************/

/* Switch database context */
USE Employee

/* Turn off query row count displays */
SET NOCOUNT ON

/* Declare cursor to select a list of employees */
DECLARE c_RandomEmployee CURSOR READ_ONLY STATIC SCROLL FOR
  SELECT Employee_ID,
         First_Name + ' ' + Last_Name AS EmpName
    FROM tbl_Employee (NOLOCK)

/* Declare variables */
DECLARE @v_EmpID INT,
        @v_EmpName varchar(40),
        @v_EmpCount INT,
```

```
            @v_WinnerRow INT,
            @v_MailMsg VARCHAR(1000)

/* Open the cursor */
OPEN c_RandomEmployee

/* Get the number of employees qualified by the cursor */
SELECT @v_EmpCount = @@CURSOR_ROWS

/* If we have at least one employee, then we can continue processing */
IF (@v_EmpCount <> 0)
  BEGIN
  /* Select the row for our random winner */
  SELECT @v_WinnerRow = CONVERT(INT,RAND() * @v_EmpCount) + 1

  /* Fetch the winner's record */
  FETCH ABSOLUTE @v_WinnerRow FROM c_RandomEmployee INTO @v_EmpID,
                                                         @v_EmpName

  /* Create an email message to notify the HR Director */
  /* of the selected winner                            */
  SELECT @v_MailMsg = 'The lucky winner for ' +
                      CONVERT(VARCHAR, GETDATE(), 107) +
                      ' is ' + @v_EmpName + ' Employee # ' +
                      CONVERT(VARCHAR, @v_EmpID)

  /* Display the email message for debugging. The PRINT can */
  /* be removed when you are satisfied the code is working  */
  /* properly.                                              */
  PRINT @v_MailMsg

  /* Use xp_sendmail to send the message to the HR Director */
  EXEC master..xp_sendmail @Recipients = 'HRDirector',
                           @Message = @v_MailMsg,
                           @Subject = 'PTO Winner'
  END

/* Close and deallocate the cursor */
CLOSE c_RandomEmployee
DEALLOCATE c_RandomEmployee
GO
```

# Chapter 14

# Stored Procedures and External Stored Procedures

(continued)

# *In Depth*

Stored procedures are supported in one form or another on most major database platforms. Microsoft SQL Server supports stored procedures in many forms. In this chapter, custom procedures, system procedures, remote procedures, and external stored procedures are discussed at length. The scope of stored procedure use varies greatly across many enterprises and is typically not embraced as much as it should be.

## Consistent Data Manipulation

Programmers have struggled for years to provide a bulletproof method of manipulating data. This endeavor has brought about many changes in the way applications are written and designed. Although each application takes a slightly different approach to managing data, one methodology remains constant for all applications: Use a consistent procedure for access, additions, modifications, or deletions of data, and you will have far fewer problems in the long run. Troubleshooting and performance tuning your applications become easier by orders of magnitude.

### Enter Stored Procedures

Adopting a standard method of data access is not difficult. Each company may choose a different path, but all have the same end result in mind. Use one way to do things, with as few "special case" changes as possible. Following the same procedures for inserting data or error checking across all your code ensures that anyone looking at the code can easily figure out what must be done to add data to one of your systems. As long as every programmer follows the guidelines that you have established for that particular system, he or she will not create problems for other applications or processes running in your production environment.

Most of the standards presented in this chapter are gleaned from many production environments. Only you can be the absolute authority on your system, because you have a thorough understanding of your specific needs. Therefore, take what is discussed in this chapter, apply what works for you, and put the remaining information into memory for later consumption. After working with these standards and realizing what standards can do for you, you might find that you can devise standards and methodologies that precisely meet your needs.

# Establishing Standards

Many standards are offered in this chapter; however, you must decide for yourself whether to adopt them in whole or in part. Any standard you can formulate will probably work for your environment. Keep in mind that each enterprise has unique requirements that might cause a suggested standard to be invalid. It is recommended that you create a standards and practices document for database manipulation and keep that document up-to-date.

**WARNING! Many companies have created a document to manage the database access and provide programmers with the guidance they need to work with the database. In most cases, the document becomes out of date or new programmers are not required to become familiar with it. Do not allow this to happen in your environment!**

It is best to use standard naming conventions with database objects, just as it is with programs that you write. See Table 14.1 for some sample naming conventions. The naming conventions help you recall the function or purpose of the object if you have not looked at it for a few months, or give you a filtering condition for queries against system tables. You should also use standard methods for manipulating data. Using a certain method to edit data ensures that consistent client manipulation is used across all programs.

**Table 14.1    Naming conventions.**

| Object Type | Prefix |
| --- | --- |
| Table | **tbl_** |
| View | **vw_** |
| Clustered Index | **cidx_** |
| Unique Index | **uidx_** |
| Index | **idx_** |
| Cursor | **c_** |
| Local Variable | **@v_** |
| Parameter | **@p_** |
| Stored Procedure | **usp_** |
| Insert Trigger | **inst_** |
| Update Trigger | **updt_** |
| Delete Trigger | **delt_** |
| Rule | **rul_** |
| Default | **def_** |
| Function | **fn_** |

**NOTE:** *You should not use* ***sp_*** *to preface your user-defined procedures. If a stored procedure name begins with* ***sp_***, *it is assumed to be a system procedure that is automatically checked against the master database before being checked against the user database.*

## Getting Data

When a client application needs data, whether in a true client/server environment or in a multitiered system, the act of reading data usually is different than the act of making changes or additions. Therefore, getting data to client applications can be easily managed with a stored procedure. You can mask the underlying data structure from the application via stored procedures and isolate the storage from the presentation layer.

Data access procedures are usually called something similar to **usp_GetMessage**, **usp_GetOrder**, or **usp_LookupRecord**. The **usp_** prefix is used for a few reasons. First, in an alphabetical list, these names show up separately from any system or external procedures, because the latter procedures are prefaced with **sp** and **xp**, respectively. Second, each of these objects, along with many others, exists in your server's system tables on your server. You can distinguish easily between a stored procedure and another object by looking at the prefix.

It is well worth the time to develop a good naming convention for all your server objects. Having a standard prefix for each object in your system and publishing them among all programmers avoids any potential confusion and can be a time-saver for developing against your server. In a multiple programmer environment, consistent naming conventions are practically a requirement. Keep in mind that these are only suggestions; they should be thought out thoroughly before being adopted in any environment. If your enterprise has an existing naming convention in use, try to mirror that as closely as possible to reduce confusion.

Another benefit of using stored procedures to transfer data between client applications is the security associated with stored procedures. User or groups of users can be granted permission to run only those procedures to which they need access. If no permission is granted to modify the underlying tables, the data is protected from accidental or intentional modifications. It is rarely recommended that you give users direct access to query or modify tables on production systems. Because ad hoc query tools make maintaining data security much more difficult, using stored procedures as a method of accessing data is invaluable. Occasionally, direct access to read views is a good idea for reporting and support issues.

For performance reasons, you should typically not allow general queries to run against tables. If a database programmer or administrator writes the queries that get data from the server and allow others to run that code through stored procedures, he or she ensures that no long-running or system resource-killing query can be introduced while production is running its queries. Ad hoc query tools should not be turned loose against your tables as a general rule. These types of tools can create contention and blocking conditions on your production data, which slows the processing of mission-critical data. Instead, a preferred approach is to create a reporting server and allow people to query against that server for reporting and analysis needs.

You can better spend your time tuning the queries for speed and maintaining data integrity. Most client applications that use stored procedures to get data need to know only the name of the procedure and the data type of any parameters required to execute the procedure. If you change the underlying code of the procedure without changing the parameter list or names, you can update and improve your stored procedures without having to rebuild any client applications. Improving performance without changing or affecting client code is an important reason to use stored procedure instead of standard SQL in a client/server environment.

## Modifying Data

All systems must have the capability to add, change, or delete records on an ongoing basis. Stored procedures are valuable in this area as well. They provide the additional security of not allowing anyone to modify data who doesn't have permission to run a particular procedure and the built-in integrity of each client using the same code and method to perform any modification task.

In addition, stored procedures allow you to mask, from your client applications, the complexity of the underlying data structure. If a procedure requires derived or table-driven data to complete a task, you can look up what is needed in your stored procedures without the user ever having to know what is happening. Concealing the complexity of your data structure from the user and client applications has many benefits. It typically reduces the amount of traffic between the client and the server and gives you much more control over potential locking issues.

## Modular Programming

Stored procedures not only provide the client developer with a standard method of dealing with the server, they also give the SQL programmer the ability to write modular code. For instance, in many systems you will need to develop a standard set of string functions. The method of parsing tokens from a string could be written as a stored procedure and called from both the client applications and from other stored procedures.

---

**NOTE:** *Client-side string manipulation is usually preferred over passing strings back and forth between client and server. This method can be used to reduce round-trip traffic and allow the server to perform a task that is typically done on the client side.*

---

By analyzing your existing stored procedures or SQL statements and looking for redundant code that performs the same task in many places, you can usually find candidates for utility functions. Consider writing a stored procedure that performs the task with as few parameters as possible while returning a standard response. Once you have created the new procedure, you can easily replace the redundant code with a call to the new procedure.

Using stored procedures can greatly reduce the amount of actual SQL code you have to write because you can call other stored procedures to perform like functions. This feature appears in all popular programming languages and allows for more reliable, error-free SQL code.

---

**NOTE:** *You can nest stored procedure calls up to 32 levels with SQL Server 2000.*

---

Once a procedure is written and tested, you can call that procedure from many places and it will work the same way in each case. If you need to enhance the feature set of stored procedures, you make the change in one place, debug the change, and you're done. In addition, stored procedures can dramatically cut the development cycle of your applications. A library of standard stored procedures can be developed once and reused many times by many different client applications.

## Reduced Client Processing

There is one feature of stored procedures that even hard-core, talented client programmers often miss. In earlier applications, the programmer was responsible for determining all the related and supporting code for modifying data. Primary keys, lookup tables, and calculations were maintained by the applications individually. With server-side processing becoming more prevalent, stored procedures can reduce the amount of client-side processing by looking up data and maintaining key values and internal integrity (reducing round-trips to the server for validation of data).

Server-based stored procedures allow you to develop "thin" client applications—applications concerned only with displaying data in a manner that meets the user's needs. Very little data logic is needed in client applications with strong server-side processing. With the speed and power of database servers today, you can offload the time-consuming tasks to the server and let users perform the tasks of data input faster with less network traffic.

## Network Traffic

Network bandwidth is typically in the 10 to 100Mb range in most enterprises. Unless you are developing an application for modem dial-up or Internet connection to the database, you should have plenty of throughput to support your applications. If you do support modems or Internet access to your applications, the amount of traffic that goes across the pipe is very important.

If you analyze the number of characters that must be sent to a server for a typical **SELECT** statement, you begin to see the difference that a stored procedure can make. See Listing 14.1 for a standard **SELECT** statement of 223 characters, including formatting, and approximately 155 characters without spaces. The stored procedure called to get the same results takes a total of 27 characters. You can imagine what the size of a 3- to 4-table join with many columns and a complicated **WHERE** clause would be versus the size of a stored procedure in this case.

**Listing 14.1    Character count example.**

```
/* Phone list in Alpha order (CA) */
SELECT 'Name'  = UPPER(au_lname) + ', ' +
                 UPPER(au_fname),
       'Phone' = '(' + SUBSTRING(phone,1,3) + ') ' +
                 SUBSTRING(phone,5,8)
  FROM authors (NOLOCK)
 WHERE state = 'CA'
 ORDER BY au_lname

/* Stored Procedure call */
EXEC usp_GetAuthorPhoneList 'CA'
```

If the query in Listing 14.1 was called by 50 different client applications 20 times per day, you would see a reduction in character-based traffic of 193,000 characters on your network. Although you would still have the same traffic volume returned from each query, you would see reduced traffic with regard to the actual requests.

If you add a modem or even the bandwidth of a full T1 line to the equation, you can begin to see the impact. Remember, a full T1 line can reach a speed of just over 1Mbps, and that even a fast modem can reach only 56,000bps in perfect conditions. By using stored procedures and a well-designed client application in tested dial-in modem access, client/server remote applications have attained speeds almost equal to regular network applications.

Keep in mind that to get a high level of performance across a modem, you must keep network traffic to a minimum. The benefit of using stored procedures in your applications is that they respond very well over your network compared to fat client applications that pay no regard to how much traffic is passed between the client and the server.

# Calling a Stored Procedure

As Listing 14.1 shows, a call to a stored procedure is not very complicated. The **EXECUTE**, or **EXEC**, statement followed by the stored procedure name and any parameter is about all you need. You can return a result set, output parameter, or a single record with a stored procedure. The beauty of stored procedures is that the code is hidden from the client application. The client developer does not need to know much about SQL to use stored procedures in his or her application. You can edit the structure of the underlying tables without impacting the client application.

---

**NOTE:** *For more information on the many uses of the **EXECUTE** statement, see Microsoft SQL Server Books Online.*
***EXECUTE** can be used in many ways to create powerful SQL scripts, dynamic SQL, and stored procedures.*

---

Stored procedures can be nested and can call other stored procedures to return the results to the client. In fact, you can even use recursion in a controlled environment to make your code more flexible. Some programmers have developed stored procedures that literally process hundreds of records in many separate tables to return a single value to the client. Cursors and control-of-flow language features can be used in your stored procedures for added functionality and can perform complex operations that would typically require multiple round-trips to the server.

## Query Optimizer

Microsoft SQL Server uses a cost-based Query Optimizer that determines the best method with which to return the data that you request to the client. Indexes, join conditions, **WHERE** clauses, **ORDER BY** statements, and optimizer hints all come into play when determining the best way to access data. You should look for any known resource-intensive item in your queries to help reduce the amount of time it takes for the Query Optimizer to determine the best plan for retrieving data. Whenever possible, you should avoid the following items when writing queries:

---

**NOTE:** *See Chapter 11 for an in-depth look at performance tuning and optimization of queries and stored procedures in SQL.*

---

- Large result sets
- **IN**, **NOT IN**, and **OR** queries
- <> (not equal)
- Row aggregate functions, such as **SUM, AVG, MAX,** and so on.
- Local variables, expressions, or data conversions in **WHERE** clauses

- Highly nonunique **WHERE** clauses or no **WHERE** clause at all
- Complex views with **GROUP BY** or **ORDER BY** statements

Remember that the Query Optimizer looks at the current state of the indexes and data distribution to choose the best plan possible. If you do not keep the statistics and integrity of your data current by periodically rebuilding indexes and updating statistics, the optimizer will recognize this and create worktables even when indexes exist and should have been used to return the data faster.

## Query Plan

For each query, SQL Server creates a query plan that includes all the information required to return the data effectively to the client. If the query is a stored procedure, this plan is stored in cache when it is compiled, so that it can be used during subsequent executions (saving time over repeated raw SQL statements being submitted to the server).

Understand that when the query plan is stored in cache, only one user can access the plan at a time. If two users request the same query plan for a stored procedure, SQL Server creates a new, second plan and stores it in cache as well. This second query plan might even be different than the first due to the integrity of the available indexes and data at the time of execution.

To better understand how query plans work, let's look at the steps involved in executing a query. When your SQL statement is first submitted to SQL Server, it performs the following steps:

1. Parses the raw SQL code to determine if there is any syntax error to be reported.
2. Checks for aliases referenced in the **FROM** clause for use later in the process and checks for valid object references (**SELECT LIST**, **FROM**, and **WHERE** clauses).
3. Generates the query plan based on available data, statistics, and indexes (sometimes referred to as the "optimization step").
4. Compiles the query and places it into cache if it is a stored procedure.
5. Executes the compiled query plan and returns the data to the client.

Once the query plan for a procedure is cached, it remains in cache until it is pushed out by other more active procedures. If a procedure's query plan is pushed out of the cache on SQL Server, it is recompiled and a new query plan created the next time it is called. If the procedure is in cache, the user requesting data through a stored procedure must have the parameters used in the procedure checked; the user then has the plan reexecuted to return data. This reduces the amount of overhead on the server for the process of returning data to the clients. In many situations where a standard set of procedures is used and constantly cached, the users see marked improvement over raw SQL code execution.

Stored procedures also enhance performance with regard to object references. In raw SQL, every time a query is executed, each object reference is checked when it is passed to the server. With stored procedures, the objects are checked when compiled and stored in the query plan. Each subsequent call to the stored procedure does not trigger the object reference check on the server, thus reducing overhead.

In addition, permissions are handled differently with stored procedures. When a stored procedure is written, the security context of the author is used. Typically, the owner of the underlying objects and the stored procedure is the same. When this is the case, object ownership checks are bypassed.

---

**NOTE:** *If the ownership of any underlying objects is different, breaking the chain, then the access of each object is checked for the current user to have permission to perform the operation. This allows for the integrity of any referenced objects to be maintained.*

---

Once the stored procedure is created and the object owner is the same, anyone calling the procedure assumes the permissions of the author inside the stored procedure. This way, the users of a stored procedure can be granted permission to run a procedure, but not to do anything else to the underlying data. Users are not able to see or change the code within a stored procedure, so the underlying objects and data are protected, and users are allowed to perform only the tasks specified. Stored procedures can greatly reduce the occurrence of security problems on your SQL server.

## Parameters

The maximum number of parameters you can use with a stored procedure is 2100 in SQL Server 2000. Most programmers have never written a stored procedure that even comes close to this limit, but you can bet that someone will test this limit at some point. When possible, you should limit the number of parameters by using table lookups internally in the stored procedure to get the data you need. This reduces the amount of parameter traffic on the network and keeps the client application as "thin" as possible. Parameters are data type-specific and should be defined to the correct size and precision as needed inside the stored procedure. You can use the **CONVERT( )** function to change any data types once they are passed into a stored procedure. You should stay away from variant data-type parameters because they typically require that you typecast them to manipulate the data inside a stored procedure.

You also can use output parameters with stored procedures. These parameters basically are passed into the procedure marked as output parameters, modified internally within the stored procedure, and returned in the modified state to the calling procedure. Output parameters can be useful in complex client applications that require multiple return values from a stored procedure as well as the result sets.

## Variables

Another great feature of stored procedures is the ability to use local variables. You can create as many local variables as needed within your stored procedures, providing you have set aside enough memory on the server for Microsoft SQL Server. Local variables are designated by the **@** sign preceding the variable name. You must declare all variables before they are referenced and use data type-specific declarations, so that Microsoft SQL Server knows how to use the variables.

*NOTE: You cannot declare global server variables.*

To be consistent, it is suggested that you use the **@v_** lowercase prefix when naming your variables. With this method, you can easily distinguish between variables, parameters, and column names. You can use **@p_** for parameters for additional clarity. The following partial list of global variables, now referred to as functions in SQL Server 2000, can be accessed from within your SQL code. Note that this is only a partial list of functions. See Microsoft SQL Server Books Online for complete information on variables. Global variables or functions have an **@@** prefix to distinguish them from local variables.

Many of the functions in the following list can be combined with queries against the system tables in Microsoft SQL Server to create a more intelligent set of stored procedures:

- **@@CONNECTIONS**—Contains the number of logins since SQL Server was last started.

- **@@CPU_BUSY**—Holds the amount of time the server has spent executing SQL statements since the last time SQL Server was started. (Data is in ticks, which are one three-hundredth of a second, or 3.33 milliseconds.)

- **@@ERROR**—Holds the return code or status of the last SQL statement executed on Microsoft SQL Server. This variable is maintained on a per connection basis. (A value of 0 means success.)

- **@@FETCH_STATUS**—Contains the result of a cursor's **FETCH** command. This value is **0** if the **FETCH** is successful, **-1** if the **FETCH** failed or the row requested is beyond the record set defined for the cursor, and **-2** if the row fetched is missing or no longer in the scope of the cursor.

- **@@IDENTITY**—Holds the value of the last identity value generated by an **INSERT** statement. Microsoft SQL Server generates identity values automatically for each table that has an identity column, and this value is unique for each record in that table. This value is maintained on a connection-by-connection basis.

- **@@IDLE**—Specifies the amount of time, in ticks, that SQL Server has been idle since it was last started.

- **@@IO_BUSY**—Contains the time, in ticks, that SQL Server has spent performing input and output operations since it was last started.

- **@@MAX_CONNECTIONS**—Holds the maximum count of simultaneous connections that can be made with the server at one time. This is not the amount of client licenses that you have purchased. One client can acquire more than one connection in a multithreaded application.

- **@@NESTLEVEL**—Holds the current count of how many levels you are nested within your stored procedures. The maximum nesting level is 32. If you exceed the maximum level, your transaction is terminated.

- **@@OPTIONS**—Returns the current **SET** options that are considered user options. The integer value returned represents the combination of option values currently set. You need to refer to the SQL Server Books Online topic "User Options Option" for each option value to determine which options have been set to **ON**.

- **@@PROCID**—Holds the stored procedure ID of the current stored procedure.

- **@@ROWCOUNT**—Specifies the number of rows affected by the statement immediately preceding it. Set to **0** for statements such as **IF** or control-of-flow statements. Caution should be taken when relying on this variable; assignments can set this value to another number and mislead you.

- **@@SPID**—Provides the server process ID number of the currently executing procedure. This value can be used for looking up information about a stored procedure in the **sysprocesses** system table.

- **@@TRANCOUNT**—Specifies the number of the currently active or nested transactions for the current user. This value is maintained on a connection-by-connection basis.

Often, you may find that using variables to create a stored procedure to perform a highly complex task can save hours of programming. Spend some time in

Microsoft SQL Server Books Online and view some of the sample code to become more familiar with how local and global variables can be used in your code.

# Windows NT Server Registry

When you require server-based global variables that are static with regard to the server operation, you have another option available to you: the Windows NT Registry on the server itself. This location is a static repository many client applications use on each local machine for startup and runtime parameters. This option is recommended for experienced programmers with a good knowledge of the Windows NT Registry and how it works.

---

**NOTE:** *In Chapter 8, an easier and faster method of performing Registry-based operations against a SQL Server table was discussed: the table method. The table method is faster than direct Windows NT Registry manipulation.*

---

You can make calls to the Windows NT Registry by using external stored procedures available with Microsoft SQL Server (see Table 14.2). If you use the Windows NT Registry on your server, you should adopt a very strict standard of writing, reading, and deleting these values, so that you do not leave a lot of stray entries floating around in the Registry. These externals are *not* well documented in the Books Online and should be tested thoroughly if used. You can pick up bits and pieces as well as the syntax from looking up **xp_regwrite** and finding a related topic with some examples.

---

**NOTE:** *Great care should be taken any time you access the registry on your system. Do not manipulate any keys that you did not create yourself for use in your applications!*

---

As with any other application, adopting a standard of using a specific key value structure is a good idea when using these procedures. Typically, you should create and document a Registry key, where you should place all your subkeys. Use a well-thought-out, descriptive name for your keys. This makes finding your custom Registry entries with an application like regedt32.exe easier. See Listing 14.2 for an example of how to add a key, read the new key, and remove the key within a SQL script or stored procedure.

**Table 14.2    Registry external procedures.**

| Name | Function |
| --- | --- |
| **xp_regread** | Reads a key value or data from the Registry |
| **xp_regwrite** | Writes a key value or data to the Registry |
| **xp_regdeletevalue** | Removes a key from the Registry |

### Listing 14.2    Registry examples.

```
/* Sample registry script */
SET NOCOUNT ON

/* Local Variables                   */
DECLARE @v_AuthorID    VARCHAR(11),
        @v_StateName   VARCHAR(11)

/* Get a Michigan author             */
SELECT @v_AuthorID = au_id
  FROM pubs..authors (NOLOCK)
 WHERE state = 'MI'

/* Write this value to the registry  */
EXEC master.dbo.xp_regwrite
  'HKEY_LOCAL_MACHINE',
  'SOFTWARE\MyApplication\Global_Keys',
  'Michigan',
  'REG_SZ',
  @v_AuthorID

/* Return the registry value         */
EXEC master.dbo.xp_regread
  'HKEY_LOCAL_MACHINE',
  'SOFTWARE\MyApplication\Global_Keys',
  'Michigan',
  @param = @v_StateName OUTPUT

/* Check the value from the registy  */
PRINT @v_StateName

/* Remove the key                    */
EXEC master.dbo.xp_regread
  'HKEY_LOCAL_MACHINE',
  'SOFTWARE\MyApplication\Global_Keys',
  'Michigan'
```

Notice that each **EXEC** line in Listing 14.2 references the stored procedure with the database, owner, and name of the stored procedure separated by periods (three-part name). This allows you to be in the Pubs database and run a procedure stored in another database without changing the current active database context.

Each procedure lists the sample syntax to perform the basic tasks of getting data into and out of the Registry. You can use the samples as a template and modify them for your environment by replacing the key values and the data types of the keys on a case-by-case basis. The listing is provided only to illustrate the use of these external stored procedures to create pseudo-global variables on your server. This method can be used to store many different types of data, such as a server error-state or the steps of a long-running process. The only real drawback to using the Registry in this manner is that you are creating additional disk I/O for each call.

## Maintenance

Stored procedures allow you to centralize your code management. You can easily maintain and/or debug your SQL code on the server and be sure that all the clients that call the stored procedures are not going to run into SQL errors or introduce problems in the server environment. You may want to print out or place online each of your stored procedures for reference, so that developers can use them when writing client applications. That way, you can make changes to a stored procedure in one location to provide additional features to all the clients that use your stored procedure, and update the documentation for everyone at once.

Periodically, you should recompile each of your stored procedures to ensure that the underlying data structure and query are up-to-date and error-free. You can create a procedure that sets the recompile flag for all your procedures by using the table looping sample code in Chapter 6 and running **sp_recompile** against all the user tables. The next time the procedure is run, the query and execution plans will be rebuilt based on current data and index distribution.

---

**NOTE:** *An alternative to using **sp_recompile** is to use the **DBCC FLUSHPROCINDB(<dbid>)** command. SQL Server uses this DBCC command internally to set the recompile flag for all stored procedures in a database.*

---

When performing maintenance on your procedures, you might occasionally see an error message stating that you cannot change a stored procedure that is in use. Do not be alarmed; this is normal. To solve this problem, make sure you are not the one that has the procedure loaded in another window, and try to recompile the procedure again. (Scheduled recompiles work best during off hours when nobody is connected to the server.) Users do not have to disconnect for you to replace or rebuild a stored procedure. However, they must not be accessing them at the time of recompile. You can actually update a stored procedure in real time to replace code or update a procedure. The window of contention is actually very small and usually does not keep you from recompiling a stored procedure. Remember that users load the procedure into cache the first time it is called and use the cached information from that point on until it is purged from cache or recompiled with the **RECOMPILE** option.

As far as procedure maintenance goes, you might consider creating a master script file containing all your procedures for a database, and then back it up on tape or disk. This allows you to re-create all your stored procedures in a single step on the same server or on another server should the need arise. The only prerequisite to running the master script is that all the underlying dependent objects that are referenced in the procedures exist prior to running the script.

## Return Codes

Stored procedures can return result sets and return codes to signal the success or failure state of the execution. The **RETURN** statement terminates the execution of a stored procedure and optionally returns an integer value that can be checked by the client application or another stored procedure. You can create a coded return value to communicate additional information from within your stored procedures to a calling application.

Output parameters offer another useful method of returning values to calling procedures or clients. Using SQL statements, you can specify that a particular parameter in a stored procedure is an output parameter, call the procedure, and then modify the value of the parameter passed into the stored procedure from within. The resulting changes can be viewed by the calling procedure. This is a powerful and often underutilized feature. For more information on return stats and output parameters, check Microsoft SQL Server Books Online.

## Additional Rules

The following list contains some additional rules to keep in mind when creating stored procedures on Microsoft SQL Server:

- **CREATE PROCEDURE** statements cannot be combined with other SQL statements in a single batch and must be the first statement in your batch. This means that you cannot use multiple batches inside a stored procedure (only one **GO** statement is allowed per stored procedure).

- The **CREATE PROCEDURE** definition can include any number and type of SQL statements, with the exception of the **CREATE VIEW**, **TRIGGER**, **DEFAULT**, **PROCEDURE**, and **CREATE RULE** statements.

- Other database objects can be created within a stored procedure. However, you can reference these new objects only if they are created before being referenced. (Take care when doing this so that you do not generate errors in the stored procedure during execution.)

- Within a stored procedure, you cannot create an object, later drop it, and then create a new object with the same name. The compiler will return an Object Already Exists error.

- You can reference temporary tables from within your stored procedures.

- If you execute a procedure that calls another procedure, the called procedure can access all objects created by the first procedure.

- If you create a private temporary table inside a procedure, the temporary table exists only for the purposes of the procedure and is dropped when you exit the stored procedure.

- The maximum number of local variables in a procedure is limited by the available memory on your server (not on the client).

- You can create private and public temporary stored procedures in the same manner as temporary tables by adding # and ## prefixes to the stored procedure name.

## Nesting and Recursion

Microsoft SQL Server 2000 supports nesting calls of stored procedures to a maximum of 32 levels. Say, for instance, you have a transaction that calls stored procedures, which internally calls other stored procedures, and so on. If the transaction count exceeds 32 levels, Microsoft SQL Server terminates the process and returns an error (code 217). This limit is not usually a problem; most systems nest procedures only three to six levels deep on average. However, you should be aware of this limitation when creating stored procedures and making internal calls to other procedures.

Transact-SQL supports recursion in a controlled manner. Again, you are limited to the 32-level rule for stored procedures. In most situations, recursions can be used to process small amounts of hierarchical data in order to reduce the amount of code you must write.

It is recommended that you use temporary tables, table variables, or join conditions to reduce the recursion to a minimum. Recursive calls typically need to run many times to be effective and may cause nesting level errors to crop up in unexpected situations.

**NOTE:** *Plan the use of recursion with caution to make sure you don't violate the 32-level nesting rule.*

## System Stored Procedures

Microsoft SQL Server ships with literally hundreds of procedures designed to make your life as a database administrator or programmer more pleasant. Many of these procedures perform specific tasks on your server that help in day-to-day server management. These stored procedures are located in the master database and can be viewed in the Enterprise Manager.

To view the list of procedures, go to the tree view of your server in the Enterprise Manager, and click on the plus sign next to your server. Repeat the process of clicking on the plus sign again to open the database node, and then open the stored procedures folder. Double-click on any of the procedures in the list to open the Stored Procedure Properties window as shown in Figure 14.1 (the **sp_ blockcnt** stored procedure.)

---

**NOTE:** *You can also create a stored procedure in the model database, so that each time a new user database is created, it will contain the stored procedures you have defined.*

---

Each of the procedures on the server has a **CREATE PROCEDURE** statement and **GO** statement that delimit the bounds of the stored procedure. All of the code within a stored procedure is written in standard SQL control-of-flow statements. Stored procedure code appears in this easy-to-read format unless you encrypt it with the **WITH ENCRYPTION** option in the **CREATE PROCEDURE** statement. (See Microsoft SQL Server Books Online for more information on encrypting stored procedures. The set of procedures that ships with Microsoft SQL Server can also serve as templates for future stored procedures.)

You can even modify the behavior of existing stored procedures to better fit your environment. It is strongly recommended that you make a copy of an existing system procedure and modify the copy. Call the new copy to perform your tasks and leave the original intact, so that you do not accidently change a procedure that the server uses and break a critical process.

Many of the system procedures in the master database are covered on Microsoft certification exams; therefore, any database administrator or programmer who works with Microsoft SQL Server should be familiar with those procedures. The

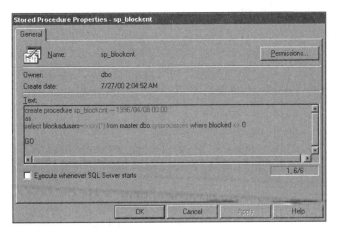

Figure 14.1   Stored Procedure Properties dialog.

following list contains some of the more important system procedures and their uses. Because of space limitations in this book, all of the 999 system stored procedures shipped with SQL Server 2000 cannot possibly be covered. Be sure to thoroughly review the following list before taking the Microsoft SQL certification exam. Each of these procedures, along with the ones not listed, is covered in depth in the Microsoft SQL Server Books Online.

- **sp_addextendedproc**—Adds the name and dynamic link library of an extended stored procedure to SQL Server's **sysobjects** and **syscomments** tables in the master database. Once registered with the SQL server, an extended procedure can be called from within your SQL code and used to extend the functionality of your server.

- **sp_addextendedproperty**—Adds an extended property to a database object so that additional data elements, such as caption or format information, can be associated directly to objects in SQL Server. This procedure is especially useful for Internet applications.

- **sp_addlogin**—Adds a user to the list of users that can log in to SQL Server and gain a connection to the server. This procedure does not grant any user permissions to databases or data objects.

- **sp_addmessage**—Can be used to add user-defined messages to your server. (See Chapter 12 for more on error handling and user-defined messages.)

- **sp_adduser**—Adds a user to a database and allows access to data. This procedure does *not* allow the user to connect to the server. See **sp_addlogin** for granting server access.

- **sp_attach_db**—Attaches the database files that house the database and data to the server.

- **sp_attach_single_file_db**—Attaches a database to a server that only has the data file (.mdf) available. The log file is automatically rebuilt for a database attached with **sp_attach_single_file_db**.

- **sp_changedbowner**—Changes the owner of a database in the event that the user is no longer required in that capacity.

- **sp_changeobjectowner**—Reassigns the ownership of a database object to a new owner.

- **sp_columns**—Displays the columns of a single object, either a table or view, that can be queried in the current environment. This procedure is useful in determining which columns are available for a custom query builder or a user-definable query tool.

- **sp_configure**—Displays or changes current SQL Server options. Some options are dynamic and can be changed without stopping and starting the

SQL Server service, whereas others are static and can be changed only by restarting the SQL Server service.

- **sp_cycle_errorlog**—Closes and moves the current SQL Server error log down one level in storage. The new log will not have the server startup information. Calling this procedure or **DBCC ERRORLOG** places an entry in the current log and in the new error log stating that the error log has been cycled.

- **sp_databases**—Lists any databases available through your connection to SQL Server.

- **sp_dbcmptlevel**—Lists or changes the database compatibility level for a database. Changing the compatibility level of a database changes performance characteristics of SQL statements run in a database. Only change the compatibility level of a database after thorough testing of *all* procedures, triggers, and client code that run against the database.

- **sp_dboption**—Displays or changes the database options for a database on SQL Server.

- **sp_depends**—Returns a list of all objects that are dependent upon the object passed into the procedure.

- **sp_detach_db**—Detaches the database from the server, removes the data and log files from the server, and allows them to be copied or deleted from the operating system. If any active user connections exist in the database when the **sp_detach_db** command is issued, an error is returned.

- **sp_dropextendedproc**—Removes the reference to an external procedure from the server.

- **sp_executesql**—Executes a Unicode string statement with optional parameters. There are some specific rules that should be followed when using **sp_executesql**. Check the SQL Server Books Online for more information on this procedure before attempting to use it in your environment.

- **sp_getapplock**—Allows for an application-level locking semaphore to be instituted by a client application. Many third-party applications have been developed to provide this functionality prior to SQL Server 2000. Using **sp_getapplock** adds a user-defined locking level to client applications that is managed by the SQL Server Lock Manager. This procedure does not impact object locks on the server in any way.

- **sp_help**—Reports information about any database object in the **sysobjects** table. There are a number of help-type procedures listed in the Books Online. You should become familiar with many of the help-type procedures before attempting to take the certification exam.

- **sp_lock**—Reports information about locks on the server. Individual process ID numbers can be passed to this procedure for more detailed lock reporting.

- **sp_monitor**—Displays 13 different server diagnostic variables used to track statistics on the current session of SQL Server.

- **sp_oacreate**—Allows stored procedures to instantiate Object Linking and Embedding (OLE) automation objects via SQL statements to extend the functionality of SQL Server. There are a number of OLE class stored procedures available in SQL Server that allow for all the required access and dispatch methods. See the SQL Server Books Online for more information on the OLE stored procedures.

- **sp_password**—Allows for the management of login passwords for SQL Server access.

- **sp_recompile**—Flags an object (table, stored procedure, or trigger) so that the next time the procedure or trigger is requested to be run, the query and execution plan is recompiled. This procedure is useful when new indexes are added or data distribution changes.

- **sp_releaseapplock**—Calling this procedure releases the lock placed with **sp_getapplock**, allowing other connections to acquire an application level lock. This procedure does not affect server object locks in any way.

- **sp_rename**—Changes the name of a user-defined object in a database.

- **sp_resetstatus**—Resets a suspect database status on SQL Server, allowing user access to the database. (Any damage that may have caused the database to be flagged as suspect is not repaired by this procedure.)

- **sp_runwebtask**—Triggers the execution of a previously defined Web job that produces a Hypertext Markup Language (HTML) document.

- **sp_spaceused**—Computes and displays the current usage of space by a table or an entire database on SQL Server.

- **sp_start_job**—Starts a previously defined SQL Server job.

- **sp_statistics**—Returns a list of all indexes and statistics for a particular table in a database.

- **sp_stored_procedures**—Displays a list of all current stored procedures in a database with information about the owner and names of the procedures.

- **sp_tables**—Returns a list of tables that can be queried in the **FROM** clause of a SQL statement.

- **sp_who**—Reports information about all current database users and their processes to include blocking processes and user's I/O information. The stored procedure **sp_who** does not place additional contention or yield to current processes for blocks and typically returns information when **sp_who2** does not due to blocking.

- **sp_who2**—Similar to **sp_who** but formatted a bit differently, **sp_who2** returns additional information about the current users of your server. Occasionally running **sp_who2** during heavy processing on the server could result in other processes being blocked on the server. If you do not get results back from **sp_who2** quickly, cancel the query and try **sp_who**.

Most of these procedures can be combined into a server management report stored procedure or used in nightly scheduled tasks to report on the state of your server. Create a proactively managed server with messages and, in some cases, even pages to warn system operators of any potential problems before they become critical.

## Custom Stored Procedures

You can create your own custom stored procedures based on the needs of your particular environment. Almost any SQL script can be modified to run as a stored procedure. As mentioned earlier, to select queries as candidates for stored procedures, look for redundant SQL code. If you are running the same queries repeatedly, you should consider using stored procedures to improve the performance and portability of your queries.

Listing 14.3 shows a query for returning a list of authors based on a match of a string passed to the procedure as a parameter. The query checks to see if the parameters are **NULL**, and if so, the entire table contents are returned to the client rather than just the specified record. In some situations, you might want to let the user know that some kind of value must be supplied for the parameter by making the appropriate changes to the conditional check for good data. The example uses the **LIKE** operator instead of the equal sign (=) operator to allow partial matches to be passed in and results returned. The techniques of using **LIKE** instead of the equal operator are useful for search routines and find procedures. If you want to allow only for exact matches and desire a slightly speedier procedure, you could replace **LIKE** with an equal sign (=), and skip appending the percent to the string in the procedure.

**Listing 14.3   Custom procedure example in the Pubs database.**

```
IF EXISTS (SELECT name
             FROM sysobjects (NOLOCK)
            WHERE name = 'usp_GetAuthors'
              AND type = 'P')
BEGIN
  DROP PROCEDURE usp_GetAuthors
END
GO

CREATE PROC usp_GetAuthors
  @p_String   VARCHAR(20) = NULL,
```

```
        @p_SearchBY VARCHAR(20) = 'ID'
    AS
    SET NOCOUNT ON

    /* Declare local variables           */
    DECLARE @v_ErrorString VARCHAR(100)

    /* Check Params                       */
    IF (@p_String IS NULL)
    BEGIN
      SELECT @p_String = '%'
    END -- Null
    ELSE
    BEGIN
      SELECT @p_String = @p_String + '%'
    END -- Not Null (Add for LIKE match)

    /* Check search for type of search    */
    IF (@p_SearchBY = 'ID')
    BEGIN
      SELECT 'ID'         = au_id,
             'Last Name'  = au_lname,
             'First Name' = au_fname
        FROM authors (NOLOCK)
       WHERE au_id LIKE @p_String
      RETURN
    END -- ID Search

    IF (@p_SearchBY = 'State')
    BEGIN
      SELECT 'ID'         = au_id,
             'Last Name'  = au_lname,
             'First Name' = au_fname
        FROM authors (NOLOCK)
       WHERE state LIKE @p_String
      RETURN
    END -- State Search

    /* Add additional search logic here   */

    /* Unknown Search = Log Error         */
    SELECT @v_ErrorString =
      'Unkown SearchBY parameter :' + @p_SearchBY

    EXEC utility.dbo.usp_ErrorLog
      0,
```

```
'usp_GetAuthors',
'MyAppliction',
60000,
@v_ErrorString

GO
```

The stored procedure returns rows to the client with formatted headers for enhanced readability. The optional parameter **@p_SearchBY** provides for various values that allow for multiple search conditions from one procedure. If you prefer, you may omit the second parameter from the **EXEC** line and the default value of **ID** will be used. In this example, a default value for each parameter has been assigned so that if one is left off, the procedure will still run. You can add as many search conditions as needed to extend the flexibility of your procedure without having to change client code or create additional procedures.

---

**NOTE:** *Each enterprise has its own needs for stored procedures. Look at your applications from the standpoint of the server and ask, "Could this data be provided faster or easier by having the body of code on the server and simply passing a parameter?" Practically every system has benefited or could benefit from server-side stored procedures. For more information on custom stored procedures, check the Microsoft SQL Server Books Online.*

---

## External Stored Procedures

In every application, you will at some point require the system to do something that it normally cannot. If modifying SQL code and recompiling a stored procedure to enhance the functionality of a program is possible, you have an easy out for this dilemma.

Many programmers have found themselves wanting to push the envelope of database applications. This has meant learning how the host applications interact with Dynamic Link Libraries (DLLs) and creating huge libraries of custom program snippets to attach to their applications. Over time, most systems have matured into well-rounded, robust applications with features and functionality that programmers could not have expected. In the old days, to enhance functionality, a programmer would have to have written a complex program in a high-level language, compiled it as a DLL, and attached it to an application. Although the same is true today, most applications require fewer custom DLLs and usually can use third-party DLLs to accomplish virtually any task.

If you want to create your own libraries to run as external procedures with SQL Server, you should be able to write your DLLs as you would any other application. Attach the DLLs to SQL Server by registering them with the server, and call them in a similar fashion to the other external procedures available with SQL Server.

---

**NOTE:** *External procedures will incur some extra overhead when used in your SQL statements. They are not always the fastest method to use to perform a task. With each release of SQL Server, you should evaluate your external procedures to determine if new server procedures or externals can replace them.*

---

A few external procedures have already been mentioned in this chapter. These functions were written to perform a task that Microsoft SQL Server was not necessarily suited to do well or efficiently. A few other external procedures are equally important. The following list contains some of the most useful externals that ship with Microsoft SQL Server. This is only a partial list; for a more complete list, check the Microsoft SQL Server Books Online.

- **xp_cmdshell**—Runs an application or command-line utility from SQL Server. This external can run executable programs or batch files that perform a wide range of tasks. Keep in mind that any command shell application must not require user interaction or be a modal window that requires user input.

- **xp_sendmail**—Sends query results, messages, and automated reports with **XP_SENDMAIL** to any Mail Application Programming Interface (MAPI) compliant mail client. You can use this procedure to warn you proactively of system problems or send reports to email recipients through SQL code. This is the most powerful and useful external procedure that is shipped with Microsoft SQL Server.

- **xp_logininfo**—Reports login and account information pertaining to your server.

- **xp_diskfree**—Returns the amount of free space available on a specified hard drive to an output parameter, which can be used to determine if there is enough free space to extend a device or create a new one on the server. This procedure can be found in the XP.DLL library and must be loaded into SQL Server before it can be used.

- **xp_logevent**—Writes a message to the Microsoft SQL Server Error log and/or the Windows NT Application log.

## Remote Stored Procedures

You can also call stored procedures on other SQL Servers you have defined as linked servers. By specifying the server name before the database name using a 4-part name, you tell SQL Server that it should run the procedure on the remote server and return the results to the client through your current server. This process allows a client application to gain connection to a single server and retrieve and modify data on multiple servers in an enterprise. The following code provides an example of a linked server stored procedure call:

```
EXEC serverx.master.dbo.sp_who
```

For more information on how to configure your local server to communicate with other servers, consult the Microsoft SQL Server Books Online and search on the keywords "linked servers" and the subtopic "configuring."

## Startup Stored Procedures

As mentioned earlier, you can set certain procedures to be executed each time you restart the SQL Server service. To view a list of startup procedures or add a new startup procedure, you would use **sp_procoption**.

---

**NOTE:** *You can disable startup procedures by starting SQL Server with the 4022 trace flag or the **–f** startup option.*

---

In many production environments you need to cache certain tables or perform a maintenance task automatically. To do this, simply write the stored procedure(s) to be run at startup and create them in the master database. Then use the **sp_procoption** stored procedure to add them to the list of startup procedures for your server.

Each procedure that is run as a startup procedure uses one connection to the server unless you create a master procedure that calls a list of other nested procedures. If you require sequential or step-by-step startup procedures, use the single master procedure approach to control the order of each startup procedure execution on your server.

**14. Stored Procedures and External Stored Procedures**

# Immediate Solutions

## Registry Procedures

In Chapter 8, a Registry table that holds system-level parameters and runtime process data was introduced. This information can be managed manually, but can be error prone and disorganized if many developers are reading and writing the data to the table. To facilitate an interface to the data in the Registry table, you can create an Application Programmer Interface (API), which can be used to access and manage the Registry data in a uniform method. You can mask the requirements for data manipulation by creating a standard set of procedures for developers. The procedures fill a number of needs that are uniform across entities in any database. Feel free to use the following set of procedures as models for your stored procedures for accessing entities, and create your own API.

### usp_GetKey

The base-level requirement of any entity is the need to get data from it. The **GET** procedure has a few forms. The **usp_GetKey** procedure takes a key value as an input parameter and returns the corresponding Registry value. The procedure masks the underlying structure from the client application and simply provides an interface to the data. Typically, in a **GET** procedure in an API, there is limited error handling because the procedure is only reading data. You could check to make sure the requested key exists and log an error if a request is made for a nonexisting key, but in most cases doing so is overkill. See Listing 14.4 for the source SQL for **usp_GetKey**. You can find the source SQL in a file called usp_GetKey.sql on the CD-ROM in the Chapter 14 directory.

---

**NOTE:** *This may seem like a great deal of work for such a simple procedure that a pass-through query could return very easily. However, do not fall for the urge to use a pass-through query. Keep the access through stored procedures! If you need to change the underlying data structure, you can change it in the stored procedure and not have to recompile client code. Using stored procedures is ultimately the best route to follow.*

---

**Listing 14.4    Source SQL for usp_GetKey.**

```
CREATE PROC usp_GetKey
  @p_RegKey VARCHAR(255)
AS
SELECT Reg_Value
```

```
   FROM tbl_Registry (NOLOCK)
  WHERE Reg_Key = @p_RegKey
GO
```

## usp_GetKeyOut

One subtle difference between **usp_GetKey** and **usp_GetKeyOut** is that with **usp_GetKeyOut** the returned value is placed in an output parameter. Client applications normally use **usp_GetKey** to access the Registry table, whereas internal stored procedures can call **usp_GetKeyOut** internally to get data items in nested procedure calls. The **usp_GetKeyOut** procedure takes a key value as an input parameter and returns the corresponding Registry value in the **@p_RegVal** output parameter. The procedure also masks the underlying structure from the client application and simply provides an interface to the data. Typically, in **GET** procedures in an API, there is limited error handling because it is only reading data. You could check to make sure the requested key exists and log an error if a request is made for a nonexisting key, but in most cases doing so is overkill. See Listing 14.5 for the source SQL for **usp_GetKeyOut**. You can find the source SQL in a file called usp_GetKeyOut.sql on the CD-ROM in the Chapter 14 directory.

---

**NOTE:** As with **usp_GetKey**, do not fall for the urge to use direct query access to the Registry table! If you need to change the underlying data structure, you can change it in the stored procedure and not have to recompile any code except the procedure.

---

### Listing 14.5   Source SQL for **usp_GetKeyOut**.

```
CREATE PROC usp_GetKeyOut
  @p_RegKey VARCHAR(255),
  @p_RegVal VARCHAR(255) OUTPUT
AS
SELECT @p_RegVal = Reg_Value
  FROM tbl_Registry (NOLOCK)
 WHERE Reg_Key = @p_RegKey
GO
```

## usp_GetKeyList

The procedure **usp_GetKeyList** is a hybrid of the **usp_GetKey** procedures. It uses the **LIKE** operator and returns a set of keys to the calling application. This stored procedure provides for a single call to get a list of values all at once. The corresponding Registry key and associated value is returned so the calling application can find the keys in a client-side cursor and make a single round-trip to the server. See Listing 14.6 for the source SQL for **usp_GetKeyList**. You can find the source SQL in a file called usp_GetKeyList.sql on the CD-ROM in the Chapter 14 directory.

### Listing 14.6    Source SQL for **usp_GetKeyList**.

```
CREATE PROC usp_GetKeyList
  @p_RegKey VARCHAR(255)
AS
SELECT Reg_Key,
       Reg_Value
  FROM tbl_Registry (NOLOCK)
 WHERE Reg_Key LIKE @p_RegKey + '%'
GO
```

## usp_UPDKey

In order to simplify the addition and update of existing keys in the Registry table, **usp_UPDKey** combines the logic to perform an **INSERT** and an **UPDATE** in the same procedure. Error handling logic is introduced in this procedure to log any problem that may occur during the data modification stages of the procedure. See the highlighted text in Listing 14.7 for the actual error handling code and the source for **usp_UPDKey**. You can find the source SQL in a file called usp_UPDKey.sql on the CD-ROM in the Chapter 14 directory.

### Listing 14.7    Source SQL for **usp_UPDKey**.

```
CREATE PROC usp_UPDKey
  @p_RegKey VARCHAR(255),
  @p_RegVal VARCHAR(255)
AS
SET NOCOUNT ON

/* Declare local variables          */
DECLARE @v_Error INT

IF EXISTS (SELECT Reg_Key
             FROM tbl_Registry (NOLOCK)
            WHERE Reg_Key = @p_RegKey)
BEGIN
  UPDATE tbl_Registry
     SET Reg_Value    = @p_RegVal,
         Date_Modified = GETDATE()
   WHERE Reg_Key    = @p_RegKey

  SELECT @v_Error = @@ERROR

  IF (@v_Error <> 0)
  BEGIN
    EXEC usp_ErrorLog
```

```
      @v_Error,
      'usp_UPDKey',
      'Registry Processing',
      NULL,
      'Failure to UPDATE existing key.'

    RETURN -1
  END -- Error Check
END -- Key Exists
ELSE
BEGIN
  INSERT INTO tbl_Registry
  VALUES (
    @p_RegKey,
    @p_RegVal,
    GETDATE(),
    NULL)

  SELECT @v_Error = @@ERROR

  IF (@v_Error <> 0)
  BEGIN
    EXEC usp_ErrorLog
      @v_Error,
      'usp_UPDKey',
      'Registry Processing',
      NULL,
      'Failure to INSERT existing key.'

    RETURN -1
  END -- Error Check
END -- Add Key
GO
```

## usp_DELKey

When the need arises to remove a key from the Registry table, the stored procedure **usp_DELKey** removes the record from the table and logs an error if a problem arises from the actual **DELETE** statement. See Listing 14.8 for the source SQL for **usp_DELKey**. You can find the source SQL in a file called usp_DELKey.sql on the CD-ROM in the Chapter 14 directory.

**NOTE:** *In the following procedure, an attempt to delete a nonexisting key is being logged to illustrate a process logic error versus the modification statement errors in previous procedures. See the highlighted code in Listing 14.8.*

### Listing 14.8  Source SQL for **usp_DELKey**.

```
CREATE PROC usp_DELKey
  @p_RegKey VARCHAR(255)
AS
SET NOCOUNT ON
/* Declare local variables        */
DECLARE @v_Error INT

/* Check for key before DELETE     */
IF EXISTS (SELECT Reg_Key
              FROM tbl_Registry (NOLOCK)
             WHERE Reg_Key = @p_RegKey)
BEGIN
  DELETE tbl_Registry
   WHERE Reg_Key  = @p_RegKey

  SELECT @v_Error = @@ERROR

  IF (@v_Error <> 0)
  BEGIN
    EXEC usp_ErrorLog
      @v_Error,
      'usp_DELKey',
      'Registry Processing',
      NULL,
      'Failure to DELETE existing key.'

    RETURN -1
  END -- Error Check
END -- Key Exists
BEGIN
  EXEC usp_ErrorLog
    NULL,
    'usp_DELKey',
    'Registry Processing',
    NULL,
    'Attempt to DELETE a non-existing registry key.'
END -- Bad Delete
```

# Code Table Procedures

The code table provides a broad range of access needs and development flexibility, and so is typically a central focus of an application and database. The **INTEGER** key makes joins back to this data very fast. The **INTEGER** key also allows for the removal of redundant data throughout tables in your database and improves storage requirements and data integrity.

To properly manage the code data, functions (Chapter 10) that allow you to use code data without greatly impacting your query structures have been supplied. You still need to populate codes and remove them if they were added in error. For the purpose of code table data, you need to develop a standard method of managing the data. In the following solutions, sample code has been supplied to do just that. Feel free to edit, copy, or implement these solutions for code table management in your enterprise.

## usp_Add_Code

Adding a code to the table requires that you know the code group ID for the code you are about to add. You should call the stored procedure **usp_Add_Code_Group** to get the code group ID of a new group, or query the code group table to get the ID value of an existing group before calling this procedure. See Listing 14.9 for an example of the stored procedure **usp_Add_Code**. You can find the file usp_Add_Code.sql on the CD-ROM in the Chapter 14 directory.

Listing 14.9   **usp_Add_Code** example.

```
CREATE PROCEDURE usp_Add_Code
  @p_Code          VARCHAR(12),
  @p_Description   VARCHAR(100) = NULL,
  @p_Code_Group_ID INTEGER
AS
DECLARE @v_Code_ID  INTEGER,
        @v_Error    INTEGER

SELECT @v_Code_ID = Code_ID
  FROM utility.dbo.tbl_Codes (NOLOCK)
 WHERE Code          = @p_Code
   AND Code_Group_ID = @p_Code_Group_ID

IF (@v_Code_ID IS NULL)
BEGIN
  INSERT INTO utility.dbo.tbl_Codes
    (Code,
     Description,
     Code_Group_ID)
```

```
      VALUES (
        @p_Code,
        @p_Description,
        @p_Code_Group_ID)

      SELECT @v_Error = @@ERROR

      IF (@v_Error <> 0)
      BEGIN
        EXEC utility.dbo.usp_ErrorLog
          @v_Error,
          'usp_Add_Code',
          'Code Processing',
          NULL,
          'Failure to INSERT code record.'
        RETURN -1
      END -- Error Check

      SET @v_Code_ID = @@IDENTITY
   END

   RETURN @v_Code_ID
   GO
```

## usp_Delete_Code

Removing a code from the code table is very simple. You should know the code ID for the code you are about to remove and call **usp_Delete_Code**. Before calling the procedure, you should ensure that all code references in associated tables have been removed or write some referential integrity code to ensure that you do not orphan codes that may be in use by removing the code. See Listing 14.10 for an example of the stored procedure **usp_Delete_Code**. You can find the file usp_Delete_Code.sql on the CD-ROM in the Chapter 14 directory.

---

**NOTE:** If you want to remove a code from the code table and it has been used to create code references in other tables, you can update the code ID in the referencing tables to match another code before removing the obsolete code.

---

**Listing 14.10  usp_Delete_Code example.**

```
CREATE PROCEDURE usp_Delete_Code
  @p_Code_ID INTEGER
AS
DECLARE @v_Error INTEGER

DELETE FROM Utility.dbo.tbl_Codes
  WHERE Code_ID = @p_Code_ID
```

```
SELECT @v_Error = @@ERROR

IF (@v_Error <> 0)
BEGIN
  EXEC utility.dbo.usp_ErrorLog
    @v_Error,
    'usp_Delete_Code',
    'Code Processing',
    NULL,
    'Failure to DELETE code record.'
  RETURN -1
END -- Error Check
GO
```

## usp_Add_Code_Group

Before you add a new code to the database, you should know which grouping mechanism you would use to group the codes. You should therefore call **usp_Add_Code_Group** to add the new group before adding any codes. See Listing 14.11 for an example of the stored procedure **usp_Add_Code_Group**. You can find the file usp_Add_Code_Group.sql on the CD-ROM in the Chapter 14 directory.

**Listing 14.11  usp_Add_Code_Group example.**

```
CREATE PROCEDURE usp_Add_Code_Group
  @p_Code_Group  VARCHAR(30),
  @p_Description VARCHAR(100) = NULL
AS
DECLARE @v_Code_Group_ID  INTEGER,
        @v_Error          INTEGER

SELECT @v_Code_Group_ID = Code_Group_ID
  FROM utility.dbo.tbl_CodeGroup (NOLOCK)
 WHERE Name = @p_Code_Group

IF (@v_Code_Group_ID IS NULL)
BEGIN
  INSERT INTO utility.dbo.tbl_CodeGroup
   (Name,
    Description)
   VALUES (
    @p_Code_Group,
    @p_Description)

  SELECT @v_Error = @@ERROR
```

```
      IF (@v_Error <> 0)
      BEGIN
        EXEC utility.dbo.usp_ErrorLog
          @v_Error,
          'usp_Add_Code_Group',
          'Code Processing',
          NULL,
          'Failure to INSERT code group record.'
        RETURN -1
      END -- Error Check

      SET @v_Code_Group_ID = @@IDENTITY
    END

    RETURN @v_Code_Group_ID
    GO
```

## usp_Delete_Code_Group

You can delete a code group and/or all associated codes using the stored procedure **usp_Delete_Code_Group**. You should remove the codes only after you have verified that all references to those codes are no longer used in any tables in your databases. See Listing 14.12 for an example of the stored procedure **usp_Delete_Code_Group**. You can find the file usp_Delete_Code_Group.sql on the CD-ROM in the Chapter 14 directory.

**Listing 14.12   usp_Delete_Code_Group example.**

```
CREATE PROCEDURE usp_Delete_Code_Group
  @p_Code_Group_ID INTEGER,
  @p_Delete_Codes  BIT = 0
AS
DECLARE @v_Error INTEGER

IF (@p_Delete_Codes = 1)
BEGIN
  DELETE FROM Utility.dbo.tbl_Codes
   WHERE Code_Group_ID = @p_Code_Group_ID

  SELECT @v_Error = @@ERROR

  IF (@v_Error <> 0)
  BEGIN
    EXEC utility.dbo.usp_ErrorLog
      @v_Error,
      'usp_Delete_Code_Group',
      'Code Processing',
```

```
        NULL,
        'Failure to DELETE code records.'
      RETURN -1
    END -- Error Check
  END

  DELETE FROM Utility.dbo.tbl_CodeGroup
   WHERE Code_Group_ID = @p_Code_Group_ID

  SELECT @v_Error = @@ERROR

  IF (@v_Error <> 0)
  BEGIN
    EXEC utility.dbo.usp_ErrorLog
      @v_Error,
      'usp_Delete_Code_Group',
      'Code Processing',
      NULL,
      'Failure to DELETE code group record.'
    RETURN -1
  END -- Error Check
  GO
```

| Related solutions: | Found on page: |
|---|---|
| Using a Codes Table | 385 |
| Implementing Error Handling in Stored Procedures and Triggers | 552 |

# Address Procedures

Rather than having you write the entire set of procedures to manage address data, the following sections provide examples of a few of the procedures you would need to manage address data effectively. The combination of activities in the following solutions makes sense from the standpoint of managing address data. Use these examples as templates for your own address management routines in your enterprise.

## usp_Add_Address

At the root of the address management tree is the need to add an address to the database. This example consists of a highly normalized structure, so a good deal of the data needed for an address is known based upon the presentation of the address, not the storage. Therefore, later in this section, stored procedures have been created to look up the underlying structure data and fill in the blanks, when adding an address. The additional stored procedures highlighted in listing 14.14 are created in various sections of this chapter and used here to complete the stored procedure. See Listing 14.13 for the source SQL for **usp_Add_Address**.

### Listing 14.13   usp_Add_Address example.

```
CREATE PROCEDURE usp_Add_Address
    @p_Line1      VARCHAR(50),
    @p_Line2      VARCHAR(50),
    @p_City       VARCHAR(50),
    @p_State_Code VARCHAR(2),
    @p_Zip5       CHAR(5),
    @p_Zip4       CHAR(4)      = NULL,
    @p_State_Name VARCHAR(30) = NULL
AS
DECLARE @v_State_ID   INTEGER,
        @v_City_ID    INTEGER,
        @v_Zip_ID     INTEGER,
        @v_Address_ID INTEGER,
        @v_Error      INTEGER

EXEC @v_State_ID = usp_Get_State_ID @p_State_Code, @p_State_Name
EXEC @v_City_ID  = usp_Get_City_ID @p_City, @v_State_ID
EXEC @v_Zip_ID   = usp_Get_Zip_ID @p_Zip5, @v_State_ID

SELECT @v_Address_ID = Address_ID
  FROM address.dbo.tbl_Address (NOLOCK)
 WHERE Line1 = @p_Line1
   AND Line2 = @p_Line2
   AND COALESCE(Zip4, '') = COALESCE(@p_Zip4, '')
   AND City_ID = @v_City_ID
   AND Zip_ID = @v_Zip_ID

IF (@v_Address_ID IS NULL)
BEGIN
  INSERT INTO address.dbo.tbl_Address
    (Line1,
     Line2,
     Zip4,
     City_ID,
     Zip_ID)
  VALUES (
     @p_Line1,
     @p_Line2,
     @p_Zip4,
```

```
      @v_City_ID,
      @v_Zip_ID)

  SELECT @v_Error = @@ERROR

  IF (@v_Error <> 0)
  BEGIN
    EXEC utility.dbo.usp_ErrorLog
      @v_Error,
      'usp_Add_Address',
      'Address Processing',
      NULL,
      'Failure to INSERT address record.'
    RETURN -1
  END -- Error Check

  SET @v_Address_ID = @@IDENTITY
END

RETURN @v_Address_ID
GO
```

The calls to the **GET** procedures look up the associated ID values for a city, state, or ZIP code and return that code to the calling procedure, so they can be added when the attributes of the address are added to the address table. If the associated lookup data is not already in the system, the **GET** procedure adds a record returning the new data to the stored procedure.

## usp_Get_Zip_ID

The procedure **usp_Get_Zip_ID** returns the key value of the normalized ZIP code to the calling procedure. If a record does not exist, it adds a new record, returning the ID value of the new record. See Listing 14.14 for the source SQL of **usp_Get_Zip_ID**, which can also be found on the CD-ROM in the Chapter 14 directory.

Listing 14.14    **usp_Get_Zip_ID** example.

```
CREATE PROCEDURE usp_Get_Zip_ID
  @p_Zip      CHAR(5),
  @p_State_ID INTEGER
AS
DECLARE @v_Zip_ID  INTEGER,
        @v_Error   INTEGER

SELECT @v_Zip_ID = Zip_ID
  FROM address.dbo.tbl_ZipCode (NOLOCK)
```

```
       WHERE Zip5 = @p_Zip
         AND State_ID = @p_State_ID

   IF (@v_Zip_ID IS NULL)
   BEGIN
     INSERT INTO address.dbo.tbl_ZipCode
       (Zip5,
         State_ID)
     VALUES (
        @p_Zip,
        @p_State_ID)

     SELECT @v_Error = @@ERROR

     IF (@v_Error <> 0)
     BEGIN
       EXEC utility.dbo.usp_ErrorLog
         @v_Error,
         'usp_Get_Zip_ID',
         'Address Processing',
         NULL,
         'Failure to INSERT zip code record.'
       RETURN -1
     END -- Error Check

     SET @v_Zip_ID = @@IDENTITY
   END

   RETURN @v_Zip_ID
   GO
```

## usp_Get_State_ID

The procedure **usp_Get_State_ID** returns the key value of the normalized state table to the calling procedure. If a record does not exist, it adds a new record, returning the ID value of the new record. See Listing 14.15 for the source SQL of **usp_Get_State_ID**, which can also be found on the CD-ROM in the Chapter 14 directory.

### Listing 14.15   **usp_Get_State_ID** example.

```
CREATE PROCEDURE usp_Get_State_ID
  @p_State_Code CHAR(2),
  @p_State_Name VARCHAR(30) = NULL
AS
DECLARE @v_State_ID  INTEGER,
        @v_Error     INTEGER
```

```
SELECT @v_State_ID = State_ID
  FROM address.dbo.tbl_State (NOLOCK)
 WHERE State_Code = @p_State_Code

IF (@v_State_ID IS NULL)
BEGIN
  INSERT INTO address.dbo.tbl_State
    (State_Code,
     Name)
  VALUES (
    @p_State_Code,
    COALESCE(@p_State_Name, @p_State_Code))

  SELECT @v_Error = @@ERROR

  IF (@v_Error <> 0)
  BEGIN
    EXEC utility.dbo.usp_ErrorLog
      @v_Error,
      'usp_Get_State_ID',
      'Address Processing',
      NULL,
      'Failure to INSERT state record.'
    RETURN -1
  END -- Error Check
  SET @v_State_ID = @@IDENTITY
END

RETURN @v_State_ID
GO
```

## usp_Get_City_ID

The procedure **usp_Get_City_ID** returns the key value of the normalized city table to the calling procedure. If a record does not exist, it adds a new record, returning the ID value of the new record. See Listing 14.16 for the source SQL of **usp_Get_City_ID**, which can also be found on the CD-ROM in the Chapter 14 directory.

**Listing 14.16   usp_Get_City_ID example.**

```
CREATE PROCEDURE usp_Get_City_ID
  @p_City VARCHAR(50),
  @p_State_ID INTEGER
AS
DECLARE @v_City_ID  INTEGER,
        @v_Error    INTEGER
```

```
SELECT @v_City_ID = City_ID
  FROM address.dbo.tbl_City (NOLOCK)
WHERE Name      = @p_City
  AND State_ID = @p_State_ID

IF (@v_City_ID IS NULL)
BEGIN
  INSERT INTO address.dbo.tbl_City
    (Name,
     State_ID)
  VALUES (
    @p_City,
    @p_State_ID)

  SELECT @v_Error = @@ERROR

  IF (@v_Error <> 0)
  BEGIN
    EXEC utility.dbo.usp_ErrorLog
      @v_Error,
      'usp_Get_City_ID',
      'Address Processing',
      NULL,
      'Failure to INSERT city record.'
    RETURN -1
  END -- Error Check

  SET @v_City_ID = @@IDENTITY
END

RETURN @v_City_ID
GO
```

## usp_Delete_Address

The procedure **usp_Delete_Address** removes the address record from the address table, but leaves the related lookup data alone because it is most likely used by other addresses. See Listing 14.17 for the source SQL of **usp_Delete_Address**, which can also be found on the CD-ROM in the Chapter 14 directory.

### Listing 14.17   **usp_Delete_Address** example.

```
CREATE PROCEDURE usp_Delete_Address
  @p_Address_ID INTEGER
AS
DECLARE @v_Error INTEGER
```

```
DELETE FROM Address.dbo.tbl_Address
 WHERE Address_ID = @p_Address_ID

SELECT @v_Error = @@ERROR

IF (@v_Error <> 0)
BEGIN
  EXEC utility.dbo.usp_ErrorLog
    @v_Error,
    'usp_Delete_Address',
    'Address Processing',
    NULL,
    'Failure to DELETE address record.'
  RETURN -1
END -- Error Check

GO
```

| Related solutions: | Found on page: |
|---|---|
| Installing the Book Databases from Scripts | 369 |
| Implementing Error Handling in Stored Procedures and Triggers | 552 |
| Creating **INSTEAD OF** Triggers for Inserts and Updates to a View | 780 |

# Utility Procedures and Scripts

The following procedures and scripts are utilities in nature and provide you with some tools that can improve your troubleshooting skills. They also provide insight into some of the more obscure SQL Server procedures that are available. With these techniques, you can begin to use SQL Server as a programming and management tool rather than a simple data repository.

---

*TIP: Take some time to understand how each procedure works. There are many ways to perform the same tasks described in the following sections. These examples may not be exactly what you need for your enterprise, but may lead you in the right direction.*

---

## usp_BlockingProcs

Blocked processes are a common occurrence on SQL Servers. From a user's perspective, a blocked process seems just like an application lockup. In fact, when the hourglass cursor appears with the SQL letters underneath and just sits there for a second or two during a normally quick query, you may be blocked by another process that has locked a page for a bit longer than anticipated. Concurrency checks and long-running processes go hand-in-hand. The tool **usp_BlockingProcs** helps troubleshoot these blocks by providing you with the current input buffer for the blocking process(es). See Listing 14.18 for the source SQL for **usp_ BlockingProcs**. You can find usp_BlockingProcs.sql, the source file for the procedure, on the CD-ROM in the Chapter 14 directory.

**Listing 14.18    Source SQL for usp_BlockingProcs.**

```
CREATE PROC dbo.usp_BlockingProcs
AS
SET NOCOUNT ON
SET DEADLOCK_PRIORITY LOW
SET CURSOR_CLOSE_ON_COMMIT OFF

DECLARE @v_BlockingSPIDS TABLE (
  SPID     INT          NULL,
  HOST     VARCHAR(30)  NULL,
  Login    VARCHAR(30)  NULL,
  DBNAME   VARCHAR(30)  NULL,
  InputCMD VARCHAR(255) NULL)

INSERT INTO @v_BlockingSPIDS
SELECT a.spid,
       CONVERT(VARCHAR(30),a.hostname),
       CONVERT(VARCHAR(30),a.loginame),
       CONVERT(VARCHAR(30),DB_NAME(a.dbid)),
       NULL
  FROM master.dbo.sysprocesses a (NOLOCK)
  JOIN master.dbo.sysprocesses b (NOLOCK)
    ON a.spid = b.blocked
 WHERE a.blocked = 0

IF (@@ROWCOUNT > 0)
BEGIN
  DECLARE @v_SPID      INT,
          @v_InputCMD VARCHAR(255),
          @v_SQL       NVARCHAR(255)

  CREATE TABLE #tbl_InputBuffer (
    EventType VARCHAR(30)  NULL,
    Params    INT          NULL,
    EInfo     VARCHAR(255) NULL)
```

```
DECLARE c_SPIDS CURSOR FAST_FORWARD FOR
 SELECT spid
   FROM @v_BlockingSPIDS

OPEN c_SPIDS
FETCH NEXT FROM c_SPIDS INTO @v_SPID

WHILE (@@FETCH_STATUS <> -1)
BEGIN
  IF (@@FETCH_STATUS <> -2)
  BEGIN
    SELECT @v_SQL = 'DBCC inputbuffer(' +
           CONVERT(VARCHAR,@v_SPID) + ') WITH NO_INFOMSGS'

    INSERT INTO #tbl_InputBuffer
      EXEC (@v_SQL)

    UPDATE @v_BlockingSPIDS
       SET InputCMD = EInfo
      FROM #tbl_InputBuffer
     WHERE spid = @v_SPID

    TRUNCATE TABLE #tbl_InputBuffer
  END -- -2
  FETCH NEXT FROM c_SPIDS INTO @v_SPID
 END -- -1
 DROP TABLE #tbl_InputBuffer
 SELECT * FROM @v_BlockingSPIDS
END -- Rows EXIST
ELSE
BEGIN
  PRINT 'No blocking processes exist...'
END
```

The highlighted code in Listing 14.18 will draw your attention to the two **SET** statements that ensure this procedure acts as expected. Setting the **CURSOR_ CLOSE_ON_COMMIT** to **OFF** disables the ANSI 92 behavior of a cursor during the execution of the procedure. If a transaction is committed during the cursor loop, the cursor is automatically closed, causing the process to error on the subsequent **FETCH** statement. The **DBCC INPUTBUFFER( )** function causes the transaction commit to occur. The first **SET** command allows this process to volunteer as the deadlock victim. The **(NOLOCK)** additions to the **sysprocesses** table reduce the chances of contention with current processes on the server. These techniques for programming a contention-friendly procedure can be used in many

14. Stored Procedures and External Stored Procedures

places to ensure that you do not experience an abundance of blocking and dead-locks in your SQL statements. You can test the procedure to ensure that it works properly by following these steps.

1. Connect to the server in the Query Analyzer. Select the Utility database.

2. In the initial window, type "BEGIN TRAN", and execute it.

3. In that same window, remove BEGIN TRAN, and type in a select statement against a table with the optimizer hint (**TABLOCKX**), and run it.

```
SELECT * FROM tbl_Codes (TABLOCKX)
```

4. Open a new window in the Query Analyzer. This establishes a new connection to the server.

5. Type in the same select statement without the optimizer hint and execute it.

```
SELECT * FROM tbl_Codes
```

6. The globe should continue to spin, and results should then be returned. Open a third window in the Query Analyzer.

7. Run the procedure **usp_BlockingProcs** in this new window. You should see at least a single row returned as a blocking process. If you scroll to the right side of the output, you see the command being executed as a blocking process with the optimizer hint.

8. Go back to the first window (where the **BEGIN TRAN** was executed), type "ROLLBACK TRAN", and execute that line of code.

9. Switch back to the third window, rerun the stored procedure **usp_BlockingProcs**, and no blocking should be listed. (You can check window 2 in this process, and you should see the results returned, proving that once the block was released, the query continues to completion.)

## usp_GetToken

String manipulation can rear its ugly head in processes more often than you real-ize. You can reduce round-trips to the server by passing a list of ID values to a procedure. In some applications, named pairs are passed around to designate key values in an application. To facilitate passing a list to a server-side process with the flexibility to handle a varied number of uses, a procedure called **usp_GetToken** has been created in the following example. See Listing 14.19 for the source syn-tax of **usp_GetToken**. You can find the source file called usp_GetToken.sql on the CD-ROM in the Chapter 14 directory.

**Listing 14.19  Source SQL for usp_GetToken.**

```
CREATE PROC usp_GetToken
  @p_List      VARCHAR(4000) = NULL OUTPUT,
  @p_Item      VARCHAR(255)  = NULL OUTPUT,
  @p_Delimiter VARCHAR(10)   = ','
AS
IF CHARINDEX(@p_Delimiter,@p_List) > 0
BEGIN
  SELECT @p_Item =
        SUBSTRING(@p_List,
                  1,
                  (CHARINDEX(@p_Delimiter,@p_List)-1))
  SELECT @p_List =
        SUBSTRING(@p_List,
                  (CHARINDEX(@p_Delimiter,@p_List) +
                   DATALENGTH(@p_Delimiter)),
                   DATALENGTH(@p_List))
END
ELSE
BEGIN
  SELECT @p_Item = @p_List
  SELECT @p_List = NULL
END
```

The delimiter parameter is flexible in width and can actually have any number of character-based separators passed in to delimit a string. Multiple character delimiters are supported because of the **DATALENGTH( )** function. The source string is truncated with each pass so that the list eventually becomes empty as items are removed from the list. See Listing 14.20 for sample uses of **usp_GetToken**. You can load the test script TestGetToken.sql from the Chapter 14 directory on the CD-ROM. The highlighted code lines show each of the different lists and delimiters that this script tests.

**Listing 14.20  Testing usp_GetToken.**

```
SET NOCOUNT ON
DECLARE @v_List VARCHAR(2000),
        @v_Item VARCHAR(255)

SELECT @v_List = 'a,bc,def'

WHILE (DATALENGTH(@v_List) > 0)
BEGIN
  EXEC usp_GetToken @v_List OUTPUT, @v_Item OUTPUT
```

```
          SELECT Item = @v_Item
        END -- WHILE

        SELECT @v_List = 'a|bc|def'

        WHILE (DATALENGTH(@v_List) > 0)
        BEGIN
          EXEC usp_GetToken @v_List OUTPUT, @v_Item OUTPUT, '|'

          SELECT Item = @v_Item
        END -- WHILE

        SELECT @v_List = 'a|*|bc|*|def'

        WHILE (DATALENGTH(@v_List) > 0)
        BEGIN
          EXEC usp_GetToken @v_List OUTPUT, @v_Item OUTPUT, '|*|'

          SELECT Item = @v_Item
        END -- WHILE

        /* Results for each pass are combined */
        Item
        ------------
        a

        Item
        ------------
        bc

        Item
        ------------
        def
```

Each **WHILE** loop returns the same results because the actual data items are identical. The only difference is the delimiter used for each string.

---

**NOTE:** *If needed, the data type of the list can be increased to 8000 characters to accommodate a larger list.*

---

## sp_MSforeachdb

In server management, you often need to loop through the available databases on a server and perform some sort of activity. In Chapter 6, we demonstrated the cursor method of managing the database when you need to filter the database list to a specific list. Microsoft has provided a little-known stored procedure that automatically loops through all databases on a server and executes up to three commands against each database. The procedure is called **sp_MSforeachdb**. See Listing 14.21 for an example of a call to **sp_MSforeachdb**.

---

**NOTE:** *You should not modify a supplied Microsoft procedure directly, but rather make a copy of that procedure with your own name, and then modify your copy. This procedure is a prime example of one that can be used as a template for database looping routines that mask the cursor manipulation from the user.*

---

**Listing 14.21    Example sp_MSforeachdb use.**

```
/*
EXEC sp_MSforeachdb
        @command1       nvarchar(2000),
        @replacechar  nchar(1)        = N'?',
        @command2       nvarchar(2000) = null,
        @command3       nvarchar(2000) = null,
        @precommand   nvarchar(2000) = null,
        @postcommand nvarchar(2000) = null

@replacechar = Databasename identifier
@precommand  = Before processing list command
@postcommand = Post processing list command

*/

/* If CCOC is ON, procedure breaks    */
SET CURSOR_CLOSE_ON_COMMIT OFF

EXEC sp_MSforeachdb
        'Print ''?'''

EXEC sp_MSforeachdb
        'Print ''$''',
        '$'
```

The additional commands for pre- and post-loop runs are helpful for preliminary code that should be run to set up the environment for the loop or for logging start and stop times. You can pass only single statement commands to this procedure. Should you need to execute multiple commands against each database, create a stored procedure that performs the commands based on database context and call the procedure with **sp_MSforeachdb**. You can find the source file sp_MSforeachdb.sql on the CD-ROM in the Chapter 14 directory.

| Related solutions: | Found on page: |
| --- | --- |
| Useful Server Administration SQL | 236 |
| DBCC Commands | 245 |

## sp_MSforeachtable

Similar to **sp_MSforeachdb**, **sp_MSforeachtable** loops through each table in a database and allows you to perform a command against each table. You can optionally filter the table list with the additional **@whereand** parameter. The **foreach** procedures allow for three commands along with pre- and post-execution commands to be executed through the procedure interface. See Listing 14.22 for an example of **sp_MSforeachtable**, and on the CD-ROM see the source file called sp_MSforeachtable.sql for the test script.

---

**NOTE:** Do not modify this procedure if you want to make a change to it. Make a copy, and edit your copy of the stored procedure.

---

Listing 14.22    Example of **sp_MSforeachtable** and its use.

```
/*
EXEC  sp_MSforeachtable
        @command1      nvarchar(2000),
        @replacechar nchar(1)        = N'?',
        @command2      nvarchar(2000) = null,
        @command3      nvarchar(2000) = null,
        @whereand      nvarchar(2000) = null,
        @precommand    nvarchar(2000) = null,
        @postcommand nvarchar(2000) = null

@replacechar = Databasename identifier
@whereand    = Provides filtering of the where clause
@precommand  = Before processing list command
@postcommand = Post processing list command

*/

/* If CCOC is ON, procedure breaks    */
SET CURSOR_CLOSE_ON_COMMIT OFF

EXEC sp_msforeachtable
        'Print ''?'''

EXEC sp_msforeachtable
        'Print ''$''',
        '$'
```

| Related solutions: | Found on page: |
| --- | --- |
| Useful Server Administration SQL | 236 |
| DBCC Commands | 245 |

### sp_Msuniquename

Running the stored procedure **sp_MSuniquename** creates a unique name for sysobjects used based on the seed value and the optional start parameter. You get back a valid object name in the context of the **sysobjects** table for the database context you are in when you execute the procedure. See Listing 14.23 for an example of **sp_MSuniquename**. You can find the source for Listing 14.23 in the file sp_MSuniquename.sql in the Chapter 14 directory on the CD-ROM.

**Listing 14.23  Sample sp_MSuniquename uses.**

```
/*
EXEC sp_MSuniquename
      @seed   nvarchar(128),
      @start int          = null

@seed  = Base text for name
@start = An integer to use as suggested start
*/
EXEC sp_MSuniquename
      ''

EXEC sp_MSuniquename
      'tbl_Address'

EXEC sp_MSuniquename
      'tbl_Address',
      10
/* Results (Abridged) */
Name                        Next
------------------------- ----------
1__54                       2

Name                        Next
------------------------- ----------
tbl_Address1__54            2

Name                        Next
------------------------- ----------
tbl_Address10__54           11
```

## sp_MSindexspace

When you need to know how much space a table's indexes are taking up, the stored procedure **sp_MSindexspace** can be a very helpful tool. You can specify a single table name to see a list of all indexes and statistics sets for the given table as well as their corresponding sizes; or optionally, you can pass an index name as a second parameter to the procedure and get just the size for that index returned to you. See Listing 14.24 for an example of **sp_MSindexspace**. You can find the sample file sp_MSindexspace.sql on the CD-ROM in the Chapter 14 directory.

**Listing 14.24  Sample use of sp_MSindexspace.**

```
/*
EXEC sp_MSindexspace
      @tablename  nvarchar(517),
      @index_name nvarchar(258) = NULL
*/
EXEC sp_MSindexspace
      'tbl_codes'

EXEC sp_MSindexspace
      'tbl_codes',
      'IDX_CodeGroup'

/* Results (Abridged) */
IndexID Index Name                          Size(KB) Comments
------  ----------------------------------- -------- ---------------------------
1       IDX_CodeGroup                       16       Size excludes actual data.
2       _WA_Sys_Code_Group_ID_75D7831F      0        (None)
3       _WA_Sys_Code_ID_75D7831F            0        (None)
4       _WA_Sys_Code_75D7831F               0        (None)


Size (KB)
----------
16
```

## sp_MStablespace

Knowing how much storage a table is taking up is practically an every-other-day occurrence for some enterprises. Some tables become hot spots and sore points in development, and space requirements are usually at the root of many discussions. Microsoft has supplied another undocumented procedure for the task of determining the space a table is taking up. The **sp_MStablespace** procedure returns the number of rows, the data and index space used by the table, and index objects. See Listing 14.25 for an example of how to use **sp_MStablespace**, which can also be found on the CD-ROM in the Chapter 14 directory.

### Listing 14.25   Example of **sp_MStablespace**.

```
/*
EXEC sp_MStablespace
      @name nvarchar(517),
      @id int = null
*/

EXEC sp_MStablespace
      'tbl_codes'

EXEC sp_MStablespace
      '',
      @id = 1977058079
/* Results */
Rows        DataSpaceUsed IndexSpaceUsed
----------  ------------- --------------
19          8             16


Rows        DataSpaceUsed IndexSpaceUsed
----------  ------------- --------------
19          8             16
```

## xp_dirtree

The need to determine the directory structure under a particular folder is actually fairly common in the database management environment. Many procedures need to know the path for output or input files. You can determine that information in a number of ways. You could use **xp_cmdshell** to determine if a directory or file exists, but shelling out to the operating system and making a call to "dir c:\temp" is a bit clunky and requires some creative programming. Alternately, you could use an external procedure called **xp_dirtree** to get the folder(s) structure and nesting level very easily. See Listing 14.26 for an example of **xp_dirtree** and its return data. You can also find the source file xp_dirtree.sql for Listing 14.26 on the CD-ROM in the Chapter 14 directory. Microsoft provides this function to return directory tree information within the Enterprise Manager tree view for times when you are looking for directories for backup or restore files or other directory-based activities.

### Listing 14.26   Example of **xp_dirtree**.

```
/*
EXEC master.dbo.xp_dirtree
      '<drive>:\<directory>'
*/

EXEC master.dbo.xp_dirtree
      'C:\temp'
```

```
EXEC master.dbo.xp_dirtree
     'C:\temp\TestSub1'

/* Results */
subdirectory                                          depth
---------------------------------------------------- ----------
TestSub1                                              1
TestSub1_1                                            2
TestSub2                                              1

subdirectory                                          depth
---------------------------------------------------- ----------
TestSub1_1                                            1
```

The depth column in the output lets you know that **TestSub1_1** is actually an extra level off the root path passed into **xp_dirtree**. The second example shows how you can pass a subdirectory to **xp_dirtree** to get a more granular result. The output is limited to directories only and does not include file references.

## xp_subdirs

When the only data you need is the immediate subdirectory off of a specific path, use the **xp_subdirs** external procedure. The use is identical to **xp_dirtree** except for the limitation of the output to the maximum depth of one level. See Listing 14.27 for an example of the external procedure **xp_subdirs**. You can find the source file xp_subdirs.sql for Listing 14.27 on the CD-ROM in the Chapter 14 directory.

**Listing 14.27  Example of xp_subdirs.**

```
/*
EXEC master.dbo.xp_subdirs
     '<drive>\<directory>'
*/

EXEC master.dbo.xp_subdirs
     'C:\temp'

EXEC master.dbo.xp_subdirs
     'C:\temp\TestSub1'

/* Results */
subdirectory
---------------------------
TestSub1
TestSub2
```

```
subdirectory
-------------------------
TestSub1_1
```

## xp_fixeddrives

Occasionally, you will need to know what fixed drive letters are available on a SQL server or how much free space is available on each of the fixed drives. The external procedure **xp_fixeddrives** returns the fixed drive letters and the available space in megabytes on the server in a tabular format:

```
EXEC master.dbo.xp_fixeddrives

/* Results */
drive MB free
---- ----------
C    3855
```

## xp_fileexist

Nightly or scheduled data importing often requires polling a directory for a particular named file. Setting up a scheduled job to run a procedure is a very simple task with the Enterprise Manager. You can use the external procedure **xp_fileexist** to test not only for the existence of a file or parent directory but whether the file is a directory or not. See Listing 14.28 for an example of the external procedure **xp_fileexist**. You can find the source for Listing 14.28 on the CD-ROM in the Chapter 14 directory.

### Listing 14.28   Example of **xp_fileexist**.

```
/*
EXEC master.dbo.xp_fileexists
     '<drive>:\<directory>\<filename>'
*/

EXEC master.dbo.xp_fileexist
     'C:\temp\test.txt'

/* Results */
File Exists File is a Directory Parent Directory Exists
---------- ------------------- -----------------------
1           0                   1
```

The ones and zeros let you know in a code of true and false if each condition is met based on the input file parameter. The value of 1 is true and the value of 0 is false. In the example in Listing 14.28, the file test.txt does exist in the specified location, and the parent directory "C:\temp\" exists as well.

## ChangePassword.sql

Occasionally, users forget their passwords, and you cannot supply the old ones to the system stored procedure **sp_password**. In those situations, you would normally override the existing passwords through the Enterprise Manager to give users new passwords. There is an alternative method that demonstrates an undocumented internal function called **PWDENCRYPT( )**. The **PWDENCRYPT( )** function uses the same encryption as the internal SQL Server engine for storing passwords. You can actually use this function to overwrite passwords in the system catalog to effect changes without going through the Enterprise Manager or the stored procedure **sp_password**. See Listing 14.29 for the ChangePassword.sql file example. You can find the ChangePassword.sql file on the CD-ROM in the Chapter 14 directory.

---

**NOTE:** If you only want to encrypt data, you can use the **ENCRYPT( )** function. Microsoft does not support decrypting data and passwords!

---

**Listing 14.29   ChangePassword.sql example.**

```
/* Fix a forgotten password        */
/* ONLY RUN AS SA                   */

EXEC sp_Configure 'allow updates', 1
GO
RECONFIGURE WITH OVERRIDE
GO

/* Replace 'Test' with target login  */
UPDATE sysxlogins
   SET password = PWDENCRYPT('newpwd')
  WHERE name = 'Test'

EXEC sp_Configure 'allow updates', 0
GO
RECONFIGURE WITH OVERRIDE
GO
```

**WARNING! This is very dangerous code to leave lying around non-database administrators with sa privileges. To prevent others from using SQL statements like the preceding ChangePassword.sql example to destroy your server, do not generally grant sa or server administration privileges to unknowledgeable users. Secure your server and the sa login to ensure you have a safe database server.**

# Chapter 15
## BCP

# In Depth

The Bulk Copy Program (BCP) is a command-line copy utility that ships with Microsoft SQL Server. The BCP utility is used to import and export large amounts of data to and from operating system files. The most common use of BCP is to copy information from a table to a data file, and then reload the data file contents into a table on a different database or server. It can also be used to generate a file to be imported by another application into another database management platform.

The BCP utility is overlooked in many SQL Server environments. Administrators that utilize this tool find it to be an invaluable asset for moving large volumes of data quickly between databases or servers. Many administrators who have used BCP to a limited degree refer to their experience as a love/hate relationship. The tool is extremely fast for moving portions of a database rather than resorting to backup and restore techniques or moving the entire database. The major complaint that many administrators voice about the BCP utility is the fact that it is somewhat confusing and very few good references exist to help an administrator become familiar with the various options and features available. It can be an extremely time-consuming task to learn by trial and error everything that you need to know about this utility. Many of the features that can provide an easy solution to a particular task are ignored because administrators don't know they are available.

The basic functionality of the BCP program is fairly straightforward. A table is copied out of a table or query into a data file or copied into a table from a data file. The capability to copy data in and out of a database in a fast and efficient manner is what this utility was designed for. Over time the utility has evolved to include a host of options that allow the user to control various behavioral and environmental aspects of this process. The multitude of switches available to make this control possible causes the syntax to look extremely convoluted. The first time administrators look at the utility and see the sheer volume of available switches, they easily become overwhelmed and shy away from attempting to work with it. This is unfortunate because most basic operations will use only four or five of these switches and all of them are easy to use and understand. The remaining switches extend the functionality and flexibility of the BCP utility to meet the needs of more advanced users. The fact that both the novice and the expert can use the BCP utility successfully makes it an extremely useful tool in any environment.

# Starting Simple

In most environments, 80 to 90 percent of the work you do with BCP requires only a handful of the available features. Before you dive into the entire list of available switches and options, it is a good idea to become familiar with the basic functionality required to perform simple copy operations with BCP. The most common options for using BCP are shown in Listing 15.1, which includes the minimum required switches to perform most tasks.

**NOTE:** *BCP switches are case sensitive, so some care must be exercised to supply the switches using the correct case.*

### Listing 15.1   BCP simple syntax.

```
BCP { dbtable | dbview } { IN | OUT } datafile
    [-n native type] [-S server name] [-U username] [-P password]
```

The parameters and switches needed to perform a basic copy operation with BCP are limited to the source or destination, the operation, the data file to import or export, and the necessary switches to connect to the SQL Server. The only additional switch that applies to most operations is **-n**, which is used to specify the native SQL Server format for the data file. Using the native format is faster than character formats and is easier to work with. The parameters shown in Listing 15.1 are explained in Table 15.1.

**NOTE:** *Native mode export files can only be used by another SQL Server.*

You can specify either a table or a view as the source of a **BCP OUT** operation. The ability to specify a view adds a great deal of flexibility to the data that can be exported. You can create a view to join tables, compute values, or perform other data manipulations before the data is exported from the server. A view can also be used as the destination of a **BCP IN** operation, but all columns in the view must refer to a single table. It is not possible to import data to columns that are computed or built with an expression.

### Table 15.1   Basic BCP options.

| Option | Definition |
|---|---|
| dbtable | The target table that is used to copy into or the source table when data is copied out. |
| dbview | The name of the view that is used to copy into or the source when data is copied out. |
| IN | This option specifies that data is copied into the table or view from a data file. |
| OUT | This option specifies that data is copied to a data file from a table or view. |
| datafile | This is the path and name of the file that is used to hold the data that the BCP utility reads to import data or write to when exporting data. |

# BCP OUT

The first parameter that you need to provide on the BCP command line to copy data out of the server is a fully qualified table or view name. A fully qualified table (or view) name begins with the database name followed by a period. The owner of the table or view is the next part of a fully qualified name. The owner name is optional, but even if it is omitted, a second period indicating the end of the owner name must still be supplied. The final part of the fully qualified name is the actual name of the table or view. Listing 15.2 provides an example of specifying a fully qualified table name in a **BCP OUT** command. The fully qualified table name appears between **BCP** and **OUT** in the listing.

---

**NOTE:** *If the table or view resides on a Linked Server, the server name needs to be included before the database name. For more information on Linked Servers, refer to Chapter 10.*

---

**Listing 15.2    Example of a fully qualified table name.**

```
BCP address.dbo.tbl_address OUT C:\TEMP\Address.bcp -n -Ssneezy -Usa -P
-- OR --
BCP address..tbl_address OUT C:\TEMP\Address.bcp -n -Ssneezy -Usa -P
```

When either of the examples provided in Listing 15.2 is executed from a command prompt, an output file is created in the C:\TEMP directory named Address.bcp. This file contains the raw data from the **tbl_Address** table in the SQL Server native data format.

# BCP IN

**BCP IN** works exactly the same way as the **BCP OUT** command. The same switches and options apply to both of these commands except the **IN** option is substituted in place of the **OUT** option in the command line. Listing 15.3 shows the **BCP IN** command, which copies back in the data that was copied out in the example for **BCP OUT**. If you want to test this example, you need to truncate the **tbl_Address** table before performing the **BCP IN** command to prevent duplicate entries in the table.

**Listing 15.3    Example of a BCP IN command.**

```
BCP address.dbo.tbl_address IN C:\TEMP\Address.bcp -n -Ssneezy -Usa -P
```

# Entering the Big Leagues

Now that you have reviewed the minimal syntax required to utilize the BCP utility, it is time to examine the other available switches and options. There are a total of 4 options and 27 switches in the full BCP syntax. This section provides the information you need to begin experimenting with the extended functionality available when using the remaining switches and options. The switches are divided into logical groups to help you find those that apply to your tasks. To keep the switch descriptions centrally accessible, the switches in the simple syntax are also explained in detail in this section.

The full syntax for the BCP command is provided in Listing 15.4. If you compare this listing to the simple syntax for the BCP command, you can easily see why many people are overwhelmed the first time they attempt to use this utility.

**Listing 15.4  Full BCP syntax.**

```
BCP {dbtable | dbview | "query"} {IN | OUT | QUERYOUT | FORMAT} datafile
  [-m maxerrors]           [-f formatfile]         [-e errfile]
  [-F firstrow]            [-L lastrow]            [-b batchsize]
  [-n native type]         [-c character type]     [-w wide char. type]
  [-N keep non-text native] [-V file format version] [-q quoted identifier]
  [-C code page specifier] [-t field terminator]   [-r row terminator]
  [-i inputfile]           [-o outfile]            [-a packetsize]
  [-S server name[\instance name]]
                           [-U username]           [-P password]
  [-T trusted connection]  [-v version]            [-R regional enable]
  [-k keep null values]    [-E keep identity values]
  [-h "load hints"]
```

The parameters available for the full BCP command syntax are explained in Table 15.2. This table provides a description for each of the parameters to help you understand when and how to use them effectively. The **QUERYOUT** and **FORMAT** options are explained in greater detail in the "**QUERYOUT**" and "Format Files" sections later in this chapter.

**Table 15.2  Full BCP options.**

| Option/Switch | Definition |
| --- | --- |
| **dbtable** | The target table that is used as the source or destination of the **BCP IN** or **BCP OUT** operation. |
| **dbview** | The name of the view that is used as the source or destination of the **BCP IN** or **BCP OUT** operation. |
| **query** | A Transact-SQL statement that returns data to be copied to the data file. The query string must be enclosed in double quotes (" ") and is only valid with the **QUERYOUT** option. |
| **IN** | This option specifies that data is copied into the table or view from a data file. |
| **OUT** | This option specifies that data is copied out to a data file from a table or view. |
| **QUERYOUT** | This option is used to copy a result set from a **QUERYOUT** to a data file. |
| **FORMAT** | This option is used to create a format file that has been customized according to the specific needs of the administrator. |
| **datafile** | This is the path and name of the file that is used to hold the data that the BCP utility either imports data from or exports data to. |

**Table 15.3   BCP switches that control authentication.**

| Switch | Definition |
|--------|------------|
| -S | Server name; \Instance name |
| -U | User name; the name of the login used to connect to SQL Server to perform the BCP operation |
| -P | Password; the password of the login |
| -T | Trusted Connection; uses the permissions of the network user for servers that support NT Authentication |

## Authentication Switches

This section provides information about the switches used to establish a connection to the SQL Server from the BCP utility. Table 15.3 contains a list of the switches used to connect to a SQL Server as well as a description of each. BCP supports connecting to SQL Server using either NT Authentication with the **-T** switch or SQL Server Authentication with the **-U** and **-P** switches. The **-S** switch is needed for either verification mode to specify the server name to establish a connection with. You can also specify the TCP/IP address for the SQL Server instead of the name of the server you want to connect to.

## Cross-Version Migration Switches

BCP has the capability to migrate data between multiple versions of SQL Server. To facilitate moving data between servers of different versions when the data is exported in native format, two switches allow you to specify the native format version for the data file being imported or exported. Refer to Table 15.4 for the available switches that allow you to control the native data file format version for importing and exporting data from SQL Server. The **-6** switch is provided for backward compatibility and supports only the SQL Server 6.0 and 6.5 native data file formats. The -V switch supports specifying the native data file formats for SQL Server versions 6.0, 6.5, and 7.0 and is the preferred method of specifying the native data file format.

Each major release of SQL Server has provided a new BCP utility that makes use of a different native format. These switches allow creating native format data files that can be imported to or exported from a version of SQL Server other than the one the BCP utility was shipped with. The version control switches do not provide 100-percent reliable results when working with older versions of SQL Server, so you may need to use the older BCP when accessing an older server or consider using an alternate format and a format file if you run into problems.

## Switches for Error Handling

Two switches are supplied to allow you to control the behavior of the BCP utility when errors occur during the import or export process. These switches and their

**Table 15.4   BCP switches that support cross-version migration.**

| Switch | Definition |
|--------|------------|
| **-V** | Version. This switch takes one of three arguments enclosed within **( )** parentheses. The three supported arguments are **60**, **65**, and **70**. |
| **-6** | Version. This switch is the same as the **-V** and is provided for backward compatibility only. The sole difference is that **-6** supports only versions 6.5 and 6.0, whereas **-V** supports versions 6.0, 6.5, and 7.0. |

descriptions are shown in Table 15.5. The **-m** switch can be used to specify an allowable number of errors that can occur without terminating the BCP operation. This can be useful for allowing an import or export operation to continue past corrupted records to save as many rows as possible.

## Switches for Partitioning the Data

In some situations, it may be desirable or even necessary to partition the data you are copying out of the server into more than one data file. The BCP utility provides two switches that allow you to select the beginning and ending rows of the **BCP OUT** operation. These switches are described in Table 15.6. By default, the operation copies all data from the specified source in a single operation and places the output in a single data file. This works well for small copy operations, but what if you need to put the data on a CD for transfer to a remote location, and the size of the source data exceeds the capacity of your transfer media? In this case, you can specify data in a range of rows to output into multiple files for transfer to your media. Whether the media is 3.5" floppy disks or writable CDs, this process generally requires a minimal amount of experimentation to determine the row count needed to produce the desired output file size.

These switches can also come in handy when trying to recover data from a corrupted table. If you can determine the rows that are corrupted, it is possible to skip them using these switches, which allows you to recover the remaining "good" data.

**Table 15.5   BCP switches that control error handling.**

| Switch | Definition |
|--------|------------|
| **-m** | Max Errors. The # of errors before the action is canceled. |
| **-e** | Error File. The path of an error file. |

**Table 15.6   BCP switches that support data partitioning.**

| Switch | Definition |
|--------|------------|
| **-F** | First row. Used to specify where the operation is to start. The default is **1**, which is the first row. |
| **-L** | Last row. Used to specify where the operation is to end. The default is **0**, which is the last row. |

## Input and Output File Format Switches

In order to make the BCP utility usable for more than just moving data to and from SQL Server, a number of switches are available to control the format of the data being imported or exported. The switches that control formatting the data files are described in Table 15.7. The formatting switches allow the importing of text files and other file formats produced in other applications into SQL Server. It is also possible to use these switches to format the output of the data into a format that can be used by another application or database platform. The use of the formatting switches and format files provides a wide range of possibilities for moving data to and from SQL Server.

## Optimization Switches

One of the main advantages of the BCP utility is the speed with which it can move data to and from the server. In an effort to keep this performance as high as possible, a few switches are available to help control certain factors that influence performance, such as the network packet size used in the transfer and the number of rows that are copied in a single batch (transaction). The two available switches for optimization are shown in Table 15.8.

**Table 15.7   BCP switches that specify input and output file formats.**

| Switch | Definition |
| --- | --- |
| -f | Format file. Used to specify the full path and file names of the format file. |
| -n | Native format. Allows the BCP operation to use the native format for SQL Server data types. This is the fastest format for both data import and export. |
| -c | Character data type. Usually used when specifying the data file (formatting the file) using **CHAR** as the data type. Unless specified by another switch, a tab is used as the column separator, and a new line is used as the row terminator. |
| -w | Unicode data type. Used like the **-c** switch but supports Unicode (**NCHAR**) values. |
| -N | Performs the bulk copy operation using the native data types of the data for noncharacter data and Unicode characters for character data (MSSQL 7.0 or later). |
| -t | Used to define the field terminator. The default is **\t** (tab). |
| -r | Used to define the row terminator. The default is **\n** (new line). |

**Table 15.8   BCP switches that control optimization.**

| Switch | Definition |
| --- | --- |
| -b | Used to specify how many rows are copied in a batch. The default behavior is to copy all rows in a single batch. |
| -a | Used to specify the size in bytes of network packets sent to and from the server. |

## Special Insert Handling

There are two switches that can be used to provide some special insert handling for importing data into SQL Server with the **BCP IN** command. These switches can be used to override the default behavior of the BCP utility in order to preserve the state of specific data columns. Table 15.9 provides a description of these two switches. These switches allow you to determine when to preserve **NULL** and identity values in the data being inserted.

## Using Hints

The BCP utility has its own set of hints, which allow an administrator to control the flow of the BCP. Hints are specified via the **-h** switch and its arguments. The six arguments available with the **-h** switch are as follows:

- **ORDER**—Specifies the sort order of the data in the data file. The default is no sort order.
- **ROWS_PER_BATCH**—Specifies the number or rows in a batch. By default this number is unknown.
- **KILOBYTES_PER_BATCH**—Specifies the approximate number of kilobytes in a batch. By default this number is unknown.
- **TABLOCK**—Specifies that a table lock should be acquired on the target table. This can be used to eliminate unnecessary lock escalation overhead for inserts that will populate the entire table. This lock also limits access to the inserted data until the operation is completed.
- **CHECK_CONSTRAINTS**—Specifies that constraints should be checked before inserting data into the target table during a **BCP IN** operation. By default, constraints are ignored for **BCP IN** operations.
- **FIRE_TRIGGERS**—Tells SQL Server to execute triggers when data is being inserted. By default a table will not fire triggers on a bulk copy operation.

The **ORDER** hint is used to optimize the performance of copying data into a target table. The performance is only improved if the **ORDER** hint is used to insert data according to a clustered index created on the table. If the sort order column

**Table 15.9  BCP switches that control special insert handling.**

| Switch | Definition |
|--------|-----------|
| **-k** | Keep **NULL**. Specifies that an empty column should be populated with **NULL** rather than inserting a default value. |
| **-E** | Identity. Specifies that existing identity values can be preserved when copying data back into the server. |

(or columns) is different than the columns included in the index, then the **OR-DER** hint is ignored. The syntax for the **ORDER** hint is shown in Listing 15.5. When more than one column is used in the **ORDER** hint, a comma is used to separate the columns. Ascending or descending order can optionally be specified for each column.

**Listing 15.5   ORDER hint syntax.**

```
BCP dbTable IN datafile -S<server> -U<user> -P -n
-hORDER(column [asc|desc][, column [asc|desc]...])
```

The number of rows exported or inserted at a time can be assigned with the **ROWS_PER_BATCH** hint. The **ROWS_PER_BATCH** hint functions like the **-b** switch. Because the **ROWS_PER_BATCH** hint and the **-b** switch perform the same function, they cannot be utilized at the same time. The syntax for specifying the **ROWS_PER_BATCH** hint is shown in Listing 15.6.

**Listing 15.6   BCP ROWS_PER_BATCH hint syntax.**

```
BCP dbTable IN datafile -S<server> -U<user> -P -n
-hROWS_PER_BATCH=<# of rows ex: 5000>
```

The **KILOBYTES_PER_BATCH** hint is usually used when copying data across a network. When bandwidth is limited, this hint can be used to control the amount of data that is being transferred at a time. Listing 15.7 provides the syntax for using the **KILOBYTES_PER_BATCH** hint.

**Listing 15.7   BCP KILOBYTES_PER_BATCH hint syntax.**

```
BCP dbTable IN datafile -S<server> -U<user> -P -n
-hKILOBYTES_PER_BATCH=<# of Kilobytes per batch>
```

## Miscellaneous Switches

Some additional switches that do not fall into any of the previously discussed categories are also available to provide miscellaneous extensions to the BCP utility's functionality. These switches are described in Table 15.10.

**Table 15.10   Miscellaneous BCP switches.**

| Switch | Definition |
|---|---|
| **-q** | Quoted Identifiers. Specifies that quotation marks (" ") are being used to enclose object names with embedded spaces or quotation marks. |
| **-C** | Code Page. Specifies a code page in the data file (supported for backward compatibility only). |
| **-i** | Input File. Specifies the path to an input file that is to be used as a response to prompts from the BCP. |

*(continued)*

15. BCP

**Table 15.10  Miscellaneous BCP switches (continued).**

| Switch | Definition |
|---|---|
| -o | Output File. Specifies the path and file names of the output file that receives the data exported from SQL Server. |
| -v | Version. Displays the version number of the BCP utility. |
| -R | Regional Settings. Uses the settings of the client computer. The default is to ignore regional settings. |

# QUERYOUT

The **BCP QUERYOUT** command is used to copy a result set from a query rather than a table or view. The query is a Transact-SQL statement enclosed in double quotes (" ") on the command line. One of the many advantages of the **QUERYOUT** option is the ability to set the order of columns in which the data is exported. When a BCP operation is executed, the order in which rows are written to the data file is not guaranteed. By using the **QUERYOUT** option, the order of the rows in the data file can be specified using an **ORDER BY** clause on the **SE-LECT** statement. This allows for a performance boost when inserting the data into a target table with the **ORDER** hint. The **ORDER** hint can significantly improve BCP performance.

The **QUERYOUT** option processes only the first result set returned by the query. If a statement is executed that returns multiple result sets, the result from the first statement is written to the data file and the rest are ignored. A statement that contains a **COMPUTE BY** clause causes the BCP operation to write only the results of the **SELECT** statement. The results of the **COMPUTE BY** clause are ignored.

The **QUERYOUT** option can also be used to join multiple tables or use aggregate functions in the result set. In addition, this option can be used to partition the data being read either horizontally or vertically. This can be useful when data has to be exported to a third party or consultant and there is sensitive data on the table that should not be viewed for security reasons. A view can be created for the same process, but if the data is sent only one time and will never be sent again, creating a view would result in unnecessary overhead.

The syntax of the **QUERYOUT** option is a little different than the **OUT** option syntax. The main difference is that the **QUERYOUT** option requires a query string, rather than a table or view name, be supplied in the command line. Listing 15.8 shows an example of using the **QUERYOUT** option. All of the switches that are valid in the **OUT** and **IN** options apply to the **QUERYOUT** option. This allows the administrator to manipulate the data file by selecting not only the data itself, but also creating the format of the data file where the data will reside.

15. BCP

**NOTE:** Depending on the operating system you are using, this option may require a command longer than what you can actually type from the command prompt. If the command is too long, you can create a view instead and retrieve the data using a standard **BCP OUT** operation.

Listing 15.8    **BCP QUERYOUT** example.

```
BCP "SELECT Address_ID, Line1 FROM address.dbo.tbl_address (NOLOCK)
ORDER BY address_id" QUERYOUT C:\TEMP\small_address.bcp
-Ssneezy -Usa -P -n
```

# BCP Errors

Errors can occur within any application and the BCP utility is no exception. The BCP utility has two switches that allow an administrator to exercise control over the handling of errors generated by the BCP utility.

The first switch causes the errors generated by a BCP operation to be saved in an error file. This file captures the errors for review in a text editor (like Notepad) as well as provides an easy way to email them to coworkers or other resources who might be able to assist in the process of identifying the cause of the errors and how to resolve them. The switch to save the errors generated by the BCP command-line utility is **-e**. To use the switch, simply add the switch and an appropriate file name to the command. An example of using the **-e** switch is provided in Listing 15.9.

Listing 15.9    BCP error file example.

```
BCP address.dbo.tbl_address OUT C:\TEMP\tbl_address.bcp
-Ssneezy -Usa -P -n -eC:\TEMP\bcperror.txt
```

The second switch allows an administrator to achieve a successful BCP operation even when errors occur during the operation, without affecting the integrity of the copied data. For instance, if an administrator uses a BCP command to import data from a data file that fails due to an error but determines that the operation will produce the desired results in spite of the error, he can use the **-m** switch to force the BCP utility to ignore a specified number of errors without terminating the operation. Listing 15.10 provides an example of using the **-m** switch to specify that six errors should be allowed before terminating the copy operation.

Listing 15.10    BCP max errors example.

```
BCP address.dbo.tbl_address IN c:\temp\tbl_address.bcp
-Ssneezy -Usa -P -n -m6
```

# Format Files

Format files are used to specify the structure of the data file used in the BCP operation. The format file either specifies the format of the file being created by a **BCP OUT** operation or indicates the format of the file being imported by a **BCP**

**IN** operation. Format files allow the BCP utility to work with files that are not in the SQL Server native data format. This allows for the exporting of files in a format that can be read by other applications, such as Microsoft Excel, text editors, accounting packages, and so on. This also allows you to import data saved by other applications into your SQL Server databases. In addition, format files allow you to alter the data types of the data being imported or exported.

A format file is actually just a text file that contains the structure information used to allow the BCP utility to understand the format of the data file being imported or exported. The BCP utility only deals internally with SQL Server native data types and must be provided with this additional information to be able to read or write data in any other format. Without a format file, the data file must be provided in the native SQL Server format, and the columns must be in the same order as the structure used as the source or destination on the server.

As an example, let's assume that a used car dealership maintains a simple table of the cars on the lot. Let's also assume that a minimal amount of data is kept in the table. The table will have four columns: year, make, style, and color. Listing 15.11 provides the script to create the **CarList** table and populate it with sample data.

### Listing 15.11   **CarList** sample data.

```
CREATE TABLE CarList
        ( Year   CHAR(4) NOT NULL,
          Make   CHAR(10) NOT NULL,
          Model  CHAR(20) NOT NULL,
          Color  CHAR(10) NOT NULL )

INSERT INTO CarList
  VALUES ('1998','Ford','Mustang','Red')
INSERT INTO CarList
  VALUES ('1999','Chevrolet','Malibu','Blue')
INSERT INTO CarList
  VALUES ('1997','Chrysler','Dakota','Green')
INSERT INTO CarList
  VALUES ('1995','Toyota','Camry','Silver')
```

If the data in the **CarList** table is exported in SQL Server native format, the result is a text file with all rows placed end to end and no row or field separators in the file. The fixed-length fields used in the example do not require any special encoding of data, so the resulting export file is at least marginally readable. If you export just the first row from the table, the output would look like the data shown in Listing 15.12.

### Listing 15.12   Native export file from **CarList** table.

```
1998Ford      Mustang             Red
```

Assuming that you exported this row, what could you do with it? You could open the file with a text editor, and you would be able to reasonably interpret the contents, especially because it is only a single row. However, what if there were 500 or even 1000 rows? The data is not really useful in this format for anything other than reimporting it into SQL Server. This problem is magnified tremendously as soon as you interject **VARCHAR** or any type of binary data in the data file. In order to produce output from this table that is useful in other applications, you need to use a format file for the **BCP OUT** operation to produce a more friendly output file. First, let's examine a format file generated from the **address.dbo. tbl_address** table, which represents the SQL Server native data format. Listing 15.13 shows the contents of such a format file.

**Listing 15.13   Sample format file.**

```
8.0
6
1 SQLINT    0  4   ""       1  address_ID   ""
2 SQLCHAR   0  50  ""       2  Line1        SQL_Latin1_General_CP1_CI_AS
3 SQLCHAR   0  50  ""       3  Line2        SQL_Latin1_General_CP1_CI_AS
4 SQLINT    0  4   ""       4  City_ID      ""
5 SQLINT    0  4   ""       5  State_ID     ""
6 SQLINT    0  4   ""       6  Zip_ID       ""
```

The first line of the format file indicates the version of the BCP utility that was used to create the file. In this example, the version is 8.0, which is the BCP utility included in MSSQL Server 2000. The second line indicates the number of column format rows in the format file. This format file has six rows, one for each column in the table. The third line of the format file starts to define the structure for how data is stored within the data file when this format file is used. The following list provides a description of each of the columns used to specify the column format in the format file:

- *Host File Column Order*—The order of each column in the data file. Since this format represents the SQL Server native format, the Host File Column Order will match the Server Column Order for each column. This column specifies which columns from the data file should be imported by a **BCP IN** operation. Using a format file to specify specific columns, it is possible to import data into multiple tables from a single import file.

- *Host File Data Type*—The data type used for storage in the import or export data file. It differs from the default data type only slightly. The **CHAR** data type is referenced as **SQLCHAR**, and the **INT** data type is referenced as **SQLINT**. An excellent table showing all the available data types and their matching storage data type can be found in Books Online by searching for "File Storage Type."

- *Prefix Length*—Length prefix characters for the field.
- *Host File Data Length*—The length of the data type.
- *Column Terminator*—The symbol used to distinguish where the field ends. In this case, no field terminator is specified.
- *Server Column Order*—The order in which columns exist in the source or destination table (or view).
- *Server Column Name*—The server column name does not actually have to be the column name that exists in the source or destination table. The column name can contain any name as long as it is not blank.
- *Collation*—The collation used to store data in the bulk copy data file.

Once you have created a format file that matches the import or export operation you need to perform, you can use it as often as you need it. You should create a repository for your format files, so that you can easily retrieve one if you have a need for it again in the future.

A format file can be generated without actually exporting any data to a data file. Executing the BCP utility with the **FORMAT** option is used to create a format file. The **FORMAT** option must be used with the **-f** switch. To create the format file shown in Listing 15.13, the following BCP command should be used:

```
BCP address.dbo.tbl_address FORMAT -Ssneezy -Usa -P -n -fc:\temp\format.fmt
```

The file name and path for the format file are specified using the **-f** switch. This command generates a format file that specifies the SQL Server native structure. It is possible to edit the generated format file to create an altered output format. This can be handy when only minimal changes are desired. When a format file is created and no formatting switches are specified on the command line, the format file is created by prompting the user for the desired format of each column. This process allows the user to specify data types, data lengths, prefix lengths, and terminators for each column. After all the prompts have been answered, the file is saved in the path specified using the **-f** switch.

# BULK INSERT

The Transact-SQL **BULK INSERT** statement is very similar to the BCP command-line utility using the **IN** option. The **BULK INSERT** statement only supports importing data to SQL Server from a data file. There is no Transact-SQL equivalent to copy data out to a data file from SQL Server. One advantage of using the **BULK INSERT** statement rather than the BCP utility is that it is often faster.

---

**NOTE:** *You need to enable the Select Into/Bulkcopy database option in order to use this command as well as some BCP operations.*

---

The speed difference is especially noticeable if the data file being imported is not located on a drive local to the client performing the insert. The **BULK INSERT** command is executed at the server, so as long as the SQL Server login account has access to the data file either on a drive local to the server or a network share, the import operation does not require copying the data from the share to the client and then to the server. When the BCP utility is used, the client processor controls the transfer, which means that all data transferred to the server must first pass through the memory of the client computer. To import a data file on a network share, the process involves copying the data across the network twice, once into the client computer's memory, and then again to the SQL Server.

The **BULK INSERT** can also be used to encapsulate the importing of data from a data file in a user-defined transaction. This ability is useful if you need to repeatedly perform an import during regular processing operations. Not only is the **BULK INSERT** command easier to automate in a server-based process, but it can also be rolled back as part of the transaction if an error occurs elsewhere in the transaction.

Another advantage that the **BULK INSERT** statement has over the BCP utility is that a Data Transformation Services (DTS) package can be customized to use the **BULK INSERT** functionality. A DTS package can in turn be set up as a scheduled task that allows a data file to be copied to a target table/view on a regular basis without requiring any manual intervention on the part of the database administrator (DBA).

The **BULK INSERT** statement also supports using a format file created with (or for) the BCP utility. This means that the BCP utility and the **BULK INSERT** statement can be used together, performing exports with the BCP utility, and then using the **BULK INSERT** statement to import the data into the desired location. The syntax of the **BULK INSERT** statement is shown in Listing 15.14.

### Listing 15.14   **BULK INSERT** syntax.

```
BULK INSERT [ { 'table_name' FROM 'data_file' }
    [ WITH
        (
            [ BATCHSIZE [ = batch_size ] ]
            [ [ , ] CHECK_CONSTRAINTS ]
            [ [ , ] CODEPAGE [ = 'ACP' | 'OEM' | 'RAW' | 'code_page' ] ]
            [ [ , ] DATAFILETYPE [ =
                { 'char' | 'native' | 'widechar' | 'widenative' } ] ]
            [ [ , ] FIELDTERMINATOR [ = 'field_terminator' ] ]
            [ [ , ] FIRSTROW [ = first_row ] ]
```

```
          [ [ , ] FIRE_TRIGGERS ]
          [ [ , ] FORMATFILE = 'format_file_path' ]
          [ [ , ] KEEPIDENTITY ]
          [ [ , ] KEEPNULLS ]
          [ [ , ] KILOBYTES_PER_BATCH [ = kilobytes_per_batch ] ]
          [ [ , ] LASTROW [ = last_row ] ]
          [ [ , ] MAXERRORS [ = max_errors ] ]
          [ [ , ] ORDER ( { column [ ASC | DESC ] } [ ,...n ] ) ]
          [ [ , ] ROWS_PER_BATCH [ = rows_per_batch ] ]
          [ [ , ] ROWTERMINATOR [ = 'row_terminator' ] ]
          [ [ , ] TABLOCK ]
      )
  ]
```

Most of the arguments for the **BULK INSERT** statement are similar to switches and options available for the BCP utility. The **BULK INSERT** statement only supports a subset of the available functionality of the BCP utility, but most of the **BCP IN** functionality is available. Table 15.11 provides descriptions for the options that are used to customize the functionality of the **BULK INSERT** statement.

## BULK INSERT Default File Format

As discussed previously, the default format for exporting data from SQL Server using the BCP utility is the SQL Server native format. Because the **BULK INSERT** statement is the Transact-SQL equivalent of the **BCP IN** command, you would generally assume that it would expect SQL Server native format input files by default. Unfortunately, this is not the case and can prove somewhat confusing when working with this statement for the first time. The default data file format expected by the **BULK INSERT** statement is, in fact, *character* format. The SQL

**Table 15.11   BULK INSERT arguments.**

| Argument | Definition |
|---|---|
| **table_name** | Specifies the target table/view that is used to copy the data into from the data file. |
| **data_file** | Specifies the path and name of the file that is used to hold the data that the BCP utility reads to import data or writes to when exporting data. |
| **BATCHSIZE** | Specifies how many rows are copied in a batch. The default is that the action looks at all rows as one batch. |
| **CHECK_CONSTRAINTS** | Tells the **BULK COPY** statement to check the target table/view for any constraints that exist on the object. By default, the constraints on an object are ignored. |
| **CODEPAGE** | Specifies a code page in the data file. |

*(continued)*

15. BCP

**Table 15.11    BULK INSERT** arguments *(continued)*.

| Argument | Definition |
|---|---|
| DATAFILETYPE | Tells the **BULK INSERT** statement to perform the copy action using a specific format (character format is the default). |
| FIELDTERMINATOR | Defines the field terminator. The default is \t (tab). |
| FIRSTROW | Specifies where the operation is to start. The default is **1**, which is the first row. |
| FIRE_TRIGGERS | Allows MSSQL Server to execute a trigger when data is being inserted. By default, a table will not fire triggers on a bulk copy operation. |
| FORMATFILE | Specifies the full path of the file that has been customized for the target object where the data is inserted. |
| KEEPIDENTITY | Retains the value of an identity column. |
| KEEPNULLS | Determines that an empty column is **NULL** instead of inserting a default value. |
| KILOBYTES_PER_BATCH | Specifies the approximate number of kilobytes in a batch. By default, this number is unknown. |
| LASTROW | Specifies where the operation is to end. The default is **0**, which is the last row. |
| MAXERRORS | Specifies the number of errors before the action is canceled. |
| ORDER | Specifies the sort order of the column in the data file. The default is no sort order. |
| ROWS_PER_BATCH | Specifies how many rows are copied in a batch. The default is that the action looks at all rows as one batch. |
| ROWTERMINATOR | Defines the row terminator. The default is **\n** (new line). |
| TABLOCK | Creates a table level lock on the table involved with the operation. |

Server native format is supported, but must be specified by using either the **DATAFILETYPE** option or providing an appropriate format file using the **FORMATFILE** option.

## BULK INSERT Permissions

The **BULK INSERT** statement must be executed under a login that has the appropriate permissions. The sysadmin and bulkadmin roles are the only two fixed database roles that have permission to execute the **BULK INSERT** statement. The bulkadmin role is provided to allow the DBA to assign access to this functionality without the need to grant full sysadmin privileges to the user.

## Executing the BULK INSERT Statement

Once you are familiar with the BCP command-line utility, it should be easy to understand the syntax required for the **BULK INSERT** statement, because the operation is fundamentally the same, and the options required to complete the action successfully are similar as well. As mentioned previously in this chapter, the **BULK INSERT** statement can be used only to import data into a target object, so in most cases, the BCP utility is still used to export data from the source table/view into a data file. Listing 15.15 shows an example of exporting data from the **tbl_Address** table in character format (the default for the **BULK INSERT** statement) using the **BCP OUT** command. It is a good idea to provide the field and row terminators even if the terminators are the default for the particular action. In this case, commas are used as field delimiters, and a new line is used to separate each.

**Listing 15.15   BCP tbl_Address Out in character format.**

```
BCP address.dbo.tbl_address OUT c:\temp\tbl_address.bcp
-Ssneezy -Usa -P -E -c -t, -r\n
```

After executing the code in Listing 15.15 to export the address data in character format, you can use the **BULK INSERT** command to reinsert the data into a table. The **BULK INSERT** command to perform this insert is provided in Listing 15.16.

**Listing 15.16   Import address data from character format file using BULK INSERT.**

```
BULK INSERT address.dbo.tbl_address
  FROM 'c:\temp\tbl_address.bcp'
  WITH ( FIELDTERMINATOR = ',',
         ROWTERMINATOR  = '\n' )
```

Even though the default data file format for the **BULK INSERT** statement is character format, it is important to keep in mind that SQL Server native format is always the fastest option if you have a choice. It would be more efficient to modify the previous examples to perform the export in native format, and then specify native format using the **DATAFILEFORMAT** option.

# BULK INSERT and DTS

**BULK INSERT** can be executed in a variety of ways. It can be used in SQL batches executed in the Query Analyzer, stored procedures, scheduled jobs, and within DTS packages. DTS is a powerful tool that administrators use to transfer data from a source to a target object. **BULK INSERT** tasks can be used in a DTS package to provide high-speed data import functionality.

15. BCP

The DTS Designer provides a Bulk Insert Task Properties dialog to allow you to specify the **BULK INSERT** options using a simple graphical interface. The Bulk Insert Task Properties dialog has two tabs: General and Options. The General tab contains five fields, which are described in the following list:

- *Description*—This field is where you provide a name for the task to allow you to keep track of the various tasks in the package.

- *Existing Connection*—This field must be assigned to the connection for the server and database that will receive the imported data. (In order to configure a Bulk Insert Task, at least one SQL Server connection must already be created.)

- *Destination Table*—This field contains the target object into which data is imported from the data file.

- *Source Data File*—This field contains the path and file names of the source data file.

- *Format*—This field provides a choice between using an existing format file by specifying the path and file names of the format file or specifying the format in the Designer by designating the field and row terminator information within the DTS package.

The Options tab allows you to configure most of the common options available for the **BULK INSERT** statement. The options that can be configured on this tab are explained in the following list:

- *Check Constraints*—This option tells the **BULK COPY** statement to check the target table/view for any constraints that exist on the object. By default, the constraints on an object are ignored.

- *Enable Identity Insert*—This option retains the value of an identity column.

- *Sorted Data*—With this option, a dialog box is provided for the Sort order of the column in the data file. The default is no sort order.

- *Keep Nulls*—This option determines that an empty column is **NULL** instead of inserting a default value.

- *Table Lock*—This option creates a table level lock on the table involved with the operation.

- *Code Page*—With this option, a dialog box is provided to specify the code page in the data file. The options are: ANSI Code Page (ACP), Original Equipment Manufacturer (OEM), and RAW.

- *Data File Type*—This option tells the **BULK INSERT** statement to perform the copy action using a specific format (character format is the default). A dialog box is provided with a list of choices from a drop-down box. These choices are: **CHAR**, **NATIVE**, **WIDECHAR**, and **WIDENATIVE**.

- *Insert Batch Size*—This option is used to specify how many rows are copied in a batch. It is not selected by default, which means that the entire operation is normally done in a single batch. If a specific batch size is desired, select the option checkbox and provide the batch size as rows per batch.

- *Only Copy Selected Rows*—When this option is selected, you can specify a set number of rows. The Only Copy Selected Rows option allows you to specify the first and last rows to be used in the **BULK INSERT** operation.

Once the options are saved, the Bulk Insert Task has all the necessary information to complete the task when the DTS package is executed. DTS packages using the Bulk Insert Task can be scheduled to run just like other DTS packages. The Bulk Insert Task is the fastest method of importing data in a DTS package. This performance comes at the cost of removing the capability to perform data transformations during the import. For more information on creating and working with DTS packages, refer to Chapter 7.

# Performing High-Speed BCP Operations

This section provides some guidelines and general information for optimizing the performance of BCP operations. This information will help you get the maximum possible performance from the BCP utility and the **BULK INSERT** statement. The BCP command-line utility has been optimized for exporting and importing large volumes of data between a database object and an operating system data file. It also provides a variety of switches that can be used to customize the performance for your task and environment. Before implementing a BCP solution, you should review the following list of issues that can affect the performance of your BCP operations:

- *Drop the indexes on the target object*—One of the biggest performance hits that a BCP operation encounters is importing data into a table/view that has an index. Unless you are importing a small amount of data or your import only accounts for a relatively small percentage of the data in the table, you will often achieve better performance by dropping the indexes prior to the import, and then re-creating them when the import has finished. If the target table has more than two indexes, it will almost always be faster to drop the indexes, execute the BCP task, and then re-create the indexes.

- *Minimally Logged Bulk Copy operations outperform a Logged Bulk Copy*— A Logged Bulk Copy operation means that all rows that are inserted into the target object are logged, which allows the operation to be rolled back if an error occurs. A Minimally Logged Bulk Copy operation only logs the new extent allocations that occur to accommodate the data being inserted, which greatly reduces the amount of overhead required to perform the insert operation.

15. BCP

**695**

---

**TIP:** *You should always perform a full database backup prior to performing a Minimally Logged Bulk Copy operation.*

---

- *Use native or Unicode format*—If the Bulk Copy Task is working only with data generated by and for SQL Server, using the native or Unicode format will maximize the performance of import and export operations.

- *Use a Sort Order*—If the target object has a clustered index, then sort the import data by the field(s) specified in the index to increase the performance. If a bulk copy operation has to be performed in a logged environment, then it is definitely beneficial to sort the data to match the clustered index order.

- *Execute a BCP task locally*—In most cases, the best performance can be achieved by executing the BCP program that is local to the machine where the import or export file is stored. This avoids an additional network trip for the data before reaching its destination.

To perform a Minimally Logged Bulk Copy operation, the following conditions must be true:

- The database option Select Into/Bulkcopy has to be turned on in the database that the target object was created in.

- The target database is not being replicated.

- The target object does not have any indexes.

- The bulk copy operation uses the **TABLOCK** hint to specify locking the entire table at the beginning of the operation rather than forcing the lock manager to escalate the lock level during the insert.

---

**TIP:** *It is recommended that you enable the Truncate Log On Checkpoint option for the database when using a Minimally Logged Bulk Copy operation. Even though it is not absolutely necessary, the log backups are virtually useless, and if a Bulk Copy Task has a large amount of data to import into the target object, the log could fill up and cause the bulk copy operation to terminate with an error.*

---

# *Immediate Solutions*

## Dropping and Creating Indexes

One way to speed up the performance of a **BCP IN** operation is to remove the indexes from the target table before beginning the copy, and then replace them after the copy is finished. This example walks you through creating a stored procedure that performs this work for you.

1. You need to start with a basic **CREATE PROCEDURE** command that specifies two variables to be passed to the procedure. The two input parameters are the table name and the input file name.

2. The stored procedure first needs to build a list of the indexes on the table and save the index name and the field list used to create the index. The code needed to accomplish this can be borrowed from the **sp_helpindex** system stored procedure and modified to suit your needs.

---

**NOTE:** *The stored procedures that ship with Microsoft SQL Server 2000 contain a wealth of useful code. For more information on stored procedures, refer to Chapter 14.*

---

3. Once you have gathered enough information about an index to be able to re-create it and have stored the information in a table variable, you can drop the index.

4. You should also output the names of the dropped indexes, so that you can see that the procedure does what you expect it to.

5. Once the indexes have been dropped, you can perform the **BCP IN** operation.

6. The final step is to loop through the index information that you saved before you dropped the indexes and re-create them.

7. You should also output the names of the indexes being re-created along with the field list, so that you can see that the procedure does what you expect it to.

8. Once you have created the stored procedure, you are ready to test it. Start the process by using BCP to export the data from the **tbl_Address** table, so that you can import it for your test. The following code produces the desired output file for your import.

```
BCP Address..tbl_Address OUT C:\TEMP\Address.bcp -n -Ssneezy -Usa -P
```

9. Once the **BCP OUT** operation has been completed successfully, you are ready to proceed.

10. Truncate the **tbl_Address** table so that when you import the data you do not generate duplicate records.

11. Use the following code to add a pair of indexes to the **tbl_Address** table, to create the necessary condition to exercise the code to drop and re-create the index.

```
CREATE INDEX IDXTest ON tbl_Address (Address_ID)
CREATE INDEX IDXTest2 ON tbl_Address (City_ID, Zip_ID)
```

12. Now you can execute the stored procedure you created to import the data back into the table.

13. Assuming that your test was successful, you are ready to start using this procedure to perform **BCP IN** operations that automatically drop and re-create the indexes on the table. A complete listing of the code for this procedure is provided in Listing 15.17.

### Listing 15.17 Create **usp_bcpin** stored procedure.

```
IF EXISTS (SELECT name
             FROM sysobjects
             WHERE name = 'usp_bcpin'
               AND type = 'P')
  DROP PROCEDURE usp_bcpin
GO

CREATE PROCEDURE usp_bcpin @p_TableName SYSNAME,
                           @p_InFile VARCHAR(250)
AS
/*********************************************************************/
/* This procedure is used to drop the indexes from the target table, */
/* perform a BCP IN operation to import the specified data file,     */
/* and then re-create the indexes that were dropped originally.      */
/*********************************************************************/
/* NOTE: The input file is expected to be provided in SQL Server     */
/*       native format                                               */
/*********************************************************************/

/* Turn off rowcount display */
SET NOCOUNT ON

/* Declare needed variables */
DECLARE @v_DBName  VARCHAR(100),
```

```
          @v_IndID    INT,
          @v_IndName  SYSNAME,
          @v_ObjID    INT,
          @v_IndKeys  VARCHAR(2078),
          @v_i        INT,
          @v_ThisKey  SYSNAME,
          @v_Keys     NVARCHAR(2078),
          @v_SQL      VARCHAR(500)

/* Declare a table variable to hold index information */
DECLARE @v_IdxList TABLE
     ( Index_Name    SYSNAME          NOT NULL,
       Index_Keys    NVARCHAR(2078)   NOT NULL )

/* Get current database name and target table's object ID */
SELECT @v_DBName = DB_NAME(),
       @v_ObjID=OBJECT_ID(@TableName)


/************************************************************/
/* Get List of indexes, save the needed information so we */
/* can re-create them, and drop the indexes              */
/************************************************************/

/* Declare cursor to get index information */
DECLARE c_IdxList CURSOR FAST_FORWARD FOR
  SELECT indid,
         name
    FROM sysindexes (NOLOCK)
    WHERE id = @v_ObjID
      AND IndID > 0
      AND IndID < 255
      -- Ignore Statistic Sets
      AND (status & 32) = 0
      AND (Status & 64) = 0
      AND (Status & 8388608) = 0
      -- Can't drop primary key
      AND (status & 2048) = 0
    ORDER BY indid

/* Open index info cursor */
OPEN c_IdxList

/* Fetch first index ID & name */
FETCH NEXT FROM c_IdxList INTO @v_IndID, @v_IndName
```

```
/* Loop through indexes */
WHILE (@@fetch_status <> -1)
  BEGIN
  /* Skip missing rows */
  IF (@@fetch_status <> -2)
    BEGIN
    /* Get information about first field in the index */
    SELECT @v_Keys = INDEX_COL(@v_TableName, @v_IndID, 1),
          @v_i = 2

    /* Get information about next field in the index (if any) */
    SELECT @v_ThisKey = INDEX_COL(@v_TableName, @v_IndID, @i)

    /* If there was another field, add it and check again */
    WHILE (@v_ThisKey IS NOT NULL)
      BEGIN
      /* Add additional field(s) to the list */
      SELECT @v_Keys = @v_Keys + ', ' + @v_ThisKey,
            @v_i = @v_i + 1

      /* Get information about next field in the index (if any) */
      SELECT @v_ThisKey = INDEX_COL(@v_TableName, @Iv_ndID, @v_i)
      END

    /* Save index name and field list in table variable */
    INSERT INTO @v_IdxList
      VALUES(@v_IndName, @v_Keys)

    /* Now that we can re-create it, it's OK to drop it */
    EXEC('DROP INDEX ' + @v_TableName + '.' + @v_IndName)

    /* Show that we got rid of it... */
    PRINT 'Index ' + @v_TableName + '.' + @v_IndName + ' removed.'
    END

  /* Fetch next index ID & name */
  FETCH NEXT FROM c_IdxList INTO @v_IndID, @v_IndName
  END

/* Close and deallocate Index cursor */
CLOSE c_IdxList
DEALLOCATE c_IdxList


/********************************/
/* Perform actual BCP IN command */
/********************************/
```

```
/* Build BCP IN command string */
SELECT @v_SQL = 'BCP ' + @v_DBName + '..' + @v_TableName + ' IN ' +
                @v_InFile + ' -n -S' + RTRIM(@@ServerName) + ' -Usa -P'

/* Perform BCP Operation */
EXEC master..xp_cmdshell @v_SQL


/**************************************************/
/* Re-create Indexes using the list in @v_IdxList */
/**************************************************/

/* Declare a cursor to loop through our index list */
DECLARE c_Indexes CURSOR FAST_FORWARD FOR
  SELECT Index_Name,
         Index_Keys
    FROM @v_IdxList

/* Open index list cursor */
OPEN c_Indexes

/* Fetch first index to rebuild */
FETCH NEXT FROM c_Indexes INTO @v_IndName, @v_IndKeys

/* Loop through list of indexes */
WHILE (@@Fetch_status <> -1)
  BEGIN
  /* Skip missing rows */
  IF (@@fetch_status <> -2)
    BEGIN
    /* Recreate index */
    EXEC('CREATE INDEX ' + @v_IndName + ' ON ' + @v_TableName +
        ' (' + @v_IndKeys + ')')

    /* Show that we put it back... */
    PRINT 'Index ' + @v_TableName + '.' + @v_IndName + ' recreated.'
    PRINT '    (' + @v_IndKeys + ')'
    END

  /* Fetch next index to rebuild */
  FETCH NEXT FROM c_Indexes INTO @v_IndName, @v_IndKeys
  END

/* Close and deallocate index list cursor */
CLOSE c_Indexes
DEALLOCATE c_Indexes
GO
```

15. BCP

# Creating a Login Data File with BCP

Many administrators eventually find themselves faced with the problem of transferring the security information on one server to one or more additional servers. In most cases, the DBA is then forced to manually set up the user accounts and passwords for each new server. This example provides a method for creating an import file that can be used to apply the user account and password information to new servers in an automated fashion.

1. You first need to create a data file that contains a list of user accounts with the user names, passwords, and database access information.

2. Because you cannot move encrypted password information between servers, the passwords need to be stored in an unencrypted character format. This can create a security risk, so the file should be carefully protected. The existing password information cannot be unencrypted and extracted, so you will be forced to supply this information by hand before importing the users into the new server. This script will actually supply the user name as a default password for each user.

3. Once you have captured the user list into a temporary table, you need to loop through a list of the users to check for which databases they need access to. You then need to create a **FORWARD_ONLY** cursor that allows updates to the **dblist** field in the temporary table.

4. In addition to looping through the list of users, you need to be able to loop through a list of databases for each user to see if the user has access to the database. You need to create a **SCROLL** cursor for the database list, so that you can repeat the loop for each user in the user list.

5. For each iteration through the database loop, you need to check for the user in the **sysusers** table of the database, and add the database name to the **dblist** column of your users table if the user has access to the database.

6. Once you have updated the **dblist** column for each user, you are ready to **BCP OUT** the temporary table to create a character format import file to be used in re-creating this information on other servers.

The complete script for this procedure is provided in Listing 15.18. After the user list has been generated and exported, you will need to edit the import file to provide the correct password information for each user. Once the passwords are entered in the file, you need to keep the file in a secure location to prevent this information from being accessed by nonadministrators.

---

**NOTE:** *This script creates the login file in the C:\TEMP directory on the SQL Server. To change the location of the output file, edit the* **BCP OUT** *command located near the bottom of the script.*

---

### Listing 15.18    Create a BCP login data file.

```
/**********************************************************************/
/* This script is used to capture login information to an export      */
/* that can be used to automate the task of adding the users to a     */
/* new server.                                                        */
/**********************************************************************/
/* NOTE: This script cannot capture the user's passwords, so the      */
/*       output file will have to be manually altered to include      */
/*       this information. The information is stored in character     */
/*       format, so the finished output file must be carefully        */
/*       guarded to ensure the security of the information.           */
/**********************************************************************/


/* Turn off row count display */
SET NOCOUNT OFF


/* DECLARE Variables */
DECLARE @v_Login     VARCHAR(255),
        @v_DBName    VARCHAR(255),
        @v_DBString  VARCHAR(500),
        @v_TpDB      VARCHAR(50),
        @v_SQL       VARCHAR(8000)


/* Create a global temporary table */
CREATE TABLE ##UserInfo
      ( Login     VARCHAR(255) NOT NULL,
        Password  VARCHAR(255) NULL,
        DBList    VARCHAR(500) NULL )


/* Load user names and default passwords */
INSERT INTO ##UserInfo
  SELECT name,
         name,
         ''

    FROM master..sysxlogins (NOLOCK)
    WHERE name NOT IN ('sa', 'null', 'BUILTIN\Administrators')
    ORDER BY name


/* Create a cursor to retrieve a list of database names */
DECLARE c_DBList CURSOR STATIC SCROLL FOR
  SELECT name
    FROM master..sysdatabases (NOLOCK)
    ORDER BY name


/* Open database list cursor */
OPEN c_DBList
```

```
/* Create cursor to retrieve a list of user names */
DECLARE c_UserList CURSOR FORWARD_ONLY FOR
  SELECT login
    FROM ##UserInfo
  FOR UPDATE OF dblist

/* Open User List Cursor */
OPEN c_UserList

/* Get first User Login ID */
FETCH NEXT FROM c_UserList INTO @v_Login

/* Loop through users */
WHILE (@@FETCH_STATUS <> -1)
  BEGIN
  /* Skip missing rows */
  IF (@@FETCH_STATUS <> -2)
    BEGIN
    /* Get first Database Name */
    FETCH FIRST FROM c_DBList INTO @v_DBName

    /* Loop through databases */
    WHILE (@@FETCH_STATUS <> -1)
      BEGIN
      /* Skip missing rows */
      IF (@@FETCH_STATUS <> -2)
        BEGIN
        /* Build update statement to add database user's */
        /* list if needed                               */
        SELECT @v_SQL =
          'IF EXISTS (SELECT name ' +
                     'FROM ' + @v_DBName + '..sysusers (NOLOCK) ' +
                     'WHERE name = ''' + @v_Login + ''') ' +
            'BEGIN ' +
            'UPDATE ##UserInfo ' +
              'SET dblist = dblist + ''' + @v_DBName + ''' + '';'' ' +
              'WHERE CURRENT OF c_UserList ' +
            'END'

        /* Execute the update code */
        EXEC(@v_SQL)
        END

      /* Get next database name */
      FETCH NEXT FROM c_DBList INTO @v_DBName
      END
    END
```

```
    /* Get Next User Login ID */
    FETCH NEXT FROM c_UserList INTO @v_Login
    END

/* Close and deallocate User List cursor */
CLOSE c_UserList
DEALLOCATE c_UserList

/* Close and deallocate Database List cursor */
CLOSE c_DBList
DEALLOCATE c_DBList

/* Build BCP Command String */
SELECT @v_SQL = 'BCP ##UserInfo OUT C:\TEMP\Logins.bcp ' +
                '-Ssneezy -Usa -P -c -t, -r\n'

/* Execute BCP Command string to copy out user info. */
EXEC xp_cmdshell @v_SQL

/* Drop the global temporary table */
DROP TABLE ##UserInfo
```

# Deploying Logins on a New Server

The "Create a Login Data File with BCP" immediate solution provided the details for creating an import file that can be used to import the logins into a new server. If you have not created the login import file, go back and follow the instructions in the "Create a Login Data File with BCP" section before attempting to use this solution.

Once you have a login import file created, you can create a script to import the login information into a new server. For simplicity, this example assigns all imported users to the database owner (DBO) role for each database listed in the import file. You can modify this to suit your environment if needed.

1. The first step for adding the database logins from your import file is to create a temporary table to import the user information into.

2. Once the temporary table has been created, you can import the data file.

3. Next, you need to create a **FAST_FORWARD** cursor to loop through the users in the temporary table.

4. You also need to create a **STATIC SCROLL** cursor to loop through the database names.

5. For each user in the user list, you need to check to see if the login name exists and add it if needed.

6. Once the login has been added, you need to loop through the databases to see if they are in the database list for the user.

7. If the database is in the database list for the user, you need to grant access to the database for that user.

8. Once you have processed all the users in the list, you can deallocate the cursors and drop the temporary table. The complete listing for the script to perform this solution is available in Listing 15.19.

**Listing 15.19   Import login information.**

```
/**********************************************************************/
/* This script is used to import login information captured on        */
/* another server to simplify the process of creating user accounts   */
/* on a new server.                                                    */
/**********************************************************************/

/* Set database context to the master database */
USE master

/* Turn off row count displays */
SET NOCOUNT OFF

/* Create global temporary table to hold user info */
CREATE TABLE ##UserList
     ( login      VARCHAR(255) NOT NULL,
       password   VARCHAR(255) NULL,
       dblist     VARCHAR(500) NULL )

/* Declare Variables */
DECLARE @v_Login      VARCHAR(255),
        @v_Password    VARCHAR(255),
        @v_DBName      VARCHAR(255),
        @v_DB          VARCHAR(255),
        @v_DBString    VARCHAR(255),
        @v_DBStringx   VARCHAR(255),
        @v_SQL         VARCHAR(8000)

/* Build BCP IN command string */
SELECT @v_SQL = 'BCP ##UserList IN c:\temp\Logins.bcp '+
                '-Ssneezy -Usa -P -c -t, -r\n'

/* Perform BCP IN operation */
EXEC xp_cmdshell @v_SQL
```

```
/* Create cursor to loop through databases */
DECLARE c_DBList CURSOR STATIC SCROLL FOR
  SELECT name
    FROM master..sysdatabases (NOLOCK)
    ORDER BY name

/* Open database list cursor */
OPEN c_DBList

/* Create cursor to loop through user information */
DECLARE c_UserInfo CURSOR FAST_FORWARD FOR
  SELECT login,
         password,
         dblist
    FROM ##UserList (NOLOCK)
    ORDER BY login

/* Open user list cursor */
OPEN c_UserInfo

/* Fetch first user from user list cursor */
FETCH NEXT FROM c_UserInfo into @v_Login,
                                @v_Password,
                                @v_DBString

/* Loop through user list */
WHILE (@@fetch_status <> -1)
  BEGIN
  /* Skip missing rows */
  IF (@@fetch_status <> -2)
    BEGIN
    /* Check to see if the login exists */
    IF NOT EXISTS (SELECT name
                     FROM sysxlogins (NOLOCK)
                     WHERE name = @v_Login)
      BEGIN
      /* If not, we need to add it */
      EXEC sp_addlogin @v_Login, @v_Password
      END

    /* Fetch first database name from database list cursor */
    FETCH FIRST FROM c_DBList INTO @v_DBName

    /* Loop through databases */
    WHILE (@@FETCH_STATUS <> -1)
```

```
        BEGIN
        /* Skip missing rows */
        IF (@@FETCH_STATUS <> -2)
          BEGIN
          /* Check to see if the current database is in the */
          /* user's list                                    */
          IF (@v_DBString LIKE '%;' + @v_DBName + ';%') OR
             (@v_DBString LIKE @v_DBName + ';%')
            BEGIN
            /* Build dynamic SQL to grant access to the user since */
            /* the database was found in the user's list           */
            SELECT @v_SQL ='IF NOT EXISTS (SELECT name ' +
                           'FROM ' + @v_DBName + '.dbo.sysusers '+
                               '(NOLOCK) ' +
                           'WHERE name = ''' + @v_Login + ''') ' +
                        'BEGIN ' +
                        'EXEC(''' + @v_DBName +
                               '.dbo.SP_GRANTDBACCESS ''''' +
                            ' ' + @v_Login + ''''''') ' +
                        'EXEC(''' + @v_DBName +
                               '.dbo.sp_addrolemember '''+
                               '''db_owner'''', ''''' +
                            ' ' + @v_Login + ''''''') ' +
                        'END'

            /* Execute dynamic SQL to grant database access */
            EXEC(@v_SQL)
            END
          END

      /* Fetch next database name from database list cursor */
      FETCH NEXT FROM c_DBList INTO @v_DBName
      END
    END

  /* Fetch next user from user list cursor */
  FETCH NEXT FROM c_UserInfo into @v_Login,
                                  @v_Password,
                                  @v_DBString
  END

/* Close and deallocate user list cursor */
CLOSE c_UserInfo
DEALLOCATE c_UserInfo
```

```
/* Close and deallocate database list cursor */
CLOSE c_DBList
DEALLOCATE c_DBList

/* Drop the global temporary table */
DROP TABLE ##UserList
```

| Related solution: | Found on page: |
|---|---|
| usp_bcp | 237 |

## Using **QUERYOUT**

The **QUERYOUT** option of the BCP utility can be used to create a data file from the result set of a query rather than requiring a fixed table or view. In this example, you use the Employee and Address databases to create an export file containing employee names and addresses that can be used to populate a denormalized name and address table. You will include the following information in this table: the employee's first name, last name, address line 1, address line 2, city, state, and ZIP code. This solution can also be used to produce a mailing list that you could transfer to another database for reporting and sending out mailings without impacting your production database.

1. The first step in this process is to construct the query that you need to retrieve the address information in the format you want to export. The easiest way to accomplish this is to create the query in the Query Analyzer.

2. Because you are creating the query in the Query Analyzer, you can use dynamic SQL to execute the BCP command from within the Query Analyzer. Load the query into a variable, and then EXEC the variable to make sure the query still works.

3. Once the SQL is in a variable, add the needed BCP syntax around the query. When this is accomplished, you should have a functional BCP command in the variable.

4. The final step is to use the **xp_cmdshell** extended stored procedure to execute the BCP command. The complete script for this task is shown in Listing 15.20.

Listing 15.20 **QUERYOUT** for denormalized address data.

```
/* Declare variable */
DECLARE @SQL VARCHAR(8000)
```

15. BCP

```
/* Build BCP Command to QUERYOUT address information */
SELECT @SQL = 'BCP "SELECT e.first_name, '+
                        'e.last_name, '+
                        'a.line1, ' +
                        'a.line2, '+
                        'a.zip4, ' +
                        'c.name, ' +
                        's.state_code, ' +
                        'z.zip5 ' +
                'FROM employee.dbo.tbl_employee e (NOLOCK)' +
                'JOIN employee.dbo.tbl_EmployeeAddressXref  x ' +
                  'ON x.employee_id = e.employee_id ' +
                'JOIN address.dbo.tbl_address a (NOLOCK) ' +
                  'ON x.address_id = a.address_id ' +
                'JOIN address.dbo.tbl_city c (NOLOCK) ' +
                  'ON a.city_id = c.city_id ' +
                'JOIN address.dbo.tbl_zipcode z (NOLOCK) ' +
                  'ON a.zip_id = z.zip_id ' +
                'JOIN address.dbo.tbl_state s (NOLOCK) ' +
                  'ON z.state_id = s.state_id" ' +
            'queryout c:\temp\name_address.bcp ' +
            '-Ssneezy -Usa -P -c -t, -r\n '

/* Perform BCP QUERYOUT command */
EXEC master..xp_cmdshell @SQL
```

# Using Format Files

There will be times when you find it necessary to import data into a structure that does not match the structure from which it was originally exported. Without format files, you would be forced to create a temporary table with the original structure, import the data to the temporary file, and then use the temporary table to retrieve the data you need. This section explains how you can use a format file to solve this problem. A format file allows you to import the data directly into the new structure without the need to involve a temporary structure.

This example uses the export file generated in the "Using **QUERYOUT**" Immediate Solution. If you did not create the c:\temp\name_address.bcp export file in the previous section, you should do so before continuing with this solution.

1. You first need to create the new structure that you want to load the data into. Listing 15.21 provides a script that creates the new table in the Address database.

**Listing 15.21    Create tbl_Name_Address in the Address database.**

```
/* Switch context to the address database */
USE Address

/* Create the table*/
CREATE TABLE tbl_address_new
        ( line1      VARCHAR(50),
          line2      VARCHAR(50),
          city       VARCHAR(50),
          state      CHAR(2),
          zip5       CHAR(5),
          zip4       CHAR(4) )
```

2. Once you have a new table, you can use it to create a format file for your import. The following code illustrates the **BCP FORMAT** command that creates this file for you.

```
BCP employee.dbo.tbl_name_address FORMAT -t, -r\n -t,
-Ssneezy -Usa -P -c -fc:\temp\new_address.fmt
```

---

**NOTE:** *The **BCP FORMAT** command can be extremely finicky about the switch ordering. The errors reported by BCP when the switches are supplied in the wrong order do not sound like a switch ordering problem. You may receive errors such as "Cannot open database requested in login 'address'. Login failed." and "Unable to open BCP host-data file." The errors vary with the switches specified and the order in which they are listed. In order to get the preceding code to function correctly, the **-t** and **-r** switches have to be specified first, and the **-c** and **-f** switches have to be moved to the end. You may also be forced to specify the **-t** switch twice in order to get the field delimiter in the format file to come out as a comma instead of a tab.*

---

3. Open the format file created by the **BCP FORMAT** command using Notepad or some other text editor.

4. The format file generated by this command will not quite match the data in your original export file. The order of the **Zip4** column has changed in the table created to move it next to the **Zip5** column. You need to move the **Zip4** line in the format file up to the line after the entry for the **Line2** field, so that it matches the export file. This requires that you change the field terminator for the **Zip4** column from "\r\n" to "," and perform the opposite substitution on the **Zip5** column because it is now the last column in the list.

5. You also have to add entries to the format file for the two name lines that were included in the export file, even though you will not be importing them. The easiest way to include these lines is to duplicate the entry for **Line1** for each of the name lines and change the field names to first and last. In addition, you need to change the table ordinal values and the data length for these columns to 0.

6. The final step is to number the file column ordinal values consecutively and adjust the column counter (the second line of the format file) to reflect the fact that you now have eight entries in the file instead of six.

Listing 15.22 shows the format file generated by the **BCP FORMAT** command and the alteration needed to make it work for the data you are importing. Both the original format file and the modified version are shown in the listing, so that you can see the changes that needed to be made to map the import file to the new structure properly.

### Listing 15.22   Format file modification.

```
--Before:
8.0
6
1    SQLCHAR    0    50    ","        1    line1    SQL_Latin1_General_CP1_CI_AS
2    SQLCHAR    0    50    ","        2    line2    SQL_Latin1_General_CP1_CI_AS
3    SQLCHAR    0    50    ","        3    city     SQL_Latin1_General_CP1_CI_AS
4    SQLCHAR    0    2     ","        4    state    SQL_Latin1_General_CP1_CI_AS
5    SQLCHAR    0    5     ","        5    zip5     SQL_Latin1_General_CP1_CI_AS
6    SQLCHAR    0    4     "\r\n "    6    zip4     SQL_Latin1_General_CP1_CI_AS

--After:
8.0
8
1    SQLCHAR    0    0     ","        0    First    SQL_Latin1_General_CP1_CI_AS
2    SQLCHAR    0    0     ","        0    Last     SQL_Latin1_General_CP1_CI_AS
3    SQLCHAR    0    50    ","        1    line1    SQL_Latin1_General_CP1_CI_AS
4    SQLCHAR    0    50    ","        2    line2    SQL_Latin1_General_CP1_CI_AS
5    SQLCHAR    0    4     ","        6    zip4     SQL_Latin1_General_CP1_CI_AS
6    SQLCHAR    0    50    ","        3    city     SQL_Latin1_General_CP1_CI_AS
7    SQLCHAR    0    2     ","        4    state    SQL_Latin1_General_CP1_CI_AS
8    SQLCHAR    0    5     "\r\n"     5    zip5     SQL_Latin1_General_CP1_CI_AS
```

**NOTE:** *The format file column widths have been reduced to make this listing readable in the book.*

Once the format file modifications have been made, you can use the **BCP IN** command with your new format file to import the name_address.bcp file into the new **tbl_name_address** table. The **BCP IN** command to perform the insert is shown in Listing 15.23.

### Listing 15.23   BCP IN name and address information using a format file.

```
BCP address.dbo.tbl_address_new IN c:\temp\name_address.bcp
-fc:\temp\new_address.fmt -Ssneezy -Usa -P
```

An alternative to using the **BCP IN** command would be to use the **BULK INSERT** statement to perform this operation. Because the **BULK INSERT** statement also supports the use of a format file, this operation is simple. Listing 15.24 provides the equivalent **BULK INSERT** statement to perform the insert for **tbl_Name_Address**.

**Listing 15.24   BULK INSERT name and address information using a format file.**

```
BULK INSERT address.dbo.tbl_address_new
  FROM 'c:\temp\name_address.bcp'
  WITH (FORMATFILE = 'c:\temp\new_address.fmt')
```

15. BCP

# Chapter 16

## Database Design

# In Depth

Database design can play such a huge role in the performance of an application. A poor design can turn even a simple application into a poor performing, hard to maintain, problem child. So often you hear the phrase, "This is to allow for acceptable performance."

There are a number of legitimate reasons for application's problems. The database design may or may not be directly related to all problems, but may be able to directly solve many of the problems. Often, the decision is made to attempt less invasive solutions in hopes of buying time or saving money. In the long run, deciding not to make the needed design changes to the database ends up costing more and requiring a greater amount of effort.

This chapter is intended to help you make the right choices in database design *before* or *after* you have a database design to work with. The solutions and techniques in this chapter will help you make the right choices in modeling your data, so that peak performance and storage techniques can be used in your application designs. It will mean a bit more work for the smaller applications, but in the long run will save you hours of headaches and reworking your code.

## ERA Model

The easiest technique to employ when analyzing your database needs is to use the Entities, Relationships, and Attributes (ERA) methodology. This methodology provides you with a simple process that can be followed when defining or redefining your tables in your database. The following sections are referenced from Chapter 8.

### Entities

The entities created in any database are essentially the nouns or items that you describe when talking about a process. A person, place, or thing can be an entity in a data model. Entities are in essence tables in database design. Each table should have a unique identifier that allows each record to be identified within a set of records returned when querying the table. You should limit the number of columns (attributes), so that you can keep the performance high across each entity you are querying.

## Relationships

Relationships are how entities relate to each other, so that records can be associated with each other in queries or view definitions. A relationship is similar to a parent and a child within a family. The parent entity has a key value *(primary key)* that uniquely identifies a record in one table with any other tables or entities that are considered children. The child table or entity has what is called a *foreign key*. This key is a column that holds the value of the parent entity, so that you can join the two entities during the query process.

## Attributes

Attributes (or columns) describe the entity. They contain the details of the entity and make each record unique in relation to other records stored in the same table. For example, the **Employee** entity can be described by attributes such as first and last names. These columns allow you to "describe" the entity by supplying individual values that make up the employee record.

# Data Integrity

Ensuring the quality of the data in a database should be the number-one priority of any developer or database administrator. If you have poor integrity rules, your reports and processes can produce invalid results or require far too complex programming techniques to maintain any level of quality.

## Entity Integrity

Entity integrity is enforced through the unique keys that identify a row in a table or entity, so that it can be identified without question. Entity integrity of parent and child records is of paramount importance in a database. Orphaned records cause space problems and **JOIN** condition problems that drive database administrators crazy.

Entity integrity allows you to rely upon the fact that one and only one record exists within the scope of an entity. That entity may be a child record with associated records, but still relates to a unique row in either table. Duplicated rows with identical matching data elements are useless in the database model and take up space.

## Domain Integrity

Domain integrity relates to the individual columns of data in an entity or table. Ensuring that values allowed in a column meet specific requirements can guarantee that you do not have to clutter client-side code with extra logic to ensure that the data presented is valid. You can enforce domain integrity through key definitions, check constraints, defaults, and nullability in the declaration of the table, or through stored procedure and trigger logic.

## Relational Integrity

In a normalized structure, the relational integrity of data can be the most important integrity check in the database. Only allowing the addition of child records that have a corresponding parent record or removing the child records when the parent is removed allows you to ensure that you do not orphan records in the database.

Cascading record manipulation has been enhanced in SQL Server 2000 to support automatic cascading of data changes through related tables. The internal processing for this kind of integrity is typically handled by triggers and stored procedure logic and should be designed into the database and maintained as the database grows.

Defining proper primary and foreign key relationships in the data model also uncovers potential design issues and additional normalization requirements. In some situations, it may be necessary to define relationships that are many-to-many in nature. In those situations, you may want to consider a cross-reference table that holds the key relationships and the type of relationship. An example of this technique of dealing with cross-reference data can be seen in the Employee database. The employee-address cross-reference table holds the key for each employee, his or her associated address key, and the type of address that key represents. The table design allows for many employees to be associated with many addresses and yet only store the required data needed to satisfy the join logic. See Chapter 8 for more information on the Employee and Address database examples.

# Estimating Database Size

One often-overlooked area of design is space consideration. When designing a database, you need to understand how the server is going to store the data and how much data you plan on placing in the new structure. Your design may dictate more storage than you anticipate.

In your calculations to determine how much space is needed, you must consider all objects that will consume disk space. Indexes, materialized views, and maintenance tasks place additional space requirements on your design. There are a few discrete steps you should follow when estimating the size of a database:

1. Determine how many rows of data will exist in the table, index, or view.

2. Determine the number of bytes each row will use in a data or index page (allow for the maximum value of any variable length columns, not an average).

3. Add 5 bytes to the row size calculation to allow for the data row header or 9 bytes for index row information.

4. Calculate the number of rows that will fit on a page (there are 8096 free bytes per page) and round down to the nearest whole number. (Partial records are not allowed in a page.)

5. If you are estimating the size of an index, be sure to take fill factor into account. Subtract the appropriate amount of page storage for the index from 8096 before determining how many index keys can fit on a page of storage.

6. Calculate the number of pages required to store all of the rows of an index key and data for a table or view. Round up to the nearest whole number to ensure that you have the total number of pages required to store the table and indexes.

7. Multiply the number of pages by 8192 to determine how much space is needed for the object.

8. Use the **CEILING( )** function to round up the value to ensure that you allow adequate space in your estimates.

The numbers in the preceding steps only represent a guide for estimating. Depending on null values and key data composition, the formulas are slightly different. See the Microsoft SQL Server Books Online topic "Estimating table size" for a more exact method of calculating sizes of tables, views, and indexes. In most situations, the preceding formula will at least approximate your storage requirements. For example, let's assume that you have a table that is 345 bytes wide. That table has a primary key of 8 bytes, two supporting indexes of 12 bytes each, and a 90 percent FILLFACTOR for indexes. To calculate the space requirements, you would follow an example like the one shown in Table 16.1. See the CD-ROM in the Chapter 16 directory for a sample spreadsheet that can be used to estimate table sizes based on this formula. The Excel spreadsheet is called SpaceEstimate.xls.

**NOTE:** *See the "Immediate Solutions" section of this chapter for a stored procedure that uses existing structures and records counts along with index information to estimate sizes of tables at various row counts or estimates the size of an entire database based on a percentage of growth.*

**Table 16.1   Estimating space example.**

| Rows | Data Width | Index Width | Data Pages | Index Pages | Space Required |
|---|---|---|---|---|---|
| 250,000 | 345 | 32 | 10,870 | 1,413 | 95.96 MB |

# Rules of Normalization

There are countless experts when it comes to normalizing data. Many college courses teach various techniques that follow Boyce-Codd Normal Form (BCNF), Domain-Key Normal Form (DKNF), or even Projection-Join Normal Form (PJNF). Each has a level of practical application in an enterprise data model and may provide you with the level of normalization that best fits your needs. Remember that there are *no* experts in your data except *you*! Your enterprise may require something that is a blend of normal and denormalized data in order to provide the best solution.

The ultimate goal of any normalization of a database should be a mix between performance and storage reasoning. Essentially, normalization is simply a process of organizing the data in a database. In order to satisfy a query, you must perform disk operations that take time. You must design your database to allow for the maximum amount of data per operation to be retrieved from the disk. Once the data is in memory, most operations are fast and only bound by the amount of memory and processor horsepower you have on your server. Disk operations are the slowest operation in any database. The main goals to keep in mind when modeling your database are:

- Store as little redundant data as possible.
- Allow for multiple values of data as efficiently as possible.
- Provide an efficient data modification structure (**INSERT**, **UPDATE**, and **DELETE**).
- Avoid the accidental loss of data.
- Try to keep your table width as small as possible to increase the number of records that are returned from each disk operation.

Most databases realize great performance and storage gains by taking the normalization process to third normal form. The following sections detail each step in normalization through fifth normal form. You should *always* normalize your data first and only denormalize the data on a case-by-case basis. Do not start by establishing denormalized data requirements. You will ultimately fail in producing a solid data model if you fall prey to this temptation. If you store redundant data, you will have to write extra code to maintain that data any time it must be changed, which is a waste of disk operation time.

## First Normal Form

A table or entity is considered in first normal form if the data elements meet the following criteria (row or column order is irrelevant):

- There are no duplicated rows in the table data.

- Each column in the row is of a single value (no repeating groups, named pairs, or arrays of values).
- Column values are of the same data type and kind.

You can accomplish these criteria by ensuring that your table has a primary key value that is guaranteed to be unique for each row and eliminate any repeating groups from the data set. Repeating groups of data point toward a separate related entity that should be considered.

## Second Normal Form

The second normal form stage of normalization is perhaps the most misunderstood in the process of normalization. Each level of normalization assumes the preceding forms have been applied to the data before applying the rules for that level. In first normal form, you should have removed repeating groups of data to create separate entities. This stage of normalization requires that you remove redundant data from the entity. The column level data should be removed if it is repeated many times in the data set. You are essentially removing any nonkey attribute that repeats and creating a separate entity for that repeating information. You are also separating data and relating it to the primary or parent table with a foreign key.

## Third Normal Form

Third normal form is commonly referred to as BCNF. This level of normalization includes the previous two levels plus the additional requirement that no attribute of the entity fails to describe the key of that entity. If an attribute does not directly describe the key for the entity, it should be removed and placed in a new separate entity or in one that already exists. The description part of this step typically confuses designers most. If a column of data cannot be used to define the key row of data, it may be a candidate for removal from that entity. When a definition is transitive and not directly linked to the key value, it should be removed.

This level of normalization may be enough to get your model to a good starting point for application development and storage. You should look for places where the forth and fifth normal forms may apply on a case-by-case basis, but you may not need to apply those levels in every situation.

## Fourth Normal Form

Fourth normal form includes levels one through three and applies the isolation of independent multiple relationships. This level of normalization only applies when you have one-to-many or many-to-many relationships in your model. You should remove any multiple sets of data that are not directly related, and separate them into independent entities.

16. Database Design

## Fifth Normal Form

The final stage of normalization is fifth normal form, also referred to as PJNF. This level of normalization is accomplished when candidate keys within the entity accommodate each join dependency. Many developers refer to this type of entity as a join-table. If each column or domain of the entity is derived from a constraint placed on the entity to support a join, it can be referred to as DKNF.

This level of normalization may be where you might take groups of related information and horizontally segment them based on join conditions. You essentially look at the set of data that an entity represents and determine whether or not it is best represented as a separate entity. These types of relationships are referred to as semantically related multiple relationships.

# Key Values

Determining the key value for an entity is often confused with creating a unique identifier column for the row. Typically, an identity or ID is generated and represents a unique row number. This is often true of key values, but not always required. You may have data elements that are already going to be unique to the row of data, and creating an additional key value would be redundant and wasteful.

The question of what data type is best suited for a key value is often asked, and the answer is typically a numeric value (**INTEGER** or **NUMERIC**). The reason these data types make such good keys in the model is actually driven by the database engine itself. If you create a character-based key and are going to join based on that key, the character values must be converted in order to be compared for join condition use.

You should always provide an index to support join conditions. This means that key columns are fine candidates for indexes. (Remember that a clustered index may not be the best choice for a key value.) When you create an entity, you should make an attempt to identify which columns, other than keys, are candidates for indexes, and include them in your design early.

---

**NOTE:** *Make sure you take index space into account when estimating the size requirements of an entity.*

---

Compound keys are valid for some child entities and should be indexed appropriately to support not only the join, but also any filtering conditions that may be used to access the information.

# Indexing Decisions

The number of indexes that are created to support queries against an entity can affect performance. Indexes are primarily used to provide a **JOIN** condition path to the data and improve the read performance of data. Having too many indexes defined for a table can slow the **INSERT**, **UPDATE**, or **DELETE** operations because each index affected by the modification must also be maintained.

There is no real method of determining how many indexes are too many. You have to weigh the importance of data retrieval versus data modification on a case-by-case basis. A rule of thumb that may help is to create an index to support **JOIN** conditions and **WHERE** clauses used in transaction processing routines, and then address reports and other processes related to SQL traffic after determining the optimal performance needed to process your transactional activity.

*NOTE: You may want to look at the autogenerated statistics to help determine where additional indexes may be helpful. You can determine how much space changing the autogenerated statistics into indexes will take by using the stored procedure **usp_EstimateDBSize** or **usp_EstimateSize** with the parameter **@p_StatsToIDX** set to **1**.*

With the increased logic in the SQL Server 2000 query optimizer, you can see performance gains by creating a *covering index* that holds the column information for every portion of the query being parsed. A number of single column indexes may provide better performance, however, because they will support a greater number of queries rather than a single-purpose covering index. You should place a test query in the Query Analyzer, and execute it showing the execution plan chosen by the query optimizer. The output from that test tells you if you have created an index strategy to support that query or not. You can find more information on performance tuning and optimization in Chapter 11.

*NOTE: Not all queries processed through the Query Analyzer will perform the same way when in a stored procedure. Thorough testing is the only sure way to know that you have created a good indexing strategy for your entities.*

# Sort Order Selection

The default sort order for SQL Server is dictionary case insensitive. This allows the most flexibility when writing stored procedures or client pass-through SQL, but does come at a cost. If you are designing a database for an application from the ground up, you may want to consider using a different sort order. The binary sort order is the fastest sort order that you can use. There are, however, rules that you should know before undertaking a development effort. Naming conventions and capitalization play an important role in your development efforts. When you use a binary sort order, the case of every character is used to determine a match. "Atable" does not equal "aTable" when you use a binary sort order. The upside of the binary sort order is that it is faster for query and index processing.

If you can develop your application in a controlled environment that respects the case-sensitive nature of object names, you will be able to take advantage of the increased performance the binary sort order provides.

---

**NOTE:** *Remember that each table, column, index, or string manipulation under a binary sort order is case sensitive!*

---

# *Immediate Solutions*

## Database Design Steps

The following solutions are intended to provide an example of the design steps that are required to generate a data model that can be used in a development environment. Once you have created a model, you should be able to identify the steps, based on these solutions, to add entities or perform updates to your data model. The data model is an evolutionary piece of work. It will never be finished. You consistently need to review the design and look for improvements based on data distribution and usage methods. It is not uncommon for a data model to undergo dramatic changes over the course of application development and maintenance. Use the rules and guidelines discussed in this chapter to manage that change, and your model will become predictable and stable.

Any good design has a discrete set of steps that takes it from the drawing board to reality. If you can follow these steps during the design phase and apply them when you must change the model, you will create a very scalable and enterprise-level solution.

### Research and Information Gathering

Many systems are born out of necessity and have evolved into the problematic state that you are presented with during the redesign process. You can take any existing data model and gather enough information to create a solid replacement. If you are replacing a paper-based system with an automated system, then the paper-based system can provide valuable insight into how the data should be organized.

You should include end-user information in the design process. The user's perspective is very important for gaining insight about how the data is perceived by the user. You should not let the user or developer dictate how the data is organized. The underlying structure of the database should be designed to accommodate storage and performance, *not* ease of programming or user concepts. You can provide users with views and reporting entities that then can be queried in a more user-friendly manner.

Follow these rules for your planning and research stages of modeling:

• Get the user involved to determine what data is required for presentation.

- Presentation, processing, and storage should be considered separately and should not place extra requirements on the database structure.

- Model the entities and attributes in abstract forms, and then provide sample data to test the design.

- Collect enough sample data so that your modeling has some test-case data.

- If you are remodeling an existing or a portion of an existing database, *avoid* incorporating existing design rules into the new model.

- When you create your new model, you must also define the rules for modifying, enhancing, or adding to the model.

- Create a standard interface for the database to abstract or separate the storage structure from the application access method (stored procedures or views).

## Identify the Objects

Most entities can be identified easily by looking for the who and what types of entities. The nouns represent the primary objects in a database. The more difficult objects are the ones that are not usually thought of as entities. Codes, states, or repeatable groups of attributes are usually the objects that do not get modeled in the first pass of the design. Follow these guidelines when identifying objects:

- Follow a top down approach of identifying the objects. Start at the 30,000 foot view and *slowly* work down to the 10,000 and 3,000 foot views of the objects.

- Stay abstract as long as possible. Developers, some database administrators, and programmers tend to model the "details" and attributes far too early in the process and complicate the modeling tasks.

- Do not be afraid to call something an object! In many situations, you might hear someone say, "That is not an object" or "That should be combined with another object." From a modeling perspective, those questions would be the exception rather than the rule.

- Only use sample data for an object after you have identified it. The tendency is to use the data early to help you identify the entities. Resist that tendency as long as possible.

## Create a Model of the Objects

If you cannot afford a more industrial-strength modeling tool, the built-in database designer in the Enterprise Manager can provide an adequate tool for creating a picture of the model and its associated attributes and relationships. Many tools exist on the market today that provide an exceptional graphical modeling tool. The first edition of the *Microsoft SQL Server Black Book* (The Coriolis Group, 1997, ISBN 1-57610-149-5), featured tool sets from Embarcadero Technologies as an alternative to the standard tool set offered by Microsoft. These tools still exist and do provide a great deal of functionality. Microsoft has closed the gap with the current release of SQL Server to provide tools that are adequate for most small- to medium-size database projects. When choosing a tool to create and manage your database, follow these guidelines:

- Use the tool to manage change, not react to it. If the tool does not allow you to manage the change within your environment, do not use it.

- If the tool does not provide a mechanism to generate reports and electronic output for developer use, you may want to consider another tool. Check the sample reporting and output formats carefully, and make sure they match your expectations.

- Do *not* take a salesman's word for functionality. Test the application against your database to ensure that it works as advertised before buying it. You may need some training in order to get it to perform the way you want, but you should know that in advance.

One final note on data modeling: You should continue to maintain the data model after you have finished the application or initial process. Once the model and the physical tables get out of synchronization, it becomes very difficult to get them back in sync without thorough knowledge of the original model and the list of changes that have been made to the database. The longer you wait to synchronize them, the harder the job will be.

## Identify the Attributes of Each Object

Once you have developed the model, you should identify the attributes of each entity. Take them one at a time and ask the question, "Does this attribute describe the key?" If you can answer yes, chances are you have done a good job modeling entities. If you cannot answer that question positively, you may need to revisit the entity definition process to ensure that you have not overlooked something important.

Each attribute falls into a specific category, such as key values, relational values, or attributes that directly describe the entity. You can often perform the attribute modeling phase after the relationship modeling phase. They are basically interchangeable, but should not be combined into one step.

**NOTE:** *You should use sample data for this step. Use enough rows of data to determine the structure validity and the design. You will often uncover new entities if you use actual sample data and not hypothetical data.*

## Identify the Relationships Between the Objects

Relationships and attributes can be modeled in either order, but should not be combined into the same step. If you combine the steps, you will start to think about attributes rather than the relationship as a separate and critical portion of the model.

You should identify the parent-child relationships first. Then look at one-to-one, one-to-many, and many-to-many relationships. Many-to-many relationships may not be present in the final model, depending upon what level of normalization you are applying to your model. Remember the following details when modeling the relationships between entities:

- Some relationships are defined by user-based or business rules.

- Many relationships are dictated by the modeling technique you are using.

- Check the graphic model to ensure that any entity in the model that has no relationships should be in the model without having any defined relationship.

- When you believe you are done, go through each relationship and make sure you have not duplicated or missed any relationships. Some models have over a dozen relationships for some entities, and they can be confusing.

## Repeat and Review All Design Steps

Repeating the steps of modeling one last time is often overlooked in the modeling process. Duplicating these steps will more often than not generate one if not many edits or changes that will be beneficial to your data model.

First, it allows you to uncover any missed entities, attributes, or relationships that may have been glossed over or missed during the initial phase. Second, it gives you a thorough review of the scope of your model. You will know each entity and determine if any redundancy exists. This step can prove very valuable prior to engaging in application development processes or data migration programming.

The graphic model printed out as a hard copy is best for this step. You should highlight each entity, attribute, and relationship as you check it in the final pass. You will then be able to identify any missing information easily.

# Creating Primary and Foreign Keys to Support Your Data Model

Some applications are designed as they are written. Following the create-as-you-go method can be dangerous. You will find that you must write code to protect against integrity problems at many levels of the application. A potential downfall is the eventual (I say eventual, but it usually ends up being guaranteed) missed integrity check and the corruption of the data.

There are various reasons that keys are not created, and none are really valid if you apply the rule that data integrity should come first. Properly implemented, keys can ensure the integrity of the data, and in most cases, provide better performance of the application. The following list contains a few rules to keep in mind when creating your keys:

- Each entity should have some sort of key that has a corresponding index to support the **JOIN** conditions and referential lookups during data manipulation.

- Primary keys will create a unique index to support the key (clustered by default if a clustered index does not already exist). You can specify whether the index for the primary key should be clustered or nonclustered during the definition of the key.

- A primary key cannot be deleted if a forcign key references it.

- Foreign keys do not automatically create a supporting index. You must do that manually.

- To modify a key, you must drop the existing key first, and then add a new one.

- SQL Server 2000 now supports automatic cascading of data manipulation through defined keys.

Refer to Appendix A for an example of the relationships in the address database that have corresponding primary and foreign keys to support the integrity of the data. Keys are considered declarative referential integrity. Declarative refers to the fact that you are defining the keys when you create the table or binding the integrity checks directly to a table. This method of integrity management allows any and all applications that interact with the data to follow the rules defined for the data. Many applications create a database application but do not provide integrity checks for tools, like the ad hoc SQL tools or third-party tools, developed to manipulate the data. Using keys to enforce integrity provides a greater degree of protection from *any* data manipulation.

For your convenience, a copy of the Address database with key relationships defined and displayed in the database diagram that is saved in the database is included on the CD-ROM in the Chapter 16 directory. You can attach this copy of the database to view the key relationships for the sample address data.

| Related solutions: | Found on page: |
|---|---|
| Query Analyzer | 193 |
| Installing the Book Databases from Scripts | 369 |
| Joining Tables | 431 |
| Changing the Execution Plan of a Query | 524 |
| Book Database Schema | 921 |

16. Database Design

# Indexing Strategies to Support the Data Model

Once you have defined the keys for your entities, you must address the additional indexes required for the fast access of the data. Not all queries are determined by a key-value match. Some queries, reports, and stored procedures require ranges of data to be searched or grouped for processing. You should look at the data stored in an entity, identify attributes that will be part of **WHERE** clause filtering, and supply indexes to support those queries as well. The following list contains a few guidelines for creating indexes in your data model:

- Analyze queries that modify rows of data to determine the impact of indexes on those tables. (Try to modify groups of rows rather than individual rows to improve performance.)

- Use **INTEGER** or **NUMERIC** columns for index keys wherever possible.

- When possible, avoid indexing columns that allow **NULL** values. (This is not always possible, but should be avoided.)

- Use clustered indexes to support queries that need to search ranges of sequential data and nonclustered indexes for **JOIN** and filter operations. (Primary keys are not always best used as clustered indexes.)

- Place a sample query in the Query Analyzer and turn on the Show Execution Plan (Ctrl+K) feature. Look at the plan to determine where you may need to create an index to improve performance.

- Use the Index Tuning Wizard to determine if you have provided adequate indexing for your queries.

- Avoid index hints in your SQL statements. As the index and data distribution change, the index that you have specified may actually be slower than an alternative plan the query optimizer may choose.

- Carefully consider covering indexes for queries. A covering index may improve performance for read operations, but can slow performance of write operations if too many columns or indexes exist.

- If you see a bookmark lookup in the execution plan of a query, you may benefit from changing that index (the one feeding the bookmark) to a clustered index. (Test the change to verify it before accepting the change at face value. Not all indexes that use bookmark lookups will be good clustered indexes.)

Microsoft recommends using the Index Tuning Wizard to determine proper indexing of tables in a database. You should use this as one of the many tools that will help you create a properly indexed database. Do not become dependent upon the wizard to cure your performance problems. Only good troubleshooting and analysis skills will provide you with the total solution to your indexing needs.

It is also important to note that queries submitted through the Query Analyzer do not always run the same when you plug them into a stored procedure. If the procedure has a great deal of control-of-flow logic and a large number of operations, you could see different results from testing a query in a stored procedure.

For your convenience, a copy of the Address database with key relationships and index changes to support a few types of queries is included in the Chapter 16 directory on the CD-ROM. You can attach this copy of the database to view the key relationships for the sample address data.

| Related solutions: | Found on page: |
| --- | --- |
| Query Analyzer | 193 |
| Installing the Book Databases from Scripts | 369 |
| Joining Tables | 431 |
| Changing the Execution Plan of a Query | 524 |

# Estimating Database Size

In order to estimate the size of a database, you must know the data and index distributions. If you are starting from scratch and do not have any sample data or an existing database to choose, you can use the EstimateSize.xls spreadsheet on the CD-ROM in the Chapter 16 directory. You will be able to fill in the tables and the estimated number of rows along with the width of data and index columns to determine the amount of space a table or database requires.

This solution focuses on an existing model that may have some or all of the tables populated with data, but needs to account for future growth. The following procedures allow you to determine the impact of increased row counts or percentage of growth that you may need to plan for during your design process. Depending upon the type of growth you are trying to account for, you may be able to use **usp_EstimateSize** for individual tables or **usp_EstimateDBSize**, which looks at an entire database.

## usp_EstimateSize

The stored procedure **usp_EstimateSize** performs in a few modes. You can pass a table name to the procedure along with an anticipated row count or an optional growth multiplier to calculate the amount of disk space the table will take up. The optional parameter **@p_StatsToIdx** determines the amount of space that would be added to the storage requirements should you convert statistics to indexes. (That conversion is a manual step and should only be done once you have tested the impact of that change against your query performance.)

**Usp_EstimateSize** uses the system catalog information to find out how wide the table and index columns are and applies the same computations as the EstimateSize.xls spreadsheet. All values are rounded appropriately to ensure that the estimate is in line with what the actual figure will be, taking into account that you want to estimate high rather than low. See Listing 16.1 for the source SQL for **usp_EstimateSize**. You can find the file usp_EstimateSize.sql on the CD-ROM in the Chapter 16 directory.

**Listing 16.1    Source SQL for usp_EstimateSize.**

```
CREATE PROC usp_EstimateSize
  @p_TableName  SYSNAME       = NULL,
  @p_NumRows    INTEGER       = 0,
  @p_Growth     NUMERIC(16,6) = 0.0,
  @p_StatsToIDX BIT           = 0
AS
IF (@p_TableName IS NULL)
BEGIN
  PRINT 'You must supply a table name...'
  RETURN
END -- TableName IS NULL

SET NOCOUNT ON
DECLARE @v_DataWidth  INTEGER,
        @v_IndexWidth INTEGER,
        @v_DataPages  INTEGER,
        @v_IndexPages INTEGER,
        @v_FillFactor NUMERIC(3,2)

IF (@p_NumRows = 0)
BEGIN
  CREATE TABLE #Count (NumRows INT)

  EXEC('INSERT INTO #Count ' +
       'SELECT COUNT(*) ' +
         'FROM ' + @p_TableName)

  SELECT @p_NumRows = NumRows
    FROM #Count
END -- NumRows = 0

/* Account For Growth Param          */
IF (@p_Growth > 0.0)
BEGIN
  SELECT @p_NumRows = @p_Numrows * @p_Growth
END -- Growth > 0.00
```

```
/* Get the table width               */
SELECT @v_DataWidth = COALESCE((SUM(col.length) + 5),0)
  FROM sysobjects obj (NOLOCK)
  JOIN syscolumns col (NOLOCK) ON obj.id = col.id
 WHERE obj.type = 'U'
   AND obj.name = @p_TableName

/* Get the index width                */
IF (@p_StatsToIDX = 0)
BEGIN
  SELECT @v_IndexWidth = COALESCE((SUM(col.length) + 9),0)
    FROM sysobjects    obj (NOLOCK)
    JOIN sysindexes    idx (NOLOCK) ON obj.id    = idx.id
    JOIN sysindexkeys idk (NOLOCK) ON obj.id    = idk.id
                                  AND idx.indid = idk.indid
    JOIN syscolumns    col (NOLOCK) ON obj.id    = col.id
                                  AND idk.colid = col.colid
   WHERE obj.type = 'U'
     AND obj.name = @p_TableName
     AND idx.name NOT LIKE '_WA_Sys%'
END -- No stats in calc
ELSE
BEGIN
  SELECT @v_IndexWidth = COALESCE((SUM(col.length) + 9),0)
    FROM sysobjects    obj (NOLOCK)
    JOIN sysindexes    idx (NOLOCK) ON obj.id    = idx.id
    JOIN sysindexkeys idk (NOLOCK) ON obj.id    = idk.id
                                  AND idx.indid = idk.indid
    JOIN syscolumns    col (NOLOCK) ON obj.id    = col.id
                                  AND idk.colid = col.colid
   WHERE obj.type = 'U'
     AND obj.name = @p_TableName
END -- Calc Stats to IDX size

/* Get an index fillfactor            */
SELECT @v_FillFactor = CASE AVG(idx.OrigFillFactor)
                       WHEN 0 THEN
                         1
                       ELSE
                         MAX(idx.OrigFillFactor) / 100.00
                       END
  FROM sysobjects    obj (NOLOCK)
  JOIN sysindexes    idx (NOLOCK) ON obj.id    = idx.id
 WHERE obj.type = 'U'
   AND obj.name = @p_TableName
```

```
        /* Avoid Divide by Zero              */
        SELECT @v_DataWidth = CASE @v_DataWidth
                            WHEN 0 THEN
                              1
                            ELSE
                              @v_DataWidth
                            END,
            @v_IndexWidth = CASE @v_IndexWidth
                            WHEN 0 THEN
                              1
                            ELSE
                              @v_IndexWidth
                            END

        SELECT @v_DataPages  = CEILING(@p_NumRows/
                                FLOOR(8096.0/@v_DataWidth)),
            @v_IndexPages = CEILING(@p_NumRows/
                                FLOOR((8096.0 * @v_FillFactor)/
                                    (@v_IndexWidth)))

        SELECT CEILING(((@v_DataPages + @v_IndexPages)* 8.0)/1024.0)
            AS 'NewSize (MB)'
        GO
```

The use of the **CEILING()** and **FLOOR()** functions ensures that you are rounding values in the proper direction. You can also see, in the highlighted code in Listing 16.1, that you are not using a full-page size (8192) in the calculation to allow for page header information. You can adjust the values in the stored procedure to meet your estimation rules as you see fit, but you should not adjust the rounding and page size information, because changes to those pieces of information could throw off the calculations and render them incorrect. The following sample code is used to call **usp_EstimateSize** and the address table along with the output from the stored procedure. The **10.0** parameter tells the procedure that you would like to see how large the storage requirements for 10 times the number of rows would be.

```
exec usp_EstimateSize 'tbl_address',0,10.0,1

/* Results */
NewSize (MB)
----------------------
147
```

| Related solutions: | Found on page: |
|---|---|
| Query Analyzer | 193 |
| Joining Tables | 431 |
| Utility Procedures and Scripts | 661 |

## usp_EstimateDBSize

The stored procedure **usp_EstimateDBSize** assumes that you have an existing database that is populated with data and uses the row counts from the existing tables along with a percentage of growth factor to determine how much space you need.

This procedure depends on a version of **usp_EstimateSize** called **usp_Estimate SizeOUT**. The procedure **usp_EstimateSizeOUT** should exist in the database before running **usp_EstimateDBSize**. The only difference between the estimate size and estimate size out procedures is the use of output parameters in the code to simplify the passing of data between procedures. You can find the source for **usp_EstimateSizeOUT** in a file called usp_EstimateSizeOUT.sql on the CD-ROM in the Chapter 16 directory.

The stored procedure estimates the database size by looping through the user tables in a database, performing a size estimate for each one of those tables, and storing that information in a table variable called **@v_TblSizes**. At the bottom of the stored procedure (see the highlighted code in Listing 16.2), you see the **SELECT** statements that actually return the summary information to the user. The stored procedure **usp_EstimateDBSize**, shown in Listing 16.2, also accepts the **@p_StatsToIDX** parameter to use statistics in determining the amount of space required for the database.

The stored procedures are installed in the sample Address database on the CD-ROM in the Chapter 16 directory. You can attach that database to your server and run the procedures with a number of different parameters to see the impact of growing or upsizing the Address database.

Listing 16.2   Source SQL for **usp_EstimateDBSize**.

```
IF (OBJECT_ID('usp_EstimateDBSize') IS NOT NULL)
BEGIN
  DROP PROC usp_EstimateDBSize
END
GO
/* Create in each database that it is used in */
CREATE PROC usp_EstimateDBSize
  @p_Growth    NUMERIC(16,6) = 1.0,
  @p_StatsToIDX BIT          = 0
```

```
            AS
            SET NOCOUNT ON
            /* Declare Variables                    */
            DECLARE @v_table SYSNAME,
                    @v_Size  NUMERIC(16,6)

            DECLARE @v_TblSizes TABLE (
              TableName SYSNAME NOT NULL,
              NewSize   NUMERIC(16,6) NOT NULL)

            /* Declare the Table Cursor (Identity) */
            DECLARE c_Tables CURSOR
              FAST_FORWARD FOR
             SELECT obj.name
               FROM sysobjects obj (NOLOCK)
              WHERE obj.type = 'U'
                AND name LIKE 'tbl_%'

            OPEN c_Tables

            FETCH NEXT FROM c_Tables INTO @v_Table
            WHILE (@@fetch_status <> -1)
            BEGIN
              IF (@@fetch_status <> -2)
              BEGIN
                EXEC usp_EstimateSizeOUT @v_Table,
                                         0,
                                         @p_Growth,
                                         @p_StatsToIDX,
                                         @v_Size OUTPUT

                IF (@v_Size IS NULL)
                BEGIN
                  SELECT @v_Size = 0.0
                END -- Size is NULL
                INSERT INTO @v_TblSizes VALUES (@v_Table, @v_Size)
              END -- -2
              FETCH NEXT FROM c_Tables INTO @v_Table
            END -- While

            CLOSE c_Tables
            DEALLOCATE c_Tables

            PRINT 'Individual Table Sizes'
            SELECT CONVERT(VARCHAR(15),TableName) AS TableName,
                   CEILING(NewSize) AS 'NewSize (MB)'
              FROM @v_TblSizes
```

```
PRINT 'Total Database Size'
SELECT SUM(CEILING(NewSize)) AS 'NewSize (MB)'
  FROM @v_TblSizes
GO
```

The calling syntax and sample output are shown in Listing 16.3. Note that the **2.0** parameter tells the stored procedure that you want to see the space requirements for the Address database at two times the current number of rows. The additional parameter, **1**, tells the procedure that it should use any statistics stored in the current database as indexes for the new structure.

**Listing 16.3    Sample call to usp_EstimateDBSize.**

```
EXEC usp_EstimateDBSize 2.0,1

/* Results */
Individual Table Sizes
TableName       NewSize (MB)
-------------- -------------------

tbl_Address     30
tbl_addressDN   59
tbl_City        1
tbl_State       1
tbl_ZipCode     1

Total Database Size
NewSize (MB)
-----------------------------------------
92
```

| Related solutions: | Found on page: |
|---|---|
| Query Analyzer | 193 |
| Joining Tables | 431 |
| Utility Procedures and Scripts | 661 |

**16. Database Design**

# Chapter 17
## Triggers

# In Depth

Microsoft SQL Server 2000 provides two main methods for enforcing business rules and data integrity at the server: constraints and triggers. This chapter focuses on the second of these two methods. A trigger is a special type of stored procedure that is automatically invoked when the data in a specified table or view is modified. The **INSERT**, **UPDATE**, and **DELETE** statements can all cause a trigger to be invoked. A trigger has the capability to query other tables and include complex Transact-SQL statements. A trigger can be used to reference or update data in another database or even on another server. When a trigger is fired, it becomes part of the transaction from which the original data modification was made. If a server error occurs, the entire transaction is rolled back automatically.

The main benefit of triggers over constraints is the capability to perform complex processing logic using Transact-SQL code. Even though triggers are powerful tools, it does not mean that triggers are always the best choice for enforcing business rules and integrity. For performance reasons, triggers should only be used in place of foreign keys and **CHECK** constraints when their functionality fails to meet your processing needs.

## Creating Triggers

Triggers are created using the **CREATE TRIGGER** Transact-SQL command. The syntax for using this command is shown in Listing 17.1. Beginning with SQL Server 2000, two enhancements have been made to this command. The **AFTER** and **INSTEAD OF** options have been added to extend the functionality of triggers. The **INSTEAD OF** option causes the invoking action to be overridden by the logic contained in the trigger. The keyword **AFTER** is used to specify the original trigger behavior rather than the **INSTEAD OF** behavior added in SQL Server 2000.

**Listing 17.1    CREATE TRIGGER syntax.**

```
CREATE TRIGGER trigger_name
ON { table | view }
[ WITH ENCRYPTION ]
{
    { { FOR | AFTER | INSTEAD OF } {[ DELETE ][ , ] [ INSERT ] [ , ]
                                    [ UPDATE ] }
```

```
        [ WITH APPEND ]
        [ NOT FOR REPLICATION ]
        AS
        [ { IF UPDATE ( column )
            [ { AND | OR } UPDATE ( column ) ]
                [ ...n ]
        | IF ( COLUMNS_UPDATED ( ) { bitwise_operator } updated_bitmask )
                { comparison_operator } column_bitmask [ ...n ]
        } ]
        sql_statement [ ...n ]
    }
}
```

The arguments involved in trigger creation are explained in greater detail in the following list. A description of the significance and allowable values for each argument is provided. There is also an explanation of the dependencies and limitations imposed by using certain options in the **CREATE TRIGGER** statement.

- *trigger_name*—The name of the trigger. A trigger name must conform to the rules for identifiers and must be unique within the database. The trigger owner name can optionally be specified as well.

- *Table | view*—The table or view on which the trigger is executed. The owner name of the table or view can be optionally prepended to the name of the table or view being referenced.

- **WITH ENCRYPTION**—This optional clause encrypts the syscomments entries that contain the text of **CREATE TRIGGER** to prevent the trigger from being published as part of SQL Server replication. This option also prevents others from being able to view the source code used to generate the trigger.

- **AFTER**—This keyword stipulates that the trigger is fired only when all operations specified in the triggering SQL statement, including any referential cascade actions and constraint checks, have executed successfully. **AFTER** is the default if **FOR** is the only keyword specified. **AFTER** triggers cannot be defined on views.

- **INSTEAD OF**—This keyword specifies that the trigger is executed in place of the triggering SQL statement. This causes the logic in the trigger to override the actions of the triggering statements. Only one **INSTEAD OF** trigger per **INSERT**, **UPDATE**, or **DELETE** statement is allowed to be defined on a table or view. It is possible, however, to define views on top of other views where each view has its own **INSTEAD OF** trigger. **INSTEAD OF** triggers are not allowed on updateable views created using **WITH CHECK OPTION**. Attempting to create a trigger to an updateable view that the **WITH CHECK OPTION** specified causes SQL Server to raise an error.

**17. Triggers**

- { [**DELETE**] [**,**] [**INSERT**] [**,**] [**UPDATE**] }—These keywords specify which data modification statements will invoke the trigger when they are executed against the specified table or view. At least one of these options must be specified for every **CREATE TRIGGER** statement. Any combination of these keywords in any order is allowed in the trigger definition, but if more than one option is being specified, the options must be separated with commas. The **DELETE** option is not allowed for **INSTEAD OF** triggers on tables that have a referential relationship that specifies a cascade action on **DELETE**. The **UPDATE** option is similarly disallowed for tables that have a referential relationship that specifies a cascade action **ON UPDATE**.

- **WITH APPEND**—This optional clause is only needed when the compatibility level of the database is set to 65 or lower. This option is used to specify that an additional trigger of an existing type should be added. When the compatibility level is 70 or higher, allowing multiple triggers of the same type is the default behavior of **CREATE TRIGGER**. **WITH APPEND** can be used only when **FOR** is specified (without **INSTEAD OF** or **AFTER**) for backward compatibility reasons. **WITH APPEND** and **FOR** will not be supported in future releases of Microsoft SQL Server.

- **NOT FOR REPLICATION**—This optional clause indicates that the trigger should not be executed when a replication process modifies the table involved in the trigger.

- **AS**—This keyword is used to indicate the actions the trigger is to perform.

- *sql_statement*—This argument is the Transact-SQL code that specifies the actions to be taken by the trigger and the conditions under which they should be performed. Trigger conditions are used to specify additional criteria to determine whether the attempted **DELETE**, **INSERT**, or **UPDATE** statements cause the trigger action to be carried out. The trigger actions specified in the Transact-SQL statements are executed when the **DELETE**, **INSERT**, or **UPDATE** operation is attempted. Triggers can include any number and kind of Transact-SQL statements. Triggers are designed to check or change data when a data modification statement is executed. The Transact-SQL statements used to define the trigger's processing should not return data to the user because the user will not expect to receive a result set when issuing **INSERT**, **UPDATE**, or **DELETE** statements. Two special tables are used in **CREATE TRIGGER** statements that are called *deleted* and *inserted*. These two tables are structurally similar to the table on which the trigger is defined and hold the old values or new values of the rows that are attempting to be changed by the user action. To retrieve the new value in either an **INSERT** or **UPDATE** trigger, join the inserted table with the original update table. If the compatibility level is 80 or higher, SQL Server allows the update of text, ntext, or image columns only through the **INSTEAD OF** trigger on tables or views.

- **IF UPDATE (*column*)**—This statement is used to test for an **INSERT** or **UPDATE** action on a specified column. This option is not used with **DELETE** operations. The table name should not be included before the field name in an **IF UPDATE** statement because the table name is specified in the **ON** clause. To test for an **INSERT** or **UPDATE** action for more than one column, you can specify a separate **UPDATE(*column*)** clause following the first one. **IF UPDATE** always returns the **TRUE** value in **INSERT** actions because the columns have either explicit values or implicit values inserted. The **IF UPDATE (*column*)** clause functions identically to an **IF**, **IF...ELSE**, or **WHILE** statement and can use the **BEGIN...END** block. **UPDATE(*column*)** can be used anywhere inside the body of the trigger.

- ***column***—This argument is the name of the column to test for either an **INSERT** or **UPDATE** action. This column can be of any data type supported by SQL Server. Computed columns cannot be used in this context.

- **IF (COLUMNS_UPDATED( ))**—This optional clause tests whether the mentioned column or columns in an **INSERT** or **UPDATE** trigger were inserted or updated. **COLUMNS_UPDATED** returns a varbinary bit pattern that indicates which columns in the table were inserted or updated. The bits are returned in order from left to right. The leftmost bit represents the first column in the table; the next bit to the right represents the second column, and so on. If the table on which the trigger is created contains more than eight columns, **COLUMNS_UPDATED** returns multiple bytes with the least significant byte being the leftmost. **COLUMNS_UPDATED** always returns the **TRUE** value for all columns in **INSERT** actions because the columns have either explicit values or implicit values inserted. **COLUMNS_UPDATED** can be used anywhere inside the body of the trigger.

- ***bitwise_operator***—This argument is the bitwise operator to use in the comparison.

- ***updated_bitmask***—This argument is the integer bitmask of those columns actually updated or inserted.

- ***comparison_operator***—This argument is the comparison operator used to determine which columns were updated. Use the equal sign to check whether certain columns specified in **updated_bitmask** are actually updated. It is also possible to perform range checking by using the greater than or less than symbols for this comparison.

- ***column_bitmask***—This argument is the integer bitmask of the columns in the table (or view) being updated, which can be used to check whether the columns are being updated or inserted.

- ***n***—This argument is a placeholder indicating that multiple Transact-SQL statements can be included in the trigger. For the **IF UPDATE (*column*)** statement, multiple columns can be included by repeating the **UPDATE** (*column*) clause.

Before you create a trigger, there are some items that you should consider. The following list provides the rules that govern trigger creation and usage:

- The **CREATE TRIGGER** statement must be the first statement in the batch, and all other statements in the batch are considered part of the trigger definition.

- Permission to create triggers on a table or view defaults to the owner of the table or view.

- Triggers can only be created in the current database, although they can reference objects outside the current database.

- Triggers cannot be created on a temporary or system table. Temporary tables can be created and referenced by a trigger. Instead of referencing system tables, you should reference the Information Schema Views. Refer to the Books Online for more information about the Information Schema Views.

- If a table contains a foreign key with an **UPDATE** or **DELETE** cascading action defined, then no **INSTEAD OF UPDATE** or **INSTEAD OF DELETE** triggers are allowed to be defined on the table.

- The **TRUNCATE TABLE** statement will not fire a **DELETE** trigger because this action is not logged.

- The **WRITETEXT** statement will not file **UPDATE** or **INSERT** triggers.

# Transact-SQL Limitations

There are some limitations on the Transact-SQL commands that can be executed by a trigger. The following list contains the commands that cannot be included in the SQL statement used to define your trigger:

- **ALTER DATABASE**
- **CREATE DATABASE**
- **DISK INIT**
- **DISK RESIZE**
- **DROP DATABASE**
- **LOAD DATABASE**
- **LOAD LOG**
- **RECONFIGURE**
- **RESTORE DATABASE**
- **RESTORE LOG**

Given the nature of these commands, it is unlikely that you will run into many situations where this limitation is an issue. It is important to understand that these commands are not only disallowed in the actual trigger SQL code, but also in any dynamic SQL executed by the trigger as well as any stored procedures called by the trigger. If any of these commands are referenced in the context of a trigger execution, the trigger returns an error and the transaction is rolled back.

# Altering Existing Triggers

To modify an existing trigger, you can either drop and re-create the trigger or use the **ALTER TRIGGER** Transact-SQL command. One main advantage to the **ALTER TRIGGER** command is that in the event of a problem with the new trigger code, the existing trigger has not been removed from the table. The only time the drop and re-create method is required to change a trigger definition is when you want to rename the trigger. The syntax for the **ALTER TRIGGER** command is shown in Listing 17.2. The arguments used in this command are identical to the **CREATE TRIGGER** command arguments described in the "Creating Triggers" section.

Listing 17.2   **ALTER TRIGGER** syntax.

```
ALTER TRIGGER trigger_name
ON ( table | view )
[ WITH ENCRYPTION ]
{
    { ( FOR | AFTER | INSTEAD OF ) { [ DELETE ] [ , ] [ INSERT ] [ , ]
                                        [ UPDATE ] }
        [ NOT FOR REPLICATION ]
        AS
        sql_statement [ ...n ]
    }
    |
    { ( FOR | AFTER | INSTEAD OF ) { [ INSERT ] [ , ] [ UPDATE ] }
        [ NOT FOR REPLICATION ]
        AS
        { IF UPDATE ( column )
        [ { AND | OR } UPDATE ( column ) ]
        [ ...n ]
        | IF ( COLUMNS_UPDATED ( ) { bitwise_operator } updated_bitmask )
        { comparison_operator } column_bitmask [ ...n ]
        }
        sql_statement [ ...n ]
    }
}
```

# Deleting Triggers

At some point, you will find that a trigger that you have created is no longer useful or desirable. In this situation, you need to remove the trigger from the table or view on which it was created. This is accomplished using the **DROP TRIGGER** Transact-SQL command. Listing 17.3 shows the syntax for the **DROP TRIGGER** command.

Listing 17.3    **DROP TRIGGER** syntax.

```
DROP TRIGGER { trigger } [ ,...n ]
```

The arguments used in the **DROP TRIGGER** command are explained in the following list:

- *trigger*—The name of the trigger(s) to remove. Trigger names must conform to the rules for identifiers. You may optionally specify the owner name of the trigger to be dropped.

- *n*—This argument is a placeholder indicating that multiple triggers can be specified in the same **DROP TRIGGER** statement. It allows you to remove multiple triggers in a single statement.

# Creating Multiple Triggers

A table can have multiple **AFTER** triggers defined for each action (**INSERT**, **UPDATE**, and **DELETE**), but only one **INSTEAD OF** trigger is allowed for each action on a given table or view. Each trigger must have a unique name and can be defined for only one table or view, but it can reference data in other tables or views and even other databases or servers. A trigger can be defined for any subset of the three actions.

# Specifying the Execution Order for AFTER Triggers

When you have multiple **AFTER** triggers defined on a table, you have the option to specify that a trigger should be fired First or Last. You can have only one First and one Last trigger defined. All other **AFTER** triggers are fired in an undefined order between the First and Last triggers. The First and Last triggers *cannot* be the same trigger. To specify the order in which **AFTER** triggers should be fired, use the **sp_settriggerorder** stored procedure. An example of using this procedure is shown in Listing 17.4. The following list provides the valid values that can be passed to the **@order** parameter of this stored procedure:

- **First**—Specifies that the trigger should be the first **AFTER** trigger fired for a triggering action.

- **Last**—Specifies that the trigger should be the last **AFTER** trigger fired for a triggering action.
- **None**—Used mainly to reset a trigger from being either first or last. It specifies that there is no specific order in which the trigger should be fired.

A table may have **INSERT**, **UPDATE**, and **DELETE** triggers defined on it at the same time, and each statement type can have its own first and last triggers, but they cannot be the same triggers. If the first or last trigger defined for a table does not cover a triggering action, such as not covering **FOR UPDATE**, **FOR DELETE**, or **FOR INSERT**, then there is no first or last trigger for the missing actions.

**INSTEAD OF** triggers cannot be specified as first or last triggers because **INSTEAD OF** triggers are fired before updates are made to the underlying tables. If updates are made by an **INSTEAD OF** trigger to underlying tables, the updates occur after triggers are fired on the table, including the first trigger. For example, if an **INSTEAD OF** trigger on a view updates a base table in the view and the base table contains three **UPDATE** triggers, the three **UPDATE** triggers in the table are fired before the data is actually inserted by the **INSTEAD OF** trigger.

If an **ALTER TRIGGER** statement changes a first or last trigger, the First or Last attribute is dropped and the order value is set to None. You will have to reset the order by using the **sp_settriggerorder** stored procedure.

If you are publishing a table with replication, it is important to understand that replication generates a first trigger automatically for any table that is an immediate or queued update subscriber. Replication requires that its trigger is always the first trigger. An error is raised if you try to make a table that has a first trigger an immediate or queued update subscriber. Also, an error is returned from **sp_settriggerorder** if you try to make a user-defined trigger a first trigger after a table has been made an immediate or queued update subscriber. If you use **ALTER** on the replication trigger or use **sp_settriggerorder** to change the replication trigger to a **Last** or **None** trigger, the subscription will no longer work correctly.

Listing 17.4   **sp_settriggerorder** example.

```
sp_settriggerorder @triggername = 'tr_aTrigger', @order = 'first',
                   @stmttype = 'UPDATE'
```

# INSTEAD OF Triggers

The primary advantage of **INSTEAD OF** triggers is that they allow views that would not be updateable to support updates. A view that has multiple base tables must use an **INSTEAD OF** trigger to support inserts, updates, and deletes. **INSTEAD OF** triggers also allow you to code logic that can reject parts of a batch and allow the rest to succeed.

**INSTEAD OF** triggers override the triggering statement (**INSERT**, **UPDATE**, or **DELETE**). For example, an **INSTEAD OF** trigger can be defined to perform error or value checking on one or more columns as well as any needed additional actions before inserting or updating a record. For instance, when the value being updated in a sale price column in a sales table is below a specified minimum value, a trigger can be defined to produce an error message and roll back the transaction or insert a new record into the audit log before inserting the record.

**INSTEAD OF** triggers are most useful for extending the types of updates that a view can support. For example, **INSTEAD OF** triggers can provide the logic to modify multiple base tables through a view or to modify base tables that contain these columns:

- **TIMESTAMP** data type
- Computed columns
- Identity columns

## INSTEAD OF DELETE

**INSTEAD OF DELETE** triggers can be defined on a view or table to replace the standard behavior of the **DELETE** statement. An **INSTEAD OF DELETE** trigger is usually defined on a view to facilitate removing data from one or more base tables. **DELETE** statements do not specify modifications to existing data values, only the rows that are to be deleted. The inserted table passed to a **DELETE** trigger is always empty, whereas the deleted table contains an image of the rows as they existed before the **DELETE** statement was issued. If the **INSTEAD OF DELETE** trigger is defined on a view, the format of the deleted table is based on the select list defined for the view.

## INSTEAD OF INSERT

**INSTEAD OF INSERT** triggers can be defined on a view or table to replace the standard behavior of the **INSERT** statement. An **INSTEAD OF INSERT** trigger is usually defined on a view to allow the insertion of data into one or more base tables. Columns in the view select list can be nullable or not nullable. If the view column does not allow nulls, an **INSERT** statement must provide a value for the column. The following list helps you determine the columns that allow nulls in a view:

- Any base table column that allows nulls
- Arithmetic operators
- Functions
- **CASE** or **COALESCE( )** with a nullable subexpression
- **NULLIF( )**

The **AllowsNull** property reported by the **COLUMNPROPERTY** function can be used to positively determine whether or not a particular column in a view allows nulls. The **sp_help** stored procedure also reports which view columns allow nulls. An **INSTEAD OF INSERT** trigger must supply values for every view column that does not allow nulls including view columns that reference columns in an underlying table for which input values cannot normally be specified, such as:

- Computed columns
- Identity columns for which **IDENTITY INSERT** is turned off
- Columns with the **TIMESTAMP** data type

The **INSTEAD OF INSERT** view trigger must ignore the values for these columns when generating the actual **INSERT** against the base table(s) using the data in the inserted table. The original **INSERT** statement can use dummy values of the applicable data type for these columns.

## INSTEAD OF UPDATE

**INSTEAD OF UPDATE** triggers can be defined on a view or table to replace the standard behavior of the **UPDATE** statement. An **INSTEAD OF UPDATE** trigger is usually defined on a view to allow the modification of data in one or more base tables. **UPDATE** statements that reference views with **INSTEAD OF UPDATE** triggers must supply values for every view column that does not allow nulls including view columns that reference columns in the base table for which input values cannot normally be specified, such as:

- Computed columns
- Identity columns for which **IDENTITY INSERT** is off
- Columns with the **TIMESTAMP** data type

These columns must be included in the **UPDATE** statement to meet the **NOT NULL** requirement of the column. Because the **UPDATE** statement references a view with an **INSTEAD OF UPDATE** trigger, the logic defined in the trigger must bypass these columns to avoid generating an error. This is done by not including the columns in the **SET** clause of the **UPDATE** statement(s) used in the trigger. When a record is processed from the inserted table, the computed, identity, or **TIMESTAMP** column will contain a dummy value to meet the **NOT NULL** column requirement, but the trigger must ignore those columns and allow the correct values to be set by SQL Server.

This solution works because an **INSTEAD OF UPDATE** trigger does not have to process data from the inserted columns that are not updated. In the inserted table passed to an **INSTEAD OF UPDATE** trigger, the columns specified in the **SET** clause follow the same rules as the inserted columns in an **INSTEAD OF INSERT** trigger. For columns not specified in the **SET** clause, the inserted table contains the original values in the columns before the **UPDATE** statement was issued. The **IF UPDATED(*column*)** clause can be used in the trigger to test whether a specific column has been updated. Values supplied for computed, identity, or **TIMESTAMP** columns should only be used in search conditions or control-of-flow logic.

# Nested Triggers

Triggers are nested when a trigger performs an action that initiates another trigger. Triggers can be nested up to 32 levels. The "nested triggers" option of the server is used to control whether or not this behavior is allowed. If nested triggers are allowed and a trigger in the chain starts an infinite loop, the trigger terminates when the nesting level is exceeded.

Using nested triggers in an order-dependent sequence is not recommended. You should use separate triggers to cascade data modifications across multiple tables. Because triggers execute within a transaction, a failure at any level of a set of nested triggers cancels the entire transaction. When this happens, all data modifications are rolled back. You can use **PRINT** statements in your triggers to help you determine where the failure occurred.

Unless the **RECURSIVE_TRIGGERS** database option is set, a trigger will not call itself recursively. There are actually two types of recursion relating to triggers:

- *Direct recursion*—Occurs when a trigger is fired and performs an action that causes the same trigger to be fired again. For example, TblA is updated, which causes trigger TrgrA to fire. TrgrA updates table TblA again, which causes trigger TrgrA to fire again.

- *Indirect recursion*—Occurs when a trigger is fired and performs an action that causes a trigger on another table to be fired. The second trigger performs an action on the original table, which causes the original trigger to be fired again. For example, TblB is updated, which causes trigger TrgrB to be fired. TrgrB updates table TblC, which causes trigger TrgrC to be fired. TrgrC in turn updates table TblB, which causes TrgrB to be fired again.

---

**NOTE:** *Only direct recursion is prevented when the **RECURSIVE_TRIGGERS** database option is set to **OFF**. To disable indirect recursion, set the "nested triggers" option on the server to 0.*

---

# When *Not* to Use Triggers

Complex or poorly written triggers can create a real problem in terms of system performance. When it comes to performance, it is helpful to remember that less is more. The more triggers you define, the more actual work has to be performed by the server when the actions you have defined triggers for are executed. Triggers can hold open locks and create additional transaction log overhead for the transactions that cause the trigger to be fired. Triggers can also prevent updates in place. For more information about updates in place, see Chapter 11. Triggers should always be avoided when a stored procedure or application program can perform the same work with minimal overhead. Triggers should never be used for simple Declarative Referential Integrity (DRI) or data validation. The standard features built into SQL Server to perform these types of tasks consume fewer resources and produce less impact on the performance of your database. It is always better to stick with the simplest option that will actually perform the needed validations for maintaining your data integrity.

# Federated Data

The first step in building a set of federated database servers is to horizontally partition the data in a set of tables across multiple servers. This refers to dividing a table into multiple smaller tables, where each member table has the same format as the original table, but only a portion of the rows. Each table is placed on a separate resource (devices or servers) to spread the processing load across these resources. For example, a company may assign seven-digit numeric customer IDs ranging from 1000000 through 9999999. The Customers table could be partitioned into three member tables, giving each one an equal customer ID range: 10000000 – 3999999, 4000000 – 6999999, and 7000000 – 9999999.

Without using views, horizontal partitioning would require applications to have logic to determine which member tables have the data requested by the user and dynamically build SQL statements referencing the tables on the correct resources. The application might require complex queries joining the member tables to retrieve all the required data. Any alteration to the distribution of the member tables would also require recoding the application to handle the new distribution. You can use views to solve this problem by making the member tables look like a single table to the application. The **UNION** operator is used to combine result sets with identical formats into a single result set. Because all the member tables have the same format, the result of **SELECT \*** statements for each table will have the same format and can be combined using the **UNION** clause to form a single result set that operates similarly to the original table. Because the data is partitioned in such a way that the rows in the member table are unique, you can use **UNION ALL** in the view to return all rows without the overhead of duplicate checking.

Once the data has been partitioned and the views are created, the read access to the data is easily satisfied by using these views in the application to retrieve the data. Another problem that must be addressed is adding, updating, and deleting data in these partitioned tables. The easiest way to make this side of the processing transparent to the application is to create **INSTEAD OF** triggers for these operations on the views that you created to hide the member tables from the application. These triggers can contain the business logic needed to determine which member table should be affected by each of these statement types depending on the rules originally used to partition the tables. In this way, if the partitioning changes in the future for any reason, the only recoding work that you have to perform is in the views and triggers that reside on the server. The application remains blissfully unaware of the physical separation of the data behind the structures it is using for database access. The process of creating and coding the views and triggers required to make this possible takes some work, but the benefits generally far outweigh the effort.

The benefits of generating the code required for handling the partitioned data quickly becomes apparent when you want to partition an existing set of tables that you already have applications running against. In this case, you can easily rename the existing tables and replace them with the views and triggers necessary to make this change transparent to the application. This allows you to partition the data easily without affecting your existing application code, and all needed business rules to enforce your new structure can be coded on the server.

# Auditing

Auditing is an important consideration that might lead you to create triggers on one or more tables. If you need to track changes made to the data to allow for auditing them later, you can easily create a trigger that writes audit records for each modified record to a separate table to review at a later time. You can code logic into the trigger to store any information that you might want in your audit table. You have access to information such as the user name, host machine, application name, date and time of the change, and so on, that can be included in your audit log along with the actual before and after pictures of the affected data.

When setting up auditing on a table using triggers, the most important outcome to watch for is the performance impact of the additional processing. If you attempt to capture a large amount of information about the changes being made, it may slow your system to an unacceptable level of performance. You should always do some benchmark testing before and after making a change of this proportion to your database to ensure that your system is able to handle the additional load without causing considerable grief to your users. Nothing moves you to the top of the "Most Popular" list quicker than a sudden noticeable drop in overall system performance. It is a good idea to refer to Chapter 11 for information on optimizing your queries before implementing triggers for any reason, but auditing can often carry one of the highest price tags in terms of performance.

# Monitoring and Notifications

Another feature that can be facilitated through the use of triggers is monitoring certain types of changes and sending an email notification to the appropriate user when they occur. You might need to monitor an automated processing system for changes to a particular record or set of records during a debugging session. You could create a trigger on the table (or a trigger for each table) that you need to monitor and use the **xp_send_mail** extended stored procedure to send an email to the interested user. You can construct the message in the trigger to give any appropriate details about the type of modification as well as the columns affected if needed.

Triggers can also be used to send notifications to a database administrator (DBA) or other responsible party when certain errors occur in processing. This can help you to create a proactive support system rather than a reactive one. If you are notified as soon as an error occurs, you may be able to prevent further errors from cascading through your processing run. Software vendors can make use of this type of notification to allow their support staff to get involved in resolving problems before the client is even aware that the problem exists. This type of proactive support is rare and generally well received by the affected client. Such a high level of attentiveness from the vendor can help raise customer confidence in the product.

Notifications using **xp_send_mail** require that SQL Mail be configured. Refer to Chapter 6 for details on using SQL Mail and the **xp_send_mail** extended stored procedure to send notifications.

# Running Totals

In some environments, it is necessary to keep running totals for various items that can be used in reporting and point-in-time decision making. Triggers can be used to keep these totals updated without having to put code in every client application that has the ability to change the underlying numbers in the source tables. Using a trigger for this type of updating also prevents inconsistencies caused by direct modification to the underlying data using tools such as the Query Analyzer. If you have a trigger in place to keep the totals up-to-date, almost all means of data modification are covered. (Data corruption and use of the **TRUNCATE TABLE** statement are two notable exceptions.) In order to keep a set of running totals, you need to define a trigger that handles all three of the possible actions (**INSERT**, **UPDATE**, and **DELETE**) because any one of them will affect the actual totals in your data. You need to determine whether data is being added, removed, or changed by the action that fires the trigger and update your totals accordingly. Listing 17.5 shows an example of creating the two triggers needed to keep the total sale amount for all order detail records in a table called **SalesTots**.

**Listing 17.5    Example triggers to keep running totals.**

```
IF EXISTS (SELECT name
              FROM sysobjects (NOLOCK)
              WHERE name = 'inst_UpdateTotSales'
                AND type = 'TR')
  DROP TRIGGER inst_UpdateTotSales
GO


CREATE TRIGGER inst_UpdateTotSales
  ON OrderDetail FOR INSERT, UPDATE
  AS
  BEGIN
  /* Declare variable for price */
  DECLARE @v_Price MONEY

  /* Check to see if the UnitPrice or Quantity is being updated */
  If UPDATE(UnitPrice) OR UPDATE(Quantity)
    BEGIN
    /* Get total price of all added records */
    SELECT @v_PRICE = SUM( COALESCE(UnitPrice, 0) *
                           COALESCE(Quantity, 0) )
      FROM inserted

    /* Deduct total price of all removed records */
    SELECT @v_PRICE = @v_PRICE - SUM( COALESCE(UnitPrice, 0) *
                                      COALESCE(Quantity, 0) )
      FROM deleted

    /* Update the TotSales table with the change in total sales price */
    UPDATE TotSales
      SET TotOrderPrice = TotOrderPrice + @v_PRICE
    END
  END
GO


IF EXISTS (SELECT name
              FROM sysobjects (NOLOCK)
              WHERE name = 'delt_UpdateTotSalesD'
                AND type = 'TR')
  DROP TRIGGER delt_UpdateTotSalesD
GO

CREATE TRIGGER delt_UpdateTotSalesD
  ON OrderDetail FOR DELETE
  AS
```

```
   BEGIN
   /* Declare variable for price */
   DECLARE @v_Price MONEY

   /* Get the total price and  */
   SELECT @v_PRICE = SUM( COALESCE(UnitPrice, 0) *
                          COALESCE(Quantity, 0) )
     FROM deleted

   /* Update the TotSales table with the change in total sales price */
   UPDATE TotSales
     SET TotOrderPrice = TotOrderPrice - @v_PRICE
   END
GO
```

# Inserting Master Records

Normally, when a foreign key is defined on a table, an insert is not permitted unless the referenced key exists in the master table. In some cases, it may be desirable or necessary to allow inserts to the child table on the fly. If so, you could create a trigger to insert the needed information in the master table. An **INSTEAD OF INSERT** trigger could be used to check each child row against the master table. If the needed master row is missing, the trigger could use the information contained in the child row to create a master record to maintain referential integrity but still allow the insert to take place on the child table. Once the needed master records are inserted by the trigger, the insert can proceed normally. Note that when setting up this type of trigger, the insert will probably not contain sufficient information to populate the entire row in the master table. This requires either leaving the remaining values **NULL** or relying on default values to fill in the missing information. For this reason, this method should be employed with care and only in exceptional circumstances.

# Cascading Referential Integrity Constraints

Cascading Referential Integrity Constraints is a new feature in SQL Server 2000, which allows you to define the action taken by SQL Server when a user attempts to delete or update a key with an existing foreign key reference. This is implemented using the **REFERENCES** clause of the **CREATE TABLE** and **ALTER TABLE** commands. The following list shows the syntax of the two available options for defining cascading actions:

- [ ON DELETE { CASCADE | NO ACTION } ]
- [ ON UPDATE { CASCADE | NO ACTION } ]

The default, if these options are not specified, is **NO ACTION**. This causes the same behavior as previous versions of SQL Server. If you attempt to perform a delete or update of a key value that is referenced by a foreign key for existing rows in another table, an error is raised, and the operation is rolled back.

Specifying **CASCADE** causes deletions or updates of key values to cascade through the tables that have foreign key relationships that can be traced back to the table on which the modification is performed. **CASCADE** is not allowed for foreign keys or primary keys that contain a **TIMESTAMP** column.

## ON DELETE CASCADE

The **ON DELETE CASCADE** option specifies that when an attempt is made to delete a row with a key that is referenced by foreign keys in existing rows in other tables, all rows containing those foreign keys should also be deleted. If cascading referential actions have also been defined on the target tables, the specified cascading actions are also taken for the rows deleted from those tables. This provides a much simpler mechanism for managing this type of delete than what was previously available in SQL Server.

## ON UPDATE CASCADE

The **ON UPDATE CASCADE** option specifies that if an attempt is made to update a key value in a row, where the key value is referenced by foreign keys in existing rows in other tables, all of the foreign key values are also updated to the new value specified for the key. If cascading referential actions have also been defined on the target tables, the specified cascading actions are also taken for the key values updated in those tables

# Cascading Updates

There are two reasons to create a trigger for cascading updates. The first is to allow you to change a key field and propagate the change to all affected child records. The second is to maintain denormalized data, which you have determined is necessary to help system performance.

The first example can be a little tricky. If the field that you are updating is referenced by a foreign key, you should use the **ON UPDATE CASCADE** option previously referenced to implement this action. It is much simpler and requires less overhead than creating a trigger. If the field is not referenced by a foreign key constraint (such as a cross-database dependency), you may need to resort to a trigger to manage this type of update. Using the inserted and deleted tables, you can update the referencing tables that match the deleted table entry with the new key value from the inserted table. Listing 17.6 provides a simple example between the **tbl_Address** table and the **tbl_EmployeeAddressXref** table for managing this type of update. This example does not account for multiple rows being updated at the same time. You could implement a loop to manage updating multiple rows and checking each one for an update to the **Address_ID** field.

**Listing 17.6    Cascading update for ID column.**

```
USE Address
GO

IF EXISTS (SELECT name
              FROM sysobjects (NOLOCK)
              WHERE name = 'updt_cascade_upd_id'
                AND type = 'TR')
  DROP TRIGGER updt_cascade_upd_id
GO


CREATE TRIGGER updt_cascade_upd_id
  ON address.dbo.tbl_Address AFTER UPDATE
AS
BEGIN
  /* Check to see if we are updating the Address_ID column */
  IF UPDATE(Address_ID)
    BEGIN
    /* Update the tbl_EmployeeAddressXRef rows with the new ID value */
    UPDATE Employee.dbo.tbl_Employee_Address_Xref
      SET Address_ID = (SELECT Address_ID
                          FROM inserted)
      FROM deletes d
      WHERE Address_ID = d.Address_ID
    END
END
GO
```

The second example, managing denormalized data, is a little simpler, but still requires careful implementation. The biggest issue that you need to watch for in constructing a trigger for maintaining denormalized data is that the trigger needs to be kept up-to-date as new fields are denormalized in the database. You either need to update the existing trigger or add additional triggers to modify the data. In this case, an **AFTER** trigger is probably the best choice for implementation. When a field is updated, your trigger must check the field (or fields) that it is monitoring to see if it was modified by the current action. In the event that it was modified, all occurrences of the original value in other tables should be updated to the new value. To simplify this process, all tables that contain the value should also contain the key field(s) to reference the record that contains the master copy of the data. A simple example for this type of cascading update is provided in Listing 17.7.

**Listing 17.7    Cascading update for denormalized data.**

```
USE Address
GO

IF EXISTS (SELECT name
             FROM sysobjects (NOLOCK)
             WHERE name = 'updt_cascade_upd_dn'
               AND type = 'TR')
  DROP TRIGGER updt_cascade_upd_dn
GO

CREATE TRIGGER updt_cascade_upd_dn
  ON address.dbo.tbl_ZipCode AFTER UPDATE
AS
BEGIN
  /* Update the denormalized address table when Zip Code */
  /* changes occur.                                      */
  UPDATE tbl_AddressDN
    SET Zip5 = i.Zip5
    FROM deleted d
    JOIN inserted i ON d.Zip_ID = i.Zip_ID
    WHERE tbl_AddressDN.Zip5 = d.Zip5
END
GO
```

# Cascading Deletes

If the record key for the record(s) you are deleting is referenced by a foreign key, you should use the **ON DELETE CASCADE** option previously referenced to implement this action. It is much simpler and requires less overhead than creating a trigger. If the field is not referenced by a foreign key constraint (such as a cross-database dependency), you may need to resort to a trigger to manage this type of delete. Using the deleted table, you can delete the referencing tables that match the deleted table entry. Listing 17.8 provides a simple example for managing a cascading delete of records from the **tbl_EmployeeAddressXref** table when the corresponding rows are deleted from the **tbl_Addtess** table. It removes any referencing rows from the **tbl_EmployeeAddressXref** table when a row is deleted from the **tbl_Address** table.

**Listing 17.8    Cascading delete trigger.**

```
USE Address
GO

IF EXISTS (SELECT name
            FROM sysobjects (NOLOCK)
            WHERE name = 'delt_cascade_delete'
              AND type = 'TR')
  DROP TRIGGER delt_cascade_delete
GO

CREATE TRIGGER delt_cascade_delete
  ON address.dbo.tbl_Address AFTER DELETE
AS
BEGIN
  /* Delete the tbl_EmployeeAddressXRef rows with the old ID value */
  DELETE FROM Employee.dbo.tbl_Employee_Address_Xref
    FROM deletes d
    WHERE Address_ID = d.Address_ID
END
GO
```

# Triggering External Processing Actions

In some environments, triggers can provide the functionality to initiate certain event-based processes. For example, let's suppose you have a computer store where you build computers to sell, and you also sell the same parts used in the building of computers to your customers separately. You have constructed two applications to assist you in keeping track of your inventory. Your technicians use the first application to keep track of the various parts used in the construction and repair of the computer systems they are working on. The second application is your cash register application, which is used to keep the inventory updated as individual parts are sold to customers. You need to keep an eye on the inventory levels of various parts to determine when to order additional supplies from your vendors. You might want to consider putting a trigger on the inventory table and creating a separate custom table that contains the minimum stock levels for your various inventory items. The trigger could be coded to compare the inventory level that is being updated with the established minimum and generate a record in an ordering table when the stock falls below a certain level. You might also want to keep a table of pending orders that the trigger could check to prevent double ordering before a new shipment is updated in the inventory database. This is a simplified example of additional processing that can be initiated by a trigger. You can also use **sp_start_job** in the msdb database to start a job from a trigger when certain events occur in your data. This should be used carefully so as not to overburden the server, but it can be an effective way to automate launching certain tasks without stopping the current transaction while they are being performed. For more information about **sp_start_job**, refer to the Books Online.

# Overriding Validation

Triggers can be used to provide validation for special override conditions that you need to enforce for specific types of updates to data. For example, you might need to allow payroll detail records to be inserted with negative amounts for earnings or taxes when an adjustment is needed in the system. Under normal circumstances, these values would not be valid for payroll processing. You could add a bit column to the table that acts as a flag to allow these records to be inserted. Assign a default of 0 to the column, and give only specific users access to change the field. An example of the code needed to make the modification to the table is shown in Listing 17.9.

**Listing 17.9   Example code to add an override column.**

```
/* Add the override column to the tax detail table */
ALTER TABLE taxdet
  ADD OvrCol BIT DEFAULT 0 NULL

/* Revoke public access to the override column */
REVOKE UPDATE ON
  taxdet(OvrCol) FROM Public

/* Grant access to HRSupervisors role to update the */
/* override column we just added                     */
GRANT UPDATE ON
  taxdet(OvrCol) TO HRSupervisors
```

When one of the configured users needs to add an adjustment record, the user would set the value of this override flag to 1. A trigger could then be employed to enforce allowing these records to be inserted only when the value of this flag column is set to 1. Listing 17.10 shows an example of a trigger that implements the logic for override checking using the new column added in the preceding example.

**Listing 17.10   Example of an override trigger.**

```
IF EXISTS (SELECT name
             FROM sysobjects (NOLOCK)
            WHERE name = 'inst_override_test'
              AND type = 'TR')
  DROP TRIGGER inst_override_test
GO
```

```
CREATE TRIGGER inst_override_test ON dbo.taxdet
  FOR INSERT, UPDATE
AS
BEGIN
  /* If no rows were affected, get out... */
  IF (@@rowcount = 0) RETURN

  /* check to see if the tax amount column was updated */
  IF UPDATE(TaxAmt)
    BEGIN
    /* Check for rows with a negative tax amount that do not */
    /* have the override flag set                            */
    IF EXISTS (SELECT *
                FROM inserted
                WHERE TaxAmt < 0
                  AND OvrCol <> 1)
      BEGIN
      /* Raise an error back to the client, roll back the */
      /* transaction, and get out...                      */
      RAISERROR ('Invalid update attempted', 16, 1)
      ROLLBACK TRANSACTION
      RETURN
      END

    /* Turn off any override flags turned on by the update */
    UPDATE taxdet
      SET OvrCol = 0
      FROM inserted
      WHERE taxamt.Rec_ID = inserted.Rec_ID
        AND taxamt.OvrCol <> 0
    END
END
GO
```

# Archiving

Archiving is another area where you might find the use of triggers handy. You can create a **DELETE** trigger that moves all or a portion of the deleted record into an archive table when a delete action is performed on the table. This can allow you to implement an archival scheme on the data without needing to modify any client application code. Once you determine the structure of the data to archive for historical purposes, you can create a trigger to perform an insert on the new table with only the fields from the original record that you want to keep. For example, you might want to allow deletes from the **tbl_Employee** table, but need to keep an archive of the basic information about the employee. Listing 17.11 provides the code to create a trimmed-down version of this table for archival purposes. Additionally, it adds the user who performed the delete and the date of the deletion as part of the historical information tracked.

**Listing 17.11    Create Employee archive table.**

```
USE Employee
GO

CREATE TABLE tbl_Employee_Archive
    ( Employee_ID  INT           NOT NULL,
      First_Name   VARCHAR(30)   NOT NULL,
      Last_Name    VARCHAR(30)   NOT NULL,
      Title        INT           NULL,
      Phone        CHAR(10)      NULL,
      Department   INT           NULL,
      Date_Hired   SMALLDATETIME NOT NULL,
      User_ID      CHAR(20)      NULL,
      Date_Deleted SMALLDATETIME NOT NULL )
GO
```

Once you have determined the structure of the table that you want to use to archive deleted employees, you can create a trigger to save this data any time a row is deleted from the Employee table. Listing 17.12 provides the source to a trigger that archives the deleted rows and adds the additional historical information you need to the table. The trigger inserts the current date using the **GETDATE( )** function and the SQL Server login name using the **SUSER_SNAME( )** function. These two functions supply the additional information needed to keep the desired historical record complete.

**Listing 17.12    Create Employee archive trigger.**

```
IF EXISTS (SELECT name
             FROM sysobjects (NOLOCK)
             WHERE name = 'delt_Archive_Emp'
               AND type = 'TR')
  DROP TRIGGER delt_Archive_Emp
GO

CREATE TRIGGER delt_Archive_Emp
  ON Employee.dbo.tbl_Employee FOR DELETE
AS
BEGIN
  /* Insert the desired information from each deleted record into the */
  /* archive table and add the current date and user information.    */
```

```
        INSERT INTO tbl_Employee_Archive (Employee_ID,
                                          First_Name,
                                          Last_Name,
                                          Title,
                                          Phone,
                                          Department,
                                          Date_Hired,
                                          User_ID,
                                          Date_Deleted)
        SELECT Employee_ID,
               First_Name,
               Last_Name,
               Title,
               Phone,
               Department,
               Date_Hired,
               CONVERT(VARCHAR(20),SUSER_SNAME()),
               GETDATE()
          FROM deleted
    END
    GO
```

# Maintaining Cross-Database Referential Integrity

Cross-database referential integrity can become a tricky issue. Because it is not possible to enforce this type of integrity using the standard constraints such as foreign keys, it is a good place to employ triggers. You will need to create triggers to handle enforcing these constraints on both sides of each link. If you want to enforce integrity between the **tbl_EmployeeAddressXref** employee table in the Employee database and the **tbl_Address** table in the Address database, you need to create triggers on both tables to properly enforce this relationship. The Employee table needs to ensure that an address with the corresponding ID exists in the **tbl_Address** table before allowing the value to be set in an insert or update statement on the **tbl_EmployeeAddressXref** table, which satisfies the integrity for adding and updating entries in the **tbl_EmployeeAddressXref** table. You then need to create an additional trigger on the **tbl_Address** table to check for any child records in the **tbl_EmployeeAddressXref** table before allowing deletes to occur on the **tbl_Address** table. Once both of these triggers are in place, the data integrity is properly secured.

Refer to the "Immediate Solutions" section of this chapter for the source to the preceding triggers as well as additional triggers needed to implement cross-database referential integrity checks for the Employee database.

**17. Triggers**

# Templates

If you are not fully familiar with the **CREATE TRIGGER** syntax, you should check out the templates in the Query Analyzer. These templates are a new feature in the Query Analyzer for SQL Server 2000. The Query Analyzer provides several templates that can assist you in setting up triggers in your database. The following is a list of the templates provided:

- Create **INSTEAD OF** Trigger Basic Template
- Create Trigger Basic Template
- Create Trigger Contained **IF COLUMNS_UPDATED**
- Create Trigger Contained **IF UPDATE**

These templates provide a basic framework for creating triggers and make it easier to start working with them. For more information about the Query Analyzer and the new templates, refer to Chapter 5.

# *Immediate Solutions*

## Creating Triggers to Maintain Cross-Database Referential Data Integrity

In this section, you create the triggers needed to maintain referential data integrity between the Employee database and the Utility and Address databases. There are a number of triggers presented in this section to maintain integrity for the various fields that reference data contained in external databases. All of the code listings contained in this section are combined in a single listing file on the CD-ROM included with this book. The complete listing file is named "Create Cross-Database RI Triggers.sql."

### The Employee Address Relationship

The first trigger you need to create is for the employee address relationship. You need to make sure that any **Address_ID** value referenced in an **INSERT** or **UPDATE** operation on the **tbl_EmployeeAddressXref** table exists in the **tbl_Address** table before allowing the operation to complete. The code to implement a trigger that makes this validation is provided in Listing 17.13.

Listing 17.13   Create Employee Address verification trigger.

```
USE Employee
GO

IF EXISTS (SELECT name
            FROM sysobjects (NOLOCK)
            WHERE name = 'inst_XDB_Emp_Addr'
              AND type = 'TR')
  DROP TRIGGER inst_XDB_Emp_Addr
GO

/* Create a trigger to validate the existence of the referenced */
/* Address_ID in the tbl_Address table                          */
CREATE TRIGGER inst_XDB_Emp_Addr
ON Employee.dbo.tbl_EmployeeAddressXref FOR INSERT, UPDATE
AS
BEGIN
  /* We only want to check this if the Address_ID field is being modified */
  IF UPDATE(Address_ID)
```

```
            BEGIN
            /* Check for the Address_ID in the tbl_Address table */
            IF NOT EXISTS (SELECT *
                            FROM Address.dbo.tbl_Address a (NOLOCK)
                            JOIN inserted i ON a.Address_ID = i.Address_ID)
                BEGIN
                /* If the Address_ID does not exist, return an error and */
                /* rollback the current operation                        */
                RAISERROR ('Address ID is invalid', 16, 1)
                ROLLBACK
                END
            END
END
GO
```

In addition to making this check when adding addresses to an employee record, you also need to perform some verification on the **tbl_Address** table for **DELETE** operations and disallow this action if an employee record is referencing the address to be deleted. For this purpose, the trigger provided in Listing 17.14 looks in the **tbl_EmployeeAddressXref** table for any records referencing the records in the deleted table and rolls back the transaction with an error if one is located.

### Listing 17.14    Create Address delete verification trigger.

```
USE Address
GO

IF EXISTS (SELECT name
            FROM sysobjects (NOLOCK)
            WHERE name = 'delt_XDB_Addr_Emp'
              AND type = 'TR')
  DROP TRIGGER delt_XDB_Addr_Emp
GO

/* Create a trigger to disallow deleting address records referenced */
/* in the tbl_EmployeeAddressXref table                             */
CREATE TRIGGER delt_XDB_Addr_Emp
ON Address.dbo.tbl_Address FOR DELETE
AS
BEGIN
  /* Check for the Address_ID in the tbl_EmployeeAddressXref table */
  IF EXISTS (SELECT *
            FROM Employee.dbo.EmployeeAddressXref e (NOLOCK)
            JOIN deleted d ON e.Address_ID = d.Address_ID)
    BEGIN
```

```
      /* If the Address_ID exists, return an error and */
      /* rollback the current operation              */
      RAISERROR ('Address referenced in Employee table', 16, 1)
      ROLLBACK
      END
END
GO
```

## The Employee Address Type Relationship

Once you have covered the verification of the address relationship, you need to verify the Address Type relationship. This verification is handled a little differently because the **tbl_Codes** table in the Utility database is used for more than one type of entry. You not only need to verify that the specified **Code_ID** exists in the table, but also that it is a member of the correct Code Group for Address Type. Listing 17.15 shows the code for the trigger, which includes the code needed to look up and verify the Code Group for the **Code_ID** being verified.

**Listing 17.15    Create Address Type verification trigger.**

```
USE Employee
GO

IF EXISTS (SELECT name
             FROM sysobjects (NOLOCK)
             WHERE name = 'inst_XDB_Emp_Addr_Typ'
               AND type = 'TR')
  DROP TRIGGER inst_XDB_Emp_Addr_Typ
GO

/* Create a trigger to validate the existence of the referenced */
/* Address_Type in the tbl_codes table                          */
CREATE TRIGGER inst_XDB_Emp_Addr_Typ
ON Employee.dbo.tbl_EmployeeAddressXref FOR INSERT, UPDATE
AS
BEGIN
  /* We only want to check this if the Address_Type field is being
     modified */
  IF UPDATE(Address_Type)
    BEGIN
    /* Get the code group for Address Type in the tbl_CodeGroup table */
    DECLARE @v_CodeGrp INT

    SELECT @v_CodeGrp = Code_Group_ID
      FROM Utility.dbo.tbl_CodeGroup (NOLOCK)
      WHERE Name = 'Addr'
```

```
            /* Check for the Address_Type in the tbl_Codes table */
            IF NOT EXISTS (SELECT *
                              FROM Utility.dbo.tbl_Codes c (NOLOCK)
                              JOIN inserted i ON c.Code_ID = i.Address_Type
                                  AND c.Code_Group_ID = @v_CodeGrp)
                BEGIN
                /* If the Address_ID does not exist, return an error and */
                /* rollback the current operation                        */
                RAISERROR ('Address Type is invalid', 16, 1)
                ROLLBACK
                END
            END
    END
END
GO
```

Next, you need to add the verification to the **tbl_Codes** table to prevent code records from being deleted that are being referenced in the **Address_Type** field in the **tbl_EmployeeAddressXref** table. The trigger code in Listing 17.16 looks up the Code Group for address types and verifies that any records being deleted that are in the address type code group are not found in the **tbl_Employee AddressXref** table before allowing the delete action to be completed. If any of the codes being deleted are found in this table, an error is raised and the transaction is rolled back.

**Listing 17.16    Create Address Type delete verification trigger.**

```
USE Utility
GO

IF EXISTS (SELECT name
             FROM sysobjects (NOLOCK)
             WHERE name = 'delt_XDB_Addr_Typ_Emp'
                AND type = 'TR')
   DROP TRIGGER delt_XDB_Addr_Typ_Emp
GO

/* Create a trigger to disallow deleting address type records */
/* referenced in the tbl_EmployeeAddressXref table            */
CREATE TRIGGER delt_XDB_Addr_Typ_Emp
ON Utility.dbo.tbl_Codes FOR DELETE
AS
BEGIN
  /* Get the code group for Address Type in the tbl_CodeGroup table */
  DECLARE @v_CodeGrp INT
  SELECT @v_CodeGrp = Code_Group_ID
    FROM Utility.dbo.tbl_CodeGroup (NOLOCK)
    WHERE Name = 'Addr'
```

```
    /* Check for the Address_Type in the tbl_EmployeAddressXref table */
    IF EXISTS (SELECT *
                  FROM Employee.dbo.EmployeeAddressXref e (NOLOCK)
                  JOIN deleted d ON e.Address_Type = d.Code_ID
                               AND d.Code_Group_ID = @v_CodeGrp)
      BEGIN
      /* If the Address_Type exists, return an error and */
      /* rollback the current operation                  */
      RAISERROR ('Address Type referenced in Employee table', 16, 1)
      ROLLBACK
      END
END
GO
```

One last detail that you need to cover in this verification to make your data integrity solid is the possibility of changing the Code Group on an Address Type. If the Code Group is changed for a **tbl_Codes** table entry that is being referenced as an Address Type, the data integrity will be broken. The code in Listing 17.17 creates a trigger that eliminates this hole by disallowing updates of the Code Group field when the **Code_ID** is referenced in the **tbl_EmployeeAddressXref** table.

### Listing 17.17    Create Address Type update verification trigger.

```
USE Utility
GO

IF EXISTS (SELECT name
              FROM sysobjects (NOLOCK)
              WHERE name = 'updt_XDB_Addr_Typ_Emp_Upd'
                AND type = 'TR')
  DROP TRIGGER updt_XDB_Addr_Typ_Emp_Upd
GO

/* Create a trigger to disallow changing the code group of address type */
/* records referenced in the tbl_EmployeeAddressXref table              */
CREATE TRIGGER updt_XDB_Addr_Typ_Emp_Upd
ON Utility.dbo.tbl_Codes FOR UPDATE
AS
BEGIN
  IF UPDATE(Code_Group_ID)
    BEGIN
    /* Get the code group for Address Type in the tbl_CodeGroup table */
    DECLARE @v_CodeGrp INT

    SELECT @v_CodeGrp = Code_Group_ID
      FROM Utility.dbo.tbl_CodeGroup (NOLOCK)
      WHERE Name = 'Addr'
```

**17. Triggers**

**769**

```
            /* Check for the Address_Type in the tbl_EmployeAddressXref table */
            IF EXISTS (SELECT *
                        FROM Employee.dbo.EmployeeAddressXref e (NOLOCK)
                        JOIN deleted d ON e.Address_Type = d.Code_ID
                                AND d.Code_Group_ID = @v_CodeGrp
                        JOIN inserted i ON d.Code_ID = i.Code_ID
                                AND d.Code_Group_ID <> @v_CodeGrp)
        BEGIN
        /* If the Address_Type exists, return an error and */
        /* rollback the current operation                   */
        RAISERROR ('Address Type referenced in Employee table', 16, 1)
        ROLLBACK
        END
    END
END
GO
```

## The Employee Title Relationship

The next relationship that you need to include a check for is on the employee title
field. Once again, you need to verify not only that the referenced **Code_ID** exists
in the table, but also that it is a member of the correct Code Group for Title.
Listing 17.18 shows the code for the trigger, which includes the code needed to
look up and verify the Code Group for the **Code_ID** being verified.

**Listing 17.18    Create Title verification trigger.**

```
USE Employee
GO

IF EXISTS (SELECT name
            FROM sysobjects (NOLOCK)
            WHERE name = 'inst_XDB_Emp_Title'
              AND type = 'TR')
  DROP TRIGGER inst_XDB_Emp_Title
GO

/* Create a trigger to validate the existence of the referenced */
/* Title in the tbl_codes table                                 */
CREATE TRIGGER inst_XDB_Emp_Title
ON Employee.dbo.tbl_Employee FOR INSERT, UPDATE
AS
BEGIN
  /* We only want to check this if the Title field is being modified */
  IF UPDATE(Title)
    BEGIN
    /* Get the code group for Title in the tbl_CodeGroup table */
    DECLARE @v_CodeGrp INT
```

```
        SELECT @v_CodeGrp = Code_Group_ID
          FROM Utility.dbo.tbl_CodeGroup (NOLOCK)
          WHERE Name = 'Title'

        /* Check for the Title in the tbl_Codes table */
        IF NOT EXISTS (SELECT *
                        FROM Utility.dbo.tbl_Codes c (NOLOCK)
                        JOIN inserted i ON c.Code_ID = i.Title
                                        AND c.Code_Group_ID = @v_CodeGrp)
          BEGIN
          /* If the Title does not exist, return an error and */
          /* rollback the current operation                   */
          RAISERROR ('Title is invalid', 16, 1)
          ROLLBACK
          END
      END
END
GO
```

You then need to add the verification to the **tbl_Codes** table to prevent code records from being deleted that are being referenced in the **Title** field in the **tbl_Employee** table. The trigger code in Listing 17.19 looks up the Code Group for titles and verifies that any records being deleted that are in the Title code group are not found in the **tbl_Employee** table before allowing the delete action to be completed. If any of the codes being deleted are found in this table, an error is raised and the transaction is rolled back.

**Listing 17.19   Create Title delete verification trigger.**

```
USE Utility
GO

IF EXISTS (SELECT name
            FROM sysobjects (NOLOCK)
            WHERE name = 'delt_XDB_Title_Emp'
              AND type = 'TR')
  DROP TRIGGER delt_XDB_Title_Emp
GO

/* Create a trigger to disallow deleting title records */
/* referenced in the tbl_Employee table                */
CREATE TRIGGER delt_XDB_Title_Emp
ON Utility.dbo.tbl_Codes FOR DELETE
AS
BEGIN
  /* Get the code group for Title in the tbl_CodeGroup table */
  DECLARE @v_CodeGrp INT
```

17. Triggers

**771**

```
          SELECT @v_CodeGrp = Code_Group_ID
            FROM Utility.dbo.tbl_CodeGroup (NOLOCK)
            WHERE Name = 'Title'

        /* Check for the Title in the tbl_Employe table */
        IF EXISTS (SELECT *
                      FROM Employee.dbo.Employee e (NOLOCK)
                      JOIN deleted d ON e.Title = d.Code_ID
                                AND d.Code_Group_ID = @v_CodeGrp)
          BEGIN
          /* If the Title exists, return an error and */
          /* rollback the current operation            */
          RAISERROR ('Title referenced in Employee table', 16, 1)
          ROLLBACK
          END
  END
GO
```

One last detail that you need to cover in this verification to make your data integrity solid is the possibility of changing the Code Group on a Title. If the Code Group is changed for a **tbl_Codes** table entry that is being referenced as a Title, the data integrity will be broken. The code in Listing 17.20 creates a trigger that eliminates this hole by disallowing updates of the Code Group field when the **Code_ID** is referenced in the **tbl_Employee** table.

**Listing 17.20   Create Title update verification trigger.**

```
USE Utility
GO


IF EXISTS (SELECT name
              FROM sysobjects (NOLOCK)
              WHERE name = 'updt_XDB_Title_Emp_Upd'
                AND type = 'TR')
  DROP TRIGGER updt_XDB_Title_Emp_Upd
GO


/* Create a trigger to disallow changing title the code group of  */
/* records referenced in the tbl_Employee table                   */
CREATE TRIGGER updt_XDB_Title_Emp_Upd
ON Utility.dbo.tbl_Codes FOR UPDATE
AS
BEGIN
  IF UPDATE(Code_Group_ID)
    BEGIN
    /* Get the code group for Title in the tbl_CodeGroup table */
```

```
        DECLARE @v_CodeGrp INT
        SELECT @v_CodeGrp = Code_Group_ID
          FROM Utility.dbo.tbl_CodeGroup (NOLOCK)
          WHERE Name = 'Title'

        /* Check for the Title in the tbl_Employe table */
        IF EXISTS (SELECT *
                      FROM Employee.dbo.Employee e (NOLOCK)
                      JOIN deleted d ON e.Title = d.Code_ID
                                   AND d.Code_Group_ID = @v_CodeGrp
                      JOIN inserted i ON d.Code_ID = i.Code_ID
                                   AND d.Code_Group_ID <> @v_CodeGrp)
          BEGIN
          /* If the Title exists, return an error and */
          /* rollback the current operation              */
          RAISERROR ('Title referenced in Employee table', 16, 1)
          ROLLBACK
          END
        END
END
GO
```

## The Employee Notification Preference Relationship

The next relationship that you need to include a check for is the Notification Preference. Once again, you need to verify not only that the referenced **Code_ID** exists in the table, but also that it is a member of the correct Code Group for Notification Preference. Listing 17.21 shows the code for the trigger, which includes the code needed to look up and verify the Code Group for the **Code_ID** being verified.

**Listing 17.21    Create Notification Preference verification trigger.**

```
USE Employee
GO

IF EXISTS (SELECT name
              FROM sysobjects (NOLOCK)
              WHERE name = 'inst_XDB_Emp_NPref'
                AND type = 'TR')
  DROP TRIGGER inst_XDB_Emp_NPref
GO

/* Create a trigger to validate the existence of the referenced */
/* Notify_Pref in the tbl codes table                           */
CREATE TRIGGER inst_XDB_Emp_NPref
```

**17. Triggers**

```
ON Employee.dbo.tbl_Employee FOR INSERT, UPDATE
AS
BEGIN
  /* We only want to check this if the Notify_Pref field is being
     modified */
  IF UPDATE(Notify_Pref)
    BEGIN
    /* Get the code group for Notify_Pref in the tbl_CodeGroup table */
    DECLARE @v_CodeGrp INT

    SELECT @v_CodeGrp = Code_Group_ID
      FROM Utility.dbo.tbl_CodeGroup (NOLOCK)
      WHERE Name = 'NotifyPref'

    /* Check for the Notify_Pref in the tbl_Codes table */
    IF NOT EXISTS (SELECT *
                     FROM Utility.dbo.tbl_Codes c (NOLOCK)
                     JOIN inserted i ON c.Code_ID = i.Notify_Pref
                              AND c.Code_Group_ID = @v_CodeGrp)
      BEGIN
      /* If the Notify_Pref does not exist, return an error and */
      /* rollback the current operation                         */
      RAISERROR ('Notification Preference is invalid', 16, 1)
      ROLLBACK
      END
    END
END
GO
```

Next, you need to add the verification to the **tbl_Codes** table to prevent code records from being deleted that are being referenced in the **Notify_Pref** field in the **tbl_Employee** table. The trigger code in Listing 17.22 looks up the Code Group for titles and verifies that any records being deleted that are in the NotifyPref code group are not found in the **tbl_Employee** table before allowing the delete action to be completed. If any of the codes being deleted are found in this table, an error is raised and the transaction is rolled back.

**Listing 17.22    Create Notification Preference delete verification trigger.**

```
USE Utility
GO

IF EXISTS (SELECT name
             FROM sysobjects (NOLOCK)
             WHERE name = 'delt_XDB_NPref_Emp'
               AND type = 'TR')
```

```
   DROP TRIGGER delt_XDB_NPref_Emp
GO


/* Create a trigger to disallow deleting notify preference */
/* records referenced in the tbl_Employee table            */
CREATE TRIGGER delt_XDB_NPref_Emp
ON Utility.dbo.tbl_Codes FOR DELETE
AS
BEGIN
  /* Get the code group for Notify Preference in the tbl_CodeGroup table */
  DECLARE @v_CodeGrp INT

  SELECT @v_CodeGrp = Code_Group_ID
    FROM Utility.dbo.tbl_CodeGroup (NOLOCK)
    WHERE Name = 'NotifyPref'

  /* Check for the Notify_Pref in the tbl_Employe table */
  IF EXISTS (SELECT *
               FROM Employee.dbo.Employee e (NOLOCK)
               JOIN deleted d ON e.Notify_Pref = d.Code_ID
                         AND d.Code_Group_ID = @v_CodeGrp)
    BEGIN
    /* If the Notify_Pref exists, return an error and */
    /* rollback the current operation                 */
    RAISERROR ('Notify Preference referenced in Employee table', 16, 1)
    ROLLBACK
    END
END
GO
```

One last detail that you need to cover in this verification to make your data integrity solid is the possibility of changing the Code Group on a Notification Preference. If the Code Group is changed for a **tbl_Codes** table entry that is being referenced as a Notification Preference, the data integrity will be broken. The code in Listing 17.23 creates a trigger that eliminates this hole by disallowing updates of the Code Group field when the **Code_ID** is referenced in the **tbl_Employee** table.

**Listing 17.23    Create Notification Preference update verification trigger.**

```
USE Utility
GO


IF EXISTS (SELECT name
             FROM sysobjects (NOLOCK)
             WHERE name = 'updt_XDB_NPref_Emp_Upd'
```

```
                           AND type = 'TR')
      DROP TRIGGER updt_XDB_NPref_Emp_Upd
   GO


   /* Create a trigger to disallow changing the code group of notify */
   /* preference records referenced in the tbl_Employee table        */
   CREATE TRIGGER updt_XDB_NPref_Emp_Upd
   ON Utility.dbo.tbl_Codes FOR UPDATE
   AS
   BEGIN
     IF UPDATE(Code_Group_ID)
       BEGIN
       /* Get the code group for Notify Preference in the tbl_CodeGroup
          table */
       DECLARE @v_CodeGrp INT

       SELECT @v_CodeGrp = Code_Group_ID
         FROM Utility.dbo.tbl_CodeGroup (NOLOCK)
         WHERE Name = 'NotifyPref'

       /* Check for the Notify_Pref in the tbl_Employe table */
       IF EXISTS (SELECT *
                    FROM Employee.dbo.Employee e (NOLOCK)
                    JOIN deleted d ON e.Notify_Pref = d.Code_ID
                            AND d.Code_Group_ID = @v_CodeGrp
                    JOIN inserted i ON d.Code_ID = i.Code_ID
                            AND d.Code_Group_ID <> @v_CodeGrp)
       BEGIN
       /* If the Notify_Pref exists, return an error and */
       /* rollback the current operation                 */
       RAISERROR ('Notify Preference referenced in Employee table', 16, 1)
       ROLLBACK
       END
     END
   END
   GO
```

## The Employee Department Relationship

The final relationship that you need to include a check for is the Department. Once again, you need to verify not only that the referenced **Code_ID** exists in the table, but also that it is a member of the correct Code Group for Departments. Listing 17.24 shows the code for the trigger, which includes the code needed to look up and verify the Code Group for the **Code_ID** being verified.

**Listing 17.24   Create Department verification trigger.**

```
USE Employee
GO

IF EXISTS (SELECT name
              FROM sysobjects (NOLOCK)
              WHERE name = 'inst_XDB_Emp_Dept'
                AND type = 'TR')
  DROP TRIGGER inst_XDB_Emp_Dept
GO

/* Create a trigger to validate the existence of the referenced */
/* Department in the tbl_codes table                            */
CREATE TRIGGER inst_XDB_Emp_Dept
ON Employee.dbo.tbl_Employee FOR INSERT, UPDATE
AS
BEGIN
  /* We only want to check this if the Department field is being
     modified */
  IF UPDATE(Department)
    BEGIN
    /* Get the code group for Department in the tbl_CodeGroup table */
    DECLARE @v_CodeGrp INT

    SELECT @v_CodeGrp = Code_Group_ID
      FROM Utility.dbo.tbl_CodeGroup (NOLOCK)
      WHERE Name = 'Dept'

    /* Check for the Department in the tbl_Codes table */
    IF NOT EXISTS (SELECT *
                     FROM Utility.dbo.tbl_Codes c (NOLOCK)
                     JOIN inserted i ON c.Code_ID = i.Department
                                    AND c.Code_Group_ID = @v_CodeGrp)
      BEGIN
      /* If the Department does not exist, return an error and */
      /* rollback the current operation                        */
      RAISERROR ('Department is invalid', 16, 1)
      ROLLBACK
      END
    END
END
GO
```

Next, you need to add the verification to the **tbl_Codes** table to prevent code records from being deleted that are being referenced in the Department field in the **tbl_Employee** table. The trigger code in Listing 17.25 looks up the Code Group for titles and verifies that any records being deleted that are in the Dept code group are not found in the **tbl_Employee** table before allowing the delete action to be completed. If any of the codes being deleted are found in this table, an error is raised and the transaction is rolled back.

**Listing 17.25    Create Department delete verification trigger.**

```
USE Utility
GO


IF EXISTS (SELECT name
              FROM sysobjects (NOLOCK)
              WHERE name = 'delt_XDB_Dept_Emp'
                AND type = 'TR')
  DROP TRIGGER delt_XDB_Dept_Emp
GO


/* Create a trigger to disallow deleting department records */
/* referenced in the tbl_Employee table                    */
CREATE TRIGGER delt_XDB_Dept_Emp
ON Utility.dbo.tbl_Codes FOR DELETE
AS
BEGIN
  /* Get the code group for Department in the tbl_CodeGroup table */
  DECLARE @v_CodeGrp INT

  SELECT @v_CodeGrp = Code_Group_ID
    FROM Utility.dbo.tbl_CodeGroup (NOLOCK)
    WHERE Name = 'Dept'

  /* Check for the Department in the tbl_Employe table */
  IF EXISTS (SELECT *
              FROM Employee.dbo.Employee e (NOLOCK)
              JOIN deleted d ON e.Department = d.Code_ID
                        AND d.Code_Group_ID = @v_CodeGrp)
    BEGIN
    /* If the Department exists, return an error and */
    /* rollback the current operation                */
    RAISERROR ('Department referenced in Employee table', 16, 1)
    ROLLBACK
    END
END
GO
```

One last detail that you need to cover in this verification to make your data integrity solid is the possibility of changing the Code Group on a Department. If the Code Group is changed for a **tbl_Codes** table entry that is being referenced as a Department, the data integrity will be broken. The code in Listing 17.26 creates a trigger that eliminates this hole by disallowing updates of the Code Group field when the **Code_ID** is referenced in the **tbl_Employee** table.

**Listing 17.26    Create Department update verification trigger.**

```
USE Utility
GO

IF EXISTS (SELECT name
             FROM sysobjects (NOLOCK)
             WHERE name = 'updt_XDB_Dept_Emp_Upd'
               AND type = 'TR')
  DROP TRIGGER updt_XDB_Dept_Emp_Upd
GO

/* Create a trigger to disallow changing the code group of department */
/* records referenced in the tbl_Employee table                      */
CREATE TRIGGER updt_XDB_Dept_Emp_Upd
ON Utility.dbo.tbl_Codes FOR UPDATE
AS
BEGIN
  IF UPDATE(Code_Group_ID)
    BEGIN
    /* Get the code group for Department in the tbl_CodeGroup table */
    DECLARE @v_CodeGrp INT

    SELECT @v_CodeGrp = Code_Group_ID
      FROM Utility.dbo.tbl_CodeGroup (NOLOCK)
      WHERE Name = 'Dept'

    /* Check for the Department in the tbl_Employe table */
    IF EXISTS (SELECT *
                 FROM Employee.dbo.Employee e (NOLOCK)
                 JOIN deleted d ON e.Department = d.Code_ID
                           AND d.Code_Group_ID = @v_CodeGrp
                 JOIN inserted i ON d.Code_ID = i.Code_ID
                           AND d.Code_Group_ID <> @v_CodeGrp)
      BEGIN
      /* If the Department exists, return an error and */
      /* rollback the current operation                */
      RAISERROR ('Department referenced in Employee table', 16, 1)
      ROLLBACK
```

```
        END
      END
    END
  GO
```

# Creating **INSTEAD OF** Triggers for Inserts and Updates to a View

In order to facilitate allowing client applications to use a view of the normalized address data to reference the address in a denormalized form, the **vw_Address** view was created to present the information in a denormalized structure. This view allows the application to read the information in a denormalized format, but you need to implement **INSTEAD OF** triggers on the view to allow **INSERT**, **UPDATE**, and **DELETE** operations to be performed against this view. In this section, you construct an **INSTEAD OF** trigger for each of these three operations, which allows updates to the underlying tables when performing these operations against the view from a client application.

## Inserting Address Information

The first trigger that you add is the **INSTEAD OF INSERT** trigger. This trigger allows the client application to perform inserts on the **vw_Address** view. Because this is an insert, you will definitely be adding a record to the **tbl_Address** table, but you may or may not need to add records to the **tbl_City**, **tbl_State**, or **tbl_ZipCode** tables. The trigger shown in Listing 17.27 defines variables to hold the IDs for each of these three tables that will either be populated by looking up an existing record or adding a new record if needed. The trigger checks for the state before the city because if you need to add a record for the city, the **State_ID** field is needed. Once the IDs have been obtained or created for all three of the referenced tables, an insert is performed on the **tbl_Address** table to add the new record.

**Listing 17.27    Create INSTEAD OF INSERT trigger for vw_Address.**

```
USE Address
GO

IF EXISTS (SELECT name
            FROM sysobjects (NOLOCK)
```

```
                    WHERE name = 'inst_vw_Addr_Insert'
                       AND type = 'TR')
    DROP TRIGGER inst_vw_Addr_Insert
GO

CREATE TRIGGER tr_vw_Addr_Insert
  ON address.dbo.vw_Address INSTEAD OF INSERT
AS
BEGIN
  DECLARE @v_CityID INT,
          @v_StateID TINYINT,
          @v_ZipID INT

  /* Get the State ID */
  SELECT @v_StateID = s.State_ID
    FROM tbl_State s (NOLOCK)
    JOIN inserted i ON s.State_Code = i.State

  /* If we don't have a valid StateID, we'll have to add the state */
  IF (@v_StateID IS NULL)
    BEGIN
    INSERT INTO tbl_State (Name,
                             State_Code)
      SELECT State,
             State
        FROM inserted

    /* The new ID is now a valid StateID */
    SELECT @v_StateID = @@IDENTITY
    END

  /* Get the city ID */
  SELECT @v_CityID = c.City_ID
    FROM tbl_City c (NOLOCK)
    JOIN tbl_State s (NOLOCK) ON c.State_ID = s.State_ID
    JOIN inserted i (NOLOCK) ON c.Name = i.City
                            AND s.State_Code = i.State

  /* If the city did not exist, we need to add it... */
  IF (@v_CityID IS NULL)
    BEGIN
    INSERT INTO tbl_City (Name,
                            State_ID)
      SELECT City,
             @v_StateID
        FROM inserted
```

```
            /* The new ID is now a valid CityID */
            SELECT @v_CityID = @@IDENTITY
            END


    /* Get the Zip ID */
    SELECT @v_ZipID = z.Zip_ID
      FROM tbl_ZipCode z (NOLOCK)
      JOIN inserted i ON z.Zip5 = i.Zip5


    /* If we don't have a valid ZipID, we'll have to add the Zip Code */
    IF (@v_ZipID IS NULL)
      BEGIN
      INSERT INTO tbl_ZipCode (Zip5,
                                  State_ID)

        SELECT Zip5,
               @v_StateID
          FROM inserted


        /* The new ID is now a valid ZipID */
        SELECT @v_ZipID = @@IDENTITY
        END


    /* Once we have a valid CityID, StateID, and ZipID, we can */
    /* add the Address record                                 */
    INSERT INTO tbl_Address (Line1,
                                Line2,
                                Zip4,
                                City_ID,
                                Zip_ID)

        SELECT Line1,
               Line2,
               Zip4,
               @v_CityID,
               @v_ZipID
          FROM inserted i
END
GO
```

## Deleting Address Information

The **INSTEAD OF** trigger for handling deletes is much simpler than the other
two. Because the city, state, and ZIP code information can be used for multiple
records, a delete for these records is not implemented in the trigger. If you want
to delete these records when they are no longer referenced in another address,
the code to do so can easily be added to this trigger. If you modify the trigger to

delete information for the city, state, and zip tables, remember to delete the address record first, the city next, and then the order of the other two won't matter. The trigger provided in Listing 17.28 provides the code to remove the referenced record from the **tbl_Address** table.

**Listing 17.28   Create INSTEAD OF DELETE trigger for vw_Address.**

```
USE Address
GO

IF EXISTS (SELECT name
             FROM sysobjects (NOLOCK)
             WHERE name = 'delt_vw_Addr_Delete'
               AND type = 'TR')
  DROP TRIGGER delt_vw_Addr_Delete
GO

CREATE TRIGGER delt_vw_Addr_Delete
  ON address.dbo.vw_Address INSTEAD OF DELETE
AS
BEGIN
  /* Remove the row from the tbl_Address table with */
  /* the Address_ID found in the deleted table      */
  DELETE FROM tbl_Address
    FROM deleted d
    WHERE tbl_Address.Address_ID = d.Address_ID
END
GO
```

## Updating Address Information

The most complex of the three triggers is the **INSTEAD OF UPDATE** trigger. This trigger needs to check which fields are being updated and process the information accordingly. Listing 17.29 provides the source to this trigger for reference. Like the **INSERT** trigger, you need to define variables for the city, state, and ZIP code IDs. If Line1 or Line2 is being updated, you can update the **tbl_Address** table with these fields immediately. If the state is being updated, you need to check and see if the new state already exists in the **tbl_State** table and add it if necessary. Save the StateID and update the new value in the **tbl_Address** record. Next, check to see if the city is being updated. The state will already have been added if needed. If the state was not updated, you need to look up the StateID. You can then look up the city, and add the record if necessary. Once you have a valid CityID, you can update the **tbl_Address** record with it. The final check is for an update to the ZIP code. As with the other tables, look up the ZIP code first, and add it if it does not already exist. The new ZipID is updated in the **tbl_Address** record.

**Listing 17.29    Create INSTEAD OF UPDATE trigger for vw_Address.**

```
USE Address
GO


IF EXISTS (SELECT name
             FROM sysobjects (NOLOCK)
            WHERE name = 'updt_vw_Addr_Update'
              AND type = 'TR')
  DROP TRIGGER updt_vw_Addr_Update
GO

CREATE TRIGGER updt_vw_Addr_Update
  ON address.dbo.vw_Address INSTEAD OF UPDATE
AS
BEGIN
  DECLARE @v_CityID INT,
          @v_StateID TINYINT,
          @v_ZipID INT

  /* Check for updates to the tbl_Address table */
  IF UPDATE(Line1) OR UPDATE(Line2) OR UPDATE(Zip4)
    BEGIN
    /* Simply update the address Line1 & Line2 information */
    UPDATE tbl_Address
      SET Line1 = i.Line1,
          Line2 = i.Line2,
          Zip4 = i.Zip4
      FROM inserted i
      WHERE tbl_Address.Address_ID = i.Address_ID
    END

  /* Check for updates to the tbl_State table */
  IF UPDATE(State)
    BEGIN
    /* Get the State ID */
    SELECT @v_StateID = s.State_ID
      FROM tbl_State s (NOLOCK)
      JOIN inserted i ON s.State_Code = i.State

    /* If we don't have a valid StateID, we'll have to add the state */
    IF (@v_StateID IS NULL)
      BEGIN
      INSERT INTO tbl_State (Name,
                             State_Code)
```

```
        SELECT State,
              State
          FROM inserted


      /* The new ID is now a valid StateID */
      SELECT @v_StateID = @@IDENTITY
      END
   END

/* Check for updates to the tbl_City table */
IF UPDATE(City) OR UPDATE(State)
  BEGIN
  IF (@v_StateID IS NULL)
    BEGIN
    /* Get the State ID */
    SELECT @v_StateID = s.State_ID
      FROM tbl_State s (NOLOCK)
      JOIN inserted i ON s.State_Code = i.State
    END

  /* Get the city ID */
  SELECT @v_CityID = c.City_ID
    FROM tbl_City c (NOLOCK)
    JOIN tbl_State s (NOLOCK) ON c.State_ID = s.State_ID
    JOIN inserted i ON c.Name = i.City
                   AND s.State_Code = i.State

  /* If the city did not exist, we need to add it... */
  IF (@v_CityID IS NULL)
    BEGIN
    INSERT INTO tbl_City (Name,
                          State_ID)
      SELECT City,
             @v_StateID
        FROM inserted

    /* The new ID is now a valid CityID */
    SELECT @v_CityID = @@IDENTITY
    END

  /* Once we have a valid CityID, we can update the tbl_Address table */
  UPDATE tbl_Address
    SET City_ID = @v_CityID
    FROM inserted i
    WHERE tbl_Address.Address_ID = i.Address_ID
  END
```

```
        /* Check for updates to the tbl_ZipCode table */
      IF UPDATE(Zip5) OR UPDATE(State)
        BEGIN
        /* Get the Zip ID */
        SELECT @v_ZipID = z.Zip_ID
          FROM tbl_ZipCode z (NOLOCK)
          JOIN tbl_State s (NOLOCK) ON z.State_ID = s.State_ID
          JOIN inserted i ON z.Zip5 = i.Zip5
                        AND s.State_Code = i.State

        /* If we don't have a valid ZipID, we'll have to add the Zip Code */
        IF (@v_ZipID IS NULL)
          BEGIN
          INSERT INTO tbl_ZipCode (Zip5,
                                   State_ID)
            SELECT Zip5,
                   @v_StateID
              FROM inserted

          /* The new ID is now a valid ZipID */
          SELECT @v_ZipID = @@IDENTITY
          END

        /* Once we have a valid ZipID, we can update the tbl_Address table */
        UPDATE tbl_Address
          SET Zip_ID = @v_ZipID
          FROM inserted i
          WHERE tbl_Address.Address_ID = i.Address_ID
        END
    END
    GO
```

# Chapter 18

## Meta Data

# In Depth

Using the most basic definition, meta data is data that describes data. Meta data is a collection of terms organized to define objects. These terms can range from the most abstract theories to the simplest entities that symbolize a physical order. Abstract meta data is used in our day-to-day conversations to describe physical characteristics, like weather. Weather itself is only a word, but it is used to define how conditions, like hot, cold, rain, and so on, affect other people. All of these descriptive references form an abstract classification that people can relate to and understand. On the other end of the spectrum is a more physical kind of meta data, like lettered tabs ranging from A through Z in an address book. If the owner of the address book follows the standard format of alphabetized organization, this physical meta data can be used to quickly find an object of importance rather than going from start to finish one page at a time. SQL Server uses the latter definition of meta data to organize objects in a way that is systematic in order to retrieve data in a quick and efficient manner.

## Fundamentals

Meta data is used to describe the structure and meaning of data. It can also describe the structure and meaning of applications and processes. Meta data can include items like project documentation, data models, and specifications. It can exist in both electronic and physical forms depending on the environment. This chapter focuses on the meta data used and managed by the SQL Server 2000 Meta Data Services. However, it is important to begin with a basic understanding of what meta data is and how it is used before attempting to make use of the meta data management facilities included in SQL Server. Meta data has three primary characteristics, which are described in the following sections.

### Meta Data Is Abstract

Abstract information that qualifies as meta data can be generated by the simple act of describing the world around us. Describing a sunset or a snowstorm requires abstractions like the concepts of beauty or weather. These concepts can be further abstracted by defining concepts such as temperature and luminescence. This abstraction of real-world concepts carries into data design as well. People may be classified as employees, and then grouped as a department, and then as a company. Each employee is a combination of various pieces of information ranging from name and address to salary and job description.

The application and database structures used to represent and store data can be abstracted into meta data classification schemes that make sense to developers and analysts. The basic table or form is derived from an object, which is derived from a class. These concepts are heavily used in object-oriented programming environments. Meta data can have multiple levels of abstraction. You can describe a specific data element, and then describe that description, and continue describing the resulting description to as many levels as you need. In most environments, the levels of meta data abstraction used in software and database development only extend to two or three levels. A real-world example of this is an "address table," which can be described as the **tbl_Address** table in the Address database. This table can further be described as being a database table object. An abstract class that defines the fixed set of characteristics that all derived objects must conform to could be used to further describe this object.

The modeling of information is generally done from the top down. In other words, when creating a model for a solution, you start with the most abstract concepts, and then get more specific. Keeping the upper levels of the model as abstract as possible increases the flexibility and reusability of the model. In the previous example, if you start by defining the **tbl_Address** table in a model, the definition is in no way helpful when you need to design a storage system for inventory items. On the other hand, if you start from the most abstract level, and create the set of characteristics that all objects must conform to, it can be reused when you need to solve an inventory problem. The more abstract the definition, the more often a model can be used in various differing projects.

## Meta Data Has a Context

The distinction between data and meta data is context sensitive. What is considered meta data at one level becomes data at another level. For example, in SQL Server, a system catalog is used to describe the tables and columns that contain your data. In this case, the data in the system catalog can be thought of as meta data because it describes data definitions. However, this data can be manipulated like any other data if you use the right software tools. Numerous examples of manipulating this meta data have been presented throughout this book. Writing a cursor to loop through some or all of the tables in a database to perform a maintenance task or gathering information about column properties using standard SQL **SELECT** statements are examples of how this meta data can become data that you can manipulate like any other data.

It is possible to design an application that is completely meta data driven. You could generate meta data that is used to describe the presentation of the data and functionality of the application when it is presented to the user. The tools used to manipulate the meta data and the framework application itself would treat the

18. Meta Data

meta data as simply data for the purpose of processing and manipulating it directly. Any of the tools designed to assist you in the creation and manipulation of meta data operate on the meta data being manipulated in the context of data.

---

**NOTE:** *Many homegrown solutions have been developed to manage meta data. The advent of the Repository and Meta Data Services in SQL Server simply allows for a standard method of collection and management of that data.*

---

## Meta Data Has More Than One Use

You can work with meta data information just as you would with any kind of application or data design elements. Using standard meta data to express design information opens up new possibilities for reuse, sharing, and multiple tool support. For example, using meta data to define data objects enables you to see how the objects are constructed and versioned. Support for versioning provides a way to view, branch, or retrieve any historical version of a particular Data Transformation Services (DTS) package or data warehousing definition. Basing your code development on meta data allows you to define a structure once, and then reuse it to create multiple instances that can be versioned for specific tools and applications. New relationships can also be created among existing meta data types to support a new application design.

Keeping your designs more abstract also eliminates placing limitations on the initial design for hardware, operating system, and platform-specific issues. This means that although the completed design at the lowest level may rely on Windows 2000, SQL Server 2000, and Visual Basic, the higher-level design pieces could be reused to create a new design that would specify replacements to account for any or all of these specific considerations for a new environment. This separation between the abstract and the reality is often referred to as a *conceptual model* versus a *physical model*.

It is a good idea to keep the conceptual issues separate from the physical issues in the design process whether you are designing a database or an application. This not only allows you the flexibility to change platforms and operating systems, but it also allows you to more easily absorb the changes brought by product upgrades in your existing platform and operating systems. Numerous companies have shied away from adopting a new version of a database server, operating system, or programming language because it would require too much effort to revamp their applications to take advantage of the new technologies. There are almost always some compatibility issues raised when making the move from one version to the next in any technology. The use of a conceptual model can help ease the work involved to absorb the physical changes required when you decide to change or update your existing tools.

# SQL Server Meta Data Services

SQL Server 2000 Meta Data Services provides a way to store and manage information system and application meta data using an object-oriented repository technology. This technology serves as a hub for data warehousing descriptions, data and component definitions, development and deployment models, and reusable software components. It can be integrated with enterprise information systems or with applications that process meta data.

You can use Meta Data Services for your own purposes as a component of an integrated information system, as a native store for custom applications that process meta data, or as a storage and management service for sharing reusable models. Meta Data Services can also be extended to provide support for new tools for resale or customized to satisfy internal tool requirements. Integrating a meta data management service requires understanding what meta data is and how it is used. The topics in this chapter describe fundamental concepts and usage strategies that help identify ways in which meta data management technology can be applied.

A number of Microsoft products and technologies use Meta Data Services to store object definitions and use it as a platform for deploying meta data. Versioned DTS packages are stored using the Meta Data Services in SQL Server 2000. Meta Data Services in Microsoft Visual Studio is used to support the exchange of model data with other development tools.

The next few sections deal with the underlying standards used by Meta Data Services to provide a high level of interoperability between applications that make use of this technology. Although you are not required to follow these standards, you should spend some time understanding what they are and how they can help you make better use of your own meta data repository.

# Meta Data Coalition

The Meta Data Coalition (MDC) is an independent organization of vendors and users who volunteer time and resources to pursue agreed-upon goals related to the standardization of enterprise meta data for the mutual benefit of all interested parties. The Open Information Model (OIM) is an information model published by the Meta Data Coalition and widely supported by software vendors. The definition, implementation, and evolution of the OIM and its support mechanisms are driven by the MDC. Proposals for new OIM models and extensions are made available to members for in-depth review. From this process, agreed upon models are formally adopted into the OIM specification and published through the MDC Web site. For more information about the MDC, see the MDC Web site at **www.mdcinfo.com**.

18. Meta Data

The OIM is described in Unified Modeling Language (UML) and is organized into subject areas that are easy to use and easy to extend. Industry standards, such as SQL, UML, and Extensible Markup Language (XML), form the basis for the data model. Over 300 companies have reviewed the OIM. The following is a list of the current subject areas that are covered by the OIM:

- Analysis and Design Models
- Objects and Components Models
- Database and Data Warehousing Models
- Knowledge Management Models
- Business Engineering Models

# Information Model

Many people read about the OIM and realize that it could possibly be a great benefit to them if they only knew more about information models in general. This section provides you with a basic understanding of information models, what they consist of, and how they are used.

A set of meta data types that describe a tool, application, data structure, or information system is an information model. An information model for a database application describes the tables and columns supported by the application. Information models describe types of data rather than instances of data. The information model for a database application describes tables, keys, constraints, and stored procedures, but not the actual data that these elements store and manipulate.

## Building Blocks

Classes, relationships, and properties are the building blocks that describe an information model. A template that defines the characteristics of one or more objects is a class. Classes represent entities in an information model. A table, a key, a constraint, and a stored procedure would be examples of different classes. Relationship types define a template to which stored relationships must conform. You can define the type of relationship between a schema and a table, a table and a column, or a column and a data type. A relationship type defines the set of criteria that describes how two objects relate to one another. The template to which stored property values must conform is a property. When you store the description of an inventory item, for example, you must store a character value.

## Open Information Model

SQL Server 2000 Meta Data Services distributes an implementation of the OIM that provides standard meta data types that can be used by various OIM-compliant tools and applications. As mentioned earlier in this chapter, the OIM provides a generic set of information models that describe object modeling, database modeling, and component reuse. You can add your own custom elements to extend the OIM, which means that if you are creating an application that requires elements that are not included in the OIM, you can add those elements to complete your design. Although compliance with the OIM standard is not required, deploying an OIM-based strategy provides integration possibilities that would not be achievable otherwise.

## Information Model Importance

In SQL Server 2000 and other Microsoft products that integrate with Meta Data Services, OIM-based models are predefined, installed, and operational. No action is required on your part to use the functionality provided by these standard models. A good working knowledge of information models is a necessity for successfully building your own tools and applications that work with meta data types or for creating an extended information model. Information models are the key to integrating Meta Data Services with other tools and technologies.

# Using Meta Data Services

SQL Server 2000 Meta Data Services is a technology that is used via tools that integrate the technology. These tools vary depending on whether you are designing meta data, programming with meta data, or accessing meta data at runtime. The diagram provided in Figure 18.1 shows the ways in which you can interact with Meta Data Services. The interaction is divided into design time, development time, and runtime phases. The distinction between these phases is not actually

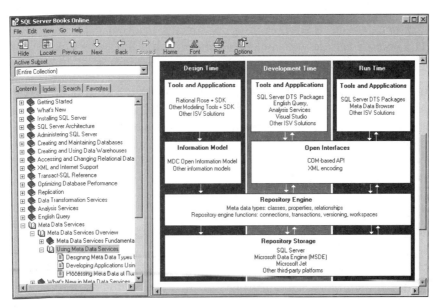

Figure 18.1   Meta Data Services interaction diagram.

very precise in practice, but using these distinctions helps make the various ways you can work with Meta Data Services clearer.

During the design process, the focus is naturally on model creation. Meta data can be created using modeling tools and the Meta Data Services Software Development Kit (SDK) and stored in the repository database. Once the design phase is completed and the model information is stored in the database, the development process can begin. XML encoding can be used to exchange data with other repositories. You can use the repository application programming interface (API) program against the meta data. You can create custom solutions based on Meta Data Services. You can also use browser tools that work directly with the repository contents.

## Using Information Models to Design Meta Data Types

An information model is the starting point for deploying the SQL Server 2000 Meta Data Services technology. Meta Data Services is intended to be used with information models that provide type information about meta data. The repository engine, repository API, add-on tools, and SDK are designed to work with information models. The meta data types defined in an information model are used to provide the design data that interacts with development tools, applications, and browsers. Information models of some type are the basis for integration to Meta Data Services used by all integrated Microsoft products.

The information models you use to build an application with Meta Data Services should completely describe the data, tool, or application structure that you will code later. If you are using the OIM, your design elements are predefined. The OIM can be extended to support any tool-specific or other meta data types required by your design, so you can use a subset of the OIM elements and supplement your model with any additional elements you require.

Although the OIM provides significant advantages in terms of tool and programming support, its use is not required. You can use UML to create custom information models that are completely unrelated to the OIM, but custom or OIM extended information models must conform to the abstract classes provided through the repository API. You should use the Meta Data Services SDK, which includes a model compiler, to build your custom information models or extended OIM models. The compiler provided with the SDK validates your model against the repository API.

## Using Meta Data in Application Development

Although using an information model does not eliminate the need for coding, it does change the role that coding plays in the application development process. In a model driven environment, code is used to provide the implementation strategy.

Once an information model has been installed in a repository database, you can begin to program against it using the repository API.

Before you begin programming, it is important to understand how the information model is constructed. The information model should completely describe at least a portion (if not all) of the code that you must provide. Your code should create instances for the objects that the information model describes. The model driven development process does not place limits on what functionality can be included in your application. Regardless of whether or not it is described by a model, your application code can support whatever structures and behavioral characteristics are required to accomplish the task it is created for. If you want your information models to be truly useful, however, they must contain the most complete set of meta data types that is possible for your situation. The key to using information models successfully is to understand that they provide the minimum design that must be implemented in your code.

## Development Scenarios

The samples and tools provided with the Meta Data Services SDK can be used and incorporated to speed up your development process. These samples and tools assist you in generating program files from your information model.

Meta Data Services provides a basis for integrating tools and managing tool meta data, which is especially useful for tool vendors. Output from one tool can be converted to input for another tool by using Meta Data Services as an intermediate storage medium. Meta Data Services can be used to provide a way to create variants of a specific application. This means that different workgroups can simultaneously pursue new application development or maintain an existing application. Functions that allow you to track this type of development activity and then synchronize or merge the versions later are also included in the Meta Data Services.

Application development methodologies can be improved by using meta data. The use of meta data separates the design and implementation aspects of application development. With the use of meta data, your design becomes portable and reusable rather than specific to the implementation you are working on. This means that a design can be created once, and then implemented using different tools and platforms to suit the needs of various customers. The use of meta data types allows for redirecting the design to a specific operating system, database, or network by using the repository data to drive your implementation tools.

## Processing Meta Data at Runtime

Application designers and tool vendors rely on processed meta data in their applications to support interoperability. The SQL Server Meta Data Services repository technology can be deployed in runtime scenarios, although it is not necessarily a common (or obvious) implementation. Meta data can be retrieved and processed

**18. Meta Data**

at runtime to produce DTS packages, queries, and cleansed data for queries. Data warehousing professionals can use the Meta Data Services for single sourcing and tool integration of data warehousing definitions that can be used to produce cleansed data.

The Meta Data Browser is an example of a tool that processes meta data at runtime. The Meta Data Browser allows you to view existing meta data and how it is defined. It provides application developers with a way to scan the contents of the repository for the right objects to use for a particular purpose. By using the Meta Data Services SDK and the repository API, you can create custom browsers or analysis tools for studying the meta data content stored in a repository database. You can also create full-featured applications that manage the meta data types used by your organization.

The previously discussed examples provide some insight into a few of the possible uses of processed meta data. You can create custom tools based on the ideas presented in this section, or devise entirely new and innovative ways to incorporate the use of meta data in your applications. In either case, the development tools provided with the Meta Data Services can be invaluable assets to your development endeavors.

# Meta Data Services Architecture

The SQL Server 2000 Meta Data Services architecture is based on a set of integrated components. The key components of the Meta Data Services are presented in the diagram shown in Figure 18.2. In Meta Data Services architecture, the tools and applications connect to the core engine and storage components through open standards. Information models define type information that is used to determine the structure and behavior of the meta data exposed by the tools and applications at the top layer.

## Tools and Applications

The Meta Data Services technology provided with SQL Server 2000 is designed for use by tools and applications. A tool is any software program designed to assist software developers as they design, implement, deploy, and maintain their applications. An application is a program that is designed to perform (or assist in the performance of) a specific task. Applications include word processors, accounting software, payroll processing software, spreadsheets, and so on.

In the Meta Data Services architecture, tools and applications are programs that you build or provide and that exist outside of the core engine and storage components. These programs connect to the core components through open standards.

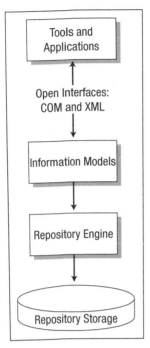

**Figure 18.2** Meta Data Services architecture diagram.

These programs range from modeling software that can be used to build information models at design time to application development tools that use or transform existing meta data at runtime. The type of applications and tools that can be used with Meta Data Services is open-ended.

There are many ways in which independent software vendors (ISVs) have integrated Meta Data Services in their tools and offerings. The following list provides some examples of how the Meta Data Services repository is being applied by Microsoft and other vendors:

- SQL Server 2000, SQL Server 2000 Analysis Services, English Query, and Microsoft Visual Studio use Meta Data Services to store meta data and to exchange meta data with other tools. Meta Data Services can also provide versioning capability to the tools that support meta data creation.

- ISV providers use Meta Data Services in their commercial product offerings to store predefined, value-added information models that can be used by their customers.

- Software developers have incorporated Meta Data Services into their development environments to facilitate deploying application designs across a variety of development tools.

For the most up-to-date information about how the Meta Data Services technology is currently being deployed by third-party vendors, visit the SQL Server page on Microsoft's Web site.

# Meta Data Services Open Standards: OIM, COM, and XML

Open standards are publicly available specifications that provide a description of the characteristics of a particular technology. The object of providing open standards is to promote interoperability between various tools and applications. For platforms like SQL Server 2000 where integration is a key ingredient in its use, interoperability is essential. This is why open interfaces and specifications are provided wherever possible for the Meta Data Services architecture.

There are three open standards supported by Meta Data Services: the OIM, the Component Object Model (COM), and XML Encoding. These multiple open standards ensure that there will be an appropriate open standard to provide integration at each phase in the life cycle of your application.

### Using OIM for Design-Time Integration

The OIM provides a standard information model that can be shared, reused, and extended. The OIM is published by the MDC and is widely supported by the tool vendor market. This wide support makes it possible to use the same information model design in a variety of implementation tools. You can use the OIM as a framework on which to build type information in Meta Data Services. Although the API or the repository engine does not require using the OIM, you cannot take full advantage of the resources and features provided in the Meta Data Services SDK unless you use the OIM. These resources and features are provided to simplify your development efforts. Using the OIM also allows you to use your information models in other OIM-compliant tools.

### Using COM Interfaces for Program-Level Integration

COM interfaces are binary specifications for building, using, and evolving component software. Numerous programming languages, such as Microsoft Visual Basic, Microsoft Visual C++, and Delphi, support COM. The COM architecture and supporting infrastructure are developed and maintained by Microsoft. You can use the COM interfaces defined in the repository API to access both the repository engine and your information model from your application code. Because both the repository engine and information models are exposed as COM objects, you only have to use the COM implementation strategy that matches your development tools to make use of this technology.

### *Using XML for Runtime and Storage-Level Integration*

XML is a World Wide Web Consortium (W3C) standard for the representation of information as structured documents. XML is increasingly being used to transport data between heterogeneous systems. The Meta Data Services repository engine supports XML Encoding to provide the capability to import and export stored meta data in an XML format. XML Encoding also enables the exchange of meta data between various OIM-compliant tools and repositories.

# Information Models

Information models define the meta data types that are stored in the repository database and used by various tools and applications. The information models used with Meta Data Services must be described using UML. A set of standard information models called the OIM is distributed by the Meta Data Services. The standard information models that describe DTS packages, data warehousing definitions, and online analytical processing (OLAP) cubes are preinstalled into the msdb database by SQL Server 2000. No modification of these information models is required in order to perform the functions for which they are intended.

These standard information models can also be used as a framework for building new applications. New information models can also be created using the Meta Data Services SDK. Any information model that is defined in UML can be used in the Meta Data Services.

Although information models can be created programmatically, most are created using modeling tools like Rational Rose. Any custom information models you create must conform to the repository API. The repository API includes abstract classes that formally describe what elements can be included in an information model. You should review the repository API for more information about the type of information objects that the repository engine supports before attempting to create a custom information model.

Once you have defined and tested your information model, you can install it in a repository database. The installation of the model creates the storage structure for your meta data. The storage can be populated with instance data about the model definitions by tools and applications that use the model. The repository reads the meta data at runtime and uses it to instantiate COM objects in a tool or application that corresponds to the objects, relationships, and members defined in the information model. The COM interfaces used in the tool or application are derived from an information model installed in a repository database. The information model is used as a blueprint for the COM objects exposed by the repository engine. XML can also be used to exchange meta data between platforms, tools, and applications.

**18. Meta Data**

# The Repository Engine

The repository engine is the service that provides basic functions for storing and retrieving objects and maintaining the relationships between them. The repository engine performs these functions within the context of an information model. It can be thought of as a model-driven interpreter. The repository engine processes user-defined model information to determine how to store and support various objects, relationships, and actions. The engine only manipulates an instance of an information model to the extent allowed by the model structure. For example, an object relationship is established only if the underlying information model supports it.

The repository engine handles all interaction with the storage layer by generating the SQL commands to execute specific actions, but you control how and when the transactions occur. The engine executes as a class library and buffers instance data from repository databases in a cache. The objects you manipulate in your code actually point to this cached data. Row caching is used to maintain state information about the objects, properties, and relationships that you instantiate.

# The Repository API

The repository API is the programming interface used to drive the repository engine from within your applications. The repository API is based on an object model that describes the type definitions and repository engine functionality that correspond to information models. The repository engine functionality includes connection services, transactions, and workspace management. Type definitions include class, property, interface, and relationship definitions. The distinction between the two parts of the object model is artificial. You can invoke objects of either type in your code whenever and wherever you need to in order to meet the requirements of your application.

The API is exposed COM and COM Automation interfaces, which support an open standard for application development. You can use any COM-compliant programming language to write applications that make use of these interfaces. The Meta Data Services SDK can be used to create information models that conform to the type definitions that are supported in the repository API. Once you create and install an information model, you can instantiate the objects and invoke the interfaces in your application code. The interfaces supported by the instantiated objects can have single-valued properties and collections of relationships.

# Repository Databases

A repository database is used to store physical data, such as repository type libraries, that contain type information or object instance data. These databases can also store tables that are used to map or otherwise manage relationships. In the SQL Server 2000 Meta Data Services distributed by Microsoft, this storage is provided via SQL Server, Microsoft Jet, or the SQL Server Runtime Engine.

Meta Data Services is an installed component of SQL Server 2000. A repository database already exists for your use if you have installed SQL Server 2000. The repository tables are predefined in the msdb database by default. These tables are used to store the data warehousing meta data used by SQL Server and add-on components. Every repository database includes a minimum set of standard tables. Additional tables are created as needed to store custom interface definitions. The repository engine stores properties and relationships within its tables.

At a minimum, a repository database includes standard tables that are present in every repository database. Additional tables are created for custom interface definitions. Within its tables, the repository engine stores properties and relationships. You can choose to add your custom meta data to the msdb database. If you store all of your existing meta data in one database, you can combine the existing definitions in new ways by creating relationships.

### Managing Repository Databases

The repository engine manages all transactions and determines the storage structures used in repository databases. Meta Data Services sometimes eliminates redundant data definitions to save space in the database. It may store a single copy of a property value, even though that property value describes many object versions. Meta Data Services can also store a single copy of a relationship when many different objects have that same relationship.

Multiple information models can be stored in the same repository database. You can connect to a repository database using Open Database Connectivity (ODBC) drivers. The repository API can be used to access a specific information model in the database.

### Other Database Types

If you are using Meta Data Services as an add-on component to SQL Server, the physical storage of your meta data is implemented as a SQL Server database. Meta Data Services is also distributed with other Microsoft products. If, for example, you are using Meta Data Services as an add-on to Microsoft Visual Studio, you can choose to implement the physical storage as SQL Server-based tables using Microsoft Jet or the SQL Server Runtime Engine. The SQL Server Runtime Engine is a SQL Server-compatible data engine that can be used to provide local data storage. For more information about Microsoft Jet or the SQL Server Runtime Engine, refer to the MSDN Library.

Some third-party vendors currently support using Meta Data Services on non-Microsoft database platforms. Future third-party development will most likely

18. Meta Data

expand the number of database platforms that can be integrated with Meta Data Services. This will provide even more benefits in terms of increasing the portability and reusability of the models that you create today.

## The Repository SQL Schema

The repository SQL schema is a mapping of information model elements to SQL schema elements, which consist of standard and extended schema elements. The repository engine uses the data in these tables to instantiate and manage COM objects. If you are using the Meta Data Services shipped with SQL Server 2000, the repository SQL schema tables are stored in the msdb database.

The standard schema consists of the tables that contain the core information necessary to manage all of the repository objects, relationships, and collections. The standard schema also contains the tables used by Meta Data Services to store the definition information for information models. These standard schema tables are prefixed with "**RTbl**."

The extended schema consists of the tables automatically generated by the repository engine when an information model is created or extended. An interface can only be mapped to a single table in the repository database. The table contains the instance data for persistent properties attached to the interface. A column is created in the table for each interface property. If a defined interface has no properties, then no table is created.

Data is added to the repository SQL schema when you install an information model or create one programmatically. When SQL Server is used for the repository storage, the repository engine creates stored procedures that are used to insert the data.

You can construct queries using standard SQL syntax to extract specific information from a repository database. Queries can be performed through generated views, or you can manually build a query to extract information from more than one information model at the same time. You must be familiar with the repository tables in order to construct queries to read this data directly.

Experienced model designers can tune the extended schema that is generated automatically when a model is created to optimize the performance and retrieval of this data. Even though the properties of each interface are stored in a separate SQL table, it is possible to map the properties of multiple interfaces to a single table. You also have the ability to specify the column names and data types used to store the property data for an interface. Indexes can be added to these tables, but you must not remove any indexes that are automatically created by Meta Data Services.

# The Meta Data Services SDK

The Meta Data Services SDK contains numerous resources for model designers and programmers. The SDK includes the Modeling Development Kit (MDK), modeling documentation, sample code, and add-on tools. The SDK provides essential resources for building new models, extending and customizing existing models, and programming against models. The following list describes the components that are distributed with the SDK:

- *The MDK*—Includes documentation, resource files, and programming extensions that can be used to validate information models and generate programming resources for Microsoft Visual Basic and Microsoft Visual C++.

- *The OIM*—Contains standard information models organized by subject area. Each subject area is distributed as a separate file, which has a set of ready-to-use modeling files associated with it to help you get started.

- *The Model Installer*—Is used to automate the process of adding information models to a repository database. It prepares models for installation by compiling them into Repository Distributed Model files.

- *Development Samples*—Provides sample files and documentation that explain how to use the files. These samples allow you to practice working with Meta Data Services. Working with the sample files helps you develop the skills needed to create and manage your own files.

The Meta Data Services SDK can be downloaded from Microsoft's Web site on the Meta Data Services page. Meta Data Services must already be installed to use the SDK. More information about the Meta Data Services SDK is available from the SQL Server page on Microsoft's Web site.

---

**NOTE:** *At the time of production of this book, the Meta Data Services SDK for SQL Server 2000 is not yet available. Some of the information in this chapter is subject to change based on the features and functionality provided by these tools when they are released. It appears that Visual Studio 6 may not support the enhanced functionality of some features in SQL Server 2000 including Meta Data Services. There is a warning in a document on Microsoft's Web site not to use any of the database design tools provided in Visual Studio 6 against SQL Server 2000 databases. The new version of Visual Studio should be released in the near future, and presumably the new SDK will be released around the same time.*

---

# Specifications and Limits

The Meta Data Services memory and storage limits depend on the amount of RAM and disk storage available on the server that is used to provide database storage services. You can fine-tune the performance of the repository engine

**18. Meta Data**

by following the performance hints provided under "Optimizing Repository Performance" in the Books Online.

There is no practical limit imposed on database size by SQL Server 2000. Whether you are using the msdb database or a new repository database, you can configure the database size appropriately when you need more storage. You can also configure the repository database to expand dynamically, and then you are limited only by the available disk space on your server. Because the repository engine uses available RAM to process transactions and instantiate model information, the more RAM you have available, the better the engine performs.

# XML Encoding

The SQL Server 2000 Meta Data Services uses XML encoding in native mode. This allows you to import, export, and publish repository meta data in a format that more closely matches your information model. XML encoding allows you to exchange meta data between two repository databases, between a repository database and an application, or between two applications that can interpret the XML format.

Meta Data Services encodes, decodes, and exchanges XML documents for you. Dual interfaces are used to provide this functionality, so that you can manage these operations from your applications. Meta Data Services supports the XML format defined by the Meta Data Coalition Open Information Model XML encoding format. The rules for generating XML based on an information model are defined by the Open Information Model XML encoding format. The application of these rules enables Meta Data Services to generate XML that corresponds to your information model. These rules also allow you to convert an existing XML document back into repository meta data.

The new XML encoding replaces the XML Interchange Format (XIF) that was part of pervious versions of the software, but Meta Data Services still recognizes models that are based on earlier versions of the OIM. You can still use XIF to import and export repository meta data if you need to, but XML Encoding can be used to achieve the same objective. You cannot combine both the XIF and the XML Encoded formats in the same operation. You must select either XIF or XML Encoding to perform an import or export.

XML Encoding supports an XML format that most closely corresponds to the most recent version of the OIM, but the import and export features of XML Encoding can also be used to map previous versions of OIM-based models to the newest version of the OIM. This mapping is done automatically during the import or export operation without modifying the information model. This mapping allows you to exchange data between information models that are based on different versions of the OIM.

---

**NOTE:** *The XML Encoding mapping correspondence is not possible for new UML and OIM elements that are not defined by previous versions of the OIM. If you attempt to transfer data from an information model that uses new definitions to an information model that uses an older definition, you will lose data in the conversion. The portion of the new model that cannot be converted is logged to an error file.*

---

## About Open Information Model XML Encoding

The MDC defines both the OIM and the Open Information Model XML Encoding format. Your meta data must conform to the most recent version of the OIM in order to make the best use of the XML Encoding functionality. The Open Information Model XML Encoding format used by Meta Data Services is optimized for the most recent version of the OIM. Using the version of the OIM that best matches the XML Encoding format allows for generating richer and more accurate XML.

Even if your information model is not based on the OIM, it is possible to generate valid and well-formed XML for the model. The Open Information Model XML Encoding rules are still used to determine which tag elements are used to structure your repository data even if you are not encoding an information model based on the OIM. The Meta Data Services MDK can be used to see which elements will be created for your information model. This is accomplished by using the MDK to generate an XML Document Type Definition. XML Document Type Definitions define the structure that an XML document can assume.

## Using XML in Meta Data Services

Having XML support for OIM-based meta data opens up new possibilities for publishing and sharing meta data. You can build an application that creates XML and use the repository engine to manage it. XML support also allows you to exchange meta data with other repositories and tools that use meta data. Any two applications that understand the same XML format can exchange meta data directly without the need to interact with the repository database or the repository engine.

# The Meta Data Browser

There is a new tool provided with SQL Server 2000 called the Meta Data Browser, which allows you to browse the contents of a repository database. The Meta Data Browser can be accessed from within the Enterprise Manager or as a separate stand-alone snap-in that can be added to the Microsoft Management Console (MMC). The features available in the browser are determined by whichever of these two methods is used to access it.

# Using the Meta Data Browser in SQL Server Enterprise Manager

To run the Meta Data browser from within the Enterprise Manager, select the Meta Data Services node in the tree view under the server your repository database is located on. Meta Data Services provides the meta data storage for SQL Server including any DTS and OLAP meta data. The standard repository tables needed to support storage and management of meta data are included in the msdb database.

From within the Enterprise Manager, you can use the Meta Data Browser to view meta data that you have created and stored in msdb. You can view this data from the Contents folder. You function in End User mode while you are using the Meta Data Browser from within the Enterprise Manager. This mode limits you to read-only access to the repository database. You are able to view information about any meta data that you store in the repository, but you are unable to make modifications of any kind.

The functionality restrictions placed on the Meta Data Browser when it is run from the Enterprise Manager are intended to protect the meta data that it uses. Your SQL Server installation could be corrupted by careless modification or deletion of the meta data it uses. Due to this potential risk factor, actions that could lead to problems are not supported in this mode.

## Running the Meta Data Browser Separately

Meta Data Services can also be run as a stand-alone MMC snap-in. Adding Meta Data Services as a separate snap-in allows you to work with other SQL Server repository databases and use a wider range of functionality within the tool itself. Once you have added Meta Data Services to the MMC, you can run it to register the various repository databases you need to work with. The Meta Data Browser works with any SQL Server repository database created in SQL Server 6.5, 7.0, or 2000, but you must use version 3.0 of the repository engine, which is shipped with SQL Server 2000.

# DTS and Meta Data

The DTS Designer provides features for saving package meta data and information about data lineage to Microsoft SQL Server 2000 Meta Data Services. You can store the catalog meta data for databases referenced in a package as well as accounting information about the package version used to modify a particular row of data in your data warehouse. The DTS Information Model is used for structuring and storing this information to the Meta Data Services. The DTS Browser found in the Enterprise Manager can be used to browse the meta data and data lineage information generated by the DTS Designer. You can use the DTS Browser to examine the meta data and version history of a package. This tool also provides a means to look up the specific package version that generated a particular row of data.

The DTS Information Model is based on the Transformation package of the OIM. The DTS Information Model describes the types of data accessed as well as the data transformations and how they are grouped into larger execution units. This model allows for the storage of data transformation meta data in one central location, so existing transformation can be reused when rebuilding a data warehouse. This central storage of meta data also facilitates sharing data transformation information across multiple tools. It is possible to use tools from multiple vendors to share this information during the building and maintenance of a data warehouse.

Data lineage can be tracked at the row level, the column level, or both. Before implementing this feature, you should take the time to design a plan for the information you need to track. There are several factors that should be carefully considered before putting this tracking in place:

- Determine your auditing needs.
- Determine the amount of lineage information that can be managed.
- Consider the performance impact of this tracking.
- Determine whether you need to track changes at the row level, column level, or both.

Row-level data lineage can be tracked at the package and row level of a table to provide a complete audit trail of data transformation and package execution information. Row-level data lineage reveals the source of each piece of data and the transformations applied to it. The information contained in an object associated with this type of lineage contains the package execution Globally Unique Identifiers (GUIDs), the user name and server name for package execution, and the execution time.

Column-level data lineage provides information about a package version as well as the tables and columns the package uses as a source or destination. You can check to see if a specific column is used as a source or destination for any package saved in the Meta Data Services. You can also browse packages and package versions that use the column as a source or destination.

18. Meta Data

# *Immediate Solutions*

## Adding the Meta Data Browser as a Stand-Alone MMC Snap-In

In order to do more than view the repository information in a repository database, it is necessary to install the Meta Data Browser as a stand-alone MMC snap-in. The following instructions in this example allow you to complete this task quickly and easily:

1. Select Start|Run.

2. Enter "MMC" to open this file.

3. Click on OK. This launches the MMC with no snap-ins.

4. Select the Add/Remove Snap-in from the Console menu.

5. The Add/Remove Snap-in dialog shown in Figure 18.3 appears.

6. Click on Add to display the Add Standalone Snap-in dialog.

7. Scroll down, and select Meta Data Services as illustrated in Figure 18.4.

8. Click on Add.

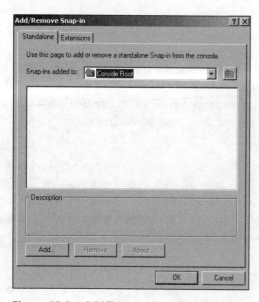

Figure 18.3    Add/Remove Snap-in dialog.

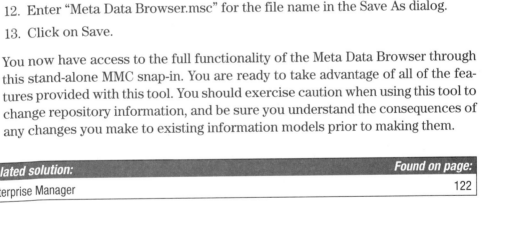

Figure 18.4   Add Standalone Snap-in dialog.

9.  Click on Close.

10. Click on OK on the Add/Remove Snap-in dialog.

11. Select Save As from the Console menu.

12. Enter "Meta Data Browser.msc" for the file name in the Save As dialog.

13. Click on Save.

You now have access to the full functionality of the Meta Data Browser through this stand-alone MMC snap-in. You are ready to take advantage of all of the features provided with this tool. You should exercise caution when using this tool to change repository information, and be sure you understand the consequences of any changes you make to existing information models prior to making them.

| Related solution: | Found on page: |
| --- | --- |
| Enterprise Manager | 122 |

# Registering a Repository Database

Before you can use a repository database in the Meta Data Browser, you must register it. This functionality is only available when using the Meta Data Browser as a stand-alone MMC snap-in. If you have not already done so, you must perform the steps outlined in the preceding immediate solution "Adding the Meta Data Browser As a Stand-Alone MMC Snap-In." To register a repository database, perform the following steps:

1. Open the stand-alone copy of the Meta Data Browser in the MMC.

18. Meta Data

2. Right-click on Meta Data Services in the tree, and select Register Database from the context menu.

3. The Database Registration Properties dialog shown in Figure 18.5 appears.

4. Enter the server name where your repository database is located.

5. Enter the authentication information required to connect to the server you chose.

6. Select the database that holds (or will hold) your repository information. The default database for repository information is the msdb database.

7. Click on Test Connection to verify that the connection and database information you have entered is valid.

8. If the settings are correct, a message box will display "Test connection succeeded." If you receive an error, go back and make any necessary corrections, and then repeat this test until the connection tests successfully.

9. Click on OK to clear the message box.

10. Select the appropriate Browse Mode. You can obtain details about each of the Browse Mode options by pressing F1 or clicking on Help at the bottom of the dialog.

11. Click on OK to complete the registration process.

12. The newly registered database appears in the tree.

| Related solution: | Found on page: |
|---|---|
| Registering a Server Using the Registered SQL Server Properties Dialog | 180 |

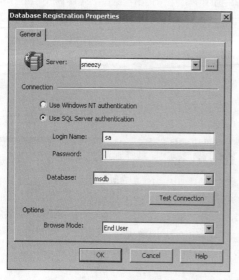

Figure 18.5   Database Registration Properties dialog.

# Chapter 19

# Advanced Techniques

**19. Advanced Techniques**

# *In Depth*

For most of this book, various elements of SQL Server management, database design, and Transact-SQL have been discussed. Now it's time to roll up your sleeves and get your hands dirty. This chapter is not for the faint of heart, and it requires a solid understanding of the basics of relational database design and SQL programming. This chapter provides you with the techniques that can move your system to the next level in database functionality.

## The Power of Transact-SQL

Most database administrators (DBAs) and developers fail to take full advantage of the power of Transact-SQL. There seems to be a mental block that prevents them from realizing that it is far more than just a query language. It is, in fact, a fairly powerful server-side programming language. The fact that it does not provide a user interface does not make it a toy. It can be used very effectively to perform the tasks for which it was designed. Transact-SQL is a backend processing, data retrieval, and data manipulation language. It has conditional branching, functions, procedures, loops, variables, and a host of built-in functions.

Taking full advantage of this language requires the ability to combine the thought processes of both a DBA and a developer. In most situations, Transact-SQL is limited only by the thought processes of the person writing the code. One of the keys to making the most of Transact-SQL (or any programming language) is to push the limits of its capability and your understanding of the language on a regular basis. In the process, you will find the true limits of the language and your own creative ability.

## Don't Reinvent the Wheel

Keep in mind that you always have access to a large code base of procedures that contain a variety of tricks and techniques that you can use in your own code. In addition to the code you have written and any code samples contained in books and magazines you may have purchased, SQL Server 2000 ships with a host of stored procedures that contain code that you can view and copy into your own procedures. It is a good idea to review this available code base to see what routines and techniques you can use to benefit your projects.

A good place to start is in Chapter 14 of this book, which provides information about many of these procedures and the types of tasks they perform. In addition, the Books Online has information about most of the stored procedures that ship with SQL Server 2000. The only tricky part can be figuring out which parts of the code to "borrow" for your particular need. This can generally be accomplished with a little experimentation. The knowledge you gain in these endeavors will help you become a more effective Transact-SQL developer and also allow you to perform tasks with ease that others consider extremely difficult (if not impossible) using this powerful language.

# List Driven Processing

There are times when you need to perform the same processing for multiple items in a list. This processing can be data retrieval, updates, or inserts. In many cases, the solution that has been used for this type of problem involves duplicating the code for each item in the list. This is generally not the most efficient approach and can create a maintenance headache when you need to change the conditions of the action being performed for each item. The **IN** operator can provide the solution to this problem. Although it may be easier to think of each item as an individual operation, the set-based logic provided by the **IN** operator generally yields better performance from SQL Server.

## Using an IN List

Look at the code shown in Listing 19.1. The code uses a group of **SELECT** statements combined with **UNION** operations to generate a list of federal tax codes missing from employee paychecks. This is an internal audit check to make sure that all employees have the required federal tax codes present on each paycheck. The tax code table contains a list of all tax codes that are configured for the company, which allows you to verify and only report missing codes for the ones that should have been generated.

**Listing 19.1   Find missing tax codes.**

```
/* Find Missing Federal Tax Records */
SELECT tc.TaxCodeID,
       pc.DocID,
       pc.EmpID,
       pc.CompID
  INTO #MissingTaxCodes
  FROM TaxCode tc (NOLOCK)
  JOIN PayChecks pc (NOLOCK) ON pc.CompID = tc.CompID
  LEFT JOIN TaxDetail td (NOLOCK) ON pc.DocID = td.DocID
                                 AND tc.TaxCodeID = td.TaxCodeID
 WHERE tc.TaxCode = 'FED_TAX'
   AND td.DocID IS NULL
```

```
/* Find Missing Employee Social Security Tax Records */
UNION ALL
SELECT tc.TaxCodeID,
       pc.DocID,
       pc.EmpID,
       pc.CompID
  FROM TaxCode tc (NOLOCK)
  JOIN PayChecks pc (NOLOCK) ON pc.CompID = tc.CompID
  LEFT JOIN TaxDetail td (NOLOCK) ON pc.DocID = td.DocID
                                 AND tc.TaxCodeID = td.TaxCodeID
  WHERE tc.TaxCode = 'EMPLOYEE_SOC'
    AND td.DocID IS NULL

/* Find Missing Employer Social Security Tax Records */
UNION ALL
SELECT tc.TaxCodeID,
       pc.DocID,
       pc.EmpID,
       pc.CompID
  FROM TaxCode tc (NOLOCK)
  JOIN PayChecks pc (NOLOCK) ON pc.CompID = tc.CompID
  LEFT JOIN TaxDetail td (NOLOCK) ON pc.DocID = td.DocID
                                 AND tc.TaxCodeID = td.TaxCodeID
  WHERE tc.TaxCode = 'EMPLOYER_SOC'
    AND td.DocID IS NULL

/* Find Missing Employee Medicare Tax Records */
UNION ALL
SELECT tc.TaxCodeID,
       pc.DocID,
       pc.EmpID,
       pc.CompID
  FROM TaxCode tc (NOLOCK)
  JOIN PayChecks pc (NOLOCK) ON pc.CompID = tc.CompID
  LEFT JOIN TaxDetail td (NOLOCK) ON pc.DocID = td.DocID
                                 AND tc.TaxCodeID = td.TaxCodeID
  WHERE tc.TaxCode = 'EMPLOYEE_MED'
    AND td.DocID IS NULL

/* Find Missing Employer Medicare Tax Records */
UNION ALL
SELECT tc.TaxCodeID,
       pc.DocID,
       pc.EmpID,
       pc.CompID
```

```
FROM TaxCode tc (NOLOCK)
JOIN PayChecks pc (NOLOCK) ON pc.CompID = tc.CompID
LEFT JOIN TaxDetail td (NOLOCK) ON pc.DocID = td.DocID
                                AND tc.TaxCodeID = td.TaxCodeID
WHERE tc.TaxCode = 'EMPLOYER_MED'
  AND td.DocID IS NULL
```

At first glance, this seems like a reasonable approach to generating the list of missing tax codes. This approach has been used for similar problems a number of times. Although this approach produces the desired results, it is not necessarily the best method to accomplish the task. Performance aside, the amount of code required to implement this solution makes it undesirable, and the fact that the **SELECT** statements are nearly identical makes matters even worse. If you need to change the selection criteria, you have to be sure to duplicate the change for each **SELECT** statement to maintain this compatibility.

By using the **IN** operator to look for all of the tax codes at once, most of this code can be eliminated. The resulting code is not only much simpler and easier to maintain, but it generally is more efficient as well. You simply use the **IN** operator to provide a list of tax codes to check for in the **TaxCode** table rather than using multiple **SELECT** statements and **UNION** operators. Listing 19.2 provides the revised SQL code that can be used to produce the same results as the previous example, but in a much more concise and efficient manner.

Listing 19.2    Find missing tax codes with an **IN** list.

```
/* Find missing tax records */
SELECT tc.TaxCodeID,
       pc.DocID,
       pc.EmpID,
       pc.CompID
  INTO #MissingTaxCodes
  FROM TaxCodes tc (NOLOCK)
  JOIN PayChecks pc (NOLOCK) ON pc.CompID = tc.CompID
  LEFT JOIN TaxDetail td (NOLOCK) ON pc.DocID = td.DocID
                                 AND tc.TaxCodeID = td.TaxCodeID
  WHERE tc.TaxCode IN ( 'FED_TAX', 'EMPLOYEE_SOC', 'EMPLOYER_SOC',
                        'EMPLOYEE_MED', 'EMPLOYER_MED' )
     AND td.DocID IS NULL
```

One catch to using the **IN** operator is the fact that the query optimizer does a much better job of correctly selecting the best query plan when you provide a list of fixed values for the **IN** operator. The use of a subquery or variables in this list can lead to poor performance in some instances. There are situations where it is beneficial to build the SQL dynamically in order to provide a hard-coded list of values rather than using a subquery. It is usually possible to convert an **IN** operation on a subquery into a join, but even a join may prove less efficient than providing a fixed list of values.

## Using a Cross-Join

Cross-joins are generally thought of as resulting from missing a join predicate in a Transact-SQL style **JOIN** statement. Although this situation is easily eliminated by the use of the ANSI Join syntax, it has still left many SQL developers with a negative opinion of cross-joins. If you are new to SQL programming, you might ask, "If cross-joins are such a bad thing, why does the ANSI Join syntax provide explicit support for them?"

The answer to this question is simple, although it may take a novice programmer several years to discover it. A cross-join can save you a great deal of work and provide some very efficient code if applied properly. Cross-joins can be applied to situations similar to the List Driven Processing example in Listing 19.2. If, for example, you did not have the **TaxCode** table and you needed to perform the check for all of the listed tax codes, you might need to make use of a cross-join. The code in Listing 19.3 shows a modified version of the **IN** list query that makes use of a cross-join. This example assumes that there is no **TaxCode** table, so the tax codes would be included in the **TaxDetail** rather than making use of a **TaxCodeID** reference to the **TaxCodes** table.

Listing 19.3   Find missing tax codes with a cross-join.

```
/* Declare table variable to hold list of tax codes */
DECLARE @v_TaxCodeList TABLE ( TaxCode   VARCHAR(15) )

/* Populate list of tax codes into table variable */
INSERT INTO @v_TaxCodeList (TaxCode) VALUES ('FED_TAX')
INSERT INTO @v_TaxCodeList (TaxCode) VALUES ('EMPLOYEE_SOC')
INSERT INTO @v_TaxCodeList (TaxCode) VALUES ('EMPLOYER_SOC')
INSERT INTO @v_TaxCodeList (TaxCode) VALUES ('EMPLOYEE_MED')
INSERT INTO @v_TaxCodeList (TaxCode) VALUES ('EMPLOYER_MED')

/* Find missing tax records */
SELECT tc.TaxCode,
       pc.DocID,
       pc.EmpID,
       pc.CompID
  INTO #MissingTaxCodes
  FROM PayChecks pc (NOLOCK)
  CROSS JOIN @v_TaxCodeList tc
```

```
LEFT JOIN TaxDetail td (NOLOCK) ON pc.DocID = td.DocID
                                AND tc.TaxCode = td.TaxCode
WHERE td.DocID IS NULL
```

Although this example focuses on a **SELECT** statement, it is important to remember that the same technique can be applied to **UPDATE** and **INSERT** operations. If you need to perform an insert into a table to produce a **TaxDetail** record for every employee for each of the federal tax codes, a similar **SELECT** to the one used in the preceding code could be used to populate the table. The cross-join can be an important tool that should not be overlooked.

# Using Derived Tables

Derived tables have been around for quite a while, but are not used on a wide scale. A derived table can be used to replace a temporary table (or table variable) in many instances. They provide the ability to use a subquery in the **FROM** or **JOIN** clause of a query. They can be especially handy in **UPDATE** operations where you need an aggregate value that would otherwise require creating a view or temporary table to obtain. A simple example of using a derived table is shown in Listing 19.4. This query returns the books in the Pubs database, giving the percentage of the book's price compared to the average price for other books of the same type. This operation normally requires creating a view or a temporary table to perform the **GROUP BY** and aggregate function to get the average price per type.

Listing 19.4    Derived table example.

```
SELECT t.Title,
       t.Type,
       COALESCE(t.Price,0),
       CONVERT(DECIMAL(7,2),
         CASE WHEN tav.AvgPrice <> 0
           THEN (COALESCE(t.price,0) / tav.AvgPrice) * 100
           ELSE 0 END) as "% of Average"
  FROM pubs..titles t (NOLOCK)
  JOIN (SELECT AVG(COALESCE(ti.Price,0)) as AvgPrice,
               ti.Type
          FROM pubs..titles ti (NOLOCK)
          GROUP BY ti. Type) tav ON t.Type = tav.Type
```

The key to using a derived table is that you *must* provide an alias for the table name in the **FROM** or **JOIN** clause because the subquery does not have a name by default. Once you have used derived tables a couple of times, you will find them to be an extremely simple technique that can be applied in a wide variety of situations that would otherwise need a temporary table.

# Getting More from WHILE Loops

**WHILE** loops are used in most cursor implementations to loop through each row in the cursor and perform the desired processing. Unfortunately, this is where their use stops in many environments. SQL developers (especially those that do not have a programming background) fail to see that the **WHILE** loop is an extremely helpful tool for other uses.

In many cases, the work performed in a cursor can actually be replaced by simply using a **WHILE** loop instead. The **WHILE** loop can retrieve one row at a time using a primary or unique key to advance to the next record. You may want to experiment with this technique because in some cases, it will be faster and produce less locking contention on the data being manipulated. The code in Listing 19.5 shows an example of using a cursor to update table statistics, and then shows an alternate implementation that uses a **WHILE** loop to perform the same task.

**Listing 19.5   Cursor replaced by WHILE loop.**

```
/*************************/
/* Cursor Implementation */
/*************************/


/* Declare a cursor to get a list of tables */
DECLARE c_TableList CURSOR FAST_FORWARD FOR
  SELECT so.Name
    FROM sysobjects so (NOLOCK)
    WHERE so.Name LIKE 'tbl_Emp%'
    ORDER BY so.Name

/* Declare a variable to hold the table names */
DECLARE @v_TblName VARCHAR(40)

/* Open the cursor */
OPEN c_TableList

/* Get the first table name */
FETCH NEXT FROM c_TableList INTO @v_TblName

/* Loop through the tables */
WHILE (@@fetch_status <> -1)
  BEGIN
  /* Skip deleted rows if needed */
  IF (@@fetch_status <> -2)
    BEGIN
    /* Display the operation that is being performed */
    PRINT 'UPDATE STATISTICS ' + @v_TblName
```

```
    /* Update the statistics for each table */
    EXEC('UPDATE STATISTICS ' + @v_TblName)
    END

  /* Get the next table name from the cursor */
  FETCH NEXT FROM c_TableList INTO @v_TblName
  END

/* Close and deallocate the cursor */
CLOSE c_TableList
DEALLOCATE c_TableList
GO


/****************************/
/* WHILE Loop Implementation */
/****************************/

/* Declare variables */
DECLARE @v_TblName VARCHAR(40),
        @v_OldTblName VARCHAR(40)

/* Get first table name */
SELECT TOP 1 @v_TblName = so.Name
  FROM sysobjects so (NOLOCK)
  WHERE so.Name LIKE 'tbl_Emp%'
  ORDER BY so.Name

WHILE (@v_TblName <> COALESCE(@v_OldTblName,''))
  BEGIN
  /* Save previous value of table name */
  SELECT @v_OldTblName = @v_TblName

  /* Display the operation that is being performed */
  PRINT 'UPDATE STATISTICS ' + @v_TblName

  /* Update the statistics for each table */
  EXEC('UPDATE STATISTICS ' + @v_TblName)

  /* Get next table name */
  SELECT TOP 1 @v_TblName = so.Name
    FROM sysobjects so (NOLOCK)
    WHERE so.Name LIKE 'tbl_Emp%' and so.name > @v_OldTblName
    ORDER BY so.Name
  END
```

**WHILE** Loops can also be used in random data generation, calculations, timing loops, to wait for another task to complete, and so on. Any looping task that needs to be done programmatically can be performed using a **WHILE** loop. This next example would not normally be done with SQL code, but it will stretch your perception of what can be accomplished with **WHILE** loops and the Transact-SQL programming language in general. Listing 19.6 shows a routine used to calculate compound interest and provides a detailed listing of each compounding period.

**Listing 19.6   Calculating compound interest.**

```
/* Turn off row count display */
SET NOCOUNT ON

/* Declare needed variables */
DECLARE @v_InitialInvestment MONEY,
        @v_NumberOfYears INTEGER,
        @v_PeriodsPerYear INTEGER,
        @v_AnnualInterestRate DECIMAL(16,6),
        @v_PeriodicRate DECIMAL(16,6),
        @v_PeriodicInterest MONEY,
        @v_AccumulatedInterest MONEY,
        @v_CurrentBalance MONEY,
        @v_i INTEGER,
        @v_Rpt VARCHAR(80)

/* Set initial values (these could be passed into an SP) */
SELECT @v_InitialInvestment = 10000,
       @v_NumberOfYears = 30,
       @v_PeriodsPerYear = 12,
       @v_AnnualInterestRate = 7.5

/* Initialize additional values needed for calculation and loop counter */
SELECT @v_AccumulatedInterest = 0,
       @v_CurrentBalance = @v_InitialInvestment,
       @v_PeriodicRate = (@v_AnnualInterestRate / 100) / @v_PeriodsPerYear,
       @v_i = 1

/* Loop for the specified number of periods */
WHILE @v_i <= (@v_NumberOfYears * @v_PeriodsPerYear)
  BEGIN
  /* Calculate interest for the current period */
  SET @v_PeriodicInterest = @v_CurrentBalance * @v_PeriodicRate

  /* Keep track of accumulated interest */
  SET @v_AccumulatedInterest = @v_AccumulatedInterest + @v_PeriodicInterest
```

```
/* Compute the current balance */
SET @v_CurrentBalance = @v_CurrentBalance + @v_PeriodicInterest

/* Output results of current period calculations */
SELECT CONVERT(INTEGER, ((@v_i -1) / 12)) + 1 AS "Year",
       ((@v_i - 1) % 12) + 1 AS "Month",
       @v_PeriodicInterest AS "Periodic Interest",
       @v_AccumulatedInterest AS "Accumulated Interest",
       @v_CurrentBalance AS "Current Balance"

/* Increment loop counter */
SET @v_i = @v_i + 1
END
```

# Padding and Justifying Data

There are a number of situations where it is necessary or desirable to control the padding of elements of your data. If all you need is trailing spaces, then converting the data to a **CHAR** data type of the appropriate length will provide the desired results. If you want to pad with a character other than a space or you need to right justify the data, the task is a bit more complicated. Using the **REPLICATE( )** function in conjunction with the **DATALENGTH( )** function will do the trick with a minimum of code. Listing 19.7 provides two examples of padding a randomly generated number to the required number of digits. The first example uses **IF** statements to establish the correct padding, and the second example accomplishes the same task in a more concise manner using the **REPLICATE( )** and **DATALENGTH( )** functions. This example would be ideal for generating test ZIP codes because they must be five digits long.

**Listing 19.7    Padding a random number to five digits.**

```
/****************/
/* Pad using IF */
/****************/

/* Delcare variables */
DECLARE @v_Zip      INTEGER,
        @v_ZipCode  CHAR(5)

/* Generate Random Number up to 5 digits long */
SELECT @v_Zip = CONVERT(INT, (RAND() * 99999) + 1)

/* Check for 1 digit zip and pad accordingly */
IF (@v_Zip < 10)
  SELECT @v_ZipCode = '0000' + CONVERT(VARCHAR, @v_Zip)
```

```
/* Check for 2 digit zip and pad accordingly */
IF (@v_Zip > 9) AND (@v_Zip < 100)
  SELECT @v_ZipCode = '000' + CONVERT(VARCHAR, @v_Zip)

/* Check for 3 digit zip and pad accordingly */
IF (@v_Zip > 99) AND (@v_Zip < 1000)
  SELECT @v_ZipCode = '00' + CONVERT(VARCHAR, @v_Zip)

/* Check for 4 digit zip and pad accordingly */
IF (@v_Zip > 999) AND (@v_Zip < 10000)
  SELECT @v_ZipCode = '0' + CONVERT(VARCHAR, @v_Zip)

/* Check for 5 digit zip and pad accordingly */
IF (@v_Zip > 9999)
  SELECT @v_ZipCode = CONVERT(VARCHAR, @v_Zip)

/* Display our new zip code */
PRINT @v_ZipCode
GO


/***********************************/
/* Pad using REPLICATE and DATALENGTH */
/***********************************/

/* Declare variables */
DECLARE @v_Zip      VARCHAR(5),
        @v_ZipCode  CHAR(5)

/* Generate Random Number up to 5 digits long */
SELECT @v_Zip = CONVERT(VARCHAR, CONVERT(INT, (RAND() * 99999) + 1))

/* Pad zip code to 5 digits */
SELECT @v_ZipCode = REPLICATE('0', 5 - DATALENGTH(@v_Zip)) + @v_Zip

/* Display our new zip code */
PRINT @v_ZipCode
```

# Formatting Output

Output formatting is another technique that can be beneficial in certain instances. It is possible to use this technique to provide a client application with a result set that does not resemble the way that information is actually stored in the tables. It can be useful for providing output that would otherwise require either additional data storage in the database or additional business logic in every application that accesses the data.

# Building a Report String

In order to clean up the output of the query example that calculates compound interest using a **WHILE** loop, you need to build a report string for each iteration through the loop. This allows you to print headings once at the top, and then provide the output lines underneath instead of having the headings inserted for each line of the report. This makes the report smaller and easier to read. Listing 19.8 provides the compound interest example rewritten to format the output by building a string of the proper width for each column and then combining the strings for each column into a report line. The headings are actually copied in from the output of the previous version and cleaned up to suit the output that is desired. Note the use of the **REPLICATE( )** function to right justify the **Year** and **Month** column values. The remaining columns are simply converted to a **CHAR** field of the appropriate length.

**Listing 19.8   Compound interest with output formatting.**

```
/* Listing 19.8 - Compound Interest With Output Formatting */
/* Turn off row count display */
SET NOCOUNT ON

/* Declare needed variables */
DECLARE @v_InitialInvestment MONEY,
        @v_NumberOfYears INTEGER,
        @v_PeriodsPerYear INTEGER,
        @v_AnnualInterestRate DECIMAL(16,6),
        @v_PeriodicRate DECIMAL(16,6),
        @v_PeriodicInterest MONEY,
        @v_AccumulatedInterest MONEY,
        @v_CurrentBalance MONEY,
        @v_i INTEGER,
        @v_Yr VARCHAR(4),
        @v_Mo VARCHAR(5),
        @v_Rpt VARCHAR(80)

/* Set initial values (these could be passed into an SP) */
SELECT @v_InitialInvestment = 10000,
       @v_NumberOfYears = 30,
       @v_PeriodsPerYear = 12,
       @v_AnnualInterestRate = 7.5

/* Initialize additional values needed for calculation and loop counter*/
SELECT @v_AccumulatedInterest = 0,
       @v_CurrentBalance = @v_InitialInvestment,
       @v_PeriodicRate = (@v_AnnualInterestRate / 100) / @v_PeriodsPerYear,
       @v_i = 1
```

```
/* Print column headings */
PRINT 'Year Month Current Interest Total Interest Balance'
PRINT '---- ----   ---------------- -------------- ---------------'

/* Loop for the specified number of periods */
WHILE @v_i <= (@v_NumberOfYears * @v_PeriodsPerYear)
  BEGIN
  /* Calculate interest for the current period */
  SET @v_PeriodicInterest = @v_CurrentBalance * @v_PeriodicRate

  /* Keep track of accumulated interest */
  SET @v_AccumulatedInterest = @v_AccumulatedInterest + @v_PeriodicInterest

  /* Compute the current balance */
  SET @v_CurrentBalance = @v_CurrentBalance + @v_PeriodicInterest

  /* Right justify Year and Month counters for display purposes */
  SET @v_Yr = CONVERT(VARCHAR(4), CONVERT(INTEGER, ((@v_i -1) / 12)) + 1)
  SET @v_Mo = CONVERT(VARCHAR(5), ((@v_i - 1) % 12) + 1)

  /* Build report line */
  SELECT @v_Rpt = REPLICATE(' ', 4 - DATALENGTH(@v_Yr)) + @v_Yr + ' ' +
                  REPLICATE(' ', 5 - DATALENGTH(@v_Mo)) + @v_Mo + ' ' +
                  CONVERT(CHAR(16),@v_PeriodicInterest) + ' ' +
                  CONVERT(CHAR(14),@v_AccumulatedInterest) + ' ' +
                  CONVERT(CHAR(15),@v_CurrentBalance)

  /* Print report line */
  PRINT @v_Rpt

  /* Increment loop counter */
  SET @v_i = @v_i + 1
  END
```

## Using a CASE Statement to Translate Code Values

The **CASE** statement can be handy for providing code translations prior to returning the query output. The code shown in Listing 19.9 was taken from Listing
13.16 (Chapter 13 of this book). The **CASE** statements are used to translate the
numeric code values retrieved from the **sp_describe_cursor_tables** stored procedure into a more useful description of the value. This reporting saves time by
eliminating the need to look in the Books Online to determine the meaning of the
code values for each column. The **CASE** statement evaluating the **@Hints** variable uses a bitwise operator to check for each possible bit flag and produces the
correct output string for the flag that is turned on.

There are two syntax variations used for the **CASE** statements in this example. The first uses an expression for each **WHEN** clause to check each bit mask position to see if it is turned on. The second specifies the variable after the **CASE** keyword, and then specifies a value for the variable after each **WHEN** clause. The fact that both of these syntax forms can be used for the **CASE** statement makes it extremely flexible and easy to use.

Listing 19.9    Translating encoded values using **CASE**.

```
PRINT CONVERT(CHAR(30), COALESCE(@v_Owner, '')) + ' ' +
      CONVERT(CHAR(30), COALESCE(@v_TableName, '')) + ' ' +
      /* Create list of applied hints */
      CONVERT(CHAR(70),
          CASE WHEN (@v_Hints &    1) =    1 THEN 'ROWLOCK ' END +
          CASE WHEN (@v_Hints &    4) =    4 THEN 'PAGLOCK ' END +
          CASE WHEN (@v_Hints &    8) =    8 THEN 'TABLOCK ' END +
          CASE WHEN (@v_Hints &   16) =   16 THEN 'TABLOCKX ' END +
          CASE WHEN (@v_Hints &   32) =   32 THEN 'UPDLOCK ' END +
          CASE WHEN (@v_Hints &   64) =   64 THEN 'NOLOCK ' END +
          CASE WHEN (@v_Hints &  128) =  128 THEN 'FASTFIRSTROW ' END +
          CASE WHEN (@v_Hints & 4096) = 4096 THEN 'HOLDLOCK ' END) +
      ' ' +
      /* Convert Lock type to readable form */
      CASE @v_LockType WHEN 0 THEN 'None       '
                       WHEN 1 THEN 'Shared     '
                       WHEN 3 THEN 'Update     '
                       ELSE 'UNKNOWN    ' END + ' ' +
      CONVERT(CHAR(30), COALESCE(@v_ServerName, '')) + ' ' +
      CONVERT(CHAR(30), COALESCE(@v_DBName, ''))
```

# Using the HAVING Clause

The **HAVING** clause can provide a simple way of performing tasks that involve aggregates that would otherwise be difficult. The most common usage of this clause is to locate duplicates in a list. Listing 19.10 provides the syntax for using the **HAVING** clause to locate authors' first names where there is more than one occurrence of the first name in the **Authors** table. This is an extremely simple example to introduce you to the use of the **HAVING** clause.

Listing 19.10    Find duplicate author first names.

```
SELECT au_Fname,
       COUNT(*)
  FROM pubs..authors (NOLOCK)
  GROUP BY au_Fname
  HAVING COUNT(*) > 1
```

Now let's look at a slightly more involved problem: You need to move records to an archive from a payroll table containing employee paycheck records. You can only perform this process for a pay group if all checks in the pay group meet certain criteria. You need to generate a list of the pay groups where all checks have either been printed or are "post only," which means they do not need to be printed. Listing 19.11 provides the code to locate this list using a **NOT IN** with a subquery in the **WHERE** clause. This does work, but it causes a great deal of overhead in the processing. After this example, the same condition being checked using a **HAVING** clause is shown. The **HAVING** example not only contains slightly shorter code, but also produces a more efficient query plan as well.

### Listing 19.11    Locate pay groups to archive.

```
/* Find checks that are OK to archive using NOT IN */
SELECT pc.PayGroup_ID,
       MAX(pg.PayGroupDescription),
       MAX(PayDate) AS PayDate,
       MAX(PeriodEndDate) AS PeriodEndDate
  FROM PayChecks pc (NOLOCK)
  JOIN PayGroups pg (NOLOCK) ON pc.PayGroup_ID = pg.PayGroup_ID
  WHERE pc.PayGroup_ID NOT IN
       (SELECT DISTINCT PayGroup_ID
          FROM PayChecks (NOLOCK)
          WHERE Printed = 'N'
            AND PostOnly = 'N')
  GROUP BY PayGroup_ID


/* Find checks that are OK to archive using CASE and HAVING */
SELECT pc.PayGroup_ID,
       MAX(pg.PayGroupDescription),
       MAX(PayDate) AS PayDate,
       MAX(PeriodEndDate) AS PeriodEndDate
  FROM PayChecks pc (NOLOCK)
  JOIN PayGroups pg (NOLOCK) ON pc.PayGroup_ID = pg.PayGroup_ID
  GROUP BY PayGroup_ID
  HAVING MIN(CASE WHEN Printed='N' AND PostOnly='N'
                  THEN 'N' ELSE 'Y' END) = 'Y'
```

# Generating Test Data

Creating test data is a task common to most environments. It can be tedious and time-consuming to produce test data, especially if you need a large amount of it. The database population script used in Chapter 8 to populate the Address database makes use of pseudorandom data generation, which creates a large volume of address data without the need to individually specify each address. This technique can be modified for use in almost any environment. Listing 19.12 shows the code used to generate the random addresses. In this case, a specific number of city, state, and ZIP code records are added manually and then attached to the randomly generated address records. The number of address records generated by this code is controlled by the value assigned to the **@v_Max** variable. Technically, this technique does not generate random addresses, but it produces the appearance of random addresses by using the modulo operator (%) to generate data for certain columns only at intervals.

**Listing 19.12  Generating address information.**

```
DECLARE @v_i      INTEGER, -- Loop counter
        @v_n      INTEGER, -- House number
        @v_Max    INTEGER, -- Number of addresses to populate
        @v_Line1  VARCHAR(50),
        @v_Line2  VARCHAR(50),
        @v_Street VARCHAR(30),
        @v_CityID INTEGER,
        @v_StateID INTEGER,
        @v_ZipID  INTEGER,
        @v_Zip4   CHAR(4),
        @v_Str    VARCHAR(255)

SELECT @v_i       = 1,
       @v_n       = 100,
       @v_Max     = 100000, -- Target number of addresses
       @v_Street  = ' Main St.',
       @v_CityID  = 1, -- Pre-populated City
       @v_StateID = 1, -- Pre-populated State
       @v_ZipID   = 2  -- Pre-populated Zip

PRINT 'Adding new addresses...'

WHILE (@v_i <= @v_Max)
  BEGIN
  IF (@v_i % (@v_Max/10)) = 0
    BEGIN
    SELECT @v_Str = CONVERT(VARCHAR, @v_i) + '...'
    PRINT @v_Str
    END
/* Build the Record */
  SELECT @v_Line1 = CONVERT(VARCHAR(10), @v_n) + @v_Street,
         @v_Line2 = CASE
                      WHEN (@v_i % 3) = 0 THEN
                        'Apt. ' + CONVERT(VARCHAR(10),@v_i)
```

```
                                    ELSE
                                    NULL
                                    END,
              @v_Zip4  = CASE
                            WHEN (@v_i % 7) = 0 THEN
                            REPLICATE('0',(4 - DATALENGTH(CONVERT(VARCHAR, @v_n))))
       +
                                CONVERT(VARCHAR, @v_n)
                            ELSE
                                NULL
                            END

/* Add the Record   */
  INSERT INTO tbl_Address
  VALUES (
    @v_Line1,
    @v_Line2,
    @v_Zip4,
    @v_CityID,
    @v_ZipID)
/* Increment Counters */
  SELECT @v_i = @v_i + 1,
         @v_n = @v_n + 1


/* Assign Strings */
/* Cities         */
  SELECT @v_CityID =
    CASE
      WHEN (@v_i % 7) = 0 THEN 2
      WHEN (@v_i % 5) = 0 THEN 3
      WHEN (@v_i % 3) = 0 THEN 4
      WHEN (@v_i % 2) = 0 THEN 5
      ELSE 1
      END
/* Zip Code       */
  SELECT @v_ZipID =
    CASE @v_CityID
      WHEN 1 THEN 2
      WHEN 2 THEN 1
      WHEN 3 THEN 3
      WHEN 4 THEN 4
      WHEN 5 THEN 5
      END
/* Streets        */
  SELECT @v_Street =
```

```
    CASE
      WHEN (@v_i % 7) = 0 THEN ' Main St.'
      WHEN (@v_i % 5) = 0 THEN ' Atlantic Blvd.'
      WHEN (@v_i % 3) = 0 THEN ' Arvida Pkwy.'
      WHEN (@v_i % 2) = 0 THEN ' West 4th.'
      ELSE ' Bonaventure'
      END
END -- While
```

In order to generate actual random data, the **RAND( )** function can be used to generate a random number rather than using the modulo technique to alter the data based on certain intervals. Let's assume that you need to generate a list of random Social Security numbers to use in an application. The code provided in Listing 19.13 makes use of the **RAND( )** function to generate these numbers. The code additionally employs a table variable to make sure that you do not get duplicates in your list, which would cause the application you are generating the data for to fail. Each Social Security number is built in three sections, which are then put together with dashes between them. The main reason for building the sections independently is that it provides less chance for a large number of leading zeroes in the Social Security number. The **REPLICATE( )** function is used to provide any needed leading zeroes for each section when they are combined. Notice that the loop counter is incremented only for nonduplicate values. If you increment the counter outside the **IF**, you end up short by the number of duplicates generated. This code was used to generate 10,000 unique Social Security numbers in about 30 seconds.

### Listing 19.13   Generating random Social Security numbers.

```
/* Turn off row count display */
SET NOCOUNT ON

/* Declare table variable to check for duplicates */
DECLARE @v_SSNList TABLE (SSN CHAR(11))

/* Declare needed variables */
DECLARE @v_SSN3     VARCHAR(3),
        @v_SSN2     VARCHAR(2),
        @v_SSN4     VARCHAR(4),
        @v_SSN      CHAR(11),
        @v_SSNItm   INTEGER,
        @v_SSNMax   INTEGER

/* Set number to generate */
SELECT @v_SSNMax = 100
```

```
/* Initialize the loop counter */
Select @v_SSNItm=0

/* Loop until we have generated the specified number */
While @v_SSNItm < @v_SSNMax
  begin
  /* Generate the SSN in pieces */
  SELECT @v_SSN3 = CONVERT(VARCHAR(3), CONVERT(INT,(RAND() * 999) + 1))
  SELECT @v_SSN2 = CONVERT(VARCHAR(2), CONVERT(INT,(RAND() * 99) + 1))
  SELECT @v_SSN4 = CONVERT(VARCHAR(4), CONVERT(INT,(RAND() * 9999) + 1))

  /* Build the completed SSN including dashes */
  SELECT @v_SSN = REPLICATE('0',(3 - DATALENGTH(@v_SSN3))) + @v_SSN3 +
                  '-' +
                  REPLICATE('0',(2 - DATALENGTH(@v_SSN2))) + @v_SSN2 +
                  '-' +
                  REPLICATE('0',(4 - DATALENGTH(@v_SSN2))) + @v_SSN4

  /* Check for duplicates */
  IF NOT EXISTS (SELECT *
                    FROM @v_SSNList
                    WHERE SSN = @v_SSN)
    BEGIN
    /* Display the new SSN */
    PRINT @v_SSN

    /* Add the new SSN to the table variable */
    INSERT INTO @v_SSNList (SSN) VALUES(@v_SSN)

    /* Increment the loop counter */
    Select @v_SSNItm = @v_SSNItm + 1
    END
END
```

# Finding Orphaned Records

In databases where relationships exist that are not enforced by referential integrity constraints, it is possible to have orphaned records. This can also happen when the relationships exist across database boundaries, which can make the integrity more difficult to enforce. In these situations, it is sometimes necessary to perform periodic checks on the data to locate orphaned records.

If your database does not have referential integrity constraints, but you are planning to add them, it is a good idea to locate and deal with any orphaned records prior to attempting to implement these constraints. If you know the relationships that exist in the data, this task is not particularly difficult to accomplish.

The same technique used to locate orphaned records can be used to locate master records that may no longer be needed. Depending on your business logic, a parent record that no longer has child records associated with it may be rendered obsolete. In this case, the same logic that is used to locate orphaned child records can be applied to locate childless master records.

The code in Listing 19.14 shows how to locate employee-address cross-reference records that do not point to a valid address record. In your database design, records meeting this condition can be considered to be orphans. This situation cannot be covered by the standard referential integrity constraints because the tables are in different databases. The logic in this query could be reversed to find addresses that are not cross-referenced to an employee by swapping the position of the tables in the join.

Once these records are located, you have to determine whether they need to be corrected or deleted in order to reinstate your data integrity. Depending on the required action, the data may have to be manipulated manually to make the required corrections. Your business logic and environmental needs will determine the proper way to correct the data.

**Listing 19.14  Find orphaned employee-address cross-reference records.**

```
SELECT ea.*
  FROM employee..tbl_EmployeeAddressXref ea (NOLOCK)
  LEFT JOIN address..tbl_Address a (NOLOCK)
       ON ea.Address_ID = a.Address_ID
 WHERE a.Address_ID IS NULL
```

# Using Binary Sort Order

Most installations of SQL Server use the default sort order (Collation), which is generally case insensitive. Although this is desirable in the majority of installations and provides the benefit of case-insensitive string matching and sorting, it comes at a cost. There is a great deal of overhead associated with making case-insensitive comparisons. This can be especially burdensome if you use **CHAR** or **VARCHAR** fields in indexes. In order to match character fields in a search or join condition, SQL Server must first perform a conversion to ensure matched cases on both sides of the comparison, and then perform the actual comparison. This overhead must be incurred even if the two values being compared already use the same case (or no case if the values are numeric) because SQL Server has no way of knowing this without examining the data.

One way to improve the performance of your database is to always perform **JOIN** operations on binary index values. This eliminates the conversion overhead in the index matching used to perform the join. A good database model should provide integer or other binary values as the key values used to relate tables to one another.

Even if all your joins are performed on binary index values, you will most likely have other character-based index columns for searching the database. You will want indexes to speed searching for names, ZIP codes (these don't even need a case conversion, but SQL Server doesn't know any better unless you use a numeric data type), departments, and so on. The performance of these searches is impacted by the case-insensitive comparisons used to locate the row(s) you need.

The alternative is to use a binary (case-insensitive) sort order. This yields approximately 20 to 30 percent performance gains in most databases, but it also comes at a cost. If you specify a binary sort order, all sorting and searching becomes case sensitive. This is manageable if you enforce the case of your character data properly in all applications that access your data. In installations where performance is a premium consideration, it may be worth the pain and trouble to enforce case guidelines and live with the necessity of case matching for data searches.

---

**NOTE:** The use of binary sort order can make some searches difficult. This sort order will not work in all situations and should be considered carefully before implementing it. Keep in mind that there is always a workaround for the exception cases, such as using the **UPPER( )** or **LOWER( )** functions to simplify searching in cases where case guidelines cannot be strictly enforced.

---

# Debugging SQL Code

The more complex your SQL code becomes, the more difficult it is to debug effectively. One technique that you may want to use in development is to build the code in small pieces and use **PRINT** statements and **SELECT** statements to output data at various points to make sure the code is behaving the way you expect it to. You can also write status records to a log table at various points in a procedure to allow you to determine where a process is failing. This method can also be used to log procedure performance if you add a time component to each step written to the table.

The Profiler allows you to trace user-defined events, which can also help you keep track of the flow of a complex procedure. This can be especially useful if you are trying to debug nested stored procedures that are several levels deep. The new Profiler also indicates the success or failure of each statement to allow you to more easily determine where a long process is breaking down.

Debugging dynamic SQL can be very challenging. You may find it easier to print the generated code rather than executing it, and then pull the resulting code into another query window to execute it. This allows you to use the Query Analyzer to find any syntax problems in the generated code. Incorrect quote and parenthesis nesting are two areas where this technique can really make it easier to find the problem in your generated code.

# Immediate Solutions

## Building and Executing Dynamic SQL

There are times when you need to perform a task in which portions of the information will not be available when you write your SQL code. This leads many developers to move the task into client code rather than using a stored procedure or other server-based feature to perform the task. The technique of building and executing dynamic SQL code in your scripts and procedures allows you to keep the business logic for these tasks on the server where it is easier to change and maintain.

This example presents a method for using a stored procedure in one database to create a stored procedure in another database. Because the table name is not known prior to the procedure being executed, a table is created in another procedure using the technique of executing dynamic SQL, which presents a problem. You need to check to see if the table has any rows in it, but the **@@rowcount** variable will not reliably return a usable value for the number of rows that were added to the table by using the **EXEC** statement to execute dynamic SQL. To accomplish this, you can create a temporary stored procedure in the worktable and use it to return the row count to your procedure. Because this table name is not known until it is created by the other procedure, it will have to be supplied to your procedure as a passed parameter.

There are a couple of catches to this process. One is the fact that you cannot directly create a stored procedure in a database other than the current database, and you cannot change database context within a stored procedure. The other interesting gotcha is that the **CREATE PROCEDURE** statement must be the first line in the batch, and the **EXEC** statement, which is used to execute dynamic SQL, does not support using the **GO** keyword to execute multiple batches at the same time. With these additional issues in mind, let's put together a stored procedure that will do what you need:

1. Start by generating the **CREATE PROCEDURE** code for a stored procedure with two parameters. The first parameter is the table name being passed in, and the second is an **OUTPUT** parameter to return the record count from the table.

2. You first need to declare a couple of variables inside the procedure: one to hold the name of the new stored procedure and one to hold dynamic SQL.

3. Next, build a dynamic SQL string. The string needs to contain an **EXEC** statement that executes an embedded dynamic string to create the new stored procedure. The embedded **EXEC** statement allows you to get around the batch limitations mentioned earlier.

4. Now you can use the **EXEC** statement to execute a **USE** command to switch database context, and then execute your dynamic string that contains an **EXEC** command to create the procedure. These two items can be combined in a single **EXEC** statement to create the procedure in an alternate database.

5. Once the new stored procedure has been created, you can build a string that contains the new procedure name qualified with the database in which it was created.

6. Using the variable that has the procedure name, you can once again use the **EXEC** statement to execute the procedure and store the return value in the output parameter you created to hold the record count.

Listing 19.15 provides the complete code for the **usp_Rows_Exist** procedure that returns the record count from a table in your Work database. Although you may never need this particular stored procedure in your environment, you should study the techniques used in this listing to determine if any of them might be useful for projects you are working on.

### Listing 19.15    usp_Rows_Exist.

```
/* Drop the procedure if it already exists */
if exists (select *
           from sysobjects
           where id = object_id('dbo.usp_Rows_Exist'))
  drop procedure dbo.usp_Rows_Exist
GO

CREATE PROCEDURE usp_Rows_Exist @p_TableName VARCHAR(60),
                                @p_RecCount INTEGER OUTPUT

AS
BEGIN
/* Declare needed variables */
DECLARE @v_NewSPName VARCHAR(90),
        @v_SubExecStatement VARCHAR(255)

/* Build create procedure nested dynamic SQL */
SELECT @v_SubExecStatement =
        '    EXEC('' Create Procedure dbo.tmpSp' + @p_TableName +
        '      AS ' +
        ' DECLARE @v_HowMany INTEGER ' +
        '  SELECT @v_HowMany=COUNT(*) FROM ' + @p_TableName +
        '  RETURN @v_HowMany '') '
```

```
/* Use exec to switch database context and create the procedure */
EXEC( 'USE WORK  ' + @v_SubExecStatement )

/* Build fully-qualified procedure name */
SELECT @v_NewSPName = 'WORK.DBO.tmpSp' + @p_TableName

/* Exec the procedure to get the row count */
EXEC @p_RecCount = @v_NewSPName

/* Build nested dynamic SQL to get rid of the temp SP */
SELECT @v_SubExecStatement =
       '    EXEC('' DROP PROCEDURE dbo.tmpSp' + @p_TableName + ''') '

/* Use exec to switch database context and drop the procedure */
EXEC( 'USE WORK  ' + @v_SubExecStatement )
END
```

| Related solution: | Found on page: |
|---|---|
| Identifying Autogenerated Statistics on All User Tables | 604 |

# Importing Data from a Denormalized Table to a Normalized Structure

In this example, you look at the need to take data from a denormalized structure, like the **tbl_AddressDN** table, and convert it to a normalized structure. Let's assume that you receive address information from an outside source (like a mailing list) that is provided in a denormalized format. You need to take this information and import it into your normalized address structure. For this purpose, you have created the **tbl_Address_DN** table that was used to hold the denormalized address information imported using **BCP IN** or **BULK INSERT**. It requires a bit of manipulation to make the denormalized address information properly match the normalized structure you created in the Address database. Because this is a situation that you know will come up regularly when you receive new addresses from the list provider, follow these steps to generate a stored procedure to transfer the information between the **tbl_AddressDN** table and the normalized structure:

1. Declare the variables you need for the process. You need a variable for each column in the **tbl_AddressDN** table and one for each of the ID fields that will be used in the various inserts.

2. Next, declare a cursor to loop through the **tbl_AddressDN** table one row at a time to allow you to process the information into the normalized structure.

3. You must initialize the ID variables to **NULL** at the beginning of each loop iteration, because the queries used to retrieve the IDs will not change the existing value of the ID variable if an existing record is not found.

4. For each row, you need to first look up the State ID because it is part of both the City and ZIP Code records. If the state does not exist in the table, you need to add it by inserting the new state into the **tbl_State** table. The **@@IDENTITY** system variable provides you with the State ID for your newly inserted record.

5. Next, look up the City ID, which will be part of the address record. If the city does not exist in the table, you need to add it by inserting the new city into the **tbl_City** table. The **@@IDENTITY** system variable provides you with the City ID for your newly inserted record.

6. Next, look up the Zip ID, which will also be part of the address record. If the ZIP code does not exist in the table, you need to add it by inserting the new ZIP code into the **tbl_ZipCode** table. The **@@IDENTITY** system variable provides you with the Zip ID for your newly inserted record.

7. Once you have the necessary IDs for the address record, you can check to see if the address record already exists. If the address is not found in the table, you can insert a new record.

8. Steps 3 through 7 are repeated to add each address in the table. The complete source code for your stored procedure is provided in Listing 19.16.

Listing 19.16   **usp_add_addresses**.

```
/* Turn off record count display */
SET NOCOUNT ON

/* Set context to the master database */
USE MASTER
GO

/* Drop the procedure if it already exists */
IF EXISTS (SELECT name
            FROM master..sysobjects (NOLOCK)
           WHERE name = 'usp_add_addresses'
             AND type = 'p')
  BEGIN
  DROP PROC usp_add_addresses
```

```
      END
   GO


   CREATE PROC usp_add_addresses
   AS
   /* DECLARE Variables */
   DECLARE @v_state      CHAR(2),
           @v_stateid    TINYINT,
           @v_zip5       CHAR(5),
           @v_zip4       CHAR(4),
           @v_zipid      TINYINT,
           @v_city       VARCHAR(50),
           @v_cityid     TINYINT,
           @v_line1      VARCHAR(30),
           @v_line2      VARCHAR(30),
           @v_addressid TINYINT


   /* DECLARE Cursor */
   DECLARE c_Address CURSOR FAST_FORWARD FOR
     SELECT line1,
            line2,
            city,
            state,
            zip5,
            zip4
       FROM address.dbo.tbl_AddressDN (NOLOCK)


   /* Open address cursor */
   OPEN c_Address


   /* Fetch first address */
   FETCH NEXT FROM c_Address into @v_line1,
                                  @v_line2,
                                  @v_city,
                                  @v_state,
                                  @v_zip5,
                                  @v_zip4


   /* Loop through address records */
   WHILE (@@FETCH_STATUS <> -1)
     BEGIN
     /* Skip missing rows */
     IF (@@FETCH_STATUS <> -2)
       BEGIN
```

```
/* Clear the ID variables */
SELECT @v_StateID = NULL,
       @v_CityID = NULL,
       @v_ZipID = NULL,
       @v_AddressID = NULL

/* Look up the state ID */
SELECT @v_stateid = state_id
  FROM address.dbo.tbl_state (NOLOCK)
  WHERE state_code = @v_state

/* If the state was not found, we need to add it */
IF @v_stateid is NULL
  BEGIN
  /* Insert new state record */
  INSERT INTO address.dbo.tbl_state
    (name, state_code)
    VALUES (@v_state, @v_state)

  /* Save the state ID for our new record */
  SELECT @v_stateid = @@identity
  END

/* Look up the zip code ID */
SELECT @v_zipid = zip_id
  FROM address.dbo.tbl_zipcode (NOLOCK)
    WHERE zip5 = @v_zip5
      AND state_id = @v_stateid

/* If the zip code was not found, we need to add it */
IF @v_zipid is NULL
  BEGIN
  /* Insert new zip code record */
  INSERT INTO address.dbo.tbl_zipcode
    (zip5, state_id)
    VALUES (@v_zip5, @v_stateid)

  /* Save the zip code ID for our new record */
  SELECT @v_zipid = @@identity
  END

/* Look up the city ID */
SELECT @v_cityid = city_id
  FROM address.dbo.tbl_city (NOLOCK)
  WHERE name = @v_city
    AND state_id = @v_stateid
```

```
      /* If the city was not found, we need to add it */
      IF @v_cityid is NULL
        BEGIN
        /* Insert new city record */
        INSERT INTO address.dbo.tbl_city
          (name, state_id)
          VALUES (@v_city, @v_stateid)

        /* Save the city ID for our new record */
        SELECT @v_cityid = @@identity
        END

      /* See if the address already exists */
      SELECT @v_addressid = address_id
        FROM address.dbo.tbl_address (NOLOCK)
        WHERE line1 = @v_line1
          AND line2 = @v_line2
          AND zip4 = @v_zip4
          AND city_id = @v_cityid
          AND zip_id = @v_zipid

      /* If the address was not found, we need to add it */
      IF @v_addressid is NULL
        BEGIN
        /* Insert new address record */
        INSERT INTO address.dbo.tbl_address
          (line1, line2, zip4, city_id, zip_id)
          VALUES (@v_line1, @v_line2, @v_zip4, @v_cityid, @v_zipid)
        END
      END

    /* Fetch next address */
    FETCH NEXT FROM c_Address into @v_line1,
                                  @v_line2,
                                  @v_city,
                                  @v_state,
                                  @v_zip5,
                                  @v_zip4

  END

/* Close and deallocate address cursor */
CLOSE c_Address
DEALLOCATE c_Address
```

After the stored procedure **usp_add_addresses** has been executed, there is one cleanup step that you may want to perform. The **tbl_AddressDN** information did not contain long state names for the states. It only had the postal abbreviations. For your normalized structure, you want to add the full state names to be used in certain reporting applications. To accomplish this, you need to find the states that were just added and update the long names accordingly. The code in Listing 19.17 looks for states that have the same entry for the state code and the state name. Sample output is also provided in the listing to show you what the new state rows would look like. Once you have this list, you can perform an update for each of these rows to set the state name column to the full state name.

**Listing 19.17  Find new state records.**

```
SELECT State_ID,
       Name,
       State_Code
  FROM tbl_state (NOLOCK)
 WHERE Name = State_Code


/* results */
State_ID Name                                 State_Code
-------- ------------------------------       ----------
6        TX                                   TX
7        LA                                   LA
8        IN                                   IN
```

| Related solution: | Found on page: |
|---|---|
| Using Format Files | 710 |

# Consolidating Worktable Values Using a **CASE** Statement

For this example, you are working on a process to post adjustments to your PayChecks file for amounts that were calculated incorrectly due to legislative changes that were not included in the original calculations. You have already created two worktables: One holds a list of the document IDs and tax codes that need to be adjusted, the other holds a list of the adjustments. The list of adjustments stores the document ID, the tax code, the adjustment amount, and a character field indicating which field in the tax detail records needed the adjustment.

In order to process the adjustments correctly, you need to combine the adjustments by document ID and tax code so that you have one adjustment record for each original record in the **TaxDetail** table. This is not a simple process, so the code in Listing 19.18 uses a series of temporary tables to hold the adjustments for each field. These are then joined using an outer join and the adjustment list table to produce a consolidated adjustment record for each document ID and tax code combination.

**Listing 19.18    Combining adjustments using temporary tables.**

```
/* Get adjustments to Gross Wages */
select Doc_ID,
       TaxCode,
       Adjustment
  INTO #GrossWages
  FROM #AdjKey ak (NOLOCK)
  JOIN #AdjWrk aw (NOLOCK) ON aw.Doc_ID = ak.Doc_ID
                          AND aw.TaxCode = ak.TaxCode
                          AND aw.AdjustmentField = 'GrossWages'


/* Get adjustments to Taxable Wages */
select Doc_ID,
       TaxCode,
       Adjustment
  INTO #TaxableWages
  FROM #AdjKey ak (NOLOCK)
  JOIN #AdjWrk aw (NOLOCK) ON aw.Doc_ID = ak.Doc_ID
                          AND aw.TaxCode = ak.TaxCode
                          AND aw.AdjustmentField = 'TaxableWages'


/* Get adjustments to Excess Wages */
select Doc_ID,
       TaxCode,
       Adjustment
  INTO #ExcessWages
  FROM #AdjKey ak (NOLOCK)
  JOIN #AdjWrk aw (NOLOCK) ON aw.Doc_ID = ak.Doc_ID
                          AND aw.TaxCode = ak.TaxCode
                          AND aw.AdjustmentField = 'ExcessWages'


/* Get adjustments to Exempt Wages */
select Doc_ID,
       TaxCode,
       Adjustment
  INTO #ExemptWages
  FROM #AdjKey ak (NOLOCK)
```

```
    JOIN #AdjWrk aw (NOLOCK) ON aw.Doc_ID = ak.Doc_ID
                            AND aw.TaxCode = ak.TaxCode
                            AND aw.AdjustmentField = 'ExemptWages'

/* Combine adjustments by Doc_ID and TaxCode */
SELECT ak.Doc_ID,
       ak.TaxCode,
       COALESCE(gw.Adjustment, 0) AS GrossWages,
       COALESCE(tw.Adjustment, 0) AS TaxableWages,
       COALESCE(ew.Adjustment, 0) AS ExcessWages,
       COALESCE(xw.Adjustment, 0) AS ExemptWages
   INTO #Consolidate
   FROM #AdjKey ak (NOLOCK)
   LEFT JOIN #GrossWages gw (NOLOCK) ON ak.Doc_ID = gw.Doc_ID
                                    AND ak.TaxCode = gw.TaxCode
   LEFT JOIN #TaxableWages tw (NOLOCK) ON ak.Doc_ID = tw.Doc_ID
                                      AND ak.TaxCode = tw.TaxCode
   LEFT JOIN #ExcessWages ew (NOLOCK) ON ak.Doc_ID = ew.Doc_ID
                                     AND ak.TaxCode = ew.TaxCode
   LEFT JOIN #ExemptWages xw (NOLOCK) ON ak.Doc_ID = xw.Doc_ID
                                     AND ak.TaxCode = xw.TaxCode

/* Get rid of work tables */
DROP TABLE #GrossWages
DROP TABLE #TaxableWages
DROP TABLE #ExcessWages
DROP TABLE #ExemptWages
```

Although the use of temporary tables will produce the desired results, this process becomes more complex as additional fields are added to your list of adjustments. The original example of this technique required 12 temporary tables to handle the various adjustment fields. Although SQL Server 2000 supports up to 256 tables in a single **SELECT** statement, you will start seeing significant performance issues long before that limit is reached, especially when you have to use a **LEFT JOIN** for each of these work tables. An alternative to the work table approach is to use the **SUM( )** function and **CASE** statements in conjunction with a **GROUP BY** clause to combine the adjustment amounts appropriately without needing to create additional work tables. As shown in Listing 19.19, you can use a **CASE** statement to feed the **SUM** function either the amount in the **Adjustment** column or zero for each row based on the value of the **AdjustmentField** column. Then, using a **GROUP BY** for the **Doc_ID** and **TaxCode** will cause the proper field adjustments to be put together for each **TaxDetail** record. This code is shorter and more efficient, but it may be a bit harder to understand if you are not familiar with using **CASE** statements in this manner.

**Listing 19.19   Combining adjustments using CASE.**

```
SELECT ak.Doc_ID,
       ak.TaxCode,
       SUM(CASE WHEN aw.AdjustmentField = 'GrossWages'
                   THEN aw.Adjustment ELSE 0 END) AS GrossWages,
       SUM(CASE WHEN aw.AdjustmentField = 'TaxableWages'
                   THEN aw.Adjustment ELSE 0 END) AS TaxableWages,
       SUM(CASE WHEN aw.AdjustmentField = 'ExcessWages'
                   THEN aw.Adjustment ELSE 0 END) AS ExcessWages,
       SUM(CASE WHEN aw.AdjustmentField = 'ExemptWages'
                   THEN aw.Adjustment ELSE 0 END) AS ExemptWages
  INTO #Consolidate
  FROM #AdjKey ak (NOLOCK)
  JOIN #AdjWrk aw (NOLOCK) ON aw.Doc_ID = ak.Doc_ID
                          AND aw.TaxCode = ak.TaxCode
                          AND aw.AdjustmentField in ( 'GrossWages',
                                                      'TaxableWages',
                                                      'ExcessWages',
                                                      'ExemptWages' )

  GROUP BY ak.Doc_ID, ak.TaxCode
```

# Creating an Impact Analysis Stored Procedure

When making database structure changes, it is important to consider the impact on existing code. This section provides the framework for doing a basic impact analysis of changes to tables and/or columns. You will create a stored procedure to search all stored procedures, views, and triggers in the database to see if the table or column being changed affects them. The names of all affected objects will be returned so that you will know which procedures need to be checked and/ or modified to be sure they will continue to function correctly after the change. Follow these steps to create the procedure:

1. Create a procedure with two input parameters. The first parameter is the table being changed, which is required. The second parameter is an optional column name affected by the change. The default for the column name should be **NULL** if it is not supplied.

2. Your procedure should first display the table and column information to verify that the correct information was searched. If the column name is **NULL**, this should be indicated in the output using the **COALESCE( )** function.

3. Next, count and display the number of objects that reference the table name by searching for the table name in the **syscomments** table.

4. Next, count and display the number of objects that reference the column name by searching for the column name in the **syscomments** table.

5. Next, you need to display each object referencing the table name and a count of the number of lines in the object that contain a reference. This information is found by searching the **syscomments** table.

6. You then need to display each object referencing the column name and a count of the number of lines in the object that contain a reference. This information is found by searching the **syscomments** table.

7. Finally, you need to determine which (if any) indexes on the table contain the specified column.

8. For cleaner output, all column-related searching should be wrapped in **IF** *column name* **IS NOT NULL** checks to bypass them if no column name is passed to the procedure.

Listing 19.20 provides the full source for this simple impact analysis procedure. If you have a database that makes use of meta data, you can adapt the code in this procedure to perform a more complete impact analysis based on your meta data and any business rules that apply. You can also expand this code to look for foreign key constraints that reference the specified table or column.

**Listing 19.20    usp_Impact_Analysis.**

```
/* Drop the procedure if it currently exists */
IF EXISTS (SELECT name
             FROM sysobjects (NOLOCK)
             WHERE name = N'usp_Impact_Analysis'
               AND type = 'P')
  DROP PROCEDURE usp_Impact_Analysis
GO

CREATE PROCEDURE usp_Impact_Analysis
    @p_TgtTable  NVARCHAR(30),
    @p_TgtColumn NVARCHAR(30) = NULL
AS

/* Turn off row count display */
SET NOCOUNT ON

/* Display table and column information */
PRINT 'Checking Table  : ' + @p_TgtTable
PRINT 'Checking Column : ' + COALESCE(@p_TgtColumn, '** NONE **')
PRINT ''

/* Get count of objects containing a reference to the table */
SELECT COUNT(*) AS 'Total Table Hits'
```

```
        FROM syscomments scm (NOLOCK)
        JOIN sysobjects  obj (NOLOCK) ON scm.id = obj.id
        WHERE scm.text LIKE '%' + @p_TgtTable + '%'

    /* Get count of objects containing a reference to the column */
    IF @p_TgtColumn IS NOT NULL
      SELECT COUNT(*) AS 'Total Column Hits'
        FROM syscomments scm (NOLOCK)
        JOIN sysobjects  obj (NOLOCK) ON scm.id = obj.id
        WHERE scm.text LIKE '%' + @p_TgtColumn + '%'

    /* Display objects referencing the table */
    PRINT 'Table'
    SELECT CONVERT(VARCHAR(7),COUNT(obj.name)) AS 'Count :',
            obj.name                           AS 'Object Name'
      FROM syscomments scm (NOLOCK)
      JOIN sysobjects  obj (NOLOCK) ON scm.id = obj.id
      WHERE scm.text LIKE '%' + @p_TgtTable + '%'
      GROUP BY obj.name
      ORDER BY 1 DESC

    /* Display objects referencing the column */
    IF @p_TgtColumn IS NOT NULL
      BEGIN
      PRINT 'Column'
      SELECT CONVERT(VARCHAR(7),COUNT(obj.name)) AS 'Count :',
              obj.name                           AS 'Object Name'
        FROM syscomments scm (NOLOCK)
        JOIN sysobjects  obj (NOLOCK) ON scm.id = obj.id
        WHERE scm.text LIKE '%' + @p_TgtColumn + '%'
        GROUP BY obj.name
        ORDER BY 1 DESC

    PRINT 'Index Summary...'
    PRINT ''

    /* Display indexes on the table referencing the column */
    SELECT CONVERT(VARCHAR(30),idx.name) AS 'Index Name',
            col.name                     AS 'Column Name'
      FROM sysobjects    obj (NOLOCK)
      JOIN sysindexes    idx (NOLOCK) ON obj.id    = idx.id
      JOIN sysindexkeys ixk (NOLOCK) ON obj.id    = ixk.id
                                   AND idx.indid = ixk.indid
      JOIN syscolumns    col (NOLOCK) ON ixk.colid = col.colid
                                   AND obj.id    = col.id
```

```
    WHERE obj.id   = OBJECT_ID(@p_TgtTable)
      AND obj.type = 'U'
      AND col.name LIKE '%' + @p_TgtColumn + '%'
    ORDER BY 1,2
  END

PRINT 'Done.'

GO
```

| Related solution: | Found on page: |
|---|---|
| Utility Procedures and Scripts | 661 |

# Data Scrubbing Techniques

Any time you bring data into your database from an outside source, you need to perform basic data cleanup. This can even apply to merging data from other parts of the same organization that do not necessarily share the same business logic and data handling rules that your system has. Before beginning the process of merging this data into your database, it is a good idea to verify the integrity of the data you will be adding to ensure that it does not create duplicate or unusable records in your database.

Let's revisit the idea of getting a list of addresses from an outside source that needs to be added to your database. Once the data has been imported into the **tbl_AddressDN** table, you first need to verify the integrity of the addresses and make sure that they conform to the standards you have applied to your own data. For example, your address data expects the apartment number to appear in the second address line. You need to scan the imported data to see if there are any cases where the apartment number is included in the first address line so that you can correct the data before transferring the data to your normalized structure. Listing 19.21 provides a query that scans the table and identifies suspect records. Notice that several checks are used to find what may be apartment number references. It is important to understand that data scrubbing is not an exact science because you have no control over the business rules and standards used on data outside of your organization. The three forms searched for are the ones you have encountered in the past, so include all of them in your search. It is also important to note that if either of the last two forms are located, then the apartment reference needs to be changed to conform to your standard of "Apt." for the apartment number in addition to being moved to the second address line.

**Listing 19.21   Locate bad apartment references.**

```
SELECT *
  FROM tbl_AddressDN (NOLOCK)
  WHERE Line1 LIKE '%apt%'
    OR Line1 LIKE '%apartment%'
    OR Line1 LIKE '%#%'
```

You also have a rule that street references should be abbreviated (Lane = Ln., Street = St., etc.), which means you need to search for references that are not abbreviated in the new address data. Listing 19.22 provides a scan for all the cases that you should check for, but it may need to be expanded to suit your needs.

**Listing 19.22   Locate missing abbreviations.**

```
SELECT *
  FROM tbl_AddressDN (NOLOCK)
  WHERE Line1 LIKE '%street%'
    OR Line1 LIKE '%lane%'
    OR Line1 LIKE '%drive%'
    OR Line1 LIKE '%road%'
    OR Line1 LIKE '%boulevard%'
    OR Line1 LIKE '%parkway%'
    OR Line1 LIKE '%terrace%'
    OR Line1 LIKE '%circle%'
    OR Line1 LIKE '%court%'
    OR Line1 LIKE '%avenue%'
```

You may also need to check for abbreviations that do not have a period at the end. This is common in many organizations, but does not match your standard. To accomplish this check, you have to combine a **LIKE** with a **NOT LIKE** to locate rows with the abbreviation that does not have a period after it. The code for this check is provided in Listing 19.23. The inclusion of a space before the abbreviation in the code helps prevent rows from being returned when these letter combinations appear in the street name (i.e., Bon**av**enture, We**st**, etc.).

**Listing 19.23   Locate missing periods for abbreviations.**

```
SELECT *
  FROM tbl_AddressDN (NOLOCK)
  WHERE (Line1 LIKE '% st%' AND Line1 NOT LIKE '% st.%')
    OR (Line1 LIKE '% ln%' AND Line1 NOT LIKE '% ln.%')
    OR (Line1 LIKE '% dr%' AND Line1 NOT LIKE '% dr.%')
    OR (Line1 LIKE '% rd%' AND Line1 NOT LIKE '% rd.%')
    OR (Line1 LIKE '% blvd%' AND Line1 NOT LIKE '% blvd.%')
    OR (Line1 LIKE '% pkwy%' AND Line1 NOT LIKE '% pkwy.%')
    OR (Line1 LIKE '% terr%' AND Line1 NOT LIKE '% terr.%')
```

```
OR (Line1 LIKE '% cir%' AND Line1 NOT LIKE '% cir.%')
OR (Line1 LIKE '% ct%' AND Line1 NOT LIKE '% ct.%')
OR (Line1 LIKE '% av%' AND Line1 NOT LIKE '% av.%')
```

Unfortunately, due to the fact that it is impossible to guarantee that you will fail to find an address that matches one of your checks, but is still valid, the data must be manually examined and cleaned up. These queries can help you locate suspect records, but it would be unwise to convert them into a script that performs an automatic correction. It is possible to create scripts to perform the automatic correction, and these can even be useful at times, but you must verify that all rows that these scripts correct actually need to be changed. Listing 19.24 provides an example script to change all occurrences of "Street" to the proper abbreviated version (St.). The **REPLACE( )** function makes this substitution extremely easy to code.

### Listing 19.24    Abbreviate "Street" if needed.

```
UPDATE tbl_AddressDN
  SET Line1 = REPLACE(Line1, 'street', 'St.')
  WHERE Line1 LIKE '%street%'
```

You should keep a library of your data scrubbing routines and update them when you locate new data conditions in the imported data. Over time, this library allows you to streamline your data scrubbing process. This library is also a good place to start when evaluating data from a new source. You should never rely on the library 100 percent, however, even for sources you have received data from in the past. New rules and standards inevitably pop up from time to time that affect the validity of the data you receive.

# Chapter 20

# XML

# In Depth

This chapter provides you with detailed information on how to make use of the XML extensions provided by SQL Server 2000. The chapter begins with a brief background and explanation of XML, why it exists, and how it is used. This information is provided as a starting point for those of you who are not familiar with XML. In order to fully utilize the XML support included with SQL Server 2000, you will need to do some additional research and reading to become more familiar with XML.

---

**NOTE:** *For the examples in this chapter, you will need to change the maximum column width allowed in the Query Analyzer. The maximum column width defaults to 255, which truncates many of these examples. The truncation occurs even if you set the Results To File option for your results. Before attempting to run the examples in this chapter, you should first follow the steps in the "Setting the Maximum Column Width in the Query Analyzer" section in this chapter to adjust the maximum width to a more usable value.*

---

## Introduction to XML

Extensible Markup Language (XML) is a subset of Standard Generalized Markup Language (SGML), as is Hypertext Markup Language (HTML). XML was created to overcome the limitations of HTML and to address future concerns for electronic document creation and delivery. Although it was not created as an attempt to replace HTML, XML addresses issues that are either impractical for HTML to handle or beyond its scope.

HTML was introduced to address document structure (how a page is broken down and grouped by elements), and from that structure, to deduce the formatting (if this text is in the header, then make it bold, etc.). The strength of HTML (at least initially) was to guarantee, or attempt to guarantee, that the document would look identical on various platforms. This is also a concern of XML. However, XML takes a different approach that has further reaching applications than HTML alone. XML was created to share a document's data between various platforms and applications without regard to the visual presentation of the information. Sharing data using well-established XML formatting will enable an enterprise to move data easily between applications from various vendors, even across heterogeneous platforms.

## Markup Languages

The term "mark up" comes from paper publishing. A traditional manuscript is annotated with formatting instructions for the typesetter and printer. These instructions occur after the content creation, but before the finished product. They are a middle step for explaining the layout of a document that has nothing to do with its content. When you type a document in a word processor and apply formatting to a word (say, making it bold), the word processor inserts formatting commands into the text itself that tells it how to display the boldfaced word. This is called a procedural markup because its purpose is to output the document in a specific way (screen, printer, Web, etc.). An example of a document in a markup language is provided in Listing 20.1.

**Listing 20.1    RTF markup example (edited for space).**

```
{\rtf1\mac\ansicpg10000\uc1
\deff0\deflang1033\deflangfe1033{\upr{\fonttbl{\f0\fnil\fcharset256\fprq2
{\*\panose
02020603050405020304}Times New Roman;}{\f4\fnil\fcharset256\fprq2{\*\panose
02000500000000000000}Times;} {\f6\fnil\fcharset256\fprq2{\*\panose
02000500000000000000}Courier;}}{\*\ud{\fonttbl{\f0\fnil\fcharset256\fprq2
{\*\panose
02020603050405020304}Times New Roman;}{\f4\fnil\fcharset256\fprq2{\*\panose
02000500000000000000}Times;} {\f6\fnil\fcharset256\fprq2{\*\panose
02000500000000000000}Courier;}}}}{\colortbl;\red0\green0\blue0;
\red0\green0\blue255;\red0\green255\blue255;\red0\green255\blue0;
\red255\green0\blue255;\red255\green0\blue0;\red255\green255\blue0;
\red255\green255\blue255;\red0\green0\blue128;\red0\green128\blue128;
\red0\green128\blue0;\red128\green0\blue128;\red128\green0\blue0;
\red128\green128\blue0;\red128\green128\blue128;\red192\green192\blue192;}
{\stylesheet{\widctlpar\adjustright
\f4\cgrid \snext0 Normal;}{\*\cs10 \additive Default Paragraph
Font;}{\s15\widctlpar\adjustright \f4\fs28\cgrid \sbasedon0
\snext15 Body Text;}}{\info{\title Memo:}{\author Brad Haarer}
{\operator Brad Haarer}{\creatim\yr1956\mo9\dy6\hr4\min27}
{\revtim\yr1956\mo9\dy6\hr4\min30}{\version1}{\edmins3}{\nofpages1}
{\nofwords0}{\nofchars0}{\*\company
BCC/CHSE}{\nofcharsws0}{\vern99}}\widowctrl\ftnbj\aenddoc\formshade
\viewkind4\viewscale100\pgbrdrhead\pgbrdrfoot
\fet0\sectd \linex0\endnhere\sectdefaultcl
)}}\pard\plain \widctlpar\adjustright \f4\cgrid {\b\f6\fs28 Memo: \par }
{ \par This is to show you how a procedural markup language looks.
These tags are the ones used for }{\i Rich Text Format Documents (RTF}{).
\par \par }\pard\plain
\s15\widctlpar\adjustright \f4\fs28\cgrid RTF is a procedural markup
```

language developed by Microsoft to give some formatting options to
generic text files.
\par \pard\plain \widctlpar\adjustright \f4\cgrid { \par }\pard
\qc\widctlpar\adjustright {As you can see, it\rquote s all done by tags
that give the formatting  directions, but have nothing to do with the
content they describe. \par }}

This example works fairly well, but is limited in what it can do. For example, it does not record the structure of the document, only its appearance. This means that any change to the structure of the document requires a manual editing of the file itself. This can become a problem when dealing with a large number of documents that should follow a similar structure if part of that structure needs to change.

These limitations led to the creation of SGML. SGML does not impose a document structure or set of tags, but it gives authors the ability to describe the structure of their documents and mark them up according to their own needs. HTML is an example of this (in fact, the best known example of SGML). The tags in HTML describe the structure of a hypertext document as shown in Listing 20.2.

### Listing 20.2    HTML example (edited for space).

```
<HTML>
<HEAD>
<META HTTP-EQUIV="Content-Type" CONTENT="text/html; charset=iso-8859-1">
<TITLE>Memo:</TITLE>
</HEAD>
<BODY>

<B><FONT FACE="Courier" SIZE=4><P>Memo:</P>
</B></FONT>
<P>This is to show you how HTML looks. These tags are the ones used for
<I>HTML</I> documents  </P>

<FONT SIZE=4><P>HTML is a markup language to give structure, and from that
 formatting, to hypertextual documents.</P>
</FONT>
<P ALIGN="CENTER">As you can see, it&#146;s all done by tags that give the
 formatting  directions, but have nothing to do with the content they
 describe.</P></BODY>
</HTML>
```

This example does not take into account the addition of specific formatting tags to HTML (**<font>** and **<center>**, as an example) or the addition of Cascading Style Sheets (CSS) that make HTML more of a procedural markup language.

20. XML

XML (and a subset of XML, Extensible Hypertext Markup Language [XHTML]) emerged as a successor to HTML. XML removes all the extraneous options available under SGML, but it retains the core elements that a markup language needs to define a document structure. Listing 20.3 demonstrates that XML is also a simpler language than HTML because XML does not need the CSS or other stylistic tags that HTML has added over the years.

**Listing 20.3    XML document example.**

```
<?xml version="1.0"?>
<!DOCTYPE memo SYSTEM "memo.dtd">
<memo>
        <header>
                <from> John Doe </from>
                <to> Jane Doe </from>
                <subject> XML Documents</subject>
        </header>

        <body>
                <para> Here is an example of XML document tags. As you can
                        see the tag layout and language are easy to understand.
                        Since the authors can define the tags themselves, that
                        means that the document structure is really easy to
                        comprehend, even for a casual reader.</para>
                <para> This also means that if you ever had to change any
                        part of this memo's formatting, you could change just
                        the tag definition of the part you needed to change
                        without having to edit the document directly.</para>

                <signature> John Doe</signature>
        </body>
</memo>
```

# Applications of XML

XML was developed so that an XML document would be able to be ported easily to any other type of output, such as a printer, a database, a screen, a hand-held device, and so on, without having to rework the original document. It is possible to create, edit, and save documents in XML, and then publish them automatically to different media. This capability has become even more important as publishers move toward both traditional and digital delivery systems.

Also of considerable importance to many enterprises is the publishing of data from a variety of sources and the delivery of that data in a variety of ways. SGML was designed to give document management access to development tools that were traditionally used to manage databases. XML now brings the publication of data to the data itself, making the distinction between the "data" and the "document" almost invisible.

Let's take a quick look at how this works by starting with data that is stored in a relational database. Table 20.1 represents the data that might be stored in a simple inventory table in a database.

Pretty straightforward isn't it? The database lists the item, its price, and a unique identifier. Based on what you've seen on XML so far, you can pretty much see how this data can be exported using XML. Tags that specify how the XML document recipient should interpret each field are assigned to each column. The result might look something like the code shown in Listing 20.4.

**Listing 20.4    Sample data in XML format.**

```
<?xml version="1.0"?>
<products>
      <product>
      <product id = "I1">
            <name>XML How to Book</name>
            <price>29.99</price>
      </product>
      <product>
      <product id = "I2">
            <name>DTD Creation Software</name>
            <price>69.99</price>
      </product>
      <product>
      <product id = "I3">
            <name>XML Database Suite</name>
            <price>299.99</price>
      </product>
      <product>
      <product id = "I4">
            <name>"I Love XML" coffee mug </name>
            <price>12.99</price>
      </product>
</products>
```

**Table 20.1    Sample database information.**

| Identifier | Name | Price |
|---|---|---|
| I1 | XML How to Book | $29.99 |
| I2 | DTD Creation Software | $69.99 |
| I3 | XML Database Suite | $299.99 |
| I4 | "I Love XML" coffee mug | $12.99 |

As you can see, the XML shows the structure of the document, not the formatting. This becomes important as you exchange information between systems. You want to exchange the data and the structure, not how it looks.

# XML and SQL Server

In a relational database, all data retrieval operations on the database produce a result set in the form of a table. In a client/server environment, the application executes a **SELECT** statement, and then processes the results by retrieving a row or block of rows from the tabular result set and mapping the column values into program variables. By contrast, Web applications generally work with a hierarchical representation of the data in the form of XML or HTML documents. In order to further enhance the usability of SQL Server in Web development environments, a number of new features have been added to SQL Server 2000 to better support XML. The following is a list of some of these new features:

- SQL Server 2000 can be accessed through a Universal Resource Locator (URL).
- SQL Server 2000 supports XML Data Reduced (XDR) schemas.
- SQL Server provides the capability to specify XML Path (XPath) queries against XDR schemas.
- The **FOR XML** clause has been added to the **SELECT** statement to provide the capability to retrieve XML data.
- XML data can be written to SQL Server 2000 using the **OPENXML** rowset provider.
- The SQL Server 2000 OLE DB provider has been enhanced to allow XML documents to be set as command text and to return result sets as a stream.
- The SQL Server 2000 database engine natively supports XML.

SQL Server can now be accessed over HTTP using a URL by defining a virtual root on a Microsoft Internet Information Server (IIS). This virtual root definition provides HTTP access to the data and XML functionality of SQL Server 2000. The XML functionality of SQL Server 2000 can be accessed using HTTP, ActiveX Database Objects (ADO), or OLE DB.

XML views of SQL Server databases can be defined by annotating XDR schemas to map the tables, views, and columns. These database components are associated with the elements and attributes of the XDR schema. XML views can be referenced in XPath queries, which are used to retrieve database results and return them as XML documents.

The Transact-SQL **SELECT** statement has been enhanced to support a **FOR XML** clause, which is used to specify that the result set should be returned in the form of an XML document rather than a standard result set. You can also store templates in an IIS virtual root, and execute the query by referencing the template name, which is useful for complex queries and queries that you need to make secure.

The data from an XML document can be exposed as a relational rowset using the new **OPENXML** rowset function. The new **OPENXML** rowset function can be used anywhere a rowset function is allowed in a Transact-SQL statement. It can be used in place of a table or view reference in a **FROM** clause. The **OPENXML** rowset function provides the capability to insert, update, or delete data in your database tables and includes the capability to modify multiple rows in multiple tables in a single operation.

# IIS Virtual Directories

In order to facilitate accessing SQL Server 2000 using HTTP, you must first set up an appropriate virtual directory. The easiest method of accomplishing this is to use the IIS Virtual Directory Management for SQL Server utility, which can be accessed by selecting Configure SQL XML Support In IIS from the SQL Server Tools program group. This utility is used to define and register a new virtual directory (or virtual root) on an IIS server. The utility also instructs IIS to create an association between this new virtual directory and an instance of SQL Server 2000. The URL that can be used to access SQL Server 2000 includes the name of the IIS server and the virtual directory. You can use the URL to perform the following functions:

- Access database objects, such as tables and views, directly.

- Execute template files, which are XML documents consisting of one or more SQL statements.

- Execute XPath queries, which are executed against an XDR schema.

Virtual names of the appropriate types must be created to allow access to templates, database objects, and schemas as part of a URL. Virtual names of type template, dbobject, and schema are created, which correspond to the template files, mapping schema files, and database objects you will reference using a URL. Once these virtual names have been created, they are specified as part of the URL to access the associated item. The virtual name is specified as part of the URL to access a database object directly, or execute a template file or an XPath query against a mapping schema file. The type of the virtual name specified in the URL is also used to determine the file type specified at the URL. The following example uses the virtual name MyVirtualTemplate, which is of template type, to reference a template file called MyTemplate.XML. The file is known to be a template file because the virtual name is of template type.

```
http://IISServer/address/MyVirtualTemplate/MyTemplate.XML
```

---

**NOTE:** *In order to access Microsoft SQL Server 2000 directly from queries executed at the URL, the Allow URL Queries option must be selected when the virtual root is registered.*

---

For best results, you should install the SQL Server 2000 client utilities on the server that is running your Internet server software. After you have installed the client utilities, you can use the IIS Virtual Directory Management For SQL Server utility on your Internet server to configure the virtual directories for your databases. Although it is possible to install IIS on the same server as SQL Server 2000, this is not recommended for production SQL servers. You should generally have one server running IIS and a separate server running SQL Server 2000. Development environments may benefit from the ability to install both IIS and SQL Server 2000 on the same machine, but this should be avoided elsewhere.

---

**NOTE:** *To install the SQL Server 2000 client utilities, at the very least, you must have Windows NT 4.0 Service Pack 5 and Internet Explorer 5.0 installed on your server.*

---

# Using HTTP to Access SQL Server

HTTP access to SQL Server provides the capability to perform a number of functions directly in the URL. This section provides you with more detailed information on some of these functions. The following is a list of functions that can be performed directly in the URL:

- Execute SQL queries
- Execute stored procedures
- Specify templates directly
- Specify template files
- Write XPath queries against XDR schemas
- Access database objects directly

## Accessing Database Objects

Tables, views, and other database objects can be accessed directly using a URL. XPath queries can be specified directly against the database object to obtain a result. You must specify a virtual name of type dbobject to access database objects directly in the URL. This can be useful for retrieving binary values. If a query using the **FOR XML** clause returns a reference to binary data, you can use another URL request that directly references the dbobject to return the actual value.

# SELECT Statement Enhancements

The **SELECT** statement in SQL Server 2000 has several enhancements to facilitate working with incoming and outgoing XML data. These enhancements allow you to produce XML documents from your databases as well as use XML data for **INSERT**, **UPDATE**, and **DELETE** operations against your databases. There are two major enhancements to the **SELECT** statement that are covered in more detail in the following sections:

- The **FOR XML** clause
- The **OPENXML** function

## The FOR XML Clause

The **FOR XML** clause is used to translate the results of a **SELECT** statement into an XML document, which is returned to the client application. The **FOR XML** clause is subject to the following limitations:

- The **FOR XML** clause is valid only in the **SELECT** statement.
- The **FOR XML** clause is not valid in sub-**SELECT** or nested **SELECT** statements.
- The **FOR XML** clause is not valid in a **SELECT INTO** statement.
- The **FOR XML** clause is not valid in conjunction with a **COMPUTE BY** or **FOR BROWSE** clause.
- The **FOR XML** clause is not valid in a view definition.
- The **FOR XML** clause is not valid in a user-defined function that returns a rowset.
- The **FOR XML** clause is not valid for a selection that requires further processing in a stored procedure.
- The **FOR XML** clause is not valid for use in a stored procedure that is executed as input for an **INSERT** statement.
- The **FOR XML** clause is not valid for cursor definitions.
- **GROUP BY** and aggregate functions are not supported with the **FOR XML AUTO** syntax.
- The XML document will not include the server name for a four-part name in the query when the query is executed on the local computer. The server name is returned for four-part names only when the query is executed on a network server.

- Using derived tables as part of a **SELECT** statement with **FOR XML AUTO** may not produce the results you expect.

In addition to the listed limitations, SQL Server names containing characters (such as spaces) that are not valid in XML names are translated into XML names. This translation involves changing the invalid characters into escaped numeric entity encoding. The only two nonalphabetic characters that can be used to begin an XML name are a colon and an underscore. Because the colon was already reserved for namespaces, the underscore was chosen as the escape character.

### Basic Syntax

The basic syntax of the **FOR XML** clause is fairly simple. It provides several options that are explained in Table 20.2. This syntax is added to the **SELECT** statement after the **ORDER BY** clause (if any). The following code shows the basic syntax of the **FOR XML** clause:

```
FOR XML <mode> [, XMLDATA] [, ELEMENTS][, BINARY BASE64]
```

### AUTO Mode

**AUTO** mode can be used to automatically create a hierarchical XML document that contains table and column definitions. Each table in the query, from which at least one column is returned, is represented as an XML element. The columns of the table are mapped to the appropriate attribute of each table element unless the **ELEMENTS** option is supplied. When using the **ELEMENTS** option, each column is represented as a subelement instead of an attribute. The table name (or alias) is mapped to the XML element name, and the column name (or alias) is mapped to an attribute or subelement name.

**Table 20.2   FOR XML arguments.**

| Argument | Description |
|----------|-------------|
| *<mode>* | Specifies the XML mode. The XML mode determines the format of the resulting XML document. The valid XML modes are **AUTO**, **EXPLICIT**, and **RAW**. |
| **XMLDATA** | Specifies that an XML-Data schema should be returned in addition to the XML document containing the data. The schema is prepended to the document as an inline schema. |
| **ELEMENTS** | Specifies that the columns should be returned as elements rather than being mapped to XML attributes. This option is supported only in **AUTO** mode. |
| **BINARY BASE64** | Specifies that any binary data returned by the query should be represented in base64-encoded format. This option must be specified to return binary data using the **RAW** or **EXPLICIT** modes. Binary data is returned as a reference by default in **AUTO** mode. |

The nesting hierarchy of the elements in the result set is based on the order in which the tables are identified by the columns in the **SELECT** list. This makes the order in which the columns are supplied in the **SELECT** list significant. The leftmost (first) table identified forms the top element in the XML document produced by the query. Each successive table identified in the **SELECT** list becomes a nested element of the previous table. If a column is encountered in the **SELECT** list that is from a table that was previously identified, the column is added as an attribute of the original element rather than creating a new level in the hierarchy.

Listing 20.5 provides a sample query that uses the **FOR XML AUTO** syntax along with sample output.

---

**NOTE:** *The line feeds in the sample outputs in this section were added to make the format suitable for reproducing in this book.*

---

### Listing 20.5    **FOR XML AUTO** example.

```
-- Sample Query --

SELECT Emp.First_Name,
       Emp.Last_Name,
       Addr.Line1
  FROM tbl_Employee Emp (NOLOCK)
  JOIN tbl_EmployeeAddressXRef ea (NOLOCK)
    ON Emp.Employee_ID = ea.Employee_ID
  JOIN Address..tbl_Address Addr (NOLOCK)
    ON ea.Address_ID = Addr.Address_ID
  WHERE Emp.Employee_ID IN (1,4,7)
  ORDER BY Emp.Employee_ID
  FOR XML AUTO


** OUTPUT **


XML_F52E2B61-18A1-11d1-B105-00805F49916B
-------------------------------------------
<Emp First_Name="Patrick" Last_Name="Dalton">
<Addr Line1="106 Main St."/>
</Emp>
<Emp First_Name="Paul" Last_Name="Whitehead">
<Addr Line1="142 Bonaventure"/>
</Emp>
<Emp First_Name="Fred" Last_Name="Couples">
<Addr Line1="166 Bonaventure"/>
</Emp>


(3 row(s) affected)
```

Because the **First_Name** column in the **SELECT** list identified the **tbl_Employee** table, the first element created is **Emp**, which is the table alias provided for the **tbl_Employee** table. The **First_Name** attribute is added to this element. Next, the **Last_Name** column is added as an additional attribute to the **Emp** element because it is from the same table. The **Line1** column represents a new table, so the **Addr** element is added as a subelement of the **Emp** element, and the **Line1** column is added as an attribute of the **Addr** element. Because of the way in which the hierarchical relationship is managed by the **FOR XML AUTO** translation, you can reverse the order of the **Line1** and **Last_Name** columns, as shown in Listing 20.6, and still receive the same XML document that was generated in the original query.

**Listing 20.6  FOR XML AUTO example with Line1 and Last_Name columns reversed.**

```
-- Sample Query --

SELECT Emp.First_Name,
       Addr.Line1,
       Emp.Last_Name
  FROM tbl_Employee Emp (NOLOCK)
  JOIN tbl_EmployeeAddressXRef ea (NOLOCK)
    ON Emp.Employee_ID = ea.Employee_ID
  JOIN Address..tbl_Address Addr (NOLOCK)
    ON ea.Address_ID = Addr.Address_ID
  WHERE Emp.Employee_ID IN (1,4,7)
  ORDER BY Emp.Employee_ID
  FOR XML AUTO


-- OUTPUT --

XML_F52E2B61-18A1-11d1-B105-00805F49916B
-------------------------------------------
<Emp First_Name="Patrick" Last_Name="Dalton">
<Addr Line1="106 Main St."/>
</Emp>
<Emp First_Name="Paul" Last_Name="Whitehead">
<Addr Line1="142 Bonaventure"/>
</Emp>
<Emp First_Name="Fred" Last_Name="Couples">
<Addr Line1="166 Bonaventure"/>
</Emp>

(3 row(s) affected)
```

The **ELEMENTS** option is used to make each column a subelement of the table element rather than an element. An example of a query using the **ELEMENTS** option in conjunction with the **FOR XML AUTO** syntax is provided in Listing

20.7. As you can see in the sample output, the order of the **Last_Name** and **Line1** columns does not affect how the columns are grouped in relation to the table from which they came. Once again, line feeds have been added to the output for readability.

**Listing 20.7   FOR XML AUTO example using the ELEMENTS option.**

```
-- Sample Query --

SELECT Emp.First_Name,
       Addr.Line1,
       Emp.Last_Name
  FROM tbl_Employee Emp (NOLOCK)
  JOIN tbl_EmployeeAddressXRef ea (NOLOCK)
    ON Emp.Employee_ID = ea.Employee_ID
  JOIN Address..tbl_Address Addr (NOLOCK)
    ON ea.Address_ID = Addr.Address_ID
  WHERE Emp.Employee_ID IN (1,4,7)
  ORDER BY Emp.Employee_ID
  FOR XML AUTO, ELEMENTS


-- OUTPUT --

XML_F52E2B61-18A1-11d1-B105-00805F49916B
-----------------------------------------
<Emp>
<First_Name>Patrick</First_Name>
<Last_Name>Dalton</Last_Name>
<Addr>
<Line1>106 Main St.</Line1>
</Addr>
</Emp>
<Emp>
<First_Name>Paul</First_Name>
<Last_Name>Whitehead</Last_Name>
<Addr>
<Line1>142 Bonaventure</Line1>
</Addr>
</Emp>
<Emp>
<First_Name>Fred</First_Name>
<Last_Name>Couples</Last_Name>
<Addr>
<Line1>166 Bonaventure</Line1>
</Addr>
</Emp>

(3 row(s) affected)
```

If any values compared in a **SELECT** statement **WHERE** clause are of type **text**, **ntext**, or **image**, **FOR XML** assumes the values are different even though they may be the same. This is due to the fact that SQL Server 2000 does not support comparing large objects. In this case, rows are included or excluded as if the comparison returns false.

When any column in the **SELECT** list cannot be associated with a table identified in the **FROM** clause, the column is added to the document at the deepest nesting level that currently exists in the document at the point the column is encountered in the list. These columns include aggregate and computed columns. If such a column is encountered at the beginning of the list, it is added to the highest level in the hierarchy. The use of the * wildcard character in the **SELECT** list causes the columns to be placed in the hierarchy based on the order in which the tables are encountered as explained previously.

### EXPLICIT Mode

When you use the **EXPLICIT** mode in the **FOR XML** clause, you control the format of the XML document returned by the query. The query must be written in a special way to explicitly provide additional information about the expected nesting of the data returned in the XML document. You also have the ability to specify additional configurations at the column level through the use of directives. Specifying **EXPLICIT** mode means that you must assume the responsibility for ensuring that the XML generated by the query is well formed and valid. For the **EXPLICIT** mode to produce an XML document, the rowset must have a specific format called a *universal table.*

The **EXPLICIT** mode requires the query to produce two meta data columns. The first column specified in the **SELECT** statement must be a named tag number (**Tag**). The **Tag** column stores the tag number of the current element and is of integer data type. The second column must be a named tag number of the parent element (**Parent**). This column stores the tag number of the parent element, which is also of integer data type. The Tag columns are used to determine the hierarchy of parents and children in the XML tree. This information is required for the query to produce the desired XML document hierarchy. If the **Parent** column is **NULL** or zero, then the row is placed at the top level of the hierarchy.

Using **EXPLICIT** mode requires the **SELECT** statement to specify the column names for the universal table in a certain way. The **SELECT** statement must associate the element names with tag numbers and provide the property names in the column names of the universal table. In order to get the correct child instances associated with their parent, it is necessary to order the rowset such that any children immediately follow the parent. The column names in the universal table must be encoded using XML generic identifiers and attribute names. This encoding of the element name, attribute name, and other translation information is specified in the form: ***ElementName!TagNumber!AttributeName!Directive***. Table 20.3 provides the descriptions for the arguments used to encode the column names.

The process for writing queries using **EXPLICIT** mode is complex and involved. You should spend time in the Books Online becoming familiar with the options and requirements before attempting to write this type of query. Listing 20.8 provides an example of a simple **EXPLICIT** mode query and the resulting XML document returned.

---

**NOTE:** *The ElementName and TagNumber arguments in the column name encoding correspond to the table referenced by the column. Notice that all encoded column names in the example use the same ElementName and TagNumber values because only one table is being referenced in the query.*

---

### Listing 20.8   Simple **FOR XML EXPLICIT** query example.

```
-- Sample Query --

SELECT 1             AS Tag,
       NULL          AS Parent,
       Emp.Employee_ID AS [Emp!1!EmployeeID],
       Emp.First_Name  AS [Emp!1!FirstName],
       Emp.Last_Name   AS [Emp!1!LastName]
  FROM tbl_Employee Emp (NOLOCK)
  WHERE Emp.Employee_ID IN (1,4,7)
  FOR XML EXPLICIT


-- OUTPUT --

XML_F52E2B61-18A1-11d1-B105-00805F49916B
---------------------------------------------------------
<Emp EmployeeID="1" FirstName="Patrick" LastName="Dalton"/>
<Emp EmployeeID="4" FirstName="Paul" LastName="Whitehead"/>
<Emp EmployeeID="7" FirstName="Fred" LastName="Couples"/>


(3 row(s) affected)
```

In order to reference more than one table in a query using the **FOR XML EXPLICIT** mode syntax, you have to use the **UNION** operator to combine the information from the multiple tables. An example of this is shown in Listing 20.9 along with the resulting output. It is important to understand that although the **EXPLICIT** mode provides a greater level of control over the format of the resulting XML document, it is also much more difficult to work with. It should be easy to see from these examples that even a moderately complex query requires a great

**Table 20.3    Column name encoding arguments.**

| Argument | Description |
|---|---|
| **ElementName** | This is the generic identifier of the element. |
| **TagNumber** | This is the tag number of the element. Every **TagNumber** corresponds to exactly one **ElementName**. |
| **AttributeName** | If **Directive** is not specified, this is the name of the XML attribute. If **Directive** is specified, this is the name of the contained element. In this case, **AttributeName** can be empty, which means that the value contained in the column is directly contained by the element specified by **ElementName**. |
| **Directive** | **Directive** is optional. If it is not specified, then **AttributeName** must be specified. If neither is specified, an element directive is implied. **Directive** is used to indicate how to encode ID, IDREF, and IDREFS by using the matching keywords, or it is used to specify how to map the string data to XML by using the keywords hide, element, xml, xmltext, and cdata. You can combine directives from each group, but not from the same group. |

deal of effort to format it correctly using the **FOR XML EXPLICIT** mode syntax. This functionality is great if you need it, but this mode should not be selected without a compelling reason because it is generally much more complex, and therefore, more prone to errors.

Listing 20.9    Simple **FOR XML EXPLICIT** query example.

```
-- Sample Query --

SELECT 1              AS Tag,
       NULL           AS Parent,
       Emp.Employee_ID AS [Emp!1!EmployeeID],
       Emp.First_Name  AS [Emp!1!FirstName],
       Emp.Last_Name   AS [Emp!1!LastName],
       NULL            AS [Addr!2!Line1]
  FROM tbl_Employee Emp (NOLOCK)
  WHERE Emp.Employee_ID IN (1,4,7)
UNION ALL
SELECT 2, --Tag
       1, --Parent
       Emp.Employee_ID,
       Emp.First_Name,
       Emp.Last_Name,
       Addr.Line1
  FROM tbl_Employee Emp (NOLOCK)
  JOIN tbl_EmployeeAddressXRef ea (NOLOCK)
    ON Emp.Employee_ID = ea.Employee_ID
  JOIN Address..tbl_Address Addr (NOLOCK)
    ON ea.Address_ID = Addr.Address_ID
```

```
    WHERE Emp.Employee_ID IN (1,4,7)
    ORDER BY [Emp!1!EmployeeID]
    FOR XML EXPLICIT


-- OUTPUT --

XML_F52E2B61-18A1-11d1-B105-00805F49916B
------------------------------------------------------------
<Emp EmployeeID="1" FirstName="Patrick" LastName="Dalton">
<Addr Line1="106 Main St."/>
</Emp>
<Emp EmployeeID="4" FirstName="Paul" LastName="Whitehead">
<Addr Line1="142 Bonaventure"/>
<Addr Line1="166 Bonaventure"/>
</Emp>
<Emp EmployeeID="7" FirstName="Fred" LastName="Couples"/>


(6 row(s) affected)
```

## RAW Mode

**RAW** mode is the simplest way to return an XML document from a query. It also provides the simplest XML document structure for the query results. Using **RAW** mode means that each row in the result set is transformed into an XML element with the generic identifier row. All non-**NULL** column values are mapped to an attribute of the XML element in which the attribute name is the same as the column name. You must specify the **BINARY BASE64** option in the **FOR XML** clause in order to return binary data in base64 encoded format. If you return binary data in a query that uses **RAW** mode without specifying the **BINARY BASE64** option, an error is generated. Listing 20.10 provides a sample query that uses the **FOR XML RAW** mode syntax along with the sample output.

**Listing 20.10   FOR XML RAW example.**

```
-- Sample Query --

SELECT Emp.First_Name,
       Emp.Last_Name,
       Addr.Line1
  FROM tbl_Employee Emp
  JOIN tbl_EmployeeAddressXRef ea ON Emp.Employee_ID = ea.Employee_ID
  JOIN Address..tbl_Address Addr ON ea.Address_ID = Addr.Address_ID
  WHERE Emp.Employee_ID IN (1,4,7)
  ORDER BY Emp.Employee_ID
  FOR XML RAW


-- OUTPUT --
```

```
XML_F52E2B61-18A1-11d1-B105-00805F49916B
-----------------------------------------------------------------
<row First_Name="Patrick" Last_Name="Dalton" Line1="106 Main St."/>
<row First_Name="Paul" Last_Name="Whitehead" Line1="142 Bonaventure"/>
<row First_Name="Fred" Last_Name="Couples" Line1="166 Bonaventure"/>

(3 row(s) affected)
```

### The XMLDATA Schema Option

The primary purpose of the **XMLDATA** option is to receive XML data type information that can be used when data types are necessary. If everything in an XML document is character data, generating an XML-Data schema creates unnecessary overhead on the server. This overhead is likely to negatively impact the performance of your queries. For this reason, the **XMLDATA** option should only be used when noncharacter data types need to be processed in your XML documents.

Database columns of type **sql_varient** do not generate data type information in the XML-Data schema. If more than one XML element is designated as having the same name by a query, **XMLDATA** may produce an invalid XML-Data schema. If you have two elements of the same name but different data types, element name collisions and data types are not resolved.

Listing 20.11 provides an example of a query using **FOR XML RAW** with the **XMLDATA** option specified. This returns a schema that matches the format of the data in the **RAW** mode XML document returned by the query. This schema information is always returned prepended to the XML document to provide an inline schema. In comparison to the **RAW** mode example shown previously, the **XMLDATA** option produces a much larger result set. The amount of overhead required for the schema is extremely significant for queries that return a small result set.

**Listing 20.11** **FOR XML RAW** with **XMLDATA** option example.

```
-- Sample Query --

SELECT Emp.Employee_ID,
       Emp.First_Name,
       Emp.Last_Name,
       Addr.Line1
  FROM tbl_Employee Emp
  JOIN tbl_EmployeeAddressXRef ea ON Emp.Employee_ID = ea.Employee_ID
  JOIN Address..tbl_Address Addr ON ea.Address_ID = Addr.Address_ID
  WHERE Emp.Employee_ID IN (1,4,7)
  ORDER BY Emp.Employee_ID
  FOR XML RAW, XMLDATA
```

20. XML

```
-- OUTPUT --

XML_F52E2B61-18A1-11d1-B105-00805F49916B
-------------------------------------------------------------------
<Schema name="Schema" xmlns="urn:schemas-microsoft-com:xml-data"
xmlns:dt="urn:schemas-microsoft-com:datatypes">
<ElementType name="row" content="empty" model="closed">
<AttributeType name="Employee_ID" dt:type="i4"/>
<AttributeType name="First_Name" dt:type="string"/>
<AttributeType name="Last_Name" dt:type="string"/>
<AttributeType name="Line1" dt:type="string"/>
<attribute type="Employee_ID"/>
<attribute type="First_Name"/>
<attribute type="Last_Name"/>
<attribute type="Line1"/>
</ElementType>
</Schema>
<row xmlns="x-schema:#Schema" Employee_ID="1" First_Name="Patrick"
Last_Name="Dalton" Line1="106 Main St."/>
<row xmlns="x-schema:#Schema" Employee_ID="4" First_Name="Paul"
Last_Name="Whitehead" Line1="142 Bonaventure"/>
<row xmlns="x-schema:#Schema" Employee_ID="7" First_Name="Fred"
Last_Name="Couples" Line1="166 Bonaventure"/>

(3 row(s) affected)
```

An example of the same query using **AUTO** mode and **XMLDATA** in the **FOR XML** clause is provided in Listing 20.12. Compare the output from this example with the output from the previous example to see the schema differences generated by the two XML document formats. Notice once again that there is significant overhead created in generating the schema information with a small result set.

### Listing 20.12   **FOR XML AUTO** with **XMLDATA** option example.

```
-- Sample Query --

SELECT Emp.Employee_ID,
       Emp.First_Name,
       Emp.Last_Name,
       Addr.Line1
  FROM tbl_Employee Emp
  JOIN tbl_EmployeeAddressXRef ea ON Emp.Employee_ID = ea.Employee_ID
  JOIN Address..tbl_Address Addr ON ea.Address_ID = Addr.Address_ID
  WHERE Emp.Employee_ID IN (1,4,7)
```

```
    ORDER BY Emp.Employee_ID
    FOR XML AUTO, XMLDATA

-- OUTPUT --

XML_F52E2B61-18A1-11d1-B105-00805F49916B
-------------------------------------------------------------------
<Schema name="Schema" xmlns="urn:schemas-microsoft-com:xml-data"
xmlns:dt="urn:schemas-microsoft-com:datatypes">
<ElementType name="Emp" content="eltOnly" model="closed" order="many">
<element type="Addr" maxOccurs="*"/>
<AttributeType name="Employee_ID" dt:type="i4"/>
<AttributeType name="First_Name" dt:type="string"/>
<AttributeType name="Last_Name" dt:type="string"/>
<attribute type="Employee_ID"/>
<attribute type="First_Name"/>
<attribute type="Last_Name"/>
</ElementType>
<ElementType name="Addr" content="empty" model="closed">
<AttributeType name="Line1" dt:type="string"/>
<attribute type="Line1"/>
</ElementType>
</Schema>
<Emp xmlns="x-schema:#Schema" Employee_ID="1" First_Name="Patrick"
Last_Name="Dalton">
<Addr Line1="106 Main St."/>
</Emp><Emp xmlns="x-schema:#Schema" Employee_ID="4" First_Name="Paul"
Last_Name="Whitehead">
<Addr Line1="142 Bonaventure"/>
</Emp>
<Emp xmlns="x-schema:#Schema" Employee_ID="7" First_Name="Fred"
Last_Name="Couples">
<Addr Line1="166 Bonaventure"/>
</Emp>

(3 row(s) affected)
```

# OPENXML

The **OPENXML** keyword is used to provide a rowset over in-memory XML documents. This rowset can then be used in a similar fashion to a table or view. **OPENXML** is used to provide access to an XML document as if it was a relational rowset. It provides a rowset view of the internal representation of an XML document. **OPENXML** can be used in **SELECT** and **SELECT INTO** statements anywhere the standard rowset can appear in the statement.

In order to write queries against an XML document using the **OPENXML** rowset function, you must make use of two system-stored procedures. The first is **sp_xml_preparedocument**, which is used to parse the XML document and return a document handle that can be used by the **OPENXML** rowset function. The parsed document is a tree representation of the various nodes in the original XML document. The document handle must be passed to **OPENXML** to provide a rowset view of the document based on the parameters passed to the **OPENXML** function. Once you are finished using the XML document with the **OPENXML** function, you must use the **sp_xml_removedocument** stored procedure to remove the document from memory and free the memory for other uses by SQL Server.

**OPENXML** accepts several parameters, which are explained in Table 20.4. These parameters determine how the XML document is interpreted in the rowset returned by the **OPENXML** function.

### sp_xml_preparedocument

The **sp_xml_preparedocument** system stored procedure is used to read an XML document that is provided as input. It parses the text and provides the parsed document in a state ready for consumption. This stored procedure returns a handle to the parsed document, which can be used to access the newly created internal representation of the XML document by the **OPENXML** function. The handle that is returned is valid for the duration of the connection to SQL Server or until the document is removed from memory by executing the **sp_xml_remove document** system stored procedure. The syntax for using **sp_xml_prepare document** is provided in Listing 20.13. See Table 20.5 for a description of the available parameters.

**Table 20.4   OPENXML parameters.**

| Parameter | Description |
|---|---|
| *idoc* | A document handle that is returned by using the **sp_xml_preparedocument** system stored procedure. |
| *rowpattern* | An XPath expression used to identify the nodes to be mapped to rows. |
| *flags* | A parameter that indicates the mapping that should be used between the XML data and the relational rowset. This optional parameter is also used to determine how the spillover column should be filled. |
| **WITH** *schemadeclaration* | A parameter that provides a description of the rowset to be generated as well as the mapping between rowset columns and the XML nodes. |
| **WITH** *tablename* | A parameter that is used instead of **WITH** *schemadeclaration* if a table with the desired schema already exists and no column patterns are required. |

**Table 20.5  sp_xml_preparedocument arguments.**

| Argument | Description |
| --- | --- |
| *hdoc* | The handle (an integer) to the newly created document. |
| [*xmltext*] | The original XML document. |
| [*xpath_namespaces*] | Specifies the namespace declarations that are used in row and column XPath expressions in **OPENXML**. |

Listing 20.13  **sp_xml_preparedocument** syntax.

```
sp_xml_preparedocument hdoc OUTPUT
    [, xmltext]
    [, xpath_namespaces]
```

### sp_xml_removedocument

The **sp_xml_removedocument** system stored procedure is used to remove from memory a parsed document that was loaded using the **sp_xml_preparedocument** system stored procedure. When an XML document is parsed using the **sp_xmp_preparedocument** stored procedure, it is stored in the internal cache of SQL Server 2000. The parser uses up to one-eighth of the total memory available to SQL Server. To avoid running out of memory, it is important to execute the **sp_xml_removedocument** stored procedure to free the memory used by the parsed document. The syntax for using **sp_xml_removedocument** is provided in Listing 20.14. This procedure takes only a single parameter. Refer to Table 20.5 for an explanation of the *hdoc* parameter. Providing an invalid handle will result in an error being returned from the SP.

Listing 20.14  **sp_xml_removedocument** syntax.

```
sp_xml_removedocument hdoc
```

# XML Templates

XML templates are used to specify SQL or XPath queries to eliminate the need to write long queries at the URL, which can be extremely cumbersome. Instead of the query, the template file name is specified in the URL. An XML template is a well-formed XML document that contains one or more SQL statements and XPath queries. Template files can be used for the following actions:

- Specifying SQL queries
- Specifying XPath queries along with the identification of the XDR schema file against which the query is to be executed
- Defining parameters that can be passed to SQL statements or XPath queries
- Declaring namespaces

20. XML

- Specifying an Extensible Stylesheet Language (XSL) style sheet to apply to the resulting XML document

Template files are also used to enhance security. Because a URL can be edited, so can the query contained in the URL. By specifying a template file that contains the query in the URL rather than the query itself, you can prevent users from modifying the query or obtaining information that you do not want them to see. Removing the URL query-processing service on the virtual root enforces this security, leaving only the Microsoft SQL Server XML Internet Services Application Programming Interface (ISAPI) to process the template files and return a result set. The IIS Virtual Directory Management for SQL Server utility is used to register the virtual root. A virtual name of template type must be created using the IIS Virtual Directory Management for SQL Server utility before templates can be specified in the URL. More in-depth information about XML templates is available in the Books Online.

# *Immediate Solutions*

## Setting the Maximum Column Width in the Query Analyzer

The default setting for the maximum column width is 255. Because the XML document created by using the **FOR XML** clause in your **SELECT** statements is returned as a single column, this limit is not sufficient for even relatively small test queries. The configured column-width limitation also applies when you select the Results To File option on the Query menu. In order to work with XML queries in the Query Analyzer, you need to increase this value to allow you to see the full XML document being produced. The following steps will help you to change the maximum column width to a more appropriate value for building and testing queries that use the **FOR XML** clause in the **SELECT** statement.

1. Open the Query Analyzer.

2. Select Tools|Options.

3. Select the Results tab on the Options dialog.

4. Enter 8000 for the Maximum Characters Per Column as shown in Figure 20.1.

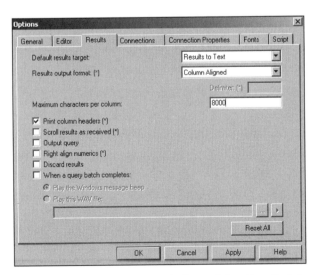

Figure 20.1   Query Analyzer Options dialog Results tab.

5. Click on Apply.

6. Click on OK to close the dialog. You are now ready to test queries using the **FOR XML** clause in the Query Analyzer.

| Related solution: | Found on page: |
|---|---|
| Changing Current Connection Properties | 195 |

# Using the IIS Virtual Directory Management for SQL Server Utility

Before you can begin accessing SQL Server 2000 using HTTP, you must set up one or more virtual directories on your IIS server to provide access to your SQL Server databases. This solution walks you through the necessary steps to create these virtual directories using the IIS Virtual Directory Management for SQL Server utility. This example assumes that you have installed the SQL Server 2000 client utilities on the server where IIS is running. If these utilities are not yet installed on the IIS server machine, you should do so before continuing with this solution. The steps in this example should be performed directly on the IIS server machine.

**NOTE:** *To install the SQL Server 2000 client utilities, you must at least have Windows NT 4.0 Service Pack 5 and Internet Explorer 5.0 installed on your server.*

1. Create a directory called Address under the inetpub\wwwroot directory.

2. Create directories called Template and Schema under the Address directory you just created.

3. Create a directory called Employee under the inetpub\wwwroot directory.

4. Create directories called Template and Schema under the Employee directory you just created.

5. Create a directory called Utility under the inetpub\wwwroot directory.

6. Create directories called Template and Schema under the Utility directory you just created.

7. Select Configure SQL XML Support in IIS from the Microsoft SQL Server menu.

8. Expand the server you want to add the new virtual directories to.

9. Right-click on the Web site you want to add the new virtual directories to, and select Virtual Directory from the New submenu on the context menu to launch the New Virtual Directory Properties dialog.

10. On the General tab of the New Virtual Directory Properties dialog, which is shown in Figure 20.2, enter Address for the Virtual Directory Name.

11. For the Local Path, enter the full path to the Address directory you created at the beginning of this solution.

12. Select the Security tab pictured in Figure 20.3.

13. Enter the appropriate login information to connect to your SQL Server 2000 server.

14. Select the Data Source tab.

15. Enter the name of your SQL Server 2000 server (including the instance name if needed) as shown in Figure 20.4.

16. Select the Address database from the drop-down list.

17. Select the Settings tab.

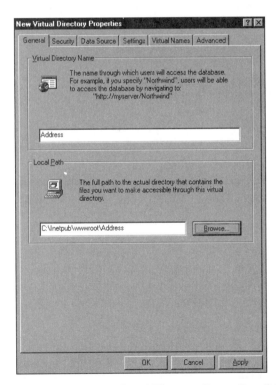

Figure 20.2   New Virtual Directory Properties dialog General tab.

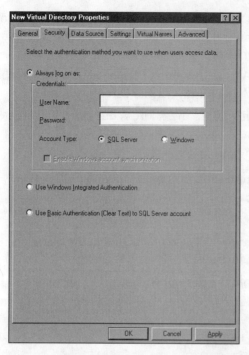

Figure 20.3    New Virtual Directory Properties dialog Security tab.

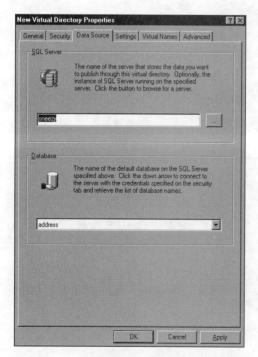

Figure 20.4    New Virtual Directory Properties dialog Data Source tab.

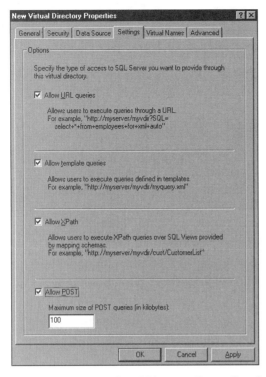

Figure 20.5   New Virtual Directory Properties dialog Settings tab.

18. Make sure that all of the available options are selected as shown in Figure 20.5.

19. Select the Virtual Names tab.

20. Click on New to launch the Virtual Name Configuration dialog shown in Figure 20.6.

21. Enter Template for the Virtual Name.

22. Select template from the Type drop-down list.

23. Enter the full path of the Template directory you created under the Address directory at the beginning of this solution.

24. Click on Save to save the new virtual name and close the dialog.

25. Click on New again.

26. Enter Schema for the Virtual Name.

27. Select schema from the Type drop-down list.

28. Enter the full path of the Schema directory you created under the Address directory at the beginning of this solution.

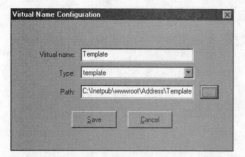

**Figure 20.6    Virtual Name Configuration dialog.**

29. Click on Save to save the new virtual name and return to the Virtual Names tab of the New Virtual Directory Properties dialog. It should show the information for the new virtual names as shown in Figure 20.7.

30. Click on OK to complete the registration of the virtual directory and return to the IIS Virtual Directory Management for SQL Server utility.

31. Repeat steps 9 through 30 for the Employee and Utility databases, making the appropriate substitutions for the virtual directory name, database selection, and path selections.

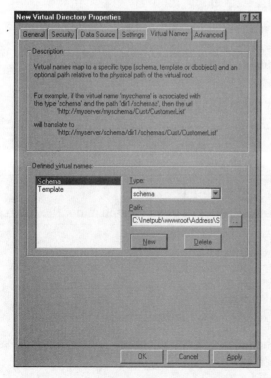

**Figure 20.7    New Virtual Directory Properties dialog Virtual Names tab.**

When you have finished registering the virtual directories for the book databases, select the Web site that you added the virtual directories under. The three virtual directories should appear in the right pane of the IIS Virtual Directory Management for SQL Server utility as shown in Figure 20.8.

| Related solution: | Found on page: |
| --- | --- |
| Registering a Server Using the Register SQL Server Wizard | 178 |
| Installing the Book Databases from Scripts | 369 |

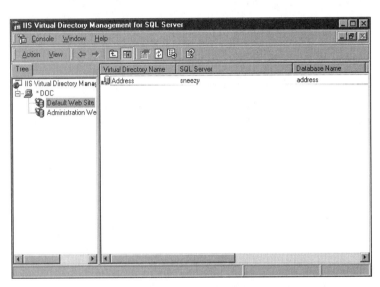

Figure 20.8    IIS Virtual Directory Management for SQL Server utility.

# Executing SQL Queries in a URL

This example assumes that you have already registered the virtual directory for the Address database on your IIS server. If you have not already done so, you should follow the steps in the "Using the IIS Virtual Directory Management for SQL Server Utility" immediate solution in this chapter to register the virtual directory.

Once you have registered a virtual directory for your database, it is possible to execute a query against the database directly from a URL. These queries will return an XML document that can be used by applications to produce an HTML document or perform other processing tasks. In this example, you will see the actual XML output directly in your browser window.

1. Open the Query Analyzer.

2. Enter the following SQL code:

```
SELECT TOP 10 Address_ID FROM tbl_Address (NOLOCK)
```

3. Execute the code to make sure it runs properly. You should get 10 address IDs from the **tbl_Address** table.

4. Add the following **FOR XML** clause to the query:

```
FOR XML RAW
```

5. Execute the query again, and look at the results.

6. Now open your Web browser.

7. Enter the following URL in the browser, substituting the appropriate server name for your IIS server. (Ignore the line breaks and enter the URL as a single line.)

```
http://<IISServer>/Address?sql=SELECT+TOP+10+Address_ID+FROM+
tbl_Address+(NOLOCK)+FOR+XML+RAW&root=ROOT
```

8. Compare the results you receive to the sample output shown in Figure 20.9.

9. Change the **FOR XML** clause in the URL to use **AUTO** mode instead of **RAW** mode.

10. Compare the results with the **RAW** mode output.

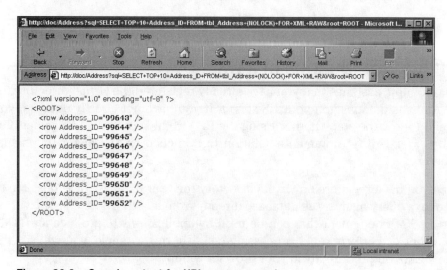

**Figure 20.9    Sample output for URL query example.**

# Using an XSL Style Sheet

This example assumes that you have already registered the virtual directory for the Address database on your IIS server. If you have not already done so, you should follow the steps in the "Using the IIS Virtual Directory Management for SQL Server Utility" immediate solution in this chapter to register the virtual directory.

It is possible to retrieve data from SQL Server 2000 in formatted HTML directly from the URL by combining an XML template and an XSL style sheet. This makes the process of retrieving data from SQL Server for use in a Web site extremely simple and does not require any special tools or processing. It is possible to create both the XSL style sheet and the XML template using a simple text editor like Notepad.

The first step is to construct the query that you want to execute in the template. It is a good idea to build and test the query in the Query Analyzer, and then plug it into the template when you are certain that it produces the desired results. Listing 20.15 shows a simple query against the **vw_Address** view that retrieves the first 10 rows from the view.

**Listing 20.15    Simple query to retrieve 10 addresses.**

```
SELECT TOP 10
       Address_ID,
       Line1,
       City,
       State,
       Zip5
  FROM vw_Address
```

Next, you need to create the template that will execute the query. Because the template is actually an XML document, you simply use XML tags to define the query that you want to run. The syntax for this template is provided in Listing 20.16. Notice that the template tags are fairly simple, and most of the template is actually the query. It is important to note the use of the root tags. These identify the output of the template as a complete XML document rather than a document fragment.

**Listing 20.16    Address query template.**

```
<?xml version ='1.0' encoding='UTF-8'?>
<root xmlns:sql='urn:schemas-microsoft-com:xml-sql'>
   <sql:query>
      SELECT TOP 10
             Address_ID,
```

```
            Line1,
            City,
            State,
            Zip5
        FROM vw_Address
        FOR XML AUTO
    </sql:query>
</root>
```

In order to convert the XML document returned by this template into an HTML document that can be used by a browser, you need to create an XSL style sheet. The XSL style sheet is actually an XML document that is used to transform another XML document. The style sheet document provided in Listing 20.17 is used to transform the XML document generated by the template into an HTML document that displays the query results in a table. In order to create a style sheet to return an HTML document, it is necessary to be familiar with the HTML tags required to generate the output you want to see. There are many good Web sites available that can teach you about the various HTML tags and how they can be used.

The style sheet defines the columns returned by the query as inputs for the template by specifying the name of the data source (in this case the view) in the template match, and then providing a definition of each column in the select as table data (the **<TD>** tags). The **<NOBR>** tag is used in the definition of the address **Line1** column to prevent the address line from wrapping in the table.

After the table data definition is complete, a definition of the table format is provided in a separate template. This template specifies the HTML tags that are used to determine how the table is formatted. The table heading and column headings are specified. After the table heading definition is complete, a tag is added to specify where the table data is to be inserted.

**Listing 20.17   Example style sheet to transform address XML document to HTML.**

```
<?xml version='1.0' encoding='UTF-8'?>
 <xsl:stylesheet xmlns:xsl="http://www.w3.org/1999/XSL/Transform"
     version="1.0">

    <xsl:template match = '*'>
        <xsl:apply-templates />
    </xsl:template>
    <xsl:template match = 'vw_Address'>
      <TR>
        <TD><xsl:value-of select = '@Address_ID' /></TD>
```

```
            <TD><NOBR><xsl:value-of select = '@Line1' /></NOBR></TD>
            <TD><xsl:value-of select = '@City' /></TD>
            <TD><xsl:value-of select = '@State' /></TD>
            <TD><xsl:value-of select = '@Zip5' /></TD>
        </TR>
    </xsl:template>
    <xsl:template match = '/'>
      <HTML>
        <HEAD>
            <STYLE>th { background-color: #CCCCCC }</STYLE>
        </HEAD>
        <BODY>
         <TABLE border='1' cellpadding='2' style='width:300;'>
           <TR><TH colspan='5'>Addresses</TH></TR>
           <TR><TH>Address ID</TH>
               <TH>Line 1</TH>
               <TH>City</TH>
               <TH>State</TH>
               <TH>Zip</TH>
           </TR>
           <xsl:apply-templates select = 'root' />
         </TABLE>
        </BODY>
      </HTML>
    </xsl:template>
</xsl:stylesheet>
```

The XML template for this example is provided in a file called GetAddresses.xml on the CD in the folder for this chapter. The template file needs to be placed in the Template directory under the root directory for the Address database on the IIS server. The XSL style sheet for this example is also provided on the CD in a file called AddressXSL.xsl, and should also be placed in the Template directory under the root directory for the Address database on the IIS server. Once these files have been placed on the IIS server in the appropriate directory, you can execute the following URL in your Web browser to view the results from the query in table form, substituting the name of your IIS server in the URL:

```
http://<IISServer>/address/template/GetAddresses.xml
?xsl=template/addressxsl.xsl
```

This code should be entered as a single line in your browser; it is separated here to allow for printing in the book. An example of the table data displayed by executing this URL is shown in Figure 20.10.

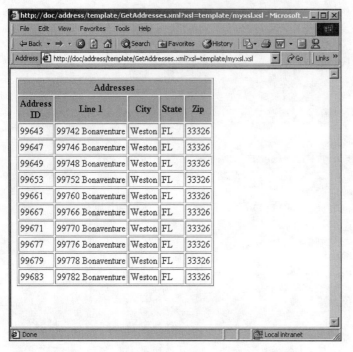

Figure 20.10    Sample **Address** table in Internet Explorer.

# Using the **OPENXML** Function

This example assumes that you have already adjusted the maximum column width in the Query Analyzer to allow working with output from queries using the **FOR XML** clause. If you have not already made this adjustment, please follow the steps in the "Setting the Maximum Column Width in the Query Analyzer" immediate solution in this chapter.

The **OPENXML** function allows you to access data in an XML document as a data source in your Transact-SQL queries. In this example, you create an XML document and use it to test this functionality. It is possible to use almost any XML document with the **OPENXML** function, but creating a test document allows all readers to work from the same basic data.

1. Open the Query Analyzer
2. Enter the SQL code shown in Listing 20.18, and execute it to generate a test XML document for this example.

**Listing 20.18    SQL code to produce sample XML document.**

```
USE Employee
GO
```

```
SELECT Emp.First_Name,
       Emp.Last_Name,
       Addr.Line1,
       City.Name AS City,
       State.State_Code AS State,
       Zip.Zip5 AS Zip
  FROM tbl_Employee Emp (NOLOCK)
  JOIN tbl_EmployeeAddressXRef ea (NOLOCK)
    ON Emp.Employee_ID = ea.Employee_ID
  JOIN Address..tbl_Address Addr (NOLOCK)
    ON ea.Address_ID = Addr.Address_ID
  JOIN Address..tbl_City City (NOLOCK)
    ON Addr.City_ID = City.City_ID
  JOIN Address..tbl_State State (NOLOCK)
    ON City.State_ID = State.State_ID
  JOIN Address..tbl_ZipCode Zip (NOLOCK)
    ON Addr.Zip_ID = Zip.Zip_ID
 WHERE Emp.Employee_ID IN (1,4,7)
 ORDER BY Emp.Employee_ID
 FOR XML AUTO
```

3. Once you have generated the XML document, copy it from the results pane, and paste it into a new query window.

4. You need to add **<ROOT>** and **</ROOT>** tags around the XML document. Without these tags, it is actually a document fragment and is not suitable for use with the **OPENXML** function.

5. You can now begin building the code to work with the document. Start by declaring two variables. The first is an **INTEGER** to hold the document handle, and the second is a large **VARCHAR** to hold the document text.

6. Assign the text of the document you created in step 2 to the **VARCHAR** variable you declared to hold the document.

7. Next, execute the **sp_xml_preparedocument** stored procedure to parse the document and get it ready for use in a query.

8. You can then start to create the **SELECT** statement to retrieve data from the XML document. Begin by creating a **SELECT** list that contains all the fields in the document (**Fname**, **Lname**, **Line1**, **City**, **State**, **Zip**).

9. Add the **FROM** clause using the **OPENXML** function. The following code opens the document and sets the rowpattern to include all nodes in the document. Flags is set to 1 to indicate attribute-centric mapping for the document.

```
FROM OPENXML(@MyDoc, 'ROOT/Emp/Addr/City/State/Zip', 1)
```

10. The next step is to provide the document column mappings for the query. The following code shows the beginning of the **WITH** clause that maps the first field in the document. Notice that the column needs to be "dereferenced" to indicate the node level where the column is stored in the document.

```
WITH(FName VARCHAR(15) '../../../../@First_Name',
```

11. The column mapping definitions need to be provided for each column included in the document that will be accessed in the query.

12. The final task that must be performed is to release the memory used by the document when you are finished working with it. This is done my executing the **sp_xml_removedocument** stored procedure and passing it the document handle.

13. Once you have finished building the script, execute and test the code. The completed code for this example is provided in Listing 20.19.

This can be a tedious task and requires patience and testing to successfully implement. It is important to understand that in most cases, this type of processing will probably be done from an application rather than the Query Analyzer. Although this task may be tedious, it is worthwhile if you need to exchange information between applications and organizations that have dissimilar system designs. Once you have created an application to work with an XML document using the **OPENXML** function, you can work with any document that shares the same XML structure. If you will be receiving data in an XML document regularly, the initial work will pay numerous dividends in the future.

Although this example focuses on using a **SELECT** statement to show the information contained within the XML document, it is also possible to use the **OPENXML** function with **INSERT**, **UPDATE**, and **DELETE** statements. This provides the flexibility to import the data contained in an XML document into your own data structures for processing by your applications.

**Listing 20.19   Executing sp_xml_preparedocument.**

```
DECLARE @v_MyDoc  INTEGER,
        @v_XMLDoc VARCHAR(8000)

SELECT @v_XMLDoc = '<ROOT>'+
                   '<Emp First_Name="Patrick" Last_Name="Dalton">'+
                   '<Addr Line1="106 Main St.">'+
                   '<City City="Ft. Lauderdale">'+
                   '<State State="FL">'+
                   '<Zip Zip="33305"/>'+
```

```
                      '</State>'+
                      '</City>'+
                      '</Addr>'+
                      '</Emp>'+
                      '<Emp First_Name="Paul" Last_Name="Whitehead">'+
                      '<Addr Line1="142 Bonaventure">'+
                      '<City City="Weston">'+
                      '<State State="FL">'+
                      '<Zip Zip="33326"/>'+
                      '</State>'+
                      '</City>'+
                      '</Addr>'+
                      '</Emp>'+
                      '<Emp First_Name="Fred" Last_Name="Couples">'+
                      '<Addr Line1="166 Bonaventure">'+
                      '<City City="Weston">'+
                      '<State State="FL">'+
                      '<Zip Zip="33326"/>'+
                      '</State>'+
                      '</City>'+
                      '</Addr>'+
                      '</Emp>'+
                      '</ROOT>'

   exec sp_xml_preparedocument @v_MyDoc OUTPUT, @v_XMLDoc

   SELECT FName,
          LName,
          Line1,
          City,
          State,
          Zip
     FROM OPENXML(@v_MyDoc, 'ROOT/Emp/Addr/City/State/Zip', 1)
          WITH(FName VARCHAR(15) '../../../../@First_Name',
               LName VARCHAR(20) '../../../../@Last_Name',
               Line1 VARCHAR(30) '../../../@Line1',
               City  VARCHAR(25) '../../@City',
               State VARCHAR(2)  '../@State',
               Zip   VARCHAR(5)  '@Zip')

   EXEC sp_xml_removedocument @v_MyDoc
```

| Related solution: | Found on page: |
|---|---|
| Utility Procedures and Scripts | 661 |

# Chapter 21

# English Query

# In Depth

"Hello, computer?" Does this sound a bit like Star Trek? It is not as far-fetched as it may seem. A little-used application in the Microsoft SQL Server arsenal is Microsoft English Query. This application, or its core technology, is actually used in more places than you may think. The cute little office assistant, the Internet site **www.askjeeves.com**, and voice recognition software are bringing the future of data access to you in ways only science fiction fans could dream of. We are far from the late Isaac Asimov's (1920-1992) dream of thinking and living machines, but we are well on the way toward that goal.

There are a number of uses for taking an English structured question or command and translating it into a database command. You can create applications and reports that take written or voice input and return data to the user without any structured code, or you can create a query interface that is finally as easy to use as speech itself. I (Patrick) have created speech and English Query applications of various flavors over the last few years and really only feel like I have scratched the surface of what is possible.

This chapter serves as an introduction and primer to the development and management of a data model for English Query use. You walk through the latest enhancements in the development tool set and learn how to modify your data model in this chapter. You also learn how you can use the English Query engine in your applications to improve the user experience and provide functionality that is not expected or even thought possible.

---

**NOTE:** *This chapter assumes that you have already installed the English Query support as well as a copy of Visual Studio. If you have not installed these applications, you should do so before continuing.*

---

There are a number of tutorials and examples that are shipped with English Query. You should run through each tutorial to gain the knowledge and understanding of how the tool works. The "Immediate Solutions" section of this chapter walks you through the creation of an English Query model for the Address database that ships with this book. (See Chapter 8 for more information on the Address database.)

## What Is a Model?

Recall that database modeling and design techniques were discussed in Chapters 8 and 16. With regard to English Query, you must create a supporting model of how the entities and relationships of your database relate to each other in the

English language. The models created to support English Query provide the English to data structure mapping used to satisfy the SQL statements generated by the English Query engine for submission to the database.

The model that you create is the foundation used by the English Query engine to parse and restructure the English language sentence into a SQL statement that can be submitted to a server as a query. You will build this model and evolve it over time. As more questions are asked and not answered correctly, you will have to create a more complete model to answer those questions. You can update your model very easily, and you deploy it by simply copying the new model over the old one.

You may find that over time your model will go through much iteration to really become useful in your enterprise. Only after users have submitted a broad range of questions (which you should store for testing purposes) can you really be confident in the model you have developed.

## Database Normalization Rules

There are some rules for a database that you should follow when designing your database model that will help you create a flexible English Query model. Those rules are:

- You must have a one-to-one relationship between instances of an entity and rows in a table. If you follow good database design principles, this rule is easily met by most databases.

- A field should have the same meaning for each row in the table. This particular rule is violated more often than you might think. General-purpose columns that can hold data of differing meanings should be avoided in *any* design. They are hard to manage and even harder to hold to any kind of standard for data integrity.

- Each table should represent only one entity. This rule can be confusing because you may normalize your data model to a point where the combination of different entities is actually the English language equivalent entity. You can meet this rule by creating a view to support the English language entity and not denormalizing the underlying data.

- Avoid multiple columns representing an instance of an entity. You should be creating entities with a single key value that represents the row in a table. Simplified **JOIN** conditions are an unfortunate restriction of the English Query engine.

- **JOIN** conditions should be based on primary and foreign key equality. It is difficult to relate nonequality relationships in English Query. Exact matches of rows are far easier for **JOIN** logic.

Following each of these rules is second nature for a well-designed database. If you are trying to create an English Query model for an existing database, review these rules and make sure you have followed them or can apply them to the target database.

# English Query Tools

The English Query development environment has been integrated with the Microsoft Visual Studio development environment. The look and feel of the designer is *very* similar to Visual Studio. There have been a few enhancements to better manage your English Query project, however. The SQL Project Wizard for English Query makes it a snap to create a basic model to use as a starting point. See the "Immediate Solutions" section for an example of creating an English Query model for the Address database.

**NOTE:** *For the purposes of this section of the chapter, we will focus on the examples that ship with SQL Server 2000.*

The development environment is broken down into a few areas. One area, the *model editor*, uses the Visual Studio interface and the built-in test tool to check the model by typing in questions, having them parsed, and optionally running them against your model. Another area, the *compiled model*, is distributed to the server or application where the questions are submitted (as long as the runtime engine is present). The project files associated with English Query are listed in Table 21.1.

Let's look at an English Query project using the Northwind database. Open the sample project for the Northwind database by following these steps:

1. Open the Microsoft English Query from the English Query program group.

2. Click on the Existing tab.

3. Navigate to the Samples directory in the Microsoft English Query directory that was installed on your hard drive, and select the Northwind.eqp file. Your dialog should look like Figure 21.1.

**Table 21.1    File extensions for English Query files.**

| File Extension | File Type |
| --- | --- |
| EQP | English Query project file |
| EGD | Compiled model |
| EQR | Regression source test file |
| EQO | Regression output file |
| EQM | English Query module |

4. Click on Open.

5. Click on the plus sign in the Project Explorer window next to the Northwind project to expand the tree view.

6. Double-click on the Northwind.eqm file to open it in the model designer. See Figure 21.2 to view the open Northwind module.

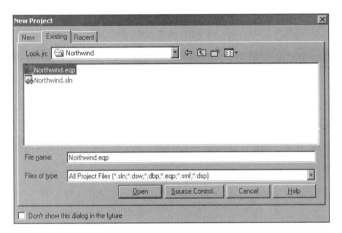

Figure 21.1    Open an existing project dialog.

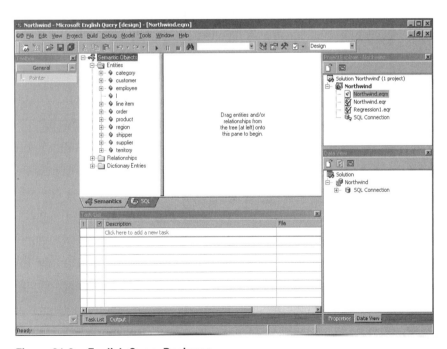

Figure 21.2    English Query Designer.

**NOTE:** *The interface and all the associated dialogs and icons are explained in detail in the Microsoft English Query Books Online (available in the English Query program group). Spend a few minutes going through the Books Online, specifically the Model Editor topic, and work through the examples to become familiar with how the tool works.*

Let's take a look at the designer in a bit more detail and review a few of the steps that you need to master in order to create and maintain an English Query model.

# Model Test Window

The model test application is launched when you press F5. Click on Run or select Debug|Start from the menu bar. This interface allows you to type in questions to be parsed and run against your model, so that you can test the logic supplied by the model. You will spend a great deal of time with this tool during the course of creating your new English Query model.

1. In the model designer, press F5 with the Northwind example model open to pull up the model test tool.

2. When the tool opens, type in the question, "How many customers are there?" and press Enter. This action submits the question to the English Query engine.

3. The question is parsed, restated, and a query is generated for submission to SQL Server. See Figure 21.3 to view the Model Test tool with the sample question submitted.

**NOTE:** *You can actually see the data returned if you type Ctrl+R or click on the View Results button on the tool bar. (A connection to a database is required to see data in the results pane, but is not required to see the generated query output.)*

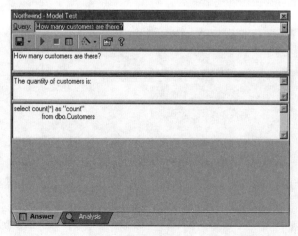

Figure 21.3    Model Test tool.

One of the nice enhancements to English Query is the capability to save questions to a regression test file. The Save button on the Model Test tool stores the question in Extensible Markup Language (XML) format to a regression test file (covered later in this chapter under "Regression Testing"). Click on Save to add the customer sample question to the regression file.

Before continuing to the next section, try each of the following questions or commands in the Model Test tool to see how the questions are parsed as well as the queries they generate:

- How many orders has each customer placed?
- Show the employees over 50.
- Who is the oldest manager?
- Show the employees that sell in the southern region.
- Show the salespeople and their territories and regions.
- Who covers the Boston territory?
- When was each order shipped?
- How old is each employee?

## Suggestion Wizard

If you type in questions that consistently return answers and data, you know you have created a model that will handle most questions well. There will be instances when the model is not prepared for a question that is submitted. When these instances occur, you can turn to the Suggestion Wizard to create the entities and relationships required to answer those questions.

---

**NOTE:** *The Suggestion Wizard will not deal with all situations in one pass. You may have to submit a question a few times and use the wizard multiple times to get the model to successfully answer the question. (There will be some situations that the wizard will have difficulty dealing with. If you try the wizard a few times for a particular question and it cannot resolve that question, you may have to manually model the entities and relationships.)*

---

In order to see how the Suggestion Wizard helps you in your modeling tasks, type in the following question, "Who are the consumers of our products?" The sample model will not know how to answer this question because it does not know enough based on the model to formulate a response. The output of submitting the consumer question is:

```
I haven't been given any information on things.
```

You can call the Suggestion Wizard by clicking on the magic wand icon on the toolbar or by typing Ctrl+W. Figure 21.4 shows the Suggestion Wizard with the consumer question loaded.

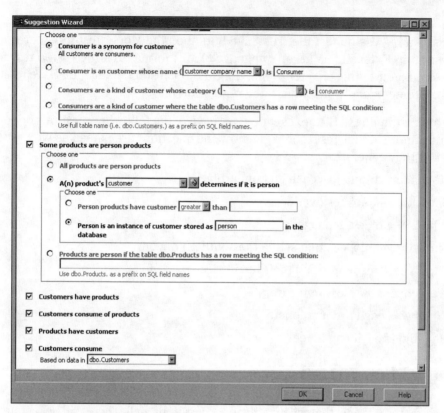

**Figure 21.4   Suggestion Wizard.**

Each time the Suggestion Wizard is loaded, it tries to analyze the question and looks at the question differently each time it is called. The wizard asks a number of various questions and tries to clarify any ambiguous references or relationships that it believes will satisfy the question. At the bottom of the wizard is the Generate Diagram Of Modeled Entities And Relationships checkbox. Leave this option selected, and review the diagram that is produced to ensure that you understand and agree with the wizard's solution. See Figure 21.5 for an example of the diagram created by the Suggestion Wizard for the consumer question.

## Regression Testing

Integrated into the English Query Designer is the capability to perform regression testing of the model to ensure that any changes in the model have not introduced problems for the existing, known questions that have been tested against the model. The regression test files are stored in XML format and are saved with the project so they can be used when the model is updated. See Listing 21.1 for an excerpt of the Northwind regression file.

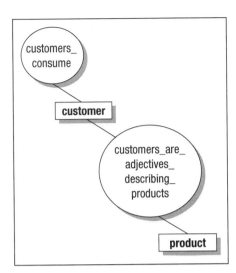

Figure 21.5    Wizard generated diagram.

---

**NOTE:** *You can have multiple regression files for each model.*

---

Listing 21.1    Sample of the Northwind regression file.

```
<?xml version="1.0"?>
<REGRESSION>
  <QUESTION>show the seafood products
    <RESTATEMENT>Which products that aren't discontinued are seafood?</
RESTATEMENT>
    <ANSWER>The seafood products that aren't discontinued are:
      <QUERY>
        <![CDATA[select dbo.Products.ProductName as "Product Name"
    from dbo.Products, dbo.Categories
    where dbo.Products.Discontinued<>'1'
    and dbo.Products.CategoryID=dbo.Categories.CategoryID
    and dbo.Categories.CategoryName in ('Seafood', 'Seafood')]]>
      </QUERY>
    </ANSWER>
  </QUESTION>
  <QUESTION>show the vegetable products
    <RESTATEMENT>Which products that aren't discontinued are vegetable?</
RESTATEMENT>
    <ANSWER>The vegetable products that aren't discontinued are:
      <QUERY>
        <![CDATA[select dbo.Products.ProductName as "Product Name"
    from dbo.Products, dbo.Categories
    where dbo.Products.Discontinued<>'1'
    and dbo.Products.CategoryID=dbo.Categories.CategoryID
```

```
        and dbo.Categories.CategoryName='Produce']]>
          </QUERY>
        </ANSWER>
      </QUESTION>
```

Each question is wrapped with the **<QUESTION>** and **</QUESTION>** tags to delimit each regression test in the file. Note the highlighted tags in Listing 21.1. To ensure that all the existing functionality is maintained, each question that the model should know how to answer based on either testing or specification should be saved in a regression test file and run against the model before it is distributed.

---

***TIP:*** *You can run a regression test by selecting the regression file in the project explorer, right-clicking on the file, and then selecting the Run Regression menu item. The status of the regression test is displayed in the lower-left corner of the screen in a status bar.*

---

You can view and compare the regression test output through the regression menu or the pop-up menu that appears when you right-click on any regression file in the project.

## Question Builder

Microsoft has provided an ActiveX control that can be used in your client applications to help the end user with English Query-enabled applications. The main purpose of the Question Builder is to provide general sample questions to help the end user become more familiar with the English Query possibilities. A help file that can be incorporated into your application is provided as well. There is a sample Active Server Page (ASP) application that can also be used as a guide for using the Question Builder. It is installed in the \Program Files\Microsoft English Query\Samples\Applications directory.

# Developing Your Model

The process of developing an English Query model is actually very simple. You create a project to manage the model, ask the model questions, and add relationships and entities to support the questions the model will be asked.

Developing a model is best described as a building block approach. You create the basic entity and relationship mapping based on the output of the SQL Project Wizard, which becomes your foundation. You then submit your target questions one after another to ensure that they work. If the question does not produce an answer, you must supply the information necessary to answer that question.

Some models are actually released with a limited set of questions as well as a facility to track the questions submitted, so that they can be modeled at a later time to enhance the functionality of the English Query model. There are a few questions that you should consider before attempting to create an English Query model and/or project.

- What is the target audience of the model? Different audiences will ask distinct kinds of questions. Users in the Accounting department may ask an entirely separate set of questions than users in the Operations department.

- What are the types of questions that users will ask? If there are specific questions that can be gathered and modeled at the outset, your model will be more useful from the beginning. Typically, you will spend more time developing the model before releasing it if the questions are very specific in nature.

- How in depth will the questions be? Depending upon the scope of the questions that will be asked, you may need to create supplemental views to add to the model to support the detail some questions may require.

## Creating an English Query Project

Before you begin, create a basic list of questions that will match what your users may ask. Keep this list simple and straightforward and use single entity kinds of questions. This will provide the relational mapping for the simple questions that will be submitted. You do not have to create a completely thorough question list at this stage in the process.

Create an enhanced list of questions that takes the more complex questions into account. This list of questions should account for the more technical and complex reporting queries that may be submitted to the English Query engine. Multiple entity questions and questions that refer to entities with optional names and actual values in the questions are candidates for this group of questions. The harder list of questions will typically require some well-thought-out modeling of the relationships and entities.

As you submit questions to the model, you will find that the selected output based on the question does not really match what you expect. You can then address this problem by changing the way the data is displayed.

You may find that in certain situations your database model does not match well to an English Query model. In that event, you can create a view and add it to your model for use as an entity. Views can easily become a crutch when you are having trouble getting a complex relationship mapped, so be careful and use them sparingly if they are to support only the English Query interface. If the view already exists in the database for some other purpose, like reporting or ad hoc queries, you can consider using the view a bit more freely because it is typically optimized for the kind of queries that English Query will submit. (Views should adhere to the same normalization rules as tables in the English Query model.)

If the data displayed from a question is incomplete, you may need to add a few remote columns to the output for that entity. The remote columns must be supported by **JOIN** conditions and can greatly improve the clarity of the data returned from some questions.

You can provide clarification information to the user through the Help Text for each entity in your English Query model. If you add a description of the entity in the Help Text area of the entity definition, like the Entity edit dialog shown in Figure 21.6, your users will be able to ask questions about the entities or ask clarification questions that may guide them in the right direction when using the model.

# Guidelines

The following list contains a few rules and guidelines that will help you create a better English Query model:

- Follow the database normalization guidelines outlined in this book. Having a normalized data set makes your English Query modeling experience much easier.

- Always provide sample questions to the users of English Query applications. Users will then be able to glean some sort of idea of sentence structure from the examples to help them submit their question.

- Save questions that fail to be translated for review and model revision purposes. This will help you update the model and clarify potentially fuzzy relationship logic.

- Create some sort of primer or explanation for what the user should expect. Some users may not understand, or the interface may not be as intuitive as

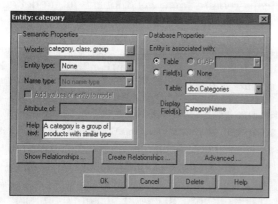

**Figure 21.6    Entity edit dialog.**

you may think. For example, imagine how hard it would be to leave a message on an answering machine if it actually talked back to you.

- Do not use the word "name" to describe an entity. This is considered a keyword and generates an error in the compile and testing modes.

- Strive to use *active* not *passive* voice. The English Query engine understands both active and passive voice questions, but is more flexible when the relationship is defined using an active voice.

- Try to avoid using the prepositions "by" and "to". They can confuse the English Query engine and may return unexpected results.

- Avoid using **NULL** data elements when possible in English Query entities. Your results for some questions may not return the rows you expect because of **NULL** masking in the **WHERE** clause of the query returned by the English Query engine.

- Do not mix the case of words when describing entities. Use all lowercase letters for describing words unless they will be submitted in uppercase or mixed case.

- There may be times when you need to create duplicate entities to support the relationships needed to answer some questions. An example might be, "Which manager reports to another manager?" or "Who moved from one country to another country in the last year?" The country or manager reference may require two different entities in the English Query model.

- Be careful of the verbs in Table 21.2 when defining command relationships. This is only a partial list. To see a complete list, look up the topic "Verbs to avoid in command relationships" in the SQL Server Books Online. (You must test any of the verbs listed to ensure they return the information you expect. They can be used, but may confuse the English Query engine.) Use of any verb in the list may return unexpected results in response to a question.

**Table 21.2   Verbs to be careful of.**

| Add | Decline | Grow | Meet | Save | Store |
|---|---|---|---|---|---|
| Average | Divide | Include | Name | Select | Subtract |
| Call | Exceed | Keep | Order | Show | Tell |
| Compare | Find | Know | Relate | Sort | Total |
| Contain | Go | Locate | Report | Stop | |

# Deploying Your Model

Once you have created a model, you then need to deploy that model so that it can be used. The typical implementation of English Query uses either a Web server or a client application to submit questions to the English Query runtime engine. The runtime engine uses the compiled model to generate SQL statements that can then be submitted as queries to a SQL Server instance as a request for records. See Figure 21.7 for an example of how the question and data flow would work for an Internet application.

The only real difference between a Web-based solution and a client application is that the runtime files, listed in Table 21.3, need to be installed only on the Web server and not each client application machine. In order to distribute the runtime files, you should copy the files listed in Table 21.3, which can be found in the \Program Files\Common\System\EQ80 directory, to the same common directory on the target machine. The compiled English Query application EQD file should then be copied to the same directory as the client application (or Web server virtual directory).

Once the files have been copied, the mseqole.dll and mseqgrqb.ocx must be registered on that machine before they can be used. You would perform this registration through an install application or manually with **regsvr32** using the following syntax (assuming you have used the default path information):

```
To Register:
Regsvr32 "\Program Files\Common Files\System\EQ80\Mseqole.dll" /s
Regsvr32 "\Program Files\Common Files\System\EQ80\Mseqgrqb.dll" /s
To Uninstall and clean up the registry:
Regsvr32 "\Program Files\Common Files\System\EQ80\Mseqole.dll" /u
```

**Table 21.3    Runtime files for an English Query application.**

| File | Description |
| --- | --- |
| Mseqole.dll | This dynamic link library (DLL) holds the object model for English Query. |
| Mseqbase.dll | Supplemental file used by the query engine. |
| Mseqsql.dll | Supplemental file used by the query engine. |
| Mseqmsg.dll | Supplemental file used by the query engine. |
| Mseqconn.dll | Supplemental file used by the query engine. |
| Mseqcore.eqd | Supplemental file used by the query engine. |
| Mseqgrqb.ocx | English Query Question Builder ActiveX control. |
| Mseqgrqb.cab | This is a cabinet file that contains the mseqgrqb.ocx file, the associated help file (CHM extension), and an INF file that tells Microsoft Internet Explorer where to copy the files during installation along with how to register and unregister the needed DLLs for the runtime environment. |

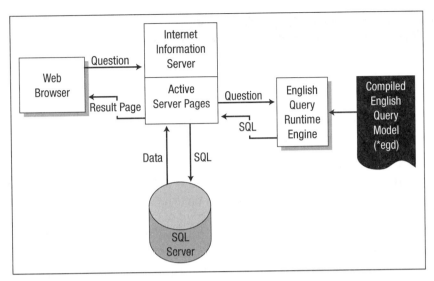

Figure 21.7    Question and data flow for an Internet application.

# Voice Recognition

This section provides a final note about English Query and the potential it can provide to the end user. I have spent a few years with voice recognition software and have used the software development kits of a few vendors to make applications voice-aware. I have even taken the time to obtain certification in the use and training of the technology because it will become more popular as the processing power of computers improves and the semantic models improve. Voice recognition is an incredible technology that is just entering the infant stages of development (in my opinion). Voice technology advances have been dramatic over the last few years. Dragon Naturally Speaking is perhaps one of the best voice recognition engines on the market. Yet it, like other engines, requires a great deal of "voice-training" to really be useful in many applications. Once trained to your voice, Dragon has a *very* good recognition level and can make conventional word processing seem ancient and outdated.

If you plan on deploying an application that couples voice technology and English Query, be sure to develop the two components separately. Make sure the English Query portion of the loop is closed before combining voice with it. Make sure the model responds correctly to type-written sentences before combining voice technology with it. Voice technology simply becomes the engine to send the sentence input to the English Query engine.

# Immediate Solutions

## English Query Tutorials

Why should you be interested in doing some silly tutorial? The English Query tutorials that ship with SQL Server 2000 are not rocket science, but they do explain the concept and walk you through the tools and processes pretty darn well! Microsoft's goal with this release of English Query was to deliver a more developer-friendly and better-documented product. It has done a good job. Although Microsoft might not have hit a home run with this release, it has definitely smacked the feature hard and is standing on second base waiting to score.

We *strongly* recommend that you walk through two tutorials before attempting to work on your own model. The basic and complex model examples are very good at getting you started. Work through them both!

One other tutorial you should consider is the ever popular "look at how someone else did it" tutorial. Open the sample models and applications. The Northwind model used in the first section of this chapter is pretty well documented and provides hours of examples for you to "use" in your design.

**NOTE:** If your model is giving you trouble, try asking the same question to the Northwind database (changing the context to match the data). You can then see how the example model supplies the answer and what relationships and entity definitions exist in that model so that you will have a basis for refining your own model.

Most developers usually jump right in to a new feature or a product without reading help files or how-to pages to determine how intuitive the application is. It is difficult to get a firm grasp on this application's nuances and features until you spend some time really looking at the documentation and examples. You will gain some valuable knowledge and produce a better model if you take this advice and work with the tutorials and samples provided.

## Creating an English Query Model from the Address Database

In addition to the sample models and the tutorials that ship with English Query, you will create a model from scratch so that you have an example of the process as it applies to your enterprise. Follow the guidelines outlined in this chapter step-by-step.

The Address database from Chapter 8 is used as an example for the following solutions. The database should already be installed and available. If it is not on your server, please refer to the "Immediate Solutions" section in Chapter 8 for the steps needed to install the Address database.

| *Related solution:* | *Found on page:* |
| --- | --- |
| Installing the Book Databases from Scripts | 369 |

**21. English Query**

## Creating the Test Questions for the Model Development Cycle

The first step in the process of developing an English Query model is to put together a list of the questions that will be submitted to the model. Because this is an Address database, you should focus on a list of questions that pertain to address information. You should develop two lists of questions. One list should cover the basic address questions, such as questions related to counts or location. The second list should be used to enhance your model and provide some additional details that create your basic English Query model, which you can release to a user community.

Both sets of questions will be saved in a regression file that is used as a baseline for testing the model during later modifications. See the following list of basic questions that will be submitted to the Address database model:

- How many addresses are there?
- How many cities are there?
- How many states are there?
- How many ZIP codes are there?

The second list of questions is typically more detailed and requires the addition of entities and relationships to the model. Using this two-phase approach allows you to save the basic model as a foundation, and then work through the second list of questions in an iterative fashion. (Save regression and model changes as you go to ensure that you do not lose any functionality.) See the following detailed list of address questions that will be used during the development of your model:

- How many cities are in Florida?
- What ZIP codes are in Florida?
- What state is Tampa in?

You can create as large a list of questions as you like for testing purposes. In fact, the larger the question list the better your model will turn out. The lists provided are short for the sake of space. A normal listing should have at least 15 to 20 sample questions of each type for a medium-sized database.

## Run the SQL Project Wizard

The second step in creating your English Query model is to run the SQL Project Wizard. You should run through the wizard to create your basic model. The wizard does a good job of determining the entities and relationships for you. You can create the entities and relationships yourself from scratch, but it is time consuming, and you may miss some of the relationships that the wizard automatically maps for you. This solution assumes that you have the Visual Studio and English Query prerequisites installed on your machine. If you do not, please refer to the English Query Books Online topic "Installation Requirements and Considerations." To create a basic model, you should follow these steps:

1. Start the English Query development environment.

2. In the New Project dialog, select the English Query Projects folder and ensure that the SQL Project Wizard is selected.

3. Supply a name for this project. For this example, use Address. Type "Address" into the Name text box.

4. Select the directory that will be used to store the project and associated files during the development of the model. For this example, use "C:\BlackBook\Ch21\Model\Address". See Figure 21.8 for the New Project dialog with the appropriate information filled in.

5. Click on Open.

6. Complete the connection properties for the model to use during the development phase. Select the Microsoft OLE DB provider for SQL Server, and click on Next.

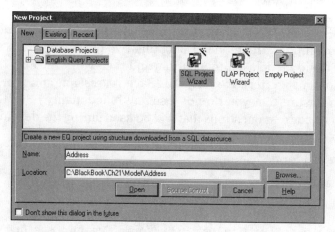

Figure 21.8    New Project dialog.

7. The Connection tab appears. This tab of the dialog is where you specify the server, user name, and database to be used for this connection. For this example, use the development server "pdalton01" and the sa login with a blank password, and then select the Address database.

8. You can click on Test Connection to verify that you have connectivity to the server with the credentials you have supplied. Your Data Link Properties dialog should look like Figure 21.9.

9. Click on OK to continue in the wizard.

10. You are then asked to select the tables that you want to include in the model. Select all the tables in the Address database *except* **tbl_AddressDN**. You can select the tables by double-clicking on them or by using the arrow buttons to move the list into the "Selected" pane. See Figure 21.10.

11. Click on OK.

12. The wizard then reads the existing data model and formulates the entities and relationships for the model.

13. Next, a wizard summary page appears, which lists the entities and relationships that the wizard recommends. Click on the plus sign next to each entity to expand the lists and show the relationships that are being suggested.

14. Review the list to become familiar with what is being presented and make any additional selections that you may want to add based on the model knowledge you possess. For the sake of this example, accept the defaults. Your Project Wizard dialog should look like Figure 21.11.

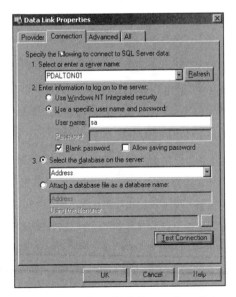

Figure 21.9    Data Link Properties dialog.

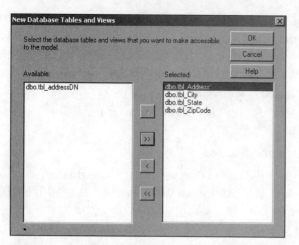

**Figure 21.10    New Database Tables And Views dialog.**

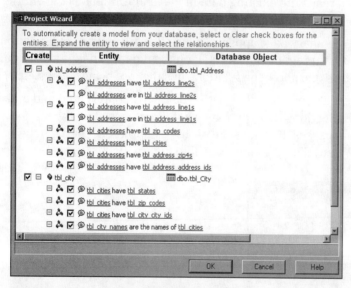

**Figure 21.11    Project Wizard dialog.**

15. Click on OK to create the model entities and complete the wizard.

16. The wizard creates the entities and relationships (under the Semantics tab on the left portion of the screen, which is shown in Figure 21.12).

17. The wizard also creates a regression file called "address.eqr" and displays that file along with the Address module and SQL connection in the Project Explorer, which is shown in the upper-right corner of Figure 21.12.

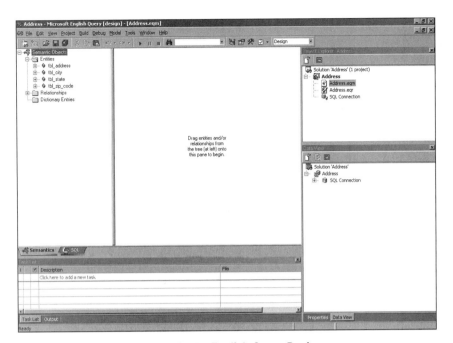

Figure 21.12    Address model in the English Query Designer.

18. You can browse through the actual tables (and eventually views) accessible through the connection in the Data View pane in the lower-right corner of Figure 21.12.

19. The task list for this project is displayed at the bottom of the screen. This list holds user-defined tasks and compiler warnings and errors when you attempt to debug the model.

20. At the center of the screen in Figure 21.12, you find the Canvas pane of the designer. (This is empty at this point in the process.)

The designer is highly customizable and can show and hide different portions of the items listed previously based on your preferences. Feel free to adjust the layout and display to fit your needs and programming habits. (The defaults for the solution are assumed in this chapter.) Once the wizard has completed, you can move on to the next step in the process, reviewing and modifying the model to make it as user-friendly as possible before testing it.

## Review and Update the Entities and Relationships Generated by the Wizard

This solution assumes you have performed the previous solution "Run the SQL Project Wizard." If you have not, please refer to that solution to get the Address model in the form expected for this solution. Look at the entities generated by the wizard and update their names to better reflect an English-language representation. When you edit the entities, the relationships each entity participates in are automatically updated to reflect the changes.

The SQL Project Wizard created four entities for this model. With the Address project open in the English Query Model Designer, ensure that the Semantics tab is selected before you begin the following steps:

1. Select the address entity under the Semantics entities folder.

2. Right-click on **tbl_address** to bring up the pop-up menu. Select Edit from the menu to bring up the Entity Properties dialog.

3. The words *text box* are selected. Click on the word in the text box "tbl_address".

4. The drop-down list that is displayed is shown in Figure 21.13. Select the word "tbl_address" and remove the "tbl_" portion of the word. This action renames the entity and any associated relationship.

5. Click on OK to save the change for the address entity.

6. Click on the plus sign next to the Relationships folder in the tree view to verify that the relationships have been updated to say "addresses" and not "tbl_addresses". Note that the other entities have not yet been updated and are displayed with the "tbl_" prefix.

7. Select the city entity and right-click on the entity to bring up the pop-up menu. Select Edit from the menu.

8. Change the entity name to read "city" just as you did for the address entity.

9. You should also specify some help text to provide users with a definition of this entity should they ask what it is. In the Help text box, type in "A city used in the display of an address."

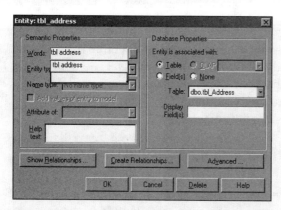

Figure 21.13    Address entity dialog with the Words drop-down list expanded.

10. Click on OK to update the entity and relationships for the city entity.

11. Double-click on the state entity (**tbl_State**) to bring up the Entity Properties dialog. (This is the same as right-clicking and selecting Edit from the pop-up menu.)

12. Change the name of the entity by modifying the word just as you did before.

13. Click on OK to update the state entity.

14. Double-click on the zip code entity.

15. This entity requires a few words to describe it. Change the tbl_zip_code entry to "zip code". Click on the word again, and add an additional word "zip" in the empty box under zip code. This allows users to type in the word "zip" instead of zip code and get the same results. Additionally, you can add the word "zipcode" in case users type it as a combined word in a question. See Figure 21.14 to verify that your zip code entity matches this example.

16. Click on OK to save the changes to the zip code entity.

17. Notice in the tree view that some of the relationships have not been completely updated to match the entity name changes that have been made so far. This happens because the field mapping reference places the table and column name in the word list for each column or attribute of an entity.

18. To change the column mappings, click on the plus sign next to the address entity.

19. In the column or attribute list, double-click on the Address_ID attribute. You will find two word entries for the attribute. The Address_ID entry is the one that you want to keep, so delete the tbl_address_ address_ID entry from the list.

20. Click on OK to update the attribute and relationships.

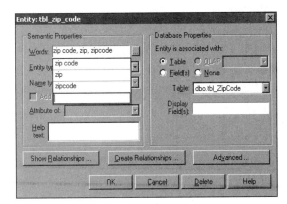

Figure 21.14   Zip code entity.

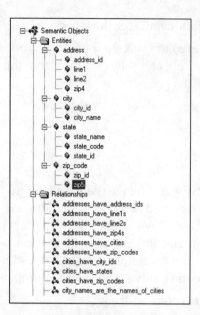

**Figure 21.15   Semantic tree view after updating the entity and attribute names.**

21. Repeat the preceding two steps for each column or attribute of each entity. See Figure 21.15 for the finished tree view representing the name updates.

You are now ready to begin the process of testing the model with the sample questions that you have collected for the Address English Query model.

## Run the Basic Questions through the Model Test Tool

This solution assumes that you have completed the previous two solutions and have the Address model open in the English Query Designer.

To open the Model Test tool, press F5 in the English Query designer. You are presented with the Model Test tool. Use the following steps to test your model:

1. Type in the first of your test questions in the Query text box, "How many addresses are there?" and press Enter. The question is submitted to the English Query engine to be rephrased and a query is generated.

2. Press Ctrl+R to add the View Results pane to the window. You must have a defined database connection (described in an earlier solution) in order to see data output for each question. You should see results similar to those shown in Figure 21.16.

3. To add this successful question and response to your XML-based regression file, click on Save on the Model Test toolbar.

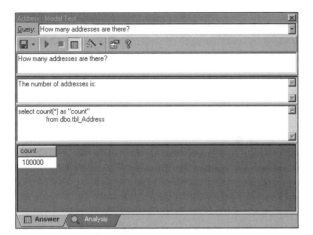

Figure 21.16    Model Test tool.

4. Notice that the Designer View behind the tool changes to the Regression File View and that the question you typed in the tool is placed in the file. See Listing 21.2 for the regression file entries.

Listing 21.2    Regression file entry for the first question.

```
<?xml version="1.0"?>
<REGRESSION>
  <QUESTION>How many addresses are there?
    <RESTATEMENT>How many addresses are there?</RESTATEMENT>
    <ANSWER>The number of addresses is:
      <QUERY>
        <![CDATA[select count(*) as "count"
    from dbo.tbl_Address]]>
      </QUERY>
    </ANSWER>
  </QUESTION>
</REGRESSION>
```

Repeat the previous steps for each of the basic questions listed in the first step of the model design process. (Create test questions for the model development cycle.) Remember to save the successful test of each question to the regression test file.

Once you have submitted each of the basic questions to the model, you are ready to move on to the more difficult questions in the modeling process.

---

**NOTE:** *In your own model development, you should use the basic questions for this stage of the model only. If you type in a question and that question does not get answered correctly on the first try, move it to the second set of questions. The second set of questions is used when you enhance the model to answer the more ambiguous questions.*

---

## Run the Complex Questions through the Model Test Tool

You should have successfully submitted the test questions from the basic list to the model and saved each question to the regression file before submitting the more difficult questions to your model. You may find that some of the questions that you thought were more difficult for the model to answer may in fact work without any additional effort. The following steps will provide a more thorough test of your model:

1. Using the same techniques as in the previous solution, press F5 to open the Model Test tool (if it is not already open).

2. In the Query text box, type in the first question, "How many cities are in Florida?" and press Enter.

3. You should see the following message stating that the English Query engine does not know enough about the entities to answer the question.

```
Based on the information I've been given about this database,
I can't answer:
  "What are the unspecified things addresses are in?".
```

4. You can use the Suggestion Wizard to give you a starting point for the model enhancements. Call the Suggestion Wizard by clicking on the Wizard button on the toolbar, or press Ctrl+W.

5. You are presented with a window that holds all the details that the Suggestion Wizard believes will add enough information to the model to effectively answer the question.

6. Tell the wizard that Florida refers to a state name by selecting the state name value from the drop-down list next to the Florida Refers To checkbox. See Figure 21.17 for the Suggestion Wizard output for the question, "How many cities are in Florida?"

7. Ensure that the States Have Cities checkbox is selected.

8. Ensure that the Cities Are In States checkbox is selected.

9. Click on OK to close the New Relationship dialog.

10. The Canvas pane should now have the entities and a connecting relationship displayed similar to the one in Figure 21.18.

11. You can retest the question by pressing F5. The previous question is filled in for you, so press Enter to submit the question.

12. You should see that the question has successfully been submitted and answered.

13. Click on Save to add this question to the regression test file.

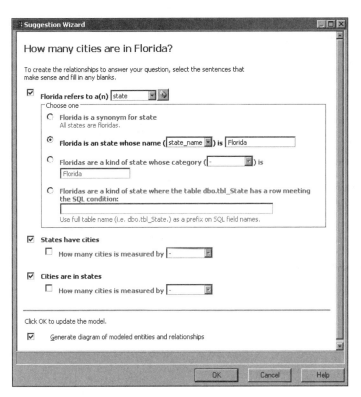

Figure 21.17    Suggestion Wizard output.

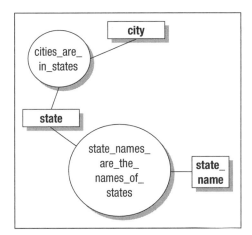

Figure 21.18    Canvas pane display showing graphic wizard output.

14. Type the next question into the Model Test tool. Type the question, "What state is Tampa in?" and press Enter.

15. Notice that this question is answered correctly without modifying the model.

16. Click on Save to add this question to the regression file.

You are now ready to compile and distribute your English Query data model for use by an application.

## Add a View to an English Query Data Model

In this solution, you create a view to answer additional questions. You first need to create a view that joins the state and zip code tables in the Address database. See Listing 21.3 for the syntax to create the **vw_StateZips** view.

### Listing 21.3    Source SQL for **vw_StateZips**.

```
CREATE VIEW dbo.vw_StateZips
AS
SELECT z.Zip_ID,
       z.Zip5,
       s.Name AS State_Name,
       s.State_Code,
       s.State_ID
  FROM tbl_ZipCode z
  JOIN tbl_State s ON z.State_ID = s.State_ID
```

Next, you need to import the new view into the English Query data model. To perform this task, follow these steps:

1. From the Model menu in the English Query Designer, select the Import Tables menu item.

2. Any tables and views not already in the model are displayed in the Tables And Views dialog. Select the **vw_StateZips** view by double-clicking in it, and then click on OK.

3. In order to use the view, it must have a primary key value to be used for join purposes. Select the SQL tab at the bottom of the Designer to display the tables and views.

4. Double-click on **vw_StatZips**. You are presented with a dialog similar to the one in Figure 21.19.

5. Specify the key column for the view. For this example, use the **zip_ID** column. Highlight the **zip_ID** attribute, and right-click on the gray box to the immediate left of the row. Select Primary Key from the pop-up menu.

6. Click on OK.

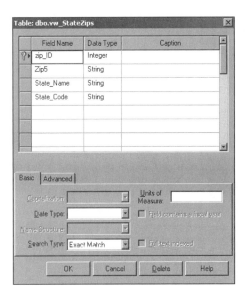

Figure 21.19    Table properties dialog.

7. Create a **JOIN** condition between zip codes and this new entity. Right-click on the Joins folder, and select Add Join.

8. In the New Join dialog, select the **tbl_ZipCode** from the Destination Table drop-down list.

9. Click on Add.

10. Select **zip_ID** for both tables as a join column, and click on OK.

11. Click on OK to close the New Join dialog.

12. Add the entity to the Semantics tab. Select the Semantics tab, right-click on the Entities folder, and choose Add Entity.

13. Fill in the Entity Property dialog reflecting the data items in Figure 21.20. The word to describe this entity is "statezips", the entity type is None, and the table displayed is **vw_StateZips**. (**Zip5** and **State_Name** attributes are the Display Fields.)

14. Click on OK.

15. Next, you need to create a relationship mapping for the new entities. Select both the statezips and zip_code entities by holding down the Shift key and dragging them onto the Canvas pane.

16. Right-click on either of the entities in the Canvas pane, and select Add Relationship.

17. In the New Relationship dialog, click on Add, which is next to the phrasings text box.

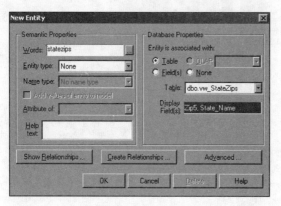

**Figure 21.20   Statezips entity properties.**

18. In the Select Phrasing dialog, select the Trait/Phrasing option, and click on OK.

19. In the Trait Phrasing dialog, select the zip_code entity in the Source drop-down list and the statezips in the Destination dialog, and click on OK.

20. The previous step adds phrasings for the relationship. See Figure 21.21 for an example of what your dialog should look like.

21. Click on OK.

| Related solution: | Found on page: |
|---|---|
| Query Analyzer | 193 |

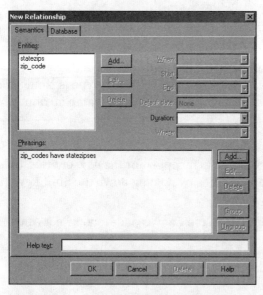

**Figure 21.21   The new relationship for zip_code to statezips.**

# Appendix A
## Book Database Schema

The databases provided on the CD for use in the examples in this book are described in detail in Chapter 8. These databases are provided as a learning tool and a practice area for your use in learning more about SQL Server 2000. You can experiment with these databases without the need to worry about causing harm to any important information on your server. These databases can be deleted and re-created by using the scripts provided with Chapter 8 or by bringing in a new copy of the completed databases from the CD.

These databases are provided to give all readers a common data set to run the majority of the examples in this book against. The Utility database in particular is a useful model for adding functionality to your own databases and servers. Whether you choose to create the Utility database on your server, or just use some of the structures in your own databases, it provides a model for creating and experimenting with new techniques and ideas.

This appendix includes a graphical representation of the three databases described in Chapter 8 (See Figures A.1, A.2, and A.3). These graphical representations will allow you to more easily see the manner in which the various entities in these databases relate to one another. It is a good idea to create this type of diagram for your own databases to allow you to clearly look at the whole picture. A diagram is also an excellent way of sharing this information with other DBAs and developers in a clear and concise manner.

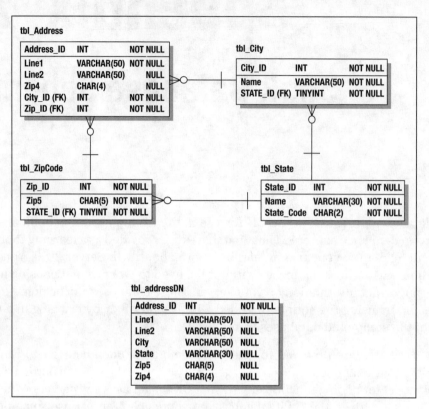

Figure A.1    The Address example database.

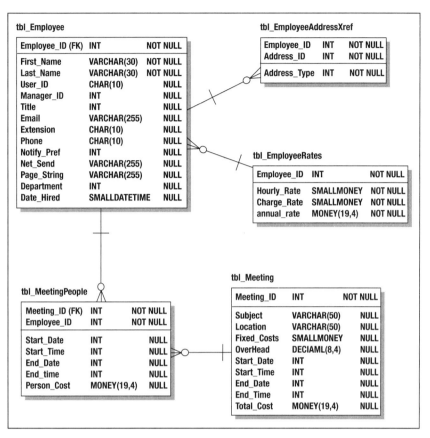

Figure A.2  The Employee example database.

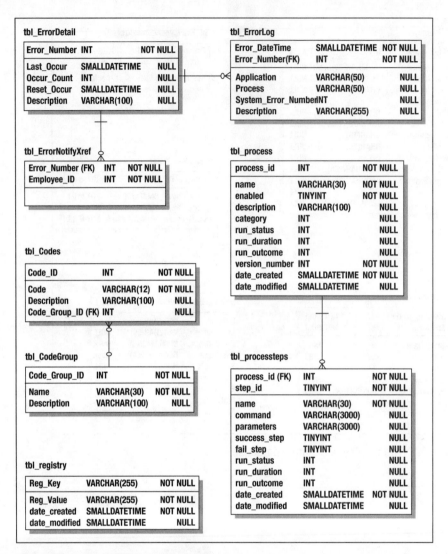

**Figure A.3    The Utility example database.**

# Appendix B
## Newsgroups and the Internet

Perhaps one of the most overlooked resources available for troubleshooting is the Internet. You have access to more information than ever before through the Internet and the newsgroups that can be accessed for the cost of a dial-up connection. Today, most companies already have some form of Internet access, and it is up to the database administrators and developers to make sure they make the most of this valuable resource. Throughout this book, there are numerous references to the Microsoft SQL Server Books Online. There are many other resources available on the Internet to help supplement and fill in the gaps that exist in the standard documentation provided in the Books Online.

Newsgroups can be very useful tools for troubleshooting problems or finding out what's new with Microsoft SQL Server. Some very good database administrators are active in the newsgroups and are more than willing to help you with any problem.

**WARNING! Not all of the users in the newsgroups are experts. No one is an expert on your system except you. Do not take advice from anyone as the ultimate fix for your system and apply changes blindly to your server without first testing to make sure the comments and suggestions work the way you expect them to.**

Another valuable resource available through the Internet is the Microsoft Knowledge Base. You can get good, current information directly from the Microsoft SQL Server source anytime, day or night, through your Internet connection. You can also subscribe to the TechNet CD, which includes a smaller version of the Knowledge Base, without the need for an Internet connection.

This appendix is not intended to change your view of any service, product, or vendor. Statements made in this appendix are the opinions of the authors and should be treated as suggestions. The companies mentioned possess many fine qualities and are all good at what they do. In no way should anything in this appendix be taken to mean that the authors feel these companies do not provide quality services and products.

# Search Engines

Searching the Internet can be as easy as typing a word or phrase and clicking the Search button. Many search engines are available on the Internet: Yahoo!, Lycos, DogPile, Iwon, and Excite, just to name a few. Most search engines are very friendly and offer step-by-step guides to getting your request processed. Not all search engines store the same information. If you do not get the results you expect from a search, you can try different sites. After a little research, you will be able to determine which search engines return the most Web site matches for the topics you are interested in. You should also identify which search engines bring the most relevant entries for your needs to the top of the list. This varies depending on the matching algorithm used by each engine.

An important consideration when performing a search is the keyword(s) you use. The more precise your keyword selection, the more accurate and relevant the Web sites returned by the search are likely to be. It is important to try alternative phrasing and spelling options when you are having trouble locating a topic. Various people post information using different ways of saying the same thing. In some cases, you may want to start with a broad search (like "SQL"), and then narrow the list by providing additional keywords in the search. Depending on the search engine, the syntax for supplying additional keywords may vary, and you may have multiple options to control how the search is performed. It is a good idea to become familiar with the available options for the search engine(s) you will be using frequently.

# Knowledge Base

The Microsoft Knowledge Base, whether the Internet version or the one available on the TechNet CD, is an up-to-the-minute source for current problems and solutions other people are experiencing with all Microsoft products. The Knowledge Base also contains current fixes or service packs you can download and apply to your software. Locating the Knowledge Base on the Internet is simple: Just use a search engine or go to the Microsoft home page at **www.microsoft.com**. When you get to the Microsoft home page, follow the links to the Knowledge Base.

The Knowledge Base has its own search engine to allow you to search the content directly. Each search returns all available articles concerning your topic. You will definitely have to try multiple ways of wording your search in order to find the relevant information. The results are returned at a default of 25 per page, or you can specify a different value. Contained within each article are tips and information regarding error messages, bugs, and bug fixes.

# Service Packs and Patches

You can obtain information relating to service packs, and in some cases, you can link directly to a patch or service pack from the Knowledge Base Web site or from the TechNet CD. Once installed on your system, the service packs should fix the problems you are having, and they might prevent error messages in the future. Read the installation instructions for the service pack or patch carefully before applying them to your production machine. As a general rule, you might want to check the newsgroups before applying a patch to make sure other people are not having trouble with the software you are about to apply to your production server.

# TechNet CD

TechNet CDs are a very useful Microsoft product. Each month, Microsoft gathers all of the articles from the Knowledge Base and any new information regarding Microsoft products and compiles them on a CD for distribution. Developers and programmers will find these CDs to be a valuable tool for staying current with any Microsoft product. By subscribing to this service (pricing available from Microsoft's Web site), you not only receive current information from the Knowledge Base, but you also have access to past articles and white papers.

You search TechNet just as you do the Knowledge Base. Click on the Find icon (the pair of binoculars on the toolbar) and enter a keyword. TechNet comes on multiple CDs and may prompt you to insert the CD it needs to complete your request. You can also use the left pane of the search engine to browse through documents by product or by category.

# Microsoft SQL Server Books Online

Microsoft SQL Server Books Online is such an important tool in developing a solid production server that it may have been mentioned in some chapters of this book more than SQL Server itself. It is included with the SQL Server software package and is an optional installation component displayed the first time you install Microsoft SQL Server or the client utilities. Microsoft SQL Server Books Online works exactly like the Microsoft TechNet CD. The main screens look the same and provide much the same search capability. Microsoft SQL Server Books Online is SQL Server-specific and carries over 30MB of data on Microsoft SQL Server and how it functions.

You might want to install Microsoft SQL Server Books Online on development machines only. Because Books Online contains the "key to the kitchen," you might be asking for problems down the road if you put the books in the wrong hands.

# Newsgroups

Newsgroups on the Internet are probably the second most useful reference tool at your disposal. A newsgroup is a group of people sending and receiving information in a single forum relating to a particular subject. You have access to thousands of newsgroups on the Internet, relating to subjects from A through Z. Let's look at what is available pertaining to Microsoft SQL Server in the newsgroups.

---

**NOTE:** *This section uses Microsoft Outlook Express, which is installed with Microsoft Internet Explorer, to browse the newsgroups. There are a number of newsreaders available that you can use for this purpose, but most readers have access to Outlook Express, so it is used in the following example.*

---

Many Internet Service Providers (ISPs) provide access to a news server as part of their service. If you do not have a news server with your Internet account, you can use the Microsoft news server (**msnews.microsoft.com**) free of charge to access the newsgroups mentioned in this section. Once you have accessed the news servers and have downloaded a list of the newsgroups, you need to locate the newsgroups that pertain to SQL Server. These newsgroups begin with "microsoft.public.sqlserver." These are the newsgroups listed on Microsoft's Web site and the ones that generally provide the most useful and "safe" information. The following is a list of newsgroups specifically pertaining to SQL Server:

- **microsoft.public.sqlserver.clients**
- **microsoft.public.sqlserver.clustering**
- **microsoft.public.sqlserver.connect**
- **microsoft.public.sqlserver.datamining**
- **microsoft.public.sqlserver.datawarehouse**
- **microsoft.public.sqlserver.dts**
- **microsoft.public.sqlserver.fulltext**
- **microsoft.public.sqlserver.misc**
- **microsoft.public.sqlserver.mseq**
- **microsoft.public.sqlserver.odbc**
- **microsoft.public.sqlserver.programming**
- **microsoft.public.sqlserver.replication**
- **microsoft.public.sqlserver.server**
- **microsoft.public.sqlserver.setup**
- **microsoft.public.sqlserver.tools**
- **microsoft.public.sqlserver.xml**

Once you have located the newsgroup that applies to your topic, you can use the Go To button to retrieve the current messages. Microsoft personnel frequent these areas quite often, so the information can be very useful. Once you are in a newsgroup, you can read and reply to messages and send out a request for information to the whole group. Be prepared; once you post a request, you might receive several email messages a day in reply. You should check the newsgroup periodically for answers to your postings because they are not really addressed to you specifically, but rather to the group.

Once you have chosen a newsgroup to read, the newsreader downloads the available message headers. You can choose which messages you want to read by looking at the subject. When you highlight a message, the newsreader downloads it for you to read. In Outlook Express, a preview pane is displayed by default, which allows you to read the message without having to open it. Short messages can be read in their entirety in this pane without needing to open or scroll the message. Messages with one or more replies are indicated by a plus (+) to the left of the subject. Clicking on the plus expands the message thread and allows you to select additional messages in the thread.

You also have the ability to subscribe to the newsgroups that you find interesting or helpful. Subscribing to one or more newsgroups using Outlook Express is very simple. Select Tools|Newsgroups. On the All tab, highlight the newsgroup(s) you want to subscribe to. Click on Subscribe to subscribe to the selected newsgroup(s). You can unsubscribe to a newsgroup just as easily by highlighting the newsgroup on the Subscribed tab and clicking on Unsubscribe.

**WARNING! Do not overload yourself with newsgroups. If you select too many newsgroups, you won't be able to keep up with the traffic. Take your time and build a set of newsgroups that you can handle on a daily or every-other-day basis.**

# Newsgroup Etiquette

Many people think that newsgroups are just for hotshot programmers. That is just not true anymore. Many beginners and intermediate users are venturing into the newsgroups and posting questions. Computer professionals are beginning to welcome novices, seeing this as an opportunity to foster a better understanding of the products they use. Unfriendly responses to "simple" questions are uncommon. (They may occur, so do not take a poor attitude or response in the wrong way.)

Newsgroup etiquette calls for participants to be patient and polite and to pose their questions clearly. It is helpful to supply as much background information as possible when posing a question to potential respondents. The more information you provide in the initial posting, the better. If possible, you can include table

Appendix B
Newsgroups and
the Internet

**929**

structure and SQL code examples to illustrate your problem or question. If there are no responses after the first day or so, it is worthwhile to repost the message and see what happens. After all, nobody is being paid to spend time in the newsgroups answering all the questions that are posted. (Although some people draw a paycheck while in the newsgroup!)

When answering any questions in the newsgroup, keep the user in mind. He or she might not have the same level of understanding that you do. Spend an extra minute or two and be more specific than usual. Thousands of people each day read newsgroup messages and take their content to heart. Therefore, be careful and check your facts as much as possible.

Finally, make sure you post to the newsgroup that is designated for the topic your question falls in. Do not post installation questions in the data warehouse group or vice versa. Check to make sure the group topics match the question, and then post as much detail as possible to ensure that you get a good answer.

# Glossary

**Active Directory**—New to Microsoft Windows 2000 Server, Active Directory stores information about resources on a network and makes it available to users and applications.

**Ad hoc query**—A query created for immediate execution. You can create an ad hoc query from scratch or modify an existing query that is saved in a text file.

**Address database**—A sample database distributed with this book to be used as a learning tool.

**Aggregate function**—A function that performs a calculation on a column in a group of rows and returns a single value.

**Alert**—A programmed response to a SQL Server event.

**Alias**—An alternative name for an entity. It is used to shorten entity references and to prevent ambiguous references.

**ANSI (American National Standards Institute)**—An organization of American industry and business groups that administers and coordinates the U.S. private sector voluntary standardization system.

**API (Application Programming Interface)**—A set of routines, protocols, and procedures provided to facilitate application development.

**Archiving**—Moving data from "current" to historical storage. This process sometimes involves eliminating portions of the data to conserve space.

**Atomic**—Describes a transaction that either performs all of its data modifications or performs none of its data modifications.

**Attributes**—Columns or fields that describe an entity.

**Auditing**—Tracking changes to data. Audit information can include date and time information, the user who made the modification, and even the specific edits that were made.

**Authentication**—The process of establishing a security access level for a user based on a user name and password. SQL Server supports NT Authentication and SQL Server Authentication for user logins.

**Autogenerated Statistics**—Statistic sets created automatically by the query optimizer to aid in the generation of a query plan. These statistics can be identified by the fact that they are prefixed with _WA_Sys_.

**AWE (Address Windowing Extensions) Memory**—An API used to support extremely large amounts of physical RAM by dynamically mapping views of nonpaged memory into the standard 32-bit address space.

**Bandwidth**—The amount of data that can be transmitted across a network or other connectivity device in a fixed amount of time. The bandwidth of a connection is generally expressed in bits per second (bps).

**BCP (Bulk Copy Program)**—A command-line utility that allows an administrator or developer to migrate data in and out of tables.

**Binary Sort Order**—A sort order that specifies how sorts and comparisons should be done based on binary bit patterns. This is a case-sensitive sorting method and results in the fastest sorts and comparisons of character data.

**Books Online**—An invaluable set of documentation that is supplied for Microsoft SQL Server.

**Bottleneck**—Excessive demand on a system resource.

**BULK INSERT**—A Transact-SQL command used to import data from an operating system file into a database table or view using a user-specified format.

**Bus**—Systems used to transfer data in a computer system.

**Cascading**—A process by which changes applied to data are automatically applied to any related fields in other tables as in cascading updates or cascading deletes.

**Check constraint**—The standard, preferred way to restrict the values allowed for a column.

**Client Network Utility**—A tool that allows you to configure how the clients on the current workstation connect to the various servers in your environment.

**Glossary**

**Client/server**—A standard two-tier application model with a front-end client that handles processing and a backend server for data storage.

**Client-side cursor**—A cursor implemented by the client application. This generally involves retrieving the entire record set and storing it locally on the client. The client-side cursor is then used to traverse the data and allow any required processing on a row-by-row basis.

**Clustered index**—An index in which the physical order of data is the same as the key values in a table.

**Collation**—A collation is very similar to a sort order. It is used to define the physical storage of character data in SQL Server 2000. The collation determines the bit patterns used to store each character.

**Column**—Also known as a field. This is a single piece of information contained within a row in a database table.

**Column terminator**—The character used to indicate the end of the column data for each column in a BCP file, which can be specified in a format file or on the BCP command line. This also applies to the **BULK INSERT** statement.

**COM (Component Object Model)**—A model developed by Microsoft to allow developers to create objects that can be used by any COM-compliant application.

**Compatibility level**—The behaviors exhibited by a database compatible with previous versions of SQL Server. The compatibility level is database-specific and is not server-wide. Compatibility levels can be changed by the use of the **sp_dbcmptlevel** stored procedure.

**Concurrency**—The ability of multiple users to access a system at the same time. Concurrency errors occur when multiple users attempt to lock or modify the same piece of data at the same time.

**Configuration**—The way a system is set up.

**Constraint**—A restriction placed upon the value that can be entered into a column. It is used to enforce integrity.

**Covering index**—An index that includes every column referenced for a particular table in a query.

**Cross-database referential integrity**—Enforcing data dependencies that exist across multiple databases.

**Cross-reference table**—A table used to define a relationship between two or more other tables.

**Cursor**—Database objects with which applications manipulate data by rows instead of by sets. Using cursors, multiple operations can be performed row-by-row against a result set with or without returning to the original table.

**Cursor variable**—Variables that can contain a reference to a cursor.

**Data Scrubbing**—The process of cleaning up data that was received from an outside source before importing it into your production database. This technique is applied to prevent importing data that would violate your data integrity rules.

**Database**—A collection of information, data tables, and other objects that are organized and presented to serve a specific purpose, such as facilitation of searching and sorting data.

**Database diagram**—A graphical representation of the structure and relationships of a database. This is an important piece of documentation in most development environments and allows a clear picture of how the various entities in the database are intended to interact.

**DB Library**—The original call-level API that allows access to SQL Server. This API has not been enhanced beyond the functionality available in SQL Server 6.5, so although it can still be used, it does not support any of the new features introduced starting with SQL Server 7.0.

**DBCC (Database Consistency Check)**—Statements that check the physical and logical consistency of a database. Several of the DBCC statements can fix problems as they detect them.

**Deadlock**—A situation that arises when two users, each having a lock on one piece of data, attempt to acquire a lock on the other's piece. Each user waits for the other to release his or her lock. SQL Server detects deadlocks and kills one user's process, returning error code 1205.

**Deallocate**—To free the memory resources associated with an in-memory object or variable.

**Declare**—To define and if necessary allocate resources for a variable, cursor, and so on.

**Default**—A value assigned automatically if one is not specified.

**Default instance**—An instance of SQL Server 2000 that is referenced solely by the name of the computer on which it is installed. Only one default instance of SQL Server 2000 is allowed per machine.

**Derived table**—A derived table is a subquery that is used in a **FROM** or **JOIN** clause in place of a table, which has an alias specified that can be used as a table identifier.

**Development server**—A server that is used by software developers and testers to develop and verify applications. A development server is not used to operate actual production databases.

**DHCP (Dynamic Host Configuration Protocol)**—A protocol used to assign IP addresses dynamically to the devices connected to a network.

**Differential backup**—A backup where only the changes that have been committed since the last full backup was performed.

**Distributed Partitioned View**—A technique used to join horizontally partitioned data across multiple servers. This technique is required to implement a Federated Server.

**DNS (Domain Name Service)**—An Internet service used to translate domain names into IP addresses.

**Domain**—A group of computers on a network that are administered using a common set of rules and procedures.

**DRI (Declarative Referential Integrity)**—Defining database referential integrity using primary keys, foreign keys, and other common database constraints to allow the server to manage data integrity regardless of the application used to access the data.

**DTS (Data Transformation Services)**—A powerful tool that allows you to transform, extract, and consolidate data from multiple sources.

**Dynamic cursor**—Dynamic cursors reflect all changes made to the underlying data in the rowset defined by the cursor. When using a dynamic cursor, there is no guarantee that the rowset will be the same from one fetch to the next, and it is possible to step across the same row multiple times if modifications to the data change their position in the result set.

**Dynamic SQL**—SQL that is built "on the fly" by applications or other SQL statements.

**English Query**—SQL Server component that allows end users to pose questions in English instead of forming a query with a SQL statement.

**Enterprise Manager**—The graphical utility that represents the primary interface for most SQL Server and database-related maintenance and configuration activities.

**Entities**—Tables in a database design.

**ERA Model**—This model covers the entities, relationships, and attributes and is one of the easiest tools to use for analyzing your database graphically.

Glossary

**Error handling**—Trapping errors and raising the errors to the next level for handling in applications and Transact-SQL code.

**Error log**—Stores information about errors that occur in the system, which can be used as aids in the troubleshooting process.

**Event log**—Stores information about various events that occur in the system. These can be informational messages, warnings, or errors.

**Export**—To take data out of a system in such a way that it can be used by another application.

**Failover cluster**—The grouping of two or more physical machines as a single server that allows the additional machine(s) to take over in the event that the primary server machine fails. This technique safeguards mission-critical systems from downtime resulting from hardware failure.

**Fault tolerance**—The capability of a computer system to maintain data integrity in the event of hardware failure.

**Federated data**—Horizontally partitioned data spread across multiple Federated Servers.

**Federated Servers**—A group of servers that are administered separately, but work together to process a work load. This is accomplished by creating horizontal partitions in the data to spread it across multiple servers using Distributed Partitioned Views to access the data from a single server.

**Fiber Channel**—A serial data transfer architecture that was developed by a consortium of mass storage device and computer manufacturers. This architecture is now being standardized by ANSI.

**Filter**—A set of criteria that determines which rowset is returned when a query is executed. A filter can also determine the sequence in which a rowset is returned.

**Foreign Key**—A reference to a primary key in another table that is used to maintain referential integrity.

**Format file**—A format file is used to specify the format of the operating system file referenced in an import or export operation by the BCP program or in an import operation by the **BULK INSERT** command.

**Fragmentation**—Distributing parts of the same file over different areas of the disk. It occurs as files are deleted and new files are added. Fragmentation can lead to slower disk access and can possibly degrade disk operation performance.

**Full database backup**—A complete copy or backup of a database.

**Full duplex**—The transmission of data in two directions at the same time.

**Full-Text Search**—A service provided with Microsoft SQL Server that allows you to create and maintain full-text indexes, which can be used to implement text searches that would otherwise be difficult to achieve.

**Global**—Refers to the scope of an object or variable. A global object or variable is available to multiple procedures in the same connection or to multiple connections on the same server.

**Global variable**—System supplied, predeclared variables. Global variables are distinguished from local variables by two symbols (**@@**) preceding their names.

**GUID (Globally Unique Identifier)**—A guaranteed unique identifier.

**Half duplex**—The transmission of data in only one direction at a time.

**HCL (Hardware Compatibility List)**—Microsoft's list of compatible hardware that indicates which hardware is supported for various Microsoft products. You should always attempt to verify that your hardware is on this "approved" list before installing Microsoft server products on it.

**Heterogeneous**—A database system other than Microsoft SQL Server.

**Hints**—Hints are used to override the default behavior of the query optimizer. There are hints available that affect locking behavior as well as various other aspects of query plans.

**Horizontal partition**—Division of a table involving defining multiple ranges of rows based on some key value that can be stored in separate tables (possibly on separate servers) to distribute the workload required to process the data.

**HTML (Hypertext Markup Language)**—The authoring language used to create Web pages.

**Hub**—A connection point for devices in a network.

**IDE (Integrated Drive Electronics)**—A drive interface in which the controller is actually located on the disk drive itself.

**Identity column**—An auto-increment column that can be used as a primary key column to uniquely identify a row.

**IIS (Microsoft Internet Information Services)**—Microsoft's Web server that runs on Windows NT and Windows 2000 platforms.

**Import**—The act of placing data produced by another application or server into Microsoft SQL Server.

**ISV (Independent Software Vendor)**—A company that produces software independently of the manufacturer of the server platform.

**Index**— An index is a database object that provides access to data in the rows of a table based on key values. Indexes provide quick access to data and can enforce uniqueness on the rows in a table.

**Indexed View**—A new feature in SQL Server 2000 that supports creating a clustered index on a view to speed query processing.

**Indexing strategies**—Determining the best set of indexes to apply to a database to achieve maximum performance for all database applications.

**Information Models**—Definitions of the meta data types stored in a repository database and used by applications.

**Instance**—An installation of Microsoft SQL Server 2000.

**INSTEAD OF trigger**—An **INSTEAD OF** trigger is used to override the standard actions of the triggering statement. This is a new feature in SQL Server 2000 that greatly enhances the functionality of database triggers.

**Integrity**—The quality or correctness of data.

**I/O (Input/Output)**—Refers to the number of hard disk read and/or write operations required to perform a task.

**IP address**—A unique identifier for a computer or device on a TCP/IP network.

**ISAM (Indexed Sequential Access Method)**—A prerelational database method for managing how a computer accesses records and files stored on a hard disk. The data is stored sequentially and direct record access is provided via an index. This is strictly a row-based access method.

**ISAPI (Internet Server API)**—An API that allows developers to create applications that are more tightly integrated with the Web server.

**Join**—The act of associating multiple tables in a SQL query. This is the technique used to create a single result set from multiple tables in a relational database.

**Join condition**— A segment of a query that specifies how two tables are joined or related to each other in a query.

**Keyset cursor**—A keyset cursor reflects changes in the underlying data in the rowset defined by the cursor, but the number and order of the rows are determined when the cursor is opened and do not change based on the changes to the underlying data.

**Knowledge Base**—A large, searchable database of information maintained by Microsoft about its various products. The Knowledge Base is available from Microsoft's Web site as well as from the TechNet CDs.

**LAN (Local Area Network)**—A computer network that spans a relatively small area, like a single building or complex.

**LDF**—The default file extension used by SQL Server 2000 for database transaction log files.

**Linked server**—A configuration that is established to allow queries against OLE DB data sources on different servers. This provides the capability to run distributed queries, transactions, updates, and commands across an entire enterprise on heterogeneous data sources

**Local**—Refers to the scope of an object or variable. A local object or variable is only available to the current procedure or connection.

**Lock**—A restriction on accessing a resource, such as a table, page, or row.

**Log shipping**—The process of backing up the transaction logs routinely on a source database, and then copying and restoring them to a destination database.

**Login**—The user name used to log on to the server.

**MAPI (Messaging API)**—A messaging system built into Microsoft Windows to enable multiple email systems to work together to distribute mail.

**Markup Language**—A set of codes that the writer inserts into a document that describes the structure and content of the document (for example, HTML).

**Master database**—A system database that records the system and configuration information for SQL Server including login accounts, system configuration settings, the existence of other databases and their file locations, and initialization information for SQL Server. You should *always* have a recent backup of this database for recovery purposes.

**MDAC (Microsoft Data Access Components)**—A set of components designed to provide common data access for a variety of data sources, which is provided by Microsoft as part of its universal data access strategy.

Glossary

**MDC (Meta Data Coalition)**—An alliance of software vendors and users with the common goal of driving forward the definition, implementation, and evolution of a meta data interchange format standard and its support mechanisms.

**MDF**—The default file extension used by SQL Server 2000 for database data files.

**MDK (Modeling Development Kit)**—A part of the Meta Data Services SDK, which includes modeling documentation, sample code, and add-on tools to aid in the process of building, extending, customizing, and programming against information models in the Meta Data Services repository database.

**Member server**—A single server participating in a federation for storing horizontally partitioned data.

**Member table**—A table referenced in a Distributed Partitioned View that contains a portion of the horizontally partitioned data located on multiple servers.

**Meta data**—Describes the structure and meaning of data as well as the structure and meaning of applications and processes.

**Microsoft Search Service**—A full-text indexing and search engine that runs as a Windows service.

**MMC (Microsoft Management Console)**—Provides a common console framework for server and network management applications.

**MSCS (Microsoft Clustering Service)**—A service built into Windows NT and Windows 2000, which is used to provide support for failover clustering.

**MSDB database**—A system database where jobs, alerts, and scheduling information (among other things) are stored in SQL Server.

**MSDN (Microsoft Developer Network)**—A subscription service available from Microsoft that delivers monthly updates of the latest Microsoft software, tools, and programming information on CD or DVD.

**MTS (Microsoft Transaction Server)**—A component-based transaction processing system that is designed for developing, deploying, and managing high-performance, scalable, and robust enterprise, Internet, and intranet server applications.

**Multi-Tiered**—A three or more tiered application architecture that makes use of a "thin" client that provides the interface, one or more middleware servers that store the business logic, and a backend server that provides data access.

**Named instance**—A new feature of SQL Server 2000 that allows you to have more than one instance of SQL Server 2000 running on a single server machine.

You must specify the instance name in addition to the computer name in order to access a named instance of SQL Server 2000.

**Named Pipes**—An interprocess protocol used to exchange information between two applications on a network.

**NAS (Network Attached Storage) devices**—Large, single-purpose servers that plug into your network. They can be thought of as high-speed file servers.

**Native format**—The fastest format for importing and exporting data using the BCP utility or **BULK INSERT** command. Native format specifies that all data in the operating system file is stored in SQL Server's native storage format for each data type.

**Nesting**—Embedding one object or procedure inside another of the same type. This is a common practice in most programming environments.

**NetBIOS** (Network Basic Input/Output System)—An API that augments the DOS BIOS by adding special functions for supporting and accessing LANs.

**Nonclustered index**—An index in which the physical order of the data is different than the logical order of the key values.

**Normalization**—The separation of data into multiple, related tables. A normalized database will have several more narrow tables rather than a few wide tables.

**n-Tiered**—*See* Multi-Tiered.

**NTFS (NT File System)**—A file system designed for the Windows NT operating system to enhance reliability and security of the information stored on your hard disk.

**NULL**—An entry that has not explicitly been assigned a value. **NULL** is not equal to zero or blank. A **NULL** value is not greater than, less than, or equal to any other value, not even another **NULL** value.

**ODBC (Open Database Connectivity)**—A set of drivers provided by different manufacturers that allows client applications to connect to database servers without regard to the native database language. These drivers interpret data requests and translate those requests into a format that the database understands.

**OIM (Open Information Model)**—A formal specification of meta data produced by the MDC that provides common ground for defining standard meta data.

**OLAP (Online Analytical Processing)**—The technology that enables client applications to efficiently access the data contained in data warehouses and data marts.

Glossary

**OLE DB**—A COM-based application programming interface that provides access to any data source for which an OLE DB provider is available. OLE DB supports data access in any format including databases, spreadsheets, text files, and so on.

**Operator**—A person who is notified of the status of a SQL Server event.

**Optimistic Locking**—A method or approach to locking behavior on the server. Data is not locked when it is read. Instead, the application or server must check to see if the data has been updated since it was read before allowing an update to proceed.

**Optimization**—Fine-tuning a program or process so that it runs more quickly or requires less storage space.

**Oracle**—Generally used as a reference to the relational database system produced by Oracle Corporation, which is the largest software company whose primary business is database products. Oracle and Microsoft SQL Server are competing database platforms.

**Orphaned records**—A child record that no longer has a valid parent entry in the database. This can generally be prevented by the use of referential integrity constraints and other server-side mechanisms to enforce data integrity.

**Parameters**—An item of information passed to a procedure or function by the calling process.

**Partition**—A division of a disk drive.

**PCI (Peripheral Component Interconnect)**—A local bus standard developed by Intel Corporation that is available in most all modern PCs. PCI is a 64-bit bus (usually implemented as a 32-bit bus) that can run at speeds of 33 or 66MHz.

**Permissions**—Specific access rights granted to a user or role for a database object.

**Precedence constraint**—A constraint that determines the order in which the steps in a DTS Package are processed.

**Production server**—A production server is used to house and provide access to "live" databases in a production environment. A production server must be properly maintained and secured to protect the mission-critical information that it contains.

**Profiler**—A tool that captures SQL Server events either to the screen or to a trace file.

**Query**—A request for information from a database.

**Query Analyzer**—A graphical query tool that allows you to write queries and view their results.

**Query optimizer**—The portion of the SQL Server engine that is used to determine the optimum execution plan for a query submitted against a database.

**Query plan**—The specific course of action that is taken by SQL Server to gather the data requested by a query and deliver the result set to the requesting application.

**Quorum disk**—A special shared disk in a failover cluster used to store cluster configuration database checkpoints and log files that help manage the cluster.

**RAID (Redundant Array of Independent Disks)**—A disk system that consists of multiple drives in combination for fault tolerance and performance.

**RAM (Random Access Memory)**—The physical memory existing on a server or workstation.

**Recursion**—A programming technique in which a routine calls itself. This is a powerful technique, but it can be dangerous and resource-intensive if used incorrectly.

**Recursive trigger**—A trigger that is executed whose actions cause the same trigger to be executed again. The Recursive_Triggers database option must be set in order for this to happen.

**Referential integrity**—A feature provided by relational database management systems that is used to prevent users from entering inconsistent data.

**Registry**—A database where information about a computer's configuration is stored.

**Relationship**—A modeling term that defines how the data in two or more tables is related. Can be equated to the relationship between parents and children. Relationships are used to eliminate redundant data in a normalized database.

**Role**—A method used to group multiple users into a single unit for the purpose of assigning database permissions.

**Row**—A group of columns that defines a logical record in a database. A single horizontal unit in a table.

**Row terminator**—The character used to indicate the end of the row data for each row in a BCP file, which can be specified in a format file or on the BCP command line. This character appears after the data for the last column in each row in the file. The row terminator also applies to the **BULK INSERT** statement.

**Rowset**—A set of rows containing columns of data that is returned by a SQL query.

**RPC (Remote Procedure Call)**—A type of protocol used to enable a program on one computer to execute a program on another computer.

**RTF (Rich Text Format)**—A standard formalized by Microsoft for formatting documents. The file is actually an ASCII file with special commands to indicate formatting options, such as fonts and margins.

**SAN (Storage Area Network)**—Multiple server, multiple storage networks that can grow to very large sizes. They can be thought of as a private network separate from the LAN.

**Schema**—The structure of a database described in a formal language supported by the relational database management system.

**Scrollable**—The capability to move through the rows in a cursor either forward or backward. Defining a scrollable cursor provides the ability to access the rows by moving to an absolute row position.

**SCSI (Small Computer System Interface)**—An interface used to connect computers to peripheral devices.

**SDK (Software Development Kit)**—A package that contains one or more APIs and documentation to aid programmers in developing applications for a particular platform.

**Self-join**—The technique of joining a table to itself as both parent and child. The key elements for the join must exist in the same table. For instance, selecting an employee's manager, which is also stored in the Employee table.

**Self-referencing**—A self-join of a table to itself through the use of alias references. *See* self-join.

**Server-side cursor**—A cursor implemented by the server. These cursors are normally exposed to the client application via an API. The Transact-SQL language also provides an implementation of server-side cursors for SQL Server.

**Set-based**—Working with row-sets rather than individual rows for processing and manipulating data.

**SGML (Standard Generalized Markup Language)**—A system for organizing and tagging the elements of a document with tags that can be interpreted to format the elements in different ways. Developed by the International Organization for Standards in 1986.

**SP (Stored Procedure)**—Transact-SQL statements stored under a name and processed as a unit. Stored procedures are stored within a database and can be executed on request from an application. A stored procedure can also allow user-declared variables, conditional execution, and other powerful programming features.

**Speed**—A measure of the amount of time that it takes a process to run.

**SQL (Structured Query Language)**—A database query and programming language originally developed by IBM for mainframe computers. It is widely used for accessing data in database systems.

**SQL-92**—The version of the SQL standard published in 1992.

**SQL DMO (Distributed Management Object)**—An API that encapsulates the objects found in SQL Server 2000 databases. This is the API that is used by the Enterprise Manager, so any COM-compliant programming language can use SQL DMO to produce applications that contain the same functionality as all or portions of the Enterprise Manager.

**SQL Mail**—This external procedure provides a way to send and receive e-mail messages generated by SQL Server, which can be used as notifications of errors, job completions, and so on.

**SQL Server Agent**—A windows service that checks for jobs to execute on a scheduled basis.

**Standards**—A definition or format that has been approved by a recognized standards organization or is accepted as a *de facto* standard by the industry. Standards enable technology to be used by various products and vendors. Whether sharing database information, or having a common basis for the development of PC peripherals, standards play an extremely important role in today's IT marketplace.

**Static cursor**—The complete result set for the cursor is created in tempdb when the cursor is initially opened, and modifications to the underlying data are not reflected in the data as it is traversed using the cursor.

**Static IP address**—An IP address that is hard coded into the setup for the network device or computer rather than being dynamically assigned using DHCP.

**Statistics**—Information about the distribution of values in a column.

**Switch**—A device that filters and forwards messages between network segments.

**System tables**—Tables that store meta data information about the other objects in a database. These tables should generally not be accessed directly, and should definitely not be modified directly except by extremely skilled database administrators (DBAs) or developers.

**Table**—A database entity that has rows and columns which are used to store data.

Glossary

**Table variable**—A special data type introduced in SQL Server 2000 that can be used to hold a result set for later processing.

**TCP/IP (Transmission Control Protocol/Internet Protocol)**—The suite of communication protocols used to connect hosts on the Internet.

**Tempdb database**—A system database that is used to store temporary database objects created by a connection to SQL Server. This is also where temporary storage is allocated by some sorting and grouping operations required to complete a query.

**Template**—The basic structure of a SQL statement.

**Temporary table**—A table that is created in tempdb by specifying the # or ## prefix when the table is created. The ## prefix is used to make the temporary table available to all connections, but it will not be automatically removed from tempdb when the creating connection closes, so it must be managed carefully.

**Terminal services**—An environment that allows users to remotely manage servers and connections through administrative tools.

**Test server**—Generally, a mirror of the production server with respect to hardware and software installation. It should also contain a reasonably current copy of all production databases. This is where any changes to software and hardware configurations as well as any upgrades should be tested prior to applying them to a production server. This server can also be used as a backup if the production server fails.

**Thin client**—A client application designed to be extremely small by offloading the processing to the backend server or middle tier.

**Thread**—A portion of a program that can execute independently. Operating systems that support multi-threaded applications allow developers to create programs that have threaded portions that can operate concurrently.

**Throughput**—The amount of data that can be transferred or processed in a specified amount of time.

**Torn page**—A page that was written incorrectly possibly due to power failure or other system outages.

**Transaction**—A transaction is a single unit of work. A transaction can consist of one or numerous SQL commands that should logically be grouped as a single unit. Transactions are used to roll back any work performed when a step in the transaction fails to execute successfully.

**Transaction Isolation Level**—A locking method used to establish the locking requirements for a particular transaction. The Transaction Isolation Level determines which locks are created by a transaction as well as which locks are respected.

**Transaction log**—A serial record of all modifications that have occurred in the database as well as the transaction that performed each modification, which can be used to recover the information in the event that a server error occurs. This log also provides the ability to roll back a transaction that did not complete successfully.

**Transaction log backup**—A complete copy of the transaction log. After a transaction log backup is completed, all committed transaction entries are removed from the log to save space.

**Trigger**—A special form of a stored procedure that goes into effect when data within a table is changed. Triggers are often created to enforce integrity or consistency among logically related data in different tables.

**UML (Unified Modeling Language)**—A general-purpose notational language for specifying and visualizing complex software that is especially useful for large, object-oriented projects.

**Unicode**—A standard for representing characters as 16-bit integers rather than the 8 bits allowed by ASCII. Unicode provides the ability to reference over 65,000 characters, which is overkill for English, but needed for many other languages like Chinese and Greek.

**Union**—A statement that combines the results of multiple queries into one result set that contains all of the rows belonging to all of the queries in the union.

**URL (Universal Resource Locator)**—The global address used to locate documents and other resources on the World Wide Web.

**User-Defined Data Type**—A data type defined by a user based on a system data type. It is set up when several tables have similar columns that must all be defined in exactly the same way.

**User-Defined Function**—A new feature of SQL Server 2000 that allows the user to design new functions using the Transact-SQL programming language, which can be called from various scripts and procedures.

**Variables**—A placeholder that allows you to store information of a specified type in memory to assist in the processing of information in your scripts and procedures.

Glossary

**View**—A stored query plan that is presented to the user or query engine as a table.

**Virtual server**—A technique used in failover and load-balancing clusters to present a single server to the client, which may actually be a group of servers acting as one to complete the task. The use of a virtual server eliminates the need to change the client configuration when servers are added or removed from the cluster.

**Volatile data**—Information that changes constantly.

**WAN (Wide Area Network)**—A system of LANs connected over telephone lines or radio waves.

**Windows service**—A process that performs system functions to support other programs.

**WINS (Windows Internet Naming System)**—A system used to determine the IP address of a computer on a Windows network.

**Wizard**—An intuitive step-by-step process that is provided for assistance in performing several associated tasks that a user may not be familiar with.

**XML (Extensible Markup Language)**—A parsed down version of SGML designed specifically to facilitate data interchange between various platforms over the Internet.

**XP (Extended Stored Procedure)**—Allows the creation of external programs using programming languages like Delphi or C, which can be accessed via Transact-SQL commands on SQL Server.

# Index

# T

# Other Coriolis Technology Press Titles

### Open Source Development with CVS

By Karl Fogel
ISBN: 1-57610-490-7
Price: $39.99 U.S. • $58.99 CAN
Media: None • Available Now

Learn the best practices of open source software development with CVS— a tool that allows several individuals to work simultaneously on the same document. CVS is covered in detail, as is the GNU license, software design and development, coding styles, documentation procedures, testing, release of software, and troubleshooting.

### HTML Black Book

By Steven Holzner
ISBN: 1-57610-617-9
Price: $59.99 U.S. • $89.99 CAN
Media: CD-ROM • Available Now

Explores HTML programming thoroughly, from the essentials up through issues of security, providing step-by-step solutions to everyday challenges. This comprehensive guide discusses HTML in-depth, as well as covering XML, dynamic XML, JavaScript, Java, Perl, and CGI programming, to create a full Web site programming package.

### Java Black Book

By Steven Holzner
ISBN: 1-57610-531-8
Price: $49.99 U.S. • $74.99 CAN
Media: CD-ROM • Available Now

A comprehensive reference filled with more than 500 examples, tips, and problem-solving solutions. Discusses the Java language, Abstract Windowing Toolkit, Swing, Java 2D, advanced java beans, the Java Database Connectivity Package, servlets, internalization and security, streams and sockets, and more.

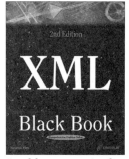

### XML Black Book, 2nd Edition

By Natanya Pitts
ISBN: 1-57610-783-3
Price: $49.99 U.S. • $74.99 CAN
Media: CD-ROM • Available Now

This comprehensive reference guide to XML covers the latest versions of the XML specification and related specifications, tips, techniques, and examples. It addresses topics from markup and DTD design, to the most popular XML-based applications and the latest software tools available for working with XML.

### 3D Game Programming with C++

By John De Goes
ISBN: 1-57610-400-1
Price: $49.99 U.S. • $74.99 CAN
Media: CD-ROM • Available Now

Create games for PC platforms and graphics accelerators and harness the power of DirectX. It explains mathematical models for programming flat-shaded polygons, 3D transformations, light-sourced polygons, and texture mapping. Includes a foreword by Andre LaMothe and full source code game engine.

### Visual C++ 6 Core Language Little Black Book

By Bill McCarty
ISBN: 1-57610-389-7
Price: $24.99 U.S. • $36.99 CAN
Media: None • Available Now

This book summarizes the syntax and grammar of C++, the routines of the C/C++ libraries, and procedures and techniques for using the Visual C++ development environment and tools. It will help you program more efficiently by putting thousands of facts and procedures at your fingertips.

---

**THE CORIOLIS GROUP, LLC**  Telephone: 480.483.0192 • Toll-free: 800.410.0192 • In Canada: 905.477.0722 • www.coriolis.com
Coriolis books are also available at bookstores and computer stores nationwide.

# Windows® 2000 Titles from Coriolis

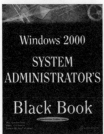
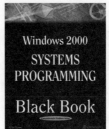
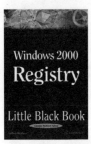
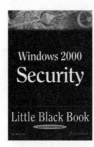

# Other Coriolis Technology Press Titles

### Active Server Pages Solutions

By Al Williams, Kim Barber, and Paul Newkirk
ISBN: 1-57610-608-X
Price: $49.99 US • $74.99 CAN
Media: CD-ROM • Available Now

Explores all the components that work with Active Server Pages, such as HTML (including Dynamic HTML), scripting, Java applets, Internet Information Server, Internet Explorer, and server-side scripting for VBScript, Jscript, and ActiveX controls. Offers practical examples using commonly used tools.

### Windows® 2000 TCP/IP Black Book

By Ian McLean
ISBN: 1-57610-687-X
Price: $49.99 US • $74.99 CAN
Media: CD-ROM • Available Now

Covers the TCP/IP Protocol Suite and tools, utilities, and client services. Takes you through configuration and implementation step by step. Explores Active Directory/TCP/IP integration, new Dynamic Domain Name Services, the latest version of Internet Protocol, Internet Protocol Security, and more.

### Windows® 2000 Professional Upgrade Little Black Book

By Nathan Wallace
ISBN: 1-57610-748-5
Price: $29.99 US • $44.99 CAN
Media: None • Available Now

This book includes complete guidance on newly introduced technologies to help administrators upgrade or migrate users of Windows 9x, NT 4, Unix, and Macintosh. Covers advanced features of Windows 2000 Professional using a concise task-oriented approach for quickly accessing solutions.

### Windows® Admin Scripting Little Black Book

By Jesse M. Torres
ISBN: 1-57610-881-3
Price: $29.99 US • $44.99 CAN
Media: None • Available Now

This book takes the reader through the basics of scripting to advanced topics such as debugging and integrating with other applications and scripting languages. Teaches the Windows administrator to quickly write complex logon scripts without requiring any expertise in programming.

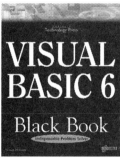

### Visual Basic 6 Black Book

By Steven Holzner
ISBN: 1-57610-283-1
Price: $49.99 US • $69.99 CAN
Media: CD-ROM • Available Now

Completely explains the crucial Visual Basic tool set in detail. Jam-packed with insight, programming tips and techniques, and real-world solutions. Covers everything from graphics and image processing to ActiveX controls, database development and data-bound controls, multimedia, OLE automation, Registry handling, error handling and debugging, Windows API, and more.

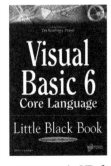

### Visual Basic 6 Core Language Little Black Book

By Steven Holzner
ISBN: 1-57610-390-0
Price: $24.99 US • $36.99 CAN
Media: None • Available Now

Provides a detailed reference on all Basic control structures, data types, and other code mechanisms. Includes step-by-step instructions on how to build common code structures in VB, from simple if statements to objects and ActiveX components. Not merely a syntax summary, but a detailed reference on creating code structures with VB6 code and data elements.

**THE CORIOLIS GROUP, LLC**   Telephone: 800.410.0192 • www.coriolis.com
Coriolis books are also available at bookstores and computer stores nationwide.

# Related Coriolis Technology Press Titles

### DATA MODELING ESSENTIALS, 2nd Edition

Revised and updated by Graham C. Witt & Graeme C. Simsion
ISBN: 1-57610-872-4 • Media: None • Price: $49.99 U.S. • $74.99 CAN

Written by expert practitioners, this highly anticipated second edition has been fully updated to cover data warehouse design, business rules, corporate data modeling, and object-oriented approaches. It explores the difference between modeling business data requirements and designing and maintaining the resulting database, including the impact of universal server and data distribution. The book takes a clear, practical approach to data modeling and includes many practical examples.

### SOFTWARE PROJECT MANAGEMENT: From Concept to Deployment

By Kieron Conway
ISBN: 1-57610-807-4 • Media: CD-ROM • Price: $49.99 U.S. • $74.99 CAN

Written specifically for programmers and developers, this book follows a real-world small-scale project from beginning to end. Covers both object-oriented and non-object-oriented technologies, multimedia, and image handling, and ultimately provides a basic set of development skills to help developers complete projects on time and under budget. Introduces the reader to planning and costing software developments and demonstrates how to formalize and analyze requirements. Explores modular design and development and tackles issues of setting up software support. Presents the need for progress monitoring and the vital importance of change handling. This book helps bridge the gap between traditional development and genuine object-oriented development.

### ACCESS 2000 CLIENT/SERVER SOLUTIONS

By Lars Klander
ISBN: 1-57610-417-6 • Media: CD-ROM • Price: $49.99 U.S. • $74.99 CAN

Designed for the intermediate to advanced Access developer, author Lars Klander shows you how to expand your existing Access skill set to enter the powerful world of true client/server development. This book is divided into logical segments designed to simplify your transition to client/server and n-tier development. You will learn to create client/server applications using multiple development tools including SQL Server and Oracle8. This book will help you master DAPs, ADOs, and ADPs; use Visual InterDev to develop Internet-based client/server applications; and much more.

**The Coriolis Group, LLC**     Telephone: 480.483.0192 • Toll-free: 800.410.0192 • In Canada: 905.477.0722 • www.coriolis.com
Coriolis books are also available at bookstores and computer stores worldwide.

# What's on the CD-ROMs

## What's on CD-ROM 1

The **SQL Server 2000 Black Book** companion CD-ROM contains elements specifically selected to enhance the usefulness of this book, including:

- Source code from the book examples that you can use royalty free!
- Server management procedures
- Sample test scripts
- BCP examples
- Cursor and trigger sample code
- Error handling routines and procedures
- Example databases and test data generation routines
- Useful links to popular Internet sites
- Electronic copies of the database diagrams from the book
- English query enabled database examples

## What's on CD-ROM 2

### Microsoft Product
SQL Server 2000 120-Day Enterprise Evaluation Edition

### Product Name and Associated Trademarks
Microsoft SQL Server 2000

### Environment
Microsoft Windows

### System Requirements

- PC with an Intel or compatible Pentium 166MHz or higher processor
- Microsoft Windows NT Server 4.0 with Service Pack 5 or later, Windows NT Server 4.0 Enterprise Edition with Service Pack 5 or later, Windows 2000 Server, Windows 2000 Advanced Server, or Windows 2000 Datacenter Server operating system
- Minimum of 64MB of RAM (128 MB or more recommended)
- Hard-disk space required:
  - 95-270MB for database server; approximately 250MB for typical installation
  - 50MB minimum for Analysis Services; 130MB for typical installation
  - 80MB for Microsoft English Query (supported on Windows 2000 operating system but not logo certified)

*(continued)*

# What's on the CD-ROMs

*(continued)*

- Microsoft Internet Explorer 5.0 or later
- CD-ROM drive
- VGA or higher resolution monitor
- Microsoft Mouse or compatible pointing device

### Difference from Retail Product

Product expires 120 days after installation; restricted license rights.

### Documentation

No printed documentation.

### Copyright Notice